Mathematica Cookbook

Sal Mangano

Beijing · Cambridge · Farnham · Köln · Sebastopol · Taipei · Tokyo

Mathematica Cookbook
by Sal Mangano

Published by O'Reilly Media, Inc., 1005 Gravenstein Highway North, Sebastopol, CA 95472.

O'Reilly books may be purchased for educational, business, or sales promotional use. Online editions are also available for most titles (*http://my.safaribooksonline.com*). For more information, contact our corporate/institutional sales department: (800) 998-9938 or *corporate@oreilly.com*.

Editor:	Mike Loukides
Production Editor:	Adam Witwer
Production Services:	Precision Graphics
Cover Designer:	Karen Montgomery
Interior Designer:	David Futato

Printing History:

May 2010:	First Edition

ISBN: 978-0-596-52099-1

[S]

To Wanda, Leonardo and Salvatore:
My life would not compute without you.

Included with this book is a free 30 day trial of the Wolfram Mathematica ® software. To access your free download, simply go to http://www.wolfram.com/books/resources and enter license number L3294-005. You will be guided to download and install the latest version of Mathematica.

Table of Contents

Preface xv

1. Numerics 1

    1.0 Introduction   1
    1.1 Controlling Precision and Accuracy   4
    1.2 Mixing Different Numerical Types   9
    1.3 Representing Numbers in Other Bases   12
    1.4 Extracting the Digits of a Number   13
    1.5 Working with Intervals   16
    1.6 Converting Between Numerical Types   18
    1.7 Displaying Numbers in Alternate Forms   20

2. Functional Programming 23

    2.0 Introduction   23
    2.1 Mapping Functions with More Than One Argument   32
    2.2 Holding Arbitrary Arguments   36
    2.3 Creating Functions That Automatically Map Over Lists   37
    2.4 Mapping Multiple Functions in a Single Pass   38
    2.5 Keeping Track of the Index of Each Item As You Map   41
    2.6 Mapping a Function over a Moving Sublist   43
    2.7 Using Prefix and Postfix Notation to Produce More Readable Code   48
    2.8 Defining Indexed Functions   51
    2.9 Understanding the Use of Fold As an Alternative to Recursion   53
    2.10 Incremental Construction of Lists   57
    2.11 Computing Through Repeated Function Application   59
    2.12 Building a Function Through Iteration   62

    2.13 Exploiting Function Composition and Inverse Functions   63

    2.14 Implementing Closures   66

    2.15 Currying in Mathematica   73

    2.16 Creating Functions with Default Values   77

    2.17 Creating Functions That Accept Options   79

3. Data Structures **85**

    3.0 Introduction   85

    3.1 Ensuring the Most Efficient Representation of Numerical Lists   95

    3.2 Sorting Lists   97

    3.3 Determining Order Without Sorting   100

    3.4 Extracting the Diagonals of a Matrix   102

    3.5 Constructing Matrices of Specific Structure   103

    3.6 Constructing Permutation and Shift Matrices   105

    3.7 Manipulating Rows and Columns of Matrices   110

    3.8 Using Sparse Arrays to Conserve Memory   112

    3.9 Manipulating Deeply Nested Lists Using Functions with Level Specifications   114

    3.10 Implementing Bit Vectors and Using Format to Customize Their Presentation   119

    3.11 Implementing Trees and Traversals Using Lists   121

    3.12 Implementing Ordered Associative Lookup Using a Red-Black Tree   125

    3.13 Exploiting Mathematica's Built-In Associative Lookup   130

    3.14 Constructing Graphs Using the Combinatorica` Package   134

    3.15 Using Graph Algorithms to Extract Information from Graphs   140

4. Patterns and Rule-Based Programming **145**

    4.0 Introduction   145

    4.1 Collecting Items That Match (or Don't Match) a Pattern   151

    4.2 Excluding Items That Match (or Don't Match) a Pattern   153

    4.3 Counting Items That Match a Pattern   155

    4.4 Replacing Parts of an Expression   157

    4.5 Finding the Longest (or Shortest) Match for a Pattern   159

    4.6 Implementing Algorithms in Terms of Rules   161

    4.7 Debugging Infinite Loops When Using ReplaceRepeated   165

    4.8 Preventing Evaluation Until Replace Is Complete   168

    4.9 Manipulating Patterns with Patterns   169

4.10 Optimizing Rules   170

4.11 Using Patterns As a Query Language   171

4.12 Semantic Pattern Matching   177

4.13 Unification Pattern Matching   178

5. String and Text Processing **181**

5.0 Introduction   181

5.1 Comparing Strings   187

5.2 Removing and Replacing Characters from Strings   188

5.3 Extracting Characters and Substrings   192

5.4 Duplicating a String   196

5.5 Matching and Searching Text   198

5.6 Tokenizing Text   201

5.7 Working with Natural Language Dictionaries   202

5.8 Importing XML   209

5.9 Transforming XML Using Patterns and Rules   213

5.10 Transforming XML Using Recursive Functions (à la XSLT)   218

5.11 Writing Parsers and Grammars in Mathematica   227

6. Two-Dimensional Graphics and Plots **237**

6.0 Introduction   237

6.1 Plotting Functions in Cartesian Coordinates   238

6.2 Plotting in Polar Coordinates   247

6.3 Creating Plots Parametrically   249

6.4 Plotting Data   252

6.5 Mixing Two or More Graphs into a Single Graph   255

6.6 Displaying Multiple Graphs in a Grid   258

6.7 Creating Plots with Legends   260

6.8 Displaying 2D Geometric Shapes   263

6.9 Annotating Graphics with Text   269

6.10 Creating Custom Arrows   270

7. Three-Dimensional Plots and Graphics **275**

7.0 Introduction   275

7.1 Plotting Functions of Two Variables in Cartesian Coordinates   276

7.2 Plotting Functions in Spherical Coordinates   283

7.3 Plotting Surfaces in Cylindrical Coordinates   285

7.4 Plotting 3D Surfaces Parametrically   290

7.5   Creating 3D Contour Plots   292
7.6   Combining 2D Contours with 3D Plots   295
7.7   Constraining Plots to Specified Regions   296
7.8   Plotting Data in 3D   298
7.9   Plotting 3D Regions Where a Predicate Is Satisfied   301
7.10 Displaying 3D Geometrical Shapes   302
7.11 Constructing Wireframe Models from Mesh   306
7.12 Controlling Viewing Geometry   309
7.13 Controlling Lighting and Surface Properties   313
7.14 Transforming 3D Graphics   317
7.15 Exploring Polyhedra   320
7.16 Importing 3D Graphics from CAD and Other 3D Software   326

8. Image Processing **329**
8.0   Introduction   329
8.1   Extracting Image Information   332
8.2   Converting Images from RGB Color Space to HSV Color Space   335
8.3   Enhancing Images Using Histogram Equalization   341
8.4   Correcting Images Using Histogram Specification   347
8.5   Sharpening Images Using Laplacian Transforms   351
8.6   Sharpening and Smoothing with Fourier Transforms   356
8.7   Detecting Edges in Images   361
8.8   Image Recognition Using Eigenvectors (Eigenimages)   365

9. Audio and Music Processing **373**
9.0   Introduction   373
9.1   Creating Musical Notes   374
9.2   Creating a Scale or a Melody   375
9.3   Adding Rhythm to a Melody   376
9.4   Controlling the Volume   377
9.5   Creating Chords   378
9.6   Playing a Chord Progression   379
9.7   Writing Music with Traditional Chord Notation   380
9.8   Creating Percussion Grooves   384
9.9   Creating More Complex Percussion Grooves   386
9.10 Exporting MIDI files   389
9.11 Playing Functions As Sound   390

9.12   Adding Tremolo   392

9.13   Adding Vibrato   393

9.14   Applying an Envelope to a Signal   394

9.15   Exploring Alternate Tunings   397

9.16   Importing Digital Sound Files   403

9.17   Analyzing Digital Sound Files   405

9.18   Slicing a Sample   408

10. Algebra **413**

10.0   Introduction   413

10.1   Solving Algebraic Equations   414

10.2   Finding a Polynomial from a Given Root   415

10.3   Transforming Expressions to Other Forms   416

10.4   Generating Polynomials   419

10.5   Decomposing Polynomials into Their Constituent Parts   420

10.6   Dividing Polynomials by Other Polynomials   422

11. Calculus: Continuous and Discrete **425**

11.0   Introduction   425

11.1   Computing Limits   426

11.2   Working with Piecewise Functions   427

11.3   Using Power Series Representations   429

11.4   Differentiating Functions   431

11.5   Integration   435

11.6   Solving Differential Equations   438

11.7   Solving Minima and Maxima Problems   441

11.8   Solving Vector Calculus Problems   443

11.9   Solving Problems Involving Sums and Products   447

11.10 Solving Difference Equations   450

11.11 Generating Functions and Sequence Recognition   452

12. Statistics and Data Analysis **455**

12.0   Introduction   455

12.1   Computing Common Statistical Metrics of Numerical
       and Symbolic Data   456

12.2   Generating Pseudorandom Numbers with a Given Distribution   459

12.3   Working with Probability Distributions   461

12.4   Demonstrating the Central Limit Theorem   464

12.5 Computing Covariance and Correlation of Vectors
and Matrices 466

12.6 Measuring the Shape of Data 468

12.7 Finding and Adjusting for Outliers 471

12.8 Fitting Data Using a Linear Model 472

12.9 Fitting Data Using a Nonlinear Model 475

12.10 Creating Interpolation Functions from Data 477

12.11 Testing for Statistically Significant Difference Between
Groups Using ANOVA 479

12.12 Hypothesis Testing with Categorical Data 483

12.13 Grouping Data into Clusters 486

12.14 Creating Common Statistical Plots 492

12.15 Quasi-Random Number Generation 496

12.16 Creating Stochastic Simulations 499

13. Science and Engineering **505**

13.0 Introduction 505

13.1 Working with Element Data 507

13.2 Working with Chemical Data 510

13.3 Working with Particle Data 513

13.4 Working with Genetic Data and Protein Data 516

13.5 Modeling Predator-Prey Dynamics 519

13.6 Solving Basic Rigid Bodies Problems 522

13.7 Solving Problems in Kinematics 524

13.8 Computing Normal Modes for Coupled Mass Problems 530

13.9 Modeling a Vibrating String 533

13.10 Modeling Electrical Circuits 537

13.11 Modeling Truss Structures Using the Finite Element Method 539

14. Financial Engineering **549**

14.0 Introduction 549

14.1 Leveraging Mathematica's Bundled Financial Data 552

14.2 Importing Financial Data from Websites 557

14.3 Present Value of Future Cash Flows 559

14.4 Interest Rate Sensitivity of Bonds 561

14.5 Constructing and Manipulating Yield Curves 563

14.6   Black-Scholes for European Option Pricing   565

14.7   Computing the Implied Volatility of Financial Derivatives   573

14.8   Speeding Up NDSolve When Solving Black-Scholes and Other PDEs   574

14.9   Developing an Explicit Finite Difference Method for the Black-Scholes Formula   578

14.10   Compiling an Implementation of Explicit Trinomial for Fast Pricing of American Options   583

14.11   Modeling the Value-at-Risk of a Portfolio Using Monte Carlo and Other Methods   585

14.12   Visualizing Trees for Interest-Rate Sensitive Instruments   587

15. Interactivity **593**

15.0   Introduction   593

15.1   Manipulating a Variable   594

15.2   Manipulating a Symbolic Expression   598

15.3   Manipulating a Plot   600

15.4   Creating Expressions for Which Value Dynamically Updates   604

15.5   Intercepting the Values of a Control Attached to a Dynamic Expression   607

15.6   Controlling Updates of Dynamic Values   609

15.7   Using DynamicModule As a Scoping Construct in Interactive Notebooks   611

15.8   Using Scratch Variables with DynamicModule to Balance Speed Versus Space   613

15.9   Making a Manipulate Self-Contained   615

15.10   Remembering the Values Found Using Manipulate   618

15.11   Improving Performance of Manipulate by Segregating Fast and Slow Operations   619

15.12   Localizing a Function in a Manipulate   622

15.13   Sharing DynamicModule Variables across Cell or Window Boundaries   624

15.14   Creating Your Own Custom Controls   625

15.15   Animating an Expression   627

15.16   Creating Custom Interfaces   630

15.17   Managing a Large Number of Controls in Limited Screen Real Estate   633

16. Parallel Mathematica 641

   16.0 Introduction   641

   16.1 Configuring Local Kernels   643

   16.2 Configuring Remote Services Kernels   646

   16.3 Sending a Command to Multiple Kernels for Parallel Evaluation   648

   16.4 Automatically Parallelizing Existing Serial Expressions   651

   16.5 Distributing Data Segments in Parallel and Combining
the Results   653

   16.6 Implementing Data-Parallel Algorithms by Using ParallelMap   654

   16.7 Decomposing a Problem into Parallel Data Sets   656

   16.8 Choosing an Appropriate Distribution Method   658

   16.9 Running Different Algorithms in Parallel and Accepting
the First to Complete   661

   16.10 Sharing Data Between Parallel Kernels   662

   16.11 Preventing Race Conditions When Multiple Kernels
Access a Shared Resource   663

   16.12 Organizing Parallel Processing Operations Using
a Pipeline Approach   665

   16.13 Processing a Massive Number of Files Using
the Map-Reduce Technique   669

   16.14 Diagnosing Parallel Processing Performance   678

   16.15 Measuring the Overhead of Parallelization
in Your Environment   686

17. Interfacing Mathematica 689

   17.0 Introduction   689

   17.1 Calling External Command Line Programs from Mathematica   690

   17.2 Launching Windows Programs from Mathematica   691

   17.3 Connecting the Frontend to a Remote Kernel   692

   17.4 Using Mathematica with C and C++   694

   17.5 Using Mathematica with Java   700

   17.6 Using Mathematica to Interact with Microsoft's
.NET Framework   707

   17.7 Using the Mathematica Kernelfrom a .NET Application   709

   17.8 Querying a Database   711

   17.9 Updating a Database   714

   17.10 Introspection of Databases   715

18.   Tricks of the Trade **719**

    18.0 Introduction   719

    18.1 Cleaning Up During Incremental Development   720

    18.2 Modifying Built-in Functions and Constants   721

    18.3 Locating Undocumented Functions   723

    18.4 Packaging Your Mathematica Solutions into Libraries
for Others to Use   725

    18.5 Compiling Functions to Improve Performance   727

    18.6 Automating and Standardizing the Appearance
of Notebooks Using Stylesheets   728

    18.7 Transforming Notebooks into Other Forms   733

    18.8 Calling into the Mathematica Frontend   736

    18.9 Initializing and Cleaning Up Automatically   737

    18.10 Customizing Frontend User Interaction   739

19.   Debugging and Testing **741**

    19.0 Introduction   741

    19.1 Printing as the First Recourse to Debugging   743

    19.2 Debugging Functions Called Many Times   746

    19.3 Stack Tracing to Debug Recursive Functions   747

    19.4 Taming Trace to Extract Useful Debugging Information   749

    19.5 Creating a Poor Man's Mathematica Debugger   753

    19.6 Debugging Built-In Functions with Evaluation
and Step Monitors   756

    19.7 Visual Debugging with Wolfram Workbench   758

    19.8 Writing Unit Tests to Help Ensure Correctness of Your Code   762

    19.9 Creating MUnit Tests Where Success Is Not Based
on Equality Testing   765

    19.10 Organizing and Controlling MUnit Tests and Test Suites   767

    19.11 Integrating Wolfram Workbench's MUnit Package
into the Frontend   769

Index. **777**

Preface

Introduction

If you were stranded on a desert island with only your laptop (and presumably a large solar panel), what software would you want to have with you? For me the answer definitely includes the latest version of Wolfram Mathematica. Whether you are a scientist, engineer, or mathematician, a Wall Street quant, a statistician or programmer, or even an artist or musician, you will be a better one if you have this tool at your disposal. Of course, having a tool and knowing how to use it well are quite different things. That is why I wrote the *Mathematica Cookbook*.

I am a big fan of O'Reilly cookbooks, as these books are designed to help you solve real-world problems. Mathematica is an ideal candidate for a cookbook because it is so vast, deep, and full of traps for the novice. I was ecstatic to learn that O'Reilly was looking to publish a Mathematica cookbook and even more excited when I was chosen to be its author. I have been a user of Mathematica since version 3.0. Although that was over 13 years ago, I still remember the frustration of trying to solve problems in this system. I don't mean this in a derogatory way. The frustration a newbie experiences when trying to learn Mathematica comes from the knowledge that you are sitting in front of a highly advanced computational platform that eventually will magnify your productivity tenfold—if you can only wrap your mind around its unfamiliar idioms. If you are a new (or even not-so-new) user of Mathematica today, you are simultaneously in a better and a much worse position than I was with version 3.0. You are in a better position because Mathematica 7.0 is vastly more powerful than 3.0 was back then. Not only has the number of available functions doubled, but Mathematica has fundamental new capabilities including dynamic interactivity, curated data sources, parallel processing, image processing, and much more. You are in a worse position because there is much more to learn!

As Mathematica grows, it remains largely unchanged in its core principles. This book is designed to help you master those core principles by presenting Mathematica in the context of real-world problems. However, my goal is not just to show you how to solve problems in Mathematica, but to show you how to do so in a way that plays to Mathematica's strengths. This means there is an emphasis on symbolic, functional, and pattern-based styles of programming. Mathematica is a multi-paradigm programming language; you can easily write code in it that a Fortran or C programmer would have little trouble following. However, the procedural style that this entails is not likely to give you good performance. More importantly, it will often cause you to write more code than necessary and spend more time adapting that code to future problems. Stephen Wolfram has said that a correct Mathematica program is often a short Mathematica program. There is much truth to this. The truth comes from the idea that good Mathematica programs leverage the capabilities of the vast built-in library of both general-purpose and highly specialized functions. Programming in Mathematica is a search for the right combination of primitives. My hope is that this cookbook will play a role as your guide.

MathematicaCookbook.com

One risk of authoring a cookbook is that it is almost inevitable that something someone finds important will be left out. With Mathematica, this risk is a certainty because even as I wrote the book, Mathematica's capabilities grew. However, even if you drew a line at, say, version 6.0, you would find that there are still many topics that I do not cover in the book, for various reasons. To remedy this and to create a living resource that I hope the Mathematica community will help nourish, I am launching *http://mathematicacookbook.com*. Here you will find recipes that did not make it into this book, and more importantly, you will be able rate recipes, contribute your own, or provide alternative implementations to those found in the book or on the site.

Structure of This Book

The *Mathematica Cookbook* is not necessarily meant to be read from start to finish like a conventional book (although you are certainly welcome to do so!). Having said that, the chapters are organized in a purposeful way. Chapters 1 through 8 present general techniques that all users of Mathematica should know. These chapters are largely self-contained, but sometimes it is necessary to use features in one chapter that are covered more deeply in another. Cross-references within each recipe should prevent you from getting stuck. However, keep in mind that a cookbook is not the same as a tutorial, and you should also make frequent use of the Mathematica reference, tutorials, and guides that are integrated into Mathematica's help system. Chapters 9 through 14 cover specific domains of Mathematica application. If you are the type of person who learns best by examples from your area of expertise, you will benefit from seeing the techniques of the first chapters leveraged in problems related to physics, engineering, calculus, statistics, music, finance, and more. Finally, Chapters 15 through 19 cover important techniques, extensions, and tools that make Mathematica unrivaled as a technical software development tool.

Chapter 1 covers numerics. For the most part, Mathematica simply does the right thing when computing numeric results, as you would expect. In pure mathematics, numbers are formal objects that are well behaved, but when you represent numbers in a finite discrete device like a computer, often you will need to understand issues of precision and accuracy in order to get reasonable results on certain classes of problems. Further, numbers have different representations in Mathematica (Integers, Rationals, Complex, and some exotic types like Intervals). Then there is an issue of input and presentation: Mathematica supports different base representations and different display formats. This chapter has recipes that cover all these issues, and it is wise to have some familiarity with them before using any of the numeric algorithms.

Functional programming is a style of Mathematica development that most seasoned users prefer. Chapter 2 dives deeply into functional programming, Mathematica style. Because Mathematica was designed to support multiple development paradigms, its functional programming abilities are not as pure as languages like Haskell. This is actually a big plus, because if you are using Mathematica chances are you are solving a problem, and it's the solution rather than the aesthetics that is foremost in your mind. Mathematica programmers prefer the functional style because it leads to efficient programs. It also leads to elegant programs. In the context of programming, elegant means the combination of brevity, power, and clarity. There is an amazing sense of intellectual satisfaction that comes from finding a concise functional solution, and this feeling creates the positive feedback that will draw you into Mathematica. However, this style is often mysterious to people who come to Mathematica from other languages like Fortran, C, Mathlab, or Microsoft Excel. I think this chapter will help you discover the rewards of the functional style.

Chapter 3 presents Mathematica data structures, which are largely built on the foundation of lists. From lists, Mathematica derives matrices and higher order tensors, sparse matrices, and more. Knowing how to manipulate these structures is essential for almost any application of Mathematica. This is obvious if you are doing linear algebra, but list processing is integral to almost every facet of use. This chapter also shows how to implement other types of data structures, such as a dictionary that leverages the fast associative look-up that is part of Mathematica's evaluation engine.

Pattern-based programming revolves around pattern matching and transformation. Chapter 4 introduces Mathematica's rich pattern-based techniques. Patterns are not a feature of most mainstream languages, but they are tremendously powerful and essential if you hope to accomplish anything nontrivial in Mathematica. Of all the techniques at your disposal, pattern matching and replacement is the one most likely to yield the "wow" reaction you get when you see a seemingly simple looking piece of code do something not so simple. To whet your appetite, here is one of my favorites.

```
In[190]:=  runEncode[l_List] := Map[{#, 1} & , l] //.
                {head___, {x_, n_}, {x_, m_}, tail___} :> {head, {x, n + m}, tail}
```

In this little ditty by Frank Zizza (which won a programming contest at the 1990 Wolfram conference), the goal is to take a list and return the list in run length encoded form. Don't worry if this code seems cryptic; it won't after you have recipes from Chapters 2 and 4 under your belt. For example, input {1, 1, 2, 2, 2, 1, 3, 3, 3, 3} should produce {{1, 2}, {2, 3}, {1, 1}, {3, 4}}.

```
In[191]:=  runEncode[{1, 1, 2, 2, 2, 1, 3, 3, 3, 3}]
Out[191]=  {{1, 2}, {2, 3}, {1, 1}, {3, 4}}
```

Although you can create small solutions to this problem in languages like Python or Ruby, I find this solution compelling because it contains no explicit looping construct and, once you learn to read it, contains a very explicit statement of the problem.

Chapter 5 covers string manipulation, which is more important than you might think for a language that is primarily associated with numeric and symbolic mathematics. Mathematica has a rich set of string manipulation primitives that include all the typical functions you expect (StringLength, StringReplace, StringInsert, and so forth), plus an extension of its pattern language specifically designed for strings and including regular expression-based transformations.

The next two chapters explore one of Mathematica's best capabilities, integrated graphics. Chapter 6 dives into two-dimensional plots and graphics. There are many packages that let you create plots, but few are so seamlessly integrated into the same development environment where you write code. This integration is an amazing productivity tool. I frequently find myself using Plot and other graphing functions simply as a means to help me understand an equation or algorithm I am developing and not necessarily because I am creating a presentation to be viewed by others. The fact that functions like Plot, ListPlot, and ParametricPlot give good results with little effort means they can become part of your day-to-day interaction with Mathematica. But if you need professionally designed graphics for an important paper or presentation, you will not be disappointed, because there are options to customize every aspect of the presentation.

Chapter 7 builds on the preceding chapter by moving into the more sexy domain of 3D graphics and plots. Plotting in 3D provides you with additional visualization and interaction capabilities. All 3D graphics can be rotated, panned, and zoomed interactively. There are also many sophisticated options that let you adjust every aspect of the plot, including shading, mesh, coloring, camera angles, how light reflects off the surface, and so on. Not every user will want to tweak all of these settings, but if you are a graphic artist or aficionado you will have a lot of fun once you master all the options. This chapter will give you a leg up on this important dimension of Mathematica's power.

Chapter 8, the first of the special-purpose chapters, covers image processing. Native image processing functions were added in Mathematica 7.0, and you can have quite a bit of fun transforming images programmatically as you do by hand with software such as Photoshop. This chapter also shows some advanced image-processing techniques for which I wrote a large part of the algorithms in Mathematica rather than relying on the built-in functions. This provides readers who are interested in image processing with a guide to approaching image algorithm development in Mathematica, and also provides some deeper insight for those who know little about these algorithms

Chapter 9 will give you respite from all the eye-candy by providing some ear-candy. You may not know it, but Mathematica is quite the musician, and I was happy to have John Kiehl, a professional musician and recording studio owner, write this chapter for you. Mathematica can turn functions into sound to play notes, chords, and electronic versions of a variety of musical instruments. Further, it can import MIDI files and other audio formats. You can even perform various operations on sound such as Fourier transforms. There really are few limits, and John is an experienced guide who provides lots of recipes for the musically inclined to expand upon and the not-so-musically inclined to educate themselves with (or just play with for fun). This chapter is available for your immediate listening pleasure at *http://www.oreilly.com/catalog/9780596521004*.

Chapter 10 returns to more mathematical fare by exploring Mathematica's formidable abilities in symbolic math. This chapter focuses on algebraic manipulation and solutions to equations. Many of the recipes show techniques for massaging results produced by Mathematica into equivalent but sometimes more desirable forms.

Symbolic and numerical calculus is what most people think about when they think about Mathematica, and Chapter 11 dives into Mathematica's formidable (many say unrivaled) capabilities in this domain. Here you will see recipes related to computing limits, derivatives, integrals, vector calculus, and the solutions to differential equations. The chapter also covers the increasingly important domain of discrete calculus, including sums, products, and difference equations.

There is high probability that the average technical person will need to do some statistics! Puns aside, Chapter 12 has recipes that will help you get a handle on Mathematica's formidable statistical capabilities, which rival those of specialized stats packages. This chapter has recipes for common statistical measures, probability distributions, data fitting, interpolation, and more sophisticated tools like ANOVA. It also introduces stochastic simulation.

Chapter 13 enters the realm of applied math by showcasing physics and engineering. These domains are extremely broad, so rather than attempting to cover a large swath, I cherry pick recipes that show applications of the mathematical tools discussed in preceding chapters. I also include recipes that demonstrate general techniques for organizing programs that have many variables. In addition, this chapter shows how educators and others can draw on Mathematica's access to curated data related to physics, chemistry, and biology.

Chapter 14 jumps bravely into the risky business of numerical finance. The goal of this chapter is to show quants and others interested in mathematical finance how to leverage Mathematica's strengths in applying common financial algorithms. This chapter presents problems of mild to moderate sophistication so that the illustration of Mathematica techniques is not lost in the complexity of modern computational finance. A large part of this chapter is the result of the efforts of Andreas Lauschke, who is expert in both computational finance and Mathematica.

Version 6.0 brought new excitement to the Mathematica world with the addition of dynamic interactivity. For the first time a Mathematica user had the capability to create notebook output that changed in response to changes in underlying variables. In many ways this ability parallels the new types of dynamic web pages that emerged around the same time (so-called Web 2.0)—but I digress. Chapter 15 introduces the primitives underlying this new dynamic interactivity. Amazingly, there are just three main ingredients to this capability: `Manipulate`, `Dynamic` and `DynamicModule`. As with many of Mathematica's advanced features, you will master the easy use cases immediately, because the primitives just do the right thing. More advanced application will require some steep learning, but this chapter has many recipes that will help you get there. For your immediate gratification, this chapter is available at *http://www.oreilly.com/catalog/9780596521004*.

Computers with multiple cores (processing elements) are commonplace; there is a good chance you own a computer with at least two cores, and if you bought one recently, perhaps even four or more. My Mac Pro has eight. Mathematica stays ahead of this trend by bundling Parallel Processing with version 7.0. Chapter 16 contains recipes that show you how to use these features. Mathematica makes it easy to add parallelism to your programs, but this does not mean your algorithms will run four times faster if you have four processors. To get any speed increase at all, you need to understand how the parallel primitives work and how they can be tuned. The recipes in this chapter show you how to configure parallelism, parallelize existing serial programs, and also implement more sophisticated parallel techniques like Map-Reduce and parallel pipelines.

As powerful as Mathematica is, there are times when you need something else. Chapter 17 will show you how to interface Mathematica with other languages and programs. Here, programmers will learn how to integrate code written in C, Java, and .NET languages. This chapter also has recipes for integrating Mathematica with database systems and third-party tools like spreadsheets.

Chapter 18, "Tricks of the Trade," includes material that every Mathematica user should know but that did not quite fit anywhere else in the book. Here I introduce recipes on performance, packaging, stylesheets, and other important techniques.

Last but by no means least, you will want to know how to debug your way out of those nasty situations where you just can't figure out why you are getting strange error messages or bizarre results. Chapter 19 presents debugging techniques and, possibly more important, unit testing techniques. An important part of this chapter is Wolfram Workbench, the alternative development environment based on Eclipse (an open source IDE designed to be customizable to different languages).

Acknowledgments

The *Mathematica Cookbook* was one of my most challenging projects and it is not something I could have accomplished without the support of many people. Although I would have never survived without this help, any problems, errors, or omissions in the final product are mine alone.

First I must thank Maryka Baraka of Wolfram Research for turning me on to this project, arranging my first visit to Wolfram Research, and most importantly, for introducing me to many valuable people on the Wolfram staff. Over the course of this project, Maryka fielded dozens of queries and directed them to where they needed to go in the Wolfram organization. Her advice and support were invaluable. Maryka, you're the best!

Theo Gray of Wolfram answered many questions and provided much support, including a personal tutorial of some of the advanced features of Mathematica's Manipulate and Dynamic functionality. He was also instrumental in my visiting Wolfram so that I could preview Mathematica 7 before its release. This improved the book tremendously.

Many other Wolfram folks answered questions and provided valuable suggestions and support. So many, in fact, that I fear I may leave someone out. At the risk of that, I must personally acknowledge Larry Adelston, Chris Carlson, Joy Costa, Lou D'Andria, John Fultz, Roger Germundsson, Bradley Harden, Jason Harris, Tom Wickham Jones, Andre Kuzniarek, Misty Moseley, Peter Overmann, Schoeller Porter, Michael Trot, and Eric W. Weisstein. Also, thanks to Stephen Wolfram for creating and nurturing Mathematica for all these years.

Working with O'Reilly for the second time has proved to be just as rewarding as the first. First and foremost, a big thank you to my editor, Michael Loukides, whose support and patience were without bound (even when I whined about this and that as we nitpicking authors so often do!). Michael provided great perspective as he read and commented on each chapter, and he helped me to understand many points that were awkward or would trip up a beginner. In addition, Abby Fox, Keith Fahlgren, and Adam Witwer provided valuable help in the early stages of production. Also thanks to Simon St. Laurent, the editor of my first cookbook, for his glowing recommendation.

Instrumental to improving the quality of many recipes were the technical critique and corrections from Larry Stead, Gregory Frascadore, and Andreas Lauschke. Not only did these reviewers correct mistakes, they also offered better implementations for several recipes. Again, remaining defects or inadequacies are the fault of the author alone.

Portions of this book would simply not exist without generous contributions from Thomas Weber (Weber and Partner), Chris Carlson (Wolfram), and Ulises Cervantes-Pimentel (Wolfram). Special thanks to John Kiehl (Soundtrack Studios), whose unique combination of musical and Mathematica abilities resulted in the entertaining and educational music and audio processing chapter. Special thanks also to Andreas Lauschke (Andreas Lauschke Consulting) for much of the material in the financial engineering chapter.

I must also thank Kirsten Dennison and her staff at Precision Graphics for arriving to solve the final production issues and seeing this book into print. Also, thanks again to Larry Adelston of Wolfram for assisting Kirsten's team with stylesheet production and other automation.

Thanks also to my colleagues who offered both moral and technical support during this project. In particular I would like to thank Doug Finke, whose conversations are always uplifting, and Kalani Thielen, who always seems to know what I need every time I ask.

Although the folks above were crucial, the most important ingredients that went into this cookbook were the love, patience, and support of my family. In particular, thanks to my wonderful wife Wanda, for enduring a second book project that never seemed to be coming to an end, and for all the things small and large that she did for me and our family when I was busy working on it. She deserves more than I can ever put into words. Also to my two boys, Leonardo and Salvatore, who had to give up quite a bit of our personal play time so I could get this beast out the door. This book is dedicated to you guys. Thanks also to my parents, family, and friends who provided so much support throughout my life and who cheered me on and lifted my spirits.

Conventions Used in This Book

The following typographical conventions are used in this book :

Italic

> Indicates new terms, URLs, email addresses, filenames, and file extensions.

`Constant width`

> Used for program listings, as well as within paragraphs to refer to program elements such as variable or function names, databases, data types, environment variables, statements, and keywords.

`Constant width bold`

> Shows commands or other text that should be typed literally by the user.

`Constant width italic`

> Shows text that should be replaced with user-supplied values or by values determined by context.

 This icon signifies a tip, suggestion, or general note.

 This icon indicates a warning or caution.

Using Code Examples

This book is here to help you get your job done. In general, you may use the code in this book in your programs and documentation. You do not need to contact us for permission unless you're reproducing a significant portion of the code. For example, writing a program that uses several chunks of code from this book does not require permission. Selling or distributing a CD-ROM of examples from O'Reilly books does not require permission. Answering a question by citing this book and quoting example code does not require permission. Incorporating a significant amount of example code from this book into your product's documentation does require permission.

We appreciate, but do not require, attribution. An attribution usually includes the title, author, publisher, and ISBN. For example: "*Mathematica Cookbook* by Salvatore Mangano. Copyright 2010 O'Reilly Media, Inc., 978-0-596-52099-1."

If you feel your use of code examples falls outside fair use or the permission given above, feel free to contact us at permissions@oreilly.com.

Safari® Enabled

Safari Books Online is an on-demand digital library that lets you easily search over 7,500 technology and creative reference books and videos to find the answers you need quickly.

With a subscription, you can read any page and watch any video from our library online. Read books on your cell phone and mobile devices. Access new titles before they are available for print, and get exclusive access to manuscripts in development and post feedback for the authors. Copy and paste code samples, organize your favorites, download chapters, bookmark key sections, create notes, print out pages, and benefit from tons of other time-saving features.

O'Reilly Media has uploaded this book to the Safari Books Online service. To have full digital access to this book and others on similar topics from O'Reilly and other publishers, sign up for free at *http://my.safaribooksonline.com*.

How to Contact Us

Please address comments and questions concerning this book to the publisher:

O'Reilly Media, Inc.
1005 Gravenstein Highway North
North Sebastopol, CA 95472
800-998-9938 (in the United States or Canada)
707-829-0515 (international or local)
707 829-0104 (fax)

We have a web page for this book, where we list errata, examples, and any additional information. You can access this page at:

http://www.oreilly.com/catalog/9780596521004

To comment or ask technical questions about this book, send email to:

bookquestions@oreilly.com

For more information about our books, conferences, Resource Centers, and the O'Reilly Network, see our web site at:

http://www.oreilly.com

CHAPTER 1

Numerics

Jenny I've got your number
I need to make you mine
Jenny don't change your number
Eight six seven five three oh nine
Eight six seven five three oh nine
Eight six seven five three oh nine
Eight six seven five three oh nine

Tommy Tutone, "867-5309/Jenny"

1.0 Introduction

Numerical Types

Mathematics is a huge, almost all-encompassing subject, and the average layperson often fails to appreciate the types of exotic objects that are in the mathematician's domain. Yet every person on the street perceives math is about numbers. So even though numbers only scratch the surface of math and Mathematica, it makes sense to begin with their representation.

Mathematica supports four numerical types: Integer, Rational, Real, and Complex. In the following examples we use Mathematica's comment notation (*comment*).

```
1        (*The integer one*)
1 / 2    (*The rational one half*)
1.2 ^ 8  (*The real 1.2 x 10^8*)
3 + 2 I  (*The complex number 3+2i*)
```

There is no need to take my word that these expressions have the specified types. You can ask Mathematica to tell you using the function **Head[ ]**, which returns the head of an expression (i.e., head of a list).

```
In[2]:=  Head[1]
Out[2]=  Integer
```

```
In[3]:=  Head[1 / 2]
Out[3]=  Rational

In[4]:=  Head[1.2 ^ 8]
Out[4]=  Real

In[5]:=  Head[3 + 2 I]
Out[5]=  Complex
```

Although Mathematica does not internally store numbers as lists, it provides the illusion that a number has a head indicating its type. This is consistent with the fact that everything in Mathematica is an expression and every expression must have a head. It is also common for Mathematica to use the head to indicate type when constructing more complex objects. See Recipe 1.5, for example. If you are confused by this, for now, just think of Head as returning a type name when presented with an *atomic expression* (expressions that can't be divided into subexpressions).

Exact and Approximate Results

Mathematica is unique in comparison to most mathematical tools and programming languages in that it will usually produce exact results unless you tell it otherwise. The following examples show the difference between exact and approximate results. Recipes 1.1 and 1.2 show you how to make Mathematica use the appropriate form.

Exact results are displayed in their entirety when possible or symbolically when full display would be impossible due to the infinity of the exact representation.

```
In[6]:=  3 ^ 1000
Out[6]=  1 322 070 819 480 806 636 890 455 259 752 144 365 965 422 032 752 148 167 664 920 368 226 ⁖
         828 597 346 704 899 540 778 313 850 608 061 963 909 777 696 872 582 355 950 954 582 100 ⁖
         618 911 865 342 725 257 953 674 027 620 225 198 320 803 878 014 774 228 964 841 274 390 ⁖
         400 117 588 618 041 128 947 815 623 094 438 061 566 173 054 086 674 490 506 178 125 480 ⁖
         344 405 547 054 397 038 895 817 465 368 254 916 136 220 830 268 563 778 582 290 228 416 ⁖
         398 307 887 896 918 556 404 084 898 937 609 373 242 171 846 359 938 695 516 765 018 940 ⁖
         588 109 060 426 089 671 438 864 102 814 350 385 648 747 165 832 010 614 366 132 173 102 ⁖
         768 902 855 220 001

In[7]:=  Sqrt[2]
Out[7]=  √2
```

Approximate numeric results are represented in machine precision floating point by default. On most modern computers, this means *double-precision* floating-point numbers, which contain a total of 64 binary bits, typically yielding 16 decimal digits of mantissa. You can also specify numbers with greater than machine precision (see

Recipe 1.1) but there is a performance cost: Mathematica must switch from the native hardware-based floating-point algorithms to software-based ones.

```
In[8]:= 3. ^ 1000
Out[8]= 1.322070819480807 × 10^477

In[9]:= Sqrt[2.]
Out[9]= 1.41421
```

By adding a decimal point to a number, you force Mathematica to treat it as approximate. These approximate numbers will be machine precision by default, but there are several ways to force higher precision. Recipes 1.1 and 1.2 in this chapter will elaborate on these differences.

Numerical Expressions

The previous examples show simple numerical expressions. In practice, Mathematica follows general mathematical notation, but in many cases this means that there are multiple ways to express the same thing. Let's consider each of the common operations that arise in algebra. There are several ways to express multiplication, division, and other arithmetic operations. A single space between expressions (e.g., variables, numbers) implies multiplication, as is the typical convention among mathematicians. You can evaluate typeset mathematics using special symbols, such as ×. You can also use *Full Form* (e.g., Plus, Times, Divide), but for arithmetic this is unnecessarily verbose.

```
In[10]:= 9 + 8
Out[10]= 17

In[11]:= Plus[9, 8]
Out[11]= 17

In[12]:= 9 × 8
Out[12]= 72

In[13]:= a = 9; b = 8;
         a b
Out[14]= 72

In[15]:= Times[9, 8]
Out[15]= 72

In[16]:= 8 / 9
Out[16]= 8
         ─
         9
```

```
In[17]:=  8
          -
          9

Out[17]=  8
          -
          9

In[18]:=  Divide[8, 9]

Out[18]=  8
          -
          9
```

The various representations are known as "forms" in Mathematica (e.g., InputForm, OutputForm, TraditionalForm, etc.). Recipe 1.7 shows you how to control what form is used for output of results. Controlling what form is used for input is a function of using the various features of the Mathematica frontend (palettes, shortcut keys, etc.). This book will not discuss the use of the frontend, since its main focus is programming, and there are numerous other resources (the best being the integrated help system) for mastering the frontend.

Numerical Approximations

Mathematica is famous for its symbolic abilities; however, when it comes to numerical methods it is also no slouch! The core functions for numerical solutions are NSum, NProduct, NSolve, NIntegrate, and NDSolve. These are covered in Chapters 10 and 12.

1.1 Controlling Precision and Accuracy

Problem

You want numerical results that are to a specified numerical precision and accuracy.

Solution

Use N[] to convert from exact to approximate form while controlling precision and accuracy to the desired amount.

```
In[19]:=  N[1 / 5]
Out[19]=  0.2
```

You can explicitly specify the precision as a second argument to N[ ].

```
In[20]:= N[1 / 17, 10]
Out[20]= 0.05882352941
```

You can also explicitly specify both the precision and accuracy, but this is less common. You might do this to guarantee a fixed number of decimal places independent of the size of the actual number.

```
In[21]:= N[{17, 1 / 17}, {Infinity, 10}]
Out[21]= {17.000000000, 0.0588235294}
```

To drive this point home, I ask you to consider the following. The first column uses fixed precision, whereas the second uses infinite precision and fixed accuracy.

```
In[22]:= Table[With [{x = 10^n + 1 / 17}, {N[x, 10], N[x, {Infinity, 10}]}],
              {n, 0, 5}] // TableForm
Out[22]//TableForm=
            1.058823529    1.058823529
            10.05882353    10.058823529
            100.0588235    100.058823529
            1000.058824    1000.058823529
            10000.05882    10000.0588235294
            100000.0588    100000.0588235294
```

Discussion

For most purposes, treat precision as the total number of digits in the decimal representation of a number and accuracy as the total number of digits after the decimal. As such, precision is a measure of relative uncertainty (given a precision p a larger number will have more uncertainty than a smaller number). Accuracy is an absolute measure of uncertainty because the number of places after the decimal is independent of the magnitude of the number. Typically you only need to control precision in most applications.

There are two common syntaxes for using N[ ]. You already saw the functional syntax in the solution section. The second uses Mathematica's postfix notation. See the sidebar "Mathematica Expressions" on page 6 for a discussion of postfix and other notations.

```
In[29]:= Sqrt[2] // N
Out[29]= 1.41421
```

Mathematica Expressions

Mathematica contains quite a bit of syntactic sugar that gives users the flexibility to enter expressions in a variety of ways. Developers of traditional languages (C+, Java, Ruby, etc.) are not typically used to this much flexibility. The flexibility stems partly from mathematics itself, which often provides many notations to express the same concepts. It also derives from Mathematica's aim to be a platform for publishing mathematical ideas as much as a computer-aided mathematics tool and programming language.

At this point in the book, I do not go over all possible ways Mathematica can display input and output. Rather, I introduce the reader to four basic syntaxes for Mathematica expressions. This was a point of confusion for me when I first learned Mathematica, so I believe it is best to attend to it now.

Functional notation
> This is the most common notation. When we use N[value,precision], we are using the functional notation for N.

Infix notation
> Infix notation is most common for operators such as +, -, *, etc. However, infix notation can be used for any function f by using the syntax ~f~.

Postfix notation
> Some operators, like ! for Factorial[], use postfix notation, but as we already saw with N, postfix notation can be generally applied for function f using //f.

Prefix notation
> Some operators, like - (unary Minus), use prefix notation, but there is also a general way to use prefix notation for any function f using the syntax f@.

Here are some examples using N. Notice that when you use prefix or postfix and need to supply an argument, you must use Mathematica's syntax for pure functions where # is used as a placeholder for the input and & is added as a postfix operator alias for Function[].

```
N[1 / 2, 10] (*Function*)
0.5000000000

1 / 2 ~N~ 10 (*Infix*)
0.5000000000

1 / 2 // N (*Postfix*)
0.5

1 / 2 // N[#, 10] & (*Postfix with argument*)
0.5000000000

N@1 / 2 (*Prefix*)
0.5

N[#, 10] &@1 / 2 (*Prefix with argument*)
0.5000000000
```

It is common to use this notation to force Mathematica to convert an exact or symbolic result to an approximate result as the last step in a computation. When you use postfix notation, you can explicitly specify the precision, but it is a bit awkward.

```
In[30]:=  Sqrt[2] // N[#, 10] &
Out[30]=  1.414213562
```

When you don't specify precision, Mathematica uses MachinePrecision, which is a built-in symbol that denotes the precision native to your computer's floating-point capabilities. The numerical value of MachinePrecision is stored in a variable $MachinePrecision.

```
In[31]:=  $MachinePrecision
Out[31]=  15.9546
```

There is another notation that is less common but you may come across it in Mathematica output. If a literal number is displayed with a trailing ` (backtick) followed optionally by a number, this indicates the number is either in machine precision or is in the precision specified by the number following the backtick.

```
In[32]:=  20` (*20 in machine precision*)
Out[32]=  20.
```

```
In[33]:=  20`20 (*20 with high precision of 20 digits*)
Out[33]=  20.000000000000000000
```

In a complex expression with a lot of high-precision numbers, you can avoid specifying each precision individually by using SetPrecision[].

```
In[34]:=  SetPrecision[20. + 1/3 * 12.3 / 37.8 + Pi, 20]
            (*All numbers will be set to a precision of 20.*)
Out[34]=  23.250058262055400604
```

 You may find it surprising that $MachinePrecision is not an integer. The reason stems from the formal definition of *precision*, which is derived from considering a number x and its uncertainty dx and using the expression - Log[10, dx/x]. Accuracy is defined as - Log[10, dx].

If you have an expression and need to know the precision or accuracy, you can use the following functions.

```
In[35]:=  Precision[2.]
Out[35]= MachinePrecision

In[36]:=  Precision[2`20]
Out[36]= 20.
```

Exact results have infinite precision.

```
In[37]:=  Precision[Sqrt[2]]
Out[37]= ∞

In[38]:=  Precision[Sqrt[2.]]
Out[38]= MachinePrecision

In[39]:=  Accuracy[2.]
Out[39]= 15.6536
```

You are not guaranteed the accuracy you specify if the precision is too small.

```
In[40]:=  Accuracy[N[30, {20, 20}]]
Out[40]= 18.5229
```

With enough precision, however, you will get accuracy.

```
In[41]:=  Accuracy[N[30, {30, 20}]]
Out[41]= 20.
```

And precision can even be specified as infinite!

```
In[42]:=  Accuracy[N[30, {Infinity, 20}]]
Out[42]= 20.
```

Mathematica also defines two internal variables: $MinPrecision, whose default value is minus infinity, and $MaxPrecision, whose default value is plus infinity.

```
In[43]:=  {$MinPrecision, $MaxPrecision}
Out[43]= {0, ∞}
```

You can control precision within a complex calculation (without using N[] on every intermediate result) by changing these values; however, you should only do so within a Block (a local context). For example, compare the difference between a calculation with automatic precision for intermediate results to the same calculation with fixed precision (obtained by making $MinPrecision == $MaxPrecision). Note that we must still start out the calculation with base values of at least

$MinPrecision, otherwise the value will revert to the lowest precision, as explained in Recipe 1.2.

```
In[44]:= SetPrecision[(1 + Exp[Sqrt[2] + Sqrt[3]]) / 2^25, 32]
Out[44]= 7.2267807426125846688404521114476 × 10⁻⁷
```

```
In[45]:= Block[{$MinPrecision = 32, $MaxPrecision = 32},
            SetPrecision[(1 + Exp[Sqrt[2] + Sqrt[3]]) / 2^25, 32]]
Out[45]= 7.2267807426125846688404521144759 × 10⁻⁷
```

However, unless you have a very specific reason to control precision yourself, it is generally best to let Mathematica automatically handle this for you.

See Also

The Wolfram documentation for N[] is here: *http://bit.ly/XVe2E*.

Discussions of precision and accuracy can be found at *http://bit.ly/15qq2N* and *http://bit.ly/icrh1*.

The most thorough discussions of precision and accuracy in Mathematica can be found in Chapter 8 of *An Introduction to Programming with Mathematica* (Cambridge University Press) and *The Mathematica GuideBook for Numerics* (Springer).

A nice essay by David Goldberg called "What Every Computer Scientist Should Know About Floating-Point Arithmetic" can be found at *http://bit.ly/1EJ23y*.

1.2 Mixing Different Numerical Types

Problem

You need to predict what Mathematica will do with expressions containing mixed types and representations.

Solution

The general rule of thumb is that the least precise type will determine the type of the result.

Mixing exact values and symbols

When expressions containing exact numeric values (integers and rationals) are mixed with symbols, Mathematica will keep all results in the most general form, possibly reducing rationals to integers but leaving symbolic values in symbolic form.

```
In[46]:=  (2 Pi) /3 + Pi /3
Out[46]=  π
```

```
In[47]:=  Sqrt[Sin[2 Pi E] / 1/2 E^2]
```

$$Out[47]=\ e\ \sqrt{\frac{1}{2}-Sin[2\,e\,\pi]}$$

Mixing exact values and approximate values

When an approximate value is used in an otherwise symbolic expression, it forces
Mathematica to convert to approximate values.

```
In[48]:=  (2.0 Pi) /3 + Pi /3
Out[48]=  3.14159
```

```
In[49]:=  1. + (2 Pi) /3 + Pi /3
Out[49]=  4.14159
```

Mixing values of different precision and accuracy

When you mix values of different precision and accuracy, the lower precision and accuracy will determine the result. For multiplication, the precision of the result will
be exactly the minimum of the precision of each term, whereas the accuracy will be
somewhat less.

```
In[50]:=  x = N[Sqrt[2], 30] * N[Sqrt[3], 10]
Out[50]=  2.449489743
```

```
In[51]:=  Precision[x]
Out[51]=  10.
```

```
In[52]:=  Accuracy[x]
Out[52]=  9.61092
```

For addition, the accuracy of the result will be exactly the minimum of the accuracy
of each term; the precision will be somewhat more.

```
In[53]:=  x = N[Sqrt[5], {Infinity, 30}] + N[Sqrt[7], {Infinity, 10}]
Out[53]=  4.8818192886
```

```
In[54]:=  Precision[x]
Out[54]=  10.6886
```

```
In[55]:=  Accuracy[x]
Out[55]=  10.
```

Discussion

When mixing exact values with inexact values, it is possible to gain precision.

```
In[56]:= Precision[N[Sqrt[2], 20]]
Out[56]= 20.
```

```
In[57]:= Precision[2 + N[Sqrt[2], 20]]
Out[57]= 20.3828
```

The gain in precision will be greater when the magnitude of the exact number dominates that of the inexact number, as we see in this generated table.

```
In[2]:= TableForm[Table[
            {2^n + N[Sqrt[2], 20], Precision[2^n + N[Sqrt[2], 20]]}, {n, 0, 10}],
            TableHeadings -> {None, {"Result", "Precision"}}]
Out[2]//TableForm=
```

Result	Precision
2.4142135623730950488	20.2323
3.4142135623730950488	20.3828
5.4142135623730950488	20.583
9.4142135623730950488	20.8233
17.4142135623730950488	21.0904
33.4142135623730950488	21.3734
65.4142135623730950488	21.6652
129.4142135623730950488	21.9615
257.4142135623730950488	22.2601
513.4142135623730950488	22.56
1025.4142135623730950488	22.8604

See Also

The most thorough discussions of Mathematica's numerical rules can be found in Chapter 8 of *An Introduction to Programming with Mathematica* and *The Mathematica GuideBook for Numerics*.

1.3 Representing Numbers in Other Bases

Problem

Your application calls for a different numerical base than 10.

Solution

Mathematica uses notation of the form *base^^digits* to represent numbers in different bases. There must not be any internal whitespace in this representation.

```
In[59]:=  2^^101   (*Binary*)
Out[59]= 5
```

```
In[60]:=  16^^FFFF  (*Hexidecimal*)
Out[60]= 65535
```

Discussion

In addition to expressing numbers in other bases, you can convert numbers to other bases with BaseForm[*digits, base*]. The base must be an integer between 2 and 36 when using either ^^ or BaseForm[]. Mathematica uses the letters a through z to represent digits higher than 10.

```
In[61]:=  BaseForm[2^^1010101, 16]
Out[61]//BaseForm=
        55₁₆
```

If you do math in another base, the output will still default to decimal, but you can use BaseForm to convert the output of a function to hex.

```
In[62]:=  16^^A0 + 16^^0F // BaseForm[#, 16] &
Out[62]//BaseForm=
        af₁₆
```

```
In[63]:=  Hash["Hello, my name is Sal", "MD5"] // BaseForm[#, 16] &
Out[63]//BaseForm=
        a275144453239f0279228469f2296881₁₆
```

You can also convert real and complex numbers to other bases.

```
In[64]:=  123.777 // BaseForm[#, 16] &
Out[64]//BaseForm=
        7b.c6f₁₆
```

```
In[65]:=  12.1 + 67.2 I // BaseForm[#, 16] &
Out[65]//BaseForm=
        c.199a₁₆ + 43.333₁₆ i
```

See Also

Recipe 1.5 shows how to extract digits of a number in alternate bases.

1.4 Extracting the Digits of a Number

Problem

You want to extract the individual digits of a number to manipulate them individually.

Solution

The functions IntegerDigits[] and RealDigits[] make this task easy.

IntegerDigits[] returns a list of digits in base 10. See the "Discussion" section, next, for additional options.

```
In[66]:=  IntegerDigits[12 345]
Out[66]=  {1, 2, 3, 4, 5}
```

RealDigits[] returns a two-item list with the first item being the digits in base 10 and the second being the position of the decimal point. See the "Discussion" section for additional options. First consider the digits display with N[] alone.

```
In[67]:=  N[1 / 31]
Out[67]=  0.0322581
```

Notice how RealDigits[] automatically extracts more precision to return the number of digits necessary to get to the point at which they begin to repeat in the decimal expansion.

```
In[68]:=  RealDigits[N[1 / 31], 10]
Out[68]=  {{3, 2, 2, 5, 8, 0, 6, 4, 5, 1, 6, 1, 2, 9, 0, 3}, -1}
```

Discussion

Both RealDigits[] and IntegerDigits[] take the desired base and the number of desired digits (length) as optional second and third arguments, respectively.

```
In[69]:=  12 !
Out[69]=  479 001 600
```

```
In[70]:= IntegerDigits[12!, 10, 5]
Out[70]= {0, 1, 6, 0, 0}
```

```
In[71]:= 12! // BaseForm[#, 16] &   (*Consider 12! in base 16.*)
Out[71]//BaseForm=
            1c8cfc00₁₆
```

```
In[72]:= IntegerDigits[12!, 16]    (*Notice how IntegerDigits
            with base 16 gives the digit values in base 10.*)
Out[72]= {1, 12, 8, 12, 15, 12, 0, 0}
```

```
In[73]:= IntegerDigits[12!, 16] // BaseForm[#, 16] &
            (*But you can easily force them to base 16.*)
Out[73]//BaseForm=
            {1₁₆, c₁₆, 8₁₆, c₁₆, f₁₆, c₁₆, 0₁₆, 0₁₆}
```

RealDigits can take an additional fourth argument that specifies where in the decimal expansion to start. If b is the base, then the fourth argument n means to start the counting at the coefficient signified by $b\hat{\ }n$. The following examples should clarify.

```
In[74]:= N[Pi, 10]       (*Pi to 10 digits of precision.*)
Out[74]= 3.141592654
```

```
In[75]:= RealDigits[Pi, 10, 3]
            (*Extract first three digits. Decimal place is indicated as 1.*)
Out[75]= {{3, 1, 4}, 1}
```

Start at 10^-2 = 0.01, or the second digit after the decimal.

```
In[76]:= RealDigits[Pi, 10, 3, -2]
            (*Extract third to fifth digit. Decimal place is indicated as -2.*)
Out[76]= {{4, 1, 5}, -1}
```

Start at 10^-5 = 0.00001, or the fifth digit after the decimal.

```
In[77]:= RealDigits[Pi, 10, 3, -5]
Out[77]= {{9, 2, 6}, -4}
```

```
In[78]:= N[Pi, 10] // BaseForm[#, 2] &
Out[78]//BaseForm=
            11.0010010000111111011010101000100₂
```

Here we get the digits of pi in base 2.

```
In[79]:= RealDigits[Pi, 2, 5, -2]
Out[79]= {{0, 1, 0, 0, 1}, -1}
```

Here is an interesting application in which IntegerDigits is combined with the Tuples function and a bit of pattern matching to get all n digits without calling

IntegerDigits[] more than once. We used Short to elide the full list. (Short places <<n>> in the output to indicate *n* missing items.)

```
In[80]:= Tuples[IntegerDigits[43 210], 4] // Short[#, 4] &
Out[80]//Short=
        {{4, 4, 4, 4}, {4, 4, 4, 3}, {4, 4, 4, 2}, {4, 4, 4, 1}, {4, 4, 4, 0}, {4, 4, 3, 4},
         {4, 4, 3, 3}, {4, 4, 3, 2}, {4, 4, 3, 1}, {4, 4, 3, 0}, {4, 4, 2, 4},
         {4, 4, 2, 3}, {4, 4, 2, 2}, {4, 4, 2, 1}, {4, 4, 2, 0}, {4, 4, 1, 4},
         {4, 4, 1, 3}, {4, 4, 1, 2}, {4, 4, 1, 1}, {4, 4, 1, 0}, {4, 4, 0, 4},
         {4, 4, 0, 3}, {4, 4, 0, 2}, <<579>>, {0, 0, 4, 2}, {0, 0, 4, 1}, {0, 0, 4, 0},
         {0, 0, 3, 4}, {0, 0, 3, 3}, {0, 0, 3, 2}, {0, 0, 3, 1}, {0, 0, 3, 0},
         {0, 0, 2, 4}, {0, 0, 2, 3}, {0, 0, 2, 2}, {0, 0, 2, 1}, {0, 0, 2, 0},
         {0, 0, 1, 4}, {0, 0, 1, 3}, {0, 0, 1, 2}, {0, 0, 1, 1}, {0, 0, 1, 0},
         {0, 0, 0, 4}, {0, 0, 0, 3}, {0, 0, 0, 2}, {0, 0, 0, 1}, {0, 0, 0, 0}}
```

If you do not want the cases with leading zeros, you can use DeleteCases as follows.

```
In[81]:= DeleteCases[Tuples[IntegerDigits[43 210], 4],
           {z_ /; z == 0, n__}] // Short[#, 4] &
Out[81]//Short=
        {{4, 4, 4, 4}, {4, 4, 4, 3}, {4, 4, 4, 2}, {4, 4, 4, 1}, {4, 4, 4, 0}, {4, 4, 3, 4},
         {4, 4, 3, 3}, {4, 4, 3, 2}, {4, 4, 3, 1}, {4, 4, 3, 0}, {4, 4, 2, 4},
         {4, 4, 2, 3}, {4, 4, 2, 2}, {4, 4, 2, 1}, {4, 4, 2, 0}, {4, 4, 1, 4},
         {4, 4, 1, 3}, {4, 4, 1, 2}, {4, 4, 1, 1}, {4, 4, 1, 0}, {4, 4, 0, 4},
         {4, 4, 0, 3}, {4, 4, 0, 2}, <<454>>, {1, 0, 4, 2}, {1, 0, 4, 1}, {1, 0, 4, 0},
         {1, 0, 3, 4}, {1, 0, 3, 3}, {1, 0, 3, 2}, {1, 0, 3, 1}, {1, 0, 3, 0},
         {1, 0, 2, 4}, {1, 0, 2, 3}, {1, 0, 2, 2}, {1, 0, 2, 1}, {1, 0, 2, 0},
         {1, 0, 1, 4}, {1, 0, 1, 3}, {1, 0, 1, 2}, {1, 0, 1, 1}, {1, 0, 1, 0},
         {1, 0, 0, 4}, {1, 0, 0, 3}, {1, 0, 0, 2}, {1, 0, 0, 1}, {1, 0, 0, 0}}
```

The inverse of IntegerDigits[] is FromDigits[].

```
In[82]:= FromDigits[IntegerDigits[987 654 321]]
Out[82]= 987 654 321
```

```
In[83]:= FromDigits[IntegerDigits[987 654 321, 2], 2]   (*Base 2*)
Out[83]= 987 654 321
```

FromDigits[] has the added capability of converting strings and roman numerals.

```
In[84]:= FromDigits["4750"] + 1
Out[84]= 4751
```

```
In[85]:= FromDigits["MMXIX", "Roman"] - 10
Out[85]= 2009
```

`IntegerString[]` is used to convert back to string form. I use `InputForm` only so the quotes are displayed.

```
In[86]:= IntegerString[4750] // InputForm
Out[86]//InputForm=
         "4750"
```

```
In[87]:= IntegerString[2009, "Roman"] // InputForm
Out[87]//InputForm=
         "MMIX"
```

1.5 Working with Intervals

Problem

You need to compute with data subject to measurement errors and you need the greatest possible estimate on the final error.

Solution

As an alternative to doing math directly on numbers, Mathematica allows you to do math on *intervals* that define the uncertainty in a value.

```
In[88]:= Clear[error1, error2, mass, velocity, kineticEnergy];
         error1 = 0.01; error2 = 0.005;
         mass = Interval[{1.10 - error1, 1.10 + error1}];
         velocity = Interval[{7.50 - error2, 7.50 + error2}];
         kineticEnergy = 1/2 mass velocity ^ 2
Out[92]= Interval[{30.6154, 31.2604}]
```

By representing them as intervals, we express the idea that there are some known errors in the measurement of the value of mass and velocity. We would like to understand what that means in terms of the value we compute for kinetic energy.

You can see that the resulting error range is magnified by the combination of each error and the squaring.

```
In[93]:= Subtract @@ kineticEnergy[[1]] //
           Abs (*This computes the size of the interval.*)
Out[93]= 0.645
```

If there were only a single interval of uncertainty, the range would be smaller.

```
In[94]:= Clear[error1, mass, velocity, kineticEnergy];
         error1 = 0.01;
         mass = Interval[{1.10 - error1, 1.10 + error1}];
         velocity = 7.5;
         kineticEnergy = 1/2 mass velocity^2
Out[98]= Interval[{30.6562, 31.2188}]

In[99]:= Subtract @@ kineticEnergy[[1]] // Abs
Out[99]= 0.5625
```

Discussion

Intervals are objects with head Interval and a sequence of one or more lists that represent segments of the interval. Typically there is one list, but non-overlapping intervals can be expressed using two or more lists.

```
In[100]:= Interval[{1, 2}]
Out[100]= Interval[{1, 2}]

In[101]:= Interval[{1, 2}, {3, 4}]
Out[101]= Interval[{1, 2}, {3, 4}]
```

Intervals will automatically reorder themselves so that the least value is first.

```
In[102]:= Interval[{2, 1}]
Out[102]= Interval[{1, 2}]

In[103]:= Interval[{4, 3}, {2, 1}]
Out[103]= Interval[{1, 2}, {3, 4}]
```

Naturally, the standard mathematical operations for scalars work on intervals as well.

```
In[104]:= Interval[{1, 2}] + Interval[{3, 4}]
Out[104]= Interval[{4, 6}]

In[105]:= Interval[{1, 2}] Interval[{3, 4}] (*Implied multiplication*)
Out[105]= Interval[{3, 8}]

In[106]:= Interval[{1, 2}] / Interval[{3, 4}]
```

$$\text{Out[106]= Interval}\left[\left\{\frac{1}{4}, \frac{2}{3}\right\}\right]$$

```
In[107]:= Sqrt[Interval[{1.0, 2.0}]]
Out[107]= Interval[{1., 1.41421}]
```

There are also functions specifically for working with intervals. IntervalUnion[] gives the interval representing set of all points of the input intervals. IntervalIntersection[] gives the interval in common among the inputs and IntervalMemberQ[] tests if a value belongs to an interval.

There are some cases in which Mathematica functions can return intervals. Consider the problem of finding the limit of an oscillating function at a critical value.

```
In[108]:= Clear[x];
          Limit[Sin[x] + 1/2 Cos[x], x → Infinity]
```

$$\text{Out[109]= Interval}\left[\left\{-\frac{3}{2}, \frac{3}{2}\right\}\right]$$

```
In[110]:= Limit[2 Sin[1/x] + 1/2 Cos[x], x → 0]
```

$$\text{Out[110]= Interval}\left[\left\{-\frac{3}{2}, \frac{5}{2}\right\}\right]$$

See Also

Papers and FAQs (as well as a movie) related to the theory of interval math can be found at *http://bit.ly/lbXoE*.

1.6 Converting Between Numerical Types

Problem

You have a number of one type and need it represented in another type.

Solution

Conversion from rational to integer happens automatically, when possible.

```
In[111]:= Head[4/2]
Out[111]= Integer
```

Conversion of rational to integer can be forced by using Floor[], Ceiling[], and Round[]. (Numbers of the form $x.5$ are rounded toward the nearest even integer.)

```
In[112]:= Floor[5/2]
Out[112]= 2
```

```
In[113]:= Ceiling[5/2]
Out[113]= 3
```

```
In[114]:=  Round[5/2]
Out[114]=  2

In[115]:=  Round[7/2]
Out[115]=  4
```

We already saw in Recipe 1.1 how N[] can be used to convert exact values and symbolic constants to approximate real numbers. Rationalize[] is how you convert from approximate values to exact.

```
In[116]:=  Rationalize[3.14159]
                314159
Out[116]=  ──────
               100000
```

The single argument version of Rationalize will only succeed if a sufficiently close (see "Discussion" section, next) rational number exists.

```
In[117]:=  Rationalize[3.1415927]
Out[117]=  3.14159
```

You can provide a second argument specifying your tolerance for error, in which case the operation will always succeed.

```
In[118]:=  Rationalize[3.1415927, 10^-8]
                121033
Out[118]=  ──────
               38526
```

And you can force an exact rational by indicating a maximum error of zero.

```
In[119]:=  Rationalize[3.1415927, 0]
               31415927
Out[119]=  ────────
              10000000
```

Discussion

On the surface, the solutions here are rather simple. In day-to-day usage, numeric conversion will not present many challenges. However, there are subtle issues and interesting theory underlying the apparent simplicity. Let's consider rounding. Suppose you need to round a set of numbers, but the numbers still must satisfy some constraint after the rounding. Consider percentages or probabilities. One would want percentages to still add to 100 and probabilities to still sum to 1. Another context is in statistics, where we want to round while preserving certain statistical properties, such as the variance. Various forms of stochastic rounding can be used in these cases. One form of stochastic rounding that gives good results is the *unbiased rounding rule*. According to this rule, a number of the form $x.v$ is rounded up with the probability $v/10$ and rounded down with probability $(10-v)/10$. So, for example, 10.5 would have equal probability of going to 10 as to 11, whereas 10.85 would have probability of 0.85 of rounding up and 0.15 of rounding down.

```
In[120]:= UnbiasedRound[x_] := Block[{whole = Floor[x], v},
            v = 10 * (x - whole); whole + Floor[v / 10 + RandomReal[]]]

In[121]:= Table[UnbiasedRound[10.5], {20}]
Out[121]= {11, 11, 10, 11, 10, 10, 10, 11, 11, 11, 10, 11, 11, 10, 10, 11, 11, 11, 11, 11}

In[122]:= Table[UnbiasedRound[10.1], {20}]
Out[122]= {10, 10, 10, 10, 10, 10, 10, 10, 10, 10, 10, 11, 10, 10, 10, 10, 11, 10, 10, 10}

In[123]:= Table[UnbiasedRound[10.8], {20}]
Out[123]= {11, 11, 11, 10, 11, 11, 11, 11, 11, 10, 11, 10, 11, 11, 10, 11, 11, 11, 11, 11}
```

The main disadvantage of stochastic rounding is that the results are not repeatable.

See Also

An Examination of the Effects of Rounding on the Quality and Confidentiality of Tabular Data by Lawrence H. Cox and Jay J. Kim (*http://bit.ly/I7JdA*).

1.7 Displaying Numbers in Alternate Forms

Problem

You don't like the format that Mathematica chooses to display a particular numerical result.

Solution

Use one of the alternative forms: AccountingForm, EngineeringForm, NumberForm, PaddedForm, and ScientificForm. The default form is usually the most compact way to represent the number, but if you are outputting values that have specific user expectations or if you are trying to convey a specific accuracy, you may want to force a different form.

```
In[124]:= number = 3.50 * 1000000
Out[124]= 3.5 × 10^6
```

Accounting form does not use scientific notation and shows negative numbers in parentheses. Here it is traditional to use the form as a postfix (//) operation.

```
In[125]:=  number // AccountingForm
Out[125]//AccountingForm=
        3500000.
```

```
In[126]:=  -number // AccountingForm
Out[126]//AccountingForm=
        (3500000.)
```

Alternatively, NumberForm allows you to control the digits of precision and the number of digits after the decimal.

```
In[127]:=  NumberForm[number, {6, 4}]
Out[127]//NumberForm=
        3.5000 × 10^6
```

Discussion

Forms have an extensive set of options to provide fine-grained control over the output. Here I use AccountingForm to display a column of numbers. DigitBlock specifies the grouping factor and NumberPadding allows control of the characters used to pad out the display on the left (shown here as spaces) and right (shown as zeros).

```
In[128]:=  AccountingForm[Column[{100 000.00, 1 000 000.00, 10 000 000.00}],
              {9, 1}, DigitBlock → 3, NumberPadding → {" ", "0"}]
Out[128]//AccountingForm=
           100,000.00
         1,000,000.00
        10,000,000.00
```

Contrast this to AccountingForm without the options.

```
In[129]:=  AccountingForm[Column[{100 000.00, 1 000 000.00, 10 000 000.00}]]
Out[129]//AccountingForm=
        100000.
        1000000.
        10000000.
```

PaddedForm is convenient when all you want to do is pad out a number with specific characters on the left and right. This is often a useful operation prior to conversion to a string to generate fixed-length identifiers.

```
In[130]:=  PaddedForm[10, 8, NumberPadding → {"0", ""}]
Out[130]//PaddedForm=
        000000010
```

```
In[131]:=  id = ToString[PaddedForm[10, 8, NumberPadding → {"0", ""}]]
Out[131]=  000000010
```

EngineeringForm forces exponents in multiples of three, provided an exponent of at least three is required.

```
In[132]:=  {10.0, 100.0, 1000.0, 10000.0, 100000.0, 1000000.0} // EngineeringForm
Out[132]//EngineeringForm=
           {10., 100., 1. × 10^3, 10. × 10^3, 100. × 10^3, 1. × 10^6}
```

ScientificForm always shows numbers with one digit before the decimal and adjusts the exponent accordingly.

```
In[133]:=  {10.0, 100.0, 1000.0, 10000.0, 100000.0, 1000000.0} // ScientificForm
Out[133]//ScientificForm=
           {1. × 10^1, 1. × 10^2, 1. × 10^3, 1. × 10^4, 1. × 10^5, 1. × 10^6}
```

You can use the option NumberFormat to get precise control of the display. NumberFormat specifies a function (see Chapter 2 for details) that accepts up to three arguments for the mantissa, base, and exponent. Here is an example that displays numbers like a calculator might. Here, the function uses Row to format the mantissa and exponent (it ignores the base).

```
In[134]:=  ScientificForm[1.77 × 10^5, NumberFormat → (Row[{#1, "E", #3}] &)]
Out[134]//ScientificForm=
           1.77E5
```

See Also

You can find information and examples on all these forms and their options in the Wolfram documentation under *tutorial/OutputFormatsForNumbers*.

Functional Programming

2.0 Introduction

Functional Programming

Many books on Mathematica tout its capabilities as a multiparadigm language. Although it's true that Mathematica supports procedural, recursive, rule-based, functional, and even object-oriented styles (to some degree), I believe it is the functional and rule-based styles that are most important to master. Some gurus may go a step further and say that if you do not master the functional style then you are not really programming in Mathematica and your programs will have a far greater chance of being inefficient and clumsy. I won't be so dogmatic, but until you are an expert it's best to stick with an approach that many Mathematica experts prefer. A practical reason to learn the functional style is that most of the recipes in this book use either functional or rule-based styles and sometimes mixtures of both. This chapter is intended as a kind of decoder key for readers who want to master the functional style and get a deeper understanding of the solutions throughout this book. There are also a few recipes at the end of the chapter that are not about functional programming proper, but rather techniques specific to Mathematica that allow you to create flexible functions. These techniques are also used throughout later recipes in the book.

The hallmark of the functional style is, of course, functions. Every high-level programming language has functions, but what makes a language functional is that functions are first-class entities (however, see the sidebar "What Is a Functional Programming Language . . ." on page 31 for more subtle points). This means you can write higher-order functions that take other functions as arguments and return functions as values. Another important feature of functional languages is that they provide a syntactic method of whipping up anonymous functions on the fly. These nameless functions are often referred to as "lambda functions," although Mathematica calls them *pure functions*.

Unless you are already a convert to functional programming, why a functional approach is considered superior may not be obvious to you. A general consensus among software developers is that given two correct solutions to a problem, the simpler solution is the superior one. Simplicity is sometimes difficult to define, but one metric has to do with the length of the solution in lines of code. You will find, almost without exception, that a high-quality functional solution will be more concise than a high-quality procedural solution. This stems partly from the fact that looping constructs disappear (become implicit) in a functional solution. In a procedural program, code must express the loop, which also introduces auxiliary index variables.

Functional programs are often faster, but there are probably exceptions. Ignoring the fact that Mathematica has a built-in function, Total, for a moment, let's contrast a procedural and functional program to sum an array of 100,000 random values.

```
In[1]:=  array = RandomReal[{-1, 1}, 100000];

In[2]:=  (*Procedural solution using For loop*)
         (sum = 0 ;
           Do[sum += array[[i]], {i, 1, Length[array]}];
         sum) // Timing
Out[2]=  {0.21406, 90.6229}

In[3]:=  (*Functional solution using Fold*)
         Fold[Plus, 0, array] // Timing
Out[3]=  {0.008291, 90.6229}
```

As you can see, the functional solution was about an order of magnitude faster. Clearly the functional solution is shorter, so that is an added bonus. Of course, one of the tricks to creating the shortest and the fastest programs is exploiting special functions when they exist. In this case, Total is the way to go!

```
In[4]:= Total[array] // Timing
Out[4]= {0.000193, 90.6229}
```

If you come from a procedural background, you may find that style more comfortable. However, when you begin to write more complex code, the procedural style begins to be a liability from a complexity and performance point of view. This is not just a case of shorter being sweeter. In a very large program, it is common to introduce a large number of index and scratch variables when programming procedurally. Every variable you introduce becomes a variable whose meaning must be tracked. I wish I had a dollar for every bug caused by a change to code that used index variable i when j was intended! It should come as no surprise that eliminating these scratch variables will result in code that is much faster. In fact, in a typical procedural language like C, it is only through the efforts of a complex optimizing compiler that these variables disappear into machine registers so that maximum speed is obtained. In an interpreted language like Mathematica, these variables are not optimized away and, hence, incur a significant overhead each time they appear. By adopting a functional approach, you get almost the equivalent of optimized machine code with the pleasure of interactive development.

There are a lot more theoretical reasons for adopting a functional approach. Some involve the ability to prove programs correct or the ability to introduce concurrency. I will not make those arguments here because they usually have only marginal value for practical, everyday development and they hinge on a language being purer than Mathematica. Readers who have interest in learning more should refer to some of the excellent resources listed in the "See Also" section on page 30.

The Elements of Functional Programming

Many functional programming languages share core primitive functions that act as the building blocks of more sophisticated functions and algorithms. The names of these primitives vary from language to language, and each language provides its own twists. However, when you learn the set of primitives of one functional language, you will have an easier time reading and porting code to other functional languages.

Table 2-1. Primary functional programming primitives

Function	Operator	Description
Map[f, expr]	/@	Return the list that results from executing the function f on each element of an expr
Apply[f, expr]	@@	Return the result of replacing the head of a list with function f
Apply[f, expr, {1}]	@@@	Applies f a level 1 inside list. In other words, replace the head of all elements.
Fold[f, x, {a1, a2, a3, ...}]	N/A	If list has length 0, return x, otherwise return $f[f[f[x, a1], a2], a3]...$
FoldList[f, x, {a1, a2, a3, ...}]	N/A	Return the list $\{x, f[x, a1], f[f[x, a1], a2], ...\}$
Nest[f, expr, n]	N/A	Return the result of $f[f[f[...f[expr]...]]]$ (i.e. f applied n times)
NestList[f, expr, n]	N/A	Return the list $\{x, f[expr], f[f[expr]], ...\}$ where f repeats up to n times

In the Mathematica documentation, you will see the verb *apply* (in its various tenses) used in at least two senses. One is in the technical sense of the function Apply[f,expr] (i.e., change the head of expr to f) and the other in the sense of invoking a function on one or more arguments (as in "applied" in the definition of Nest[], "gives an expression with f applied n times to expr"). Clearly, changing the head of the expression n times would be no different from changing it once, so it should be unambiguous in most cases. See Recipe 2.1 for syntax variations of the latter sense of function application.

There are other important Mathematica functions related to functional programming, but you should commit to memory the functions in Table 2-1, because they arise repeatedly. You should especially get used to the operator notations for

Map (/@) and Apply (@@) because they arise frequently (not only in this book but in others and in sample code you will find online). If you are unfamiliar with these functions, it is worthwhile to experiment a bit. One important exercise is to use each function with a symbol that is not defined and a list of varying structure so you can see the effects from a structural point of view. For example, pay close attention to the difference between /@ and @@@. Each iterates the function across the list, but the results are quite different.

 In this code, zz is purposefully undefined so you can visualize the effect of the operators. The ability of Mathematica to handle undefined symbols without throwing errors is both a source of power and a source of frustration to the uninitiated.

```
In[5]:= zz /@ {1, {1}, {1, 2}}

Out[5]= {zz[1], zz[{1}], zz[{1, 2}]}

In[6]:= zz @@ {1, {1}, {1, 2}}

Out[6]= zz[1, {1}, {1, 2}]

In[7]:= zz @@@ {1, {1}, {1, 2}}

Out[7]= {1, zz[1], zz[1, 2]}

In[8]:= Fold[zz, 0, {1, {1}, {1, 2}}]

Out[8]= zz[zz[zz[0, 1], {1}], {1, 2}]

In[9]:= FoldList[zz, 0, {1, {1}, {1, 2}}]

Out[9]= {0, zz[0, 1], zz[zz[0, 1], {1}],
         zz[zz[zz[0, 1], {1}], {1, 2}]}

In[10]:= Nest[zz, {1, {1}, {1, 2}}, 3]

Out[10]= zz[zz[zz[{1, {1}, {1, 2}}]]]

In[11]:= NestList[zz, {1, {1}, {1, 2}}, 3]

Out[11]= {{1, {1}, {1, 2}}, zz[{1, {1}, {1, 2}}],
          zz[zz[{1, {1}, {1, 2}}]],
          zz[zz[zz[{1, {1}, {1, 2}}]]]}
```

DownValues and UpValues

Mathematica has a flexible facility for associating symbols and their definitions. Most of the time you need not be concerned with these low-level details, but some advanced Mathematica techniques discussed in this chapter and elsewhere in the book require you to have some basic understanding. When you define functions of the form f[args] := definition or f[args] = definition you create *downvalues* for the symbol f. You can inspect these values using the function DownValues[f].

```
In[12]:=  ClearAll[f]
          f[0] := 1
          f[1] := 1
          f[n_Integer] := n * f[n - 1]

In[16]:=  DownValues[f]
Out[16]=  {HoldPattern[f[0]] :→ 1, HoldPattern[f[1]] :→ 1,
           HoldPattern[f[n_Integer]] :→ n f[n - 1]}
```

The results are shown as a list of patterns in held form (see Recipe 4.8). The order of the definitions returned by DownValues is the order in which Mathematica will search for a matching pattern when it needs to evaluate an expression containing f. Mathematica has a general rule of ordering more specific definitions before more general ones; when there are ties, it uses the order in which the user typed them. In rare cases, you may need to redefine the ordering by assigning a new order to DownValues[f].

```
In[17]:=  (*This reassignment won't affect usage of f,
          but illustrates the technique.*)
          DownValues[f] = DownValues[f][[{2, 1, 3}]]
Out[17]=  {HoldPattern[f[1]] :→ 1, HoldPattern[f[0]] :→ 1,
           HoldPattern[f[n_Integer]] :→ n f[n - 1]}
```

There are some situations in which you would like to give new meaning to functions native to Mathematica. These situations arise when you introduce new types of objects. For example, imagine Mathematica did not already have a package that supported quaternions (a kind of noncommutative generalization of complex numbers) and you wanted to develop your own. Clearly you would want to use standard mathematical notation, but this would amount to defining new downvalues for the built-in Mathematica functions Plus, Times, etc.

```
Unprotect[Plus,Times]
Plus[quaternion[a1_,b1_,c1_,d1_], quaternion[a2_,b2_,c2_,d2_]] := ...
Times[quaternion[a1_,b1_,c1_,d1_], quaternion[a2_,b2_,c2_,d2_]] := ...
Protect[Plus,Times]
```

If quaternion math were very common, this might be a valid approach. However, Mathematica provides a convenient way to associate the definitions of these operations with the quaternion rather than with the operations. These associations are called UpValues, and there are two syntax variations for defining them. The first uses operations called UpSet (^=) and UpSetDelayed (^:=), which are analogous to Set (=) and SetDelayed (:=) but create upvalues rather than downvalues.

```
Plus[quaternion[a1_,b1_,c1_,d1_], quaternion[a2_,b2_,c2_,d2_]] ^:= ...
Times[quaternion[a1_,b1_,c1_,d1_], quaternion[a2_,b2_,c2_,d2_]] ^:= ...
```

The alternate syntax is a bit more verbose but is useful in situations in which the symbol the upvalue should be associated with is ambiguous. For example, imagine you want to define addition of a complex number and a quaternion. You can use TagSet or TagSetDelayed to indicate that the operation is an upvalue for quaternion rather than Complex.

```
quaternion /: Plus[Complex[r_, im_], quaternion[a1_,b1_,c1_,d1_]] := ...
quaternion /: Times[Complex[r_, im_], quaternion[a1_,b1_,c1_,d1_]] := ...
```

Upvalues solve two problems. First, they eliminate the need to unprotect native Mathematica symbols. Second, they avoid bogging down Mathematica by forcing it to consider custom definitions every time it encounters common functions like Plus and Times. (Mathematica aways uses custom definitions before built-in ones.) By associating the operations with the new types (in this case quaternion), Mathematica need only consider these operations in expression where quaternion appears. If both upvalues and downvalues are present, upvalues have precedence, but this is something you should avoid.

Function Attributes

Mathematica will modulate the behavior of functions based on a set of predefined attributes, which users should already be familiar with as those often required to achieve proper results in users' own functions. The functions Attributes[f], SetAttributes[f,attr], and ClearAttributes[f,attr] are used to query, set, and clear attributes from functions. In the following subsections, I'll review the most important attributes. Refer to the Mathematica documentation for attributes to review the complete list.

 Attributes must be assigned to symbols before functions are defined for the symbols.

Orderless

This tells Mathematica that the function is *commutative*. When Mathematica encounters this function, it will reorder arguments into canonical order (sorted in ascending order). Orderless also influences pattern matching (see Recipe 4.1) since Mathematica will consider reordering when attempting to match.

Flat

Use `Flat` to tell Mathematica that nested applications of the function (`f[f[x,y],z]`) can be flattened out (`f[x,y,z]`). In mathematics, flat functions are called *associative*.

Listable

It is often convenient to define functions that automatically map across lists. See Recipe 2.3 for more information.

HoldFirst

Mathematica defines a function `Hold` which prevents its argument from being evaluated. The attribute `HoldFirst` allows you to give this feature to the first argument of a function. All remaining arguments will behave normally.

HoldRest

This is the opposite of `HoldFirst`; the first argument is evaluated normally, but all remaining arguments are kept in unevaluated form.

HoldAll

All arguments of the function are kept unevaluated. This is equivalent to using both `HoldFirst` and `HoldRest`.

See Also

An excellent animated introduction to the core Mathematica functions can be found at *http://bit.ly/3cuB4B*.

See *guide/FunctionalProgramming* in the documentation for an overview of Mathematica's functional programming primitives.

A classic paper on the benefits of functional programming is *Why Functional Programming Matters* by John Hughes (*http://bit.ly/4mRBYO*).

Another classic is *A Tutorial on the Universality and Expressiveness of Fold* by Graham Hutton (PDF available at *http://bit.ly/ZYDiH*).

Further discussion of upvalues and downvalues can be found at *tutorial/TheStandardEvaluationProcedure* and *tutorial/AssociatingDefinitionsWithDifferentSymbols* in the documentation.

What Is a Functional Programming Language and How Functional Is Mathematica?

Anyone who has spent time in mail groups frequented by programmers knows they like to argue. One of the favorite arguments centers around the "best programming language." Derivatives include "what language is the most [insert characteristic here]" arguments. For example, what language is the most "object-oriented," "self-documenting," or in our case, "functional." The problem is that such characteristics rarely have an objective, a priori definition; rather, their definitions emerged out of research in actual language use. Since each researcher is interested in different features, the definitions become fuzzy. It is thus difficult to give a precise definition of "functional" with which every computer scientist and programmer will agree. However, to help you discover more on your own, I provide some generally agreed-on features that are important to the theory of functional programming and discuss Mathematica's support for these features. The usefulness of features rather than the cachet of labels (like "functional") is likely the primary concern of readers of cookbooks!

All functional languages emphasize the evaluation of expressions to produce values rather than commands or statements that are executed for their side effects. Consider the language C, which has functions but also other statements (for, if-then-else, while, goto, etc.) that execute without producing a return value (although values may be computed and stored in variables as side effects of these statements). In a functional language, all constructs, even conditional logic constructs and looping constructs, are executed to compute some value, and they should generally be executed only for the value and not for other side effects. Most of Mathematica's functions produce a value, but there are exceptions, and these exceptions can lead to problems. The obvious example of this is the "function" Do[]. If Do[] appears in a context where a value is expected, it will evaluate to null. Since no one needs to set up a loop to produce null, it is clear that Do[] exists for producing some side effect. Thus Do[] is certainly not functional. Even expressions that produce values can have side effects in Mathematica, which leads to the next consideration.

Functional languages that are, by design, free of side effects are called *pure functional languages*. One hallmark of a pure functional language is *single-assignment*, where a variable within a given scope can only get a value once. Examples include Haskell and Erlang, but not Mathematica, because in most cases, a variable can be reassigned (one exception is variables introduced by With[]). If you make a concerted effort to avoid multiple assignment, you will be rewarded with programs that are often easier to debug; in this book, I'll often ignore this advice if it results in a simpler example of the particular recipe in question.

Another feature is the so-called *lambda function* or anonymous function. There is a rich mathematical theory called *lambda calculus* that underlies this idea, but from a practical point of view, whipping up a function on the fly is a very nice thing in a language centered around functions. Whenever you write something like {#1+#2}& (i.e., an anonymous function that takes two arguments and produces a list containing their sum), you are using Mathematica's syntax for a lambda function or, in Mathematica speak, a Function[].

Functional languages are also distinguished as being *strict* versus *nonstrict*. In a strict language, arguments to functions are evaluated immediately, whereas nonstrict languages use *lazy evaluation* to evaluate expressions passed as arguments only when those values are needed. Mathematica is generally a strict language and does not provide for automatic lazy evaluation. However, some nonstrictness exists by the availability of Hold and the attributes HoldAll, HoldFirst, and HoldRest. These are not the same as lazy evaluation: they allow expressions to be passed in unevaluated form, but the programmer largely controls whether a held expression gets evaluated (e.g., by using ReleaseHold[] in the case of an explicit Hold[]).

Another rather technical feature of modern functional languages is their support for *currying*. This is a feature that applies a function to multiple arguments individually. For example, a function of two arguments, A and B, is applied to A, returning a new function that is then applied to B to return a value. This definition can clearly be extended to functions that take any number of arguments. Some languages that explicitly support currying are Haskell and ML. You will not find references to currying in Mathematica documentation, but the feature is essentially present, and I discuss it in Recipe 2.15.

Finally, modern functional languages often support *closures* (a function executed in an environment that can access previously bound local values) and *continuations* (a value representing the rest of a computation that can be completed later). Closures are discussed in Recipe 2.14.

2.1 Mapping Functions with More Than One Argument

Problem

You need to map a function over a list containing sublists whose values are arguments to the function.

Solution

Use a Map-Apply idiom. A very simple example of this problem is when you want to sum the sublists.

```
In[18]:= Map[(Apply[Plus, #]) &, {{1, 2, 3}, {4, 5, 6, 7, 8}, {9, 10, 11, 12}}]
Out[18]= {6, 30, 42}
```

This can be abbreviated to:

```
In[19]:= Plus @@ # & /@ {{1, 2, 3}, {4, 5, 6, 7, 8}, {9, 10, 11, 12}}
Out[19]= {6, 30, 42}
```

Discussion

Although the solution seems very simple, this problem arises quite frequently in more complicated guises, and you should learn to recognize it by studying some of the following more interesting examples.

Consider a structure representing an order for some product with the form order[sku, qty,price]. Now imagine you have a list of such orders along with a function for computing the total cost of an order. Given a list of orders, you want to produce a list of their costs. The situation is a bit tricky because our function does not care about the sku, and rather than a list of lists we have a list of order[]. Even with these differences you still have the same basic problem. Recall that Apply does not necessarily require an expression whose head is List; it will work just as well with any head, such as order. Also, using compOrderTotCost we can easily preprocess each order to extract just the elements needed.

```
In[20]:= compOrderTotCost[qty_, price_] := qty * price
         Map[(Apply[compOrderTotCost, Rest[#]]) &, {order["sku1", 10 , 4.98],
            order["sku2", 1 , 17.99], order["sku3", 12, 0.25]}]
Out[21]= {49.8, 17.99, 3.}
```

This solution is still a bit contrived because both qty and price within order were adjacent at the end of order, so Rest made it easy to grab the needed values. The real world is rarely that accommodating. Let's complicate the situation a bit by introducing another element to order that represents a discount percent: order[sku, disc%,qty,price]. Here you use Apply with a function that takes slot specifications (#n) to pick out the proper arguments. The convention is that #n stands for the nth argument and # by itself is short for #1.

```
In[22]:= compDiscOrderTotCost[qty_, price_, disc_] :=
             qty * price * (1.0 - disc / 100.0)
          Map[ (Apply[compDiscOrderTotCost[#3, #4, #2] &, #]) &,
             {order["sku1", 5, 10 , 4.98],
              order["sku2", 0, 1 , 17.99], order["sku3", 15, 12, 0.25]}]
Out[23]= {47.31, 17.99, 2.55}
```

There is another version of Apply that takes a level specification as a third argument. If we use this version, we can often get the same effect without explicitly using Map.

```
In[24]:= Apply[Plus[##] &, {{1, 2, 3}, {4, 5, 6, 7, 8}, {9, 10, 11, 12}}, {1}]
Out[24]= {6, 30, 42}
```

Here we apply Plus using level specification {1} that restricts Apply to level one only. This uses ## (slot sequence) to pick up all elements at this level. There is also a shortcut operator, @@@, for this case of applying a function to only level one. In this case, you can also dispense with ## to create a very concise expression.

```
In[25]:= Plus @@@ {{1, 2, 3}, {4, 5, 6, 7, 8}, {9, 10, 11, 12}}
Out[25]= {6, 30, 42}
```

You will need slot sequence if you want to pass other arguments in. For example, consider the following variations.

```
In[26]:= Plus[1, ##] & @@@ {{1, 2, 3}, {4, 5, 6, 7, 8}, {9, 10, 11, 12}}
Out[26]= {7, 31, 43}
```

This says to produce the sum of each list and add in the element (hence, you use the second element twice in the sum).

```
In[27]:= Plus[#2, ##] & @@@ {{1, 2, 3}, {4, 5, 6, 7, 8}, {9, 10, 11, 12}}
Out[27]= {8, 35, 52}
```

This leads to a simplified version of the discounted order example.

```
In[28]:= compDiscOrderTotCost[ #3, #4, #2] & @@@ {order["sku1", 5, 10 , 4.98],
             order["sku2", 0, 1 , 17.99], order["sku3", 15, 12, 0.25]}
Out[28]= {47.31, 17.99, 2.55}
```

If the lists are more deeply nested, you can use larger level specifications to get the result you want. Imagine the order being nested in an extra structure called envelope.

```
In[29]:= Apply[compDiscOrderTotCost[ #3, #4, #2] &,
             {envelope[1, order["sku1", 5, 10 , 4.98]],
              envelope[2, order["sku2", 0, 1 , 17.99]],
              envelope[3, order["sku3", 15, 12, 0.25]]}, {2}]
Out[29]= {envelope[1, 47.31], envelope[2, 17.99], envelope[3, 2.55]}
```

The same result is obtained using Map-Apply because Map takes level specifications as well.

```
In[30]:= Map[(Apply[compDiscOrderTotCost[#3, #4, #2] &, #]) &,
            {envelope[1, order["sku1", 5, 10 , 4.98]],
             envelope[2, order["sku2", 0, 1 , 17.99]],
             envelope[3, order["sku3", 15, 12, 0.25]]}, {2}]
Out[30]= {envelope[1, 47.31], envelope[2, 17.99], envelope[3, 2.55]}
```

Of course, you probably want to discard the envelope. This can be done with a part specification [[All,2]], which means all parts at the first level but only the second element of each of these parts.

```
In[31]:= Map[(Apply[compDiscOrderTotCost[#3, #4, #2] &, #]) &,
            {envelope[1, order["sku1", 5, 10 , 4.98]],
             envelope[2, order["sku2", 0, 1 , 17.99]],
             envelope[3, order["sku3", 15, 12, 0.25]]}, {2}][[All, 2]]
Out[31]= {47.31, 17.99, 2.55}
```

The following does the same thing using only Map, Apply, and a prefix form of Map that brings the level specification closer. There are a lot of # symbols flying around here, and one of the challenges of reading code like this is keeping track of the fact that # is different in each function. I don't necessarily recommend writing code this way if you want others to understand it, but you will see code like this and should be able to read it.

```
In[32]:= Part[#, 2] & /@
            Map[compDiscOrderTotCost[#3, #4, #2] & @@ # &, #, {2}] &@
            {envelope[1, order["sku1", 5, 10 , 4.98]],
             envelope[2, order["sku2", 0, 1 , 17.99]],
             envelope[3, order["sku3", 15, 12, 0.25]]}
Out[32]= {47.31, 17.99, 2.55}
```

With some practice, this expression translates rather easily to English as "take the second element of each element produced by applying compDiscOrderTotCost at level two over the list of enveloped orders."

See Also

Slots (#) and slot sequences (##) are discussed in *tutorial/PureFunctions* in the documentation.

2.2 Holding Arbitrary Arguments

Problem

You want to create a function that holds arguments in different combinations than provided by HoldFirst and HoldRest.

Solution

Use Hold in the argument list. Here I create a function called arrayAssign whose objective is to accept a symbol that is associated with a list, an index (or Span), and a second symbol associated with another list. The result is the assignment of the elements of array2 to array1 that are specified by index. For this to work, arguments a and b must remain held but aIndex should not.

```
In[33]:= array1 = Table[0, {10}]; array2 = Table[1, {10}];
         arrayAssign[Hold[a_Symbol], aIndex_, Hold[b_Symbol], bIndex_] :=
          Module[{},
           a[[aIndex]] = b[[bIndex]];
           a[[aIndex]]]
         (*Assign elements 2 through 3 in array 2 to array 1.*)
         arrayAssign[Hold[array1], 2 ;; 3, Hold[array2], 1];
         array1
Out[36]= {0, 1, 1, 0, 0, 0, 0, 0, 0, 0}
```

Discussion

The attributes HoldFirst, HoldRest, and HoldAll fill the most common needs for creating functions that don't evaluate their arguments. However, if your function is more naturally implemented by keeping other combinations of variables unevaluated, then you can use Hold directly. Of course, you need to use Hold at the point of call, but by also putting Hold in the arguments of the implementation, you ensure the function will only match if the Holds are in place on the call and you also unwrap the hold contents immediately without causing evaluation.

See Also

The attributes HoldFirst, HoldRest, and HoldAll are explained in the "Introduction" on page 30.

2.3 Creating Functions That Automatically Map Over Lists

Problem

You want to write functions that act as if they are being called Map[f, list].

Solution

A Mathematica attribute called Listable indicates a function that should automatically be threaded over lists that appear as its arguments.

```
In[37]:= SetAttributes[myListableFunc, Listable]
         myListableFunc[x_] := x + 1
         myListableFunc[{1, 2, 3, 4}]
Out[39]= {2, 3, 4, 5}
```

Discussion

Log and D are examples of built-in Mathematica functions that are listable. Listability also works for operators used in prefix, infix, and postfix notation.

```
In[40]:= {10, 20, 30} ^ {3, 2, 1}
Out[40]= {1000, 400, 30}
```

```
In[41]:= {1 / 2, 1 / 3, 1 / 5, Sqrt[2]} // N
Out[41]= {0.5, 0.333333, 0.2, 1.41421}
```

Listable has a performance advantage over the explicit use of Map, so is recommended if the function will often be applied to vectors and matrices.

```
In[42]:= Timing[Log[RandomReal[{1, 1000}, 1000000]]][[1]]
Out[42]= 0.057073
```

```
In[43]:= Timing[Map[Log, RandomReal[{1, 1000}, 1000000]]][[1]]
Out[43]= 0.14031
```

2.4 Mapping Multiple Functions in a Single Pass

Problem

You want to map several functions over elements of a list in a single pass.

Solution

There is no need to make multiple passes over a list when using Map[]. In this example we compute a table that relates each number to its square and cube in a single pass.

```
In[44]:= {#, #^2, #^3} & /@ {1, 7, 3, 8, 5, 9, 6, 4, 2} // TableForm
Out[44]//TableForm=
        1  1   1
        7  49  343
        3  9   27
        8  64  512
        5  25  125
        9  81  729
        6  36  216
        4  16  64
        2  4   8
```

Here we map several functions over a generated list and add the individual results; structurally, this is the same solution.

```
In[45]:= Sin[#]^2 + # Cos[2 #] & /@ Table[N[1/i Pi], {i, 16, 1, -1}]
Out[45]= {0.219464, 0.23456, 0.251693, 0.271252, 0.293712, 0.319635, 0.349652, 0.384378,
          0.424127, 0.468077, 0.511799, 0.539653, 0.5, 0.226401, -0.570796, 3.14159}
```

Here, since Table is already being used, it would be easier to write Table[With[{p = N[1/i Pi]}, Sin[p]^2 + p Cos[2 p]], {i, 16, 1, -1}], but that misses the point. I am using Table because I need a list, but imagine the list was a given. Map applies to cases for which you are given a list and need to create a new list, whereas Table is better used when you are generating the list on the fly.

Discussion

Once you become comfortable with functional programming, you will find all sorts of really nice applications of this general pattern. Here is a slick little demonstration borrowed from the Mathematica documentation for visually identifying the first 100 primes.

```
In[46]:= Grid[Partition[If[PrimeQ[#], Framed[#], #] & /@ Range[100], 20]]
```

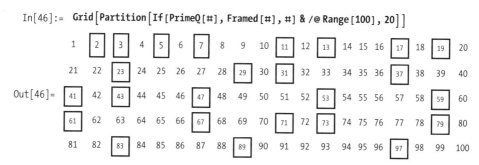

In the following, I apply the technique twice to create a presentation that shows the first 12 regular polygons, with the number of sides and the interior angles in degrees displayed in the center.

```
In[47]:= angles = Table[i 2 Pi/n, {n, 3, 14}, {i, 0, n - 1}];
         Graphics[{EdgeForm[{Thin, Black}],
             FaceForm[White], Polygon[#], Inset[{Length[#],
               (Pi - VectorAngle[#[[1]], #[[2]]]) /Degree}]}] & /@
           Map[N[{Sin[#], Cos[#]}] &, angles, {2}] //
          Partition[#, 4] & // GraphicsGrid[#, Frame → All, ImageSize → 500] &
```

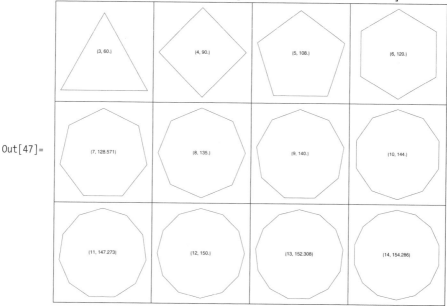

The first step is to generate a list of lists using Table. The innermost list (rows below) contains *n* equally spaced angles about a circle where *n* varies between 3 and 14. We can see this by inspecting angles in tabular form. Here, using Map is superior to Table if you want to use the computed table of angles in further steps in the computation. In my case, I just want to display them.

```
In[48]:= TableForm[angles, TableSpacing → {1, 2}]
Out[48]//TableForm=
```

0	$\frac{2\pi}{3}$	$\frac{4\pi}{3}$											
0	$\frac{\pi}{2}$	π	$\frac{3\pi}{2}$										
0	$\frac{2\pi}{5}$	$\frac{4\pi}{5}$	$\frac{6\pi}{5}$	$\frac{8\pi}{5}$									
0	$\frac{\pi}{3}$	$\frac{2\pi}{3}$	π	$\frac{4\pi}{3}$	$\frac{5\pi}{3}$								
0	$\frac{2\pi}{7}$	$\frac{4\pi}{7}$	$\frac{6\pi}{7}$	$\frac{8\pi}{7}$	$\frac{10\pi}{7}$	$\frac{12\pi}{7}$							
0	$\frac{\pi}{4}$	$\frac{\pi}{2}$	$\frac{3\pi}{4}$	π	$\frac{5\pi}{4}$	$\frac{3\pi}{2}$	$\frac{7\pi}{4}$						
0	$\frac{2\pi}{9}$	$\frac{4\pi}{9}$	$\frac{2\pi}{3}$	$\frac{8\pi}{9}$	$\frac{10\pi}{9}$	$\frac{4\pi}{3}$	$\frac{14\pi}{9}$	$\frac{16\pi}{9}$					
0	$\frac{\pi}{5}$	$\frac{2\pi}{5}$	$\frac{3\pi}{5}$	$\frac{4\pi}{5}$	π	$\frac{6\pi}{5}$	$\frac{7\pi}{5}$	$\frac{8\pi}{5}$	$\frac{9\pi}{5}$				
0	$\frac{2\pi}{11}$	$\frac{4\pi}{11}$	$\frac{6\pi}{11}$	$\frac{8\pi}{11}$	$\frac{10\pi}{11}$	$\frac{12\pi}{11}$	$\frac{14\pi}{11}$	$\frac{16\pi}{11}$	$\frac{18\pi}{11}$	$\frac{20\pi}{11}$			
0	$\frac{\pi}{6}$	$\frac{\pi}{3}$	$\frac{\pi}{2}$	$\frac{2\pi}{3}$	$\frac{5\pi}{6}$	π	$\frac{7\pi}{6}$	$\frac{4\pi}{3}$	$\frac{3\pi}{2}$	$\frac{5\pi}{3}$	$\frac{11\pi}{6}$		
0	$\frac{2\pi}{13}$	$\frac{4\pi}{13}$	$\frac{6\pi}{13}$	$\frac{8\pi}{13}$	$\frac{10\pi}{13}$	$\frac{12\pi}{13}$	$\frac{14\pi}{13}$	$\frac{16\pi}{13}$	$\frac{18\pi}{13}$	$\frac{20\pi}{13}$	$\frac{22\pi}{13}$	$\frac{24\pi}{13}$	
0	$\frac{\pi}{7}$	$\frac{2\pi}{7}$	$\frac{3\pi}{7}$	$\frac{4\pi}{7}$	$\frac{5\pi}{7}$	$\frac{6\pi}{7}$	π	$\frac{8\pi}{7}$	$\frac{9\pi}{7}$	$\frac{10\pi}{7}$	$\frac{11\pi}{7}$	$\frac{12\pi}{7}$	$\frac{13\pi}{7}$

Since Polygon requires points, I compute them by mapping the Sin and Cos functions in parallel over each sublist by giving a level specification of {2} to Map. I show only the first three results below for sake of space.

```
In[49]:= Map[N[{Sin[#], Cos[#]}] &,
          Table[i 2 Pi / n, {n, 3, 14}, {i, 0, n - 1} ], {2}][[1 ;; 3]] // Column
         {{0., 1.}, {0.866025, -0.5}, {-0.866025, -0.5}}

         {{0., 1.}, {1., 0.}, {0., -1.}, {-1., 0.}}

Out[49]=  {{0., 1.}, {0.951057, 0.309017}, {0.587785, -0.809017},
          {-0.587785, -0.809017}, {-0.951057, 0.309017}}
```

The next pass uses the technique to create both the polygon and the inset with the number of sides and the interior angles. The use of Partition and GraphicsGrid is solely for formatting purposes.

See Also

See Recipe 2.5 for a variation of Map called MapIndexed that gives you the position of an element as a second argument.

2.5 Keeping Track of the Index of Each Item As You Map

Problem

You want to apply a function over a list as with Map (/@), but the function requires the position of the item in the list in addition to its value.

Solution

Use MapIndexed instead of Map. Keep in mind that MapIndexed wraps the index in a list, so a common idiom is to use First[#2] to access the index directly. To show this, I first use an undefined function ff before showing a more useful application.

```
In[50]:= Clear[ff];
         MapIndexed[ff[#1, First[#2]] &, {a, b, c, d, e}]
Out[51]= {ff[a, 1], ff[b, 2], ff[c, 3], ff[d, 4], ff[e, 5]}
```

Imagine you want to raise the elements of a list to a power based on its position. You could not easily do this with Map, but MapIndex makes it trivial.

```
In[52]:= MapIndexed[#1^First[#2] &, {2, 0, 7, 3}]
Out[52]= {2, 0, 343, 81}
```

This is not so contrived if you consider the problem of converting a list to a polynomial.

```
In[53]:= Plus @@ MapIndexed[#1 x^First[#2] &, {2, 0, 7, 3}]
Out[53]= 2 x + 7 x^3 + 3 x^4
```

Discussion

Although MapIndexed is used less frequently than Map, it is a godsend when you need it, since it avoids the need to return to a procedural style when you want the position. I think you might agree the following procedural implementation is a bit uglier.

```
In[54]:=  Block[{poly = 0,
           list = {2, 0, 7, 3}},
          Do[
           poly = poly + list[[i]] x^i,
           {i, 1, Length[list]}
          ];
          poly]
```
Out[54]= $2 x + 7 x^3 + 3 x^4$

You may find it curious that MapIndexed wraps the position in a list, forcing you to use First to extract the index. There is a good reason for this convention: MapIndexed easily generalizes to nested lists such as matrices where the position has multiple parts. Here we use a variant of MapIndexed that takes a level specification as a third argument indicating the function ff should map over the items at level two. Here two integers are required to specify the position; thus, the list convention immediately makes sense.

```
In[55]:=  MapIndexed[ff[#1, #2] &, {{a, b, c}, {d, e, f}, {g, h, i}}, {2}]
Out[55]=  {{ff[a, {1, 1}], ff[b, {1, 2}], ff[c, {1, 3}]},
          {ff[d, {2, 1}], ff[e, {2, 2}], ff[f, {2, 3}]},
          {ff[g, {3, 1}], ff[h, {3, 2}], ff[i, {3, 3}]}}
```

As an application, consider a function for reading the positions of pieces on a chessboard. The board is a matrix with empty spaces designated by 0 and pieces designated by letters with subscripts B for black and W for white. We implement a function piecePos that can convert a piece and its position into a description that uses algebraic chess notation.

```
In[56]:= Clear[piecePos]
         chessboard = {
            {0, 0, 0, 0, 0, 0, 0, 0},
            {0, 0, 0, 0, 0, 0, 0, 0},
            {0, 0, 0, 0, 0, 0, 0, 0},
            {0, 0, 0, 0, 0, 0, 0, 0},
            {N_B, P_W, N_W, 0, 0, 0, 0, 0},
            {0, 0, 0, 0, 0, 0, 0, 0},
            {0, 0, Q_W, 0, 0, 0, 0, 0},
            {K_B, 0, 0, 0, 0, 0, 0, 0}
         };

         toColor[B] = "Black";
         toColor[W] = "White";
         toPos[{x_, y_}] :=
          Module[{file = {"a", "b", "c", "d", "e", "f", "g", "h"}},
           file[[y]] <> ToString[x]]

         piecePos[P_c_, pos_] := {toColor[c], " Pawn ", toPos[pos]}
         piecePos[N_c_, pos_] := {toColor[c], " Knight ", toPos[pos]}
         piecePos[B_c_, pos_] := {toColor[c], " Bishop ", toPos[pos]}
         piecePos[R_c_, pos_] := {toColor[c], " Rook ", toPos[pos]}
         piecePos[Q_c_, pos_] := {toColor[c], " Queen ", toPos[pos]}
         piecePos[K_c_, pos_] := {toColor[c], " King ", toPos[pos]}
         piecePos[0, _] := Sequence[]
```

MapIndexed will allow us to use piecePos to describe the whole board. Here, piecePos converts an empty space to any empty sequence, which Mathematica will automatically remove for us. Flatten is used to collapse unneeded nesting inherited from the chessboard's representation as a list of lists.

```
In[68]:= Flatten[MapIndexed[piecePos, chessboard, {2}], 1]
Out[68]= {{Black,  Knight , a5}, {White,  Pawn , b5},
          {White,  Knight , c5}, {White,  Queen , c7}, {Black,  King , a8}}
```

2.6 Mapping a Function over a Moving Sublist

Problem

You have a list and wish to apply some operation over a moving window of fixed size over that list.

Solution

Ignoring available special functions of Mathematica for a moment, you can attack this problem head-on by using Table in conjunction with a Part and Span (i.e., [[start;;end]]) to create the moving window (sublist) and Apply the desired function to each sublist. For example, use Mean if you want a moving average.

```
In[69]:= array = RandomReal[{0, 10}, 20] ;

In[70]:= Table[Mean @@ {array[[i ;; i + 4]]}, {i, 1, 16}]
Out[70]= {3.13108, 3.27291, 4.31676, 5.41289, 5.98751, 5.6219, 5.8349, 5.52834,
          5.87892, 4.7862, 5.5245, 5.36589, 4.35811, 4.09389, 4.66446, 3.87226}
```

Here is a variation using Take.

```
In[71]:= Table[Mean @@ {Take[array, {i, i + 4}]}, {i, 1, 16}]
Out[71]= {3.13108, 3.27291, 4.31676, 5.41289, 5.98751, 5.6219, 5.8349, 5.52834,
          5.87892, 4.7862, 5.5245, 5.36589, 4.35811, 4.09389, 4.66446, 3.87226}
```

A nonmathematical example uses the same technique to create successive pairs.

```
In[72]:= Table[List @@ array[[i ;; i + 1]], {i, 1, 16}]
Out[72]= {{5.14848, 4.21272}, {4.21272, 0.968604},
          {0.968604, 2.94497}, {2.94497, 2.38062}, {2.38062, 5.85762},
          {5.85762, 9.43197}, {9.43197, 6.44928}, {6.44928, 5.81804},
          {5.81804, 0.552592}, {0.552592, 6.92264},
          {6.92264, 7.89915}, {7.89915, 8.20219}, {8.20219, 0.354432},
          {0.354432, 4.24409}, {4.24409, 6.12958}, {6.12958, 2.86026}}
```

Discussion

The solution illustrates the basic idea, but it is not very general because the function and window size are hard coded. You can generalize the solution like this:

```
In[73]:= moving[f_, expr_, n_] := Module[{len = Length[expr], windowEnd },
             windowEnd = Min[n, len] - 1;
             Table[Apply[f, {expr[[i ;; i + windowEnd]]}], {i, 1, len - windowEnd}]]
```

Note that there is a built-in function, MovingAverage, that computes both simple and weighted moving averages. There is also a MovingMedian. You should use these instead of the solution given here if they are appropriate for what you need to compute.

Two special functions in Mathematica, ListConvolve and ListCorrelate, present the most general way to perform computations on sublists. These functions contain a myriad of variations, but it is well worth the added effort to familiarize yourself with them. I will present only ListConvolve because anything you can compute with one you can compute with the other, and the choice is just a matter of fit for the specific problem. Let's ease in slowly by using ListConvolve to implement a moving average.

```
In[74]:= movingAvg[list_, n_] := ListConvolve[Table[1/n, {n}], list]
```

```
In[75]:= movingAvg[array, 5]
```
Out[75]= {3.13108, 3.27291, 4.31676, 5.41289, 5.98751, 5.6219, 5.8349, 5.52834,
          5.87892, 4.7862, 5.5245, 5.36589, 4.35811, 4.09389, 4.66446, 3.87226}

The first argument to ListConvolve is called the *kernel*. It is a list that defines a set of values that determines the length of the sublists and factors by which to multiply each element in the sublist. After the multiplication, each sublist is summed. This is shown more easily using symbols.

```
In[76]:= ListConvolve[{1, 1}, {a, b, c, d, e}]
```
Out[76]= {a + b, b + c, c + d, d + e}

Here I use a simple kernel {1,1}, which implies sublists will be size 2 and each element will simply be itself (because 1 is the identity). This yields a list of successive sums. In the moving average, the kernel was simply $1/n$ repeated n times since this results in the mean.

```
In[77]:= ListConvolve[{1, 1}/2, {a, b, c, d, e}]
```
Out[77]= $\left\{ \dfrac{a}{2} + \dfrac{b}{2}, \dfrac{b}{2} + \dfrac{c}{2}, \dfrac{c}{2} + \dfrac{d}{2}, \dfrac{d}{2} + \dfrac{e}{2} \right\}$

It's easy to see how using an appropriate kernel gives a weighted moving average, but I won't continue in this vein, because my goal is to demonstrate the generality of ListConvolve and, as I already said, MovingAverage does the trick.

The first bit of generality comes from Mathematica adding a third argument to List-Convolve that can be an integer k or a list {kL,kR}. Since using just k is equivalent to using {k,k}, I'll only discuss the later case. It is best to start with some examples.

```
In[78]:= ListConvolve[{1, 1}, {a, b, c, d, e}, {1, 1}]
```
Out[78]= {a + e, a + b, b + c, c + d, d + e}

```
In[79]:= ListConvolve[{1, 1}, {a, b, c, d, e}, {1, -1}]
```
Out[79]= {a + e, a + b, b + c, c + d, d + e, a + e}

Hopefully you can guess the meaning of {kL,kR}; kL tells ListConvolve how much to overhang the kernel on the left of the list, and kR tells it how much to overhang the kernel on the right. Hence, it tells ListConvolve to treat the list as circular. The default value is {-1,1}, which means no overhang on either side.

Sometimes you do not want to treat the lists as circular, but rather as padded; hence, ListConvolve takes a fourth argument that specifies the padding.

```
In[80]:= ListConvolve[{1, 1}, {a, b, c, d, e}, {1, -1}, 1]
```
Out[80]= {1 + a, a + b, b + c, c + d, d + e, 1 + e}

I've rushed through these features a bit because the Mathematica documentation can fill you in on the details and because my real goal is to arrive at the version of ListConvolve that takes a fifth and sixth argument. This takes us back to the theme of this recipe, which is the idea of mapping arbitrary functions over moving sublists. Thus far, ListConvolve has been about mapping a very specific function, Plus, across a sublist defined by a kernel, which defines both the length of the sublist (matches length of kernel) and a set of weights to Times the individual elements (the elements of the kernel). The fifth argument allows you to replace Times with an arbitrary function, and the sixth argument allows you to replace Plus with an arbitrary function.

Here is the pair extraction function from the solution implemented using ListConvolve, shown here but using strings to emphasize that we don't necessarily need to do math. I replace Times with the function #2&, which simply ignores the element from the kernel, and I replace Plus with List because that will form the pairs.

```
In[81]:= list = {"foo", "bar", "baz", "bing"};
         ListConvolve[{1, 1}, list, {-1, 1}, {}, #2 &, List]
Out[82]= {{foo, bar}, {bar, baz}, {baz, bing}}
```

But sometimes you can make nice use of the kernel even in nonmathematical contexts. Here we hyphenate pairs using StringJoin with input kernel strings {"-",""} (consider that "" is the identity for string concatenation).

```
In[83]:= ListConvolve[{"-", ""}, list, {-1, 1}, {}, StringJoin, StringJoin]
Out[83]= {foo-bar, bar-baz, baz-bing}
```

Let's consider another application. You have a list of points and want to compute the distances between successive pairs. This introduces a new wrinkle because the input list is two levels deep. ListConvolve assumes you want to do a two-dimensional convolution and will complain that the kernel does not have the same rank as the list. Luckily, you can tell ListConvolve to remain on the first level by specifying a final (seventh) argument.

```
In[84]:= points = RandomReal[{-1, 1}, {20, 2}];
         ListConvolve[{1, 1}, points, {-1, 1}, {}, #2 &, EuclideanDistance, 1]
Out[85]= {1.49112, 0.764671, 0.789573, 0.941825, 0.933473, 1.05501,
          1.21181, 0.827185, 1.25728, 0.365742, 0.62815, 1.88344, 0.741821,
          1.13765, 0.719799, 0.643237, 1.60263, 0.93153, 1.33332}
```

Taking three points at a time, you can compute the area of successive triangles and draw them as well!

```
In[86]:= triarea[{xA_, yA_}, {xB_, yB_}, {xC_, yC_}] :=
            Abs[ (xB * yA - xA * yB) + (xC * yB - xB * yC) + (xA * yC - xC * yA)]/2
            ListConvolve[{1, 1, 1}, points, {-1, 1}, {}, #2 &, triarea, 1]
Out[87]= {0.549352, 0.064558, 0.31907, 0.228057, 0.308535, 0.561063,
            0.0457104, 0.126488, 0.164337, 0.104572, 0.107751, 0.581687,
            0.333659, 0.408676, 0.220177, 0.457996, 0.679265, 0.550845}

In[88]:= ListConvolve[{1, 1, 1}, points,
            {-1, 1}, {}, #2 &, Polygon[{##}] &, 1] // Graphics[
            {EdgeForm[Black], FaceForm[White], Opacity[0.5], #}, ImageSize → Small] &
```

Out[88]=

There is something a bit awkward about ListConvolve use cases where we essentially ignore the kernel. Readers familiar with the function Partition will immediately see a much shorter variation.

```
In[89]:= triarea @@@ Partition[ points, 3, 1]
Out[89]= {0.549352, 0.064558, 0.31907, 0.228057, 0.308535, 0.561063,
            0.0457104, 0.126488, 0.164337, 0.104572, 0.107751, 0.581687,
            0.333659, 0.408676, 0.220177, 0.457996, 0.679265, 0.550845}
```

Partition and ListConvolve have many similar features, and with a bit of programming, you can implement ListConvolve in terms of Partition and vice versa. The one observation I can make in favor of ListConvolve is that it does the partitioning and function application in one fell swoop. This inspires the following compromise.

```
In[90]:= partitionApply[func_, list_, n_] :=
            ListConvolve[Array[1 &, n], list, {-1, 1}, {}, #2 &, func, 1]
```

Above, Array is used to generate a kernel of the required size where 1& is the function that always returns 1.

```
In[91]:=  partitionApply[triarea, points, 3]
Out[91]=  {0.549352, 0.064558, 0.31907, 0.228057, 0.308535, 0.561063,
           0.0457104, 0.126488, 0.164337, 0.104572, 0.107751, 0.581687,
           0.333659, 0.408676, 0.220177, 0.457996, 0.679265, 0.550845}
```

But, lo and behold, the function we are looking for is actually buried inside the Developer` package! It's called Developer`PartitionMap.

```
In[92]:=  Developer`PartitionMap[triarea @@ # &, points, 3, 1]
Out[92]=  {0.549352, 0.064558, 0.31907, 0.228057, 0.308535, 0.561063,
           0.0457104, 0.126488, 0.164337, 0.104572, 0.107751, 0.581687,
           0.333659, 0.408676, 0.220177, 0.457996, 0.679265, 0.550845}
```

See Also

I highly recommend reviewing the documentation for Partition, ListConvolve, and ListCorrelate in succession to get insight into their relationships. I spent a lot of time in my early Mathematica experience understanding how to use Partition but viewing ListConvolve and ListCorrelate as mysterious. If you find a need to use Partition in one of its advanced forms, you might be working on a problem where ListConvolve or ListCorrelate applies.

ListConvolve and ListCorrelate are frequently used in image-processing applications. See Recipe 8.5. Also see Recipe 2.12, in which I use it for a traveling salesperson problem.

2.7 Using Prefix and Postfix Notation to Produce More Readable Code

Problem

A complicated piece of functional code can become deeply nested and, as a result, hard to read. You want to collapse some of these levels of nesting without introducing intermediate variables. Of course, readability is in the eye of the beholder, so a closely related problem is making sure you can understand this style when you see it in the wild.

Solution

Many Mathematica veterans prefer a functional style of programming that makes liberal use of prefix notation, which uses the @ symbol to compose functions, and postfix notation, which uses //. Let's consider a simple program that looks for primes of the form $2^n \pm 1$ up to some limiting value of nmax.

```
In[93]:=  somePrimes[nmax_] :=
              Select[Union[Flatten[Table[{2^n - 1, 2^n + 1}, {n, 0, nmax}]]], PrimeQ];
          somePrimes[
            5]
Out[94]=  {2, 3, 5, 7, 17, 31}
```

As a first step, you can eliminate some levels of nesting by using @.

```
In[95]:=  somePrimes[nmax_] :=
              Select[Union@Flatten@Table[{2^n - 1, 2^n + 1}, {n, 0, nmax}], PrimeQ]
          somePrimes[5]
Out[96]=  {2, 3, 5, 7, 17, 31}
```

You can further emphasize that this program is about finding primes by using functional composition with Select. This brings the PrimeQ test to the front.

```
In[97]:=  somePrimes[nmax_] := Select[#, PrimeQ] & @
              Union@Flatten@Table[{2^n - 1, 2^n + 1}, {n, 0, nmax}]
          somePrimes[
            5]
Out[98]=  {2, 3, 5, 7, 17, 31}
```

The use of postfix is perfectly valid on the left-hand side, although you are less likely to see this style widely used.

```
In[99]:=  somePrimes@nmax_ :=
              Select[#, PrimeQ] & @ Union@Flatten@Table[{2^n - 1, 2^n + 1}, {n, 0, nmax}]
```

A functional purist might go further and make somePrimes a pure function, but most would agree this goes way too far in this instance! Still, you should know how to read code like this, because you will come across it, and there are cases where it makes sense.

```
In[100]:=  Clear[somePrimes];
           somePrimes = (Select[#, PrimeQ] & @
               Union@Flatten@Table[{2^n - 1, 2^n + 1}, {n, 0, #}]) &;
           somePrimes[
             5]
Out[102]=  {2, 3, 5, 7, 17, 31}
```

Discussion

The uninitiated could make an argument that the first form of somePrimes was more understandable to them than any of the later ones. First, let me say that there is no reward in heaven for coding in a specific style, so don't feel the need to conform to a particular fashion. Your programs won't run faster just because you use a terser syntax. Having said that, I now defend the merits of this particular style. Let me repeat the version that I think strikes the right balance.

```
In[103]:=  Clear[somePrimes];
           somePrimes[nmax_] :=
             Select[#, PrimeQ] & @ Union@Flatten@Table[{2^n - 1, 2^n + 1}, {n, 0, nmax}]
```

First, use of symbols like @ should not be a real barrier. After all, such symbolic forms of expression are pervasive. Every first grader knows what 1 + 1 or $15 means. Symbolic operators are not inherently mysterious after you are exposed to them.

However, the primary goal and claim is readability. This expression can be read as "select the primes of the union of the flattening of the table of pairs {2^n-1, 2^n+1} with n ranging from 0 to nmax". As I stated in the solution, the most relevant aspect of this program is that it selects primes. Having a language that gives you the freedom to express programs in a way that emphasizes their function is really quite liberating in my opinion.

The flip side of emphasis by pushing functions forward is deemphasis by pushing ancillary detail toward the end. This is one of the roles of postfix //. Common uses include formatting and timing. Here the main idea is taking the last value of somePrime[500]. The fact that you are interested in the timing is likely an afterthought, and you may delete that at some point. Placing it at the end makes it easy to remove.

```
In[105]:=  Last@somePrimes[500] // Timing
Out[105]=  {0.113328, 170 141 183 460 469 231 731 687 303 715 884 105 727}
```

Likewise, formatting is a convention that does not change meaning, so most users tag formatting directives at the end.

```
In[106]:=  10.00 + 12.77 - 36.00 - 42.01 // AccountingForm
Out[106]//AccountingForm=
           (55.24)
```

Note that @ has high precedence and associates to the right, whereas // has low precedence and associates to the left. The precedence is suggested by the way the front-end typesets expressions with @ containing no space to suggest tight binding, while // expressions are spaced out to suggest loose binding and lower precedence.

```
In[107]:=  a@b@c // f@d // e
Out[107]=  e[f[d][a[b[c]]]]
```

It's worth mentioning that `Postfix` and `Prefix` will convert standard functional form to the shortened versions.

```
In[108]:= Prefix[f[1]]
Out[108]= Prefix[1]
```

```
In[109]:= Postfix[f[1]]
Out[109]= Postfix[1]
```

See Also

Additional perspectives on this notation can be found in the essay *The Concepts and Confusions of Prefix, Infix, Postfix and Fully Nested Notations* by Xah Lee at *http://bit.ly/t6GoC*.

Readers interested in functional programming styles should google the term *Point-free* to learn how the ideas discussed here manifest themselves in other languages, such as Haskell.

2.8 Defining Indexed Functions

Problem

You want to define a family of functions differentiated by an index or indices.

Solution

Use indexed heads or subscripts.

```
In[110]:= ClearAll[f] ;
          f[1][x_, y_] := 0.5 * (x + y)
          f[2][x_, y_] := 0.5 * (x - y)
          f[3][x_, y_] := 0.5 * (y - x)
In[114]:= Table[f[RandomInteger[{1, 3}]][3, 2], {i, 6}]
Out[114]= {2.5, -0.5, -0.5, -0.5, 2.5, 0.5}
```

The mathematician in you might prefer using subscripts instead.

```
In[115]:= ClearAll[f] ;
          f₁[x_, y_] := 0.5 * (x + y)
          f₂[x_, y_] := 0.5 * (x - y)
          f₃[x_, y_] := 0.5 * (y - x)
In[119]:= f_{RandomInteger[{1,3}]}[3, 2]
Out[119]= 0.5
```

Discussion

In Stan Wagon's *Mathematica in Action* (W.H. Freeman), there is a study of iterated function systems that are nicely expressed in terms of indexed functions. This is a variation of his code that takes advantage of the new RandomChoice function in Mathematica 6. The fernlike structure emerges out of a nonuniform distribution of function selections.

```
In[120]:= ClearAll[f]
          f[1][{x_, y_}] := Dot[{{0.85, 0.04}, {-0.04, 0.85}}, {x, y}] + {0, 1.6}
          f[2][{x_, y_}] := Dot[{{-0.15, 0.28}, {0.26, 0.24}}, {x, y}] + {0, 0.44}
          f[3][{x_, y_}] := Dot[{{0.2, -0.26}, {0.23, 0.22}}, {x, y}] + {0, 1.6}
          f[4][{x_, y_}] := Dot[{{0.0, 0.0}, {0.0, 0.16}}, {x, y}]
          ff[p_] := f[RandomChoice[{85, 7, 7, 1} → {1, 2, 3, 4}]][p]
          fern[n_] :=
           Graphics[{AbsolutePointSize[0.5], Point /@ NestList[ff, {0, 0}, n]},
            PlotRange → {{-3, 3}, {-1, 11}}, AspectRatio → 0.83, ImageSize → Small]
```

```
In[127]:= fern[10 000]
```

Out[127]=

You are not restricted to indexing functions by integers. Here are some variations that are possible.

```
In[128]:= g[1, 1][x_, y_] := x + 2 y
          g[weird][x_, y_] := Exp[Sin[x] Tan[y]]
          g[1 + 2 I] := x + 2 y I
```

2.9 Understanding the Use of Fold As an Alternative to Recursion

Problem

You want to understand and create programs that use Fold[] as an alternative to explicit recursion.

Solution

Consider the following simple recursive definition for a summation function.

```
In[131]:= mySum[{}] := 0
          mySum[l_] := First[l] + mySum[Rest[l]]

In[133]:= mySum[{1, 2, 3, 4, 5}]
Out[133]= 15
```

This function can easily be translated to a nonrecursive implementation that uses Fold[].

```
In[134]:= mySum2[l_] := Fold[#1 + #2 &, 0, l]

In[135]:= mySum[{1, 2, 3, 4, 5}]
Out[135]= 15
```

Discussion

The function Fold[f, x, {a1,a2,...,aN}] computes f[f[f[x,a1],a2],...,aN]. It is a simple enough definition to understand, but it is not always clear to the uninitiated when such a function might be useful. It turns out that there is a relationship between Fold and certain common kinds of recursive functions. Consider the following abstract recursive structure.

```
g[{}] = x
g[l_] = f[First[l], g[Rest[l]]]
```

When a function g has this recursive structure in terms of another function f, then it can easily be translated into a nonrecursive function using Fold, provided f is associative. If f is not associative, then you may need to reverse the list l before passing to Fold.

```
g[l_] = Fold[f[#1,#2]&,x,l]
```

Here is an example that shows that the functionality of Map can be implemented in terms of Fold. First start with your own recursive definition of Map.

```
In[136]:= myMap[_, {}] := {}
          myMap[f_, l_] := Prepend[myMap[f, Rest[l]], f[First[l]]]
```

The translation requires reversing the list because prepending the application of f to a list is clearly not associative.

```
In[138]:= myMap2[f_, l_] := Fold[Prepend[#1, f[#2]] &, {}, Reverse[l]]
```

Here is a test of the recursive implementation, first on an empty list, then on a nonempty one.

```
In[139]:= myMap[Sqrt, {}]
Out[139]= {}
```

```
In[140]:= myMap[Sqrt, {1, 2, 3, 4}]
```
$$Out[140]= \left\{1, \sqrt{2}, \sqrt{3}, 2\right\}$$

Now the Fold version.

```
In[141]:= myMap2[Sqrt, {}]
Out[141]= {}
```

```
In[142]:= myMap2[Sqrt, {1, 2, 3, 4}]
```
$$Out[142]= \left\{1, \sqrt{2}, \sqrt{3}, 2\right\}$$

Before considering more useful applications of Fold, I need to clear up some potential confusion with folding implementations from other languages. In Haskell, there are functions called foldl and foldr, which stand for *fold left* and *fold right*, respectively. Mathematica's Fold is like foldl.

```
In[143]:= (*This is like Haskell's foldr.*)
          foldr[f_, v_, {}] := v
          foldr[f_, v_, l_] := f[First[l], foldr[f, v, Rest[l]]]

In[145]:= (*This is like Haskell's foldl and Mathematica's Fold.*)
          foldl[f_, v_, {}] := v
          foldl[f_, v_, l_] := foldl[f, f[v, First[l]], Rest[l]]
```

These various folds will give the same answer if the function passed is associative and commutative.

```
In[147]:= foldr[Plus, 0, {1, 2, 3}]
Out[147]= 6
```

```
In[148]:= foldl[Plus, 0, {1, 2, 3}]
Out[148]= 6
```

```
In[149]:= Fold[Plus, 0, {1, 2, 3}]
Out[149]= 6
```

To visualize the difference between foldr and foldl, consider the trees produced by using the List function. Trees labeled b and c are the same, confirming the equivalence of Haskell's foldl and Mathematica's Fold.

```
In[150]:= Grid[Partition[MapIndexed[TreeForm[#, ImageMargins → 1,
             ImagePadding → 0, PlotLabel → Extract[{"a", "b", "c"}, #2]] &,
          {foldr[List, {}, {1, 2, 3}], foldl[List, {}, {1, 2, 3}],
           Fold[List, {}, {1, 2, 3}]}], 2, 2, {1, 1}, SpanFromLeft]]
```

Out[150]=

You can use the relationship between Fold and recursion to analyze more complicated use cases. For example, the Mathematica documentation provides an example of using Fold to find all the unique sums of a list of numbers.

```
In[151]:= Fold[Union[#1, #1 + #2] &, {0}, {1, 2, 7}]
Out[151]= {0, 1, 2, 3, 7, 8, 9, 10}
```

When I first saw this, it was not immediately obvious to me why the solution worked. However, by converting to the recursively equivalent solution, it is easier to analyze what is happening.

```
In[152]:= uniqueSums[{}] := {0}
          uniqueSums[l_] :=
            Union[{First[l]}, uniqueSums[Rest[l]], First[l] + uniqueSums[Rest[l]]]
In[154]:= uniqueSums[{1, 2, 7}]
Out[154]= {0, 1, 2, 3, 7, 8, 9, 10}
```

The first rule is obvious. The sum of the empty list is zero. The second rule says that the unique sums of a list are found by taking the union of the first element of the list, the unique sums of the rest of the list, and the sum of the first element and the unique sums of the rest of the list. The last part of the union (First[1] + uniqueSums [Rest[1]]) provided me with the key insight into why this example worked. It is a sum of a scalar and a vector and provides the sum of the first element with all other combinations of sums of the remaining elements. It is obvious that the recursive translation, as written, is suboptimal because the recursive call is made twice (this could easily be fixed with a local variable), but the point here was to use the recursive function as a tool to analyze the meaning of the Fold implementation.

See Also

FoldList is a variant of Fold that returns all intermediate steps of the Fold in a list. Refer to the Mathematica documentation for details.

Nest and NestList also repeatedly apply a function to an expression, but the repetitions are controlled by an integer *n*. See Recipe 2.11.

NestWhile and NestWhileList apply a function as long as a test condition remains true. See Recipe 2.11.

2.10 Incremental Construction of Lists

Problem

You need to build up a list piece by piece during an iterative or recursive computation.

Solution

An obvious solution to this problem is to use the function AppendTo[s, elem]; however, AppendTo should be avoided for performance reasons. Instead, use Reap and Sow. Here is a simple factorial function that collects intermediate results using Reap and Sow.

```
In[155]:= factorialList[n_Integer /; n ≥ 0] := Reap[factorialListSow[n]]
          factorialListSow[0] := Sow[1]
          factorialListSow[n_] := Module[{fact}, Sow[ n * factorialListSow[n - 1]]]
In[158]:= factorialList[8]
Out[158]= {40320, {{1, 1, 2, 6, 24, 120, 720, 5040, 40320}}}
```

Discussion

Reap and Sow cause confusion for some, possibly because there are few languages that have such a feature built in. Simply think of Reap as establishing a private queue and each Sow as pushing an expression to the end of that queue. When control exits Reap, the items are extracted from the queue and returned along with the value computed by the code inside the Reap. I don't claim that Reap and Sow are implemented in this way (they might or might not be), but thinking in these terms will make you more comfortable with their use.

Reap and Sow are often used as evaluation-monitoring functions for numerical algorithms. FindRoot, NDSolve, NIntegrate, NMinimize and NSum allow an optional Evaluation-Monitor or StepMonitor where Reap and Sow can come in handy.

```
In[159]:= Module[{x, y, f = Function[{x, y}, (x^3 - y^2)^2]}, Reap[
            NMinimize[f[x, y],
              {{x, -5, 5}, {y, -5, 5}}, EvaluationMonitor :> Sow[{x, y}]]]]]
Out[159]= {{2.93874×10^-39, {x$2657 → 0.0781025, y$2657 → 0.0218272}},
            {{{1.52468, 1.3307}, {1.82813, 0.663518}, {4.35202, 4.76188},
              {-0.999213, -2.76766}, {0.338596, -0.885272}, {0.0351429, -0.218087},
              {-0.861351, -0.65889}, {-1.15094, -2.43406}, {0.855774, 0.389512},
              {0.552321, 1.0567}, {0.392027, -0.39978}, {-0.428604, -1.00738},
              {0.534679, 0.0402892}, {-0.107509, -0.658156}, {0.374132, -0.134322},
              {0.0172481, 0.0473707}, {-0.170141, 0.270946}, {0.356237, 0.131136},
              {-0.000646785, 0.312828}, {0.280437, -0.0225345},
              {-0.0585518, -0.106299}, {-0.321741, -0.0363943},
              {0.129893, -0.0259995}, {0.205693, 0.127671}, {0.139632, 0.0691781},
              {0.252276, -0.00419199}, {0.0760051, 0.03448}, {0.0662664, -0.0606976},
              {0.12129, 0.0367092}, {0.0674026, 0.0971887}, {0.11427, 0.00479757},
              {0.0830251, 0.0663916}, {0.106459, 0.0201961}, {0.0908364, 0.0509931},
              {0.102553, 0.0278953}, {0.147838, 0.0301245}, {0.0939635, 0.0333911},
              {0.0752265, 0.0245773}, {0.0521947, 0.0185113}, {0.0666367, 0.0300731},
              {0.0935742, 0.0284398}, {0.0748372, 0.0196259}, {0.0931849, 0.0234884},
              {0.0797161, 0.0243051}, {0.0886953, 0.0237606}, {0.0819609, 0.024169},
              {0.100698, 0.0329828}, {0.0813024, 0.0229651}, {0.0929156, 0.027236},
              {0.0846996, 0.0249357}, {0.0901769, 0.0264692}, {0.0860689, 0.0253191},
              {0.0737971, 0.0198445}, {0.0785637, 0.0221984}, {0.0908355, 0.027673},
              {0.0780567, 0.0218016}, {0.085562, 0.0249223}, {0.0838124, 0.0242413},
              {0.0780567, 0.0218016}, {0.0780567, 0.0218016}, {0.0781026, 0.0218272},
              {0.0781025, 0.0218272}, {0.0781025, 0.0218272}, {0.0781025, 0.0218272},
              {0.0780567, 0.0218016}, {0.0780567, 0.0218016}, {0.0780545, 0.021807},
              {0.0780545, 0.021807}, {0.0780545, 0.021807}}}}
```

Reap and Sow also can be used to build up several lists by specifying tags with Sow and patterns that match those tags in Reap. Here you create a three-way partitioning function using an ordering function by sowing values with tags -1, 0, or 1, depending on the relation.

```
In[160]:= partition[l_, v_, comp_] := Flatten /@ Reap[
            Scan[
              Which[comp[#, v], Sow[#, -1],
                comp[v, #], Sow[#, 1], True, Sow[#, 0]] &, l],
            {-1, 0, 1}][[2]]
In[161]:= partition[{3, 5, 7, 9, 2, 4, 6, 8, 3, 4}, 4, Less]
Out[161]= {{3, 2, 3}, {4, 4}, {5, 7, 9, 6, 8}}
```

Our queue analogy easily extends to this case by assuming Reap establishes a separate queue for each pattern and Sow chooses the matching queue.

See Also

Reap and Sow are used in the tree traversal algorithms in Recipe 3.11.

2.11 Computing Through Repeated Function Application

Problem

You want to understand the types of computations you can perform using the Nest family of functions (Nest, NestList, NestWhile, NestWhileList).

Solution

Many problems require repeated application of a function for a specified number of times. One example that is familiar to most people is compounded interest.

```
In[162]:= compoundedInterest[principal_, rate_, years_, n_] :=
            Nest[# (1.0 + rate / n) &, principal, years n]
```

As expected, the principal grows in value quicker the more times the interest is compounded per year.

```
In[163]:= Table[compoundedInterest[1000, 0.05, 10, n], {n, {1, 2, 4, 12, 365}}]
Out[163]= {1628.89, 1638.62, 1643.62, 1647.01, 1648.66}
```

Another classic application is fractals. Here I use Nest to generate one side of the Koch snowflake. The rule for creating the snowflake is to take the line segment, divide it into three equal segments, rotate copies of the middle segment Pi/3 and -Pi/3 radians from their ends to form an equilateral triangle, and then remove the middle section of the original line segment. This is implemented literally (but not efficiently) by iterating a replacement rule using Nest. We cover these rules in Chapter 4.

```
In[164]:=  Clear[koch, snowflake]
           koch[Line[x_]] := With[{s = ScalingMatrix[{1/3, 1/3}],
               r1 = RotationMatrix[Pi/3], r2 = RotationMatrix[-Pi/3]},
              { Line[x.s], Line[x.r1.s + {{1/3, 0}, {1/3, 0}}],
               Line[x.r2.s + {{1/2, -0.289}, {1/2, -0.289}}],
               Line[s.x + {{2/3, 0}, {2/3, 0}}]}]
           snowflake[n_] := With[{g = Graphics[{Line[{{0, 0}, {1, 0}}]}]},
               Nest[# /. Line[x_] :> koch[Line[x]] &, g, n]]
           GraphicsGrid[
              {{snowflake[1], snowflake[3]}, {snowflake[2], snowflake[4]}}]
```

Out[167]=

Discussion

If you are interested in the intermediate values of the iteration, NestList is the answer. Suppose you want to see all rotations of a shape through d radians. Here I use NestList to rotate clockwise and translate a square with a dot in its corner through angle d until at least 2Pi radians (360 degrees) are covered.

```
In[168]:=  allRotations[shape_, d_] := With[{n = Ceiling[2 Pi/d]},
               Graphics[NestList[Translate[Rotate[#, -d], {1.5, 0}] &, shape, n]]]
           allRotations[{Red, Rectangle[], Black, Point[{0.90, 0.1}]}, Pi/6]
```

Out[169]=

NestWhile and NestWhileList generalize Nest and NestList, respectively, by adding a test predicate to determine if the iterative application of the function should continue. In addition to the test, an upper limit can be specified to guarantee the iteration terminates in a given number of steps if the test does not terminate it first. Here is an application that searches for a tour in a traveling salesperson problem (TSP) that is less than some specified distance. The cities are numbered 1 through n, and the distances are represented as a sparse matrix.

```
In[170]:=  (*Make random set of cities.*)
           makeCities[n_] :=
            SparseArray[Flatten[
              Table[{i, j} → If[i == j, 0, RandomReal[{1, 50}]], {i, 1, n}, {j, 1, i}]]]
           (*Given set of cities, and two particular cities,
           return distance between.*)
           distance[cities_, c1_, c2_] :=
            With[{i1 = Max[c1, c2], i2 = Min[c1, c2]}, cities[[i1, i2]]]
           (*Given a tour, compute the total distance traveled
            if you visit each city and return to the first.*)
           totalDistance[cities_, tour_] :=
            Total[ListConvolve[{1, 1}, tour,
              {-1, -1}, tour, #2 &, distance[cities, #1, #2] &]]
           (*Make an initial tour where cities are visted in
            ascending order of city number.*)
           makeOrderedTour[cities_] := Range[Length[cities]]
           (*Randomly sample tours until a tour is less
            than specified distance or maxTries is exceeded.*)
           findTourLessThan[cities_, distance_, maxTries_] :=
            Module[{n = Length[cities]},
             NestWhile[RandomSample[#, n] &, makeOrderedTour[cities],
              totalDistance[cities, #] >= distance &, maxTries]]
```

The algorithm is not very intelligent, but it nicely demonstrates NestWhile. First I make a random set of 10 cities and see the distance of the ordered tour.

```
In[175]:=  cities = makeCities[10];
           dist = totalDistance[cities, makeOrderedTour[cities]]
Out[176]=  273.898
```

Now I see if I can find a better tour that is better than 80% of the ordered tour in 100,000 tries.

```
In[177]:=  findTourLessThan[cities, 0.80 dist , 100 000]
Out[177]=  {9, 5, 10, 2, 6, 8, 3, 7, 1, 4}
```

You can see that it was successful!

```
In[178]:=  totalDistance[cities, %]
Out[178]=  300.754
```

See Also

The replacement rules used in the Koch snowflake are covered in Chapter 4.

In Recipe 12.16, NestList is used to drive a simulation.

The TSP example used ListConvolve to compute the distance of a tour. See Recipe 2.6.

2.12 Building a Function Through Iteration

Problem

You want to construct a higher-order function from explicit iteration of a lower-order function.

Solution

This is a good application for Nest. For example, you can pre-expand terms in Newton's method for $\sqrt{n}$.

```
In[179]:= Clear[f, x, y, z, n, terms];
          makeSqrtNewtonExpansion[n_, terms_Integer: 4]  :=
            Function[x,
              Evaluate[Together[Nest[Function[z, (z + n / z) / 2], x, terms]]]]
```

```
In[181]:= sqrt2 = makeSqrtNewtonExpansion[2, 4]
```

Out[181]= Function$\left[x\$, \left(256 + 15360\ x\$^2 + 116480\ x\$^4 + \right.\right.$
$256256\ x\$^6 + 205920\ x\$^8 + 64064\ x\$^{10} + 7280\ x\$^{12} + 240\ x\$^{14} + x\$^{16}\right) /$
$\left(16\ x\$\ \left(2 + x\$^2\right)\ \left(4 + 12\ x\$^2 + x\$^4\right)\ \left(16 + 224\ x\$^2 + 280\ x\$^4 + 56\ x\$^6 + x\$^8\right)\right)\right]$

We are left with a function that will converge quickly to sqrt[2] when given an initial guess. Here we see it takes just four iterations to converge.

```
In[182]:= FixedPointList[sqrt2, 1`40]
```

Out[182]= {1.000000000000000000000000000000000000000,
          1.4142135623746899106262955788901349 1012,
          1.4142135623730950488016887242096980786,
          1.4142135623730950488016887242096980079}

Discussion

Code generation is a powerful technique; the solution shows how Function and Nest can be used with Evaluate to create such a generator. The key here is the use of Evaluate, which forces the Nest to execute immediately to create the body of the function. Later, when you use the function, you execute just the generated code (i.e., the cost of the Nest is paid only during generation, not application).

Fold can also be used as a generator. Here is an example of constructing a continued fraction using Fold adapted from Eric W. Weisstein's "Continued Fraction" from MathWorld (*http://bit.ly/35rxJF*).

```
In[183]:= continuedFraction[{a0_, l_List?MatrixQ}] :=
            a0 + Fold[#2[[1]] / (#1 + #2[[2]]) &, 0, Reverse[l]]
          continuedFraction[{a0_, {}}] := a0
```

```
In[185]:= continuedFraction[{a[0], Table[{b[i], a[i]}, {i, 4}]}] /.
            x_[y_] :> Subscript[x, y]
```

$$Out[185]= a_0 + \cfrac{b_1}{a_1 + \cfrac{b_2}{a_2 + \cfrac{b_3}{a_3 + \cfrac{b_4}{a_4}}}}$$

2.13 Exploiting Function Composition and Inverse Functions

Problem

You want to compose one or more functions to produce a new function, with the added ability to easily invert the new function.

Solution

Use Composition to build a new function f1[f2[f3...[x]]] from f1, f2, f3... and InverseFunction to convert the composition to ...f3^{-1}[f2^{-1}[f1^{-1}[x]]].

```
In[186]:= f = Composition[Exp, Cos]
Out[186]= Composition[Exp, Cos]
```

```
In[187]:= result = f[0.5]
Out[187]= 2.40508
```

```
In[188]:= Exp[Cos[0.5]]
Out[188]= 2.40508
```

If the composed functions are invertible, you can compute the inverse of the composition.

```
In[189]:= InverseFunction[f][result]
Out[189]= 0.5
```

Discussion

The Mathematica 6 documentation for Composition is not very compelling. It lists the following examples of usage:

```
In[190]:= (*Create a sum of numbers to be displayed in held form.*)
          Composition[HoldForm, Plus] @@ Range[20]

          1 + 2 + 3 + 4 + 5 + 6 + 7 + 8 + 9 + 10 + 11 + 12 + 13 + 14 + 15 + 16 + 17 + 18 + 19 + 20
Out[190]= 1 + 2 + 3 + 4 + 5 + 6 + 7 + 8 + 9 + 10 + 11 + 12 + 13 + 14 + 15 + 16 + 17 + 18 + 19 + 20

Out[191]= 1 + 2 + 3 + 4 + 5 + 6 + 7 + 8 + 9 + 10 + 11 + 12 + 13 + 14 + 15 + 16 + 17 + 18 + 19 + 20

In[192]:= (*Tabulate square roots of values without using auxiliary variables.*)
          TableForm[Composition[Through, {Identity, Sqrt}] /@ {0, 1.0, 2.0, 3.0, 4.0}]
Out[192]//TableForm=
          0   0
          1.  1.
          2.  1.41421
          3.  1.73205
          4.  2.
```

Although these are certainly examples of usage, they are not compelling because the same results can be achieved without Composition and, to my tastes, more simply.

```
In[193]:= HoldForm[Plus[##]] & @@ Range[20]
Out[193]= 1 + 2 + 3 + 4 + 5 + 6 + 7 + 8 + 9 + 10 + 11 + 12 + 13 + 14 + 15 + 16 + 17 + 18 + 19 + 20
```

This is an example of Recipe 2.4.

```
In[194]:= {Identity[#], Sqrt[#]} & /@ {0, 1.0, 2.0, 3.0, 4.0} // TableForm
Out[194]//TableForm=
          0   0
          1.  1.
          2.  1.41421
          3.  1.73205
          4.  2.
```

For some time I thought that Composition was just a curiosity that might appeal to some mathematically minded folks on aesthetic grounds but otherwise did not add much value. This was before I understood how Composition can work together with InverseFunction. When you have an arbitrary composition of functions, InverseFunction will produce an inverse of the composition by inverting each component and reversing the order of application. In the case of the example in the preceding "Solution" section, you get the following:

```
In[195]:= InverseFunction[Composition[Exp, Cos]]
Out[195]= Composition[ArcCos, Log]
```

Unfortunately, mathematical functions often are not invertible, so this particular example will not always work given an arbitrary list of functions. But the really cool thing is that the functions need not be mathematical or perfectly invertible as long as you tell Mathematica you know what you're doing by defining the inverses of your custom functions!

You can see that Mathematica has no idea what the inverse of RotateRight is, even though it is obvious that for a list it is RotateLeft.

```
In[196]:= InverseFunction[RotateRight][{1, 2, 3}]
Out[196]= RotateRight^(-1)[{1, 2, 3}]
```

But you can define your own version and its inverse by using upvalues (see "DownValues and UpValues" on page 27).

```
In[197]:= ClearAll[reverse, rotateRight];
          rotateRight[list_List] := RotateRight[list]
          (*Define an UpValue for inverse of rotateRight.*)
          InverseFunction[rotateRight] ^:= RotateLeft[#1] &
          reverse[list_List] := Reverse[list]
          (*Clearly, reverse is its own inverse.*)
          InverseFunction[reverse] ^:= reverse[#] &
```

Now, given an arbitrary composition of these functions, we are guaranteed the ability to produce its inverse with no effort at all! I find that compelling, don't you?

```
In[202]:= tr1 = Composition[reverse, rotateRight, rotateRight];

In[203]:= v = tr1[{1, 2, 3, 4, 5, 6}]
Out[203]= {4, 3, 2, 1, 6, 5}

In[204]:= InverseFunction[tr1][v]
Out[204]= {1, 2, 3, 4, 5, 6}
```

The obvious implication of this simple example is that if you define a set of functions and inverses, then given an arbitrary composition of those functions, you will always have the undo operation handy. Further, you get partial undo via Drop.

```
In[205]:= (*Drop one level of undo.*)
          Drop[InverseFunction[tr1], 1][v]
Out[205]= {6, 1, 2, 3, 4, 5}
```

In Recipe 2.7 we discussed composing functions using prefix operator @. The following illustrates the relationship:

```
In[206]:= Composition[f1, f2, f3][x] === f1@f2@f3@x
Out[206]= True
```

See Also

ComposeList returns the list of results computed by successive compositions of a given list of functions. See the Mathematica documentation.

2.14 Implementing Closures

Problem

You want to create expressions with persistent private state, behavior, and identity, but Mathematica does not directly support Lisp-like closures or object-oriented programming.

 The techniques described in this section fall a bit outside garden-variety Mathematica; some purists may frown on using techniques that make Mathematica feel like a different language. They might argue that Mathematica has enough features to solve problems and that users are better off mastering these rather than trying to morph the language into something else. I think this advice is generally sound. However, Mathematica is a system for multiparadigm programming as well as a system for research and exploration. So if you are interested, as I am, in exploring software development concepts for their own sake, I think you will find this recipe useful in stimulating new ideas about what Mathematica can do.

Solution

Create a symbol called closure with attributes HoldAll and with the form closure [var_List, val_List, func_List]. Create an evaluation function for closures that executes in a private environment provided by Block and returns the result and a new closure that captures any state changes that occurred during the evaluation.

```
In[207]:=  SetAttributes[closure, HoldAll];
           SetAttributes[evaluate, HoldFirst];
           evaluate[f_, closure[vars_, vals_, funcs_]] := Block[vars, vars = vals;
             Block[funcs, {f, closure[vars, Evaluate[vars], funcs]}]]
```

You can now use this machinery to create a counter.

```
In[210]:=  ClearAll[makeCounter, counter];
           makeCounter[init_] := With[{v = init}, closure[{x}, {v},
             {incr = Function[x = x + 1], decr = Function[x = x - 1],
              reset = Function[v, x = v], read = Function[x]}]]
           counter = makeCounter[0]
Out[212]=  closure[{x}, {0}, {incr = (x = x + 1) &,
             decr = (x = x - 1) &, reset = Function[v, x = v], read = x &}]
```

From a syntactic point of view, the implementation is only half done, but it is usable (see the folllowing "Discussion" for the icing on the cake).

```
In[213]:= {val, counter} = evaluate[incr[], counter]; val
Out[213]= 1
```

When you evaluate again, you see that the state change persisted.

```
In[214]:= {val, counter} = evaluate[incr[], counter]; val
Out[214]= 2
```

Notice that even though the closure contains a free variable x, changes to x in the global environment do not impact the closure.

```
In[215]:= x = 0;
          {val, counter} = evaluate[incr[], counter]; val
Out[216]= 3
```

However, you can reset the counter through the provided interface. You can also decrement it and read its current value.

```
In[217]:= {val, counter} = evaluate[decr[], counter]; val
Out[217]= 2
```

```
In[218]:= {val, counter} = evaluate[reset[7], counter]; val
Out[218]= 7
```

```
In[219]:= {val, counter} = evaluate[read[7], counter]; val
Out[219]= 7
```

Discussion

In computer science, a closure is a function that closes over the lexical environment in which it was defined. In some languages (e.g., Lisp, JavaScript), a closure may occur when a function is defined within another function, and the inner function refers to local variables of the outer function. Mathematica cannot do this in a safe way (as discussed here), hence the solution.

The solution presented is a bit awkward to use and read and, thus, would be easy to dismiss as a mere curiosity. However, we can use an advanced feature of Mathematica to make the solution far more compelling, especially to those readers who come from an object-oriented mind-set. One problem with the solution is that you need to deal with both the returned value and the returned closure. This is easy to fix by defining a function call that hides this housekeeping.

```
In[220]:= SetAttributes[call, HoldAll];
          call[f_, c_] := Module[{val}, {val, c} = evaluate[f, c]; val]
```

This simplifies things considerably.

```
In[222]:= val = call[decr[], counter]
Out[222]= 6
```

But we can go further by adding some syntactic sugar using the Notation facility.

```
In[223]:= << Notation`
          Notation[c_ ⇒ func_ ⇔ call[func_, c_]];
```

Now you can write code like this:

```
In[225]:= counter ⇒ incr[]
Out[225]= 7
```

```
In[226]:= counter ⇒ reset[0]
Out[226]= 0
```

```
In[227]:= counter ⇒ incr[]
Out[227]= 1
```

You can use an existing closure to create new independent closures by creating a clone method. This is known as the *prototype pattern*.

```
In[228]:= clone[closure[vars_, vals_, funcs_]] :=
            clone[closure[vars, vals, funcs], vals]
          clone[closure[vars_, vals_, funcs_], newVals_] :=
            With[{v = newVals}, closure[vars, v, funcs]]
```

```
In[230]:= counter2 = clone[counter] (*Clone existing state.*)
Out[230]= closure[{x}, {1}, {incr = (x = x + 1) &,
            decr = (x = x - 1) &, reset = Function[v, x = v], read = x &}]
```

```
In[231]:= counter3 = clone[counter, {0}]
            (*Clone structure but initialize to new state.*)
Out[231]= closure[{x}, {0}, {incr = (x = x + 1) &,
            decr = (x = x - 1) &, reset = Function[v, x = v], read = x &}]
```

You can see these counters are independent from the original counters (but they do share the same functions, so they don't incur much additional memory overhead).

```
In[232]:= counter2 ⇒ incr[]
Out[232]= 2
```

```
In[233]:= counter3 ⇒ incr[]
Out[233]= 1
```

```
In[234]:= counter ⇒ read[]
Out[234]= 1
```

It is instructive to compare this solution with other languages that support closures. In JavaScript, a closure over an accumulator can be created like this:

javascript

```
function counter (n) {
    return function (i) { return n += i }
    }
```

Let's see what happens if we attempt the same approach in Mathematica.

```
In[235]:= Clear[makeCounter];
          makeCounter[n_Integer] := Function[i, n += i]
          counter = makeCounter[0];

In[238]:= counter[1]
```

AddTo::rvalue :
  0 is not a variable with a value, so its value cannot
      be changed. >>

```
Out[238]= 0 += 1
```

This was doomed from the start because *n* is not a free variable that can be closed over by Function. But let's try something else.

```
In[239]:= Clear[makeCounter, state];
          makeCounter[n_Integer] := Block[{state = n}, Function[i, state += i]]
          counter = makeCounter[0];

In[242]:= counter[1]
```

AddTo::rvalue :
  state is not a variable with a value, so its value
      cannot be changed. >>

```
Out[242]= state += 1
```

This fails because state is only defined while the block is active, because Block is a dynamic scoping construct and closures require lexical scoping. You might recall that Module is a lexical scoping construct; perhaps we would have better luck with that.

```
In[243]:= Clear[makeCounter, state];
          makeCounter[n_Integer] := Module[{state = n}, Function[i, state += i]]
          counter = makeCounter[0];

In[246]:= counter[1]
Out[246]= 1

In[247]:= counter[1]
Out[247]= 2
```

This seems to work, but it has a flaw that you can see if you inspect the value of counter.

```
In[248]:= counter
Out[248]= Function[i$, state$2811 += i$]
```

The variable we called state has now morphed into something called state$<*some number*>. The point here is that Module implements lexical scope by synthesizing a global variable that is guaranteed not to be defined already, but that variable is not protected in any way and could be changed by the user. This is not esthetically pleasing and is not at all what is happening in the JavaScript or Lisp equivalents.

The solution in this recipe uses a different tactic. It uses the HoldAll attribute to create a container for the lexical environment of the closure. Because the variables and functions are held in unevaluated form, it makes no difference if there are global symbols with the same names. When it comes time to evaluate the closure, the evaluate function builds up a Block on the fly to create local instances of the variables and another Block to create local instances of the functions. It then binds the stored values of the variables and functions to these locals and calls the appropriate locally defined function.

What practical value are closures within the context of Mathematica? Clearly, creating a counter is too trivial. However, even the simple counter example shows some promising features of this technique. First, had we implemented the counter as a simple global variable, it could be used accidentally for some purpose inconsistent with the behavior of a counter. By encapsulating the counter in the closure, we restrict access to its state and the interface exposed by the closure becomes the only way to manipulate it. Further, the interface can be easily inspected because it is carried around inside the closure.

Mathematica 6's Dynamic feature provides the context for a compelling application of closures. Let's say you want to create a graphic that can be dynamically updated under programmatic control (rather than user control, for which you would use Manipulate instead). One way to do this is to define variables for all the aspects of the graphic that you need to change and wrap the graphic in a Dynamic function.

```
In[249]:= rectX = 1; rectY = 2; rectAngle = 10 Degree; circR = 1;
         DynamicModule[{g},
           g = Graphics[{Thick, Green, Rotate[Rectangle[{0, 0}, {rectX, rectY}],
               rectAngle], Red, Disk[{0, 0}, circR]}, ImageSize → Small];
           Dynamic[
             g]]
```

Out[250]=

You then write Mathematica code that manipulates the variables as necessary to dynamically update the drawing. This is all well and good for a simple example with two shapes and four degrees of freedom, but imagine if you were doing this as part of a simulation that had hundreds of shapes with hundreds of degrees of freedom. Clearly, you would want a way to encapsulate all those variables behind an interface that made sense for the simulation. This closure facility can do just that.

```
In[251]:= ClearAll[shapeCtrl]
         shapeCtrl = closure[{rectX, rectY, rectAngle, circR}, {1, 2, 10 Degree, 1},
           {rotate = Function[a, rectAngle += a],
            grow = Function[r, rectX *= r; rectY *= r],
            rectCorner = Function[{rectX, rectY}],
            angle = Function[rectAngle],
            radius = Function[circR]}]
Out[252]= closure[{rectX, rectY, rectAngle, circR},
           {1, 2, 10 °, 1}, {rotate = Function[a, rectAngle += a],
            grow = Function[r, rectX *= r; rectY *= r],
            rectCorner = {rectX, rectY} &, angle = rectAngle &, radius = circR &}]
```

```
In[253]:= closure[{rectX, rectY, rectAngle, circR},
          {1, 2, 10°, 1}, {rotate = Function[a, rectAngle += a],
          grow = Function[r, rectX *= r; rectY *= r],
          rectCorner = {rectX, rectY} &, angle = rectAngle &, radius = circR &}]

Out[253]= closure[{rectX, rectY, rectAngle, circR},
          {1, 2, 10°, 1}, {rotate = Function[a, rectAngle += a],
          grow = Function[r, rectX *= r; rectY *= r],
          rectCorner = {rectX, rectY} &, angle = rectAngle &, radius = circR &}]
```

Here you define a closure, called shapeCtrl, over the same graphic but expose only two functions, rotate and grow, that are capable of changing the state. The other functions are strictly for returning the values for use in the graphic. You now specify the dynamic graphic in terms of the shape controller closure.

```
In[254]:= Dynamic[Graphics[{Thick, Green, Rotate[
          Rectangle[{0, 0}, shapeCtrl ⇒ rectCorner[]], shapeCtrl ⇒ angle[]], Red,
          Disk[{0, 0}, shapeCtrl ⇒ radius[]]}, Frame → True, PlotRange → All]];
```

By its nature, dynamic content does not lend itself to static print demonstration, but we compensate by showing the result of each transform in the figure.

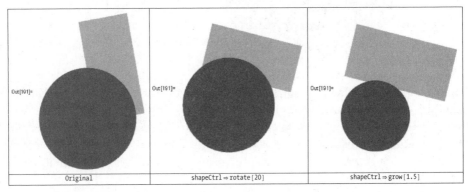

Figure 2-1. Transformations snapshots of the graphics

It could be argued that this recipe has crossed the boundary of the traditional definition of a closure and moved toward the capabilities of object-oriented programming. This is no accident, since there is a relationship between closures and objects, in that closures can be used to implement object-oriented programming, and languages like C++ can implement closures in terms of objects with operator(). However, a full-blown, object-oriented implementation would have to provide additional features not implemented by this recipe. Inheritance is the most obvious, but there are others (e.g., different access levels for functions and data). I prefer to think of this implementation as souped-up closures rather than dumbed-down objects, but you can think of them in whichever way makes the most sense to you. My feeling is that more traditional closures that act like single functions don't provide enough bang for the buck. In any case, the simpler, traditional form can be implemented in terms of the richer form demonstrated in this recipe. Here is one way to do it.

```
In[255]:= (*First define a closure with a
             single function and assign to a variable.*)
          incr = closure[{x}, {0}, {incr = Function[x = x + 1]}]
Out[255]= closure[{x}, {0}, {incr = (x = x + 1) &}]

In[256]:= (*Then define a function pattern in terms of the same closure
             but with a Blank where the state variables would reside.*)
          closure[{x}, {_}, {incr = Function[x = x + 1]}] [] := call[incr[], incr]

In[257]:= (*Now, whenever the variable is used like a function,
          it will invoke the call on the closure.*)
          incr[]
Out[257]= 1

In[258]:= incr[]
Out[258]= 2

In[259]:= incr[]
Out[259]= 3
```

See Also

The Wikipedia entry for closures (*http://bit.ly/T9vhN*) is a good place to start learning more about this concept because it contains links to some useful papers and implementations in other languages.

2.15 Currying in Mathematica

Problem

You want to emulate the ability of other functional languages to automatically convert functions of multiple arguments into higher-order functions with a single argument.

 This recipe is more of theoretical interest to functional programming aficionados than of practical use for everyday Mathematica development. The techniques employed are of more general interest, but you may need to consult Chapter 4 if you are unfamiliar with patterns and replacement rules.

Solution

Mathematica does not support implicit currying like Haskell does, but you can use this solution to create functions that curry implicitly. Refer to the next section, "Discussion," if you are unfamiliar with currying.

```
In[260]:= Clear[f, f1, f2]; Curry[f_, x__] :=
             Module[{expr}, expr = Hold[If[ValueQ[f[x]], f[x], Curry[z, ##] &]] //.
                  g_[a__][b__] -> g[a, b] /. z -> f[x]; ReleaseHold[expr]]
          f[x_, y_, z_] := x + y +
                z
```

```
In[262]:= (*Create f1 by currying f.*)
          f1 = Curry[f, 10]
Out[262]= Curry[f[10], ##1] &
```

```
In[263]:= (*f2 now can be created by implicit currying f1.*)
          f2 = f1[20]
Out[263]= Curry[f[10][20], ##1] &
```

```
In[264]:= (*f2 evaluates because all three arguments become available.*)
          f2[30]
Out[264]= 60
```

```
In[265]:= (*f1 evaluates if the remaining two arguments are supplied.*)
          f1[20, 30]
Out[265]= 60
```

```
In[266]:= (*And the curried syntax works as well.*)
          f1[20][30]
Out[266]= 60
```

Discussion

Currying is the process of transforming a function that takes multiple arguments into a function that takes just a single argument and returns another function if any arguments are still needed. In languages that implicitly curry, you can write code as follows:

```
In[267]:= f1 = f[10]
Out[267]= f[10]
```

```
In[268]:= f2 = f1[20]
Out[268]= f[10][20]
```

```
In[269]:= f2[30]
Out[269]= f[10][20][30]
```

This is legal in Mathematica, but notice that when all three arguments are supplied, the function remains in unevaluated curried form. This is not the effect that you typically want. It is possible to manually uncurry by using ReplaceAllRepeated (//.) to transform the curried form to normal form.

```
In[270]:= f2[30] //. g_[a_][b__] → g[a, b]
Out[270]= 60
```

The function Curry in the solution works as follows. It builds up an expression that says, "See if the specified function (first argument) with the specified parameters (second argument) will evaluate (ValueQ); if so, evaluate it. Otherwise, return the curried version of the function within a lambda expression using the Curry function itself." To add to the trickery, this expression needs to be built up in the context of a Hold to keep everything unevaluated until it can be transformed into a format where the ValueQ test and evaluation are in uncurried form. However, the lambda function part must remain in curried form, so we use z as a placeholder for a second round ReplaceAll (/.) that injects the curried form, instead of z.

I'll be the first to admit this is tricky, but if you are tenacious (and perhaps look ahead to some of the recipes in Chapter 4), you will be rewarded with a deeper understanding of how powerful Mathematica can be at bootstrapping new behaviors. One way to get a handle on what is happening is to execute a version of Curry that does not release the Hold. This allows you to inspect the result at each stage before it is evaluated.

```
In[271]:= CurryHold[f_, x__] :=
            Module[{expr}, expr = Hold[If[ValueQ[f[x]], f[x], Curry[z, ##] &]] //.
              g_[a_][b__] -> g[a, b] /. z → f[x]]
```

When the Hold is released, ValueQ[f[10]] will return false, so we will return a Function (&) that curries f[10] with yet to be supplied arguments ##1.

```
In[272]:= CurryHold[f, 10]
Out[272]= Hold[If[ValueQ[f[10]], f[10], Curry[f[10], ##1] &]]
```

When this Hold is released, ValueQ will also fail because there is no two-argument version of f, and we get a further currying function on f[10][20] that is ready for more arguments ##1.

```
In[273]:= CurryHold[f1, 20]
Out[273]= Hold[If[ValueQ[f[10, 20]], f[10, 20], Curry[f[10][20], ##1] &]]
```

Finally, by supplying a third argument, we get an uncurried function f[10,20,30] that will evaluate; so ValueQ succeeds, and the uncurried version is evaluated.

```
In[274]:= CurryHold[f2, 30]
Out[274]= Hold[If[ValueQ[f[10, 20, 30]], f[10, 20, 30], Curry[f[10][20][30], ##1] &]]
```

A useful addition is a function that creates a self-currying function without supplying the first argument.

```
In[275]:=  makeCurry[f_] := Curry[f, ##] &

In[276]:=  f0 = makeCurry[f]
Out[276]=  Curry[f, ##1] &

In[277]:=  f0[10] [20] [30]
Out[277]=  60
```

So now that you've suffered through this magic act, I expect you'd like to be told that there is some neat application of currying. However, as I mentioned in the warning on page 73, currying is largely of theoretical interest. This is true even in languages where it occurs transparently. For example, many new Haskell programmers don't think in terms of transformations from functions to higher-order functions, but rather, in terms of producing new functions that are specializations of existing functions (i.e., the new function is produced by binding the first argument of the general function). The reason Haskell was designed with currying functions is that its designers were concerned with formal proofs of correctness. Such proofs are easier when all functions can be thought of as having a single argument and producing a single result. If you're a mathematician, you may find these ideas interesting; please see the references in the "See Also" section on page 77.

I should emphasize that the goal of this recipe was to achieve implicit currying. Explicit currying is easy. In fact, explicit currying should really not be called currying at all, but rather, should be called partial function application. For example, if you want to manually create a function that hard codes the first parameter of f to 10, simply write f[10, ##]& . You can automate creation of such functions with the following code:

```
In[278]:=  explicitCurry[f_, v_] := Function[f[v, ##]]

In[279]:=  f1 = explicitCurry[f, 10];
           f2 = explicitCurry[f1, 20];

In[281]:=  f1[20, 30]
Out[281]=  60

In[282]:=  f2[30]
Out[282]=  60
```

The obvious difference between implicit and explicit currying is the need to explicitly use the currying function each time, hence the name "explicit."

See Also

Information on currying in Haskell can be found at *http://bit.ly/2eABAm*.

You will be impressed by the expressiveness of Mathematica by comparing the amount of code in this recipe with the code to implement implicit currying in scheme (*http://bit.ly/otB90*).

Theoretical ideas about the relationship between proofs and programs can be found at *http://bit.ly/2YrkxI*.

2.16 Creating Functions with Default Values

Problem

You want to create functions with optional arguments that specify default values.

Solution

The simplest way to define a function with default values is to use the syntax x_: default or x_h:default.

```
In[283]:= someFunc[arg1_Integer, arg2_Integer : 0] := arg1 ^ 2 + arg2
```

```
In[284]:= someFunc[10]
Out[284]= 100
```

```
In[285]:= someFunc[10, 1]
Out[285]= 101
```

Another technique is to register a global default value with Mathematica using Default. This facility is used by many built-in Mathematica functions, such as Plus. You can use Default to query or set defaults for your own functions. Defaults can apply to multiple arguments or specific arguments.

```
In[286]:= Default[Plus] (*Missing arguments to Plus default to zero.*)
Out[286]= 0
```

```
In[287]:= Plus[]
Out[287]= 0
```

```
In[288]:= Plus[1]
Out[288]= 1
```

If you ask for a default that is undefined, the function will not evaluate.

```
In[289]:= ClearAll[myFuncWithDefault]; Default[myFuncWithDefault, 2]
Out[289]= Default[myFuncWithDefault, 2]
```

You must define the default before defining the function that uses it.

```
In[290]:= Default[myFuncWithDefault, 2] = 0
Out[290]= 0
```

```
In[291]:= Default[myFuncWithDefault, 2]
Out[291]= 0
```

An argument whose default has been registered with Default is specified as x_. (the trailing period signals the default).

```
In[292]:= myFuncWithDefault[x_, y_.] := x^y - x + y
```

When you inspect the definition of a function, it shows the registered defaults.

```
In[293]:= Definition[myFuncWithDefault]
```
$$Out[293]= \text{myFuncWithDefault}[x\_, y\_.] := x^y - x + y$$

$$\text{myFuncWithDefault} /: \text{Default}[\text{myFuncWithDefault}, 2] = 0$$

```
In[294]:= myFuncWithDefault[4]
Out[294]= -3
```

```
In[295]:= myFuncWithDefault[10, 1]
Out[295]= 1
```

Discussion

Unlike in some other languages, in Mathematica, the arguments with default values need not be at the end.

```
In[296]:= someFunc2[arg1_Integer : 1, arg2_Integer] := arg1 ^ 2 + arg2
```

```
In[297]:= someFunc2[10]
Out[297]= 11
```

```
In[298]:= someFunc2[10, 1]
Out[298]= 101
```

Ambiguities are resolved by assigning values to the leftmost argument that matches.

```
In[299]:= someFunc3[arg1_Integer : 1, arg2_Integer : 0] := 2 arg1 + arg2
```

```
In[300]:= someFunc3[10]
Out[300]= 20
```

```
In[301]:= someFunc4[arg1_String : "test", arg2_Integer : 1] := StringTake[arg1, arg2]
```

```
In[302]:= someFunc4[3] (*3 does not match String
            so it is assigned to the second default.*)
Out[302]= tes
```

Having this much flexibility is sometimes useful, but if you are writing a library of functions to be used by others, it is probably best to place all parameters with defaults at the end.

You may be wondering why Mathematica provides two distinct methods to specify default values. The flippant answer is that Mathematica provides at least two ways to do everything! But there are useful differences. For functions you write for your own use, the arg_ : default does the job in most cases. The advantage of the Default method is that it separates the default definition from the function definition. This allows users to alter the defaults if they do so before loading the module containing your functions, and if you code your module to only define defaults if existing defaults are not already defined.

```
BeginPackage["SomePackage`"]

yourFunction::usage = "This function works miracles."

Begin["`Private`"]

(*If there are not already defaults defined, define them.*)
If[DefaultValues[yourFunction] == {},
    Default[yourFunction] = 0,
    Null];

yourFunction[a_,b_,c_.,d_.] := ...

End[]

EndPackage[]
```

2.17 Creating Functions That Accept Options

Problem

You need to write a function that can be customized by the user in a variety of ways.

Solution

Set up default values for the function by registering them with Options[yourFun]. Then write the function to accept an optional OptionsPattern[] as the last argument. Use the companion function OptionValue[option] to retrieve the effective value of option. I'll illustrate this technique by implementing a quick sort algorithm. There are two obvious ways to customize a quick sort. First, you can allow the user to specify the comparison function. Second, you can allow the caller to customize the function used to select the pivot element.

 This quick sort is in no way as performant as Mathematica's Sort[], so I don't recommend using it. I introduce it solely to illustrate a custom function with options.

By default, use the first element to pivot and the Less function for comparisons.

```
In[303]:= Options[qsort] = {pivot → First, compare → Less} ;
```

The options, by convention, are accepted as the last parameter.

```
In[304]:= qsort[l_List, opts : OptionsPattern[]] :=
            Module[{pivotFunc, compareFunc},
              {pivotFunc, compareFunc} = {OptionValue[pivot], OptionValue[compare]} ;
              Reap[qsort2[l, pivotFunc, compareFunc]][[2, 1]]]
```

Function qsort2 does most of the work after options are resolved. The partition is from Recipe 2.10.

```
In[305]:= qsort2[{}, _, _] := {}
            qsort2[{a_}, _, _] := Sow[a]
            qsort2[l_List, pivot_, comp_] :=
            Block[{l1, l2, l3}, {l1, l2, l3} = partition[l, pivot[l], comp];
              qsort2[l1, pivot, comp];
              Scan[Sow, l2];
              qsort2[l3, pivot, comp]]
```

Prior to version 6, OptionValue[] did not exist. The idiomatic solution used ReplaceAll (/.) to first apply user-specified options and then the default options. You may still encounter this idiom in older code.

```
        {pivotFunc, compareFunc} = {pivot, compare} /. opts /. Options[qsort];
```

Let's test the function with and without options.

```
In[308]:= unsorted = RandomInteger[{-100, 100}, 50]
Out[308]= {42, 77, 50, 98, -89, 49, 21, 70, 2, -39, 41, -100, 32, -19, -36, 99, 43,
            37, 34, 35, -98, 58, -10, -38, -80, 25, -40, -26, 3, 62, -13, 5, 15, -40,
            83, -74, -43, 31, 78, -89, 15, 60, 67, -55, -7, -45, -16, -91, 21, 16}

In[309]:= qsort[unsorted]
Out[309]= {-100, -98, -91, -89, -89, -80, -74, -55, -45, -43, -40, -40, -39, -38,
            -36, -26, -19, -16, -13, -10, -7, 2, 3, 5, 15, 15, 16, 21, 21, 25, 31,
            32, 34, 35, 37, 41, 42, 43, 49, 50, 58, 60, 62, 67, 70, 77, 78, 83, 98, 99}
```

```
In[310]:=  qsort[unsorted, compare → Greater]
Out[310]=  {99, 98, 83, 78, 77, 70, 67, 62, 60, 58, 50, 49, 43, 42, 41, 37, 35, 34, 32,
           31, 25, 21, 21, 16, 15, 15, 5, 3, 2, -7, -10, -13, -16, -19, -26, -36,
           -38, -39, -40, -40, -43, -45, -55, -74, -80, -89, -89, -91, -98, -100}

In[311]:=  (*Always pivoting on the first element leads to bad performance
           if lists are already sorted, so a random selection of pivot
           points might be safer (although there are no guarantees).*)
           qsort[unsorted, pivot → RandomChoice]
Out[311]=  {-100, -98, -91, -89, -89, -80, -74, -55, -45, -43, -40, -40, -39, -38,
           -36, -26, -19, -16, -13, -10, -7, 2, 3, 5, 15, 15, 16, 21, 21, 25, 31,
           32, 34, 35, 37, 41, 42, 43, 49, 50, 58, 60, 62, 67, 70, 77, 78, 83, 98, 99}

In[312]:=  (*Here we specify both pivot and comparison using custom functions.*)
           qsort[unsorted, pivot → (Part[#, Floor[Length[#]/2]] &),
           compare → (Less[Abs[#1], Abs[#2]] &)]
Out[312]=  {2, 3, 5, -7, -10, -13, 15, 15, -16, 16, -19, 21, 21, 25, -26, 31, 32, 34,
           35, -36, 37, -38, -39, -40, -40, 41, 42, 43, -43, -45, 49, 50, -55, 58,
           60, 62, 67, 70, -74, 77, 78, -80, 83, -89, -89, -91, 98, -98, 99, -100}
```

Discussion

Options are a better choice than default values (Recipe 2.16) when there are many different options (the Graphics function of Mathematica is a good example) or when the default option values are fine for most users and you don't want to clutter the function interface with low-level details.

Sometimes you are not interested in using options directly in your function, but merely want to pass them on to other built-in Mathematica functions. You need to be careful to pass only options that are applicable. The function FilterRules provides a convenient way to solve this problem. The Mathematica documentation provides a nice example of a function that solves a differential equation and then plots the solution.

```
In[313]:=  Clear[x, y, x0, x1];
           odeplot[de_, y_, {x_, x0_, x1_}, opts : OptionsPattern[]] :=
           Module[{sol},
             sol =
               NDSolve[de, y, {x, x0, x1}, FilterRules[{opts}, Options[NDSolve]]];
             If[Head[sol] === NDSolve,
               $Failed,
               Plot[Evaluate[y /. sol], {x, x0, x1},
                 Evaluate[FilterRules[{opts}, Options[Plot]]]]
             ]
           ]

In[315]:=  odeplot[{y''[x] + y[x] == 0, y[0] == 1, y'[0] == 0}, y[x],
           {x, 0, 10}, Method -> "ExplicitRungeKutta", PlotStyle -> Dashed]
```

Out[315]=

Without FilterOptions you would get an error.

```
In[316]:=  Clear[x, y, x0, x1];
           odeplotBad[de_, y_, {x_, x0_, x1_}, opts : OptionsPattern[]] :=
           Module[{sol},
             sol = NDSolve[de, y, {x, x0, x1}, opts];
             If[Head[sol] === NDSolve,
               $Failed,
               Plot[Evaluate[y /. sol], {x, x0, x1}, opts]
             ]
           ]
```

```
In[318]:= odeplotBad[{y''[x] + y[x] == 0, y[0] == 1, y'[0] == 0}, y[x],
            {x, 0, 10}, Method -> "ExplicitRungeKutta", PlotStyle → Dashed]
```

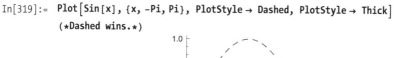

```
NDSolve::optx : Unknown option PlotStyle in
        NDSolve[{y[x] + y''[x] == 0, y[0] == 1, y'[0] == 0}, y[x],
        {x, 0, 10}, Method →
        ExplicitRungeKutta, PlotStyle → Dashing[{Small, Small}]].
    ≫
```

Out[318]= $Failed

When writing or working with functions that use options, keep in mind that Mathematica's convention is to give precedence to options that appear earlier in the list. So if two options conflict, the first wins.

```
In[319]:= Plot[Sin[x], {x, -Pi, Pi}, PlotStyle → Dashed, PlotStyle → Thick]
            (*Dashed wins.*)
```

Out[319]=

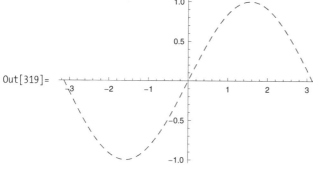

CHAPTER 3

Data Structures

Well I live with snakes and lizards
And other things that go bump in the night

Ministry, "Everyday Is Halloween"

3.0 Introduction

Higher mathematics is rich in structures and formalisms that take mathematics beyond the realm of numbers. This chapter includes a potpourri of recipes for data structures and algorithms that arise in linear algebra, tensor calculus, set theory, graph theory, and computer science. For the most part, lists form the foundation for these structures. Mathematica gains a lot of mileage by representing sets, vectors, matrices, and tensors using lists because all the generic list operations are available for their manipulation. Of course, a list, a set, and a tensor are very distinct entities from a mathematical point of view, but this distinction is handled by special-purpose functions rather than special-purpose data structures.

This introduction reviews the most common operations associated with list structures but is not an exhaustive reference. These operations will be used frequently throughout this book, so you should have some basic familiarity.

List Functions

The foundation of most data structures in Mathematica is the list. It is difficult to do much advanced work with Mathematica unless you are fluent in its functions for list processing. To this end, the initial recipes revolve around basic list processing. A list in Mathematica is constructed using the function List[elem1,elem2,...,elemN] or, more commonly, with curly brackets {elem1,elem2,...,elemN}. There is no restriction on the nature of these elements. They could be mixtures of numbers, strings, functions, other lists, or anything else Mathematica can represent (like graphic or sound data).

The first thing you need to know about lists is how to generate them. Table is the workhorse function for doing this. It has several variations that are most easily explained by example.

```
In[1]:=  (*Ten copies of an expr; in this case, the constant 1*)
         Table[1, {10}]
Out[1]=  {1, 1, 1, 1, 1, 1, 1, 1, 1, 1}

In[2]:=  (*The result of evaluation expr for i 1 to 10*)
         Table[i^2, {i, 10}]
Out[2]=  {1, 4, 9, 16, 25, 36, 49, 64, 81, 100}

In[3]:=  (*The result of evaluation expr for i 2 to 10*)
         Table[i^2, {i, 2, 10}]
Out[3]=  {4, 9, 16, 25, 36, 49, 64, 81, 100}

In[4]:=  (*The result of evaluation expr for i 2 to 10 by steps of 2*)
         Table[i, {i, 2, 10, 2}]
Out[4]=  {2, 4, 6, 8, 10}

In[5]:=  (*2 x 3 matrix of constant 1*)
         Table[1, {2}, {3}]
Out[5]=  {{1, 1, 1}, {1, 1, 1}}

In[6]:=  (*Tensor of rank three*)
         Table[i + j^2 + k^3, {i, 0, 2}, {j, 0, 2}, {k, 0, 2}] // MatrixForm
Out[6]//MatrixForm=
```

$$\left(\begin{array}{ccc} \begin{pmatrix} 0 \\ 1 \\ 8 \end{pmatrix} & \begin{pmatrix} 1 \\ 2 \\ 9 \end{pmatrix} & \begin{pmatrix} 4 \\ 5 \\ 12 \end{pmatrix} \\ \begin{pmatrix} 1 \\ 2 \\ 9 \end{pmatrix} & \begin{pmatrix} 2 \\ 3 \\ 10 \end{pmatrix} & \begin{pmatrix} 5 \\ 6 \\ 13 \end{pmatrix} \\ \begin{pmatrix} 2 \\ 3 \\ 10 \end{pmatrix} & \begin{pmatrix} 3 \\ 4 \\ 11 \end{pmatrix} & \begin{pmatrix} 6 \\ 7 \\ 14 \end{pmatrix} \end{array}\right)$$

In addition to Table, Mathematica has several special-purpose list constructors: Range, Array, ConstantArray, DiagonalMatrix, and IdentityMatrix. These functions are less general than Table but are clearer and simpler to use when applicable. For example, consider IdentityMatrix and its Table equivalent.

```
In[7]:= IdentityMatrix[3] // MatrixForm
Out[7]//MatrixForm=
        ⎛ 1  0  0 ⎞
        ⎜ 0  1  0 ⎟
        ⎝ 0  0  1 ⎠

In[8]:= (*Equivalent to IdentityMatrix*)
        Table[If[i == j, 1, 0], {i, 1, 3}, {j, 1, 3}] // MatrixForm
Out[8]//MatrixForm=
        ⎛ 1  0  0 ⎞
        ⎜ 0  1  0 ⎟
        ⎝ 0  0  1 ⎠
```

Sometimes using a special-purpose list constructor is more verbose. Consider these equivalent ways of generating an array of ten 1s. Here, 1& is the function that always returns 1.

```
In[9]:= Array[1 &, 10] == ConstantArray[1, 10]
Out[9]= True
```

Once you have one or more lists, you can compose new lists using functions like Append, Prepend, Insert, Join, and Riffle.

```
In[10]:= list1 = Range[10]
Out[10]= {1, 2, 3, 4, 5, 6, 7, 8, 9, 10}

In[11]:= list2 = list1 ^ 2
Out[11]= {1, 4, 9, 16, 25, 36, 49, 64, 81, 100}

In[12]:= (*Add elements to the end.*)
         Append[list1, 11]
Out[12]= {1, 2, 3, 4, 5, 6, 7, 8, 9, 10, 11}

In[13]:= (*Add elements to the front.*)
         Prepend[list1, 0]
Out[13]= {0, 1, 2, 3, 4, 5, 6, 7, 8, 9, 10}

In[14]:= (*Insert elements at specific positions.*)
         Insert[list1, 3.5, 4]
Out[14]= {1, 2, 3, 3.5, 4, 5, 6, 7, 8, 9, 10}

In[15]:= (*Negative offsets to insert from the end*)
         Insert[list1, 3.5, -4]
Out[15]= {1, 2, 3, 4, 5, 6, 7, 3.5, 8, 9, 10}

In[16]:= (*You can insert at multiple positions {{i1},{i2},...,{iN}}.*)
         Insert[list1, 0, List /@ Range[2, Length[list1]]]
Out[16]= {1, 0, 2, 0, 3, 0, 4, 0, 5, 0, 6, 0, 7, 0, 8, 0, 9, 0, 10}
```

```
In[17]:=  (*Join one or more lists.*)
          Join[list1, list2]
Out[17]=  {1, 2, 3, 4, 5, 6, 7, 8, 9, 10, 1, 4, 9, 16, 25, 36, 49, 64, 81, 100}

In[18]:=  (*Riffle is a function specifically designed to interleave elements.*)
          Riffle[list1, 0]
Out[18]=  {1, 0, 2, 0, 3, 0, 4, 0, 5, 0, 6, 0, 7, 0, 8, 0, 9, 0, 10}
```

The flip side of building lists is taking them apart. Here you will use operations like Part, First, Last, Rest, Most, Take, Drop, Select, and Cases.

```
In[19]:=  (*Part is frequently accessed via its operator [[expr]] equivalent.*)
          list1[[3]] == Part[list1, 3]
Out[19]=  True

In[20]:=  (*Accessing the first element. Lisp
           programmers call this operation car.*)
          First[list1]
Out[20]=  1

In[21]:=  (*Accessing the last element*)
          Last[list1]
Out[21]=  10

In[22]:=  (*All but the first element. Lisp programmers call this operation cdr.*)
          Rest[list1]
Out[22]=  {2, 3, 4, 5, 6, 7, 8, 9, 10}

In[23]:=  (*All but the last element*)
          Most[list1]
Out[23]=  {1, 2, 3, 4, 5, 6, 7, 8, 9}

In[24]:=  (*The first three elements*)
          Take[list1, 3]
Out[24]=  {1, 2, 3}

In[25]:=  (*All but the first three*)
          Drop[list1, 3]
Out[25]=  {4, 5, 6, 7, 8, 9, 10}

In[26]:=  (*The elements in which some criterion is satisfied,
          in this case odd elements*)
          Select[list1, OddQ]
Out[26]=  {1, 3, 5, 7, 9}
```

```
In[27]:=  (*The elements matching a pattern*)
          Cases[list1 /3 , a_Integer → 3 a]
Out[27]=  {3, 6, 9}
```

See Chapter 5 for more information on patterns.

You rearrange and restructure lists using functions such as Reverse, RotateLeft, RotateRight, Flatten, Partition, Transpose, and Sort.

```
In[28]:=  Reverse[list1]
Out[28]=  {10, 9, 8, 7, 6, 5, 4, 3, 2, 1}

In[29]:=  RotateLeft[list1]
Out[29]=  {2, 3, 4, 5, 6, 7, 8, 9, 10, 1}

In[30]:=  RotateRight[list1]
Out[30]=  {10, 1, 2, 3, 4, 5, 6, 7, 8, 9}
```

Partition and Flatten are very versatile functions for creating and removing structure. Flatten can be thought of as the inverse of Partition. Here, repeated partitioning using Nest converts a list to a binary tree.

```
In[31]:=  bifurcate[list_] :=
          Nest[Partition[#, 2] &, list, Floor[Log[2, Length[list]]]]
          (structured = bifurcate[list1]) // TreeForm
Out[32]//TreeForm=
```

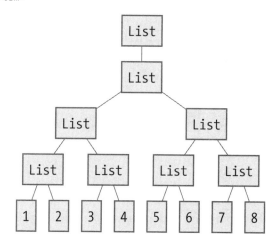

```
In[33]:=  Flatten[structured]
Out[33]=  {1, 2, 3, 4, 5, 6, 7, 8}
```

Flatten can also take a level that tells it to flatten only up to that level.

```
In[34]:= Flatten[structured, 1] // TreeForm
Out[34]//TreeForm=
```

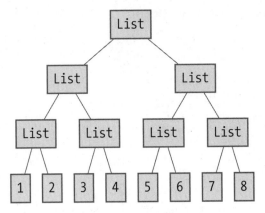

```
In[35]:= Flatten[structured, 2] // TreeForm
Out[35]//TreeForm=
```

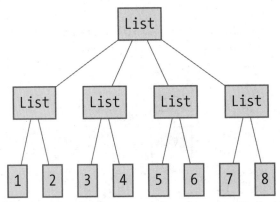

```
In[36]:= Flatten[structured, 3]
Out[36]= {1, 2, 3, 4, 5, 6, 7, 8}
```

Many of these functions have advanced features, so you should refer to the Mathematica documentation for each to understand their full capabilities. I will use these functions frequently throughout this book without further explanation, so if you are not already familiar with them, you should take some time to experiment on your own.

Set Functions

A set in Mathematica is nothing more than a list that is normalized to eliminate duplicates upon application of a set operation: Union, Intersection, or Complement. To determine duplicates, Mathematica uses an option called SameTest, which by default is the function SameQ or ===. The function Subsets constructs a list of all subsets. MemberQ is used to test membership, but this function is far more general, and I will revisit it in Chapter 4.

```
In[37]:=  Union[list1, list2]
Out[37]=  {1, 2, 3, 4, 5, 6, 7, 8, 9, 10, 16, 25, 36, 49, 64, 81, 100}

In[38]:=  Intersection[list1, list2]
Out[38]=  {1, 4, 9}

In[39]:=  (*Complement can be used with
             Intersection to implement Set Difference.*)
          Complement[list1, Intersection[list1, list2]]
Out[39]=  {2, 3, 5, 6, 7, 8, 10}

In[40]:=  Complement[list2, Intersection[list1, list2]]
Out[40]=  {16, 25, 36, 49, 64, 81, 100}

In[41]:=  (*Generating all subsets*)
          Subsets[{a, b, c}]
Out[41]=  {{}, {a}, {b}, {c}, {a, b}, {a, c}, {b, c}, {a, b, c}}

In[42]:=  MemberQ[list2, 4]
Out[42]=  True
```

Vector Functions

A vector is also represented by a list, but Mathematica has a special representation called a SparseArray that can conserve space when a vector contains many zero entries (see Recipe 3.8). Matrices and tensors are naturally represented as nested lists; these likewise can use SparseArrays.

Vector math is supported by the fact that most mathematical operations have the attribute Listable, meaning that the operations automatically thread over lists.

```
In[43]:=  (*Multiplication and subtraction of a vector by a scalar*)
          3 * list1 - 3
Out[43]=  {0, 3, 6, 9, 12, 15, 18, 21, 24, 27}

In[44]:=  (*Listable is the relevant property.*)
          Intersection[Flatten[Attributes[{Times, Plus, Minus, Divide, Power}]]]
Out[44]=  {Flat, Listable, NumericFunction,
              OneIdentity, Orderless, Protected, ReadProtected}
```

Same-sized vectors and matrices can also be added, multiplied, and so on, in an element-by-element fashion.

```
In[45]:=  Range[10] ^ Range[10, 1, -1]
Out[45]=  {1, 512, 6561, 16384, 15625, 7776, 2401, 512, 81, 10}
```

Vector-specific operations are also supported. Some of the more advanced operations are in a package called VectorAnalysis`, including CrossProduct, Norm, Div, Grad, Curl, and about three dozen others. Use ?VectorAnalysis`* after loading the package to see the full list.

```
In[47]:=  u = {-1, 0.5, 1}; v = {1, -0.5, 1};

In[48]:=  u.v
Out[48]=  -0.25

In[49]:=  Norm[u]
Out[49]=  1.5

In[50]:=  Orthogonalize[{u, v}]
Out[50]=  {{-0.666667, 0.333333, 0.666667}, {0.596285, -0.298142, 0.745356}}

In[51]:=  Projection[u, v]
Out[51]=  {-0.111111, 0.0555556, -0.111111}
```

CrossProduct is not built in, so you must load a special package.

```
In[52]:=  Needs["VectorAnalysis`"]

In[53]:=  CrossProduct[u, v]
Out[53]=  {1., 2., 0.}
```

Matrix and Tensor Functions

Vectors and matrices are familiar to most scientists, engineers, and software developers. A tensor is a generalization of vectors and matrices to higher dimensions. Specifically, a scalar is a zero-order tensor, a vector is a first-order tensor, and a matrix is a second-order tensor. Tensors of order three and higher are represented in Mathematica as more deeply nested lists. Here is an example of a tensor of order four. Note that the use of subscripting in this example is for illustration and is not integral to the notion of a tensor from Mathematica's point of view. (Mathematicians familiar with tensor analysis know that subscripts and superscripts have very definite meaning, but Mathematica does not directly support those notations [although some third-party packages do].)

```
In[54]:= (tensor4 = Table[Subscript[a, i, j, k, l],
            {i, 1, 2}, {j, 1, 2}, {k, 1, 2}, {l, 1, 2}]) // MatrixForm
Out[54]//MatrixForm=
```

$$
\begin{pmatrix}
\begin{pmatrix} a_{1,1,1,1} & a_{1,1,1,2} \\ a_{1,1,2,1} & a_{1,1,2,2} \end{pmatrix} & \begin{pmatrix} a_{1,2,1,1} & a_{1,2,1,2} \\ a_{1,2,2,1} & a_{1,2,2,2} \end{pmatrix} \\
\begin{pmatrix} a_{2,1,1,1} & a_{2,1,1,2} \\ a_{2,1,2,1} & a_{2,1,2,2} \end{pmatrix} & \begin{pmatrix} a_{2,2,1,1} & a_{2,2,1,2} \\ a_{2,2,2,1} & a_{2,2,2,2} \end{pmatrix}
\end{pmatrix}
$$

```
In[55]:= (*Using Part with a single index yields a third-order tensor.*)
         tensor4[[1]] // MatrixForm
Out[55]//MatrixForm=
```

$$
\begin{pmatrix}
\begin{pmatrix} a_{1,1,1,1} \\ a_{1,1,1,2} \end{pmatrix} & \begin{pmatrix} a_{1,1,2,1} \\ a_{1,1,2,2} \end{pmatrix} \\
\begin{pmatrix} a_{1,2,1,1} \\ a_{1,2,1,2} \end{pmatrix} & \begin{pmatrix} a_{1,2,2,1} \\ a_{1,2,2,2} \end{pmatrix}
\end{pmatrix}
$$

```
In[56]:= (*Using Part with two indices on a fourth-
           order tensor yields a second-order tensor (i.e., a matrix).*)
         tensor4[[1, 1]] // MatrixForm
Out[56]//MatrixForm=
```

$$
\begin{pmatrix}
a_{1,1,1,1} & a_{1,1,1,2} \\
a_{1,1,2,1} & a_{1,1,2,2}
\end{pmatrix}
$$

```
In[57]:= (*Using Part with three indices yields a vector.*)
         tensor4[[1, 1, 2]]
Out[57]= {a_{1,1,2,1}, a_{1,1,2,2}}
```

```
In[58]:= (*And all 4 indices gives a scalar.*)
         tensor4[[2, 1, 2, 2]]
Out[58]= a_{2,1,2,2}
```

The recipes in this chapter deal mostly with vectors and matrices, but many operations in Mathematica are generalized to higher-order tensors. A very important function central to linear algebra is the Dot product. In linear algebra texts, this is often referred to simply as *vector multiplication*. The Dot product only works if vectors and matrices have compatible shapes.

```
In[59]:= Dot[{x1, x2, x3}, {y1, y2, y3}]
Out[59]= x1 y1 + x2 y2 + x3 y3
```

```
In[60]:= Clear[x, y];
         Dot[Table[Subscript[x, i, j], {i, 1, 3}, {j, 1, 2}],
            Table[Subscript[y, i, j], {i, 1, 2}, {j, 1, 3}]] // MatrixForm
Out[61]//MatrixForm=
```

$$\begin{pmatrix} x_{1,1}\,y_{1,1} + x_{1,2}\,y_{2,1} & x_{1,1}\,y_{1,2} + x_{1,2}\,y_{2,2} & x_{1,1}\,y_{1,3} + x_{1,2}\,y_{2,3} \\ x_{2,1}\,y_{1,1} + x_{2,2}\,y_{2,1} & x_{2,1}\,y_{1,2} + x_{2,2}\,y_{2,2} & x_{2,1}\,y_{1,3} + x_{2,2}\,y_{2,3} \\ x_{3,1}\,y_{1,1} + x_{3,2}\,y_{2,1} & x_{3,1}\,y_{1,2} + x_{3,2}\,y_{2,2} & x_{3,1}\,y_{1,3} + x_{3,2}\,y_{2,3} \end{pmatrix}$$

Inner[f,m1,m2,g] is a function that generalizes Dot by allowing a function f to take the place of multiplication and g to take the place of addition. Here are some examples.

```
In[62]:= Inner[List, Table[i^j, {i, 1, 4}, {j, 1, 3}],
            Table[j! i!, {i, 1, 3}, {j, 1, 4}], Max] // MatrixForm
Out[62]//MatrixForm=
```

$$\begin{pmatrix} 6 & 12 & 36 & 144 \\ 8 & 12 & 36 & 144 \\ 27 & 27 & 36 & 144 \\ 64 & 64 & 64 & 144 \end{pmatrix}$$

```
In[63]:= Inner[List, Table[i + j, {i, 1, 3}, {j, 1, 2}],
            Table[i * j, {i, 1, 2}, {j, 1, 3}], List] // MatrixForm
Out[63]//MatrixForm=
```

$$\begin{pmatrix} \begin{pmatrix} 2 & 1 \\ 3 & 2 \end{pmatrix} & \begin{pmatrix} 2 & 2 \\ 3 & 4 \end{pmatrix} & \begin{pmatrix} 2 & 3 \\ 3 & 6 \end{pmatrix} \\ \begin{pmatrix} 3 & 1 \\ 4 & 2 \end{pmatrix} & \begin{pmatrix} 3 & 2 \\ 4 & 4 \end{pmatrix} & \begin{pmatrix} 3 & 3 \\ 4 & 6 \end{pmatrix} \\ \begin{pmatrix} 4 & 1 \\ 5 & 2 \end{pmatrix} & \begin{pmatrix} 4 & 2 \\ 5 & 4 \end{pmatrix} & \begin{pmatrix} 4 & 3 \\ 5 & 6 \end{pmatrix} \end{pmatrix}$$

```
In[64]:= Inner[List, Table[i*j, {i, 1, 2}, {j, 1, 2}],
              Table[i + j, {i, 1, 2}, {j, 1, 2}], Join] // MatrixForm
Out[64]//MatrixForm=
```

$$\left(\begin{array}{cc} \left(\begin{array}{c} 1 \\ 2 \\ 2 \\ 3 \end{array} \right) & \left(\begin{array}{c} 1 \\ 3 \\ 2 \\ 4 \end{array} \right) \\ \left(\begin{array}{c} 2 \\ 2 \\ 4 \\ 3 \end{array} \right) & \left(\begin{array}{c} 2 \\ 3 \\ 4 \\ 4 \end{array} \right) \end{array} \right)$$

```
In[65]:= Inner[And, Table[i < j, {i, 1, 3}, {j, 1, 3}],
              Table[j < i, {i, 1, 3}, {j, 1, 3}], Or] // MatrixForm
Out[65]//MatrixForm=
```

$$\left(\begin{array}{ccc} True & True & False \\ True & True & False \\ False & False & False \end{array} \right)$$

3.1 Ensuring the Most Efficient Representation of Numerical Lists

Problem

You are performing very mathematically intense computations on large vectors, matrices, or higher-order tensors and want the most efficient representation in terms of speed and space.

Solution

Make sure your lists are *packed arrays* by not mixing numerical types. This means arrays of integers should work exclusively in integers or exclusively in machine precision floating point. Use of uniform types is necessary but not sufficient for getting packed arrays. Mathematica tries to automatically use packed arrays when generating large lists of numbers, but sometimes subtle coding differences prevent it from packing the result.

Here are two very similar pieces of code, but the first generates an unpacked representation and the second generates a packed one.

```
In[66]:= array1 = N[Table[i * Pi, {i, 0, 500000}]];
         Developer`PackedArrayQ[array1]
Out[67]= False
```

```
In[68]:= array2 = Table[i * Pi, {i, 0.0, 500000.0}];
         Developer`PackedArrayQ[array2]
Out[69]= True
```

The difference is that the first Table generates a table in symbolic form and then converts it to real numbers with N. So, although the final array meets the uniform criteria, N will not pack it. In the second version, I force Table to create a list of real numbers right off the bat by using real bounds for the index i. This makes N unnecessary and causes Table to return a packed result.

Discussion

To get some insight into the superiority of packed arrays, we can ask Mathematica to tell us the size of each array from the solution.

```
In[70]:= Grid[{{"", "size", "per elem"},
           {"array1", ByteCount[array1], N[ByteCount[array1] / Length[array1]]},
           {"array2", ByteCount[array2], N[ByteCount[array2] / Length[array2]]}},
         Alignment → Right, Frame → All]
```

	size	per elem
array1	12000056	24.0001
array2	4000132	8.00025

Out[70]=

As you can see, the space saved is considerable. Essentially, packed is giving you the equivalent of a C or Fortran array. Space savings is not the only reason to work with packed arrays. Many operations are considerably faster as well. Here you see that multiplication of packed arrays is an order of magnitude faster than unpacked!

```
In[71]:= Mean@Table[Timing[array1 * array2][[1]], {100}]
Out[71]= 0.0909364
```

```
In[72]:= Mean@Table[Timing[array2 * array2][[1]], {100}]
Out[72]= 0.00625822
```

When you can get an order of magnitude improvement, it is a good idea to take it, because life is short!

The Developer` package has a function to pack an unpacked array, although it is preferable to alter your coding style as we've discussed here to get packed arrays.

```
In[73]:= array1 = Developer`ToPackedArray[array1];
         Developer`PackedArrayQ[array1]
Out[74]= True
```

If you have a very large packed array and assign a value to one of the elements that differ from the packed type, this assignment will be expensive relative to a normal assignment. Mathematica will be forced to copy the entire array into unpacked form before the assignment can be made.

See Also

The Developer` package also has a function Developer`FromPackedArray for converting a packed form back to the normal representation. Evaluating ?"Developer`*" allows you to peruse all the functions in this package, but many are undocumented.

3.2 Sorting Lists

Problem

You need to sort a list based on standard ordering (Less) or a custom-ordering relation. One common reason for sorting is to enable binary search.

Solution

Use Sort or SortBy, depending on how the ordering relation is specified. By default, Sort uses less than (<) to order elements.

```
In[76]:= list = RandomInteger[{-100, 100}, 10];
```

```
In[77]:= Sort[list]
Out[77]= {-73, -50, -45, -43, -20, 2, 42, 50, 66, 84}
```

```
In[78]:= Sort[list, Greater]
Out[78]= {84, 66, 50, 42, 2, -20, -43, -45, -50, -73}
```

SortBy does not use an ordering relation, but rather uses a function whose output is passed to Less.

```
In[79]:= SortBy[list, Abs]
Out[79]= {2, -20, 42, -43, -45, -50, 50, 66, -73, 84}
```

Discussion

If you need to sort lists containing objects more complicated than scalars, you will need to be comfortable with expressing the order relation function. Here are some examples.

```
In[80]:=  data = {
              {"21 Mar 2007 14:34:30", 10.1, 12.7, 13.3},
              {"21 Jun 2005 10:19:30", 10.3, 11.7, 11.7},
              {"21 Aug 2006 15:34:01", 11.7, 16.8, 8.6},
              {"21 Aug 2006 09:34:00", 11.9, 16.5, 8.6}
              };
          (*Sort the data by the time entry,
          which must be converted to an absolute time to be properly ordered.*)
          Sort[data,
            Less[AbsoluteTime[{#1[[1]], {"Day", "MonthNameShort", "Year", "Time"}}],
              AbsoluteTime[{#2[[1]],
                  {"Day", "MonthNameShort", "Year", "Time"}}]] &] // TableForm
Out[81]//TableForm=
              21 Jun 2005 10:19:30  10.3  11.7  11.7
              21 Aug 2006 09:34:00  11.9  16.5  8.6
              21 Aug 2006 15:34:01  11.7  16.8  8.6
              21 Mar 2007 14:34:30  10.1  12.7  13.3
```

For practical sorting, you will never need to look beyond Sort, because it is both fast
and flexible. However, if you are interested in sorting from an algorithmic perspective, Mathematica also has a package called Combinatorica`, which contains some
sorting routines that use specific algorithms (SelectionSort, HeapSort).

```
In[82]:=  Needs["Combinatorica`"]

In[83]:=  SelectionSort[list, Less]
Out[83]=  {-73, -50, -45, -43, -20, 2, 42, 50, 66, 84}
```

Of course, there is probably no practical reason to use SelectionSort since its asymptotic behavior is $O(n^2)$, whereas Sort uses a $O(n \log n)$ algorithm. You can count
the number of comparisons each sort makes using a custom comparison function.
The framed number is the comparison count.

```
In[84]:=  (*The sorted list and count of comparisons with Sort*)
          Block[{count = 0}, {Sort[list, (count ++; Less[#1, #2]) &], Framed[count]}]

Out[84]=  {{-73, -50, -45, -43, -20, 2, 42, 50, 66, 84}, | 26 |}
```

```
In[85]:=  (*Comparisons consistent with n log n*)
          Log[2.0, Length[list]] * Length[list]
Out[85]=  33.2193
```

```
In[86]:=  (*The sorted list and count of comparisons
            with SelectionSort. Roughly twice the comparisons*)
          Block[{count = 0},
            {SelectionSort[list, (count++; Less[#1, #2]) &], Framed[count]}]
Out[86]=  {{-73, -50, -45, -43, -20, 2, 42, 50, 66, 84}, [55]}


In[87]:=  (*Although better than worst case*)
          Length[list]^2
Out[87]=  100
```

Heap sort is O(n log n), but the Combinatorica` implementation is somewhat crippled because the ordering operation cannot be customized.

```
In[88]:=  HeapSort[list]
Out[88]=  {-73, -50, -45, -43, -20, 2, 42, 50, 66, 84}
```

If you are keen to do this experiment with HeapSort, you can easily make a customizable version, since the source code is available.

```
In[89]:=  genericHeapSort[{}, _] := {}
          genericHeapSort[p_List, ordering_] :=
            Module[{heap = genericHeapify[p, ordering], min},
              Append[Table[min = First[heap]; heap[[1]] = heap[[n]];
                heap = genericHeapify[Drop[heap, -1], 1, ordering]; min,
                {n, Length[p], 2, -1}], Max[heap]]] /; Length[p] > 0
          (*HeapSort is implemented in terms of a function Heapify,
          which we must customize to inject our ordering.*)
          genericHeapify[p_List, ordering_] :=
            Module[{j, heap = p}, Do[heap = genericHeapify[heap, j, ordering],
              {j, Quotient[Length[p], 2], 1, -1}]; heap]
          genericHeapify[p_List, k_Integer, ordering_] :=
            Module[{hp = p, i = k, l, n = Length[p]},
              While[(l = 2 i) ≤ n, If[l < n && ordering[hp[[l + 1]], hp[[l]]], l++];
                If[ordering[hp[[l]], hp[[i]]],
                  {hp[[i]], hp[[l]]} = {hp[[l]], hp[[i]]}; i = l, i = n + 1];]; hp]
In[93]:=  Block[{count = 0},
            {genericHeapSort[list, (count++; Less[#1, #2]) &], Framed[count]}]
Out[93]=  {{-73, -50, -45, -43, -20, 2, 42, 50, 66, 84}, [39]}
```

It is unfortunate that we have to hack HeapSort to give it customizable ordering function. When you develop your own general-purpose functions, it pays to consider facilities that allow you and other users to customize the details while leaving the essential algorithm intact. This is the essence of what is called *generic programming*. Chapter 2 has several recipes that demonstrate how to create more generic functions.

One application of sorting is performing efficient search. The Combinatorica` package provides the function BinarySearch, which requires a sorted list. BinarySearch returns the index of the first occurrence of a search key, if found. If the key is not found, it returns index + 1/2, indicating that the key belongs between index and index + 1 if it were to be inserted.

```
In[94]:= list2 = Range[1, 20, 2]
Out[94]= {1, 3, 5, 7, 9, 11, 13, 15, 17, 19}
```

```
In[95]:= BinarySearch[list2, 7]
Out[95]= 4
```

```
In[96]:= BinarySearch[list2, 6]
```
$$Out[96]= \frac{7}{2}$$

```
In[97]:= (*An example of how BinarySearch might be used to
          conditionally insert new elements into a sorted list*)
         value = 6 ;
         pos = BinarySearch[list2, value];
         If[IntegerQ[pos], pos, pos = Ceiling[pos];
            list2 = Insert[list2, value, pos]; pos];
         list2
Out[100]= {1, 3, 5, 6, 7, 9, 11, 13, 15, 17, 19}
```

See Also

Recipe 3.3 discusses how to determine sorted order without rearranging the elements of the list.

A good overview of various sorting algorithms can be found at *http://bit.ly/2bRckv*.

3.3 Determining Order Without Sorting

Problem

You need to know how the elements of a list are ordered without actually sorting them. This may be because it is too expensive to keep multiple copies of the data in various orderings.

Solution

Use `Ordering` to get a list of offsets to the elements in the order they would appear if sorted.

```
In[101]:=  unsorted = RandomInteger[{90, 99}, 10]
Out[101]=  {98, 90, 91, 98, 98, 91, 99, 99, 97, 96}
```

```
In[102]:=  Ordering[unsorted]
Out[102]=  {2, 3, 6, 10, 9, 1, 4, 5, 7, 8}
```

Discussion

`Ordering` has two variations. The first takes an integer that limits how many positions are returned. If you specify n, then the first n are returned; if you specify -n, the last n are returned. This option makes `Ordering` more useful than `Sort` when you don't need the entire list sorted.

```
In[103]:=  Ordering[unsorted, 3]
Out[103]=  {2, 3, 6}
```

```
In[104]:=  Ordering[unsorted, -3]
Out[104]=  {5, 7, 8}
```

The second variation takes both an integer and an ordering relation.

```
In[105]:=  Ordering[unsorted, Length[unsorted], Greater]
Out[105]=  {8, 7, 5, 4, 1, 9, 10, 6, 3, 2}
```

Given an ordering, it is easy to create a sorted version of the list.

```
In[106]:=  unsorted[[Ordering[unsorted]]]
Out[106]=  {90, 91, 91, 96, 97, 98, 98, 98, 99, 99}
```

Unfortunately, `Ordering` does as many comparisons as a full sort even if you only want the first few orderings.

```
In[107]:=  Block[{count = 0},
             {Ordering[unsorted, 3, (count++; Less[#1, #2]) &], Framed[count]}]
Out[107]=  {{2, 6, 3}, 23 }
```

```
In[108]:=  Block[{count = 0},
             {Ordering[unsorted, 6, (count++; Less[#1, #2]) &], Framed[count]}]
Out[108]=  {{2, 6, 3, 10, 9, 5}, 23 }
```

A heap would be superior in such an application, but rolling your version of Ordering is unlikely to yield superior results due to optimizations that go beyond minimizing comparisons. After all, it takes Ordering less than a second to do its work on a million integers on my relatively low-powered laptop.

```
In[109]:= Timing[Ordering[RandomInteger[{1, 999999}, 1000000], 2]]
Out[109]= {0.255152, {314075, 337366}}
```

See Also

Recipe 3.2 discusses sorting.

OrderedQ tests if a list is ordered, and Order compares two expressions, returning -1 (Less), 0 (Equal), or 1 (Greater).

3.4 Extracting the Diagonals of a Matrix

Problem

You want to extract the diagonal, subdiagonal, superdiagonal, or antidiagonal of a matrix.

Solution

In versions prior to Mathematica 6, use Tr with List as the combining function (the default combining function of Tr is Plus).

```
In[110]:= (matrix = {{1, 2, 3}, {4, 5, 6}, {7, 8, 9}}) // MatrixForm
Out[110]//MatrixForm=
            ⎛ 1  2  3 ⎞
            ⎜ 4  5  6 ⎟
            ⎝ 7  8  9 ⎠
```

```
In[111]:= Tr[matrix, List]
Out[111]= {1, 5, 9}
```

Mathematica 6 introduced the function Diagonal, which makes this recipe trivial.

```
In[112]:= Diagonal[matrix]
Out[112]= {1, 5, 9}
```

You can extract the antidiagonal using either of the following expressions:

```
In[113]:= Diagonal[Map[Reverse, matrix]]
Out[113]= {3, 5, 7}
```

```
In[114]:= Tr[Map[Reverse, matrix], List]
Out[114]= {3, 5, 7}
```

Discussion

The Diagonal function is more versatile than Tr in that it allows you to select off the main diagonal by proving an index.

```
In[115]:= Diagonal[matrix, 1]
Out[115]= {2, 6}
```

```
In[116]:= Diagonal[matrix, -1]
Out[116]= {4, 8}
```

Although the solutions implementation of antidiagonal is simple, it is not the most efficient: it reverses every row of the input matrix. An iterative solution using Table is simple and fast.

```
In[117]:= AntiDiagonal[matrix_] := Module[{len = Length[matrix]},
            Table[matrix[[i, len - i + 1]], {i, 1, len}]]
```

```
In[118]:= bigMatrix = Table[i * j, {i, 0, 5500}, {j, 0, 5500}];
```

```
In[119]:= Timing[AntiDiagonal[bigMatrix]][[1]]
Out[119]= 0.001839
```

```
In[120]:= Timing[Diagonal[Map[Reverse, bigMatrix]]][[1]]
Out[120]= 0.230145
```

It is always good to test a new version of an algorithm against one you already know works.

```
In[121]:= AntiDiagonal[bigMatrix] == Diagonal[Map[Reverse, bigMatrix]]
Out[121]= True
```

3.5 Constructing Matrices of Specific Structure

Problem

You want to construct matrices of a specific structure (e.g., diagonal, identity, tridiagonal).

Solution

Mathematica has built-in matrix constructions for the most common kinds of matrices.

```
In[122]:= IdentityMatrix[5] // MatrixForm
Out[122]//MatrixForm=
```

$$\begin{pmatrix} 1 & 0 & 0 & 0 & 0 \\ 0 & 1 & 0 & 0 & 0 \\ 0 & 0 & 1 & 0 & 0 \\ 0 & 0 & 0 & 1 & 0 \\ 0 & 0 & 0 & 0 & 1 \end{pmatrix}$$

```
In[123]:= DiagonalMatrix[Range[4]] // MatrixForm
Out[123]//MatrixForm=
```

$$\begin{pmatrix} 1 & 0 & 0 & 0 \\ 0 & 2 & 0 & 0 \\ 0 & 0 & 3 & 0 \\ 0 & 0 & 0 & 4 \end{pmatrix}$$

Discussion

Although identity and diagonal matrices are quite common, there are other kinds of matrices that arise frequently in practical problems. For example, problems involving coupled systems often give rise to tridiagonal matrices. SparseArray and Band are perfect for this job. These are discussed in Recipe 3.8. Here, the use of Normal to convert sparse form to list form is not essential because sparse arrays will play nicely with regular ones.

```
In[124]:= triDiagonal[sub_List, main_List, super_List] /;
            {Length[sub], Length[super]} + 1 == {Length[main], Length[main]} :=
          Module[{},
            Normal[SparseArray[{Band[{2, 1}] → sub,
              Band[{1, 2}] → super, Band[{1, 1}] → main}, Length[main]]]]

In[125]:= triDiagonal[sub_?NumericQ, main_?NumericQ, super_?NumericQ, n_Integer] :=
          Normal[SparseArray[
            {Band[{2, 1}] → sub, Band[{1, 2}] → super, Band[{1, 1}] → main}, n]]

In[126]:= triDiagonal[{-1, -1, -1}, {2, 2, 2, 2}, {1, 1, 1}] // MatrixForm
Out[126]//MatrixForm=
```

$$\begin{pmatrix} 2 & 1 & 0 & 0 \\ -1 & 2 & 1 & 0 \\ 0 & -1 & 2 & 1 \\ 0 & 0 & -1 & 2 \end{pmatrix}$$

Tridiagonal matrices are always invertible.

```
In[127]:= Inverse[triDiagonal[{-1, -1, -1}, {2, 2, 2, 2}, {1, 1, 1}]]
```

$$Out[127]= \left\{\left\{\frac{12}{29}, -\frac{5}{29}, \frac{2}{29}, -\frac{1}{29}\right\}, \left\{\frac{5}{29}, \frac{10}{29}, -\frac{4}{29}, \frac{2}{29}\right\},\right.$$
$$\left.\left\{\frac{2}{29}, \frac{4}{29}, \frac{10}{29}, -\frac{5}{29}\right\}, \left\{\frac{1}{29}, \frac{2}{29}, \frac{5}{29}, \frac{12}{29}\right\}\right\}$$

There are also functions to transform a given matrix to another. Mathematica 7 introduced LowerTriangularize and UpperTriangularize to create triangular matrices from a given matrix.

```
In[128]:= With[{m = Array[1 &, {4, 4}]}, Row[{LowerTriangularize[m] // MatrixForm,
           UpperTriangularize[m] // MatrixForm}]]
```

$$Out[128]= \begin{pmatrix} 1 & 0 & 0 & 0 \\ 1 & 1 & 0 & 0 \\ 1 & 1 & 1 & 0 \\ 1 & 1 & 1 & 1 \end{pmatrix} \begin{pmatrix} 1 & 1 & 1 & 1 \\ 0 & 1 & 1 & 1 \\ 0 & 0 & 1 & 1 \\ 0 & 0 & 0 & 1 \end{pmatrix}$$

These functions take an optional second parameter k, where positive k refers to subdiagonals above the main diagonal and negative k refers to subdiagonals below the main diagonal. This points to another way to arrive at a tridiagonal matrix from a given or synthesized matrix.

```
In[129]:= UpperTriangularize[
           LowerTriangularize[Array[# &, {4, 4}], 1], -1] // MatrixForm
Out[129]//MatrixForm=
```

$$\begin{pmatrix} 1 & 1 & 0 & 0 \\ 2 & 2 & 2 & 0 \\ 0 & 3 & 3 & 3 \\ 0 & 0 & 4 & 4 \end{pmatrix}$$

See Also

Certain important transformation matrices are accommodated by ScalingMatrix, RotationMatrix, and ReflectionMatrix. See Recipe 2.11 for a usage example.

3.6 Constructing Permutation and Shift Matrices

Problem

You want to construct a matrix that will permute or shift the rows or columns of an input matrix.

Solution

A permutation matrix is a permutation of the identity matrix. It is used to permute either the rows or columns of another matrix.

```
In[130]:= permutationMatrix[list_] := IdentityMatrix[Length[list]][[list]]
```

```
In[131]:= (m1 = Table[2 i + j, {i, 1, 3}, {j, 1, 3}]) // MatrixForm
Out[131]//MatrixForm=
```

$$\begin{pmatrix} 3 & 4 & 5 \\ 5 & 6 & 7 \\ 7 & 8 & 9 \end{pmatrix}$$

```
In[132]:= (*Create a permutation matrix that
           permutes the second and first row or column.*)
          (p1 = permutationMatrix[{2, 1, 3}]) // MatrixForm
Out[132]//MatrixForm=
```

$$\begin{pmatrix} 0 & 1 & 0 \\ 1 & 0 & 0 \\ 0 & 0 & 1 \end{pmatrix}$$

```
In[133]:= (m1p1 = Dot[m1, p1]) // MatrixForm (*Permute columns.*)
Out[133]//MatrixForm=
```

$$\begin{pmatrix} 4 & 3 & 5 \\ 6 & 5 & 7 \\ 8 & 7 & 9 \end{pmatrix}$$

```
In[134]:= (p1m1 = Dot[p1, m1]) // MatrixForm (*Permute rows.*)
Out[134]//MatrixForm=
```

$$\begin{pmatrix} 5 & 6 & 7 \\ 3 & 4 & 5 \\ 7 & 8 & 9 \end{pmatrix}$$

Whereas a permutation matrix permutes rows or columns, a shift matrix shifts rows or columns, replacing the empty elements with zeros. A shift matrix is simply a matrix with 1s on the superdiagonal or subdiagonal and 0s everywhere else. This can easily be constructed using the DiagonalMatrix function.

```
In[135]:= shiftMatrix[n_, dir_] := DiagonalMatrix[Table[1, {n - Abs[dir]}], dir]
```

```
In[136]:= Dot[shiftMatrix[4, 2], Table[1, {i, 1, 4}, {j, 1, 4}]] // MatrixForm
Out[136]//MatrixForm=
```

$$\begin{pmatrix} 1 & 1 & 1 & 1 \\ 1 & 1 & 1 & 1 \\ 0 & 0 & 0 & 0 \\ 0 & 0 & 0 & 0 \end{pmatrix}$$

```
In[137]:=  (*Shift columns right.*)
           Dot[m1, shiftMatrix[3, 1]] // MatrixForm
Out[137]//MatrixForm=
           ⎛ 0  3  4 ⎞
           ⎜ 0  5  6 ⎟
           ⎝ 0  7  8 ⎠

In[138]:=  (*Shift columns left.*)
           Dot[m1, shiftMatrix[3, -1]] // MatrixForm
Out[138]//MatrixForm=
           ⎛ 4  5  0 ⎞
           ⎜ 6  7  0 ⎟
           ⎝ 8  9  0 ⎠

In[139]:=  (*Shift rows up.*)
           Dot[ shiftMatrix[3, 1], m1] // MatrixForm
Out[139]//MatrixForm=
           ⎛ 5  6  7 ⎞
           ⎜ 7  8  9 ⎟
           ⎝ 0  0  0 ⎠

In[140]:=  (*Shift rows down.*)
           Dot[ shiftMatrix[3, -1], m1] // MatrixForm
Out[140]//MatrixForm=
           ⎛ 0  0  0 ⎞
           ⎜ 3  4  5 ⎟
           ⎝ 5  6  7 ⎠
```

Discussion

A generalized permutation matrix has the same zero entries as the corresponding permutation matrix, but the nonzero entries can have values other than 1.

```
In[141]:=  generalizedPermutationMatrix[values_List, perm_List] :=
           Dot[DiagonalMatrix[values], permutationMatrix[perm]]
In[142]:=  generalizedPermutationMatrix[{3, -1, 4}, {2, 3, 1}] // MatrixForm
Out[142]//MatrixForm=
           ⎛ 0  3   0 ⎞
           ⎜ 0  0  -1 ⎟
           ⎝ 4  0   0 ⎠
```

You can easily enumerate all n! permutation matrices of size n.

```
In[143]:=  allPermutationMatrices[n_] :=
           permutationMatrix[#] & /@ Permutations[Range[n]]
```

```
In[144]:=  Grid[Partition[MatrixForm /@ allPermutationMatrices[4], 6]]
```

$$
\begin{pmatrix} 1&0&0&0 \\ 0&1&0&0 \\ 0&0&1&0 \\ 0&0&0&1 \end{pmatrix}
\begin{pmatrix} 1&0&0&0 \\ 0&1&0&0 \\ 0&0&0&1 \\ 0&0&1&0 \end{pmatrix}
\begin{pmatrix} 1&0&0&0 \\ 0&0&1&0 \\ 0&1&0&0 \\ 0&0&0&1 \end{pmatrix}
\begin{pmatrix} 1&0&0&0 \\ 0&0&1&0 \\ 0&0&0&1 \\ 0&1&0&0 \end{pmatrix}
\begin{pmatrix} 1&0&0&0 \\ 0&0&0&1 \\ 0&1&0&0 \\ 0&0&1&0 \end{pmatrix}
\begin{pmatrix} 1&0&0&0 \\ 0&0&0&1 \\ 0&0&1&0 \\ 0&1&0&0 \end{pmatrix}
$$

$$
\begin{pmatrix} 0&1&0&0 \\ 1&0&0&0 \\ 0&0&1&0 \\ 0&0&0&1 \end{pmatrix}
\begin{pmatrix} 0&1&0&0 \\ 1&0&0&0 \\ 0&0&0&1 \\ 0&0&1&0 \end{pmatrix}
\begin{pmatrix} 0&1&0&0 \\ 0&0&1&0 \\ 1&0&0&0 \\ 0&0&0&1 \end{pmatrix}
\begin{pmatrix} 0&1&0&0 \\ 0&0&1&0 \\ 0&0&0&1 \\ 1&0&0&0 \end{pmatrix}
\begin{pmatrix} 0&1&0&0 \\ 0&0&0&1 \\ 1&0&0&0 \\ 0&0&1&0 \end{pmatrix}
\begin{pmatrix} 0&1&0&0 \\ 0&0&0&1 \\ 0&0&1&0 \\ 1&0&0&0 \end{pmatrix}
$$

```
Out[144]=
```

$$
\begin{pmatrix} 0&0&1&0 \\ 1&0&0&0 \\ 0&1&0&0 \\ 0&0&0&1 \end{pmatrix}
\begin{pmatrix} 0&0&1&0 \\ 1&0&0&0 \\ 0&0&0&1 \\ 0&1&0&0 \end{pmatrix}
\begin{pmatrix} 0&0&1&0 \\ 0&1&0&0 \\ 1&0&0&0 \\ 0&0&0&1 \end{pmatrix}
\begin{pmatrix} 0&0&1&0 \\ 0&1&0&0 \\ 0&0&0&1 \\ 1&0&0&0 \end{pmatrix}
\begin{pmatrix} 0&0&1&0 \\ 0&0&0&1 \\ 1&0&0&0 \\ 0&1&0&0 \end{pmatrix}
\begin{pmatrix} 0&0&1&0 \\ 0&0&0&1 \\ 0&1&0&0 \\ 1&0&0&0 \end{pmatrix}
$$

$$
\begin{pmatrix} 0&0&0&1 \\ 1&0&0&0 \\ 0&1&0&0 \\ 0&0&1&0 \end{pmatrix}
\begin{pmatrix} 0&0&0&1 \\ 1&0&0&0 \\ 0&0&1&0 \\ 0&1&0&0 \end{pmatrix}
\begin{pmatrix} 0&0&0&1 \\ 0&1&0&0 \\ 1&0&0&0 \\ 0&0&1&0 \end{pmatrix}
\begin{pmatrix} 0&0&0&1 \\ 0&1&0&0 \\ 0&0&1&0 \\ 1&0&0&0 \end{pmatrix}
\begin{pmatrix} 0&0&0&1 \\ 0&0&1&0 \\ 1&0&0&0 \\ 0&1&0&0 \end{pmatrix}
\begin{pmatrix} 0&0&0&1 \\ 0&0&1&0 \\ 0&1&0&0 \\ 1&0&0&0 \end{pmatrix}
$$

It is also easy to detect if a matrix is a row permutation of another matrix: simply remove each row from m1 that matches m2 and see if you are left with no rows. Of course, you must also check that the matrices are the same size. A check for column permutation is just a check for row permutations on the transpose of each matrix.

```
In[145]:=  isRowPermutation[m1_, m2_] :=
             Length[m1] == Length[m2] && Fold[DeleteCases[#1, #2] &, m1, m2] == {}
           isMatrixPermutation[m1_, m2_] := isRowPermutation[m1, m2] ||
             isRowPermutation[Transpose[m1], Transpose[m2]]
```

You can verify this on some test cases.

```
In[147]:=  (*Obviously a matrix is a permutation of itself.*)
           isMatrixPermutation[m1, m1]
Out[147]=  True
```

```
In[148]:=  (*Test a row permutation.*)
           isMatrixPermutation[m1, p1m1]
Out[148]=  True
```

```
In[149]:=  (*Test a column permutation.*)
           isMatrixPermutation[m1, m1p1]
Out[149]=  True
```

```
In[150]:=  (*A matrix and its tranpose are not permutations unless symmetric.*)
           isMatrixPermutation[m1, Transpose[m1]]
Out[150]=  False
```

You may be thinking that matrix permutations via linear algebra will only apply to matrices of numbers, but recall that Mathematica is a symbolic language and, thus, not limited to numerical manipulation. Here we do a Dot product on a matrix of graphics!

```
In[151]:= greenRook = Import[
              FileNameJoin[{NotebookDirectory[], "..", "images", "greenRook.gif"}]];
          redSq = Import[FileNameJoin[{NotebookDirectory[],
              "..", "images", "redSq.gif"}]];
          greenSq = Import[FileNameJoin[{NotebookDirectory[],
              "..", "images", "greenSq.gif"}]];
          piece[i_, j_] := Which[i == j, greenRook, OddQ[i + j],
              redSq, True, greenSq];
          (board = Table[piece[i, j], {i, 1, 4}, {j, 1, 4}]) // MatrixForm
Out[155]//MatrixForm=
```

```
In[156]:= Dot[board, permutationMatrix[{2, 3, 1, 4}]] // MatrixForm
Out[156]//MatrixForm=
```

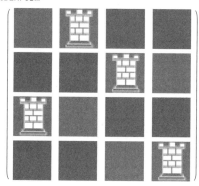

This chess demo lacks some aesthetics (the squares move along with the rooks), but it does illustrate the generality of the permutation matrix.

3.7 Manipulating Rows and Columns of Matrices

Problem

You want to add, remove, or modify entire rows or columns of a matrix in place.

Solution

Many operations on lists (including higher-order lists such as matrices) do not modify the input list but rather produce a new list with the change. For example, Append[myList,10] returns a list with 10 appended but leaves myList untouched. Sometimes you want to modify the actual value of the list associated with a symbol.

```
In[157]:=  (*Create a 5 x 5 zero matrix.*)
           (x = Table[0, {5}, {5}]) // MatrixForm
Out[157]//MatrixForm=
```

$$\begin{pmatrix} 0 & 0 & 0 & 0 & 0 \\ 0 & 0 & 0 & 0 & 0 \\ 0 & 0 & 0 & 0 & 0 \\ 0 & 0 & 0 & 0 & 0 \\ 0 & 0 & 0 & 0 & 0 \end{pmatrix}$$

```
In[158]:=  (*Set the second column to {1,2,3,4,5}.*)
           x[[All, 2]] = Range[5];
```

```
In[159]:=  x // MatrixForm
Out[159]//MatrixForm=
```

$$\begin{pmatrix} 0 & 1 & 0 & 0 & 0 \\ 0 & 2 & 0 & 0 & 0 \\ 0 & 3 & 0 & 0 & 0 \\ 0 & 4 & 0 & 0 & 0 \\ 0 & 5 & 0 & 0 & 0 \end{pmatrix}$$

```
In[160]:=  (*Set the third row to 3.*)
           x[[3, All]] = 3;
```

```
In[161]:=  x // MatrixForm
Out[161]//MatrixForm=
```

$$\begin{pmatrix} 0 & 1 & 0 & 0 & 0 \\ 0 & 2 & 0 & 0 & 0 \\ 3 & 3 & 3 & 3 & 3 \\ 0 & 4 & 0 & 0 & 0 \\ 0 & 5 & 0 & 0 & 0 \end{pmatrix}$$

```
In[162]:=  (*Set 3 x 3 interior to 9.*)
           x[[2 ;; 4, 2 ;; 4]] = 9;
```

```
In[163]:= x // MatrixForm
Out[163]//MatrixForm=
```

$$\begin{pmatrix} 0 & 1 & 0 & 0 & 0 \\ 0 & 9 & 9 & 9 & 0 \\ 3 & 9 & 9 & 9 & 3 \\ 0 & 9 & 9 & 9 & 0 \\ 0 & 5 & 0 & 0 & 0 \end{pmatrix}$$

You may also want to add elements, rows, and columns.

```
In[164]:= (*Add a row.*)
          AppendTo[x, Range[10, 14]];
```

```
In[165]:= x // MatrixForm
Out[165]//MatrixForm=
```

$$\begin{pmatrix} 0 & 1 & 0 & 0 & 0 \\ 0 & 9 & 9 & 9 & 0 \\ 3 & 9 & 9 & 9 & 3 \\ 0 & 9 & 9 & 9 & 0 \\ 0 & 5 & 0 & 0 & 0 \\ 10 & 11 & 12 & 13 & 14 \end{pmatrix}$$

```
In[166]:= (*Add a column of 9s.*)
          Do[AppendTo[x[[i]], 9], {i, 1, 6}]
```

```
In[167]:= x // MatrixForm
Out[167]//MatrixForm=
```

$$\begin{pmatrix} 0 & 1 & 0 & 0 & 0 & 9 \\ 0 & 9 & 9 & 9 & 0 & 9 \\ 3 & 9 & 9 & 9 & 3 & 9 \\ 0 & 9 & 9 & 9 & 0 & 9 \\ 0 & 5 & 0 & 0 & 0 & 9 \\ 10 & 11 & 12 & 13 & 14 & 9 \end{pmatrix}$$

Discussion

Destructive operations should generally be avoided because they can lead to annoying bugs. For one thing, they make code sensitive to evaluation order. This type of code is harder to change. Further, you need to keep in mind that these operations are being performed on symbols rather than lists. What does this mean? Let's inspect the attributes of AppendTo to gain a bit of insight.

```
In[168]:= Attributes[AppendTo]
Out[168]= {HoldFirst, Protected}
```

The relevant attribute here is HoldFirst. This means that the expression passed as the first argument is passed in unevaluated form. This has implications when you want to write your own functions that destructively change the value of a symbol. Consider trying to implement your own AppendTo.

```
In[169]:= ClearAll[myAppendTo] ;
          myAppendTo[x_, val_] := x = Append[x, val]

In[171]:= Attributes[myAppendTo]
Out[171]= {}

In[172]:= x = {} ; myAppendTo[x, 10]
```

> Set::shape : Lists {} and {10} are not the same shape. >>

```
Out[172]= {10}

In[173]:= x
Out[173]= {}
```

First notice that this generated an error message and that *x* did not change. This occurred because *x* was evaluated before the call, and you ended up evaluating AppendTo[List[], 10], which is illegal. You can remedy this by using HoldFirst.

```
In[174]:= SetAttributes[myAppendTo, {HoldFirst}]

In[175]:= myAppendTo[x, 10]
Out[175]= {10}

In[176]:= x
Out[176]= {10}
```

Now it works. As a general rule, you need to use attributes HoldFirst, HoldRest, or HoldAll, as appropriate, to pass expressions in unevaluated form to your own functions. This is covered in Chapter 2, "Introduction," on page 30, and in Recipe 2.2.

3.8 Using Sparse Arrays to Conserve Memory

Problem

You need to work with very large arrays or matrices but most of the entries are duplicates (typically 0).

Solution

Mathematica has direct support for sparse arrays and higher-order tensors using the SparseArray function. The sparse array is built from a rule-based specification that maps positions to values.

```
In[177]:= (*1000 × 1000 sparse matrix*)
          m1 = SparseArray[{{1, 1} → 1, {1000, 1000} → -1, {500, 750} → 5}]
Out[177]= SparseArray[<3>, {1000, 1000}]
```

You can also specify the positions and values in separate lists. Here is a sparse vector using this technique.

```
In[178]:= v1 = SparseArray[{1, 3, 9, 81, 6561} → {5, 10, 15, 20, 25}]
Out[178]= SparseArray[<5>, {6561}]
```

You can also convert a standard matrix to a sparse one.

```
In[179]:= dense = DiagonalMatrix[Range[1000]];

In[180]:= sparse = SparseArray[dense]
Out[180]= SparseArray[<1000>, {1000, 1000}]
```

As you can see, the memory savings is considerable.

```
In[181]:= ByteCount[dense] - ByteCount[sparse]
Out[181]= 3 987 416

In[182]:= ClearAll[dense]
```

Discussion

Very large but sparsely populated matrices arise often in applications of linear algebra. Mathematica provides excellent support for sparse arrays because most operations that are available for list-based matrices (or tensors in general) are available for sparse array objects.

Mathematica does not have sparse equivalents of the convenience functions IdentityMatrix and DiagonalMatrix, but they are easy to synthesize using Band, which specifies either the starting position of a diagonal entry or a range of positions for a diagonal.

```
In[183]:= (*100 x 100 identity matrix*)
          identity = SparseArray[Band[{1, 1}] → 1, {100, 100}]
Out[183]= SparseArray[<100>, {100, 100}]
```

```
In[184]:=  (*100 x 100 diagonal matrix with
            the values {1,2,3,...,100} on the diagonal*)
          diagonal = SparseArray[Band[{1, 1}] → Range[100], {100, 100}]
Out[184]= SparseArray[<100>, {100, 100}]
```

A general sparse diagonal function looks like this.

```
In[185]:=  sparseDiagonal[list_, k_] :=
          SparseArray[Band[If[k > 0, {1, 1 + k}, {1 - k, 1}]] → list,
            (Length[list] + Abs[k]) {1, 1}]
```

You can also produce sparse versions of the permutation matrices from Recipe 3.6.

```
In[186]:=  sparsePermutationMatrix[list_] :=
          SparseArray[Band[{1, 1}] → 1, Length[list] {1, 1}] [[list]]
          antiDiag = sparsePermutationMatrix[Range[100, 1, -1]]
Out[187]= SparseArray[<100>, {100, 100}]
```

See Also

Recipe 3.5 showed how to use SparseArray and Band to create tridiagonal matrices.

3.9 Manipulating Deeply Nested Lists Using Functions with Level Specifications

Problem

You need to extract, delete, modify, or transform content deep inside a nested list.

Solution

A level specification (or *levelspec*) is the key for surgically manipulating lists that contain many levels. Most of Mathematica's functions that deal with lists have variations that take levelspecs. Position is one such function. Consider a list of integers that has values nested up to eight levels.

```
In[188]:=  deep = {1, {2, 3, 4, 5, {1, 6, 1, 7},
            {1, {{{{1, 8}, 1}, {1}}, 1}}, 1, 1, 1, 9, 10, 11}, 12};
          Depth[
            deep]
Out[189]= 8
```

```
In[190]:=  deep // TreeForm
Out[190]//TreeForm=
```

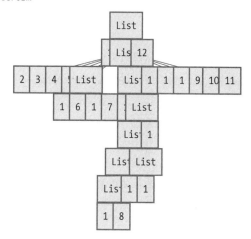

If you use Position to search for 1, you get a list of all positions that have the value 1. You can verify this using Extract.

```
In[191]:=  Position[deep, 1]
Out[191]=  {{1}, {2, 5, 1}, {2, 5, 3}, {2, 6, 1}, {2, 6, 2, 1, 1, 1, 1},
           {2, 6, 2, 1, 1, 2}, {2, 6, 2, 1, 2, 1}, {2, 6, 2, 2}, {2, 7}, {2, 8}, {2, 9}}
```

```
In[192]:=  Extract[deep, Position[deep, 1]]
Out[192]=  {1, 1, 1, 1, 1, 1, 1, 1, 1, 1, 1}
```

Suppose you do not want the 1s at every level. This is where levelspecs come in handy.

Use a single positive integer *n* to search at all levels up to and including *n*.

```
In[193]:=  (*Only search up to level two.*)
           Position[deep, 1, 2]
Out[193]=  {{1}, {2, 7}, {2, 8}, {2, 9}}
```

Enclosing the level {n} in a list restricts search to that level.

```
In[194]:=  (*Only search at level two.*)
           Position[deep, 1, {2}]
Out[194]=  {{2, 7}, {2, 8}, {2, 9}}
```

The list notation {n,m} restricts search to levels n through m, inclusively.

```
In[195]:=  (*Search at levels three through five.*)
           Position[deep, 1, {3, 5}]
Out[195]=  {{2, 5, 1}, {2, 5, 3}, {2, 6, 1}, {2, 6, 2, 2}}
```

Negative level specification of the form -n looks for objects that themselves have depth n.

```
In[196]:= Position[deep, 1, -1]
Out[196]= {{1}, {2, 5, 1}, {2, 5, 3}, {2, 6, 1}, {2, 6, 2, 1, 1, 1, 1},
          {2, 6, 2, 1, 1, 2}, {2, 6, 2, 1, 2, 1}, {2, 6, 2, 2}, {2, 7}, {2, 8}, {2, 9}}

In[197]:= (*See the discussion for why this is empty and must be empty.*)
          Position[deep, 1, -2]
Out[197]= {}
```

Discussion

We used Position to get a feel for level specifications because it is easy to judge, based on the length of each position sublist, the depth of each item found. However, you may be surprised that the last example was empty. It is easy to mistakenly think that negative level specification means searching from the bottom of the tree up because this seems analogous to the way negative indices work in functions like Part. This is not the case. A negative level specification means only looking for items with specified depth after dropping the minus sign. Any scalar (like 1) has depth 1, including complex numbers.

```
In[198]:= {Depth[1], Depth[3.7], Depth["foo"], Depth[1 + 7 I]}
Out[198]= {1, 1, 1, 1}
```

From this, it follows that a scalar will never be found by using a negative depth value less than -1.

Another important function for illustrating the use of level specifications is Level. Its function is to retrieve all objects at the specified level(s).

```
In[199]:= Level[deep, {2}]
Out[199]= {2, 3, 4, 5, {1, 6, 1, 7}, {1, {{{{1, 8}, 1}, {1}}, 1}}, 1, 1, 1, 9, 10, 11}
```

Objects at level {2} may have a variety of depths.

```
In[200]:= Depth /@ Level[deep, {2}]
Out[200]= {1, 1, 1, 1, 2, 6, 1, 1, 1, 1, 1, 1}
```

Objects at level {-2} will only have a single depth by definition.

```
In[201]:= Level[deep, {-2}]
Out[201]= {{1, 6, 1, 7}, {1, 8}, {1}}

In[202]:= Depth /@ Level[deep, {-2}]
Out[202]= {2, 2, 2}
```

A picture helps reinforce this. Note that each tree has two levels.

In[203]:= `GraphicsRow[TreeForm /@ Level[deep, {-2}], ImageSize → Large]`

Out[203]=

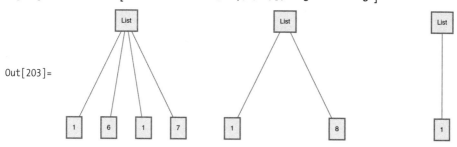

Note the difference between {-2}, meaning exactly depth 2, and -2, meaning depth 2 or more.

In[204]:= `Depth /@ Level[deep, -2]`
Out[204]= {2, 2, 3, 2, 4, 5, 6, 7}

Once you have mastered level specifications, the functions Apply, Cases, Delete, DeleteCases, Extract, FreeQ, Level, Map, MapIndexed, MemberQ, Position, Replace, and Scan take on more power and precision because they each have versions that use levelspecs.

Here are some examples in which we extract, delete, and modify the contents of a deeply nested expression. This time we use an algebraic expression.

In[205]:= `Clear[x, y];`
`deepAlg = 1 + (x + y) - 2 x^2 + (x + y)^3 + E^(x + y);`
`deepAlg = Factor[deepAlg ^ deepAlg - deepAlg]`

Out[207]= $\left(1 + e^{x+y} + x - 2 x^2 + x^3 + y + 3 x^2 y + 3 x y^2 + y^3\right)$

$\left(1 + e^{x+y} + x - 2 x^2 + y + (x + y)^3\right)^{-2 x^2} \left(-\left(1 + e^{x+y} + x - 2 x^2 + y + (x + y)^3\right)^{2 x^2} + \right.$

$\left. \left(1 + e^{x+y} + x - 2 x^2 + y + (x + y)^3\right)^{e^{x+y} + x + y + (x+y)^3}\right)$

In[208]:= `Depth[deepAlg]`
Out[208]= 8

In[209]:= `(*The three x's at levels two through three*)`
`Extract[deepAlg, Position[deepAlg, x, {2, 3}]]`
Out[209]= {x, x, x, x}

In[210]:= (*Delete the x's at two and three.*)
Delete[deepAlg, Position[deepAlg, x, {2, 3}]]

Out[210]= $\left(4 + e^{x+y} - 2 x^2 + y + 3 x^2 y + 3 y^2 + y^3\right)$

$\left(1 + e^{x+y} - 2 x^2 + y + (x + y)^3\right)^{-2 x^2} \left(-\left(1 + e^{x+y} + x - 2 x^2 + y + (x + y)^3\right)^{2 x^2} +\right.$

$\left.\left(1 + e^{x+y} + x - 2 x^2 + y + (x + y)^3\right)^{e^{x+y} + x + y + (x+y)^3}\right)$

In[211]:= (*Change those x's to z's.*)
Replace[deepAlg, x → z, {2, 3}]

Out[211]= $\left(-\left(1 + e^{x+y} + x - 2 x^2 + y + (x + y)^3\right)^{2 x^2} +\right.$

$\left.\left(1 + e^{x+y} + x - 2 x^2 + y + (x + y)^3\right)^{e^{x+y} + x + y + (x+y)^3}\right)$

$\left(1 + e^{x+y} - 2 x^2 + y + (x + y)^3 + z\right)^{-2 x^2}$

$\left(1 + e^{x+y} - 2 x^2 + y + 3 x^2 y + y^3 + z + 3 y^2 z + z^3\right)$

In[212]:= (*Sure enough, there are now four z's.*)
Count[%, z, {2, 3}]

Out[212]= 4

In[213]:= (*Replace any subexpression with depth three with z.*)
Replace[deepAlg, _ → z, {-3}]

Out[213]= $\left(1 + x + y + 3 z\right)^z \left(1 + x + x^3 + y + y^3 + 4 z\right)$

$\left(-\left(1 + x + y + 3 z\right)^z + \left(1 + x + y + 3 z\right)^{x+y+2 z}\right)$

In[214]:= (*Square all subexpressions of depth three.*)
Map[#^2 &, deepAlg, {-3}]

Out[214]= $\left(1 + e^{2 x+2 y} + x + x^3 + 4 x^4 + y + 9 x^4 y^2 + y^3 + 9 x^2 y^4\right)$

$\left(1 + e^{2 x+2 y} + x + 4 x^4 + y + (x + y)^6\right)^{4 x^4}$

$\left(-\left(1 + e^{2 x+2 y} + x + 4 x^4 + y + (x + y)^6\right)^{4 x^4} +\right.$

$\left.\left(1 + e^{2 x+2 y} + x + 4 x^4 + y + (x + y)^6\right)^{e^{2 x+2 y} + x + y + (x+y)^6}\right)$

See Also

Chapter 2, "Functional Programming," has recipes that deal with the specifics of Apply, Map, MapIndexed, and Scan.

Chapter 4, "Patterns," has recipes that deal with the specifics of Cases, DeleteCases, FreeQ, MemberQ, and Replace.

3.10 Implementing Bit Vectors and Using Format to Customize Their Presentation

Problem

You want to manipulate a vector of bits in a space-efficient fashion. You also want to give these vectors a concise default display format.

Solution

You can use Mathematica's ability to represent arbitrarily large integers as a means of implementing bit vectors. Using Mathematica's UpValue convention (see Chapter 2, "DownValues and UpValues," page 27) you can make bit vectors adopt the familiar interface used by lists. When you create custom data structures like this, you can give them an output format that hides the details of their internal representation.

```
In[215]:= (*Make a bit vector from a list of bit value.*)
          makeBitVector[bits_List] :=
           bitvec[FromDigits[Reverse[bits], 2], Length[bits]]
          (*Make a bit vector of a specified
           length. Values are initialized to 0.*)
          makeBitVector[l_: 32] := bitvec[0, l]
          (*Set bit at index to 0 or 1.*)
          setBit[bitvec[n_, l_], index_Integer, 1] :=
           Module[{n2 = BitSet[n, index - 1]}, bitvec[n2, Max[1, BitLength[n2]]]]
          setBit[bitvec[n_, l_], index_Integer, 0] :=
           bitvec[BitClear[n, index - 1], l]
          SetAttributes[setBitOf, HoldFirst]
          setBitOf[name_Symbol, index_Integer, bit_ /; bit === 0 || bit === 1] :=
           name = setBit[name, index, bit]
          (*Get the first bit value.*)
          bitvec /: First[bitvec[n_, _]] := BitGet[n, 0]
          (*Get the rest of the bits after the first as a new bit vector.*)
          bitvec /: Rest[bitvec[n_, l_]] := bitvec[Floor[n / 2], l - 1]
          (*Get bit at index.*)
          bitvec /: Part[bitvec[n_, _], index_Integer] := BitGet[n, index - 1]
          (*Get the length of the bit vector.*)
          bitvec /: Length[bitvec[n_, l_]] := l
          bitvec /: BitLength[bitvec[n_, l_]] := l
          (*Perform bitwise AND of two vectors.*)
```

```
bitvec /: BitAnd[bitvec[n1_, l1_], bitvec[n2_, l2_]] :=
  bitvec[BitAnd[n1, n2], Max[l1, l2]]
(*Perform bitwise OR of two vectors.*)
bitvec /: BitOr[bitvec[n1_, l1_], bitvec[n2_, l2_]] :=
  bitvec[BitAnd[n1, n2], Max[l1, l2]]
(*Return the complement (NOT) of a bit vector.*)
bitvec /: BitNot[bitvec[n_, l_]] :=
  bitvec[BitAnd[BitNot[n], 2^l - 1], l]
(*Create a format to print bit vectors in an abbreviated fashion.*)
Format[bitvec[n_, l_]] :=
  "bitvec"["<" <> ToString[BitGet[n, 0]] <> "..." <>
    ToString[BitGet[n, l - 1]] <> ">", l]
```

Here are some examples of usage.

```
In[229]:= bv = makeBitVector[{1, 0, 0, 0, 1}]
Out[229]= bitvec[<1...1>, 5]

In[230]:= bv[[2]]
Out[230]= 0

In[231]:= bv = setBit[bv, 2, 1]
Out[231]= bitvec[<1...1>, 5]

In[232]:= bv[[2]]
Out[232]= 1

In[233]:= bv = setBit[bv, 500, 1]
Out[233]= bitvec[<1...1>, 500]

In[234]:= bv2 = Rest[bv]
Out[234]= bitvec[<1...1>, 499]

In[235]:= bv3 = BitNot[makeBitVector[{1, 0, 0, 0, 1}]]
Out[235]= bitvec[<0...0>, 5]

In[236]:= bv3[[1]]
Out[236]= 0
```

Discussion

Even if you have no immediate application for bit vectors, this recipe provides a lesson in how you can create new types of objects and integrate them into Mathematica using familiar native functions.

See Also

See *tutorial/DefiningOutputFormats* in the Mathematica documentation for more details on Format.

3.11 Implementing Trees and Traversals Using Lists

Problem

You want to model tree data structures in Mathematica and operate on them with standard tree-based algorithms.

Solution

The simplest tree is the binary tree, and the simplest model of a binary tree in Mathematica is a list consisting of the left branch, node value, and right branch.

```
In[238]:=  (*MakeTree constructs either an empty
             tree or a tree with only a root element.*)
           makeTree[] := {}
           makeTree[value_] := {{}, value, {}}
           (*Functions for extracting the parts of a node*)
           getTreeValue[tree_] := tree[[2]]
           getTreeLeft[tree_] := tree[[1]]
           getTreeRight[tree_] := tree[[3]]
           (*We insert elements into a tree using < ordering relation.*)
           insertTree[{}, value_] := {{}, value, {}}
           insertTree[tree_, value_] := If[value < getTreeValue[tree],
             {insertTree[getTreeLeft[tree], value],
              getTreeValue[tree], getTreeRight[tree]},
             {getTreeLeft[tree], getTreeValue[tree],
              insertTree[getTreeRight[tree], value]}]
           (*Given the above primitives, it is easy to define
            some common algorithms.*)
           listToTree[list_List] := Fold[insertTree[#1, #2] &, makeTree[], list]
           (*A preorder traversal is also known as depth-first.*)
           preorder[tree_] := Reap[preorder2[tree]][[2, 1]]
           preorder2[{}] := {}
           preorder2[tree_] := Module[{}, Sow[getTreeValue[tree]];
                                  preorder2[getTreeLeft[tree]];
                                preorder2[getTreeRight[tree]]]
```

```
postorder[tree_] := Reap[postorder2[tree]][[2, 1]]
postorder2[{}] := {}
postorder2[tree_] := Module[{},
  postorder2[getTreeLeft[tree]];
  postorder2[getTreeRight[tree]];
      Sow[getTreeValue[tree]]]
(*An inorder traversal returns the values in sorted order.*)
inorder[tree_] := Reap[inorder2[tree]][[2, 1]]
inorder2[{}] := {}
inorder2[tree_] := Module[{},
  inorder2[getTreeLeft[tree]];
  Sow[getTreeValue[tree]];
  inorder2[getTreeRight[tree]]]
(*A level order traversal is also known as breadth first.*)
levelorder[tree_] := Reap[levelorder2[{tree}]][[2, 1]]
(*Breadth first is commonly implemented in terms of
 a queue that keeps track of unprocessed levels. I model
 the queue as a list.*)
levelorder2[{}] := {}  (*Stop on empty queue.*)
levelorder2[{{}}] := {} (*Stop on queue with empty tree.*)
levelorder2[queue_] := Module[{front = First[queue],
    queue2 = Rest[queue], (*Pop front of queue.*),
    left, right},
  Sow[getTreeValue[front]]; (*Visit node.*)
  left = getTreeLeft[front];
  right = getTreeRight[front];
  queue2 = If[Length[left] == 0, queue2, Append[queue2, left]];
  (*Append left if not empty.*)
  queue2 = If[Length[right] == 0, queue2, Append[queue2, right]];
  (*Append right if not empty.*)
  levelorder2[queue2]]
```

In[259]:= nodes = RandomInteger[{1, 100}, 18]

Out[259]= {62, 97, 36, 82, 76, 84, 58, 32, 79, 16, 89, 15, 45, 72, 90, 32, 12, 9}

```
In[260]:=  (tree = listToTree[nodes]) //
            TreeForm[#, PlotRangePadding → 0, ImageSize → 450] &
Out[260]//TreeForm=
```

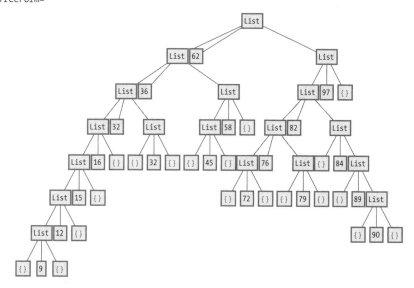

```
In[261]:=  preorder[tree]
Out[261]=  {62, 36, 32, 16, 15, 12, 9, 32, 58, 45, 97, 82, 76, 72, 79, 84, 89, 90}

In[262]:=  postorder[tree]
Out[262]=  {9, 12, 15, 16, 32, 32, 45, 58, 36, 72, 79, 76, 90, 89, 84, 82, 97, 62}

In[263]:=  inorder[tree]
Out[263]=  {9, 12, 15, 16, 32, 32, 36, 45, 58, 62, 72, 76, 79, 82, 84, 89, 90, 97}

In[264]:=  levelorder[tree]
Out[264]=  {62, 36, 97, 32, 58, 82, 16, 32, 45, 76, 84, 15, 72, 79, 89, 12, 90, 9}
```

Discussion

The tree implementation in the solution is a bit simplistic, but it is intended to illustrate basic concepts. One way to generalize the implementation is to allow a different ordering function. It makes sense to keep the ordering with each instance of the tree. For this, it is best to use Mathematica options, which are a standard convention for optional values. You need to redefine the functions for creating trees and accessing their parts, but once you do that, the existing algorithm implementations will still work.

```
In[265]:= ClearAll[makeTree, getTreeValue,
            getTreeLeft, getTreeRight, insertTree, listToTree];
          (*Use the explicit head Tree to hold the
           representation and the options.*)
          makeTree[opt : OptionsPattern[Ordering -> Less]] := Tree[{}, opt]
          makeTree[value_, opt : OptionsPattern[ordering -> Less]] :=
           Tree[{{}, value, {}}, opt]
          (*Functions for extracting the parts of a node are now overloaded for top-
           level Tree form.*)
          getTreeValue[Tree[tree_, ___]] := getTreeValue[tree]
          getTreeValue[tree_] := tree[[2]]
          getTreeLeft[Tree[tree_, ___]] := getTreeLeft[tree]
          getTreeLeft[tree_] := tree[[1]]
          getTreeRight[Tree[tree_, ___]] := getTreeRight[tree]
          getTreeRight[tree_] := tree[[3]]
          (*Insert extracts the ordering option
           using the replacement rule and passes it to
            the function that implements the insert.*)
          insertTree[Tree[tree_, opts_], value_] :=
           Tree[insertTree[tree, value, ordering /. opts], opts]
          insertTree[{}, value_, _] := {{}, value, {}}
          insertTree[tree_, value_, ordering_] :=
           If[ordering[value, getTreeValue[tree]],
             {insertTree[getTreeLeft[tree], value, ordering],
              getTreeValue[tree], getTreeRight[tree]},
             {getTreeLeft[tree], getTreeValue[tree],
              insertTree[getTreeRight[tree], value, ordering]}]
          listToTree[list_List, opt : OptionsPattern[Ordering -> Less]] :=
           Fold[insertTree[#1, #2] &, makeTree[opt], list]
In[278]:= t1 = listToTree[RandomInteger[{1, 100}, 20], ordering -> Greater];
          inorder[t1]
Out[279]= {92, 92, 91, 84, 78, 71, 68, 56, 56, 54, 41, 39, 38, 35, 34, 32, 21, 16, 11, 2}
```

Another enhancement is to generalize the so-called *visit* function of the traversal algorithms.

```
In[280]:= ClearAll[inorder, inorder2];
          inorder[tree_, visit_ : Sow] := Flatten[ Reap[inorder2[tree, visit]]]
          inorder2[{}, _] := {}
          inorder2[tree_, visit_] := Module[{},
           inorder2[getTreeLeft[tree], visit];
           visit[getTreeValue[tree]];
           inorder2[getTreeRight[tree], visit]]
```

This allows the caller the option of not receiving all the nodes. For example, rather than Sow, you can pass in a function that writes the values to a file or a filter as we do here.

```
In[284]:= inorder[t1, If[OddQ[#], Sow[#], #] &]
Out[284]= {91, 71, 41, 39, 35, 21, 11}
```

See Also

More information on trees and tree traversal can be found in any computer science data structures book or at *http://bit.ly/7xP6jQ*.

3.12 Implementing Ordered Associative Lookup Using a Red-Black Tree

Problem

You need better-than-linear associative lookup and storage to increase performance of a program. You also need the elements to remain ordered.

Solution

A red-black tree is a popular balanced tree algorithm used as the foundation for associative data structures. To implement a red-black tree in Mathematica, you create a representation of the tree and functions for creating, reading, updating, and deleting (CRUD). This implementation will use a head rbTree containing a tree and an ordering relation. The tree is modeled as either an empty list or a quadruple consisting of a color (red or black), a left subtree, an element, and a right subtree. By default, we use the function Less as the ordering relation. Storing the ordering relation as part of the tree allows for trees of varying element content.

```
In[285]:=  (*Make an empty tree with default ordering.*)
           makeRBTree[] := rbTree[{}, Less]
           (*Make an empty tree with a custom ordering.*)
           makeRBTree[ordering_] := rbTree[{}, ordering]
           (*Make a tree with given root and ordering.*)
           makeRBTree[{color_, left_, elem_, right_}, ordering_] :=
             rbTree[{color, left, elem, right}, ordering]
```

Before we can do much with these trees, we need a method for inserting new elements while keeping the tree well ordered and balanced. For this, we create a top-level insert function implemented in terms of several low-level functions that maintain all the constraints necessary for a red-black tree.

```
In[288]:=  insertRBTree[rbTree[struct_, ordering_], elem_] :=
             makeRBTree[makeBlack[insertRBTree2[struct, elem, ordering]], ordering]

In[289]:=  (*This implementation method does ordered
             insertion and balancing of the tree representation.
               Note: empty subtrees {} are considered implicitly black.*)
           insertRBTree2[{}, elem_, _] := {red, {}, elem, {}}
           insertRBTree2[{color_, left_, elem2_, right_}, elem1_, ordering_] :=
             Which[ordering[elem1, elem2],
               balance[color, insertRBTree2[left, elem1, ordering], elem2, right],
                   ordering[elem2, elem1],
               balance[color, left, elem2, insertRBTree2[right, elem1, ordering]],
                   True, {color, left, elem2, right}]

In[291]:=  (*This is a helper that turns a node to black.*)
           makeBlack[{color_, left_, elem_, right_}] := {black, left, elem, right}

In[292]:=  (*Balancing is handled by a transformation function that
               matches all red-black constraint violations
               and transforms them into balanced versions.*)
           balance[black, {red, {red, left1_, elem1_, right1_}, elem2_, right2_},
             elem3_, right3_] :=
             {red, {black, left1, elem1, right1}, elem2, {black, right2, elem3, right3}}
           balance[black, {red, left1_, elem1_, {red, left2_, elem2_, right1_}},
             elem3_, right2_] :=
             {red, {black, left1, elem1, left2}, elem2, {black, left2, elem3, right2}}
```

```
balance[black, left1_, elem1_,
  {red, {red, left2_, elem2_, right1_}, elem3_, right2_}] :=
  {red, {black, left1, elem1, left2}, elem2,
    {black, right1, elem3, right2}}
balance[black, left1_, elem1_,
  {red, left2_, elem2_, {red, left3_, elem3_, right1_}}] :=
  {red, {black, left1, elem1, left2}, elem2, {black, left3, elem3, right1}}
balance[color_, left1_, elem1_, right1_] :=
  {color, left1, elem1, right1}
```

List-to-tree and tree-to-list conversions are very convenient operations for interfacing with the rest of Mathematica.

```
In[296]:=  (*Given a list create an rbTree of the elements.*)
           listToRBTree[list_List] :=
             Fold[insertRBTree[#1, #2] &, makeRBTree[], list]
           listToRBTree[list_List, ordering_] :=
             Fold[insertRBTree[#1, #2] &, makeRBTree[ordering], list]
           (*Given a tree convert to a list while retaining ordering.*)
           rbTreeToList[rbTree[tree_, _]] :=
             Flatten[tree /. (red | black) -> Sequence[], Infinity]
           rbTreeFind[rbTree[{}, _], _] := {}
           rbTreeFind[rbTree[tree_, ordering_], elem_] :=
             rbTreeFind2[tree, elem, ordering]
           rbTreeFind2[{color_, left_, elem2_, right_}, elem1_, ordering_] :=
             Which[ordering[elem1, elem2], rbTreeFind2[left, elem1, ordering],
               ordering[elem2, elem1], rbTreeFind2[right, elem1, ordering],
               True, {elem2}]
           rbTreeMax2[{_, _, elem_, {}}] := elem
           rbTreeMax2[{_, _, _, right_}] := rbTreeMax2[right]
           removeRBTree[rbTree[{}, ordering_], elem_] := rbTree[{}, ordering]
           removeRBTree[rbTree[tree_, ordering_], elem_] :=
             makeRBTree[makeBlack[removeRBTree2[tree, elem, ordering]], ordering]
           removeRBTree2[{}, _, _] := {}
```

```
removeRBTree2[{color_, left_, elem2_, right_}, elem1_, ordering_] :=
  Which[ordering[elem1, elem2],
    balance[red, removeRBTree2[left, elem1, ordering], elem2, right],
        ordering[elem2, elem1],
    balance[red, left, elem2, removeRBTree2[right, elem1, ordering]],
        True, Which[right == {}, left,
                    left == {}, right,
                    True, With[{max = rbTreeMax2[left]},
        balance[red, removeRBTree2[left, max, ordering], max, right]]]
  ]
```

Discussion

There are several ways to approach a problem like this. One reasonable answer is to implement associative lookup outside of Mathematica using a language like C++ and then use MathLink to access this functionality. Here we will take the approach of implementing a red-black tree directly in Mathematica.

A red-black tree implemented in C may typically be hundreds of lines of code, yet we achieve an implementation in Mathematica with less than a hundred, including comments. How is this possible? The main idea is to exploit pattern matching as much as possible. Note particularly the function balance. This function directly implements the most tricky part of a red-black-tree implementation in a traditionally procedural language by stating the balancing rules in a form that is very close to the way the algorithm requirements might specify them. Let's take one of the versions as an example.

```
balance[black, {red, {red, left1_, elem1_, right1_}, elem2_, right2_}, elem3
_, right3_] :=
  {red, {black, left1, elem1, right1}, elem2, {black, right2, elem3, right3}}
```

The above says: "If you find a black node (elem3) with a red left child (elem2) that also has a red left child (elem1), then convert to a red node with two black children (elem1 and elem3, in that order). This is a case where the code speaks more clearly and precisely than any English translation. With a slight bit of editing, the code itself translates into a graphical view of before and after. I can't think of another general programming language where you can code and visualize an algorithm with so little added effort!

```
In[309]:= TreeForm[{black, {red, {red, left1, elem1, right1}, elem2, right2},
          elem3, right3} , ImageSize → Medium]
       TreeForm[{red, {black, left1, elem1, right1}, elem2,
          {black, right2, elem3, right3}}, ImageSize → 450]
```

Out[309]//TreeForm=

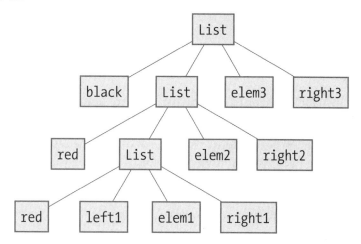

Out[310]//TreeForm=

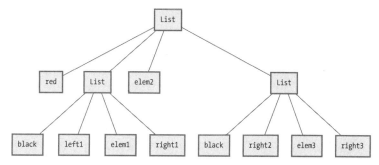

See Also

A solution to associative lookup that is more in the spirit of Mathematica can be found in Recipe 3.13.

This recipe was inspired by the book *Purely Functional Data Structures* by Chris Okasaki (Cambridge University Press), in which Haskell is used to demonstrate that data structures can be written under the constraints of a pure functional programming language.

Wikipedia provides a good basic explanation of and references to more sources for red-black trees (*http://bit.ly/3WEqrT*).

3.13 Exploiting Mathematica's Built-In Associative Lookup

Problem

You want to create a dictionary to associate keys with values, but you want Mathematica to do most of the work.

Solution

Harness the same mechanism Mathematica uses to locate the downvalues of a symbol to create the dictionary.

Here I outline the basic idea for the solution and defer the actual implementation to the discussion. The idea is simply to exploit something that Mathematica must already do well: look up a symbol's downvalues. It must do this well because it is central to Mathematica programming. Imagine you want to create a table of values associating some U.S. zip codes with towns. A reasonable way to proceed is as follows:

```
In[311]:= zipcode[11771] = {"Oyster Bay", "Upper Brookville",
              "East Norwhich", "Cove Neck", "Centere Island"};
          zipcode[11772] = {"Patchogue", "North Patchogue", "East Patchogue"};
          (*And so on...*)
          zipcode[11779] = {"Ronkonkoma", "Lake Ronkonkoma"};
```

Now, when your program needs to do a lookup, it can simply call the "function" zipcode.

```
In[314]:= With[{zip = 11771},
            Print["The number of towns in ",
              zip, " is ", Length[zipcode[zip]], ";"];]
```

```
The number of towns in 11771 is 5.
```

This is so obvious that few regular Mathematica programmers would even think twice about doing this. However, this use case is static. Most associative data structures are dynamic. This is not a problem because you can also remove downvalues.

```
In[315]:= zipcode[11779] =.
```

Now there is no longer an association to 11779. Mathematica indicates this by returning the expression in unevaluated form.

```
In[316]:= zipcode[11779]
Out[316]= zipcode[11779]
```

But this is still not enough. An associated data structure should also tell you all the keys and all the values it knows. Again, Mathematica comes through.

```
In[317]:= DownValues[zipcode]
Out[317]= {HoldPattern[zipcode[11771]] :→
             {Oyster Bay, Upper Brookville, East Norwhich, Cove Neck, Centere Island},
           HoldPattern[zipcode[11772]] :→
             {Patchogue, North Patchogue, East Patchogue}}
```

So all the building blocks are present in the core of Mathematica to create a dynamic dictionary-like data structure. All that is needed is the creation of some code to neatly tie these pieces together into a general utility.

Discussion

The first function we need is a way to construct a dictionary. In the solution, we use a symbol that makes sense for the problem at hand, but in a generic implementation what symbol is used is not significant so long as it is unique. Luckily, Mathematica has the function Unique to deliver the goods. We initialize the dictionary by creating a downvalue that maps any value to the empty list. The symbol is wrapped up in the head Dictionary and returned to the caller.

```
In[318]:= makeDictionary[] :=
            Module[{name},
                name = Unique["dict"];
                Evaluate[name][k_] := {};
                Dictionary[name]
            ]
```

You will also want a way to get rid of dictionaries and all their content. Remove does the trick.

```
In[319]:= destroyDictionary[Dictionary[name_, ___]] :=
            If[ValueQ[name[_]], Remove[name]; True, False]
```

Although we said that there is no need to know the symbol used internally, there is no harm in providing a function to retrieve it. Further, our implementation will use this function so that it is easier to change the internal representation in the future.

```
In[320]:= dictName[Dictionary[name_, ___]] := name
```

The most important function, dictStore, allows the association of a value with a key. We assume, as in the solution, that more than one value may be needed for a given key, so we store values in a list and prepend new values as they are added.

```
In[321]:= dictStore[dict_Dictionary, key_, value_] :=
            Module[{d = dictName[dict]}, d[key] = Prepend[d[key], value]]
```

The function `dictReplace` is like `dictStore`, except it guarantees value is unique. That is, there are no duplicates of value, although there might be other values for the key.

```
In[322]:= dictReplace[dict_Dictionary, key_, value_] :=
          Module[{d = dictName[dict]}, d[key] = d[key] ⋃ {value}]
```

In contrast, the function `dictRemove` ensures that there are no instances of value associated with the key (although, again, there might be other values for the key).

```
In[323]:= dictRemove[dict_Dictionary, key_, value_] :=
          Module[{d = dictName[dict]}, d[key] = Complement[d[key], {value}]]
```

If you want all values removed, then use `dictClear`.

```
In[324]:= dictClear[Dictionary[name_, ___]] :=
          If[ValueQ[name[_]], Clear[name]; Evaluate[name][k_] := {}; True, False]
```

Maintaining the dictionary is all well and good, but you also need to be able to retrieve values. The function `dictLookup` is the easiest to implement because it gets Mathematica to do all the work by simply asking for the downvalue in the usual way.

```
In[325]:= dictLookup[Dictionary[name_, ___], key_] := name[key]
```

Sometimes you might not care what the value is but rather if the key exists at all. Here I use `ValueQ`, which returns true if the evaluation of an expression returns something different than the expression itself (hence, indicating there is a value). In this implementation, I don't care that the value may be the empty list `{}` because `dictHasKeyQ` is only intended to tell the caller that the key is present.

```
In[326]:= dictHasKeyQ[Dictionary[name_, ___], key_] := ValueQ[name[key]]
```

This function tells you that the key is present but has no values.

```
In[327]:= dictKeyEmptyQ[Dictionary[name_, ___], key_] := name[key] === {}
```

In some applications, you may want to know the set of all keys; `dictKeys` provides that. It works by using `DownValues`, as shown in the solution, but transforms the results to extract only the keys. `Most` is used to exclude the special downvalue `name[k_]`, which was created within `makeDictionary`. The use of `HoldPattern` follows from the format that `DownValues` uses, as seen in the solution section. Here, `Evaluate` is used because `DownValues` has the attribute `HoldAll`.

```
In[328]:= dictKeys[dict_Dictionary] := Most[DownValues[Evaluate[dictName[dict]]]] /.
          HoldPattern[a_ :→ _List] :→ a[[1, 1]]
```

Another useful capability is to get a list of all key value pairs; `dictKeyValuePairs` does that.

```
In[329]:= dictKeyValuePairs[dict_Dictionary] :=
            Most[DownValues[Evaluate[dictName[dict]]]] /.
              HoldPattern[a_ :→ values_List] :→ {a[[1, 1]], values}
```

Before I exercise this functionality, a few general points need to be made.

You may be curious about the pattern Dictionary[name_, ___] since the representation of the dictionary, per makeDictionary, is clearly just Dictionary[name]. As you probably already know (see Chapter 4 if necessary), ___ matches a sequence of zero or more expressions. Using this pattern will future proof the functions against changes in the implementation. For example, I may want to enhance Dictionary to take options that control aspects of its behavior (for example, whether duplicate values are allowed for a key or whether a key can have multiple values all together). Keep this in mind when creating your own data structures.

A collection of functions like this really begs to be organized more formally as a Mathematica package. In fact, you can download such a package, with the source code, at this book's website, *http://oreilly.com/catalog/9780596520991/*. I cover packages in Recipe 18.4.

Here is how I might code the zip codes example from the solution if I needed the full set of create, read, update, and delete capabilities that Dictionary provides.

```
In[330]:= zipcodes = makeDictionary[];
          dictStore[zipcodes, 11771, #] & /@ {"Oyster Bay",
            "Upper Brookville", "East Norwhich", "Cove Neck", "Centere Island"};
          dictStore[zipcodes, 11772, #] & /@
            {"Patchogue", "North Patchogue", "East Patchogue"};
          dictStore[zipcodes, 11779, #] & /@ {"Ronkonkoma", "Lake Ronkonkoma"};
In[334]:= dictLookup[zipcodes, 11771]
Out[334]= {Centere Island, Cove Neck, East Norwhich, Upper Brookville, Oyster Bay}

In[335]:= dictLookup[zipcodes, 99999]
Out[335]= {}
```

Ask if a key is present.

```
In[336]:= dictHasKeyQ[zipcodes, 11779]
Out[336]= True
```

Get all the zip codes stored.

```
In[337]:= dictKeys[zipcodes]
Out[337]= {11771, 11772, 11779}
```

In Recipe 3.12, "Red-Black Trees," quite a bit more coding is required to get a similar level of functionality. This recipe is relatively easy because it leverages one of Mathematica's strengths. This is an important lesson when working with Mathematica (or any language). Always look for solutions that play to the language's strengths rather than using hack solutions designed for other programming environments. To be fair, the red-black-tree implementation has features that would be more difficult to support in this recipe. Specifically, we could control the ordering of keys with red-black tree, but here keys are ordered according to Mathematica's conventions (which are conveniently in line with the expectations one would have for a dictionary).

3.14 Constructing Graphs Using the Combinatorica` Package

Problem

You are solving a problem modeled as a graph and need to create that graph for use with Combinatorica` package's algorithms.

Solution

If your graph is almost complete, construct a complete graph and remove unwanted edges.

```
In[338]:= Needs["Combinatorica`"]

In[339]:= g1 = CompleteGraph[6];
          g1 = DeleteEdges[g1, {{1, 5}, {1, 3}}];
          ShowGraph[g1, VertexNumber → True, ImageSize → Small]
```

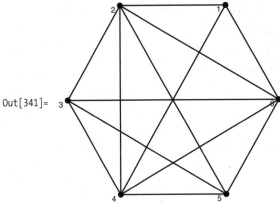

Out[341]=

If your graph is sparse, construct directly.

```
In[342]:= ShowGraph[FromUnorderedPairs[{{1, 2}, {1, 4}, {2, 3}, {3, 6}, {4, 6}}],
            VertexNumber → True, ImageSize → Small]
```

Out[342]=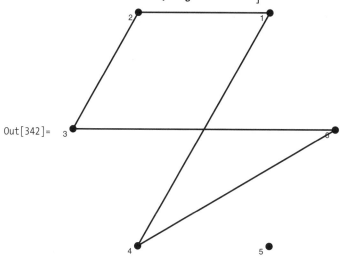

Use MakeGraph if your graph can be defined by a predicate.

```
In[343]:= ShowGraph[MakeGraph[Range[14], ! CoprimeQ[#1, #2] && #1 ≠ #2 &,
            Type -> Undirected], VertexNumber → True,
            VertexStyle → Directive[PointSize[0.01]], ImageSize → Small]
```

Out[343]=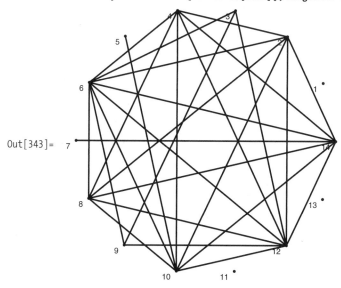

Discussion

Graphs can also be constructed from combinations of existing graphs by using GraphUnion, GraphIntersection, GraphDifference, GraphProduct, and GraphJoin. In the examples given here, I always use two graphs, but the operations are generalized to multiple graphs.

GraphUnion always creates a disjoint graph resulting from the combination of the graphs in the union.

In[344]:= ShowGraph[GraphUnion[CompleteGraph[3], CompleteGraph[3, 2]],
    VertexLabel → True]

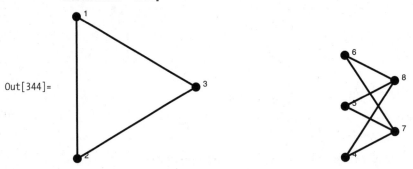

Out[344]=

GraphJoin performs a union and then links up all the vertices from the corresponding graphs.

In[345]:= ShowGraph[GraphJoin[CompleteGraph[3], CompleteGraph[3, 2]],
    VertexLabel → True]

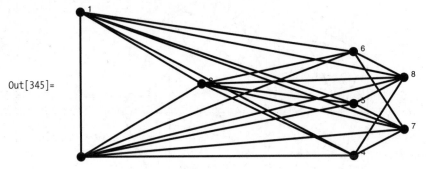

Out[345]=

GraphIntersection works only on graphs with the same number of vertices and produces a graph where the input graphs have edges in common.

```
In[346]:= g1 = DeleteEdge[CompleteGraph[5], {1, 2}];
          g2 = DeleteEdge[CompleteGraph[5], {2, 3}];
          ShowGraphArray[{g1, g2, GraphIntersection[g1, g2]}, VertexLabel → True]
```

Out[348]=

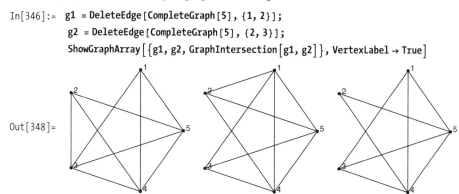

GraphDifference creates a graph with all the edges that are in the first graph but not in the second.

```
In[349]:= g1 = CompleteGraph[5];

          g2 = DeleteEdges[CompleteGraph[5], {{1, 2}, {2, 3}, {2, 5}, {4, 5}}];
          ShowGraphArray[{g1, g2, GraphDifference[g1, g2]}, VertexLabel → True]
```

Out[351]=

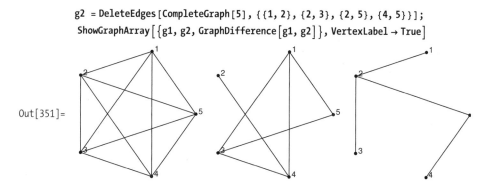

GraphProduct creates a graph by injecting copies of the first graph into the second at each vertex of the second and then connecting the vertices of the injected graphs.

Unlike a numerical product, this operation is not commutative, as demonstrated in Out[354] on page 138.

```
In[352]:= g1 = CompleteGraph[3];
          g2 = CompleteGraph[3, 2];
          ShowGraphArray[{{g1, g2}, {GraphProduct[g1, g2], GraphProduct[g2, g1]}},
            VertexLabel → True, ImageSize → Medium]
```

Out[354]=

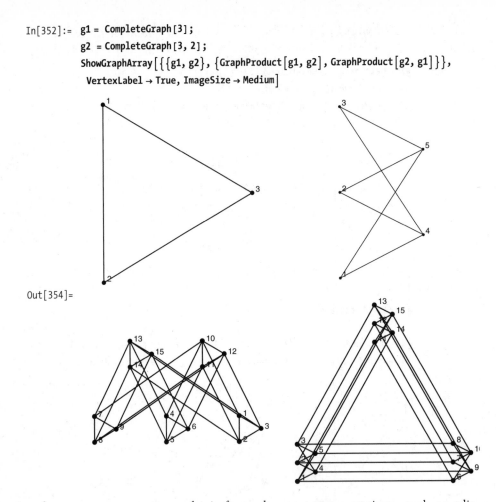

Another way to construct graphs is from alternate representations, such as adjacency matrices and adjacency lists. Out[355] on page 139 shows a graph constructed from an adjacency matrix obtained from GraphData. Normal is used to convert Sparse-Matrix, since Combinatorica does not recognize sparse-matrix representations.

```
In[355]:= ShowGraph[FromAdjacencyMatrix[Normal[
              GraphData["CubicalGraph", "AdjacencyMatrix"]]], ImageSize → Small]
```

Out[355]=

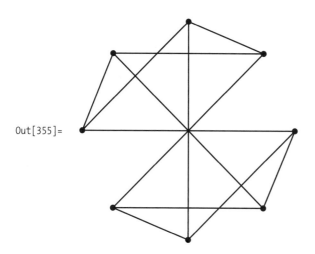

Combinatorica also supports directed graphs and graphs with weighted edges. Using SetEdgeWeights alone gives random real weights in the range [0,1]. SetEdgeWeights also accepts WeightingFunction and WeightRange options. You can also explicitly specify the weights in a list, which will be assigned to the edges in the same order as returned by the function Edges.

```
In[356]:= SeedRandom[1];
          g1 = RandomGraph[5, 0.3, Type → Directed];
          g1 = SetEdgeWeights[g1,
              WeightingFunction → RandomInteger, WeightRange → {1, 10}];
          g2 = MakeUndirected[g1];
          (*The number of weights must match
            the number of edges or you'll get garbage!*)
          g2 = SetEdgeWeights[g2, {1, 2, 3, 4, 5, 6, 7}];
          SetGraphOptions[g2, Type → Directed];
          GraphicsRow[{ShowGraph[
              SetEdgeLabels[g1, GetEdgeWeights[g1]], ImagePadding → {{40, 0}, {0, 0}}],
             ShowGraph[SetEdgeLabels[g2, GetEdgeWeights[g2]],
               ImagePadding → {{40, 0}, {0, 0}}]},
            BaseStyle → {FontSize → 10}, ImageSize → Medium]
```

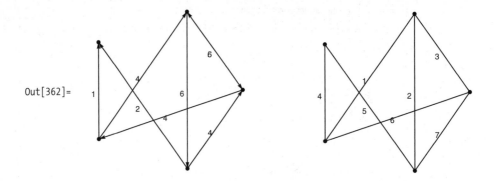

Out[362]=

See Also

The definitive reference to Combinatorica is *Computational Discrete Mathematics: Combinatorics and Graph Theory with Mathematica* by Sriram Pemmaraju and Steven Skiena (Cambridge University Press). This reference is essential if you intend to use Combinatorica in a serious way, because the documentation that comes bundled with Mathematica is very sparse.

Mathematica has an alternate graph package called `GraphUtilities`` that represents graphs using lists of rules (e.g., {a→b, a→c, b→c}). There is a conversion function to `Combinatorica`` graphs. Search for `GraphUtilities` in the Mathematica documentation.

3.15 Using Graph Algorithms to Extract Information from Graphs

Problem

You want to test a graph for specific properties or find paths through a graph with specific properties or which satisfy specific constraints.

Solution

There are many graph theoretic functions in the `Combinatorica`` package related to shortest paths, network flows, connectivity, planarity testing, topological sorting, and so on. The solutions and following discussion show a sampling of some of the more popular graph algorithms.

Out[363]a shows a graph generated from a complete graph with select edges removed. The graph in Out[363]b is the minimum spanning tree of Out[363]a, and Out[363]c is the shortest path spanning tree.

```
In[363]:=
        Module[{g, edges},
          (*Start with a complete graph.*)
          g = CompleteGraph[20];
          (*Generate some edges to remove.*)
          {dummy, {edges}} = Reap[
            Do[If[Mod[j, i] < 7, Sow[{i, j}], Null], {i, 1, 20}, {j, i + 1, 15}]];
          (g = DeleteEdge[g, #]) & /@ edges;
          (*Weight the edges randomly.*)
          SeedRandom[1]; (*Make random edge weights repeatable.*)
          SetEdgeWeights[g];
          (*Demonstrate MinimumSpanningTree and ShortestPathSpanningTree.*)
          GraphicsRow[{ShowGraph[g, PlotLabel → "a"],
            ShowGraph[MinimumSpanningTree[g], VertexNumber → True, PlotLabel → "b"],
            ShowGraph[ShortestPathSpanningTree[g, 1],
              VertexNumber → True, PlotLabel → "c"]}, ImageSize → 450]
        ]
```

Out[363]=

Discussion

Properties of graphs can be tested using a variety of functions, such as HamiltonianQ (which has a cycle that visits each vertex once), EulerianQ (which has a tour that traverses each edge once), AntisymmetricQ, ReflexiveQ, UndirectedQ, SelfLoopsQ, and so on. There are over 40 such predicates in Combinatorica.

```
In[364]:=  g1 = Hypercube[3]; g2 = CompleteGraph[4, 2];
           GraphicsRow[{ShowGraph[g1,
               PlotLabel → "HamiltonianQ == " <> ToString[HamiltonianQ[g1]]],
             ShowGraph[g2, PlotLabel → "HamiltonianQ == " <>
               ToString[HamiltonianQ[g2]]]}]
```

HamiltonianQ == True   HamiltonianQ == False

Out[365]=

```
In[366]:=  GraphicsRow[
             {ShowGraph[g1, PlotLabel → "EulerianQ == " <> ToString[EulerianQ[g1]]],
              ShowGraph[g2, PlotLabel → "EulerianQ == " <> ToString[EulerianQ[g2]]]}]
```

EulerianQ == False   EulerianQ == True

Out[366]=

A directed graph with no cycles is called a *directed acyclic graph* (DAG). The transitive closer of a DAG is the supergraph that adds directed edges from ancestors to descendants.

```
In[367]:=  g = CompleteBinaryTree[7];
           e = Reverse[Edges[g], {2}];
           g = DeleteEdges[MakeDirected[g], e];
           {AcyclicQ[g], TopologicalSort[TransitiveClosure[g]]}
Out[370]=  {True, {1, 2, 3, 4, 5, 6, 7}}
```

Out[371] shows the tree and its transitive closure. When you display highly connected graphs (like the transitive closure) with vertex labels, it often helps to use
opacity or font control to make sure vertex labels are not obscured by the edges.

```
In[371]:= Module[{opts},
            opts =
              Sequence[VertexLabel → True, BaseStyle → {FontWeight → Bold, FontSize → 12},
                LabelStyle -> {FontWeight → Medium},
                VertexStyle → Disk[0.005], EdgeStyle -> Opacity[0.4]];
            GraphicsRow[
              {ShowGraph[g, opts, PlotLabel → "Tree"], ShowGraph[TransitiveClosure[g],
                opts, PlotLabel → "TransitiveClosure"]}, ImageSize → 450]]
```

Out[371]=

See Also

See Chapters 7 and 8 in *Computational Discrete Mathematics: Combinatorics and
Graph Theory with Mathematica* by Sriram Pemmaraju and Steven Skiena.

CHAPTER 4

Patterns and Rule-Based Programming

You are an obsession
I cannot sleep
I am your possession
Unopened at your feet
There's no balance
No equality
Be still I will not accept defeat

I will have you
Yes, I will have you
I will find a way and I will have you
Like a butterfly
A wild butterly
I will collect you and capture you

Animotion, "Obsession"

4.0 Introduction

In Chapter 2, I argue that the functional style of programming is the preferred way to solve problems in Mathematica. Although functions form much of the brawn, pattern matching provides the brains. In fact, functions and patterns should be thought of as partners rather than competitors. By mastering both functional programming and pattern-based programming, you will be able to use Mathematica to its fullest potential. In fact, once you get the hang of pattern-based solutions they may become a bit of an obsession.

If you have done any programming that involves text manipulation, you have no doubt been exposed to regular expressions, a concise syntax for describing patterns in text and manipulating text. Mathematica's pattern syntax generalizes regular expressions to the domain of symbolic processing, which allows you to manipulate arbitrary symbolic structures. Patterns and rules are at the foundation of Mathematica's symbolic processing capabilities. Symbolic integration, differentiation, equation solving, and simplification are all driven by the pattern primitives explained in this chapter.

In the context of Mathematica, a *pattern* is an expression that acts as a template against which other expressions can be matched. Some of the most useful patterns contain variables that are bound to values as a result of the matching process. However, many times just knowing that a pattern matched is sufficient. Patterns are central to specifying constraints in function arguments (e.g., Integer). They also play roles in parsing, replacing, and counting, as we show in the recipes here. I defer the role of patterns in string manipulation to Chapter 5.

Rules build on patterns by specifying a mapping from a pattern to another expression that uses all or parts of the matched results. Rules pervade Mathematica, as you will see in this chapter's recipes and throughout this book. It's safe to say that Mathematica would be almost as crippled by the removal of rules as it would be by the removal of the definition for Plus.

The rest of this introduction gives a brief overview of the most important primitives associated with pattern matching. This will make the recipes a bit easier to follow if you are new to these concepts. The recipes will explore the primitives more deeply, and as usual, you should refer to the Mathematica documentation for subtle details or clarification.

Blanks

The most basic pattern constructs are Blank[] (_), BlankSequence[] (__), and BlankNullSequence[] (___). Blank[] matches any expression (_), whereas Blank[h] (_h) matches any expression with head h. BlankSequence (__) means one or more; BlankNullSequence means zero or more. Thus, ___h means zero or more expressions with head h. Here MatchQ tests if a pattern matches an expression.

```
In[1]:=  MatchQ[a, _]
Out[1]=  True

In[2]:=  MatchQ[a[1], _a]
Out[2]=  True

In[3]:=  (*By itself a has head Symbol.*)
         MatchQ[a, _a]
Out[3]=  False

In[4]:=  MatchQ[{1, 2}, _List]
Out[4]=  True
```

Blanks are more powerful when you can determine what they are matched against so you can use the matched value for further processing. This is most often done using a prefix symbol (e.g., x_, x__, x___). This syntax should be familiar since it is most commonly used for function arguments. However, as shown in this recipe, there are other contexts where binding symbols to matches comes into play.

```
In[5]:=  (*f1 will match when called with a single integer argument.*)
         f1[n_Integer] := {n}
         (*f2 will match when called with one or more integers.*)
         f2[n__Integer] := {n}
         (*f3 will match when called with zero or more integers.*)
         f3[n___Integer] := {n}

In[8]:=  f1[10] (*Match*)
Out[8]=  {10}

In[9]:=  f1[10, 20] (*No match*)
Out[9]=  f1[10, 20]

In[10]:= f2[10, 20] (*Match*)
Out[10]= {10, 20}

In[11]:= f2[] (*No match*)
Out[11]= f2[]

In[12]:= f3[] (*Match*)
Out[12]= {}

In[13]:= f3[1, 2, "3"] (*No match*)
Out[13]= f3[1, 2, 3]
```

Alternatives

Sometimes you need to construct patterns that match two or more forms. This can be done using Alternatives[p1,p2,...,pn] or, more commonly, using vertical bar p1|p2|...|pn.

```
In[14]:= Cases[{a, r, t, i, c, h, o, k, e}, a | e | i | o | u]
Out[14]= {a, i, o, e}
```

This form can also appear in functions.

```
In[15]:= Clear[f]
         f[x_Complex | x_Real | x_Integer] := x
```

```
In[17]:=  f /@ {1, 3.14, 10 + 3 I, 1/2, "foo"}

Out[17]=  {1, 3.14, 10 + 3 i, f[1/2], f[foo]}
```

Repeats

You use Repeated[p] or p.. to match one or more instances of some pattern p; you use RepeatedNull[p] or p... to match zero or more instances of p.

```
In[18]:=  Cases[{{0, 0, 0}, {0, 0, 1}, {0, 1, 0}, {0, 1, 1},
            {1, 0, 0}, {1, 0, 1}, {1, 1, 0}, {1, 1, 1}}, {1.., 0..}]
Out[18]=  {{1, 0, 0}, {1, 1, 0}}

In[19]:=  Cases[{{0, 0, 0}, {0, 0, 1}, {0, 1, 0}, {0, 1, 1},
            {1, 0, 0}, {1, 0, 1}, {1, 1, 0}, {1, 1, 1}}, {1..., 0...}]
Out[19]=  {{0, 0, 0}, {1, 0, 0}, {1, 1, 0}, {1, 1, 1}}
```

PatternSequence

Repeated (p..) matches a very specific sequence, whereas BlankSequence (x__) is very general. Sometimes you need to match a sequence of intermediate specificity. PatternSequence was introduced in Mathematica 6 to help achieve this. The following means f is a function that takes exactly two expressions.

```
In[20]:=  Clear[f];
          f[x : PatternSequence[_, _]] := Power[x]

In[22]:=  f[1] (*No match, too few*)
Out[22]=  f[1]

In[23]:=  f[2, 3] (*Match*)
Out[23]=  8

In[24]:=  f[2, 3, 4] (*No match, too many*)
Out[24]=  f[2, 3, 4]
```

Above, PatternSequence is not strictly necessary because f[x_,y_] := Power[x,y] is the more conventional notation, but consider these more interesting use cases.

```
f[0 | PatternSequence[]] := 0 (*Matches either f[0] or f[]*)
f[p : PatternSequence[_,_],___] := {p} (*Names the first two elements of a
sequence and discards the rest*)
f[p : Longests@PatternSequence[a,b]..,rest___] (*The longest repeated
sequence of a,b*)
```

Except

Often, it is easier to describe what you don't want to match than what you do. In these cases, you can use Except[p] to indicate matching for everything except what matches p.

```
In[25]:= Cases[{a, r, t, i, c, h, o, k, e}, Except[a | e | i | o | u]]
Out[25]= {r, t, c, h, k}
```

Conditions and Pattern Tests

Conditions allow you to qualify a pattern with an additional test that the matching element must pass for the match to succeed. This is a powerful construct because it extends the degree of control over the matching process to any criteria Mathematica can compute.

```
In[26]:= Cases[{{0, 0, 0}, {0, 0, 1}, {0, 1, 0}, {0, 1, 1},
          {1, 0, 0}, {1, 0, 1}, {1, 1, 0}, {1, 1, 1}}, b__ /; Total[b] > 1]
Out[26]= {{0, 1, 1}, {1, 0, 1}, {1, 1, 0}, {1, 1, 1}}
```

Pattern tests also qualify the match, but they apply to the entire pattern and, therefore, don't require pattern variables. The following lists all primes less than $2^{50} + 2$ of the form $2^n \pm 1$.

```
In[27]:= Cases[Union[Flatten[Table[{2^n - 1, 2^n + 1}, {n, 0, 50}]]], _?PrimeQ]
Out[27]= {2, 3, 5, 7, 17, 31, 127, 257, 8191, 65537, 131071, 524287, 2147483647}
```

```
In[28]:= Cases[Union[Flatten[Table[{2^n - 1, 2^n + 1}, {n, 0, 50}]]],
          _?(#1 < 127 &)]
Out[28]= {0, 1, 2, 3, 5, 7, 9, 15, 17, 31, 33, 63, 65}
```

A common mistake is to write the last example in one of two ways that will not work:

```
In[29]:= Cases[Union[Flatten[Table[{2^n - 1, 2^n + 1},
          {n, 0, 50}]]], _?(#1 < 127)&]    (*wrong!*)
Out[29]= {}
In[30]:= Cases[Union[Flatten[Table[{2^n - 1, 2^n + 1},
          {n, 0, 50}]]], _?#1 < 127&]    (*wrong!*)
Out[30]= {}
```

I still make this mistake from time to time, and it's frustrating; pay attention to those parentheses!

Rules

Rules take pattern matching to a new level of expressiveness, allowing you to perform transformations on matched expressions. Rules are an integral part of Mathematica internal operations and are used in expressing solutions to equations (see Recipe 11.6), Options (see Recipe 2.17), and SparseArrays (see Recipe 3.8). Rules are also the foundation of Mathematica's symbolic abilities. With all these applications, no serious user of Mathematica can afford to ignore them.

```
In[32]:= (*Here we use a rule to replace all (/.)
          occurrences of x with the numerical value of Pi.*)
        x - x^2 + x^3 - x ^4 + x^5 /. x → N[Pi]
Out[32]= 232.889
```

```
In[33]:= (*Convert matching binary digit list to integers. You need
          to use RuleDelayed since b is not defined until the match.*)
        Cases[{{0, 0, 0}, {0, 0, 1}, {0, 1, 0}, {0, 1, 1}, {1, 0, 0},
              {1, 0, 1}, {1, 1, 0}, {1, 1, 1}}, b : {1 .., 0 ..} :→ FromDigits[b, 2]]
Out[33]= {4, 6}
```

A good way to gain insight into the difference between → and :→ is to consider replacements of a randomly generated number.

```
In[34]:= (*With Rule, RandomInteger[] is evaluated
          immediately so is constant while the rule is applied.*)
        {x, x, x, x} /. x → RandomInteger[{0, 100}]
Out[34]= {2, 2, 2, 2}
```

```
In[35]:= (*With RuleDelayed, it is newly evaluated on each match.*)
        {x, x, x, x} /. x :→ RandomInteger[{0, 100}]
Out[35]= {36, 37, 62, 23}
```

See Also

The tutorial of pattern primitives is a useful resource: *tutorial/PatternsAndTransformationRules*. Committing most of these to memory will strengthen your Mathematica skills considerably.

4.1 Collecting Items That Match (or Don't Match) a Pattern

Problem

You have a list or other expression and want to find values that match a pattern. You may also want to transform the matching values as they are found.

Solution

Use Cases with a pattern to produce a list of expressions that match the pattern.

```
In[36]:= list = {1, 1.2, "test", 3, {2}, x + 1};
         Cases[list, _Integer]
Out[37]= {1, 3}
```

Use a rule to transform matches to other forms. Here the matched integers are squared to produce the result. This added capability of Cases is extremely powerful.

```
In[38]:= Cases[list, x_Integer :> x^2]
Out[38]= {1, 9}
```

Wrapping the pattern in Except gives the nonmatching values.

```
In[39]:= Cases[{1, 1.2, "test", 3, {2}, x + 1}, Except[_Integer]]
Out[39]= {1.2, test, {2}, 1 + x}
```

Note the use of colon syntax when capturing the value matched using Except with a rule-based transformation. Here I use a rule that demonstrates that the type of object produced does not need to be the same as the type that matched (i.e., all results here are symbols).

```
In[40]:= Cases[{1, 1.2, "test", 3, {2}, x + 1}, x : Except[_Integer] :> Head[x]]
Out[40]= {Real, String, List, Plus}
```

Discussion

Cases will work with any expression, not just lists. However, you need to keep in mind that Mathematica will rearrange the expression before the pattern is applied.

```
In[41]:= Cases[x + y - z^2 + z^3 + x^5, _^_]
Out[41]= {x^5, z^3}
```

You may have expected z^2 or -z^2 to be selected; examining the FullForm of the expression will reveal why it was not. FullForm is your friend when it comes to debugging pattern matching because that is the form that Mathematica sees.

```
In[42]:= x + y - z^2 + z^3 + x^5 // FullForm
Out[42]//FullForm=
            Plus[x, Power[x, 5], y, Times[-1, Power[z, 2]], Power[z, 3]]
```

Providing a level specification will allow you to reach down deeper. Level specifications are discussed in Recipe 3.9.

```
In[43]:= Cases[x + y - z^2 + z^3 + x^5, _^_, 2]
Out[43]= {x^5, z^2, z^3}
```

You can also limit the number of matches using an optional fourth argument.

```
In[44]:= Cases[x + y - z^2 + z^3 + x^5, _^_, 2, 1]
Out[44]= {x^5}
```

Take into account the attributes Flat and Orderless when pattern matching. Flat means nested expressions like Plus[a,Plus[b,c]] will be flattened; Orderless means the operation is communicative, and Mathematica will account for this when pattern matching.

```
In[45]:= Attributes[Plus]
Out[45]= {Flat, Listable, NumericFunction, OneIdentity, Orderless, Protected}
```

Here we select every expression that contains b +, no matter its level or order in the input expression.

```
In[46]:= Cases[{a + b, a + c, b + a, a^2 + b, Plus[a, Plus[b, c]]}, b + _]
Out[46]= {a + b, a + b, a^2 + b, a + b + c}
```

Hold will suppress transformations due to Flat and Orderless, but the pattern itself is still reordered from b + a to a + b. In Recipe 4.8 we show how to prevent this using HoldPattern.

```
In[47]:= Cases[Hold[a + b, a + c, b + a, a^2 + b, Plus[a, Plus[b, c]]], b + a]
Out[47]= {a + b}
```

An alternative to Cases is the combination of Position and Extract. Here Position locates the items, and Extract returns them. This variation would be more helpful than Cases, for example, if you needed to know the positions as well as the items, since Cases does not provide positional information. By default, Position will search every level, but you can restrict it with a levelspec as I do here.

```
In[48]:= list = {1, 1.2, "test", 3, {2}, x + 1};
         positions = Position[list, _Integer, {1}];
         Extract[list, positions]
Out[50]= {1, 3}
```

One useful application of this idiom is matching on one list and extracting from a parallel list.

```
In[51]:= names = {"Jane", "Jim", "Jeff", "Jessie", "Jezebel"};
         ages = {30, 20, 42, 16, 69} ;
         Extract[names, Position[ages, x_ /; x > 30]]
Out[53]= {Jeff, Jezebel}
```

See Also

Recipe 3.9 also discusses Position and Extract in greater detail.

4.2 Excluding Items That Match (or Don't Match) a Pattern

Problem

You have a list or other expression and want to exclude elements that do not match a pattern.

Solution

DeleteCases has features similar to Cases but excludes elements that match.

```
In[54]:= DeleteCases[{1, 1.2, "test", 3, {2}, x + 1}, _Integer]
Out[54]= {1.2, test, {2}, 1 + x}
```

Wrapping the pattern in Except makes DeleteCases work like Cases for the non-inverted pattern.

```
In[55]:= DeleteCases[{1, 1.2, "test", 3, {2}, x + 1}, Except[_Integer]]
Out[55]= {1, 3}
```

Cases and DeleteCases can be made to return the same result by using Except, but Cases should be used when you want to transform the items that remain (see Recipe 4.1).

```
In[56]:= DeleteCases[{1, 1.2, "test", 3, {2}, x + 1}, Except[_Integer]] ==
           Cases[{1, 1.2, "test", 3, {2}, x + 1}, _Integer]
Out[56]= True
```

Discussion

Most of the variations supported by Cases discussed in Recipe 4.1 apply to Delete-Cases as well. In fact, given the existence of Except, one could argue that DeleteCases is redundant. However, given the context of the problem, usually either Cases or DeleteCases will be easier to understand compared to using pattern inversions. Also, Except has some limitations since pattern variables like x_ can't appear inside of an Except.

Use levelspecs to constrain deletions to particular portions of an expression tree. Here is an expression that is nine levels deep.

In[57]:= **expr** = $\int$ **Sqrt[x + Sqrt[x]] dx**

Out[57]= $\frac{1}{12} \sqrt{\sqrt{x} + x} \left(-3 + 2\sqrt{x} + 8x\right) + \frac{1}{8} \text{Log}\left[1 + 2\sqrt{x} + 2\sqrt{\sqrt{x} + x}\right]$

In[58]:= **Depth[expr]**
Out[58]= 9

You can delete roots at level four.

In[59]:= **DeleteCases[expr, Sqrt[_], {4}]**

Out[59]= $\frac{1}{12} \sqrt{x} (-1 + 8x) + \frac{1}{8} \text{Log}\left[1 + 2\sqrt{x} + 2\sqrt{\sqrt{x} + x}\right]$

You can also delete roots at levels up to four.

In[60]:= **DeleteCases[expr, Sqrt[_], 4]**

Out[60]= $\frac{1}{12} (-1 + 8x) + \frac{1}{8} \text{Log}\left[1 + 2\sqrt{x} + 2\sqrt{\sqrt{x} + x}\right]$

Or, you delete roots at every level.

In[61]:= **DeleteCases[expr, Sqrt[_], Infinity]**

Out[61]= $\frac{1}{12} (-1 + 8x) + \frac{\text{Log}[5]}{8}$

Just as Extract plus Position is the equivalent of Cases (discussed in Recipe 4.1), Delete plus Position is the equivalent for DeleteCases. Again, remember that Position looks at all levels unless you restrict it.

```
In[62]:=  list = {1, 1.2, "test", 3, {2}, x + 1};
          Column[{
            Delete[list, Position[list, _Integer]],
            Delete[list, Position[list, _Integer, {1}]]
          }]
Out[63]=  {1.2, test, {}, x}
          {1.2, test, {2}, 1 + x}
```

This leads to a way to get the results of Cases and DeleteCases without executing the pattern match twice.

```
In[64]:=  list = {1, 1.2, "test", 3, {2}, x + 1};
          positions = Position[list, _Integer, {1}];
          Column[{
            Extract[list, positions],
            Delete[list, positions]
          }]
Out[66]=  {1, 3}
          {1.2, test, {2}, 1 + x}
```

4.3 Counting Items That Match a Pattern

Problem

You need to know the number of expressions that match a pattern by matching the expressions themselves or their position.

Solution

Use Count to count matching elements in an expression or at particular levels in an expression. Counting literal matches is perhaps the simplest application of Count.

```
In[67]:=  Count[{a, 1, a, 2, a, 3}, a]
Out[67]=  3
```

By default, Count works only on level one (levelspec {1}), but you can provide alternate levelspecs as a third argument.

```
In[68]:=  expr = 1 + 3 I + 4 + I x + x^2 + y^x^x;
          { Count[expr, x],
            Count[expr, x, Infinity]}
Out[69]=  {0, 4}
```

Count can be derived from `Position` or `Cases`, so these are handy if you need the matching items (or positions) in addition to the count.

```
In[70]:= Length[Cases[{a, 1, a, 2, a, 3}, a]]
Out[70]= 3
```

```
In[71]:= Length[Position[{a, 1, a, 2, a, 3}, a, {1}]]
Out[71]= 3
```

Discussion

Other counting functions include `LeafCount` and `Tally`. It is difficult to emulate `Leaf-Count` using `Count` because `LeafCount` treats complex numbers in their `FullForm` (e.g., `Complex[1,1]` has `LeafCount == 3`) but using `FullForm` on an expression does not provide the right answer.

```
In[72]:= {LeafCount[expr], Count[FullForm[expr], _?AtomQ, Infinity, Heads → True]}
Out[72]= {17, 14}
```

You need to eliminate the complex numbers using `ReplaceAll` before performing the count, so `LeafCount` is rather unique.

```
In[73]:= {LeafCount[expr], Count[
              expr /. Complex[r_, i_] :> complex[r, i], _?AtomQ, Infinity, Heads → True]}
Out[73]= {17, 17}
```

`Tally` counts equivalent elements in a list using `SameQ` or a user-supplied equality test. It works only on lists, so you'll need to convert expressions with other heads to `List` before using `Tally`. The output is a list of pairs showing the element and its count.

```
In[74]:= Tally[{a, x, a, x, a, a, b, y}]
Out[74]= {{a, 4}, {x, 2}, {b, 1}, {y, 1}}
```

```
In[75]:= Tally[Flatten@Apply[List, expr, {0, Infinity}]]
Out[75]= {{5 + 3 i, 1}, {i, 1}, {x, 4}, {2, 1}, {y, 1}}
```

Here is an example using a different equivalence relation (congruence module 7).

```
In[76]:= Tally[Prime[Range[100]], Mod[#1, 7] == Mod[#2, 7] &]
Out[76]= {{2, 18}, {3, 18}, {5, 18}, {7, 1}, {11, 14}, {13, 16}, {29, 15}}
```

See Also

Level specifications are covered in detail in Recipe 3.9.

4.4 Replacing Parts of an Expression

Problem

You want to transform the parts of an expression designated by an index.

Solution

Use ReplacePart, which can use indices or index patterns to limit the scope of a replacement.

```
In[77]:= (*Replace elements at position three and position seven.*)
         ReplacePart[{a, b, c, d, e, f, g, h, i}, {3 → 3, 7 → 11}]
Out[77]= {a, b, 3, d, e, f, 11, h, i}

In[78]:= Range[0, 20, 2]
Out[78]= {0, 2, 4, 6, 8, 10, 12, 14, 16, 18, 20}
```

Place an *x* at prime-numbered positions. Note that the position is being tested for primality, not for value.

```
In[79]:= ReplacePart[{a, b, c, d, e, f, g, h, i}, {i_?PrimeQ :> x}]
Out[79]= {a, x, x, d, x, f, x, h, i}
```

If you want access to the value as well, you can use the position to index into the list.

```
In[80]:= With[{list = {a, b, c, d, e, f, g, h, i}},
         ReplacePart[list, {i_?PrimeQ :> Framed[list[[i]]]}]]
Out[80]= {a, b , c , d, e , f, g , h, i}
```

Discussion

On first encounter, you might think ReplacePart and part assignment are redundant.

```
In[81]:= list1 = {1, 2, 3, 4, 5, 6};
         list1[[{1, 3}]] = 99;
         list1
Out[83]= {99, 2, 99, 4, 5, 6}
```

This seems similar to what is achieved using ReplacePart.

```
In[84]:= list1 = {1, 2, 3, 4, 5, 6};
         list2 = ReplacePart[list1, {1 → 99, 3 → 99}]
Out[85]= {99, 2, 99, 4, 5, 6}
```

However, there are a multitude of differences. First, `ReplacePart` does not modify the list but creates a new list with modified values.

```
In[86]:= {list1, list2}
Out[86]= {{1, 2, 3, 4, 5, 6}, {99, 2, 99, 4, 5, 6}}
```

A related difference is that assignment is meaningful only to symbols, not expressions. In contrast, `ReplacePart` can use either as input.

```
In[87]:= {1, 2, 3}[[2]] = 99
```

> Set::setps : {1, 2, 3} in the part assignment is not a symbol. »

```
Out[87]= 99
```

Another important difference is that it is harmless to specify an index that does not match. `ReplacePart` simply returns a new list with the same content. Contrast this to part assignment, where you get an error.

```
In[88]:= ReplacePart[{1, 2, 3}, 10 → 99]
Out[88]= {1, 2, 3}
```

```
In[89]:= list1[[10]] = 99
```

> Set::partw : Part 10 of {1, 2, 3, 4, 5, 6} does not exist. »

```
Out[89]= 99
```

Part assignment gains flexibility by supporting ranges and lists of position, whereas `ReplacePart` uses index patterns.

```
In[90]:= list1 = Range[10] ;
```

```
In[91]:= ReplacePart[Range[10], i_ ? (# > 3 && # < 7 &) → 99]
Out[91]= {1, 2, 3, 99, 99, 99, 7, 8, 9, 10}
```

```
In[92]:= list1[[4 ;; 6]] = 99;
         list1
Out[93]= {1, 2, 3, 99, 99, 99, 7, 8, 9, 10}
```

ReplacePart works on arbitrarily nested expressions, including matrices. Also note that the index patterns can be referenced on the right side of rules.

```
In[94]:= ReplacePart[IdentityMatrix[5], {i_, i_} -> i] // MatrixForm
Out[94]//MatrixForm=
```

$$\begin{pmatrix} 1 & 0 & 0 & 0 & 0 \\ 0 & 2 & 0 & 0 & 0 \\ 0 & 0 & 3 & 0 & 0 \\ 0 & 0 & 0 & 4 & 0 \\ 0 & 0 & 0 & 0 & 5 \end{pmatrix}$$

The following use case performs a transpose.

```
In[95]:= matrix = Table[x, {10}, {x, 1, 10}];
         ReplacePart[matrix, {i_, j_} :> matrix[[j, i]] ] // MatrixForm
Out[96]//MatrixForm=
```

$$\begin{pmatrix} 1 & 1 & 1 & 1 & 1 & 1 & 1 & 1 & 1 & 1 \\ 2 & 2 & 2 & 2 & 2 & 2 & 2 & 2 & 2 & 2 \\ 3 & 3 & 3 & 3 & 3 & 3 & 3 & 3 & 3 & 3 \\ 4 & 4 & 4 & 4 & 4 & 4 & 4 & 4 & 4 & 4 \\ 5 & 5 & 5 & 5 & 5 & 5 & 5 & 5 & 5 & 5 \\ 6 & 6 & 6 & 6 & 6 & 6 & 6 & 6 & 6 & 6 \\ 7 & 7 & 7 & 7 & 7 & 7 & 7 & 7 & 7 & 7 \\ 8 & 8 & 8 & 8 & 8 & 8 & 8 & 8 & 8 & 8 \\ 9 & 9 & 9 & 9 & 9 & 9 & 9 & 9 & 9 & 9 \\ 10 & 10 & 10 & 10 & 10 & 10 & 10 & 10 & 10 & 10 \end{pmatrix}$$

```
In[97]:= ReplacePart[Expand[ (x + 3) ^3], {3, 2} :> z]
Out[97]= 27 + 27 x + x^3 + 9 z
```

See Also

Chapter 3 covers list manipulation in detail, including the use of Part.

4.5 Finding the Longest (or Shortest) Match for a Pattern

Problem

A replacement rule is not working the way you think it should. In particular, it seems to work on only part of the expression. Often this is an indication that you need greedy matching provided by Longest.

Solution

By default, sequence patterns like a__ and a___ act as if they are surrounded by Shortest. This means they match as little as possible to still be consistent with the entire pattern. The following repeated replacement seems like it should shuffle items in the list until all equal values are adjacent. It almost works, but a 3 and a 1 stubbornly remain in place. This happens because on the final pass a___ matches nothing (which is shortest), b_ matches 1, c__ matches 1, b_ matches the third 1, and d___ matches the remainder. This results in a null transformation, so Replace-Repeated stops.

```
In[98]:= {1, 3, 1, 4, 1, 3, 4, 2, 7, 1, 8} //.
           {{a___, b_, c__, b_, d___} -> {b , b, a, c, d}}
Out[98]= {1, 1, 1, 3, 4, 3, 4, 2, 7, 1, 8}
```

Contrast this to the same transformation using Longest. Here we force a___ to greedily gobble up as many elements as it can and still keep the rest of the pattern matching.

```
In[99]:= {1, 3, 1, 4, 1, 3, 4, 2, 7, 1, 8} //.
           {{Longest[a___], b_, c__, b_, d___} -> {b , b, a, c, d}}
Out[99]= {1, 1, 1, 1, 3, 3, 4, 4, 2, 7, 8}
```

Forcing a___ to match as much as it can and yet still satisfy the rest of the pattern results in all sequences of identical elements separated by one or more other elements (b_, c__, b_) to be found.

Discussion

Readers familiar with regular expression will recognize the solution example as illustrating the difference between greedy and nongreedy matching. This difference is the source of infinite frustration to pattern writers because, depending on your test case, nongreedy patterns can appear to work most of the time. Always consider what will happen if patterns like a__ match only one item and a___ matches nothing. Often this is what you want, but almost as often it is not!

A reasonable question to ask is why there is a Shortest if it is the default. For string patterns (see Chapter 5), the default is reversed. You may also use Shortest to document that it is your intent, but you should probably limit this to portions of the pattern that are up front.

Also keep in mind that if multiple Shortest or Longest directives are used, the ones that appear earlier are given higher priority to match the shortest or longest number of elements, respectively.

```
In[100]:= {1, 2, 3, 4, 5} /. {Shortest[a__], Shortest[b__]} → {{a}, {b}}
Out[100]= {{1}, {2, 3, 4, 5}}

In[101]:= {1, 2, 3, 4, 5} /. {Longest[a__], Longest[b__]} → {{a}, {b}}
Out[101]= {{1, 2, 3, 4}, {5}}
```

See Also

Mastering Regular Expressions by Jeffrey E. F. Friedl (O'Reilly) has an extensive discussion of greedy versus lazy matching that is relevant to understanding Longest and Shortest. This book is a good investment if you also make use of Mathematica's regular expression syntax for string manipulation.

4.6 Implementing Algorithms in Terms of Rules

Problem

You need to implement an algorithm that can be viewed as a transformation from a start state to a goal state.

Solution

Many problems are elegantly stated in a few simple transformation rules. Here I show some simple examples; the discussion will try a few more ambitious tasks.

Imagine you have a graph of vertex-to-vertex connection rules. This is the notation used by GraphPlot and the functions in the GraphUtilities` package.

```
In[102]:=

In[103]:= Clear[a, b, c, d, e, f, g, h, x, y, z];
         graph = {a → b, b → e, b → f, f → g, a → c, a → d, e → g};
         graph2 = {a → b, b → c, c → d, d → e, b → h, h → c, c → g, g → d, d → f,
             f → e, h → i, i → g, i → f, a → x, x → y, x → z, y → z, z → a};

In[106]:= GraphPlot[graph, VertexLabeling → True, DirectedEdges → True]
```

Out[106]=

The idea in this solution is to find a path from the from node to some intermediate node x, and from x to some node y, and then add the path from→y if it does not already exist. Continue this until the graph no longer changes (hence FixedPoint). Then check if from→to is present using MemberQ.

```
In[107]:=  hasPath[graph_, from_, from_] := True
           hasPath[graph_, from_, to_] :=
           Module[{graph2 = graph, pat1},
             pat1 = {a___, from → x_, b___, x_ → y_, c___} /;
               ! MemberQ[graph2, from → y] :> {from → y, x → y, from → x, a, b, c};
             MemberQ[FixedPoint[((graph2 = ReplaceAll[#, pat1]) &, graph2], from → to]]
```

You can test hasPath on the graph in Out[106] on page 161.

```
In[109]:=  hasPath[graph, a, g]
Out[109]=  True
```

```
In[110]:=  hasPath[graph, b, d]
Out[110]=  False
```

Here is an exhaustive test of the vertex c in the graph in Out[113].

```
In[111]:=  {hasPath[graph2, c, #], #} & /@ (graph2 /. Rule[v_, _] :> v)
Out[111]=  {{False, a}, {False, b}, {True, c}, {True, d}, {False, b}, {False, h},
           {True, c}, {True, g}, {True, d}, {True, f}, {False, h}, {False, i},
           {False, i}, {False, a}, {False, x}, {False, x}, {False, y}, {False, z}}
```

Here is a related function to compute the *transitive closure* of a graph.

```
In[112]:=  transitiveClosure[graph_] :=
           Module[{graph2 = graph, pat1},
             pat1 = {a___, w_ → x_, b___, x_ → y_, c___} /;
               ! MemberQ[graph2, w → y] && w =!= y :> {a, w → x, b, x → y, c, w → y};
             FixedPoint[((graph2 = ReplaceAll[#, pat1]) &, graph2]]
```

```
In[113]:=  GraphPlot[graph2, VertexLabeling → True, DirectedEdges → True]
```

Out[113]=

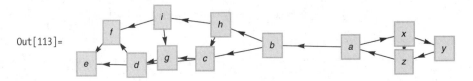

Here you compute the transitive closure of Out[113].

```
In[114]:= transitiveClosure[graph2]
Out[114]= {a → b, b → c, c → d, d → e, b → h, h → c, c → g, g → d, d → f, f → e,
           h → i, i → g, i → f, a → x, x → y, x → z, y → z, z → a, a → c, a → h,
           b → d, a → d, b → g, a → g, c → e, b → e, a → e, c → f, b → f, a → f,
           b → i, a → i, h → g, h → e, h → f, g → f, a → y, a → z, x → a, y → a, z → c,
           x → c, y → c, z → h, x → h, y → h, z → d, x → d, y → d, z → g, x → g, y → g,
           z → e, x → e, y → e, z → f, x → f, y → f, z → i, x → i, y → i, z → y}
```

Out[115] is the plot of the transitive closure of the simpler graph from Out[106] on page 161.

```
In[115]:= GraphPlot[transitiveClosure[graph],
          VertexLabeling → True, DirectedEdges → True]
```

Out[115]=

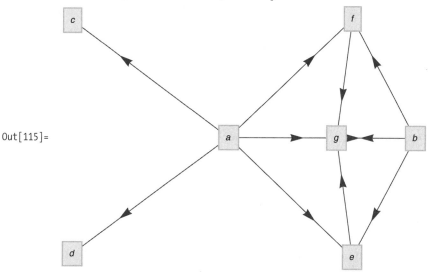

Discussion

The hasPath and transitiveClosure functions share a common property. They are implemented by repeated transformation of the input until some goal state is achieved. The search terminates when there are no more available transformations, as determined by FixedPoint. TransitiveClosure uses the final state as the result, whereas hasPath makes one more match using MemberQ to see if the goal was reached.

Although rule-driven algorithms tend to be small, they are not always the most efficient. HasPath finds all paths from the start node before making a determination.

The hasPath2 implementation here uses Catch-Throw to exit as soon as the solution is found.

```
In[116]:= hasPath2[graph_, from_, to_] :=
          Module[{graph2 = graph, pat1, pat2},
             pat1 = {___, from → to, ___} :> Throw[from → to];
             pat2 = {a___, from → x_, b___, x_ → y_, c___} /;
                 ! MemberQ[graph2, from → y] :> {from → y, from → x, x → y, a, b, c};
             Catch[FixedPoint[(graph2 = ReplaceAll[#, {pat1, pat2}]) &, graph2]];
             MemberQ[graph2, from → to]]

In[117]:= monsterGraph = Table[i → i + 1, {i, 500}];

In[118]:= Timing[hasPath[monsterGraph, 1, 250]]
Out[118]= {6.15429, True}

In[119]:= Timing[hasPath2[monsterGraph, 1, 250]]
Out[119]= {0.519091, True}
```

The main components of this solution are:

1. Localization: Module[{rules, start, next, final}, ..]

2. Rules: Enumeration of the rules with tests against next (graph2 plays the role of next in the examples). An optional Throw rule detects success for early termination.

3. Repetition: next = ReplaceAll[next, rules]

4. Stopping criteria: final = FixedPoint[.., start]. Assignment to final allows the result to undergo some post processing. In the examples, final was implicit. If a Throw rule is used, FixedPoint should be wrapped in a Catch.

5. Postprocessing: Extract results from final. Here MemberQ is used to test if the path was found.

If you have trouble following one of these solutions, Mathematica will show its work if you use FixedPointList. For example, here is the expansion of the steps in hasPath.

```
In[120]:= explainHasPath[graph_, from_, from_] := {from → from}
          explainHasPath[graph_, from_, to_] :=
            Module[{graph2 = graph, pat1},
               pat1 = {a___, from → x_, b___, x_ → y_, c___} /;
                   ! MemberQ[graph2, from → y] :> {from → y, x → y, from → x, a, b, c};
               FixedPointList[(graph2 = ReplaceAll[#, pat1]) &, graph2]]
```

```
In[122]:= explainHasPath[graph, a, g] // TableForm
Out[122]//TableForm=
        a → b    b → e    b → f    f → g    a → c    a → d    e → g
        a → e    b → e    a → b    b → f    f → g    a → c    a → d    e → g
        a → g    e → g    a → e    b → e    a → b    b → f    f → g    a → c    a → d
        a → f    b → f    a → b    a → g    e → g    a → e    b → e    f → g    a → c    a → d
        a → f    b → f    a → b    a → g    e → g    a → e    b → e    f → g    a → c    a → d
```

This shows each step in the transition from the original graph to the one with all intermediate steps filled in. Try to work out how the rule took each line to the next line. Only by working through examples like this will you begin to master the concepts.

See Also

FixedPoint usually finds application in numerical methods that use iteration, such as Newton's method (see Recipe 2.12), but any algorithm that computes until an equilibrium state is reached can use FixedPoint.

4.7 Debugging Infinite Loops When Using ReplaceRepeated

Problem

Mathematica went into an infinite loop when you used //. (ReplaceRepeated), and the reason is not immediately obvious.

Solution

ReplaceRepeated is often very handy but also dangerous because it only terminates when the result stops changing. The simplest thing to do is to test ReplaceRepeated with the option MaxIterations set to a reasonably small value (the default is 65,536).

```
In[123]:= ReplaceRepeated[{1, 2}, {a_, b_} → {{a}, {b}}, MaxIterations → 10]

        ReplaceRepeated::rrlim :
          Exiting after {1, 2} scanned 10 times. ≫

Out[123]= {{{{{{{{{{{1}}}}}}}}}}}, {{{{{{{{{{{2}}}}}}}}}}}
```

It should be clear that this will never terminate. Any transformation that adds structure is doomed. However, sometimes the end result obtained when clamping iterations does not immediately reveal the problem. In such cases, it helps to see the whole sequence of transformations. You can do that using NestList and ReplaceAll to emulate a ReplaceRepeated with a small number of iterations that return the result after each iteration.

```
In[124]:= NestList[ReplaceAll[#, {a_, b_} → {b, a}] &, {1, 2}, 10]
Out[124]= {{1, 2}, {2, 1}, {1, 2}, {2, 1}, {1, 2},
          {2, 1}, {1, 2}, {2, 1}, {1, 2}, {2, 1}, {1, 2}}
```

Here the problem is an oscillating transformation that will never settle down. You could probably see that by inspection, but seeing each step makes it obvious.

Discussion

Sometimes applying the debugging techniques in the solution can still leave you stumped. Here is an example that one would expect to terminate based on the fact that NumberQ[Infinity] is false.

```
In[125]:= ReplaceRepeated[{1, a, 2, b, 3, c},
          {_?NumberQ → F[Infinity]}, MaxIterations -> 10]
```

```
ReplaceRepeated::rrlim :
  Exiting after {1, a, 2, b, 3, c} scanned 10 times. >>
```

```
Out[125]= {F[DirectedInfinity[F[DirectedInfinity[
              F[DirectedInfinity[F[DirectedInfinity[F[DirectedInfinity[
                  F[DirectedInfinity[F[DirectedInfinity[F[DirectedInfinity[
                      F[DirectedInfinity[F[∞]]]]]]]]]]]]]]]],
          a, F[DirectedInfinity[F[DirectedInfinity[F[DirectedInfinity[
              F[DirectedInfinity[F[DirectedInfinity[
                  F[DirectedInfinity[F[DirectedInfinity[F[DirectedInfinity[
                      F[DirectedInfinity[F[∞]]]]]]]]]]]]]]]],
          b, F[DirectedInfinity[F[DirectedInfinity[F[DirectedInfinity[
              F[DirectedInfinity[F[DirectedInfinity[
                  F[DirectedInfinity[F[DirectedInfinity[F[DirectedInfinity[
                      F[DirectedInfinity[F[∞]]]]]]]]]]]]]]]], c}
```

In situations like this, you should try applying FullForm to the output to see what Mathematica sees rather than what it shows you.

```
In[126]:= FullForm[%]
Out[126]//FullForm=
        List[F[DirectedInfinity[
          F[DirectedInfinity[F[DirectedInfinity[F[DirectedInfinity[
            F[DirectedInfinity[F[DirectedInfinity[F[DirectedInfinity[F[
              DirectedInfinity[F[DirectedInfinity[
                F[DirectedInfinity[1]]]]]]]]]]]]]]]]]]]],
          a, F[DirectedInfinity[F[DirectedInfinity[F[DirectedInfinity[
            F[DirectedInfinity[F[DirectedInfinity[F[DirectedInfinity[
              F[DirectedInfinity[F[DirectedInfinity[F[DirectedInfinity[
                F[DirectedInfinity[1]]]]]]]]]]]]]]]]]]]],
          b, F[DirectedInfinity[F[DirectedInfinity[F[DirectedInfinity[
            F[DirectedInfinity[F[DirectedInfinity[F[DirectedInfinity[
              F[DirectedInfinity[F[DirectedInfinity[F[DirectedInfinity[
                F[DirectedInfinity[1]]]]]]]]]]]]]]]]]]]], c]
```

Do you see the problem? It is near the end of the output. If you can't see it, consider this.

```
In[127]:= FullForm[Infinity]
Out[127]//FullForm=
        DirectedInfinity[1]
```

The full form of Infinity contains the integer 1, which is being matched and replaced with F[DirectedInfinity[1]] and so on, ad infinitum. In this simple case, Replace-Repeated was not needed because ReplaceAll would do the trick. If Replace-Repeated is necessary, break the process into two steps, first using a proxy for the construct that has the hidden representation that is messing you up. Here I use Inf instead of Infinity.

```
In[128]:= {1, a, 2, b, 3, c} //. {_?NumberQ → F[Inf]} /. Inf → Infinity
Out[128]= {F[∞], a, F[∞], b, F[∞], c}
```

See Also

You can find a realistic example of the Infinity problem at the Wolfram Math-Group Archives: *http://bit.ly/2oRAuZ*.

4.8 Preventing Evaluation Until Replace Is Complete

Problem

You are trying to transform an expression, but the structure you want to transform is disappearing due to evaluation before you can transform it.

Solution

Use Hold and ReleaseHold with the replacement.

This does not work the way you probably intended.

```
In[129]:= 1 + 1 + 1 + 1 + 1 /. {1→2, Plus -> Times}
Out[129]= 5
```

This preserves the structure until the transformation is complete, then allows it to evaluate.

```
In[130]:= ReleaseHold[Hold[1 + 1 + 1 + 1 + 1] /. {1→2, Plus -> Times}]
Out[130]= 32
```

A related problem is wanting the left side of a replacement rule to remain unevaluated. In this case, you need to use HoldPattern.

This is equivalent to ReleaseHold[Hold[1 + 1 + 1 + 1 + 1] /. 4 :> 2 + 2 + 2 + 2].

```
In[131]:= ReleaseHold[Hold[1 + 1 + 1 + 1 + 1] /. 1+1+1+1 :> 2 + 2 + 2 + 2]
Out[131]= 5
```

```
In[132]:= (*This works as intended by preserving the structure of the pattern.*)
          ReleaseHold[
            Hold[1 + 1 + 1 + 1 + 1] /. HoldPattern[1+1+1+1] :> 2 + 2 + 2 + 2]
Out[132]= 9
```

Discussion

Keep in mind that HoldPattern[expr] differs from Hold[expr]. From a pattern-matching point of view, HoldPattern[expr] is equivalent to expr alone except it prevents evaluation. Hold[expr] includes the Hold as part of the pattern.

```
In[133]:= GO = "gone";

In[134]:= Hold[1 + 2 + 3] /. HoldPattern[1 + 2 + 3] :> GO
Out[134]= Hold[GO]

In[135]:= Hold[1 + 2 + 3] /. Hold[1 + 2 + 3] :> GO
Out[135]= gone
```

See Also

Chapter 2 discusses Hold in more detail.

4.9 Manipulating Patterns with Patterns

Problem

You need to transform a pattern expression using patterns.

Solution

Use Verbatim to allow a pattern to match another pattern. Here Verbatim tells Mathematica to treat the expression literally.

```
In[136]:= x_ → 1 /. Verbatim[x_] :> y_
Out[136]= y_ → 1
```

Here we want to split up a pattern variable into the name and the head it matches.

```
In[137]:= x_Integer /. Verbatim[Pattern][name_, head_] :> {name, head}
Out[137]= {x, _Integer}
```

Discussion

The key to understanding the solution is to consider the FullForm of pattern variables.

```
In[138]:= {FullForm[x_], FullForm[x__], FullForm[x___], FullForm[x_Integer]}
Out[138]= {Pattern[x, Blank[]], Pattern[x, BlankSequence[]],
          Pattern[x, BlankNullSequence[]], Pattern[x, Blank[Integer]]}
```

Without Verbatim, the first example in the first part of the solution would go wrong.

```
In[139]:= x_ → 1 /. x_ :> y_
Out[139]= y_
```

The second part of the solution would fail because a pattern can't have another pattern as its name.

```
In[140]:=  x_Integer /. Pattern[name_, head_] :> {name, head}
```

```
Pattern::patvar :
  First element in pattern Pattern[name_, head_] is
      not a valid pattern name. >>
```

```
Out[140]=  x_Integer
```

Verbatim[expr] says "match **expr** exactly as it appears." You will not use Verbatim often unless you find yourself writing Mathematica code to transform Mathematica code, as you might if you were writing a special interpreter or code to rewrite Mathematica code containing patterns in some other form.

See Also

The Mathematica Programmer II by Roman Maeder (Academic Press) uses Verbatim during the development of an interpreter for a Prolog-like language.

4.10 Optimizing Rules

Problem

You have a large list of frequently used rules and want to speed up processing.

Solution

Use Dispatch to create a dispatch table and use that in place of the rules.

```
In[141]:=  rules = { Inf → Infinity, sin → Sin, cos → Cos, tan → Tan, pi → Pi}
Out[141]=  {Inf → ∞, sin → Sin, cos → Cos, tan → Tan, pi → π}
```

```
In[142]:=  dispatch = Dispatch[rules]
Out[142]=  Dispatch[{Inf → ∞, sin → Sin, cos → Cos, tan → Tan, pi → π}, -DispatchTables -]
```

```
In[143]:=  cos[2 pi θ] + sin[θ^2] - sin[cos[3 z]] /. dispatch
Out[143]=  Cos[2 π θ] + Sin[θ²] - Sin[Cos[3 z]]
```

Discussion

If you do a lot of multiple-rule transformations, it is convenient to store all the rules in a single variable. This common practice makes maintenance of your code simpler since there is only a single definition to maintain for all rules. However, the penalty for doing this is that the performance of a replace decreases as the number of rules increases. This is because each rule must be scanned in turn, even if it ends up being inapplicable to a given transformation. Rule dispatch tables optimize rule dispatch so it is mostly independent of the number of rules.

To test this claim, I generate a list of 5,000 rules, called monsterRuleSet, and then optimize it to create monsterDispatch. The timing on the monsterRuleSet is very poor, whereas the dispatched version is lickety-split.

```
In[144]:= monsterRuleSet = Table[i → i + 1, {i, 5000}];
          monsterDispatch = Dispatch[monsterRuleSet];

In[146]:= Timing[{1} //. monsterRuleSet]
Out[146]= {3.29176, {5001}}

In[147]:= Timing[{1} //. monsterDispatch]
Out[147]= {0.005828, {5001}}
```

Peering into the implementation, you can see that the secret to Dispatch's success is a hash table.

```
In[148]:= monsterDispatch[[2]] // Short
Out[148]//Short=
          {HashTable[1, 5000, 1, {{10, 2856}, {}, {3110, 3440}, {}, {1245}, ≪4989≫,
             {3060}, {1008}, {912}, {879, 3696, 4165, 4971}, {545, 676, 4204}}]}
```

4.11 Using Patterns As a Query Language

Problem

You want to perform SQL-like queries on data stored in Mathematica.

Solution

Consider data of the sort one might encounter in a relational database but encoded in Mathematica form. This example is taken from the classic introduction to databases by C. J. Date.

```
In[149]:= S = {
            supplier[ "S1" , "Smith", 20, "London"],
            supplier ["S2", "Jones" , 10 , "Paris"],
            supplier ["S3", "Blake" , 30 , "Paris"],
            supplier [ "S4", "Clark", 20 , "London"],
            supplier [ "S5", "Adams" , 30 , "Athens"]
          };

        P = {
            part ["P1", "Nut" , "Red", 12, "London"],
            part [ "P2" , "Bolt" , "Green", 17, "Paris"],
            part ["P3" , "Screw", "Blue", 17, "Rome"],
            part ["P4" , "Screw", "Red", 14, "London"],
            part ["P5" , "Cam", "Blue", 12, "Paris"],
            part [ "P6" , "Cog", "Red" , 19, "London"]
          };
        INV = {
            inventory [ "S1" , "P1" , 300],
            inventory [ "S1" , "P2" , 200],
            inventory [ "S1" , "P3" , 400],
            inventory [ "S1" , "P4" , 200],
            inventory [ "S1" , "P5" , 100],
            inventory [ "S1" , "P6" , 100],
            inventory [ "S2" , "P1" , 300],
            inventory [ "S2" , "P2" , 400],
            inventory [ "S3" , "P2" , 200],
            inventory [ "S4" , "P2" , 200],
            inventory [ "S4" , "P4" , 300],
            inventory [ "S4" , "P5" , 400]
          };
```

Simple queries can be done using Cases alone.

```
In[152]:= (*Find suppliers in Paris.*)
          Cases[S, supplier[_, _, _, "Paris"] ]
Out[152]= {supplier[S2, Jones, 10, Paris], supplier[S3, Blake, 30, Paris]}

In[153]:= (*Find suppliers in Paris with status greater than 10.*)
          Cases[S, supplier[_, _, status_ /; status > 10, "Paris"] ]
Out[153]= {supplier[S3, Blake, 30, Paris]}
```

Queries involving joins can be implemented with the help of Outer.

```
In[154]:= (*Find suppliers and parts located in the same city.*)
          Flatten[Outer[
            Cases[{{#1, #2}}, {supplier[sid_, __, city_], part[pid_, __, city_]} :>
              colocated[sid, pid, city]] &, S, P]]
Out[154]= {colocated[S1, P1, London], colocated[S1, P4, London],
            colocated[S1, P6, London], colocated[S2, P2, Paris],
            colocated[S2, P5, Paris], colocated[S3, P2, Paris],
            colocated[S3, P5, Paris], colocated[S4, P1, London],
            colocated[S4, P4, London], colocated[S4, P6, London]}

In[155]:= (*Find suppliers who have the same status.*)
          Flatten[Outer[Cases[{{#1, #2}},
            {supplier[sid1_, _, s_, _], supplier[sid2_, _, s_, _]} /;
              Order[sid1, sid2] == 1 :> same[sid1, sid2, s]] &, S, S]]
Out[155]= {same[S1, S4, 20], same[S3, S5, 30]}
```

Discussion

If the data you need to query resides in a database, it makes more sense to let that database do the query work before the data is imported into Mathematica. If this is not the case, Mathematica can easily do the job, even for rather sophisticated queries. Here are some simple examples with SQL equivalents.

Find all pairs of cities where a supplier in the first city has inventory on a part in the second city.

```
SELECT DISTINCT S.CITY, P.CITY
FROM S, INV, P
WHERE S.SID = INV.SID
AND INV.PID = P.PID;
```

```
In[156]:= query = {supplier[sid_, _, _, city1_], inventory[sid_, pid_, _],
            part[pid_, _, _, _, city2_]} :> cities[city1, city2];
          Union[Flatten[Outer[Cases[{{#1, #2, #3}}, query] &, S, INV, P]]] //
            TableForm
Out[157]//TableForm=
          cities[London, London]
          cities[London, Paris]
          cities[London, Rome]
          cities[Paris, London]
          cities[Paris, Paris]
```

In this case, ReplaceRepeated can be used to implement GROUP BY. The idea is to continually search for pairs of items that match on the grouping criteria and combine them according to some aggregation method, in this case the sum of qty. Since each replacement removes an inventory item, we are guaranteed to terminate when all items are unique. A final ReplaceAll is used to extract the relevant information. The use of Null in the replacement rule is just for aesthetics, conveying that when you aggregate two inventory records you no longer have a valid record for a particular supplier.

```
SELECT PID, SUM(QTY)
FROM INV
GROUP BY PID;
```

```
In[158]:= INV //.
          {Longest[i1___], inventory[_, p_, q1_], i2__, inventory[_, p_, q2_],
           i3___} :> {i1, inventory[Null, p, q1 + q2], i2, i3} /.
          inventory[s_, p_, q_] :> totals[p, q] // TableForm
Out[158]//TableForm=
          totals[P1, 600]
          totals[P2, 1000]
          totals[P3, 400]
          totals[P4, 500]
          totals[P5, 500]
          totals[P6, 100]
```

Suppose you want the names of suppliers who have inventory in the part P1. This involves integrating information from S and INV. This can be done as a join, but in SQL it can also be done via a subquery. You can emulate that using rules. Here MemberQ implements the semantics of the SQL IN.

```
SELECT NAME
FROM S
WHERE SID IN
      (   SELECT SID
          FROM INV
          WHERE PID = 'P2')
```

```
In[159]:= Cases[S, supplier[sid_, sname_, ___] /; MemberQ[
              Cases[INV, inventory[sid1_, "P2", _] :> sid1],
              sid] :> sname]
Out[159]= {Smith, Jones, Blake, Clark}
```

In the examples given, I have demonstrated queries for which the data is in relational form. One feature of relational form is that it is normalized so that each column can hold only atomic data. However, Mathematica is not a relational database, so data can appear in just about any form with any level of nesting. This is no problem because patterns are much more flexible than SQL. Still, I find it easier to put data in a tabular form before trying to extract information and relationships with other collections of data. Let's consider an example that is more in the Mathematica domain.

GraphData and PolyhedronData are two extensive data sources that are bundled with Mathematica 6 and later versions. The relationship between these data sources is that each polyhedron has an associated graph. In PolyhedronData, the property that ties the two sources together is called SkeletonGraph. In database jargon, Skeleton-Graph is a *foreign key* to GraphData, and thus, allows us to investigate relationships between polyhedra and their associated graphs. For this example, I want to consider all graphs that are both Eulerian and Hamiltonian with their associated polyhedron being Archimedean. (An Archimedean solid is a highly symmetric, semiregular, convex polyhedron composed of two or more types of regular polygons meeting in identical vertices.)

```
In[160]:= Archimedean = Cases[{ToString[#],
              PolyhedronData[#], PolyhedronData[#, "SkeletonGraphName"],
              PolyhedronData[#, "Archimedean"]} & /@ PolyhedronData[] ,
            {name_, image_, graph_, True} :> archimedean[name, image, graph]];
        Graphs = Cases[{ToString[#], GraphData[#], GraphData[#, "Eulerian"],
              GraphData[#, "Hamiltonian"]} & /@ GraphData[] ,
            {name_, image_, True, True} :> graphEorH[name, image]];
```

It's often a good idea to see how many results you received.

```
In[162]:= {Length[Archimedean], Length[Graphs]}
Out[162]= {13, 676}
```

```
In[163]:= results =
          Flatten[Outer[Cases[{{#1, #2}}, {archimedean[pname_, pimage_, gname_],
                graphEorH[gname_, gimage_]} :>
              r[gname, pname, gimage, pimage]] &, Archimedean, Graphs]] ;
```

There are exactly 4 cases out of 13 Archimedean polyhedra that meet the criteria of having both Eulerian and Hamiltonian graphs.

```
In[164]:= TableForm[results /. { r[gname_, pname_, gimage_, pimage_] :>
            {{gname, gimage} /. Graphics[a__] :> Graphics[a, ImageSize -> 100],
             {pname, pimage} /. Graphics3D[b__] :> Graphics3D[b, ImageSize -> 100]}}]
```

CuboctahedralGraph

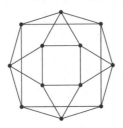

Cuboctahedron

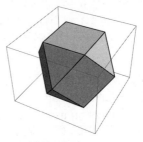

IcosidodecahedralGraph

Icosidodecahedron

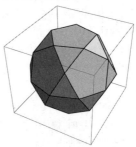

SmallRhombicosidodecahedralGraph

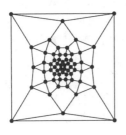

SmallRhombicosidodecahedron

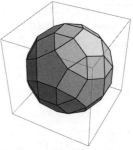

SmallRhombicuboctahedralGraph

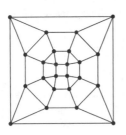

SmallRhombicuboctahedron

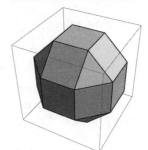

You might find more intuitive ways to solve this problem, but the solution given emphasizes pattern matching. You could also use `Intersection` with an appropriate `SameTest`, as shown here. The `r @@@` serves only to put the result in the same form as we used previously and is not strictly needed.

```
In[165]:= results = r @@@
              Intersection[Archimedean, Graphs, SameTest -> (#1[[3]] == #2[[1]] &)];
```

See Also

The supplier-parts database is a classic example borrowed from *An Introduction to Database Systems: Volume 1,* Fourth Edition, by C. J. Date (Addison-Wesley).

4.12 Semantic Pattern Matching

Problem

You want to work with patterns that reach beyond syntactic (structural) relationships to consider semantic relationships.

Solution

This solution is a simplified adaptation of concepts from "Semantica: Semantic Pattern Matching in Mathematica" by Jason Harris, published in the *Mathematica Journal,* Volume 7, Issue 3, 1999.

Pattern matching in Mathematica is strictly structural. Consider the following function f.

```
In[166]:= Clear[f]
          SetAttributes[f, HoldFirst];
          f[x_Integer^2] := 1
```

Clearly, 3^2 matches the first version of the function. However, neither f[9] nor f[10] are in the correct form, so they fail to match, even though in the second case 9 == 3^2.

```
In[169]:= {f[3^2], f[9], f[10]}
Out[169]= {1, f[9], f[10]}
```

All hope is not lost. By exploiting patterns, you can create a semantic match that uses Condition, which is commonly abbreviated as /;.

```
In[170]:= Clear[f];
          SetAttributes[f, HoldFirst];
          f[x_ /; IntegerQ[x] && (Reduce[z^2 == x, {z}, Integers] =!= False)] := 1
```

Now both the first and second cases match but not the last.

```
In[173]:= {f[3^2], f[9], f[10]}
Out[173]= {1, 1, f[10]}
```

Discussion

Mathematica deals with structural patterns simply because, in general, it is impossible to determine if two expressions are semantically equivalent. In the 1930s, Gödel, Turing, Church, and others performed the theoretical work that underlies this unfortunate truth. Still, there are many restricted cases for which semantic matching can succeed, as demonstrated in the solution.

4.13 Unification Pattern Matching

Problem

You want to emulate unification-based matching, à la Prolog.

Solution

Unification is more powerful than Mathematica pattern matching in that it allows pattern variables on both sides of the match. We can't use normal pattern variables for this purpose, so we use the syntax $[var] to denote unification variable.

```
In[174]:= ClearAll[unify]
          SetAttributes[$, HoldAll]
          Options[unify] = {bindings -> {}};
          unify[x_, y_, opt___] :=
            Block[{$bindings = bindings /. {opt} /. Options[unify]},

              Module[{unify0, boundQ, lookup},
                SetAttributes[unify0, Orderless];
                boundQ[x1_] := Module[{}, (x1 /. $bindings ) =!= x1];

                lookup[x1_] := Module[{}, x1 /. $bindings];
```

```
(*If both variables are bound, then match if values match.*)
unify0[$[x1_], $[y1_]] /; boundQ[x1] && boundQ[y1] :=
 Module[{}, lookup[x1] === lookup[y1]];
(*If one variable matches,
then bind the other to the same value and unify again.*)
unify0[$[x1_], $[y1_]] /; boundQ[x1] :=
 Module[{xval}, xval = lookup[x1];
  AppendTo[$bindings, y1 → xval]; unify0[xval, $[y1]]];

(*If neither variable is bound,
then eliminate variable by binding first to second.*)
unify0[$[x1_], $[y1_]] :=
 Module[{}, AppendTo[$bindings, x1 → y1]; True];

(*Unify a bound variable to an
 expression by unifying its value to the expression.*)
unify0[$[x1_], y1_] /; boundQ[x1] :=
 Module[{}, unify0[lookup[x1], y1]];

(*Unify an unbound variable
 to an expression by binding to the expression.*)
unify0[$[x1_], y1_] := Module[{},
  AppendTo[$bindings, x1 → y1]; True];
(*Atoms unify if they are the same.*)
unify0[x1_?AtomQ, y1_?AtomQ] := Module[{}, x1 === y1];
(*Compound expressions unify if they have the same head and
 the same length and their corresponding elements unify.*)
unify0[x1_, y1_] /; Head[x1] === Head[y1] &&
   Length[x1] == Length[y1] :=
 Module[{u}, And @@ Thread[u[x1, y1], Head[x1]] /. u → unify0];
(*Otherwise fail*)
unify0[x1_, y1_] := False;

If[unify0[x, y], {True, $bindings /. $[a_] :> a}, {False, {}}]]]
```

Test unify on various expressions:

```
In[178]:= unify[1, 1]
Out[178]= {True, {}}

In[179]:= unify[$[x], 1]
Out[179]= {True, {x → 1}}
```

```
In[180]:=  unify[1, $[x]]
Out[180]=  {True, {x → 1}}

In[181]:=  unify[f[$[x], a], f[b, $[y]]]
Out[181]=  {True, {x → b, y → a}}

In[182]:=  unify[f[$[x], a], f[b, $[x]]]
Out[182]=  {False, {}}

In[183]:=  unify[f[$[x], g[$[y]]], f[g[3], $[x]]]
Out[183]=  {True, {x → g[3], y → 3}}

In[184]:=  unify[f[g[$[y]]], f[$[x]]]
Out[184]=  {True, {x → g[y]}}
```

Here you pass in a preexisting binding so the unification fails.

```
In[185]:=  unify[1, $[x], bindings → {x → 2}]
Out[185]=  {False, {}}
```

Discussion

```
In[186]:=  Clear[unifyN]
           unifyN[x_, y_] := unify[x, y]
           unifyN[x_, y_, z__] := Module[{t, b2},
             {t, b2} = unifyN[x, z]; If[t, unify[x, y, bindings :> b2], {t, b2}]]


In[189]:=  unifyN[f[$[w], 2, 3, 4], f[1, $[x], 3, 4], f[1, 2, $[y], 4], f[1, 2, 3, $[z]]]
Out[189]=  {True, {w → 1, z → 4, y → 3, x → 2}}
```

See Also

Maeder's *Mathematica Programmer II* goes much further than this recipe by implementing a large subset of Prolog. It also allows you to use normal pattern syntax by
rewriting the variables using techniques discussed in Recipe 3.10.

CHAPTER 5

String and Text Processing

Someone will call
Something will fall
And smash on the floor
Without reading the text
Know what comes next
Seen it before
And it's painful
Things must change
We must rearrange them
Or we'll have to estrange them
All that I'm saying
The game's not worth playing
Over and over again
Depeche Mode, "The Sun and the Rainfall"

5.0 Introduction

Users who come to Mathematica for its superior mathematical capabilities are pleasantly surprised to find strong abilities in programming areas outside of mathematics proper. This is certainly true in the area of textual and string processing. Mathematica's rich library of functions for string and structured text manipulation rivals Java, Perl, or any other modern language you can tie a string around.

The sections in this introduction provide information on some of the basic tools of strings and string manipulation.

Characters and Character Encodings

Mathematica uses *Unicode* internally, but externally (e.g., when saving a notebook) it uses ASCII codes, encoding non-ASCII characters in a special form.

For example, lowercase Greek letters and other non-ASCII characters are encoded using backslash-bracketed character names (\[*name*]).

```
In[1]:= alpha = "α"
Out[1]= α
```

The function ToString will translate strings using different encoding schemes.

```
In[2]:= ToString[alpha, CharacterEncoding → "ASCII"]
Out[2]= \[Alpha]
```

The default character encoding used by Mathematica is stored in $CharacterEncoding, and the native character encoding of the underlying operating system Mathematica is running is stored in $SystemCharacterEncoding. All available encodings are stored in $CharacterEncodings.

```
In[3]:= $CharacterEncoding
Out[3]= UTF-8
```

```
In[4]:= $SystemCharacterEncoding
Out[4]= UTF-8
```

```
In[5]:= Partition[$CharacterEncodings, 4] // TableForm
Out[5]//TableForm=
```

AdobeStandard	ASCII	CP936	CP949
CP950	Custom	EUC-JP	EUC
IBM-850	ISO10646-1	ISO8859-10	ISO8859-11
ISO8859-13	ISO8859-14	ISO8859-15	ISO8859-16
ISO8859-1	ISO8859-2	ISO8859-3	ISO8859-4
ISO8859-5	ISO8859-6	ISO8859-7	ISO8859-8
ISO8859-9	ISOLatin1	ISOLatin2	ISOLatin3
ISOLatin4	ISOLatinCyrillic	Klingon	koi8-r
MacintoshArabic	MacintoshChineseSimplified	MacintoshChineseTraditional	MacintoshCroatian
MacintoshCyrillic	MacintoshGreek	MacintoshHebrew	MacintoshIcelandic
MacintoshKorean	MacintoshNonCyrillicSlavic	MacintoshRomanian	MacintoshRoman
MacintoshThai	MacintoshTurkish	MacintoshUkrainian	Math1
Math2	Math3	Math4	Math5
Mathematica1	Mathematica2	Mathematica3	Mathematica4
Mathematica5	Mathematica6	Mathematica7	PrintableASCII
ShiftJIS	Symbol	Unicode	UTF8
WindowsANSI	WindowsBaltic	WindowsCyrillic	WindowsEastEurope
WindowsGreek	WindowsThai	WindowsTurkish	ZapfDingbats

Notice how UTF-8 needs two bytes to display alpha.

```
In[6]:= ToString[alpha, CharacterEncoding → "UTF8"]
Out[6]= Î±
```

ToCharacterCode gives the numerical representation.

```
In[7]:= ToCharacterCode[ToString[alpha, CharacterEncoding → "UTF8"]]
Out[7]= {206, 177}
```

You can map from character codes back to characters using FromCharacterCode[].

```
In[8]:= FromCharacterCode[{87, 88, 89, 90}]
Out[8]= WXYZ
```

The mapping may not be one-to-one for certain encodings.

```
In[9]:= FromCharacterCode[{206, 177}, "UTF8"]
Out[9]= α
```

String and Regular Expressions

A great deal of Mathematica's prowess in text processing comes from its rich support for pattern matching. There are two basic classes of string patterns: string expressions and regular expressions. Introduced in version 5.1, each has a similar expressive power. The advantage of StringExpression is that it is less cryptic because it uses more words than symbols to express patterns. The advantage of RegularExpression is that it is more standardized with other languages such as Perl, Ruby, Java, and so on. Non-Mathematica programmers, especially those with a background in Unix, are more likely to understand regular expressions, although these expressions are cryptic to the uninitiated. You should become familiar with both if you plan to do much string manipulation. If you program frequently in languages outside of Mathematica, master the regular expression syntax. If you work strictly in Mathematica, choose the one that most appeals to you. If you learn the string expression syntax, you will have a leg up on learning Mathematica's more general pattern-matching syntax, which is used in many contexts outside text processing. You can also mix string expressions and regular expressions into compound patterns.

String expressions

StringExpressions are mostly written using the infix operator ~~, which is a syntactic shortcut for the StringExpression[] function. StringExpression uses Mathematica's blanks notation (e.g., _, __, and ___) to represent wild cards. See Chapter 4 for more on blanks.

Match "xy" followed by any character.

```
In[10]:= "xy" ~~ _;
In[11]:= StringMatchQ["xyz", "xy" ~~ _]
Out[11]= True

In[12]:= StringMatchQ["xyzz", "xy" ~~ _]
Out[12]= False
```

Match "xy" followed by one or more characters.

```
In[13]:= "xy" ~~ __;

In[14]:= StringMatchQ["xyzz", "xy" ~~ __]
Out[14]= True

In[15]:= StringMatchQ["xy", "xy" ~~ __]
Out[15]= False
```

Match "xy" followed by zero or more characters.

```
In[16]:= "xy" ~~ ___;

In[17]:= StringMatchQ["xyz", "xy" ~~ ___]
Out[17]= True

In[18]:= StringMatchQ["xy", "xy" ~~ ___]
Out[18]= True
```

Patterns can be associated with variables so that the matching portion can be referred to in a subsequent expression. For example, the following pattern will match if the string begins and ends with the same sequence of characters.

```
In[19]:= StringMatchQ["xyx", x__ ~~ ___ ~~ x__]
Out[19]= True

In[20]:= StringMatchQ["Hello. I said, hello", x__ ~~ ___ ~~ x__, IgnoreCase → True]
Out[20]= True

In[21]:= StringMatchQ["123ABC323", x : NumberString ~~ ___ ~~ x_]
Out[21]= False

In[22]:= StringMatchQ["123ABC123", x : NumberString ~~ ___ ~~ x_]
Out[22]= True
```

Table 5-1 shows some of the common raw ingredients for string expressions. If you have already read Chapter 4 on pattern matching, you can see that all the same constructs are available for strings. The full set of string expression primitives can be found in *tutorial/WorkingWithStringPatterns*.

Table 5-1. Common string patterns

Pattern	Description
`"\"string\""`	`"a literal string of characters"`
`"_"`	`"any single character"`
`"__"`	`"any substring of` `  one or more characters"`
`"___"`	`"any substring of` `  zero or more characters"`
`"x_,x__,x___"`	`"substrings given the name x"`
`"x:pattern"`	`"pattern given the name x"`
`"pattern.."`	`"pattern repeated one or more times"`
`"pattern..."`	`"pattern repeated zero or more times"`
`"patt1|patt2|..."`	`"a pattern matching` `  at least one of the patt-i"`
`"patt/;cond"`	`"a pattern for which` `  cond evaluates to True"`
`"pattern?test"`	`"a pattern for which test` `  yields True for each character"`
`"Except[pattern]"`	`"matches anything except pattern"`
`"Whitespace"`	`"a sequence of whitespace characters"`
`"NumberString"`	`"the characters of a number"`
`"DatePattern[spec]"`	`"the characters of a date"`
`"charobj"`	`"an object representing a` `  character class (see below)"`

Table 5-2 shows some of the common raw ingredients for regular expressions. The full set of regular expression primitives can be found in *tutorial/WorkingWithStringPatterns*. Here c or c*n*, where *n* is a number, is a placeholder for an arbitrary character, and p*n* is a placeholder for an arbitrary regular expression.

Table 5-2. Common regular expressions

Regular expression	Description
`"[c1c2c3]"`	`"Matches any of the characters c1, c2, or c3.`
`"[c1-c2]"`	`   For example, [AEIOUaeiou] matches vowels."`
	`"Matches characters c1 through c2. For example,`
	`   [a-z] matches all lowercase letters."`
`"[^c1c2c3]"`	`"Matches any characters EXCEPT c1, c2, c3. For`
	`   example, [^AEIOUaeiou] matches nonvowels."`
`"c*"`	`"Zero or more occurrences`
	`   of character c. Greedy version."`
`"c+"`	`"One or more occurrences`
	`   of character c. Greedy version."`
`"c?"`	`"The character c or nothing (i.e., zero`
	`   or one occurrences). Greedy version."`
`"c*?"`	`"Lazy version of c*."`
`"c+?"`	`"Lazy version of c+."`
`"c??"`	`"Lazy version of c?."`
`"p1|p2|...|pN"`	`"Matches p1 or p2 or ... pN."`
`"p1p2...pN"`	`"Matches p1, followed by p2, followed by ... pN."`
`"^p1"`	`"Matches p1 only at the start of the string."`
`"p1$"`	`"Matches p1 only at the end of the string."`
`"^p1$"`	`"Matches only if p1 matches the entire string."`
`"\\d"`	`"Any digit 0-9"`
`"\\s"`	`"Whitespace"`

See Also

The definitive reference on regular expressions is *Mastering Regular Expressions*, Second Edition, by Jeffrey E. F. Friedl (O'Reilly). If you plan to do anything nontrivial using regular expression matching, you will save yourself hours of frustration by consulting this book.

An excellent tutorial on working with string patterns in Mathematica can be found in the documentation under *tutorial/WorkingWithStringPatterns* or online at *http://bit.ly/yGbND*. Besides being a good all-around tutorial, it has a section specifically targeting Perl programmers, which is helpful for those who already have experience with string manipulation in Perl.

5.1 Comparing Strings

Problem

You want to compare strings but Less, LessEqual, Greater, and GreaterEqual do not work.

Solution

Use Order[e1,e2], which returns 1 if e1 is before e2, -1 if e1 is after e2, and 0 if they are equal.

```
In[23]:= Order["rat", "rate"]
Out[23]= 1

In[24]:= Order["rat", "cat"]
Out[24]= -1
```

Discussion

Most users of Mathematica will not find themselves doing direct string comparison since functions like Sort and Ordering do the right thing. However, if you find yourself needing to use the more natural comparison operators with strings, you can do the following:

```
In[25]:= Unprotect[Less, LessEqual, Greater, GreaterEqual];
         Less[s1_String, s2_String] := Order[s1, s2] > 0;
         LessEqual[s1_String, s2_String] := Order[s1, s2] > -1;
         Greater[s1_String, s2_String] := Order[s1, s2] < 0;
         GreaterEqual[s1_String, s2_String] := Order[s1, s2] < 1;
         Protect[Less, LessEqual, Greater, GreaterEqual];

In[31]:= "rat" < "cat"
Out[31]= False

In[32]:= "cat" < "rat"
Out[32]= True

In[33]:= "cat" <= "cat"
Out[33]= True
```

5.2 Removing and Replacing Characters from Strings

Problem

You want to strip certain characters (e.g., whitespace) or characters at certain positions from a string. You may also want to replace these characters with other characters.

Solution

Using patterns

StringReplace[] is an extremely versatile function that solves most character-oriented stripping and replacing operations. It supports a very general set of string-substitution rules, including regular expressions and Mathematica-specific string patterns.

Strip all spaces.

```
In[34]:= myString = " The quick brown  fox   jumped over the lazy programmer    ";
```

```
In[35]:= StringReplace[myString, " " → ""]
Out[35]= Thequickbrownfoxjumpedoverthelazyprogrammer
```

Strip leading and trailing whitespace.

```
In[36]:= StringReplace[myString, RegularExpression["^\\s+|\\s+$"] → ""] // InputForm
Out[36]//InputForm=
         "The quick brown  fox   jumped over the lazy programmer"
```

Normalize whitespace: strip leading, trailing, and multiple internal whitespace.

```
In[37]:= StringReplace[myString, {RegularExpression["^\\s+|\\s+$"] → "",
            RegularExpression["\\s\\s+"] → " "}] // InputForm
Out[37]//InputForm=
         "The quick brown fox jumped over the lazy programmer"
```

Literal string substitution.

```
In[38]:= StringReplace[myString, "the" → "a"] // InputForm
Out[38]//InputForm=
         " The quick brown  fox   jumped over a lazy programmer    "
```

Ignore case while matching.

```
In[39]:= StringReplace[myString, "the" → "a", IgnoreCase → True] // InputForm
Out[39]//InputForm=
         " a quick brown  fox   jumped over a lazy programmer    "
```

Use Mathematica-specific patterns instead of regular expressions.

```
In[40]:= StringReplace[myString, "ox" ~~ Whitespace → "ox "]
Out[40]= The quick brown  fox jumped over the lazy programmer
```

Using positions

Sometimes you know exactly where the characters are that you want to remove. In that case, StringDrop[] is a lot more efficient. StringDrop[] takes the string and a second argument, which can be an offset from the front, an offset from the end, specific positions, or a range of positions.

Consider:

```
In[41]:= myString = "abcdefghijklmnop";
```

Here you drop the first three characters.

```
In[42]:= StringDrop[myString, 3]
Out[42]= defghijklmnop
```

Alternatively, you drop the last three characters, like so.

```
In[43]:= StringDrop[myString, -3]
Out[43]= abcdefghijklm
```

Drop only the third character, like this.

```
In[44]:= StringDrop[myString, {3}]
Out[44]= abdefghijklmnop
```

And drop the third through fifth ("cde"), using a range list.

```
In[45]:= StringDrop[myString, {3, 5}]
Out[45]= abfghijklmnop
```

The step size in the range can even be greater than one by specifying it as the third element. Here you specify a step size of two to remove every other character. The -1 upper limit is a convenient way to specify the end of the string without having to know its length.

```
In[46]:= StringDrop[myString, {1, -1, 2}]
Out[46]= bdfhjlnp
```

You can also act on several strings at once.

```
In[47]:= otherString = "1234567890";
```

```
In[48]:= StringDrop[{myString, otherString}, {3, 5}]
Out[48]= {abfghijklmnop, 1267890}
```

The positional form for replacement is called StringReplacePart[], and it works using similar conventions for specifying positions. The difference is that you must always provide a contiguous range or a list of such ranges.

```
In[49]:= StringReplacePart[myString, "ZZZ", {3, 5}]
Out[49]= abZZZfghijklmnop
```

```
In[50]:= StringReplacePart[myString, "ZZZ", {{3, 5}, {10, 15}}]
Out[50]= abZZZfghiZZZp
```

Each range can also have its own replacement string.

```
In[51]:= StringReplacePart[myString, {"ZZZ", "WWW"}, {{3, 5}, {10, 15}}]
Out[51]= abZZZfghiWWWp
```

Discussion

As you can see from the given examples, StringReplace is quite versatile. However, the versatility is derived from Mathematica's rich support for patterns (see "Introduction" on page 181). Here are some typical text-processing problems that yield to the application of StringReplace[] and pattern matching.

Stripping comments

String expression version:

```
In[52]:= StringReplace[
            "1 + 2 * 3.14 (*precise enough for our purpose*) / 42 (*secret
                of the universe*)", "(*" ~~ ShortestMatch[___] ~~ "*)" → ""]
Out[52]= 1 + 2 * 3.14  / 42
```

Regular expression version:

```
In[53]:= StringReplace[
            "1 + 2 * 3.14 (*precise enough for our purpose*) / 42 (*secret of
                the universe*)", RegularExpression["\\(\\*.*?\\*\\)"] → ""]
Out[53]= 1 + 2 * 3.14  / 42
```

Changing delimiters

Delimited text (e.g., comma-delimited text) sounds simple at first, but many delimited formats allow a way to handle the delimiters as regular text by some quoting mechanism, as well as a way to escape quotes themselves. Furthermore, you must handle empty fields. If you want to replace a comma-delimited format with, say, a semicolon-delimited format, you must craft expressions that deal with all cases. Here, "" is used to escape a double quote. This example does not handle empty fields, but see Friedl's *Mastering Regular Expressions* for guidance.

```
In[54]:=  delimitedText = "Ten Thousand,10000,
          2710 ,\"10,000\",\"It's \"\"10 Grand\"\",baby\",10k";
       StringJoin[Riffle[StringCases[delimitedText,
          RegularExpression["([^\",]+|\"(?:[^\"]|\"\")*\")"] :→
          StringReplace["$1", "\"\"" :→ "\""]], ";"]]
Out[55]= Ten Thousand;10000; 2710 ;"10,000";"It's "10 Grand",baby";10k
```

Removing XML markup

Simple XML manipulations, such as discarding markup, can be accomplished with
StringReplace[].

```
In[56]:=  NotebookDirectory[]
Out[56]= /Users/smangano/Documents/workspace/Mathematica Cookbook/mathematica/

In[57]:=  xml = Import[FileNameJoin[
          {NotebookDirectory[], "..", "data", "ch02", "data1.xml"}], "Text"]
Out[57]= <?xml version="1.0" encoding="UTF-8"?>
       <!-- Some data to use as a test for Mathematica's XML import -->
       <?test Just for didactic purposes?>
       <data>
           <item>
               <name>Leonardo</name>
               <sex>male</sex>
               <age>8</age>
               <height>4.7</height>
           </item>
           <item>
               <name>Salvatore</name>
               <sex>male</sex>
               <age>5</age>
               <height>4.1</height>
           </item>
           <item>
               <name>Alexis</name>
               <sex>female</sex>
               <age>6</age>
               <height>4.4</height>
           </item>
       </data>
       <!-- Comment at end -->
```

```
In[58]:= StringReplace[xml,
            {Shortest["<" ~~ Except[">"] .. ~~ ">"] .. → "", Whitespace → " "}]
Out[58]=     Leonardo male 8 4.7   Salvatore male 5 4.1   Alexis female 6 4.4
```

Replacing with expression evaluation

By capturing matched substrings in variables, you can perform expression evaluation using ToExpression[] as you replace.

```
In[59]:= expr = "Is 1 + 1 in every possible universe? What about Pi / 2?";
```

```
In[60]:= StringReplace[expr,
            x : ({NumberString , "Pi"} ~~ Whitespace ... ~~ {"*","+","-","/"} ~~
                Whitespace ... ~~ {NumberString , "Pi"}) :>
            x <> " = " <> ToString[N[ToExpression[x]]]]
Out[60]= Is 1 + 1 = 2. in every possible universe? What about Pi / 2 = 1.5708?
```

Here is another example using dates.

```
In[61]:= invoice =
            "05/17/2008\nMathematica Programming: $1000.00\nInvoice is Net 30";
         Block[{datefmt = {"Month", "/", "Day", "/", "Year"}, date},
            date = StringCases[invoice, DatePattern[datefmt]];
            StringReplace[invoice, "Net " ~~ n : NumberString :> "due " <> DateString[
                DatePlus[DateList[date[[1]]], ToExpression[n]], datefmt]]]
Out[62]= 05/17/2008
         Mathematica Programming: $1000.00
         Invoice is due 06/16/2008
```

See Also

See Recipe 2.4 for use of StringPosition[], which returns sequence specification that can be fed into StringReplacePart[] and StringDrop[].

See Recipes 2.8 and 2.9 for more sophisticated forms of XML processing.

5.3 Extracting Characters and Substrings

Problem

You want to extract a substring by position or content from a string.

Solution

Using patterns

StringCases[] provides the pattern-driven means of extracting substrings. There are two major variations. In the first, you simply extract what the patterns literally match. The second variation uses rules to transform the matched substrings into other strings and return those instead.

You can extract specific words using regular expressions (here \\b matches word boundaries).

```
In[63]:= StringCases["The pig thought he was a dog and then chased the cat.",
            RegularExpression["\\b(a|the)\\b"], IgnoreCase → True]
Out[63]= {The, a, the}
```

The same can be done using string expressions.

```
In[64]:= StringCases["The pig thought he was a dog and then chased the cat.",
            WordBoundary ~~ {"a", "the"} ~~ WordBoundary, IgnoreCase -> True]
Out[64]= {The, a, the}
```

The most common reason for using rules instead of patterns is to match a substring within a specific context but return the substring alone. Here we want to return substrings bracketed by one or more occurrences of the letter *a*. This example also illustrates that regular expressions and string expressions can be mixed.

```
In[65]:= StringCases["abacbcdbdaeaaazzza",
            RegularExpression["(?<=a)"] ~~
            x : Repeated[Except["a"]] ~~
            RegularExpression["(?=a)"] → x]
            (*Return the characters surrounded by "a".*)
Out[65]= {b, cbcdbd, e, zzz}
```

Using positions

Sometimes you know exactly where the characters are that you want to remove. In that case, StringTake[] is a lot more efficient. StringTake[] takes the string and a second argument, which can be an offset from the front, an offset from the end, specific positions, or a range of positions.

Consider:

```
In[66]:= myString = "abcdefghijklmnop";
```

Here you take the first three characters.

```
In[67]:= StringTake[myString, 3]
Out[67]= abc
```

Alternatively, you take the last three characters, like so.

```
In[68]:= StringTake[myString, -3]
Out[68]= nop
```

Take only the third character, like this.

```
In[69]:= StringTake[myString, {3}]
Out[69]= c
```

And take the third through fifth ("cde") using a range list.

```
In[70]:= StringTake[myString, {3, 5}]
Out[70]= cde
```

The step size in the range can even be greater than one by specifying it as the third element. Here you specify a step size of two to take every other character. The -1 upper limit is a convenient way to specify the end of the string without having to know its length.

```
In[71]:= StringTake[myString, {1, -1, 2}]
Out[71]= acegikmo
```

Conveniently, you can also act on several strings at once.

```
In[72]:= otherString = "1234567890";
In[73]:= StringTake[{myString, otherString}, {3, 5}]
Out[73]= {cde, 345}
```

If you have read Recipe 5.2, you see that StringTake has very similar parameter variations as StringDrop[]. However, StringTake has an additional feature: it can take a list of position specifications and produce a list of the resulting extracts.

```
In[74]:= StringTake[myString, {{1}, {3}, {8, 10}}]
Out[74]= {a, c, hij}
```

This is useful for picking multiple segments from a string in one step. However, if you want a string rather than a list, simply wrap the expression in a StringJoin[].

```
In[75]:= StringJoin[StringTake[myString, {{1}, {3}, {8, 10}}]]
Out[75]= achij
```

Discussion

In the "Solution" section on page 193 we used `RegularExpression["(?<=a)"]` (look-behind) and `RegularExpression["(?=a)"]` (look-ahead) because there is no string-expression equivalent. However, there is an option for `StringCases[]` called `Overlaps`, which when set to `True`, causes the matcher to continue at the character that follows the first character of the last matched substring. In the following example, this allows a single *a* to act as both a start of pattern and end of pattern.

```
In[76]:= StringCases["abacbcdbdaeaaazzza",
            "a" ~~ x : Repeated[Except["a"]] ~~ "a" → x, Overlaps → True]
Out[76]= {b, cbcdbd, e, zzz}
```

Without `Overlaps→True`, you would not get the "cbcbd" substring.

```
In[77]:= StringCases["abacbcdbdaeaaazzza",
            "a" ~~ x : Repeated[Except["a"]] ~~ "a" → x]
Out[77]= {b, e, zzz}
```

There is a third setting, `Overlaps→All`, which causes the matcher to repeat searches from the same position until no new matches are found. To see the effect of `All`, we need to consider a different example, one in which the bracketing character is not excluded from the match. A parenthesized expression is a good example.

```
In[78]:= StringCases["((a-b) (c + d) (e / (f + g)))",
            Shortest["(" ~~ _ ~~ ")"], Overlaps → False] // TableForm
Out[78]//TableForm=
            ((a-b)
            (c + d)
            (e / (f + g)
```

```
In[79]:= StringCases["((a-b) (c + d) (e / (f + g)))",
            Shortest["(" ~~ _ ~~ ")"], Overlaps → True] // TableForm
Out[79]//TableForm=
            ((a-b)
            (a-b)
            (c + d)
            (e / (f + g)
            (f + g)
```

```
In[80]:= StringCases["((a-b) (c + d) (e / (f + g)))",
            Shortest["(" ~~ _ ~~ ")"], Overlaps → All] // TableForm
```

```
Out[80]//TableForm=
          ((a-b)
          ((a-b) (c + d)
          ((a-b) (c + d) (e / (f + g)
          ((a-b) (c + d) (e / (f + g))
          ((a-b) (c + d) (e / (f + g)))
          (a-b)
          (a-b) (c + d)
          (a-b) (c + d) (e / (f + g)
          (a-b) (c + d) (e / (f + g))
          (a-b) (c + d) (e / (f + g)))
          (c + d)
          (c + d) (e / (f + g)
          (c + d) (e / (f + g))
          (c + d) (e / (f + g)))
          (e / (f + g)
          (e / (f + g))
          (e / (f + g)))
          (f + g)
          (f + g))
          (f + g)))
```

See Also

If you have a list of strings and want to extract those that match a pattern, you want Select, using StringMatchQ with a string pattern as the test, rather than StringCases. See Recipe 4.1.

5.4 Duplicating a String

Problem

You need to synthesize a string from a fixed number of copies of a seed string.

Solution

Use StringJoin[] on the output of Table[].

```
In[81]:=  stringDup[seed_, n_: 2] := StringJoin@Array[seed &, n]

In[82]:=  stringDup["-", 10] // InputForm
Out[82]//InputForm=
          "----------"

In[83]:=  stringDup["wiki "]
Out[83]=  wiki wiki
```

Discussion

This is a simple recipe, and I include it because it's something you expect to be bundled as a native function, but it's not. For most practical applications, the solution is fine, but for very large n, a doubling approach will have better performance. Rather than doing the math to get the exact string size, we simply truncate the closest sized string obtained from pure doubling of the seed.

```
In[84]:= stringDup2[seed_, n_] :=
           StringTake[Nest[# <> # &, seed, Ceiling[Log[2, n]] ], n]

In[85]:= Mean[Table[Timing[stringDup["-", 100000]] [[1]], {10}]]
Out[85]= 0.0486878

In[86]:= Mean[Table[Timing[stringDup2["-", 100000]] [[1]], {10}]]
Out[86]= 0.0031014
```

This solution may not be obvious, so let's break it down. It should be clear that mapping the function #<>#& to a list containing a string will double that string (recall that <> is string concatenation).

```
In[87]:= # <> # & /@ {"-"}
Out[87]= {--}
```

It follows that doing this twice will quadruple it.

```
In[88]:= # <> # & /@ (# <> # & /@ {"-"})
Out[88]= {----}
```

Repeating this process m times will create a string of length 2^m. However, the input is the desired length n, not the number of doublings, so we know we need at least Ceiling[Log[2, n]] doublings; by using Nest with this number, we get exactly that. However, this overshoots the desired length in most cases, because we rarely expect n to be an exact power of 2. So we use Take to extract the correct length. The reason this is fast for large n is that it reduces a O(n) operation in terms of Table to a O(log n) operation using StringJoin.

You can bundle these versions together into one function that gives good performance across all sizes.

```
In[89]:= Clear[stringDup];
           stringDup[seed_String, n_Integer /; n >= 2^12] :=
            StringTake[Nest[# <> # &, seed, Ceiling[Log[2, n]] ], n]
           stringDup[seed_String, n_Integer: 2] := StringJoin @ Array[seed &, n]
```

See Also

Nest is discussed in Recipe 2.11.

5.5 Matching and Searching Text

Problem

You want to determine if a string contains a pattern and at what positions.

Solution

Use StringMatchQ[string,pattern] to determine if a string matches a pattern.

```
In[92]:= StringMatchQ["1234", NumberString]
Out[92]= True
```

Here I show a match on multiple strings with a pattern that is predicated.

```
In[93]:= StringMatchQ[{"1234", "1237"}, p : NumberString /; OddQ[FromDigits[p]]]
Out[93]= {False, True}
```

Use StringFreeQ[string,pattern] to determine if a string does not match a pattern.

```
In[94]:= StringFreeQ[{"1234", "abcde"}, p : NumberString]
Out[94]= {False, True}
```

Use StringPosition[string,pattern] to find the integer offsets of matches. The default behavior is to search for all occurrences of the pattern (i.e., Overlaps → True).

```
In[95]:= StringPosition["1234abcd54321", NumberString]
Out[95]= {{1, 4}, {2, 4}, {3, 4}, {4, 4},
          {9, 13}, {10, 13}, {11, 13}, {12, 13}, {13, 13}}
```

With Overlaps → False, you only get matches on substrings that don't share characters with prior matches.

```
In[96]:= StringPosition["1234abcd54321", NumberString, Overlaps → False]
Out[96]= {{1, 4}, {9, 13}}
```

Discussion

StringMatchQ[] and StringFreeQ[] very often find application in restricting inputs to functions.

```
In[97]:= classify[word_String /; StringMatchQ[word, {"I", "me", "we",
             "you", "they", "him", "her", "it"}]] := pronoun[word]
         classify[word_String /; StringMatchQ[word, {"and", "or", "nor",
             "after," "although," "as," "because," "before," "how," "if,"
              "once," "since," "than," "that," "though," "till," "until,"
              "when," "where," "whether,", "while"}]] := conjunction[word]
         classify[word_String /; StringMatchQ[word, DatePattern[{"DayName"}]]] :=
           dayofweek[word]
         classify[word_String /; StringMatchQ[word, DatePattern[{"MonthName"}]]] :=
           month[word]
         (*...*)
         classify[word_String] := other[word] ;
```

You can also use them as input to other functions, like Pick[] in the following grep implementation adapted from an example in Mathematica documentation. Recall that in the standard Unix grep, *option -v* instructs grep to return lines that don't match the pattern. Here Transpose and Range are used to number each line so the result contains a list of pairs {line, match text}. This grep function was implemented in terms of StringFreeQ rather than StringMatchQ since the latter only succeeds if the entire string matches.

```
In[102]:= grep[file_, patt_, "-v"] := grepImpl[file, patt, True ]
          grep[file_, patt_] := grepImpl[file, patt, False]
          grepImpl[file_, patt_, value_] := With[{data = Import[file, "Lines"]},
            Pick[Transpose[{Range[Length[data]], data}],
              StringFreeQ[data, RegularExpression[patt]], value]]
In[105]:= grep[FileNameJoin[{NotebookDirectory[], "greptest.txt"}], "bar"] //
             TableForm
Out[105]//TableForm=
             1  bar
             4  foo bar
             5  foobar
             6  barfo

In[106]:= grep[FileNameJoin[{NotebookDirectory[], "greptest.txt"}], "bar$"]
Out[106]= {{1, bar}, {4, foo bar}, {5, foobar}}

In[107]:= grep[FileNameJoin[{NotebookDirectory[], "greptest.txt"}], "bar", "-v"]
Out[107]= {{2, foo}, {3, baz}, {7, fo o}}
```

Both StringMatchQ[] and StringFreeQ[] support the IgnoreCase → True option. StringMatchQ also supports option SpellingCorrection → True, which allows the match to succeed even if a small number of characters are wrong. However, in many cases a small number can mean only 1, as the following example demonstrates, so I would not rely too heavily on this "feature."

```
In[108]:= StringMatchQ["mississippi", "missisippi", SpellingCorrection → True]
Out[108]= True
```

```
In[109]:= StringMatchQ["mississippi", "misisipi", SpellingCorrection → True]
Out[109]= False
```

The output of StringPosition[] can be used as the input to StringTake.

```
In[110]:= With[{str = "1234abcd54321"},
              StringTake[str, StringPosition[str, NumberString]]]
Out[110]= {1234, 234, 34, 4, 54321, 4321, 321, 21, 1}
```

If you want to use it with StringDrop[], you need to map StringDrop[] over the list returned by StringPosition[]. This will give you a list with each matching segment dropped. More than likely, you will want to set Overlaps → False in this case. Try Overlaps → True with the expression given below to see why it is undesirable.

```
In[111]:= With[{str = "1234abcd54321"}, StringDrop[str, #] & /@
              StringPosition[str, NumberString, Overlaps → False]]
Out[111]= {abcd54321, 1234abcd}
```

See Also

See Recipes 5.3 and 5.2 for usage of StringTake[] and StringDrop[].

5.6 Tokenizing Text

Problem

You want to break a string into tokens based on a character or pattern.

Solution

StringSplit[] provides a variety of options for tokenizing text. The default is simply to tokenize on whitespace.

```
In[112]:= StringSplit["The quick brown fox\njumped over the lazy programmer"]
Out[112]= {The, quick, brown, fox, jumped, over, the, lazy, programmer}
```

Other delimiters can be specified as literals or more general patterns. Here you specify comma delimiters with zero or more whitespace characters.

```
In[113]:= StringSplit["2008/01/20, test1, 100.3, 77.8,33.77",
            "," ~~ WhitespaceCharacter ...]
Out[113]= {2008/01/20, test1, 100.3, 77.8, 33.77}
```

If there are several delimiters, give each pattern in a list. Here you decide to parse the date along with the comma-delimited text.

```
In[114]:= StringSplit["2008/01/20, test1, 100.3, 77.8,33.77",
            {"," ~~ WhitespaceCharacter ..., "/"}]
Out[114]= {2008, 01, 20, test1, 100.3, 77.8, 33.77}
```

Discussion

StringSplit supports rules as well as patterns, which leads to some interesting applications, such as a means of highlighting output. Here is an example that stylizes XML by rendering directives, comments, and tags in specific font styles and colors. (The colors will not be visible in a monochrome print, but you can try the code on your own to see the effect.)

```
In[115]:= StringSplit[Import[
            FileNameJoin[{NotebookDirectory[], "..", "data", "ch02", "data1.xml"}],
            "text"], {x : ("<!--" ~~ Except[">"] .. ~~ ">") :>
            Style[x, FontSlant → Italic, FontColor → Brown],
            x : ("<?" ~~ Except[">"] .. ~~ ">") :> Style[x, FontColor → Red],
            x : ("<" ~~ Except[">"] .. ~~ ">") :>
            Style[x, FontWeight → Bold, FontColor → Blue]}] // Row

Out[115]= <?xml version="1.0" encoding="UTF-8"?>
          <!-- Some data to use as a test for Mathematica's XML import -->
          <?test Just for didactic purposes?>
          <data>
              <item>
                  <name>Leonardo</name>
                  <sex>male</sex>
                  <age>8</age>
                  <height>4.7</height>
              </item>
              <item>
                  <name>Salvatore</name>
                  <sex>male</sex>
                  <age>5</age>
                  <height>4.1</height>
              </item>
              <item>
                  <name>Alexis</name>
                  <sex>female</sex>
                  <age>6</age>
                  <height>4.4</height>
              </item>
          </data>
          <!-- Comment at end -->
```

5.7 Working with Natural Language Dictionaries

Problem

You want to do some simple linguistic processing driven by a reliable lexicon.

Solution

As of version 6, Mathematica comes bundled with many useful data sources. One of these sources is an integrated English language dictionary (dictionaries for other languages can be installed).

Look up words that begin with *th* and end with *y*.

```
In[116]:=  DictionaryLookup["th" ~~ ___ ~~ "y"]
Out[116]=  {thankfully, thanklessly, theatricality, theatrically,
           thematically, theocracy, theologically, theology, theoretically,
           theory, theosophy, therapeutically, therapy, thereby, thermally,
           thermodynamically, thermostatically, they, thickly, thievery,
           thingummy, thingy, thinly, thirdly, thirstily, thirsty, thirty, thorny,
           thoroughly, thoughtfully, thoughtlessly, thready, threateningly,
           threepenny, threnody, thriftily, thrifty, thrillingly, throatily,
           throaty, throwaway, thruway, thuggery, thunderously, thundery, thy}
```

Look up words that end in *ee*.

```
In[117]:=  DictionaryLookup[___ ~~ "ee"]
Out[117]=  {absentee, addressee, agree, Aimee, Albee, amputee, apogee, appointee,
           Ashlee, attendee, Attlee, axletree, banshee, bee, bootee, bumblebee,
           bungee, carefree, Chattahoochee, Cherokee, chickadee, chimpanzee,
           coffee, committee, conferee, consignee, coulee, Cree, debauchee, decree,
           Dee, degree, deportee, Desiree, detainee, devotee, disagree, divorcee,
           draftee, Dundee, dungaree, Elysee, emcee, employee, enlistee, entree,
           epee, escapee, evacuee, fat-free, fee, fiancee, filigree, flee, foresee,
           franchisee, free, fricassee, Frisbee, fusee, Galilee, garnishee, gee, ghee,
           glee, goatee, grandee, grantee, guarantee, gumtree, honeybee, honoree,
           Humvee, inductee, internee, interviewee, invitee, jamboree, Jaycee,
           jubilee, kedgeree, Klee, knee, lee, Lee, legatee, Legree, lessee, levee,
           licensee, manatee, marquee, matinee, McGee, McKee, melee, Menominee,
           Milwaukee, mortgagee, Murrumbidgee, Muskogee, nee, negligee, nominee,
           Okeechobee, Okefenokee, oversee, parolee, Pawnee, payee, pedigree, pee,
           peewee, Pelee, perigee, pewee, pharisee, Pharisee, pongee, prithee,
           protegee, puree, puttee, quadtree, ranee, referee, refugee, Renee,
           repartee, retiree, returnee, Rhee, rupee, Sadducee, scree, see, settee,
           Shawnee, Sheree, shoetree, singletree, sirree, Slurpee, soiree, spree,
           squeegee, standee, subcommittee, subtree, suttee, Suwanee, Swanee,
           Tallahassee, tee, Tennessee, tepee, thee, three, toffee, toll-free, topee,
           toupee, towhee, townee, Toynbee, trainee, transferee, tree, trochee,
           Truckee, trustee, Tuskegee, twee, Tweedledee, Tyree, wannabee, wee, whee,
           whiffletree, whippletree, whoopee, Yahtzee, Yankee, yippee, Zebedee}
```

Discussion

There are a lot of neat applications for an integrated dictionary.

Crossword puzzles

Here is how you might cheat at a crossword puzzle. Say you have three letters of a six-letter word and the clue is "51 down: unkeyed."

```
In[118]:= DictionaryLookup["a" ~~ _ ~~ "o" ~~ _ ~~ _ ~~ "l"]
Out[118]= {amoral, atonal, avowal}
```

Ah, *atonal* sounds right (pun intended)!

Anagrams

You can also help your second grader impress the teacher on that November worksheet for finding all the words you can make out of the letters in "Thanksgiving" (i.e., anagrams). Here we use a pattern containing all combinations of the letters in "thanksgiving" and an extra constraint function to ensure letters are contained by their availability (count). Strictly speaking, an anagram must use all the letters of the input, but I ignore that here.

```
In[119]:= thanksgivingQ[word_] := StringCount[word, "t"] < 2 &&
            StringCount[word, "h"] < 2 && StringCount[word, "a"] < 2 &&
            StringCount[word, "n"] < 3 && StringCount[word, "k"] < 2 &&
            StringCount[word, "s"] < 2 && StringCount[word, "g"] < 3 &&
            StringCount[word, "i"] < 3 && StringCount[word, "v"] < 2;

In[120]:= DictionaryLookup[
            word : ("t" | "h" | "a" | "n" | "k" | "s" | "g" | "i" | "v") .. /;
            thanksgivingQ[word], IgnoreCase -> True]
```

```
Out[120]= {a, aging, agings, Agni, ah, Aisha, akin, Akita, an, Ana, angst, Anita, ankh,
          ankhs, Ann, Anna, ans, Anshan, ant, anti, anting, antis, ants, as, ash,
          Ashanti, ashing, Asia, Asian, ask, asking, at, Atkins, Ava, Avis, gag,
          gags, gain, gaining, gains, gait, gaits, gang, gangs, gas, gash, gashing,
          gating, Gavin, ghat, ghats, Ghats, GI, giant, giants, gig, gigs, gin,
          Gina, gins, Gish, gist, git, gits, giving, givings, gnash, gnashing,
          gnat, gnats, gs, ha, hag, haggis, hags, Hahn, Haiti, Han, hang, hanging,
          hangings, hangs, hank, Hank, hanks, Hans, has, hast, hasting, hat, hating,
          hats, having, hi, Higgins, hiking, hinging, hint, hinting, hints, his,
          histing, hit, hits, HIV, hiving, I, Ian, in, Ina, ink, inking, inks, inn,
          innit, inns, ins, insight, inti, is, Isa, Isiah, it, IT, its, Iva, Ivan,
          Kan, Kans, Kant, khan, Khan, khans, kin, king, King, kings, Kings, kins,
          kit, Kit, kith, kithing, kiths, kiting, kits, knavish, knight, Knight,
          knighting, knights, knish, knit, knits, ks, nag, nags, nah, nan, Nan,
          nans, NASA, Nash, Nat, nigh, night, nights, Nikita, Nina, ninth, ninths,
          Nisan, nit, Nita, nits, nth, sag, saint, saith, Saki, Saks, San, sang,
          Sang, saning, sank, Sask, sat, SAT, satin, sating, satining, saving, sh,
          shag, shaking, shank, shat, shaving, shin, shining, shiv, Shiva, sigh,
          sighing, sight, sighting, sign, signing, Sikh, Sikhs, sin, Sinai, sing,
          singing, sink, Sinkiang, sinking, sit, siting, Siva, Sivan, ska, skating,
          ski, skiing, skin, skint, skit, skiting, skiving, snag, snaking, snit,
          stag, staging, stain, staining, staking, Stan, stank, staving, sting,
          stinging, stink, stinking, ta, tag, tags, Tahiti, taking, takings, tan,
          tang, tangs, tank, tanking, tanks, tans, task, tasking, Thai, Thais,
          than, thank, thanking, thanks, thanksgiving, Thanksgiving, Thant, thin,
          thing, things, think, thinking, thinks, thins, this, ti, Tia, tin, Tina,
          ting, Ting, tinging, tings, tining, tins, Tisha, Titan, Titans, Titian,
          TNT, ts, TV, TVs, vain, van, Van, Vang, vanish, vanishing, vans, vast,
          vat, VAT, vats, VHS, via, viking, Viking, vikings, Vikings, vining,
          visa, Visa, visaing, vising, visit, vista, vistaing, vita, Vivian, vs}
```

Using Tally[] to count letter occurrences and doing a bit of set manipulation, we can generalize this for any word. The condition checking for the empty complement at the end is not strictly needed here because we will never match a word in the dictionary that has a letter that is not in the input word. However, it is needed to make the logic if isWordSubsetQ[] is correct as a general predicate.

```
In[121]:= isWordSubsetQ[word1_, word2_] :=
            Block[{tally1 = Tally[Characters[word1]],
              tally2 = Tally[Characters[word2]]},
             And @@ MapThread[(#1[[2]] ≥ #2[[2]]) &, {Intersection[tally1,
                 tally2, SameTest → (#1[[1]] === #2[[1]] &)], Intersection[
                 tally2, tally1, SameTest → (#1[[1]] === #2[[1]] &)]}] &&
              Complement[Characters[word2], Characters[word1]] === {}]

In[122]:= isWordSubsetQ["thanksgiving", "visa"]
Out[122]= True

In[123]:= isWordSubsetQ["thanksgiving", "pork"]
Out[123]= False

In[124]:= anagrams[word_] := DictionaryLookup[
            w : Characters[word] .. /; isWordSubsetQ[word, w], IgnoreCase → True]
```

You can test the generality against other words.

```
In[125]:= anagrams["winter"]
Out[125]= {en, er, in, inert, inter, ire, it, net, new, newt, nit, niter, re, rein, rent,
           rite, ten, tern, ti, tie, tier, tin, tine, tire, twin, twine, twiner, we,
           weir, wen, went, wet, win, wine, winter, wire, wit, wren, writ, write}

In[126]:= anagrams["dog"]
Out[126]= {do, dog, go, god}
```

Palindromes

Here is a neat little palindrome finder (courtesy of the Mathematica documentation).

```
In[127]:= DictionaryLookup[x__ /; x === StringReverse[x]]
Out[127]= {a, aha, aka, bib, bob, boob, bub, CFC, civic, dad, deed, deified,
           did, dud, DVD, eke, ere, eve, ewe, eye, gag, gig, huh, I, kayak,
           kook, level, ma'am, madam, mam, MGM, minim, mom, mum, nan, non, noon,
           nun, oho, pap, peep, pep, pip, poop, pop, pup, radar, redder, refer,
           repaper, reviver, rotor, sagas, sees, seres, sexes, shahs, sis,
           solos, SOS, stats, stets, tat, tenet, TNT, toot, tot, tut, wow, WWW}
```

Spell-checker

By using all the words in the dictionary with Nearest[], you can create a rudimentary spell-checker. For our first attempt, we'll use Nearest's default distance function. We'll return a list for which the first element is True or False depending on the word's inclusion in the dictionary and the second element is a list of potential correct spellings.

```
In[128]:= nf1 = Nearest[DictionaryLookup[]];

           SpellCheck1[word_] := Module[{corrections = nf1[word, 15]},
             If[ MemberQ[ corrections, word], {True, word}, {False, corrections}]]

In[130]:= SpellCheck1["pickel"]
Out[130]= {False, {nickel, picked, picker, picket, bicker, dicker, dickey,
             hickey, kicked, kicker, licked, Michel, mickey, Mickey, nicked}}
```

We see that the default distance function used for strings (EditDistance) does not make the greatest spell-checker: the obvious suggestion of *pickle* is not among the first 15 nearest words. You can experiment with other distance functions. Here is one that penalizes more heavily for mistakes in consonants than for mistakes in vowels.

```
In[131]:= SpellDistance[a_, b_] := Module[
             {vowelpat = ("a" | "e" | "i" | "o" | "u") -> ""}, EditDistance[a, b] +
               EditDistance[StringReplace[a, vowelpat], StringReplace[b, vowelpat]]]

           nf2 = Nearest[DictionaryLookup[], DistanceFunction -> SpellDistance];

           SpellCheck2[word_] := Module[{corrections = nf2[word, 10]},
             If[ MemberQ[ corrections, word], {True, word}, {False, corrections}]]

In[134]:= SpellCheck2["pickel"]
Out[134]= {False, {nickel, picked, picker,
             picket, pickle, packed, packer, packet, pecked, pick}}
```

Here we test on some commonly misspelled words (according to the Oxford Dictionaries website: *http://bit.ly/KuIQ2*) .

```
In[135]:= SpellCheck2["accomodate"]
Out[135]= {False, {accommodate, accommodated, accommodates, accumulate, accelerate,
             accentuate, acclimate, accolade, accommodation, accordant}}

In[136]:= SpellCheck2["alcahol"]
Out[136]= {False, {alcohol, alcohols, alcoholic,
             achoo, ahchoo, algal, anchor, carol, lethal, local}}

In[137]:= SpellCheck2["mispell"]
Out[137]= {False, {misspell, Aspell, Ispell, miscall,
             respell, spell, dispel, dispels, misdeal, misplay}}
```

This returns useful results, but performance (speed) is poor.

```
In[138]:= SpellCheck2["pickel"] // Timing
Out[138]= {2.22533, {False, {nickel, picked, picker,
             picket, pickle, packed, packer, packet, pecked, pick}}}
```

We can improve the speed using a divide-and-conquer approach: pick a large but manageable number (e.g., 100) of nearest words according to simple EditDistance, and then do a second pass on the smaller set with the EditDistance sans vowels. We define a distance function called ConsonantDistance[] for the second pass.

```
In[139]:= ConsonantDistance[a_, b_] :=
            Module[{vowelpat = ("a" | "e" | "i" | "o" | "u") → ""},
              EditDistance[StringReplace[a, vowelpat], StringReplace[b, vowelpat]]]
```

```
In[140]:= SpellCheck3[word_] :=
            Module[{corrections, corrections2, nf}, corrections = nf1[word, 100];
              nf = Nearest[corrections, DistanceFunction → ConsonantDistance];
              corrections2 = nf[word, 10];
              If[MemberQ[corrections2, word], {True, word}, {False, corrections2}]]
```

```
In[141]:= SpellCheck3["pickel"] // Timing
Out[141]= {0.055973, {False, {pickle, nickel, picked,
              picker, picket, packed, packer, packet, pecked, pick}}}
```

Good results and about 43 times faster!

Mathematica also provides WordData[], which returns information about properties of words, such as parts of speech and definitions.

```
In[142]:= WordData["run"]
Out[142]= {{run, Noun, Score}, {run, Noun, Travel}, {run, Noun, RegularTrip},
            {run, Noun, ShortTrip}, {run, Noun, FootballPlay}, {run, Noun, Endeavor},
            {run, Noun, Successiveness}, {run, Noun, Flow}, {run, Noun, Damage},
            {run, Noun, Footrace}, {run, Noun, Campaign}, {run, Noun, Streak},
            {run, Noun, Stream}, {run, Noun, IndefiniteQuantity},
            {run, Noun, Liberty}, {run, Noun, TimePeriod}, {run, Verb, Disintegrate},
            {run, Verb, SplitUp}, {run, Verb, Dissolve}, {run, Verb, Treat},
            {run, Verb, Change}, {run, Verb, Get}, {run, Verb, Vie}, {run, Verb, Race},
            {run, Verb, Catch}, {run, Verb, Draw}, {run, Verb, Operate},
            {run, Verb, Function}, {run, Verb, CarryThrough}, {run, Verb, Play},
            {run, Verb, Circularize}, {run, Verb, Trip}, {run, Verb, GoThrough},
            {run, Verb, Hurry}, {run, Verb, TravelRapidly}, {run, Verb, Sport},
            {run, Verb, Accompany}, {run, Verb, Sail}, {run, Verb, SpreadOut},
            {run, Verb, Flow}, {run, Verb, GoAway}, {run, Verb, Displace},
            {run, Verb, MoveFreely}, {run, Verb, Trade}, {run, Verb, Loose},
            {run, Verb, Direct}, {run, Verb, Succeed}, {run, Verb, Implement},
            {run, Verb, Occur}, {run, Verb, Continue}, {run, Verb, Endure},
            {run, Verb, Extend}, {run, Verb, MakePass}, {run, Verb, Lean},
            {run, Verb, Incur}, {run, Verb, Go}, {run, Verb, Range}}
```

See Also

Readers interested in spell-checkers should check out this approach (written in Python) by Peter Norvig of Google: *http://bit.ly/19gyjN*.

5.8 Importing XML

Problem

You want to import and manipulate XML data in Mathematica.

Solution

Use Import[] with format "XMLObject" to import XML and convert it to a special Mathematica expression form. Consider the following XML in file *data1.xml* (available for download at the book's website).

```
<?xml version="1.0" encoding="UTF-8"?>
<!-- Some data to use as a test for Mathematica's XML import -->
<?test Just for didactic purposes?>
<data>
    <item>
        <name>Leonardo</name>
        <sex>male</sex>
        <age>8</age>
        <height>4.7</height>
    </item>
    <item>
        <name>Salvatore</name>
        <sex>male</sex>
        <age>5</age>
        <height>4.1</height>
    </item>
    <item>
        <name>Alexis</name>
        <sex>female</sex>
        <age>6</age>
        <height>4.4</height>
    </item>
</data>
```

```
In[143]:= data = Import[FileNameJoin[
            {NotebookDirectory[], "..", "data", "ch02", "data1.xml"}], "XMLObject"]
Out[143]= XMLObject[Document][
            {XMLObject[Declaration][Version → 1.0, Encoding → UTF-8],
             XMLObject[Comment][
               Some data to use as a test for Mathematica's XML import ],
             XMLObject[ProcessingInstruction][test, Just for didactic purposes]},
            XMLElement[data, {}, {XMLElement[item, {},
                {XMLElement[name, {}, {Leonardo}], XMLElement[sex, {}, {male}],
                 XMLElement[age, {}, {8}], XMLElement[height, {}, {4.7}]}],
               XMLElement[item, {}, {XMLElement[name, {}, {Salvatore}],
                 XMLElement[sex, {}, {male}], XMLElement[age, {}, {5}],
                 XMLElement[height, {}, {4.1}]}], XMLElement[item, {},
                {XMLElement[name, {}, {Alexis}], XMLElement[sex, {}, {female}],
                 XMLElement[age, {}, {6}], XMLElement[height, {}, {4.4}]}]}],
            {XMLObject[Comment][ Comment at end ]}]
```

Discussion

Mathematica imports XML into expression form. You can manipulate the expression just like you would any other Mathematica expression, but first you need to understand the structure, which is a bit unconventional. Mathematica uses two types of heads to encode XML. XMLObject["*type*"] is used to represent everything that is not an element, including the entire document (type = "Document"), comments (type = "Comment"), CDATA sections (type = "CDATASection"), processing instructions (type = "ProcessingInstruction"), declarations (type = "Declaration"), and document types (type = "Doctype"). In the XML above, you see examples for document, declaration, comment, and processing instruction. XMLElement[tag,{attr1→val1,...},{data1,...}] is used to represent element data for both simple (text values) and complex element types (those with child elements). Don't get tripped up by the XMLObject notation. The entire syntax XMLObject["type"] is the head of the expression, while the remainder is a sequence of one or more arguments that depends on the type.

```
In[144]:= Head[data] // InputForm
Out[144]//InputForm=
            XMLObject["Document"]
```

The document version consists of three arguments: a list containing the declaration and possibly other objects, the document content, and a list of any objects (such as comments) that might appear past the last XML element. A very crude way to access structure is through Part[] or, equivalently, [[n]].

```
In[145]:=  data[[1]]
Out[145]=  {XMLObject[Declaration][Version → 1.0, Encoding → UTF-8],
             XMLObject[Comment][
               Some data to use as a test for Mathematica's XML import ],
             XMLObject[ProcessingInstruction][test, Just for didactic purposes]}

In[146]:=  data[[2]]
Out[146]=  XMLElement[data, {}, {XMLElement[item, {},
             {XMLElement[name, {}, {Leonardo}], XMLElement[sex, {}, {male}],
              XMLElement[age, {}, {8}], XMLElement[height, {}, {4.7}]}],
             XMLElement[item, {}, {XMLElement[name, {}, {Salvatore}],
              XMLElement[sex, {}, {male}], XMLElement[age, {}, {5}],
              XMLElement[height, {}, {4.1}]}], XMLElement[item, {},
             {XMLElement[name, {}, {Alexis}], XMLElement[sex, {}, {female}],
              XMLElement[age, {}, {6}], XMLElement[height, {}, {4.4}]}]}]

In[147]:=  data[[3]]
Out[147]=  {XMLObject[Comment][ Comment at end ]}

In[148]:=  data[[2]][[1]] (*The tag of the root element*)
Out[148]=  data

In[149]:=  data[[2]][[3]][[1]] (*The first child*)
Out[149]=  XMLElement[item, {},
             {XMLElement[name, {}, {Leonardo}], XMLElement[sex, {}, {male}],
              XMLElement[age, {}, {8}], XMLElement[height, {}, {4.7}]}]
```

Pattern matching is much more elegant and more resilient to changes in document structure. Here we extract male elements using Cases with a pattern and an infinite level specification. This is roughly equivalent to using *XPath* in native XML processing.

```
In[150]:=  Cases[data, XMLElement[_, _, {_, XMLElement["sex", _, {"male"}], ___}],
             Infinity] // TableForm
Out[150]//TableForm=
             XMLElement[item, {}, {XMLElement[name, {}, {Leonardo}], XMLElement[sex,
             {}, {male}], XMLElement[age, {}, {8}], XMLElement[height, {}, {4.7}]}]
             XMLElement[item, {}, {XMLElement[name, {}, {Salvatore}], XMLElement[sex,
             {}, {male}], XMLElement[age, {}, {5}], XMLElement[height, {}, {4.1}]}]
```

Sometimes, the XMLObject and XMLElement notation can be a bit too heavy, and it is easier to work with simple nested lists. This can be done with Apply plus List, specifying all levels.

```
In[151]:= list = Apply[List, data, {0, Infinity}]
Out[151]= {{{{Version, 1.0}, {Encoding, UTF-8}},
          { Some data to use as a test for Mathematica's XML import },
          {test, Just for didactic purposes}}, {data, {},
          {{item, {}, {{name, {}, {Leonardo}}, {sex, {}, {male}}, {age, {}, {8}},
            {height, {}, {4.7}}}}, {item, {}, {{name, {}, {Salvatore}},
             {sex, {}, {male}}, {age, {}, {5}}, {height, {}, {4.1}}}}},
          {item, {}, {{name, {}, {Alexis}}, {sex, {}, {female}},
            {age, {}, {6}}, {height, {}, {4.4}}}}}}, {{ Comment at end }}}
```

This can shorten the patterns needed to extract content.

```
In[152]:= Cases[list, {___, {"sex", _, {"male"}}, ___}, Infinity]
Out[152]= {{{name, {}, {Leonardo}}, {sex, {}, {male}},
          {age, {}, {8}}, {height, {}, {4.7}}}, {{name, {}, {Salvatore}},
          {sex, {}, {male}}, {age, {}, {5}}, {height, {}, {4.1}}}}
```

Another useful transformation is to change all heads to the symbolic form of the element tag. Here we use //. (ReplaceAll) with rules that strip XMLObject and convert XMLElement expressions. I show the output in tree form to make it clear what this transformation does.

```
In[153]:= data //. {XMLObject["Document"][_, content_, _] :> content,
          XMLElement["data", attrs_, content_] :> XMLElement["items",
            attrs, content], XMLElement[tag_String, _, {content__}] :>
          Symbol[tag] @@ {content}} // TreeForm[#, ImageSize -> 600] &
Out[153]//TreeForm=
```

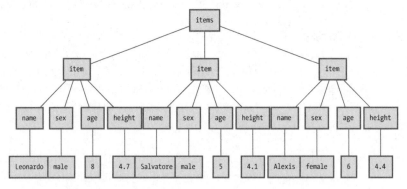

When converting strings to symbols, you need to be cognizant of whether a symbol already exists and has a value. This bit me when I was preparing this recipe, because I failed to recognize that the top-level element tag name was "data," which, of course, turned out to be the name of the variable that I was transforming. Infinite recursion! The solution was to include the transformation from XMLElement["data", attrs_, content_] to XMLElement["items", attrs, content] as the first transformation.

See Also

Recipes 5.9 and 5.10 show you how to transform imported XML into other structures.

5.9 Transforming XML Using Patterns and Rules

Problem

You want to transform imported XML into something more suitable to mathematical manipulation.

Solution

The format of imported XML is a bit heavy. You use pattern matching and ReplaceAll to transform it into something more digestible. Here we take our row-oriented XML data into a simple matrix.

```
In[154]:= data = Import[FileNameJoin[
              {NotebookDirectory[], "..", "data", "ch02", "data1.xml"}], "XMLObject"];

In[155]:= Cases[data , XMLElement["item", _, _], Infinity] /.
              XMLElement[_, _, {val_}] :> val /.
              XMLElement["item", _, list_] :> list /. {n_, s_, age_, ht_} →
              {n, s, ToExpression[age], ToExpression[ht]} // MatrixForm
Out[155]//MatrixForm=
              ⎛ Leonardo    male    8  4.7 ⎞
              ⎜ Salvatore   male    5  4.1 ⎟
              ⎝ Alexis      female  6  4.4 ⎠
```

This technique has two basic steps. First, you use Cases to extract the relevant elements. Second, you use a series of one or more transformations to massage the data into the form you want. In the first transformation, elements are taken to primitive values. Here you rely on the column position to determine when strings need conversion into numbers via ToExpression[]. The second transformation strips out the remaining XMLElement content. Until you have some experience with these types of transformations it is unlikely that you'll whip them up off the top of your head. The final form of this transformation reflects the fact that I developed it in stages. Here are the successive refinements.

Choose the relevant elements.

```
In[156]:= Cases[data, XMLElement["item", _, _], Infinity]
Out[156]= {XMLElement[item, {},
              {XMLElement[name, {}, {Leonardo}], XMLElement[sex, {}, {male}],
               XMLElement[age, {}, {8}], XMLElement[height, {}, {4.7}]}],
            XMLElement[item, {}, {XMLElement[name, {}, {Salvatore}],
               XMLElement[sex, {}, {male}], XMLElement[age, {}, {5}],
               XMLElement[height, {}, {4.1}]}], XMLElement[item, {},
              {XMLElement[name, {}, {Alexis}], XMLElement[sex, {}, {female}],
               XMLElement[age, {}, {6}], XMLElement[height, {}, {4.4}]}]}}
```

Strip out the data-level XML structure.

```
In[157]:= Cases[data, XMLElement["item", _, _], Infinity] /.
          XMLElement[_, _, {val_}] :> val
Out[157]= {XMLElement[item, {}, {Leonardo, male, 8, 4.7}],
            XMLElement[item, {}, {Salvatore, male, 5, 4.1}],
            XMLElement[item, {}, {Alexis, female, 6, 4.4}]}
```

Strip out the row-level XML structure, leaving the data in matrix form but all the primitive values as strings.

```
In[158]:= Cases[data, XMLElement["item", _, _], Infinity] /.
          XMLElement[_, _, {val_}] :> val /. XMLElement["item", _, list_] :> list
Out[158]= {{Leonardo, male, 8, 4.7}, {Salvatore, male, 5, 4.1}, {Alexis, female, 6, 4.4}}
```

Finally, do the type conversion.

```
In[159]:= Cases[data, XMLElement["item", _, _], Infinity] /.
           XMLElement[_, _, {val_}] :> val /.
           XMLElement["item", _, list_] :> list /.
           {n_, s_, age_, ht_} -> {n, s, ToExpression[age], ToExpression[ht]}
Out[159]= {{Leonardo, male, 8, 4.7}, {Salvatore, male, 5, 4.1}, {Alexis, female, 6, 4.4}}
```

Discussion

There are always many ways to solve the same transformation problem. The trade-offs involve brevity, clarity, generality, and performance. The solution has clarity, because it accomplishes the transformation in a step-by-step fashion. However, it is neither brief nor very general. The following transformation does the same thing but is more general. It will work on any two-level XML document because it does not match on specific element names (like "item"). It also does not hardcode which columns contain numeric data. However, it is a bit more cryptic because it does not mention XMLElement at all. Rather, it immediately converts the data to a list (using Apply with head List), and it uses [[n]] to pick out the relevant items.

```
In[160]:= toMatrix[xml_] :=
            Apply[List, xml[[2]], {0, Infinity}][[3]] /. {_, {}, row_} :> row /.
            {_, {}, {val_}} :>
              If[StringMatchQ[val, NumberString], ToExpression[val], val]
          toMatrix[data] // MatrixForm
Out[161]//MatrixForm=
          ⎛ Leonardo   male    8  4.7 ⎞
          ⎜ Salvatore  male    5  4.1 ⎟
          ⎝  Alexis    female  6  4.4 ⎠
```

I demonstrate the generality by processing an XML file with a different number of rows, columns, and data types.

```
In[162]:= toMatrix[Import[
            FileNameJoin[{NotebookDirectory[], "..", "data", "ch02", "data2.xml"}],
            "XMLObject"]] // MatrixForm
Out[162]//MatrixForm=
          ⎛ 1.   88.33  8  1000  4.7  ⎞
          ⎜ 2.   99.66  5  1001  4.1  ⎟
          ⎜ 3.   89.7   6  1002  4.4  ⎟
          ⎝ 1.5  99.7   6  1008  4.45 ⎠
```

XML-to-XML transformations

You may find that you need to transform XML for reasons other than using the data in Mathematica. Unless you already know a language specifically designed for this purpose (like XSLT), Mathematica is a good choice. Mathematica's pattern-matching capabilities are well suited to many types of XML transformations. Consider the problem of converting elements to attributes.

```
In[163]:= dataUsingAttr =
            data /. XMLElement["item", {}, childElements_] :> XMLElement["item",
              childElements /. XMLElement[tag_, _, {val_}] :> Rule[tag, val], {}]
Out[163]= XMLObject[Document][
            {XMLObject[Declaration][Version → 1.0, Encoding → UTF-8],
             XMLObject[Comment][
               Some data to use as a test for Mathematica's XML import ],
             XMLObject[ProcessingInstruction][test, Just for didactic purposes]},
            XMLElement[data, {},
              {XMLElement[item, {name → Leonardo, sex → male, age → 8, height → 4.7}, {}],
               XMLElement[item, {name → Salvatore, sex → male, age → 5, height → 4.1},
                 {}], XMLElement[item,
                 {name → Alexis, sex → female, age → 6, height → 4.4}, {}]}],
            {XMLObject[Comment][ Comment at end ]}]
```

It is a bit easier to see how this worked by converting back to XML text. The stripping of carriage returns (\r) is only for formatting purposes.

```
In[164]:= StringReplace[ExportString[dataUsingAttr, "XML"], "\r" → ""]
Out[164]= <?xml version='1.0' encoding='UTF-8'?>
          <!-- Some data to uses as a test for Mathematica's XML import -->
          <?test Just for didactic purposes?>
          <data>
            <item name='Leonardo'
                sex='male'
                age='8'
                height='4.7' />
            <item name='Salvatore'
                sex='male'
                age='5'
                height='4.1' />
            <item name='Alexis'
                sex='female'
                 age='6'
                height='4.4' />
          </data>
          <!-- Comment at end -->
```

A transformation from attributes to elements follows similar lines. The use of Join[ ] here is not strictly necessary, but it shows you how to handle cases in which you don't want to lose preexisting child elements at the point where you are injecting attribute content.

```
In[165]:= dataUsingElems =
            dataUsingAttr /. XMLElement["item", attrs_, childElements_] :→
              XMLElement["item", {}, Join[childElements,
                attrs /. Rule[tag_, val_] :→ XMLElement[tag, {}, {val}]]]
```

```
Out[165]= XMLObject[Document][
            {XMLObject[Declaration][Version → 1.0, Encoding → UTF-8],
             XMLObject[Comment][
                Some data to use as a test for Mathematica's XML import ],
             XMLObject[ProcessingInstruction][test, Just for didactic purposes]},
            XMLElement[data, {}, {XMLElement[item, {},
               {XMLElement[name, {}, {Leonardo}], XMLElement[sex, {}, {male}],
                XMLElement[age, {}, {8}], XMLElement[height, {}, {4.7}]}],
              XMLElement[item, {}, {XMLElement[name, {}, {Salvatore}],
                XMLElement[sex, {}, {male}], XMLElement[age, {}, {5}],
                XMLElement[height, {}, {4.1}]}], XMLElement[item, {},
               {XMLElement[name, {}, {Alexis}], XMLElement[sex, {}, {female}],
                XMLElement[age, {}, {6}], XMLElement[height, {}, {4.4}]}]}],
            {XMLObject[Comment][ Comment at end ]}]

In[166]:= StringReplace[ExportString[dataUsingElems, "XML"], "\r" → ""]
Out[166]= <?xml version='1.0' encoding='UTF-8'?>
          <!-- Some data to use as a test for Mathematica's XML import -->
          <?test Just for didactic purposes?>
          <data>
           <item>
            <name>Leonardo</name>
            <sex>male</sex>
            <age>8</age>
            <height>4.7</height>
           </item>
           <item>
            <name>Salvatore</name>
            <sex>male</sex>
            <age>5</age>
            <height>4.1</height>
           </item>
           <item>
            <name>Alexis</name>
            <sex>female</sex>
            <age>6</age>
            <height>4.4</height>
           </item>
          </data>
          <!-- Comment at end -->
```

See Also

See the tutorial *XML/tutorial/TransformingXML* in the Mathematica documentation (also at *http://bit.ly/4tS1Ce*).

Recipe 5.10 shows alternate techniques for XML transformation.

5.10 Transforming XML Using Recursive Functions (à la XSLT)

Problem

The pure pattern-based approach of Recipe 5.9 is too awkward, cryptic, or complex for your particular transformation problem.

Solution

Consider using an approach inspired by Extensible Stylesheet Language Transforms (XSLT). XSLT is a language that is specifically designed to transform XML. There are some rough similarities between XSLT and a style of Mathematica programming that exploits functions, patterns, and recursion. Here is how you use Mathematica to process XML in ways similar to XSLT. Consider the Recipe 5.9 transformation of elements to attributes. Rather than rely on replacement, we use a set of mutually recursive functions with patterns to navigate the XML tree while surgically inserting transformations at the correct places.

```
In[167]:= data = Import[FileNameJoin[
              {NotebookDirectory[], "..", "data", "ch02", "data1.xml"}], "XMLObject"]

Out[167]= XMLObject[Document][
              {XMLObject[Declaration][Version → 1.0, Encoding → UTF-8],
               XMLObject[Comment][
                 Some data to use as a test for Mathematica's XML import ],
               XMLObject[ProcessingInstruction][test, Just for didactic purposes]},
             XMLElement[data, {}, {XMLElement[item, {},
                {XMLElement[name, {}, {Leonardo}], XMLElement[sex, {}, {male}],
                 XMLElement[age, {}, {8}], XMLElement[height, {}, {4.7}]}],
               XMLElement[item, {}, {XMLElement[name, {}, {Salvatore}],
                 XMLElement[sex, {}, {male}], XMLElement[age, {}, {5}],
                 XMLElement[height, {}, {4.1}]}], XMLElement[item, {},
                {XMLElement[name, {}, {Alexis}], XMLElement[sex, {}, {female}],
                 XMLElement[age, {}, {6}], XMLElement[height, {}, {4.4}]}]}],
             {XMLObject[Comment][ Comment at end ]}]
```

```
In[168]:=  ClearAll[transform]
           transform[XMLObject["Document"][decl_, content_, rest_]] :=
            Module[{}, XMLObject[type][decl, transform[content], rest] ]
           transform[XMLObject[type_][args___]] :=
            Module[{}, XMLObject[type][args] ]
           transform[XMLElement["item", _, elements__]] :=
            Module[{}, XMLElement["item", asAttribute[#] & /@ elements, {}] ]
           transform[XMLElement[tag_String, attrs_List, child_List]] :=
            Module[{}, XMLElement[tag, attrs, transform[child]] ]
           transform[list_List] := Module[{}, transform[#] & /@ list ]
           asAttribute[XMLElement[tag_, {}, {val_}]] :=
            Module[{}, Rule[tag, val] ]
In[175]:=  transform[data]
Out[175]=  XMLObject[type][
            {XMLObject[Declaration][Version → 1.0, Encoding → UTF-8], XMLObject[
               Comment][ Some data to use as a test for Mathematica's XML import ],
             XMLObject[ProcessingInstruction][test, Just for didactic purposes]},
            XMLElement[data, {},
             {XMLElement[item, {name → Leonardo, sex → male, age → 8, height → 4.7}, {}],
              XMLElement[item, {name → Salvatore, sex → male, age → 5, height → 4.1},
               {}], XMLElement[item,
               {name → Alexis, sex → female, age → 6, height → 4.4}, {}]}],
            {XMLObject[Comment][ Comment at end ]}]
```

Discussion

A natural objection to using this style of transformation rather than using replacement rules is that it is more verbose. This verbosity comes with some advantages. The first advantage is that when things go wrong, it is generally easier to debug a set of discrete functions than a replacement pattern. Most of the action of a replacement pattern is happening under the covers. The second advantage comes in cases where you need to make many changes at different levels in the XML hierarchy. Here the overhead of the recursive approach is less bothersome. We implement a transformation that changes elements to attributes, renames the "item" element to "row", changes "sex" to "gender", and converts the height from feet to meters—all with very little extra overhead.

```
In[176]:= ClearAll[transform]
          transform[XMLObject["Document"][decl_, content_, rest_]] :=
           Module[{}, XMLObject["Document"][decl, transform[content], rest] ]
          transform[XMLObject[type_][args___]] :=
           Module[{}, XMLObject[type][args]]
          transform[XMLElement["item", _, elements__] ] :=
           Module[{}, XMLElement["row", asAttribute[#] & /@ elements, {}] ]
          transform[list_List] := Module[{}, transform[#] & /@ list ]
          transform[XMLElement[tag_String, attrs_List, child_List]] :=
           Module[{}, XMLElement[tag, attrs, transform[child]]]
          asAttribute[XMLElement["sex", {}, {val_}]] :=
           Module[{}, Rule["gender", val] ]
          asAttribute[XMLElement["height", {}, {val_}]] :=
           Module[{}, Rule["height", ToString[0.3048 * ToExpression[val]]] ]
          asAttribute[XMLElement[tag_, {}, {val_}]] := Module[{}, Rule[tag, val] ]

In[185]:= data2 = transform[data]

Out[185]= XMLObject[Document][
            {XMLObject[Declaration][Version → 1.0, Encoding → UTF-8],
             XMLObject[Comment][
               Some data to use as a test for Mathematica's XML import ],
             XMLObject[ProcessingInstruction][test, Just for didactic purposes]},
            XMLElement[data, {}, {XMLElement[row,
               {name → Leonardo, gender → male, age → 8, height → 1.43256}, {}],
              XMLElement[row, {name → Salvatore, gender → male,
                age → 5, height → 1.24968}, {}], XMLElement[row,
                {name → Alexis, gender → female, age → 6, height → 1.34112}, {}]}],
            {XMLObject[Comment][ Comment at end ]}]
```

```
In[186]:=  ExportString[data2, "XML"] // StringReplace[#, "\r" → ""] &
Out[186]=  <?xml version='1.0' encoding='UTF-8'?>
           <!-- Some data to use as a test for Mathematica's XML import -->
           <?test Just for didactic purposes?>
           <data>
            <row name='Leonardo'
               gender='male'
               age='8'
               height='1.43256' />
            <row name='Salvatore'
               gender='male'
               age='5'
               height='1.24968' />
            <row name='Alexis'
               gender='female'
               age='6'
               height='1.34112' />
           </data>
           <!-- Comment at end -->
```

One of the first things you learn about XSLT is that if you create an empty stylesheet
(XSLT's equivalent of a program), you get some default transformation rules that act
to output just the text nodes of the XML data. We can emulate that behavior in
Mathematica with the following functions.

```
In[187]:=  ClearAll[transform]
           transform[XMLObject[type_][content__]] :=
            StringJoin[transform[#] & /@ List[content]]
           transform[XMLElement[tag_, attrs_List, data_List]] :=
            StringJoin[transform[#] & /@ data ]
           transform[text_String] := text
           transform[_] := ""

In[192]:=  transform[data]
Out[192]=  Leonardomale84.7Salvatoremale54.1Alexisfemale64.4
```

So far, so good, but can we do something more interesting? Suppose we want to clone our XML document but replace all occurrences of the element "sex" with the element "gender".

```
In[193]:= ClearAll[transform]

In[194]:= transform[XMLObject[type_][content__]] :=
            Module[{}, XMLObject[type][transform[List[content]]] ]
          transform[XMLElement["sex", attrs_List, data_List]] :=
            Module[{}, XMLElement["gender", attrs, transform[data]]]
          transform[XMLElement[tag_String, attrs_List, data_List]] :=
            Module[{}, XMLElement[tag, attrs, transform[data]] ]
          transform[list_List] := Module[{}, transform[#] & /@ list ]
          transform[text_String] := Module[{}, text]


In[199]:= transform[data]

Out[199]= XMLObject[Document][{{XMLObject[Declaration][{transform[Version → 1.0],
              transform[Encoding → UTF-8]}], XMLObject[Comment][
              { Some data to use as a test for Mathematica's XML import }],
            XMLObject[ProcessingInstruction][{test, Just for didactic purposes}]},
          XMLElement[data, {}, {XMLElement[item, {},
            {XMLElement[name, {}, {Leonardo}], XMLElement[gender, {}, {male}],
             XMLElement[age, {}, {8}], XMLElement[height, {}, {4.7}]}],
           XMLElement[item, {}, {XMLElement[name, {}, {Salvatore}],
             XMLElement[gender, {}, {male}], XMLElement[age, {}, {5}],
             XMLElement[height, {}, {4.1}]}], XMLElement[item, {},
            {XMLElement[name, {}, {Alexis}], XMLElement[gender, {}, {female}],
             XMLElement[age, {}, {6}], XMLElement[height, {}, {4.4}]}]}],
          {XMLObject[Comment][{ Comment at end }]}}]
```

This recursive transformational approach is overkill in this scenario since we can more easily express this transformation using ReplaceAll.

```
In[200]:=  data /. "sex" → "gender"
Out[200]=  XMLObject[Document][
              {XMLObject[Declaration][Version → 1.0, Encoding → UTF-8],
               XMLObject[Comment][
                 Some data to use as a test for Mathematica's XML import ],
               XMLObject[ProcessingInstruction][test, Just for didactic purposes]},
              XMLElement[data, {}, {XMLElement[item, {},
                 {XMLElement[name, {}, {Leonardo}], XMLElement[gender, {}, {male}],
                  XMLElement[age, {}, {8}], XMLElement[height, {}, {4.7}]}],
                XMLElement[item, {}, {XMLElement[name, {}, {Salvatore}],
                  XMLElement[gender, {}, {male}], XMLElement[age, {}, {5}],
                  XMLElement[height, {}, {4.1}]}], XMLElement[item, {},
                 {XMLElement[name, {}, {Alexis}], XMLElement[gender, {}, {female}],
                  XMLElement[age, {}, {6}], XMLElement[height, {}, {4.4}]}]}],
              {XMLObject[Comment][ Comment at end ]}]
```

There are certain types of structure-adding transformations that were difficult to do in XSLT until a grouping construct was added (xsl:for-each-group) in XSLT 2.0. Here is a solution to a grouping problem using Mathematica's Sort[] and Split[] functions.

```
In[201]:= employees =
            Import[FileNameJoin[{NotebookDirectory[],
              "..", "data", "ch02", "employee.xml"}], "XMLObject"]

Out[201]= XMLObject[Document][
            {XMLObject[Declaration][Version → 1.0, Encoding → UTF-8]},
            XMLElement[Employees, {},
             {XMLElement[employee, {name → Jil Michel, sex → female, dept → 1001}, {}],
              XMLElement[employee, {name → Nancy Pratt, sex → female, dept → 1001}, {}],
              XMLElement[employee,
               {name → Phill McKraken, sex → male, dept → 1003}, {}],
              XMLElement[employee, {name → Ima Little, sex → female, dept → 1001}, {}],
              XMLElement[employee, {name → Betsy Ross, sex → female, dept → 1007}, {}],
              XMLElement[employee, {name → Jane Doe, sex → female, dept → 1003}, {}],
              XMLElement[employee, {name → Walter H. Potter, sex → male, dept → 2001},
               {}], XMLElement[employee,
               {name → Wendy B.K. McDonald, sex → female, dept → 2003}, {}],
              XMLElement[employee, {name → Craig F. Frye, sex → male, dept → 1001}, {}],
              XMLElement[employee, {name → Hardy Hamburg, sex → male, dept → 2001}, {}],
              XMLElement[employee, {name → Rich Shaker, sex → male, dept → 2001}, {}],
              XMLElement[employee, {name → Mike Rosenbaum, sex → male, dept → 2003},
               {}], XMLElement[employee,
               {name → Cindy Post-Kellog, sex → female, dept → 3001}, {}],
              XMLElement[employee, {name → Allen Bran, sex → male, dept → 3001}, {}],
              XMLElement[employee, {name → Frank N. Berry, sex → male, dept → 1001},
               {}], XMLElement[employee,
               {name → Jack Apple, sex → male, dept → 2001}, {}], XMLElement[
               employee, {name → Oscar A. Winner, sex → male, dept → 3003}, {}],
              XMLElement[employee, {name → Jack Nickolas, sex → male, dept → 1001}, {}],
              XMLElement[employee, {name → R.P. McMurphy, sex → male, dept → 1001}, {}],
              XMLElement[employee, {name → Tom Hanks, sex → male, dept → 2001}, {}],
              XMLElement[employee, {name → Forest Gump, sex → male, dept → 2003}, {}],
              XMLElement[employee, {name → Andrew Beckett, sex → male, dept → 3001},
               {}], XMLElement[employee,
               {name → Susan Sarandon, sex → female, dept → 1001}, {}], XMLElement[
               employee, {name → Helen Prejean, sex → female, dept → 2001}, {}]}], {}]
```

The goal of this transformation is to group all employees in the same department under a new element <Dept dept="**num**">. Notice how this is accomplished with little additional code. Helper functions define an ordering and an equivalence relation for Sort and OrderQ, respectively, and a transform[] applies the additional level of grouping when it matches the "employees" element.

```
In[202]:= ClearAll[transform]
          getDept[XMLElement[_, {__, "dept" → dept_}, {}]] := dept
          sameDeptQ[a_, b_] := Module[{}, Order[getDept[a], getDept[b]] == 0]
          orderDept[a_, b_] := Module[{}, Order[getDept[a], getDept[b]] == 1]
          transform[XMLObject["Document"][decl_, content_, rest_]] :=
           Module[{}, XMLObject["Document"][decl, transform[content], rest]]
          transform[XMLObject[type_][args___]] :=
           Module[{}, XMLObject[type][args]]
          transform[XMLElement["Employees", _, elements__]] :=
           Module[{}, XMLElement["Employees", {},
             XMLElement["Dept", {"dept" → getDept[#[[1]]]}, #] & /@
              Split[Sort[elements, orderDept], sameDeptQ]]]
          transform[list_List] := Module[{}, transform[#] & /@ list]
          transform[XMLElement[tag_String, attrs_List, child_List]] :=
           Module[{}, XMLElement[tag, attrs, transform[child]]]
```

```
In[211]:=  transform[employees]
Out[211]=  XMLObject[Document][
           {XMLObject[Declaration][Version → 1.0, Encoding → UTF-8]},
           XMLElement[Employees, {}, {XMLElement[Dept, {dept → 1001},
             {XMLElement[employee, {name → Susan Sarandon, sex → female, dept → 1001},
               {}], XMLElement[employee, {name → R.P. McMurphy,
                 sex → male, dept → 1001}, {}], XMLElement[employee,
                 {name → Jack Nickolas, sex → male, dept → 1001}, {}], XMLElement[
                 employee, {name → Frank N. Berry, sex → male, dept → 1001}, {}],
               XMLElement[employee, {name → Craig F. Frye, sex → male, dept → 1001},
                 {}], XMLElement[employee, {name → Ima Little,
                   sex → female, dept → 1001}, {}], XMLElement[employee,
                 {name → Nancy Pratt, sex → female, dept → 1001}, {}], XMLElement[
                 employee, {name → Jil Michel, sex → female, dept → 1001}, {}]}],
             XMLElement[Dept, {dept → 1003}, {XMLElement[employee,
               {name → Jane Doe, sex → female, dept → 1003}, {}], XMLElement[
                 employee, {name → Phill McKraken, sex → male, dept → 1003}, {}]}],
             XMLElement[Dept, {dept → 1007}, {XMLElement[employee,
               {name → Betsy Ross, sex → female, dept → 1007}, {}]}],
             XMLElement[Dept, {dept → 2001}, {XMLElement[employee,
               {name → Helen Prejean, sex → female, dept → 2001}, {}],
               XMLElement[employee, {name → Tom Hanks, sex → male, dept → 2001}, {}],
               XMLElement[employee, {name → Jack Apple, sex → male, dept → 2001}, {}],
               XMLElement[employee, {name → Rich Shaker, sex → male, dept → 2001}, {}],
               XMLElement[employee, {name → Hardy Hamburg, sex → male, dept → 2001},
                 {}], XMLElement[employee, {name → Walter H. Potter, sex → male,
                   dept → 2001}, {}]}], XMLElement[Dept, {dept → 2003},
               {XMLElement[employee, {name → Forest Gump, sex → male, dept → 2003}, {}],
               XMLElement[employee, {name → Mike Rosenbaum, sex → male, dept → 2003},
                 {}], XMLElement[employee,
                 {name → Wendy B.K. McDonald, sex → female, dept → 2003}, {}]}],
             XMLElement[Dept, {dept → 3001}, {XMLElement[employee,
               {name → Andrew Beckett, sex → male, dept → 3001}, {}],
               XMLElement[employee, {name → Allen Bran, sex → male, dept → 3001}, {}],
               XMLElement[employee,
                 {name → Cindy Post-Kellog, sex → female, dept → 3001}, {}]}],
             XMLElement[Dept, {dept → 3003}, {XMLElement[employee,
               {name → Oscar A. Winner, sex → male, dept → 3003}, {}]}]}], {}]
```

Of course, there are significant differences between these transformations and XSLT. For example, in XSLT, you operate on a tree and, hence, can navigate upward from child elements to parent elements. This is not the case for Mathematica's representation of XML. The tutorial mentioned in the following "See Also" section provides some guidance for working around these issues.

See Also

The tutorial *XML/tutorial/TransformingXML* in the Mathematica documentation (also at *http://bit.ly/4tS1Ce*) has a section comparing Mathematica to XSLT and can provide further help in exploiting these techniques.

You can learn more about XSLT at the XSL Working Group's website: *http://bit.ly/1fJsB*.

5.11 Writing Parsers and Grammars in Mathematica

Problem

You want to write a parser in Mathematica.

Solution

The easiest type of parser to write in Mathematica is a recursive descent parser. Before writing the parser, we need to know the grammar of the language we will parse. The most common notation for grammars is Backus-Naur Form (BNF), but for reasons that will become apparent in the discussion, I use Mathematica itself to represent the grammar. For this example, I use a simplified English grammar. The presentation here is a variation of one developed and given by Daniel Lichtblau of Wolfram Research at the Wolfram Developer's Conference in 1999. Refer to the "See Also" section on page 235 for more information.

First, we need some helper functions to make creating the grammar easier. We use two functions, sequence and choose, with attribute HoldAll to prevent them from evaluating their arguments and causing an infinite recursion. As its name would suggest, sequence[] represents a sequence of terms of the grammar. Choose represents a choice of one out of two or more possible terms. I allow choose to take an extra argument, which is a list of probabilities for the choices. More on that later.

```
In[212]:=  SetAttributes[{sequence, choose}, HoldAll]
           NILL = "";
```

This grammar is for a small subset of English.

```
In[214]:= sentence := choose[declarative, interrogative, imperative]
          declarative := sequence[subject, predicatepast]
          interrogative := sequence[qverb, subject, predicatepresent]
          imperative := sequence[actverb, subject]
          subject := choose[nounclause, sequence[nounclause, prepositionclause]]
          nounclause := sequence[adjectiveclause, noun]
          noun = {"skyscraper", "ball", "dog", "cow", "shark", "attorney", "hatter",
              "programmer", "city", "village", "buffalo", "moon", "librarian", "sheep"};
          adjectiveclause := sequence[article, adjectivelist]
          adjectivelist := choose[NILL, sequence[adjective, adjectivelist], {0.7}]
          article = {"a", "the", "this", "that"};
          adjective =
              {"big", "wet", "mad", "hideous", "red", "repugnant", "slimy", "delectable",
               "mild-mannered", "lazy", "silly", "crazy", "ferocious", "cute"};
          prepositionclause := sequence[preposition, nounclause ]
          preposition = {"in", "above", "under", "from", "near", "at", "with"} ;
          predicatepresent := sequence[verbpresent, subject]
          predicatepast := sequence[verbclause, subject]
          verbclause := sequence[adverblist, verbpast]
          adverblist := choose[NILL, sequence[adverb, adverblist ], {0.6}]
          adverb =
              {"swiftly", "unflinchingly", "smugly", "selflessly", "oddly", "mightily"};
          verbpast = {"ate", "threw", "gnashed", "boiled",
              "grated", "milked", "spanked", "jumped"};
          verbpresent = {"eat", "throw", "gnash", "boil", "grate",
              "milk", "spank", "salivate", "jump"};
          qverb = {"did", "will", "could", "should"};
          actverb = {"break", "fix", "launch", "squeeze", "fetch"};

In[236]:= ToUpperCase[StringTake[ToString[Hold[sentence]], {6, -2}]]
Out[236]= SENTENCE
```

This grammar becomes the specification for our parser. Recursive descent parsers are probably the easiest parsers to craft by hand because their structure mimics the grammar. The goal of this parser is to create a labeled parse tree from a sentence. The parser is very simple: it contains no provision for error handling and relies on the grammar being completely conflict free. For example, the major sentence types are completely determined by the first word. Real languages or even artificial languages (like programming languages) are rarely that clean.

```
In[237]:= (*Test for membership of a terminal
          symbol in a list of terminal symbols.*)
          isQ[type_, word_] := MemberQ[type, word]

          (*Get next word for parser.*)
          getNextWord[{}] := ""
          getNextWord[words_List] := First[words]

          (*Parse a single word, classifying it as head, and return length of 1.*)
          atomParse[head_, words_List] := {head[getNextWord[words]], 1}

          (*Top level parse function for
           sentences. Dispatches based on first word.*)
          sentenceParse[sentence_sentenceType] :=
           Module[{sentencelist = Apply[List, sentence], firstWord},
            firstWord = First[sentencelist];
            If[isQ[qverb, firstWord], interrogativeParse[sentencelist],
             If[isQ[actverb, firstWord], imperativeParse[sentencelist],
              declarativeParse[sentencelist]]]]

          (*declarative := sequence[subject, predicatepast]*)
          declarativeParse[words_List] :=
           Module[{subject = subjectParse[words], predicate},
            predicate = predicatepastParse[Drop[words, subject[[2]]]];
            "DECLARATIVE SENTENCE"[subject[[1]], predicate[[1]]]]

          (*interrogative := sequence[qverb, subject, predicatepresent]*)
          interrogativeParse[words_List] :=
           Module[{qverb = atomParse["QUESTION VERB", words], subject, predicate},
            subject = subjectParse[Drop[words, qverb[[2]]]];
            predicate = predicatepresentParse[
              Drop[words, qverb[[2]] + subject[[2]]]];
            "INTERROGATIVE SENTENCE"[qverb[[1]], subject[[1]], predicate[[1]]]]
            (**)

          (*imperative := sequence[actverb, subject]*)
          imperativeParse[words_List] :=
           Module[{actverb = atomParse["ACTION VERB", words], subject},
            subject = subjectParse[Drop[words, actverb[[2]]]];
            "IMPERATIVE SENTENCE"[actverb[[1]], subject[[1]]]]
```

```
(*subject :=
 choose[nounclause,  sequence[nounclause, prepositionclause]]*)
subjectParse[words_List] :=
 Module[{nounclause = nounclauseParse[words], prepositionclause},
  prepositionclause = Drop[words, nounclause[[2]]];
  If[! isQ[preposition, getNextWord[prepositionclause]],
   {"SUBJECT"[nounclause[[1]]], nounclause[[2]]},
   prepositionclause = prepositionclauseParse[prepositionclause];
   {"SUBJECT"[nounclause[[1]], prepositionclause[[1]]],
    nounclause[[2]] + prepositionclause[[2]]}]]


(*predicatepast:=sequence[verbclause,subject]*)
predicatepastParse[words_List] :=
 Module[{verbclause = verbclauseParse[words], subject},
  subject = subjectParse[Drop[words, verbclause[[2]]]];
  {"PREDICATE"[verbclause[[1]], subject[[1]]],
   verbclause[[2]] + subject[[2]]}]


(*predicatepresent:=sequence[verbpresent,subject]*)
predicatepresentParse[words_List] :=
 Module[{verb = atomParse["VERB (PRESENT TENSE)", words], subject},
  subject = subjectParse[Drop[words, verb[[2]]]];
  {"PREDICATE"[verb[[1]], subject[[1]]], verb[[2]] + subject[[2]]}]


(*verbclause:=sequence[adverblist,verbpast]*)
verbclauseParse[words_List] :=
 Module[{adverbs = adverblistParse[words], verb},
  verb = atomParse["VERB (PAST TENSE)", Drop[words, adverbs[[2]]]];
  If[adverbs[[2]] == 0, verb,
   {"VERB CLAUSE"[adverbs[[1]], verb[[1]]], adverbs[[2]] + verb[[2]]}]]


(*nounclause:= sequence[adjectiveclause, noun]*)
nounclauseParse[words_List] :=
 Module[{adjectiveclause = adjectiveclauseParse[words], noun},
  noun = atomParse["NOUN", Drop[words, adjectiveclause[[2]]]];
  {"NOUN CLAUSE"[adjectiveclause[[1]], noun[[1]]],
   adjectiveclause[[2]] + noun[[2]]}]


(*adjectiveclause := sequence[article, adjectivelist]*)
adjectiveclauseParse[words_List] :=
 Module[{art = atomParse["ARTICLE", words], adjlist},
  adjlist = adjectivelistParse[Drop[words, art[[2]]]];
```

```
    If[adjlist[[2]] == 0, art, {"ADJECTIVE CLAUSE"[art[[1]], adjlist[[1]]],
       art[[2]] + adjlist[[2]]}]]

(*Parse (possibly empty) list of adjectives.*)
(*adjectivelist :=
 choose[NILL, sequence[adjective, adjectivelist], {0.7}]*)
adjectivelistParse[words_List] :=
 Module[{words2 = words, adj, result, len = 0}, result = "ADJECTIVE LIST"[];
  While[isQ[adjective, getNextWord[words2]],
   adj = atomParse["ADJECTIVE", words2];
   len += adj[[2]];
   result = "ADJECTIVE LIST"[result, adj[[1]]];
   words2 = Drop[words2, adj[[2]]]];
  {Flatten[result, Infinity, "ADJECTIVE LIST"], len}]

(*prepositionclause := sequence[preposition, nounclause]*)
prepositionclauseParse[words_List] :=
 Module[{preposition = atomParse["PREPOSITION", words], nounclause},
  nounclause = nounclauseParse[Drop[words, preposition[[2]]]];
  {"PREPOSITION CLAUSE"[preposition[[1]], nounclause[[1]]],
   preposition[[2]] + nounclause[[2]]}]

(*Parse (possibly empty) list of adverbs.*)
(*adverblist := choose[NILL, sequence[adverb,adverblist], {0.6}]*)
adverblistParse[words_List] :=
 Module[{words2 = words, adv, result, len = 0}, result = "ADVERB LIST"[];
  While[isQ[adverb, getNextWord[words2]],
   adv = atomParse["ADVERB", words2];
   len += adv[[2]];
   result = "ADVERB LIST"[result, adv[[1]]];
   words2 = Drop[words2, adv[[2]]]];
  {Flatten[result, Infinity, "ADVERB LIST"], len}]
```

We can test the parser on a sentence that conforms to the grammar.

```
In[254]:= sentenceParse[
            sentenceType["will", "the", "wet", "programmer", "spank", "the", "moon"]]
Out[254]= INTERROGATIVE SENTENCE[QUESTION VERB[will],
            SUBJECT[NOUN CLAUSE[ADJECTIVE CLAUSE[ARTICLE[the],
                ADJECTIVE LIST[ADJECTIVE[wet]]], NOUN[programmer]]],
            PREDICATE[VERB (PRESENT TENSE)[spank],
             SUBJECT[NOUN CLAUSE[ARTICLE[the], NOUN[moon]]]]]
```

Discussion

You may wonder why I took the trouble to specify the grammar using Mathematica if I was going to write the parser by hand. First, I did not write this parser; I just prettied up a parser written by Daniel Lichtblau! The more serious answer is that the grammar can be used to easily create a language generator to go along with the parser. The generator is very useful for testing the parser. Here I based a generator on Lichtblau's implementation but made some significant improvements. The first improvement is that my implementation is more declarative than procedural because it leverages Mathematica's pattern matching. The second improvement is that the generator absorbs all the complexity so the grammar can remain very clean. In Lichtblau's original grammar, the representation was soiled by the presence of programmatic constructs, like Hold[] and his implementation of random choice. Other than the presence of probabilities, the grammar in the preceding "Solution" section is completely clean. In fact, it reads as easy as BNF. Refer to the URL in the "See Also" section on page 235 to compare this implementation with the original.

```
In[255]:=  << Combinatorica`
           (*needed for BinarySearch[]*)
           (*randomChoose[parts_List,probs_List] selects an item from
            parts_List based on a list of probabilities the length of
            which must be one less than the number of parts and the sum
            of which is less than one. The interpretation is that each
            probability corresponds to the probability of the item in the same
            position except for the last item, which gets the residual.*)
           randomChoose[parts_List, probs_List] := Module[{weights, test, pos},
             weights = N[Append[FoldList[Plus, First[probs], Rest[probs]], 1]];
             test = RandomReal[]; pos = Ceiling[BinarySearch[weights, test]];
             parts[[pos]]]
           (*randomPart[] is responsible for interpreting the grammar in
            a random manner. There is a variation for each possible term,
            and recursion is used to expand nonterminals.*)
           randomPart[sequence[parts__]] := randomPart[#] & /@ List[parts]
           randomPart[choose[parts__, probs_List]] :=
             Union[Flatten[List[randomPart[randomChoose[List[parts], probs]]]]]
           randomPart[choose[parts__]] := Module[{partList, numParts},
             partList = List[parts]; numParts = Length[partList];
             randomPart[randomChoose[partList, Table[1 / numParts, {numParts - 1}]]]]
           randomPart[terminals_List] :=
             terminals[[ RandomInteger[ {1, Length[terminals]} ] ]]
           randomPart[NILL] := {}
           (*randomSentence[] is the entry point for
            generating a random sentence of the grammar.*)
           randomSentence[] := sentenceType @@ Flatten[randomPart[sentence]]
           (*We provide a nice textual formatting for
            sentences that also takes care of punctuation.*)
           Format[sentence_sentenceType] :=
             Module[{word = First[sentence], words, punc},
               words = Map[StringJoin[#, " "] &, sentence];
               punc = If[isQ[qverb, word], "?", If[isQ[actverb, word], "!", "."]];
               words[[Length[words]]] = StringReplacePart[Last[words], punc, -1];
               words[[1]] = StringReplacePart[First[words],
                 ToUpperCase[StringTake[First[words], 1]], 1];
               Apply[StringJoin, words]]
```

Here you can see the result of generating 10 random sentences. They are, for the most part, utter gibberish, but some are kind of funny. They all conform to the grammar, as we can see by running them through the parser.

```
In[264]:= randomSentence[] // InputForm
Out[264]//InputForm=
            sentenceType["a", "city", "in", "that", "mad", "village", "threw", "the",
            "shark", "at", "a", "ball"]
```

```
In[265]:= Table[randomSentence[], {10}] // TableForm
Out[265]//TableForm=
            Launch this moon from the city!
            A skyscraper from a village ate a skyscraper in the attorney.
            "The delectable librarian above that red hatter spanked this buffalo above
            the big sheep."
            Will that programmer salivate that programmer?
            Could that mad silly ball spank this moon at that buffalo?
            This skyscraper under the cow boiled a village in that village.
            Squeeze a ball!
            "The crazy mad city in the skyscraper unflinchingly jumped this village
            above the skyscraper."
            Could a programmer spank the attorney?
            Fetch a programmer in this shark!
```

```
In[266]:= SeedRandom[2];
          sentenceParse[randomSentence[]] // TreeForm[#, ImageSize → 500] &
Out[267]//TreeForm=
```

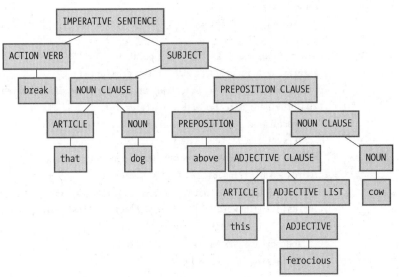

The parser we wrote by hand is an instance of a *predictive* recursive descent parser because it looks ahead wherever there is a choice so that it does not take a wrong path through the grammar. In contrast, a backtracking parser simply starts over from where it left off if a particular parse path fails. If you are ambitious, you can continue this recipe and write a backtracking parser generator in Mathematica. The references in the following "See Also" section provide some background.

See Also

See Daniel Lichtblau's original implementation at *http://bit.ly/zXhUm*.

Packrat parsing is amenable to Mathematica implementation. See *http://bit.ly/RsNCe*.

A functional approach to parsing is discussed in "Monadic Parser Combinators" by Graham Hutton and Erik Meijer, published in *Journal of Functional Programming,* Volume 8, Issue 4, 1996. See *http://bit.ly/PIVAh* (PostScript file).

CHAPTER 6

Two-Dimensional Graphics and Plots

I've been looking so long at these pictures of you
that I almost believe that they're real
I've been living so long with my pictures of you
that I almost believe that the pictures are all I can feel

The Cure, "Pictures of You"

6.0 Introduction

One of the features that places Mathematica in a class by itself among similar computer-aided mathematics tools is its advanced graphics capabilities. This chapter focuses on two-dimensional graphics. Mathematica provides a variety of plotting functions with a versatile set of options for customizing their display. The most common types of 2D graphic are the plot of a function and list plots of values. Recipe 6.1 covers Plot and Recipe 6.4 covers ListPlot. Frequently you will want to use other coordinate systems or scales. In two dimensions, PolarPlot and ParametricPlot are often used as demonstrated in Recipes 6.1 and 6.2.

True to its symbolic nature, Mathematica represents all graphics as collections of graphics primitives and directives. Primitives include objects such as Point and Line; directives provide styling information such as Thickness and Hue. Mathematica allows you to work with the low-level primitives (see Recipe 6.8), but most readers will be interested in the higher-level functions like Plot and ListPlot, which generate graphics from functions and data and display them. However, it is easy to demonstrate that these functions generate primitives by specifying InputForm.

```
In[1]:= ListPlot[{0, 1, 2, 3}] // InputForm
```

```
Out[1]//InputForm=
        Graphics[{Hue[0.67, 0.6, 0.6],
          Point[{{1., 0.}, {2., 1.}, {3., 2.}, {4., 3.}}]},
         {AspectRatio -> GoldenRatio^(-1), Axes -> True,
          AxesOrigin -> {0, Automatic},
          PlotRange -> Automatic, PlotRangeClipping -> True}]
```

This uniform representation allows graphics to be manipulated programmatically, just like any Mathematica object, and sometimes can be useful for generating custom effects. However, this representation is not entirely at the lowest level, because graphics constructs like axes are implicitly specified via options. To get to the lowest level you can use the function FullGraphics. Here I use Short to suppress some of the details.

```
In[2]:=  Short[InputForm[FullGraphics[ListPlot[{0, 1, 2, 3}]]], 10]
Out[2]//Short=
        Graphics[{{{Hue[0.67, 0.6, 0.6], Point[{{1., 0.}, {2., 1.}, {3.,
          2.}, {4., 3.}}]}, {{GrayLevel[0.], AbsoluteThickness[0.25],
          Line[{{0.2, 0.}, {0.2, 0.010112712429686845}}]}, Text[0.2,
          {0.2, -0.02022542485937369}, {0., 1.}], {GrayLevel[0.],
          AbsoluteThickness[0.25], Line[{{0.4, 0.}, {0.4,
          0.010112712429686845}}]}, Text[0.4, {0.4, -0.02022542485937369},
          {0., 1.}], {GrayLevel[0.], AbsoluteThickness[0.25],
          Line[{{0.6000000000000001, 0.}, {0.6000000000000001,
          0.010112712429686845}}]}, Text[0.6000000000000001,
          {0.6000000000000001, -0.02022542485937369}, {0., 1.}],
          {GrayLevel[0.], AbsoluteThickness[0.25], Line[{{0.8, 0.}, {0.8,
          0.010112712429686845}}]}, <<41>>, {GrayLevel[0.], <<2>>},
          {GrayLevel[0.], AbsoluteThickness[0.125], Line[{{0., 0.9}, {0.00375,
          0.9}}]}, {GrayLevel[0.], AbsoluteThickness[0.125], Line[{{0.,
          0.9500000000000001}, {0.00375, 0.9500000000000001}}]}, {GrayLevel[0.],
          AbsoluteThickness[0.25], Line[{{0., 0.}, {0., 1.}}]}}}}]
```

In the recipes that follow, I make frequent use of GraphicsRow, GraphicsColumn, and GraphicsGrid. These are handy for formatting multiple graphics outputs across the page to make maximum use of both horizontal and vertical space. Both GraphicsRow and GraphicsColumn take a list of graphics to format, whereas GraphicsGrid takes a matrix. To help generate these lists and matrices, I sometimes use Table and Partition. These functions are simple enough that I hope they do not detract from the intended lesson of the recipe. Recipe 6.6 explains the use of these grid-like formatting functions in detail.

6.1 Plotting Functions in Cartesian Coordinates

Problem

You want to graph one or more built-in or user-defined functions.

Solution

The simplest solution is to use the Plot command with the range of values to plot. Plot takes one or more functions of a single variable and an iterator of the form {var, min, max}.

```
In[3]:= GraphicsRow[{
            Plot[Erf[x], {x, -2, 2}],
            Plot[{0.5 Sin[2 x], Cos[3 x]}, {x, -Pi, Pi}]
        }]
```

Out[3]=

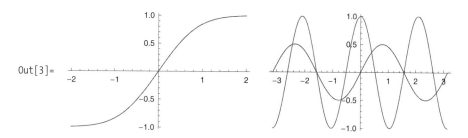

Discussion

Plot has a wide variety of options for controlling the appearance of the plot. Here are the defaults.

```
In[4]:= Partition[ Options[Plot] , 4] // TableForm
Out[4]//TableForm=
```

AlignmentPoint → Center	AspectRatio → 1/GoldenRatio	Axes → True	AxesLabel → None
AxesOrigin → Automatic	AxesStyle → {}	Background → None	BaselinePosition → Automatic
BaseStyle → {}	ClippingStyle → None	ColorFunction → Automatic	ColorFunctionScaling → True
ColorOutput → Automatic	ContentSelectable → Automatic	CoordinatesToolOptions → Automatic	DisplayFunction :→ $DisplayFunction
Epilog → {}	Evaluated → Automatic	EvaluationMonitor → None	Exclusions → Automatic
ExclusionsStyle → None	Filling → None	FillingStyle → Automatic	FormatType :→ TraditionalForm
Frame → False	FrameLabel → None	FrameStyle → {}	FrameTicks → Automatic
FrameTicksStyle → {}	GridLines → None	GridLinesStyle → {}	ImageMargins → 0.
ImagePadding → All	ImageSize → Automatic	ImageSizeRaw → Automatic	LabelStyle → {}
MaxRecursion → Automatic	Mesh → None	MeshFunctions → {#1 &}	MeshShading → None
MeshStyle → Automatic	Method → Automatic	PerformanceGoal :→ $PerformanceGoal	PlotLabel → None
PlotPoints → Automatic	PlotRange → {Full, Automatic}	PlotRangeClipping → True	PlotRangePadding → Automatic
PlotRegion → Automatic	PlotStyle → Automatic	PreserveImageOptions → Automatic	Prolog → {}
RegionFunction → (True &)	RotateLabel → True	Ticks → Automatic	TicksStyle → {}

When plotting two or more functions, you may want to explicitly set the style of each plot's lines. You can also suppress one or both of the axes using Axes, as I do in the second and fourth plots. You can label one or both of the axes using AxesLabel and control the format using LabelStyle.

```
In[5]:=  GraphicsGrid[{
            {Plot[{0.5 Sin[2 x], Cos[3 x], Sin[x] - Cos[2 x]}, {x, -Pi, Pi},
              PlotStyle → {Directive[Black, Thin], Directive[Black, Thick],
                Directive[Black, Dashed]}, ImageSize → Small],
             Plot[Erf[x], {x, -2, 2}, Axes → {False, True}]},
            {Plot[0.5 Sin[2 θ], {θ, 0, 2 π}, AxesLabel → {"Angle", "Amplitude"},
              LabelStyle → Directive[Bold], ImageSize → Small],
             Plot[0.5 Sin[2 θ], {θ, 0, 2 π}, Axes → False, ImageSize → Small]
            }}]
```

Out[5]=

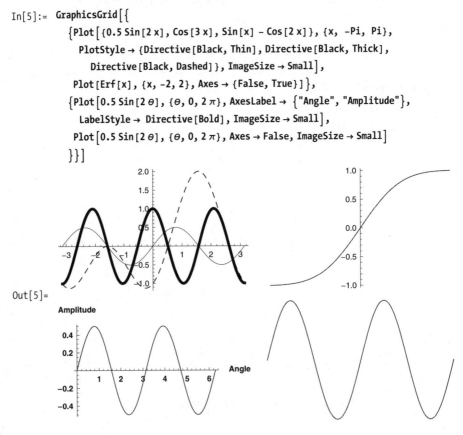

PlotLabel is a handy option for naming plots, especially when you display several plots at a time.

```
In[6]:= GraphicsRow[{
            Plot[Sin[x], {x, -2 Pi, 2 Pi}, PlotLabel → "Sin"],
            Plot[Cos[x], {x, -2 Pi, 2 Pi}, PlotLabel → "Cos"]
        }]
```

Out[6]=

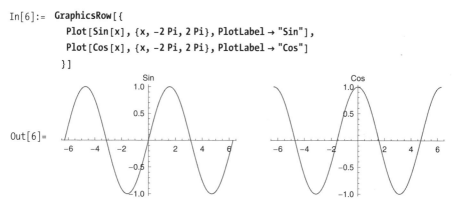

You can add grid lines with an explicitly determined frequency or a frequency determined automatically by Mathematica.

```
In[7]:= GraphicsRow[{
            Plot[Tan[x], {x, -Pi / 2, Pi / 2}, GridLines → Automatic, ImageSize → Small,
            PlotLabel → "Automatic Grid"], Plot[Tan[x], {x, -Pi / 2, Pi / 2},
            GridLines → {{-Pi / 2, -Pi / 4, 0, Pi / 4, Pi / 2}, {-6, -4, -2, 0, 2, 4, 6}},
            ImageSize → Small, PlotLabel → "Custom Grid"]
        }]
```

Out[7]=

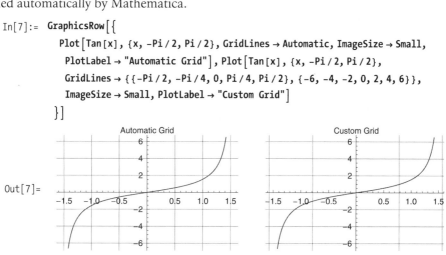

Frame, FrameStyle, and FrameLabel let you annotate the graph with a border and label. Note that FrameStyle and FrameLabel only have effect if Frame→True is also
specified.

```
In[8]:=  GraphicsRow[{
            Plot[Exp[Sin[x]], {x, 0, 2 Pi}, Frame → True, FrameLabel → "e^sin x",
              ImageSize → Small],
            Plot[Exp[Cos[x]], {x, 0, 2 Pi}, Frame → True, FrameLabel → "e^cos x",
              FrameStyle → Directive[Gray, Thick],
              ImageSize → Small]
          }]
```

Out[8]=

Mesh is an option that allows you to highlight specific points in the plot. Mesh → All
will highlight all points sampled while plotting the graph, Mesh → Full will use
regularly spaced points. Mesh → n will use n equally spaced points. The behavior of
Mesh → Automatic will vary based on the plotting primitive.

```
In[9]:=  GraphicsGrid[Partition[Table[
             Plot[0.5 Sin[2 θ], {θ, 0, 2 π}, Mesh → m,
               ImageSize → Small, Frame → True,
               PlotLabel → "Mesh → " <> ToString[m]],
             {m, {None, Automatic, All, Full, 16, 50}}], 2], Spacings → 0]
```

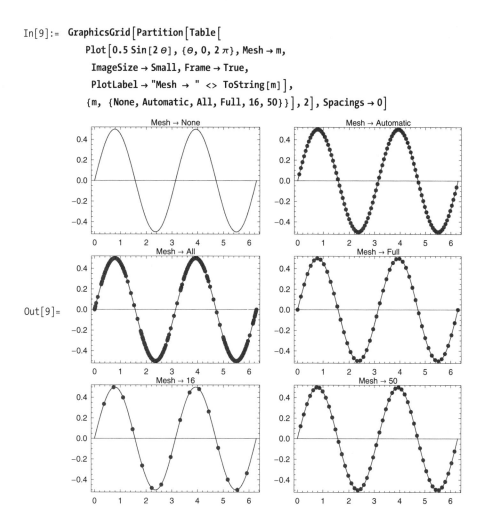

Out[9]=

PlotRange is an important option that controls what coordinates to include in the plot. Automatic lets Mathematica decide on the best choice, All specifies all points actually plotted, and Full specifies the entire range. In addition, you can supply explicit coordinates in the form {{xmin,xmax},{ymin,ymax}}.

```
In[10]:= GraphicsGrid[Partition[
          Table[
            Plot[Sqrt[100.0 - x^2], {x, 0, 100},
              PlotRange → r, ImageSize → {225, Automatic}, Frame → True,
              FrameLabel → "PlotRange → " <> ToString[r]],
            {r, {Automatic, All, Full, {{0, 20}, {0, 20}}}}], 2], Spacings → 0]
```

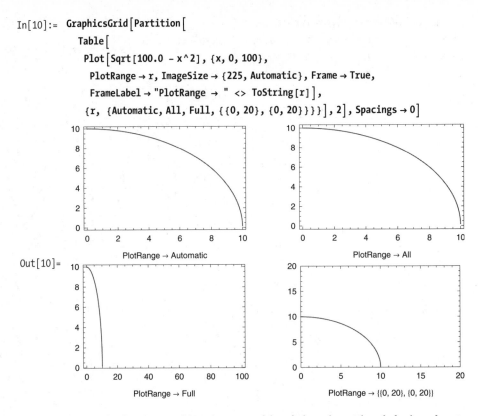

AspectRatio controls the ratio of height to width of the plot. The default value is 1/GoldenRatio (also known as φ). A value of Automatic uses the coordinate values to determine the aspect ratio.

```
In[11]:= GraphicsGrid@Partition[
          Table[
            Plot[Sqrt[100.0 - x^2], {x, 0, 10}, AspectRatio → a, Frame → True,
             FrameLabel → "AspectRatio → " <> ToString[TraditionalForm[a]]],
            {a, {GoldenRatio^-1, Automatic, 1.25, 0.75}}], 2]
```

Out[11]=

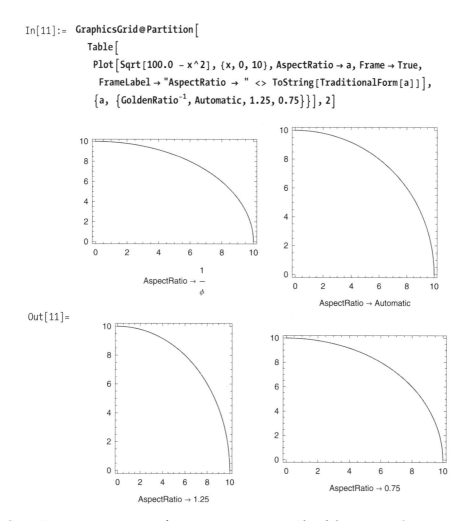

Sometimes you want to emphasize an area on one side of the curve or between two different curves. Filling can be set to Top to fill from the curve upward, Bottom to fill from the curve downward, Axis to fill from the axis to the curve, or to a numeric value to fill from the curve to that value in either *y* direction.

```
In[12]:= GraphicsGrid@Partition[Table[
            Plot[Sin[x], {x, 0, 2 Pi}, Filling → f, Frame → True,
             FrameLabel -> "Filling → " <> ToString[f],
             ImageSize → {200, Automatic}],
            {f, {Top, Bottom, Axis, 0.5}}], 2]
```

Out[12]=

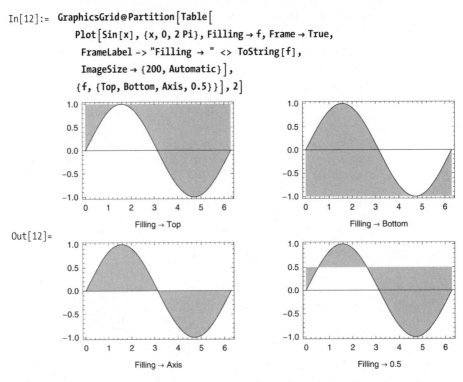

FillingStyle allows you to control the color and opacity of the filling. Specifying an opacity is useful where regions of multiple functions overlap.

```
In[13]:= Plot[{Cosh[x], Cosh[3 x]}, {x, -1, 1}, Filling → Top,
          FillingStyle → Directive[Gray, Opacity[0.5]], ImageSize → 300]
```

Out[13]=

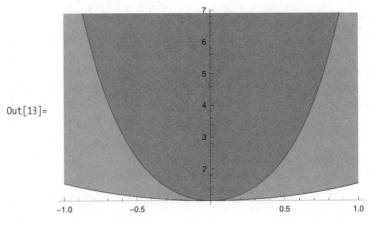

You can also use a special notation to fill the area between two curves. In this notation, you refer to a curve by {i} where i is an integer referring to the *i*th plot. You can then say something like Filling → {i → {j}} to specify that filling should be between plot **i** and plot **j**. You can also override the FillingStyle by including a graphics directive, as in the example here.

```
In[14]:= Plot[{Sin[x], 2 Sin[x + 1] + 3, 3 Sin[x + 2] + 6}, {x, 0, 2 Pi},
           Filling → {1 → {{2}, Red}, 2 → {{3}, Yellow}},
           ImageSize → 300]
```

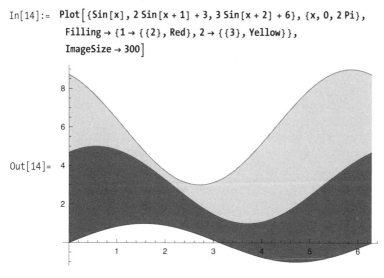

Out[14]=

See Also

Recipes 6.2 and 6.3 demonstrate PolarPlot and ListPlot, which share most of the options of Plot.

6.2 Plotting in Polar Coordinates

Problem

You want to create a plot in polar coordinates of radius as a function of angle.

Solution

Use PolarPlot, which plots the radius as the angle in polar coordinates varies counterclockwise with 0 at the x-axis, $\pi/2$ at the y-axis, and so on.

```
In[15]:=  GraphicsGrid[{
            {PolarPlot[1, {θ, 0, 2 π}, PlotLabel → "Constant"],
             PolarPlot[θ, {θ, 0, 2 π}, PlotLabel → "Spiral"]},
            {PolarPlot[Sin[5 θ], {θ, 0, 2 π}, PlotLabel → "Loops"],
             PolarPlot[1 / (1.5 + Sin[5 θ]), {θ, 0, 2 π}, PlotLabel → "Star Fish"]}
          }]
```

Out[15]=

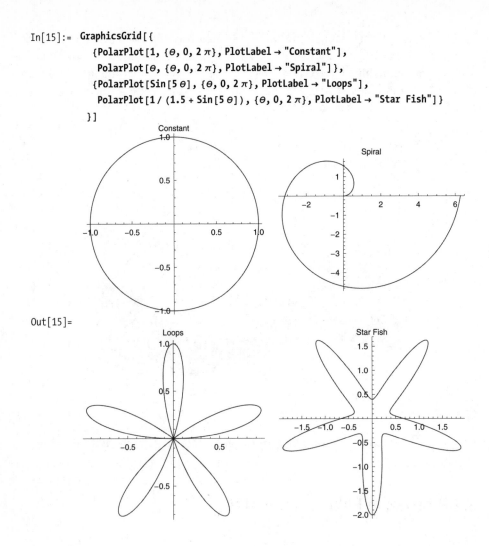

Discussion

As with Plot, you can plot several functions simultaneously.

```
In[16]:= PolarPlot[{1, 0.5 Cos[2 θ], Sin[Exp[θ / 2]]}, {θ, 0, 2 π},
    ImageSize → 300,
    PlotStyle → {Directive[Black, Dashed],
      Directive[Black, DotDashed],
      Directive[Black, Dotted]}]
```

Out[16]=

The options for PolarPlot are essentially the same as Plot. One notable exception is the absence of options related to Filling. Also note that AspectRatio is automatic by default, which makes sense because symmetry is an essential aesthetic of polar plots.

```
In[17]:= Complement[Options[PolarPlot], Options[Plot]]
Out[17]= {AspectRatio → Automatic, Axes → Automatic, AxesOrigin → {0, 0},
    MeshFunctions → {#3 &}, PlotRange → Automatic, PolarAxes → False,
    PolarAxesOrigin → Automatic, PolarGridLines → None, PolarTicks → Automatic}
```

6.3 Creating Plots Parametrically

Problem

You want to create Lissajous curves and other parametric plots where points {$fx[u]$, $fy[u]$} are plotted against a parameter u.

Solution

Here are some common Lissajous curves. Note how `ParametricPlot` takes a pair of functions in the form of a list.

```
In[18]:= GraphicsGrid[{{ParametricPlot[
            {Sin[Pi u], Sin[2 Pi u]}, {u, 0, 2}, PlotLabel → "(1:2)"],
          ParametricPlot[{Sin[2 Pi u], Sin[Pi u]},
            {u, 0, 2}, PlotLabel → "(2:1)"]},
         {ParametricPlot[{Sin[5 Pi u], Sin[4 Pi u]}, {u, 0, 2},
           PlotLabel → "(5:4)"],
          ParametricPlot[
            {Sin[9 Pi u], Sin[8 Pi u]}, {u, 0, 2}, PlotLabel → "(9:8)"]}}]
```

Out[18]=

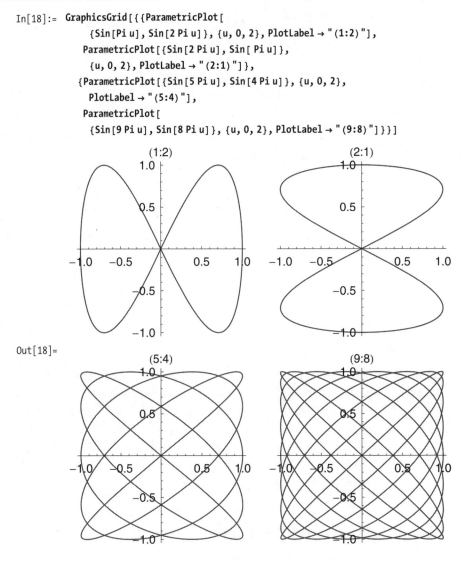

Discussion

Here is an animation showing the effect of phase shifting on signals of frequency ratio 1:1 and 2:1.

```
In[19]:=  Animate[
            GraphicsRow[{ParametricPlot[{Sin[Pi u + d], Sin[Pi u]}, {u, 0, 2}],
              ParametricPlot[{Sin[2 Pi u + d], Sin[Pi u]}, {u, 0, 2}]
            }], {d, 0, 2 Pi}]
```

Out[19]=

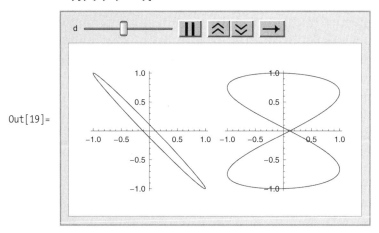

You also use ParametricPlot to create parametric surfaces. This introduces a second parameter.

```
In[20]:=  ParametricPlot[
            {r^2 Cos[Sqrt[t]], Sqrt[r] Sin[r t]}, {t, 0, 2 Pi}, {r, 1, 2}]
```

Out[20]=

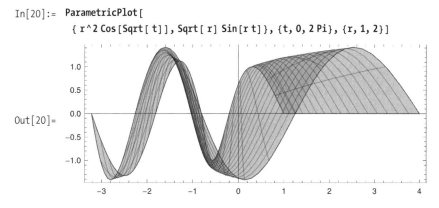

See Also

The 3D counterpart to ParametricPlot, ParametricPlot3D, is covered in Recipe 7.5.

6.4 Plotting Data

Problem

You want to graph data values that were captured outside Mathematica or previously computed within Mathematica.

Solution

Use ListPlot with either lists of *x* values or lists of (*x*,*y*) pairs. In this first plot, I generate the *y* values but let the *x* values derive from the iteration range. You can also explicitly provide the *x* and *y* values as a pair for each point plotted, as shown in the second ListPlot, which compares PrimePi to Prime.

```
In[21]:= GraphicsRow[{
            ListPlot[Table[Prime[i] / (1 + Log[Fibonacci[i]]), {i, 1, 100}],
              ImageSize → 250],
            ListPlot[Table[{PrimePi[i], Prime[i]}, {i, 1, 200}], ImageSize → 250]
          }]
```

Out[21]=

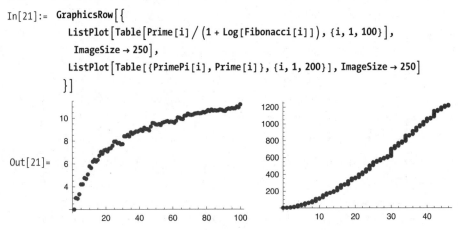

Discussion

ListPlot shares most options with Plot; instead of repeating them here, I show only the differences.

```
In[22]:= Complement[Options[ListPlot], Options[Plot]]
Out[22]= {DataRange → Automatic, InterpolationOrder → None, Joined → False,
          MaxPlotPoints → ∞, PlotMarkers → None, PlotRange → Automatic}
```

DataRange allows you to specify minimum and maximum values for the x-axis. In the first plot, the x-axis is assumed to be integer values.

```
In[24]:= data = Table[Sin[x], {x, -10, 10, 0.1}]; GraphicsRow[
            {ListPlot[data], ListPlot[data, DataRange → {-10, 10}]}, ImageSize → 500]
```

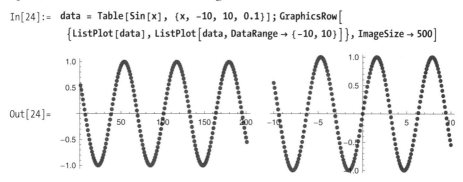

InterpolationOrder is used with Joined to control the way lines drawn between points are interpolated. A value of 1 results in straight lines; higher values result in smoothing, although for most practical purposes, a value of 2 is sufficient.

```
In[25]:=  data = RandomReal[{0, 2}, 8];
          GraphicsColumn[
           Table[ListPlot[data, Joined → True, InterpolationOrder → i,
             PlotLabel → ("InterpolationOrder" <> ToString[i]),
             ImageSize → Small], {i, {1, 2, 3}}]]
```

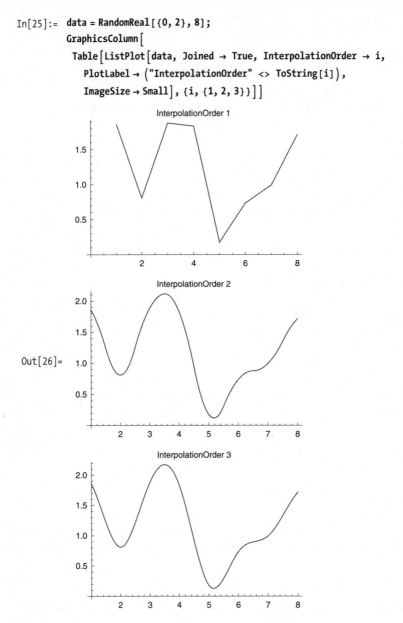

Out[26]=

See Also

Mathematica has related list plotting functions ListLinePlot, ListLogLogPlot, and ListLogLinearPlot that have similar usage to ListPlot but are specialized for certain types of data. Refer to the Mathematica documentation to learn more.

6.5 Mixing Two or More Graphs into a Single Graph

Problem

You want to mix several kinds of plots into a single graph.

Solution

Use Show to combine graphs produced by different functions.

In[27]:= `Show[Plot[x, {x, 1, 100}], ListPlot[Table[Prime[x], {x, 1, 100}]]]`

Out[27]=

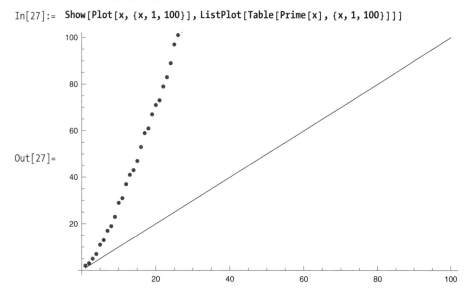

Discussion

When using Show to combine plots, you can override options used in the individual graphs. For example, you can override the position of axes, aspect ratio, and plot range.

In[28]:= `g1 = Plot[x^2 - x, {x, 1, 10}, AspectRatio → 0.6, AxesOrigin → Automatic];`
`g2 = Plot[x^2 + x, {x, 1, 10}, AspectRatio → 0.6, AxesOrigin → Automatic];`

In[30]:= `GraphicsColumn[`
`{g1, g2, Show[g1, g2, AspectRatio → 1, AxesOrigin → {0, 0}, PlotRange → All]},`
`ImageSize → 200]`

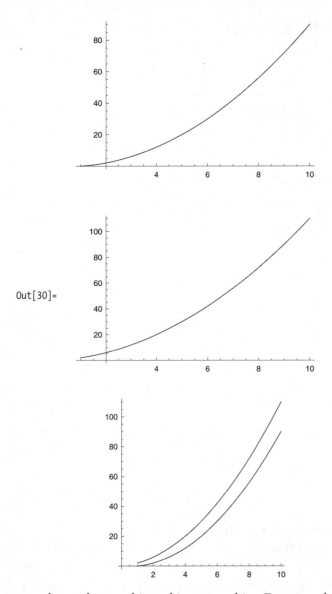

Out[30]=

Show can be used to combine arbitrary graphics. For example, you can give a graphic a background image.

```
In[31]:= g1 = Import[FileNameJoin[
            {NotebookDirectory[], "..", "images", "truck.jpg"}], "Graphics"];
        g1 = Graphics[{Opacity[0.3], g1[[1]]}];
        (*Insert opacity directive into graphics.*)
        Show[Plot[x, {x, 0, 100}, PlotStyle → Thick],
        g1, PlotRange → All, ImageSize → Small]
```

Out[32]=

One of my favorite mathematical illustrations is convergence through the iteration of a function (something I am sure many of you have done by repeatedly pressing *Cos* on a pocket calculator). Here, `NestList` performs 12 iterations. We duplicate every two and flatten and partition into pairs with overhand of 1 to yield the points for illustrating the convergence of the starting point 1 to the solution of x == Cos[x].

```
In[33]:= Show[Plot[{x, Cos[x]}, {x, 0.1, 1.1}], Graphics[
          Line[Partition[Flatten[{#, #} & /@ NestList[Cos, 1.0, 12]], 2, 1]]]]
```

Out[33]=

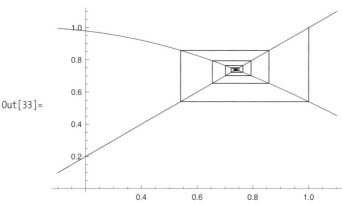

Show uses the following rules to combine plots:

- Use the union of plot intervals.
- Use the value of Options from the first plot unless overridden by Show's own options.

6.6 Displaying Multiple Graphs in a Grid

Problem

You want to display several related graphs for easy comparison.

Solution

Use GraphicsGrid in Mathematica 6 or GraphicsArray in earlier versions. You can use tables to group several plots together, but this gives you very little control of the layout of the images. GraphicsGrid gives control of the dimensions of the grid, the frame, spacing, dividers, and other options. The dimensions of the grid are inferred from the dimensions of the list of graphics passed as the first argument. You will find Partition handy for converting a linear list into the desired two-dimensional form.

```
In[34]:= With[{cols = 2},
          GraphicsGrid[
           Partition[Table[Plot[0.5 Sin[2 θ], {θ, 0, 2 π},
             Mesh → m, ImageSize → Small, Frame → True,
             FrameLabel → "Mesh → " <> ToString[m]],
            {m, {None, Automatic, All, Full, 16, 50}}],
           cols], Frame → All]
          ]
```

Out[34]=

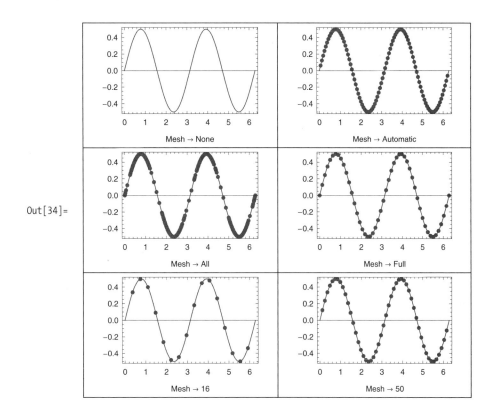

Discussion

In addition to GraphicsGrid, Mathematica provides GraphicsRow and GraphicsColumn, which are simpler to use for laying out graphics horizontally or vertically. These layout functions can be combined and nested to create more complex layouts. Here I demonstrate using GraphicsRow to show a GraphicsColumn next to another Graphics-Row. Frames can be drawn around the row or column (Frame→True) or additionally dividing all the elements (Frame→All).

```
In[35]:= With[{polygons = Table[
            Graphics[{EdgeForm[Black], FaceForm[LightGray],
              Polygon[Table[{Cos[2 Pi k / p], Sin[2 Pi k / p]}, {k, p}]]},
            ImageSize → Tiny],
            {p, 4, 8, 2}]},
        GraphicsRow[{
          GraphicsColumn[polygons, Frame → True],
          GraphicsRow[polygons, Frame → True]
          }, Frame → All, ImageSize → 450]]
```

Out[35]=

6.7 Creating Plots with Legends

Problem

You want to identify the information in a plot of multiple data sets using a legend.

Solution

Use the PlotLegends` package with the PlotLegend, LegendPosition, and LegendSize options.

```
In[36]:= Needs["PlotLegends`"];
         Plot[{Sin[x], Sin[2 x]}, {x, 0, 2 Pi},
           PlotStyle → {Directive[Black, Dotted], Directive[Black, Dashed]},
           PlotLegend → {"Sin x", "Sin 2x"},
           LegendPosition → {1, 0.1}, LegendSize → 0.75]
```

Out[37]=

Legends use their own coordinate system, for which the center of the graphic is at {0,0} and the inside is the scaled bounding region {{-1,-1},{1,1}}. LegendPosition refers to the lower left corner of the legend.

Discussion

There are a variety of options for further tweaking the legend's appearance. You can turn off or control the offset of the drop shadow (LegendShadow); control spacing of various elements using LegendSpacing, LegendTextSpace, LegendLabelSpace, and LegendBorderSpace; control the labels with LegendTextDirection, LegendTextOffset, LegendSpacing, and LegendTextSpace; and give the legend a label with LegendLabel and LegendLabelSpace.

Notice the effect of LegendTextSpace, which is a bit counterintuitive because it expresses the ratio of the text space to the size of a key box so larger numbers actually shrink the legend. LegendSpacing controls the space around each key box on a scale where the box size is 1.

```
In[38]:= plotCommonOptions = Sequence[
          PlotStyle → {Directive[Black, Dotted], Directive[Black, Dashed]},
          PlotLegend → {"Sin x", "Sin 2x"}, LegendPosition → {1, 0.1},
          LegendSize → 0.75, ImageSize → 250];

        GraphicsGrid[{
          {Plot[{Sin[x], Sin[2 x]}, {x, 0, 2 Pi},
            Evaluate[plotCommonOptions],
            LegendShadow → None,
            LegendSpacing → 1 / 2, LegendTextSpace → 10],
           Plot[{Sin[x], Sin[2 x]}, {x, 0, 2 Pi},
            Evaluate[plotCommonOptions],
            LegendShadow → None, LegendLabel → "Plots",
            LegendSpacing → 0.2, LegendTextSpace → 5]
          },
          {Plot[{Sin[x], Sin[2 x]}, {x, 0, 2 Pi},
            Evaluate[plotCommonOptions],
            LegendShadow → {-0.1, -0.1}, LegendLabel → "Plots",
            LegendSpacing → 0.2, LegendTextSpace → 5],
           Plot[{Sin[x], Sin[2 x]}, {x, 0, 2 Pi},
            Evaluate[plotCommonOptions],
            LegendShadow → {0.1, 0.1},
            LegendSpacing → 1 / 2, LegendTextSpace → 10]
          }
         },
         Dividers → All]
```

Out[39]=

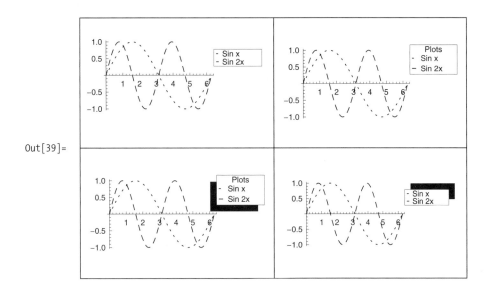

See Also

Sometimes you want to create a more customized legend. In that case, consider Legend and ShowLegend.

See the tutorial on the PlotLegends` package at *http://bit.ly/TYvfV*.

6.8 Displaying 2D Geometric Shapes

Problem

You want to create graphics that contain lines, squares, circles, and other geometric objects.

Solution

Mathematica has a versatile collection of graphics primitives: Text, Polygon, Rectangle, Circle, Disk, Line, Point, Arrow, Raster, and Point can be combined to create a variety of 2D drawings. Here I demonstrate a somewhat frivolous yet instructive function that creates a snowman drawing using a broad sampling of the available primitives. Included is a useful function, ngon, for creating regular polygons.

```
In[41]:= ClearAll[generateSnow]

In[42]:= (*Create a regular polygon.*)
         ngon[sides_Integer, center_List, size_?NumberQ, rotation_: 0 ] :=
          Polygon[Table[{size Cos[2 Pi k / sides + rotation] + center[[1]],
             size Sin[2 Pi k / sides + rotation] + center[[2]]}, {k, sides}]]
         (*Generate snow as randomly scattered pairs of
          semitransparent points of random size.*)
         generateSnow[minPoint_List, maxPoint_List, density_?NumberQ] := Module[
           {size, z = 100, j}, {Opacity[0.3], Reap[Do[Which[RandomReal[] < 0.3,
              size = RandomReal[{0.001, 0.008}];
              j = RandomReal[{-1.0, 1.0}];
              Sow[{PointSize[size / 1.3],
                If[RandomReal[] < 0.5, {Point[{x, y + z size + j}],
                  Point[{x, y - z size + j}], Point[{x + z size, y + j}],
                  Point[{x - z size, y + j}]}, {Point[{x + z size, y + z size + j}],
                  Point[{x - z size, y + z size + j}], Point[{x + z size,
                    y - z size + j}], Point[{x - z size, y - z size + j}]}]}],
                PointSize[size], Point[{x, y + j}]}]],
             {x, minPoint[[1]], maxPoint[[1]], density},
             {y, minPoint[[2]], maxPoint[[2]], density}]][[2, 1]]}]
         (*Draw a snowman whose base is of the given radius.*)
         snowman[bodyRadius_] := Module[{bodyCenter = {0, 0},
           (*Proportioning the torso and head
            based on golden ratio gives a pleasing effect.*)
           torsoRadius = bodyRadius / GoldenRatio,
           headRadius = bodyRadius / (GoldenRatio^2),
           torsoCenter, headCenter, leftShoulder, rightShoulder,
           buttonSize = bodyRadius / 10, buttonSep = bodyRadius / 3.3,
           leftHand, rightHand, mouthCenter, leftEyeCenter, rightEyeCenter},
           torsoCenter = {bodyCenter[[1]], torsoRadius + bodyRadius};
           headCenter =
            {bodyCenter[[1]], bodyRadius + 2 torsoRadius + headRadius};
           (*Position the arms at -60 and 60 degrees.*)
           leftShoulder =
            torsoCenter + {torsoRadius * Sin[-Pi / 3], torsoRadius * Cos[-Pi / 3]};
           leftHand = torsoCenter + {3 torsoRadius * Sin[-Pi / 3],
              3 torsoRadius * Cos[-Pi / 3]};
           rightShoulder = torsoCenter + {torsoRadius * Sin[Pi / 3],
              torsoRadius * Cos[Pi / 3]};
           rightHand = torsoCenter + {3 torsoRadius * Sin[Pi / 3],
              3 torsoRadius * Cos[Pi / 3]};
```

```
(*Position eyes at -45 and 45 degrees and half
  the radius of the head.*)
leftEyeCenter = headCenter + {0.5 headRadius * Sin[-Pi / 4],
    0.5 headRadius * Cos[-Pi / 4]};
rightEyeCenter = headCenter + {0.5 headRadius * Sin[Pi / 4],
    0.5 headRadius * Cos[Pi / 4]};
(*Position mouth at 180 degrees -
  bottom of circle. Also half radius of head.*)
mouthCenter = headCenter +
  {0.5 headRadius * Sin[Pi], 0.5 headRadius * Cos[Pi]};
Graphics[{
  Circle[bodyCenter, bodyRadius], (*base ciricle*)
  Circle[torsoCenter, torsoRadius], (*middle circle*)
  Circle[headCenter, headRadius], (*head*)
  Circle[mouthCenter, headRadius / 4, {-Pi, 0}],
  (*half circle for mouth*)
  (*Use disks for eyes.*)
  Disk[leftEyeCenter, headRadius / 8],
  Disk[rightEyeCenter, headRadius / 8],
  (*Make a carrot-shaped nose out of lines. The
    proportions here were worked out by trial and error.*)
  Line[{headCenter - {0, headRadius / 10}, headCenter -
      {headRadius / 2, headRadius / 5}, headCenter + {0, headRadius / 10}}],
  (*I use arrows for arms to illustrate how they
    work. See discussion for more detail.*)
  {Arrowheads[{-0.1, 0}], Arrow[{leftHand, leftShoulder}]},
  {Arrowheads[{0, 0.1}], Arrow[{rightShoulder, rightHand}]},
  {Gray, Thickness[torsoRadius / 800],
   Line[{rightHand + {-2, 2}, {rightHand[[1]] - 2, -bodyRadius / 2}}],
   Rectangle[bodyCenter + {bodyRadius / 1.4, -2},
     bodyCenter + {2.4 bodyRadius, -bodyRadius}]},
  generateSnow[{-2 bodyRadius, -bodyRadius},
    {3 bodyRadius, 3.1 bodyRadius}, 5],
  (*Use pentagons to simulate coal buttons.*)
  ngon[5, {0, torsoRadius + bodyRadius - buttonSep}, buttonSize],
  ngon[5, {0, torsoRadius + bodyRadius}, buttonSize],
  ngon[5, {0, torsoRadius + bodyRadius + buttonSep}, buttonSize]},
  ImageSize -> bodyRadius * 10]]
snowman[40]
```

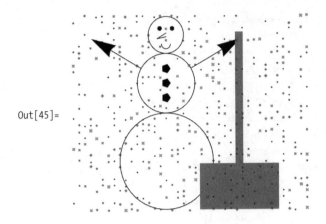

Out[45]=

Discussion

One of the keys to getting the most out of the graphics primitives is to learn how to combine them with graphics directives. Some directives are very specific, whereas others are quite general. For example, Arrowheads applies only to Arrow, whereas Red and Opacity apply to all primitives. A directive will apply to all objects that follow it, subject to scoping created by nesting objects within a list. For example, in the following graphic, Red applies to Disk and Rectangle but not Line because the line is given a specific color and thickness within its own scope.

```
In[46]:= Graphics[{Red, Disk[{-2, -2}, 0.5], Rectangle[], {Thickness[0.02],
           Black, Line[{{-1.65, -1.65}, {0, 0}}]}}, ImageSize → Small]
```

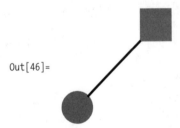

Out[46]=

Color directives can use named colors: Red, Green, Blue, Black, White, Gray, Cyan, Magenta, Yellow, Brown, Orange, Pink, Purple, LightRed, LightGreen, LightBlue, LightGray, LightCyan, LightMagenta, LightYellow, LightBrown, LightOrange, LightPink, and LightPurple. You can also synthesize colors using RGBColor or Hue, CMYKColor, GrayLevel, and Blend. In Mathematica 6 or later versions, these directives can take opacity values in addition to values that define the color or gray settings. Blend is also new to Mathematica 6.

```
In[47]:= Graphics[Table[{Hue[x], Rectangle[{x, 1}, {x + 0.1, 2}]}, {x, 0, 0.99, .1}],
         ImageSize -> Small]
```

Out[47]=

```
In[48]:= Graphics[Table[{Hue[x], Rectangle[{x, 1}, {x + 0.05, 2}]},
           Blend[{Hue[x], Hue[x + 0.05]}, 0.25], Rectangle[{x + .05, 1},
             {x + 0.1, 2}]}, {x, 0, 0.99, .1}], ImageSize -> Small]
```

Out[48]=

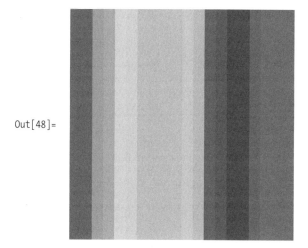

Of course, you'll need to try the code on your own to view the colors.

Thickness[r] is specified relative to the total width of the graphic and, therefore, scales with size changes. AbsoluteThickness[d] is specified in units of printer points (1/72 inch) and does not scale. Thick and Thin are predefined versions (0.25 and 2, respectively) of AbsoluteThickness. Thickness directives apply to primitives that contain lines such as Line, Polygon, Arrow, and the like.

```
In[49]:= Graphics[{Line[{{0, -1}, {0, 1}}],
            {Thin, Line[{{0.5, -1}, {0.5, 1}}]}, {Thick, Line[{{1, -1}, {1, 1}}]},
            {AbsoluteThickness[3], Line[{{1.5, -1}, {1.5, 1}}]}}]
```

Out[49]=

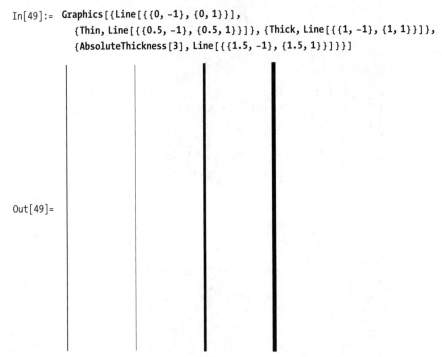

See Also

Recipe 14.12 applies Mathematica's graphics primitives to the serious task of visualizing Hull-White trees, which are used in modeling interest-rate-sensitive securities.

Recipe 13.11 shows an application in constructing finite element diagrams used in engineering.

6.9 Annotating Graphics with Text

Problem

You want to add stylized text to graphics.

Solution

Use Text with Style to specify FontFamily, FontSubstitutions, FontSize, FontWeight, FontSlant, FontTracking, FontColor, and Background.

```
In[50]:= Graphics[{Text[Style["12 Point Default Font", FontSize → 12], {0, 0}], Text[
            Style["16 Point Italic", FontSize → 16, FontSlant → Italic], {0, -.2}],
          Text[Style["14 Point Bold", FontSize → 14, FontWeight → Bold], {0, -.4}],
          Text[
            Style["14 Point Arial", FontSize → 14, FontFamily → "Arial"], {0, -.6}],
          Text[Style["14 Point Arial Narrow", FontSize → 14,
            FontFamily → "Arial", FontTracking → "Narrow"], {0, -.8}],
          Text[Style["14 Point Bold White on Black", FontSize → 14,
            FontWeight → Bold, FontColor → White, Background → Black],
            {0, -1}]}, ImageSize → Small]
```

12 Point Default Font

16 Point Italic

14 Point Bold

Out[50]=

14 Point Arial

14 Point Arial Narrow

14 Point Bold White on Black

Discussion

In this chapter, I demonstrate various plotting functions that contain options for adding labels to the entire graph, frames, and axes. These options can also be stylized.

```
In[51]:= Plot[0.5 Sin[2 θ], {θ, 0, 2 π},
         PlotLabel → Style[0.5 Sin[2 θ], FontSize → 20, FontFamily → "Arial"],
         AxesLabel → {"Radians", "Amplitude"}, LabelStyle →
          Directive[Bold, FontFamily → "Arial", FontSize → 12], Frame → True,
         FrameLabel → Style["Sine Wave", FontSlant → Italic], ImageSize → Medium]
```

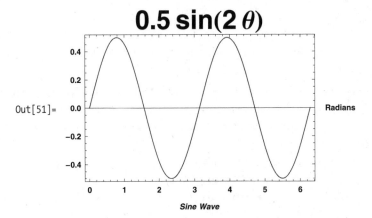

The Style directive was added into Mathematica 6 and is quite versatile. Style can add style options to both Mathematica expressions and graphics.

6.10 Creating Custom Arrows

Problem

You want to create arrows with custom arrowheads, tails, and connecting lines for use in annotating graphics.

Solution

Use Arrowheads with a custom graphic to create arbitrary arrowheads and tails.

```
In[52]:= With[{h = Graphics[{Disk[{0, 0}, 0.75]}],
         t = Graphics[{Line[{{-0.5, 0}, {0.5, 0}}],
            Line[{{0, -0.6}, {0, 0.6}}], Line[{{0.2, -0.6}, {0.2, 0.6}}]}]},
         Graphics[{Arrowheads[{{0.05, 1, h}, {0.1, 0, t}}],
          Arrow[{{0, 0}, {0.25, 0.25}}]}, ImageSize → Small]]
```

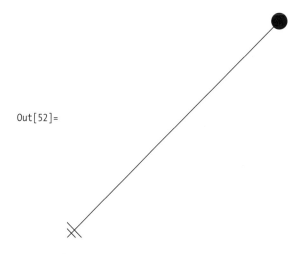

Out[52]=

Discussion

Arrowheads is quite versatile. You can easily create double-ended arrows and arrows with multiple arrowheads along the span.

```
In[53]:= Graphics[{Arrowheads[{-0.1, 0.1}], Arrow[{{0, 0}, {1, 0}}],
            Arrowheads[{0, 0.1, .1, .1, .1}], Arrow[{{0, -0.5}, {1, -0.5}}]},
          ImageSize → Small]
```

Out[53]=

You may consider using Arrowheads to label arrows, but Mathematica does not treat such "arrowheads" specially, so you may get undesirable effects.

In[54]:= Graphics[{Arrowheads[{0, {Automatic, 0.5, Graphics[
                {Text[Style["Label", FontSize → 14, FontWeight → Bold]]}]}]}, 0.1}],
        Arrow[{{0, 0}, {-0.25, 0.25}}]}, ImageSize → Small]

Out[54]=

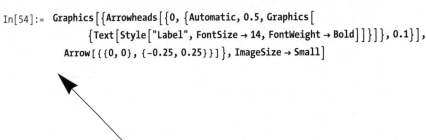

A better option is to position the text by using Rotate with Text or Inset or by using GraphPlot or related functions (see Recipe 4.6). The advantage of Inset over manually positioned Text is that you get auto-centering if you don't mind the label not being parallel to the arrow.

In[55]:= Graphics[{Arrowheads[{0.1}], Arrow[{{0, 0}, {-0.25, 0.25}}],
        Rotate[Text[Style["Label", FontSize → 14, FontWeight → Bold],
            {-0.14, 0.11}], -Pi/4]}, ImageSize → Small]

Out[55]=

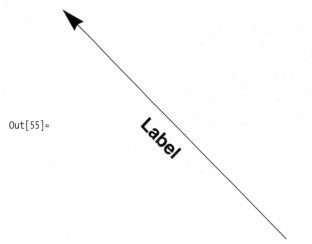

```
In[56]:= Graphics[{Arrowheads[{0.1}], Arrow[{{0, 0}, {-0.25, 0.25}}],
           Inset[Text[Style["Label", FontSize → 14, FontWeight → Bold]]]},
          ImageSize → Small]
```

Out[56]= **Label**

Three-Dimensional Plots and Graphics

7.0 Introduction

Modern mathematics demands advanced visualization tools. Although Mathematica's 2D graphics are impressive, 3D graphics is where Mathematica really distinguishes itself. As with 2D, 3D graphics are represented symbolically but with the head Graphics3D instead of Graphics. There are 3D counterparts to most 2D plotting functions. For example, Plot3D and ListPlot3D are the counterparts to the 2D functions Plot and ListPlot. There are also many functions unique to 3D space, such as SphericalPlot3D and RevolutionPlot3D.

Mathematica's 3D graphics are interactive, although it is difficult to illustrate this in book form! Any 3D plot or drawing can be rotated, flipped, and stretched, allowing you to see different perspectives. Furthermore, Mathematica 6 added a host of options for controlling lighting, camera placement, and even how light reflects off of surfaces (see Recipes 7.12 and 7.13).

The Symbolic Nature of Graphics

I think most users are quite impressed with the breadth and depth of what Mathematica 7 can achieve with plotting functions (see Recipes 7.1 through 7.9). However, as a programmer, I am even more taken with what can be achieved in Mathematica that would be next to impossible in most plotting packages outside of Mathematica. When you ask the Mathematica kernel to perform a plot, it does not produce a raster image that the frontend simply renders using the graphics hardware. Instead, it produces a symbolic representation of the plot that the frontend translates into a raster image. Why is this relevant? Imagine you were working in another domain (e.g., Microsoft Excel) and there were two plotting functions that each did half of what you wanted to render on the screen. How could you morph those two plots to achieve the desired result? You couldn't. (I'm ignoring whatever skills you might possess as a Photoshop hacker!) In Mathematica, all hope is not lost. In Recipe 7.6, a 3D plot and a 2D contour plot are combined to achieve a 3D plot with a 2D contour "shadow" underneath. Another example is Recipe 7.10: RevolutionPlot3D is used to generate a cone to compensate for the lack of a Cone primitive in Mathematica 6 (Cone is built into Mathematica 7). Achieving these results involves sticking your head under the hood and, sometimes, doing quite a bit of trial and error, but the results are within reach once you have the general principles.

See Also

In Recipe 18.5, I discuss how the attributes of 3D graphics can be controlled through stylesheets. If you intend to create publication-quality documents in Mathematica, you should familiarize yourself with stylesheets.

7.1 Plotting Functions of Two Variables in Cartesian Coordinates

Problem

You want to graph one or more built-in or user-defined functions of two variables.

Solution

Use Plot3D with the function or functions to plot and two lists specifying the ranges for the independent variables.

In[1]:= `Plot3D[Sin[x Pi Exp[-y + x]], {x, -1, 1}, {y, -1, 1}]`

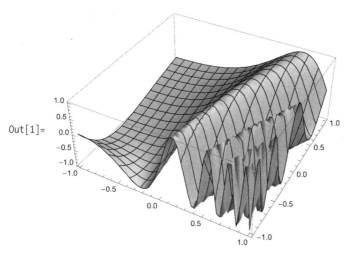

Out[1]=

As with most plots, you can provide multiple functions. However, 3D plots will become crowded quickly (Figure 7-1a), so consider placing multiple plots side by side rather than trying to shoehorn everything into a single plot. With some functions and options, this is not an issue (Figure 7-1b).

In[2]:= `GraphicsGrid[`
`{{Plot3D[{Sin[x Pi Exp[-y + x]], Cos[x Pi Exp[1 - x y]]}, {x, -1, 1},`
`{y, -1, 1}, PlotLabel → "a"], Plot3D[{x^2 + y^2, -x^2 - y^2}, {x, -2, 2},`
`{y, -2, 2}, BoxRatios → Automatic, PlotLabel → "b"]}}, ImageSize → Large]`

Out[2]=

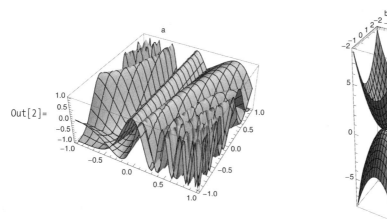

Figure 7-1. 3D plots of multiple functions

Discussion

As you might suspect, Plot3D has a variety of options for customizing presentation. Here I use Complement to list only those options that differ from the 2D Plot function in Recipe 6.1.

```
In[3]:= Complement[First /@ Options[Plot3D], First /@ Options[Plot]]
Out[3]= {AxesEdge, BoundaryStyle, Boxed, BoxRatios, BoxStyle, ControllerLinking,
         ControllerMethod, ControllerPath, FaceGrids, FaceGridsStyle,
         Lighting, NormalsFunction, RotationAction, SphericalRegion, ViewAngle,
         ViewCenter, ViewMatrix, ViewPoint, ViewRange, ViewVector, ViewVertical}

In[4]:= {AxesEdge, BoundaryStyle, Boxed, BoxRatios, BoxStyle, ControllerLinking,
         ControllerMethod, ControllerPath, FaceGrids, FaceGridsStyle,
         Lighting, NormalsFunction, RotationAction, SphericalRegion, ViewAngle,
         ViewCenter, ViewMatrix, ViewPoint, ViewRange, ViewVector, ViewVertical}
Out[4]= {AxesEdge, BoundaryStyle, Boxed, BoxRatios, BoxStyle, ControllerLinking,
         ControllerMethod, ControllerPath, FaceGrids, FaceGridsStyle,
         Lighting, NormalsFunction, RotationAction, SphericalRegion, ViewAngle,
         ViewCenter, ViewMatrix, ViewPoint, ViewRange, ViewVector, ViewVertical}
```

AxesEdge determines where the axes are drawn, and the default value of Automatic (Figure 7-2a) usually gives good results. You can override the default by proving a specification of the form {{dir y, dir z},{dir x, dir z},{dir x, dir y}} where each **dir i** must be either +1 or -1, indicating whether axes are drawn on the edge of the box with a larger or smaller value of coordinate **i**, respectively (Figure 7-2b, c, and d).

```
In[5]:= GraphicsGrid[{{Plot3D[{x^2 + y^2, -x^2 - y^2}, {x, -2, 2}, {y, -2, 2},
           BoxRatios → Automatic, PlotLabel → "a", AxesEdge → Automatic], Plot3D[
           {x^2 + y^2, -x^2 - y^2}, {x, -2, 2}, {y, -2, 2}, BoxRatios → Automatic,
           PlotLabel → "b", AxesEdge → {{-1, -1}, {-1, 1}, {-1, -1}}]},
           {Plot3D[{x^2 + y^2, -x^2 - y^2}, {x, -2, 2}, {y, -2, 2}, BoxRatios →
             Automatic, PlotLabel → "c", AxesEdge → {{1, 1}, {1, -1}, {1, 1}}],
           Plot3D[{x^2 + y^2, -x^2 - y^2}, {x, -2, 2}, {y, -2, 2}, BoxRatios →
             Automatic, PlotLabel → "d", AxesEdge → {{1, 1}, {1, 1}, {1, 1}}]}},
           ImageSize → 400, Spacings → {0.1, 0.1}]
```

Out[5]=

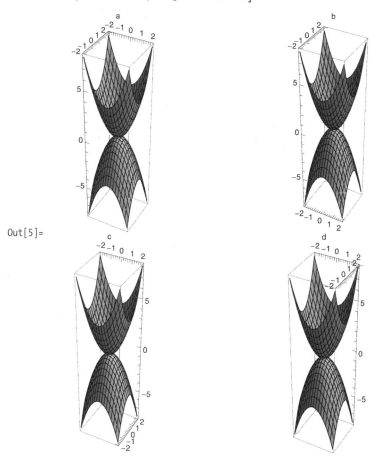

Figure 7-2. *Examples of* AxesEdge *option*

BoundaryStyle allows you to stylize the edge of a plot surface.

```
In[6]:= Plot3D[{x^2 + y^2, -x^2 - y^2}, {x, -2, 2}, {y, -2, 2},
           BoundaryStyle → Directive[Black, Thickness[0.0125]]]
```

Out[6]=
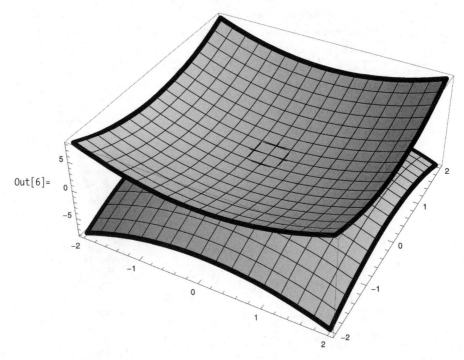

Boxed, BoxRatios, and BoxStyle control the presence, proportions, and style of the edges surrounding 3D plots. Each of the plots in Figure 7-3 is of the same function. The differences are that Figure 7-3a is not boxed, Figure 7-3b is boxed with Automatic ratios, and Figure 7-3c and Figure 7-3d have specified ratios.

```
In[7]:= GraphicsGrid[
        {{Plot3D[{x^2 + y^2, -x^2 - y^2}, {x, -2, 2}, {y, -2, 2}, PlotLabel → "a",
           Boxed → False], Plot3D[{x^2 + y^2, -x^2 - y^2}, {x, -2, 2},
          {y, -2, 2}, BoxRatios → Automatic, PlotLabel → "b"]},
         {Plot3D[{x^2 + y^2, -x^2 - y^2}, {x, -2, 2}, {y, -2, 2}, BoxRatios →
            {1, 2, 1}, PlotLabel → "c", AxesEdge → {{1, 1}, {1, -1}, {1, 1}}],
          Plot3D[{x^2 + y^2, -x^2 - y^2}, {x, -2, 2}, {y, -2, 2},
           BoxRatios → {2, 1, 2}, PlotLabel → "d"]}}, ImageSize → Medium]
```

Out[7]=

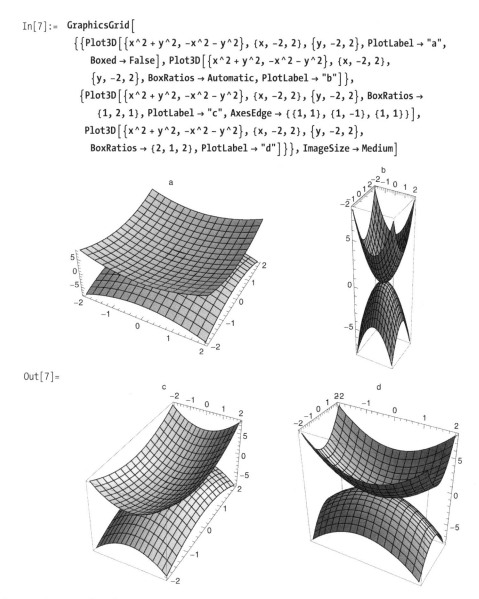

Figure 7-3. Examples of BoxRatios *option*

FaceGrids specifies grid lines to draw on the faces of the bounding box. You can specify All or specific faces using {x,y,z}, where two values are 0 and the third is either +1 (largest value) or -1 (smallest value). FaceGridsStyle allows you to stylize the grid to your liking.

```
In[8]:= GraphicsGrid[{{Plot3D[x^2 + y^2, {x, -2, 2}, {y, -2, 2},
          BoxRatios → Automatic, PlotLabel → "a", FaceGrids → All],
        Plot3D[x^2 + y^2, {x, -2, 2}, {y, -2, 2}, BoxRatios → Automatic,
          PlotLabel → "b", FaceGrids → {{0, 0, 1}}]},
       {Plot3D[x^2 + y^2, {x, -2, 2}, {y, -2, 2}, BoxRatios → Automatic,
          PlotLabel → "c", FaceGrids → {{1, 0, 0}, {0, 1, 0}}],
        Plot3D[x^2 + y^2, {x, -2, 2}, {y, -2, 2}, BoxRatios → Automatic,
          PlotLabel → "d", FaceGrids → {{-1, 0, 0}, {0, 1, 0}},
          FaceGridsStyle → Directive[Red, Thick]]}}, ImageSize → 400]
```

Out[8]=

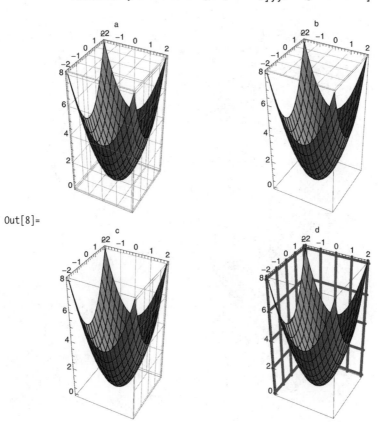

See Also

ViewAngle, ViewCenter, ViewMatrix, ViewPoint, ViewRange, ViewVector, and View-Vertical are options that give you detailed control of the orientation of the plot. These are covered in Recipe 7.12.

Recipe 6.1 demonstrates Plot, which is the 2D counterpart to Plot3D.

7.2 Plotting Functions in Spherical Coordinates

Problem

You want to plot a surface with spherical radius r as a function of rotational angles θ (latitude) and ϕ (longitude).

Solution

Use SphericalPlot3D when plotting one or more surfaces in spherical coordinates. Such plots most often arise in situations where there is some degree of rotational symmetry. For example, a sphere is fully symmetrical under all rotations and is trivially plotted using SphericalPlot3D as a constant radius.

In[9]:= SphericalPlot3D[1, {θ, 0, Pi}, {ϕ, 0, 2 Pi}, ImageSize → Small]

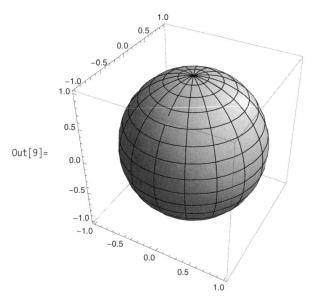

Out[9]=

Discussion

You can plot multiple surfaces by providing a list of functions and leave holes in some of the surfaces by returning the symbol None for these regions.

In[10]:= SphericalPlot3D[{1, If[ϕ < 3 Pi / 2, 2, None], If[ϕ < 3 Pi / 2, 3, None]},
          {θ, 0, Pi}, {ϕ, 0, 2 Pi}, ImageSize → Small]

Out[10]=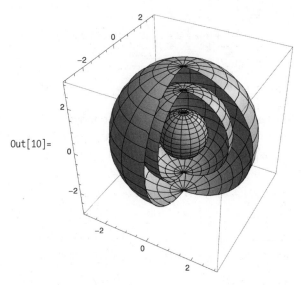

Of course, you will probably use SphericalPlot3D to plot more interesting functions too.

In[11]:= SphericalPlot3D[Exp[1 / (1 + θ) + Cos[3 ϕ]],
          {θ, 0, Pi}, {ϕ, 0, 2 Pi}, ImageSize → Small]

Out[11]=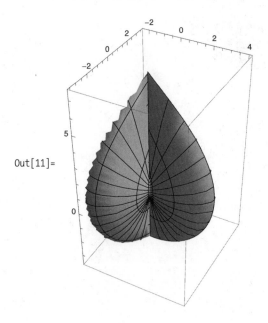

Use PlotStyle to achieve some dramatic effects. Applying the Opacity option is especially useful when specifying rotational angles greater than 2Pi radians; otherwise, the resulting interior surfaces would be hidden. Compare Figure 7-4a with Figure 7-4b.

```
In[12]:= GraphicsRow[
            {SphericalPlot3D[If[θ < Pi / 4, None, 1 / (φ + 5)], {θ, 0, Pi}, {φ, 0, 4 Pi},
               PlotStyle → Directive[Orange, Opacity[0.6], Specularity[White, 10]],
               Mesh → None, PlotPoints → 30, PlotLabel → "a"],
             SphericalPlot3D[If[θ < Pi / 4, None, 1 / (φ + 5)], {θ, 0, Pi},
               {φ, 0, 4 Pi}, PlotStyle → Directive[Orange, Specularity[White, 10]],
               Mesh → None, PlotPoints → 30, PlotLabel → "b"]}, ImageSize → 400]
```

Out[12]=
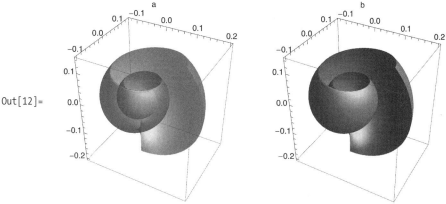

Figure 7-4. Effect of Opacity

See Also

See Recipe 7.4 for the relationship between SphericalPlot3D and ParametricPlot3D.

7.3 Plotting Surfaces in Cylindrical Coordinates

Problem

You want to visualize a surface generated via a revolution of a function or parametric curve around the z-axis.

Solution

Many common surfaces can be generated by revolving a 2D curve. The following examples illustrate the basic idea.

Revolve a parabola to create a bowl.

```
In[13]:= RevolutionPlot3D[t^2 , {t, 0, 1}, ImageSize → Small]
```

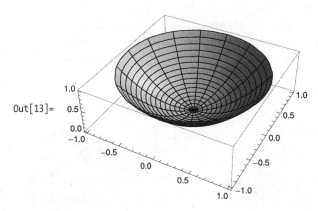

```
Out[13]=
```

Revolve a vertical line at a constant distance from the center to create a cylinder.

```
In[14]:= RevolutionPlot3D[{1, t} , {t, 0, 1}, ImageSize → Small]
```

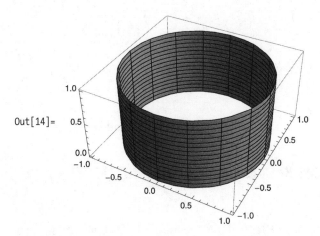

```
Out[14]=
```

Functions that incorporate the angle of revolution can create more exotic surfaces, such as the spiral shown here. Notice how the angle of revolution can be greater (or less) than 2Pi (one revolution).

In[15]:= `RevolutionPlot3D[{4 t, θ} , {t, 0, 1}, {θ, 0, 4 Pi}, ImageSize → Small]`

Out[15]=

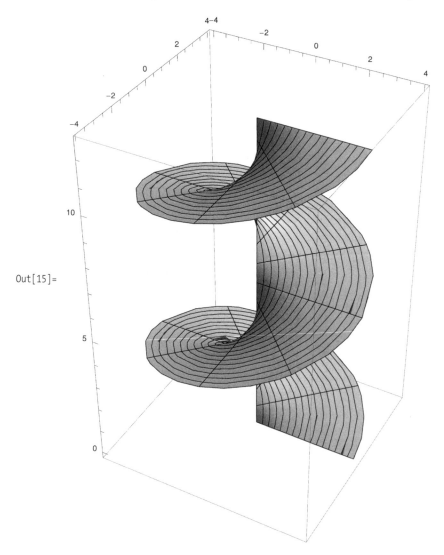

Discussion

To get a feel for RevolutionPlot3D, plot the 2D parametric version of the equation next to the 3D revolution. It is fairly easy to see how the 180-degree rotation of the 2D curve around the y-axis in Figure 7-5a will yield the 3D surface shown in Figure 7-5b.

```
In[16]:= Module[{f1, f2},
            fx[x_] := Sin[x] + Sin[9 x] / 5;
            fy[x_] := Cos[x] + Cos[9 x] / 5;
            GraphicsRow[{
              ParametricPlot[{fx[t], fy[t]}, {t, 0, Pi}, PlotLabel → "a"],
              RevolutionPlot3D[{fx[t], fy[t]}, {t, 0, Pi}, {θ, 0, Pi}, PlotLabel → "b"]
            }, ImageSize → 400]]
```

Out[16]=

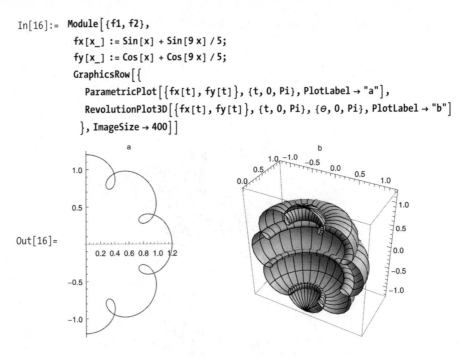

Figure 7-5. Relationship between ParametricPlot *and* RevolutionPlot3D

RevolutionPlot3D was introduced in Mathematica 6. Prior to version 6, similar surfaces could be generated with ParametricPlot3D; however, the equations one needs to plot a specific surface using RevolutionPlot3D are often simpler and more intuitive than those used when plotting parametrically. Both of the following plots yield a torus, but the RevolutionPlot3D version is simpler.

```
In[17]:= GraphicsRow[
            {ParametricPlot3D[{(2 + Cos[v]) Sin[u], (2 + Cos[v]) Cos[u], 2 + Sin[v]},
              {u, 0, 2 Pi}, {v, 0, 2 Pi}],
            RevolutionPlot3D[{2 + Cos[t], 2 + Sin[t]}, {t, 0, 2 Pi}]}, ImageSize → 400]
```

Out[17]=

As of version 6, Mathematica did not have a RevolutionAxis option, which was in a legacy package called Graphics`SurfaceOfRevolution`. The effect could be emulated by swapping axes and using ViewVertical. Here I also use ViewPoint to compensate for the different default orientations of the two plotting functions, but that is not strictly necessary. The important aspect of the code that produces Figure 7-6 is the transposition of t and t^2 in RevolutionPlot3D.

```
In[18]:=  Needs["Graphics`SurfaceOfRevolution`"]
          GraphicsRow[{RevolutionPlot3D[{t^2, t}, {t, 0, 2},
            Ticks → None, ViewVertical → {-1, 0, 0}, ViewPoint → {-2, -2, 1.1}],
            SurfaceOfRevolution[{t, t^2}, {t, 0, 2}, Ticks → None,
            RevolutionAxis → {1, 0, 0}]}, ImageSize → 400]
```

```
General::obspkg :
Graphics`SurfaceOfRevolution` is now obsolete. The
    legacy version being loaded may conflict with
    current Mathematica functionality. See the
    Compatibility Guide for updating information. ≫
```

Out[19]=

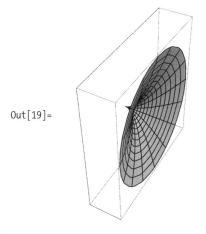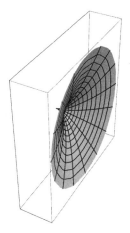

Figure 7-6. Emulating SurfaceOfRevolution

(Note: RevolutionAxis was added in version 7.)

See Also

See discussion of ParametricPlot3D in Recipe 7.4.

See Recipe 7.12 for use of the geometry options ViewVertical and ViewPoint.

7.4 Plotting 3D Surfaces Parametrically

Problem

You want to plot a 3D curve or surface parameterized over a region defined by a range.

Solution

Here you plot a curve in 3D space by specifying a single variable u over the range [-Pi,Pi]. This creates the curve in 3D space, shown in Figure 7-7.

```
In[20]:= ParametricPlot3D[{Cos[u], Sin[u], Cos[u^2] * Sin[u^2]},
            {u, -Pi, Pi}, ImageSize → Small]
```

Out[20]=

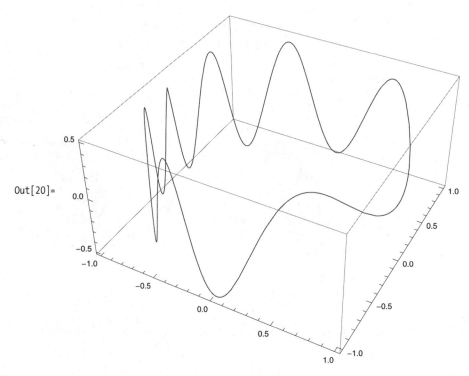

Figure 7-7. Curve in 3D space

Here you plot a surface in 3D space by specifying an area defined by variables u and v, yielding Figure 7-8.

In[21]:= `ParametricPlot3D[{Cos[u], Sin[v], Cos[u^2] * Sin[v^2]},`
        `{u, -Pi, Pi}, {v, -Pi, Pi}, ImageSize → Small]`

Out[21]=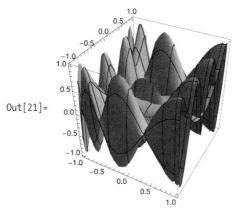

Figure 7-8. Surface in 3D space

Discussion

To get a better understanding of `ParametricPlot3D`, consider it as a generalization of the more specialized `Plot3D`. In `Plot3D`, the *x* and *y* coordinates always vary linearly over the range as it plots a specified function in the z-axis. This implies that you can mimic `Plot3D` using `ParametricPlot` (Figure 7-9). The only caveat is that you need to change the `BoxRatios`, which have different defaults in `ParametricPlot3D`.

In[22]:= `GraphicsRow[`
        `{Plot3D[Sin[x y] + Cos[x], {x, -Pi, Pi}, {y, -Pi, Pi}, PlotLabel → Plot3D],`
        `ParametricPlot3D[{x, y, Sin[x y] + Cos[x]}, {x, -Pi, Pi}, {y, -Pi, Pi},`
        `BoxRatios → {1, 1, 0.4}, PlotLabel -> ParametricPlot3D]}, ImageSize → 400]`

Out[22]=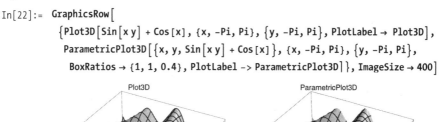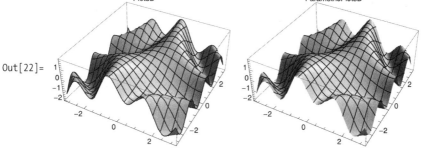

Figure 7-9. Using `ParametricPlot3D` *to emulate* `Plot3D`

The relationship between ParametricPlot3D and SphericalPlot3D can be understood in terms of the following:

$fx = f[\theta,\phi] \sin \theta \cos \phi$

$fy = f[\theta,\phi] \sin \theta \sin \phi$

$fz = f[\theta,\phi] \cos \theta$

For example, if we pick $f[\theta,\phi]$ to be the constant 1, both SphericalPlot3D and ParametricPlot3D give a sphere using this relationship.

```
In[23]:= GraphicsRow[
            {SphericalPlot3D[1, {θ, 0, Pi}, {φ, 0, 2 Pi}, PlotLabel -> SphericalPlot3D],
             ParametricPlot3D[{1 Sin[θ] Cos[φ], 1 Sin[θ] Sin[φ], 1 Cos[θ]},
              {θ, 0, Pi}, {φ, 0, 2 Pi}, PlotLabel -> ParametricPlot3D]}, ImageSize → 400]
```

Out[23]=

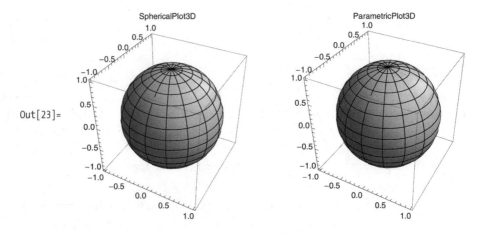

7.5 Creating 3D Contour Plots

Problem

You want to create a plot showing the surfaces where a function of three variables takes on a specific value (Figure 7-10).

Solution

Use ContourPlot3D with a function to produce evenly spaced contour surfaces for that function.

In[24]:= `ContourPlot3D[Sin[x y z], {x, -Pi, Pi},`
`{y, -1, 1}, {z, -1, 1}, ImageSize → 300]`

Out[24]=

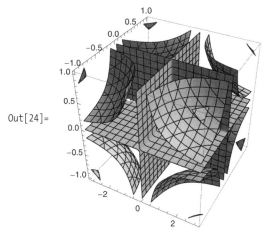

Figure 7-10. 3D contour plot example

Use `ContourPlot3D` with an equivalence relation to plot the surface where the equivalence is satisfied. In Figure 7-11, `ContourPlot3D` shows the surface where the polynomial is equal to zero.

In[25]:= `ContourPlot3D[x^3 + y^2 - z^2 == 0,`
`{x, -2, 2}, {y, -2, 2}, {z, -2, 2}, ImageSize → Small]`

Out[25]=

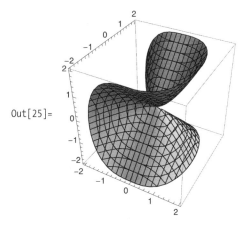

Figure 7-11. Surface where polynomial is zero

Discussion

3D contour plots show surfaces of equal value. ContourPlot3D plots several equally spaced surfaces over the specified intervals. You use the option Contours → n, where n is an integer, to control the number of surfaces.

```
In[26]:=  GraphicsGrid[
            Partition[Table[ContourPlot3D[x^3 + y^2 - z^2, {x, -2, 2}, {y, -2, 2},
              {z, -2, 2}, Contours → n, PlotLabel → "Contours->" <> ToString[n]],
              {n, 1, 4}], 2], ImageSize → 400]
```

Out[26]=

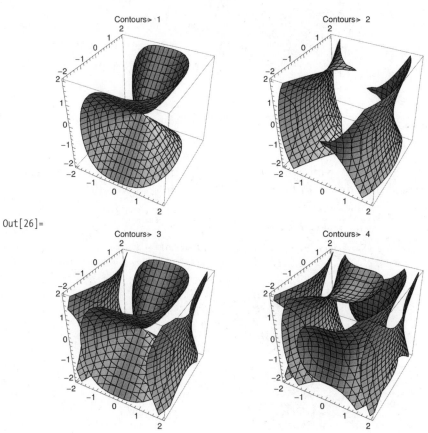

See Also

The 2D version ContourPlot is discussed in Recipe 7.6.

7.6 Combining 2D Contours with 3D Plots

Problem

You want to use a 2D contour plot to annotate the lower plane of a 3D plot.

Solution

Transform the 2D contour plot into a 3D graphic by adding a third z coordinate of constant value. Use Show to combine the new 3D graphic with a 3D plot.

```
In[27]:=  Module[{f}, f[x_, y_, z_] := 2 x^3 + 3 y^2 - 5 z; Show[
            ContourPlot3D[f[x, y, z], {x, -1, 1}, {y, -1, 1}, {z, -1, 1}, Contours → 1],
            Graphics3D[ContourPlot[f[x, y, -1], {x, -1, 1}, {y, -1, 1}][[1]] /.
              {x_Real, y_Real} → {x, y, -1}], ImageSize → 300]]
```

Out[27]=
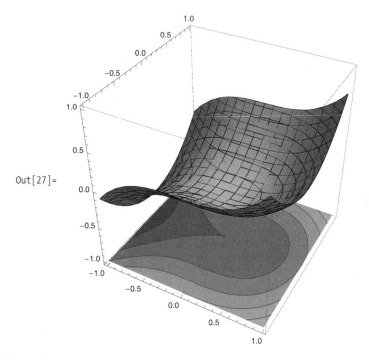

Discussion

You can apply the same technique to Plot3D. Here I use a larger PlotRange on the z-axis to provide room to see the contour. Using Opacity to add some translucence to the 3D plot also allows the contour plot to be better viewed.

```
In[28]:=  Module[{f}, f[x_, y_] := Sin[2 Pi x^3] + Cos[3 Pi y^2];
          Show[Plot3D[f[x, y], {x, -1, 1}, {y, -1, 1},
            PlotStyle → Opacity[0.7], PlotRange → {Automatic, Automatic, {-8, 2}}],
          Graphics3D[
            ContourPlot[f[x, y], {x, -1, 1}, {y, -1, 1}, Axes → False][[1]]
            ] /. {x : _Real, y : _Real} → {x, y, -8}],
          ViewPoint → {-2, -2, 1}, ImageSize → 300
          ]
        ]
```

Out[28]=

7.7 Constraining Plots to Specified Regions

Problem

You want to plot a 3D surface that includes only the points defined by a predicate.

Solution

Use the RegionFunction option with Plot3D, SphericalPlot3D, RevolutionPlot3D, ParametricPlot3D, and other 3D plots.

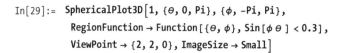

```
In[29]:= SphericalPlot3D[1, {θ, 0, Pi}, {φ, -Pi, Pi},
           RegionFunction → Function[{θ, φ}, Sin[φ θ] < 0.3],
           ViewPoint → {2, 2, 0}, ImageSize → Small]
```

Out[29]=

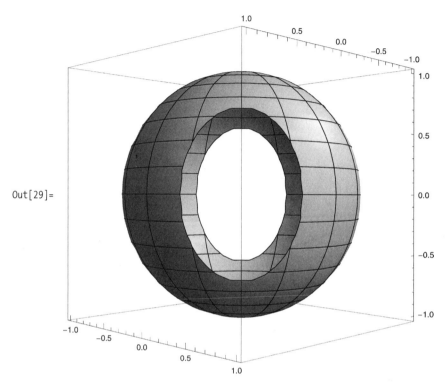

Discussion

The parameters passed to a region function vary by plot type; these are listed in Table 7-1.

Table 7-1. Region functions by plot type

Plot type	RegionFunction arguments
Plot3D, ListPlot3D, ListSurfacePlot3D	x, y, z
ContourPlot3D, ListContourPlot3D	x, y, z, f
ParametricPlot3D	x, y, z, u, v
SphericalPlot3D	x, y, z, θ, φ, r
RevolutionPlot3D	x, y, z, t, θ, r

The region function can be used to create quite exotic effects, as demonstrated in Figure 7-12.

```
In[30]:= GraphicsRow[{SphericalPlot3D[1 + Sin[5 φ] / 10, {θ, 0, Pi}, {φ, 0, 2 Pi},
            RegionFunction -> (Sin[5 (#3 + #5)] > 0 &),
              Mesh → None, BoundaryStyle → Black],
            SphericalPlot3D[1 + Sin[5 φ] / 10, {θ, 0, Pi}, {φ, 0, 2 Pi},
            RegionFunction -> (Sin[5 (#3 + #6)] > 0 &),
              Mesh → None, BoundaryStyle → Black]}, ImageSize → 400]
```

Out[30]=

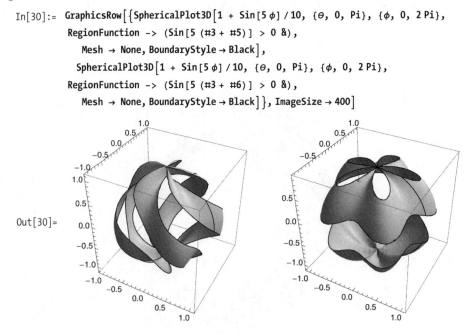

Figure 7-12. Effects of the RegionFunction *option*

7.8 Plotting Data in 3D

Problem

You have a matrix of data points that you want to plot as heights, with possible interpolation of intermediate values.

Solution

Use ListPlot3D with InterpolationOrder→0 to plot distinct levels, Interpolation-Order→1 to join points with straight lines, and InterpolationOrder→2 or higher to create smoother surfaces.

```
In[31]:= SeedRandom[1000];
          data = RandomReal[{-10, 10}, {20, 20}];
```

In[33]:= GraphicsColumn[
    Table[ListPlot3D[data, InterpolationOrder → i, Mesh → None], {i, 0, 2}],
    ImageSize → 150, Frame → All]

Out[33]=

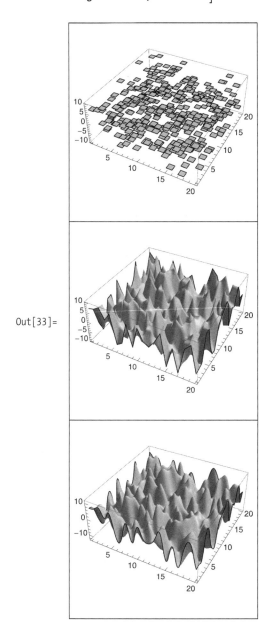

Discussion

3D list plots are often enhanced by use of a mesh. Here, in an example adapted from the Wolfram documentation, I show a plot of elevation of the state of Utah by latitude and longitude. The option MeshFunctions → {#3 &} uses the elevation data to specify the mesh giving contours (first image) that help visualize the elvation better than the default mesh (second image).

```
In[34]:= Column[{ListPlot3D[
            {CityData[#, "Longitude"], CityData[#, "Latitude"], CityData[#,
              "Elevation"]} & /@ CityData[{All, "Utah", "UnitedStates"}],
          MeshFunctions → {#3 &}, ImageSize → 300],
        ListPlot3D[{CityData[#, "Longitude"],
            CityData[#, "Latitude"], CityData[#, "Elevation"]} & /@
          CityData[{All, "Utah", "UnitedStates"}], ImageSize → 300]}]
```

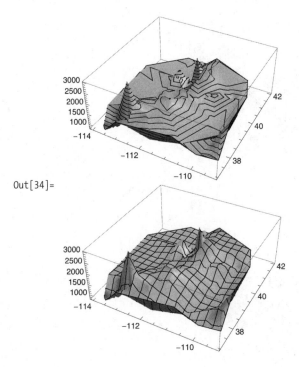

Out[34]=

See Also

ListPointPlot3D is used to create 3D scatter plots.

7.9 Plotting 3D Regions Where a Predicate Is Satisfied

Problem

You want to visualize regions where a predicate is satisfied.

Solution

RegionPlot takes a predicate of up to three variables. The predicate can use all of the relational operators (<, <=, >, >=, ==, !=) and logical connectives (&&, ||, Not).

```
In[35]:= RegionPlot3D[ x^2 + z^3 - 4 y^2 > 1 || x^2 + y^2 + z^2 < 0.5,
          {x, -2, 2}, {y, -2, 2}, {z, -2, 2}, ViewPoint → Front, ImageSize → 250]
```

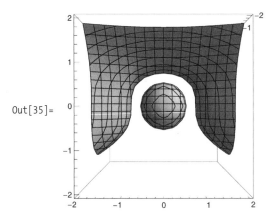

Out[35]=

Discussion

RegionPlot3D uses an adaptive algorithm that is based on the options PlotPoints and MaxRecursion. The default setting for each is Automatic, meaning Mathematica will pick what it thinks are appropriate values based on the predicate and ranges. The algorithm first samples using equally spaced points, and then subdivides those points based on MaxRecursions and the behavior of the predicate. It is possible for the algorithm to miss regions where the predicate is true. One way to gain confidence in the result is to plot with successively larger values for PlotPoints and MaxRecursion. However, of the two, PlotPoints usually has a more significant effect.

```
In[314]:= Grid[Partition[Table[
          RegionPlot3D[x^2 + y^2 + z^2 ≤ 0.75 + Sin[3 x] Sin[5 y] Sin[7 z] / 2,
            {x, -1.25, 1.25}, {y, -1.25, 1.25}, {z, -1.25, 1.25}, Mesh → None,
            MaxRecursion → 0, PlotPoints → pp], {pp, {5, 10, 15, 25}}], 2]]
```

Out[314]=

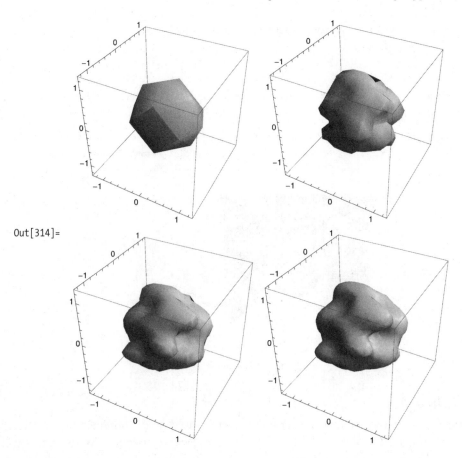

7.10 Displaying 3D Geometrical Shapes

Problem

You want to create graphics that contain spheres, cylinders, polyhedra, and other 3D shapes.

Solution

Mathematica has 3D primitives: Cuboid, Sphere, Cylinder Line, Point, and Polygon.

```
In[37]:= ClearAll[cone]

In[38]:= cone[height_, base_, {x_, y_, z_}, {ax_, ay_, az_}] :=
          Module[{c1, c2, c3, c4, c5},
            c1 = RevolutionPlot3D[{t, -height t 2}, {t, 0, base}, Mesh → None];
            c2 = Rotate[c1[[1]], ax, {1, 0, 0}]; c3 = Rotate[c2, ay, {0, 1, 0}];
            c4 = Rotate[c3, az, {0, 0, 1}];
            c5 = Translate[c4, {x, y, z + height * base}]; c5]
        torus[] := {}
        snowman3D[bodyRadius_] := Module[{bodyCenter = {0, 0, 0},
            (*Proportioning the torso and
              head based on golden ratio gives pleasing effect.*)
            torsoRadius = bodyRadius / GoldenRatio,
            headRadius = bodyRadius / (GoldenRatio^2),
            torsoCenter, headCenter, leftShoulder, rightShoulder,
            buttonSize = bodyRadius / 10, buttonSep = bodyRadius / 3.3,
            leftHand, rightHand, mouthCenter, leftEyeCenter, rightEyeCenter},
            torsoCenter =
              {bodyCenter[[1]], bodyCenter[[2]], torsoRadius + bodyRadius};
            headCenter = {bodyCenter[[1]], bodyCenter[[2]],
              bodyRadius + 2 torsoRadius + headRadius};
            (*Position the arms at -60 and 60 degrees.*)
            leftShoulder = torsoCenter +
              {torsoRadius * Sin[-Pi / 3], 0, torsoRadius * Cos[-Pi / 3]};
            leftHand = torsoCenter + {2.5 torsoRadius * Sin[-Pi / 3],
              0, 3 torsoRadius * Cos[-Pi / 3]};
            rightShoulder = torsoCenter + {torsoRadius * Sin[Pi / 3],
              0, torsoRadius * Cos[Pi / 3]};
            rightHand = torsoCenter + {2.5 torsoRadius * Sin[Pi / 3],
              0, 3 torsoRadius * Cos[Pi / 3]};
            (*Position eyes at -45 and 45 degrees and half
              the radius of the head.*)
            leftEyeCenter = headCenter + {0.5 headRadius * Sin[-Pi / 4],
              -0.8 headRadius, 0.5 headRadius * Cos[-Pi / 4]};
            rightEyeCenter = headCenter + {0.5 headRadius * Sin[Pi / 4],
              -0.8 headRadius, 0.5 headRadius * Cos[Pi / 4]};
            (*Position mouth at 180 degrees - bottom of circle,
            also half radius of head.*)
            mouthCenter = headCenter + {0.75 headRadius * Sin[Pi],
              -25, 0.75 headRadius * Cos[Pi]};
```

```
Graphics3D[{
    Sphere[bodyCenter, bodyRadius], (*Base circle*)
    Sphere[torsoCenter, torsoRadius], (*Middle circle*)
    Sphere[headCenter, headRadius],
    Cylinder[{leftShoulder, leftHand}, 1.5],
    Cylinder[{rightShoulder, rightHand}, 1.5],
    Sphere[leftEyeCenter, headRadius / 4],
    Sphere[rightEyeCenter, headRadius / 4],
    cone[headRadius / 4, headRadius / 4,
      headCenter - {headRadius / 8, 2 headRadius, 0.75 headRadius},
      {90 Degree, 180 Degree, -5 Degree}]}, Axes → True,
    AxesLabel → {"x", "y", "z"}, ImageSize → Small]];
snowman3D[30]
```

Out[41]=

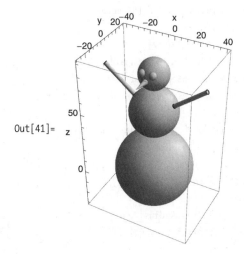

Discussion

A more mathematically inspired demonstration of graphics primitives is the Dandelin construction. Here one drops two spheres, one small and one large, into a cone such that the spheres do not touch. Consider a plane that slices through the cone tangent to the surface of both spheres. As you may know, a plane intersecting a cone traces an ellipse. What is remarkable is that the tangent points with the spheres are the foci of this ellipse. I adapt the construction from Stan Wagon's *Mathematica in Action* (W.H. Freeman), upgrading it to take advantage of the advanced 3D features of Mathematica 6, such as Opacity and PointSize. I refer the reader to Wagon's book for the derivation of the mathematics.

```
In[42]:= Block[
        {r1, r2, m, h1, h2, C1, C2, M, MC1, MC2, T1, T2, ht,
         cone, slope, plane},
        {r1, r2} = {1.4, 3.4};
        m = Tan[70. * Degree];
        h1 := r1 * Sqrt[1 + m^2];
        h2 := r2 * Sqrt[1 + m^2];
        C1 := {0, 0, h1};
        C2 := {0, 0, h2};
        M = {0, MC1 + h1};
        MC2 = MC1 * (r2 / r1);
        MC1 = (r1 * (h2 - h1)) / (r1 + r2);
        T1 = C1 + r1 * {-Sqrt[1 - r1^2/MC1^2], 0, r1/MC1};
        T2 = C2 + r2 * {Sqrt[1 - r2^2/MC2^2], 0, -(r2/MC2)};
        ht = 1.2 * (h2 + r2); cone[m_, h_] :=
        RevolutionPlot3D[{t, m * t}, {t, 0, h/m}, Mesh -> False][[1]];
        slope = (T2[[3]] - T1[[3]]) / (T2[[1]] - T1[[1]]);
        plane = ParametricPlot3D[{t, u, slope * t + M[[2]]}, {t, -2 * m, 12/m},
            {u, -3, 3}, Boxed -> False, Axes -> False][[1]];

        Graphics3D[{{Opacity[0.45], cone[m, 1.2 * (h2 + r2)]},
           {Opacity[0.5], Sphere[C1, r1], Sphere[C2, r2]},
           {Opacity[0.5], plane}, PointSize[0.0175], Point[T1], Point[T2]},
          Boxed -> False, ViewPoint -> {-1.8, -2.5, 1.5}, ImageSize -> 300]]
```

Out[42]=

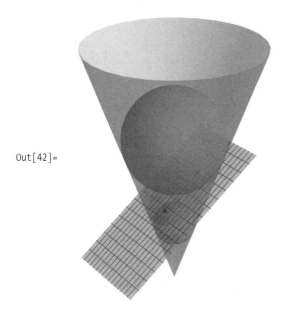

Mathematica can also deal with 3D graphics that are not necessarily of mathematical origin. You can demonstrate this using ExampleData.

```
In[43]:= GraphicsGrid[
            Partition[ExampleData /@ Take[ ExampleData["Geometry3D"], 16], 4]]
```

Out[43]=

7.11 Constructing Wireframe Models from Mesh

Problem

You want to build a wireframe model or other structural models from an existing 3D plot.

Solution

The following solution was developed by Ulises Cervantes-Pimentel and Chris Carlson of Wolfram Research. As with Recipe 7.6, the trick is to leverage Mathematica's symbolic representation of 3D graphics and to perform transformations on that representation to yield the desired result.

You begin with the shape of interest. Here Chris Carlson was interested in an architectural model of a bubblelike structure. Note the use of the Mesh option, which is central to extracting the wireframe.

```
In[44]:= bubbleModel = Module[
        {d = 1.5`, h = 5, l = 0.15`, nx = 10, ny = 10, r = 0.4`, t = 0.15`, zMin = -0.2`},
        ContourPlot3D[((x - d/2)^2 + y^2 + h z^2 - 1) ((x + d/2)^2 + y^2 + h (z + t)^2 - r),
        {x, -2, 2}, {y, -2, 2}, {z, zMin, 1}, BoxRatios → Automatic,
        PlotPoints → 20 {1, 1, 1}, Axes → None, PerformanceGoal → "Quality",
        Contours → {l}, ImageSize → 400, Mesh → {nx, ny, 0}]]
```

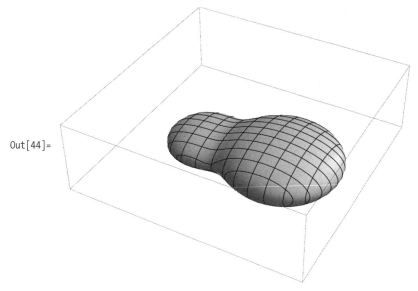

Out[44]=

You can go directly to a wireframe by simply extracting the lines.

```
In[45]:= Graphics3D[Cases[Normal[bubbleModel], _Line, ∞],
        Boxed → False, ImageSize → 400]
```

Out[45]=

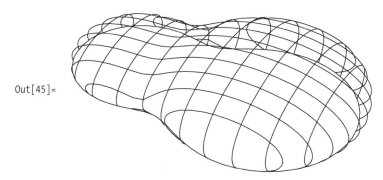

Discussion

The solution was quite simple because the transformation was a simple extraction of graphics data that was already present. However, you can take this approach much further. Here Normal is used to force the Graphics3D object into a representation of low-level primitives, and Cases is used to extract the lines. However, this time the lines are transformed to polygons to create a box model.

```
In[46]:= Graphics3D[Cases[Normal[bubbleModel], Line[pts_, ___] :> Polygon[pts], ∞],
            Boxed → False, ImageSize → 400]
```

Out[46]=

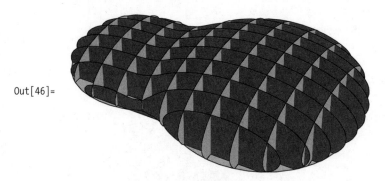

If your end goal was an architectural structure, the box model is no good. You need to open up the space. Here is an even more sophisticated transformation that turns the walls of the model into curved support beams.

```
In[47]:= InsetPoints[pts_] := Polygon[Join[pts, Reverse[
            Module[{centroid = (Plus @@ pts) / Length[pts]},
              (# + .1 (centroid - #)) & /@ pts]
            ]]]
        Graphics3D[Cases[Normal[bubbleModel],
            Line[pts_, ___] :> InsetPoints[pts], ∞], Boxed → False, ImageSize → 500]
```

Out[48]=

As a final step, you may want to show how the structure would look if it were covered with a translucent covering. Here Mathematica's sophisticated Lighting and Specularity options are used.

```
In[49]:= Graphics3D[{
            Gray,
            Cases[Normal[bubbleModel], Line[pts_, ___] :> InsetPoints[pts], ∞],

            EdgeForm[None], Opacity[.5],
            Specularity[White, 1000], Hue[.66, .75, .5], Lighting → "Neutral",
            Cases[Normal[bubbleModel], _Polygon, ∞]
          }, Boxed → False, ImageSize → 500, Lighting → "Neutral"]
```

Out[49]=

See Also

Recipe 7.13 covers Lighting and Specularity.

Chris Carlson gave a superb presentation at the 2009 International Mathematica User Conference (IMUC). This post on the Wolfram Blog covers a good portion of the talk: *http://bit.ly/291CDE*.

7.12 Controlling Viewing Geometry

Problem

You want to control the placement of a simulated camera that determines viewing perspective of a 3D graphic.

Solution

Use the ViewPoint option to control the point in space from which a 3D object is to be viewed. Here I enumerate some of the possibilities.

```
In[50]:= GraphicsGrid[
           Partition[Table[Append[ExampleData[{"Geometry3D", "Beethoven"}],
             {ViewPoint → vp, PlotLabel → ToString[vp]}], {vp, {Front, Back,
             Above, Below, Top, Left, Right, {0, -2, 2}, {2, -2, 0}}}], 3]]
```

Out[50]=

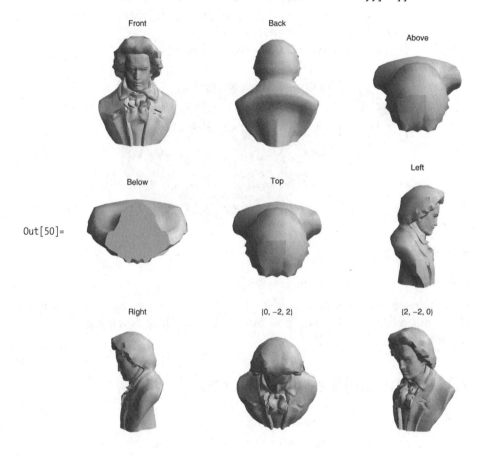

Use the ViewCenter option to control the point that should appear as the center of the displayed image. The coordinates are scaled to the range [0,1].

```
In[51]:= Grid[Partition[
        Table[Graphics3D[Cylinder[], ViewCenter → vc, SphericalRegion → True,
          PlotLabel → ToString[N[vc, 2]], ImageSize → Tiny], {vc,
          {{0, 0, 0}, {1/2, 1/2, 1/2}, {1, 0, 1}, {1, 1, 0}, {0, 1, 1}, {1, 1, 1},
           {1/3, 1/2, 1/3}, {0, 1/3, 1/3}, {1/3, 1/3, 0}}}], 3], Frame → All]
```

Out[51]=

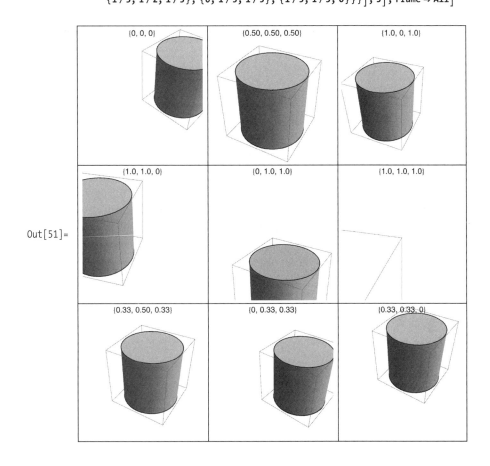

Use the ViewVertical option to control which coordinates should be vertical.

In[52]:= `GraphicsRow[Table[Graphics3D[Cylinder[], ViewVertical → vv],`
`{vv, {{1, 0, 0}, {0, 1, 0}, {0, 0, 1}, {-0.5, -1, 1}}}]]`

Out[52]=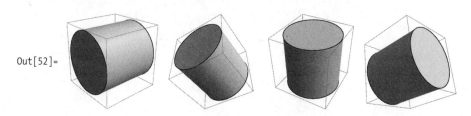

Discussion

For many users, combinations of ViewPoint, ViewCenter, and ViewVertical will create the initial spatial orientation of the 3D graphic that most suits your tastes or visual emphasis. However, there are additional options that are useful in some circumstances. ViewVector allows you to control the position and orientation of a simulated camera. ViewVector takes either a single vector that specifies the position of the camera that is pointed at ViewCenter or a pair of vectors that specify both the position of the camera and the center. ViewVector overrides ViewPoint and ViewCenter. To understand the concept of the camera, picture yourself looking through the camera as it moves around the stationary graphic.

In[53]:= `GraphicsRow[`
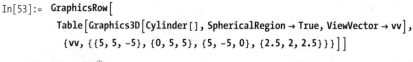
`Table[Graphics3D[Cylinder[], SphericalRegion → True, ViewVector → vv],`
`{vv, {{5, 5, -5}, {0, 5, 5}, {5, -5, 0}, {2.5, 2, 2.5}}}]]`

Out[53]=

Continuing with the camera metaphor, the option ViewAngle is analogous to zooming. The default view angle is 35 degrees. You can specify a specific angle or the symbol All, which will pick an angle that is sufficient to see everything.

7.13 Controlling Lighting and Surface Properties

Problem

You want to modulate lighting and surface characteristics to highlight important features or create artistic effects.

Solution

Mathematica provides quite sophisticated control of light via the options Lighting, Specularity, and Glow. The simplest settings for Lighting are Automatic, "Neutral", and None (Figure 7-13).

```
In[54]:= GraphicsRow[Table[Graphics3D[Sphere[], Lighting → l],
            {l, {Automatic, "Neutral", None}}]]
```

Out[54]=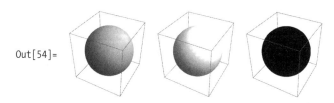

Figure 7-13. Examples of Lighting

For more sophisticated control, you can specify combinations of ambient, directional, spot, and point light sources (Figure 7-14). Try the code on your own for the full effect.

```
In[55]:= GraphicsRow[Table[Graphics3D[Sphere[], Lighting → l],
            {l, {{{"Point", Red, {0, 0, 2}}}, {{"Ambient", Green}},
                {{"Directional", Blue, {{0, 0, 1}, {-1, 1, 1}}}}}}]]
```

Out[55]=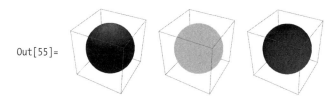

Figure 7-14. Examples of Glow

Glow is the opposite of Lighting. It specifies the color of the surface itself. Glow is also different from an object's color, as you can see in Figure 7-15. (However, Glow is not easily demonstrated in monochrome print. Please try the code on your own to see the effect.) Both the cylinder and the sphere have a green color, but the sphere also has a green glow. There is no lighting, so only the cylinder appears bright because of Glow. Another way Glow differs from Lighting is that it does not affect surrounding objects, only the objects with Glow. In other words, a glowing object is not a light source in the Graphics3D domain.

In[56]:= `Graphics3D[{{Glow[Green], Green, Cylinder[]},`
`{Green, Sphere[{2, 1.5, 0}]}}, Lighting → None, ImageSize → 300]`

Out[56]=

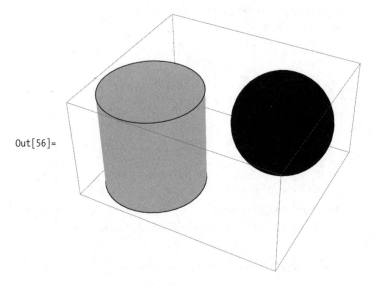

Figure 7-15. Difference between Glow and color

Discussion

As you probably would expect from your experience with colored lights, Mathematica lighting follows the additive color model (refer to the online version of the following image to appreciate its full glory: *http://bit.ly/xIgx7*).

```
In[58]:= Module[{lights, plane}, lights = {{"Spot", Red, {{3, 3, 5}, {3, 3, 0}}, Pi / 8},
            {"Spot", Green, {{7, 3, 5}, {7, 3, 0}}, Pi / 8},
            {"Spot", Blue, {{5, 6, 5}, {5, 6, 0}}, Pi / 8}};
         plane = ParametricPlot3D[{u, v, -2}, {u, 0, 10}, {v, 0, 9},
            PlotPoints → 100, MaxRecursion → 0, Mesh → None, Axes → False];
         Show[plane, Lighting → lights]]
```

Out[58]=

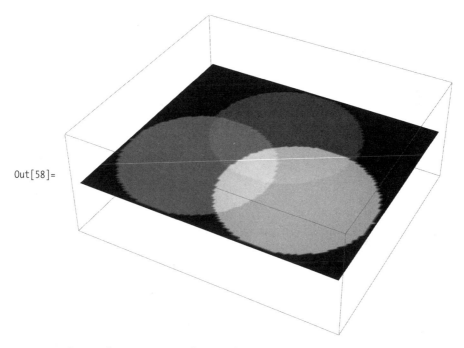

Lighting can be used as an option that applies to an entire graphic, but it also works as a graphics directive that applies to the objects that follow it within the same scope.

```
In[59]:= Graphics3D[{
            {Lighting → {{"Directional", Blue, {{0, 0, 1}, {-1, 1, 1}}},
                {"Point", Red, {1, 1, 1}}}},
              {Specularity[0.5], Sphere[{0, 0, 1}, 0.25]},
              Sphere[{1, 0, 0}, 0.25]},
              Sphere[{1, 1, 1}, 0.25]
            }, Lighting → {{"Ambient", Green}}, ImageSize → Small]
```

Out[59]=

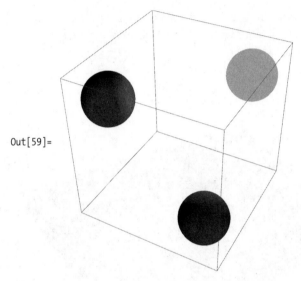

Specularity and Glow are strictly used as directives, although Specularity can be combined with Lighting.

See Also

The use cases covered in this recipe should satisfy most common uses of colored lighting, but if you are trying to achieve very specific lighting effects, you should consult the Mathematica documentation to explore the full range of forms Lighting, Specularity, and Glow can take and how they interact with color.

7.14 Transforming 3D Graphics

Problem

You want to scale, translate, or rotate graphics in 3D space.

Solution

Use Scale to stretch or shrink graphics.

```
In[60]:= GraphicsGrid[
           Partition[Table[Graphics3D[{Scale[Sphere[], {s, s, s}, {0, 0, 0}]},
             PlotRange → {{-2, 2}, {-2, 2}, {-2, 2}},
             PlotLabel → "Scale = " <> ToString[N[s]]],
             {s, {1/3, 1/2, 1, 2}}], 2], ImageSize → 300]
```

Out[60]=

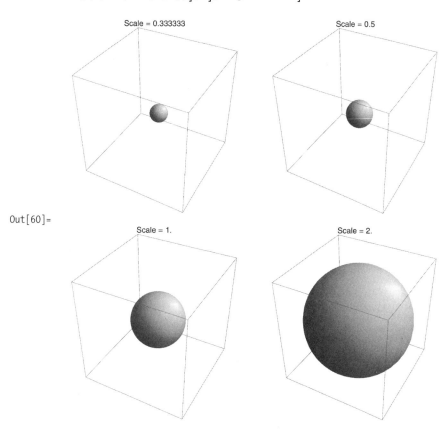

Use Translate to move graphics in 3D space. Figure 7-16 presents four translations of a sphere that is originally constructed at the origin.

```
In[61]:= GraphicsGrid[Partition[
            Table[Graphics3D[{Translate[Sphere[{0, 0, 0}, 0.75], v]}, PlotRange →
              {{-2, 2}, {-2, 2}, {-2, 2}}, PlotLabel → "Vec = " <> ToString[N[v]]],
            {v, {{-1, -1, -1}, {0, 0, 0}, {1, 1, 1}, {1 / 2, 0, -1 / 2}}}],
            2], ImageSize → 300]
```

Out[61]=

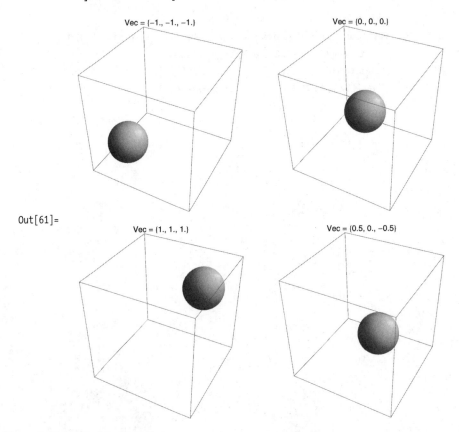

Figure 7-16. Examples of Translate

Use Rotate to change the orientation of graphics. Figure 7-17 rotates a cube through Pi/4 radians (45 degrees) but uses different vectors to define the rotation axis.

```
In[62]:= GraphicsGrid[
          Partition[Table[Graphics3D[{Rotate[Cuboid[], Pi / 4, v]}, PlotRange →
              {{-2, 2}, {-2, 2}, {-2, 2}}, PlotLabel → "Vec =" <> ToString[N[v]]],
            {v, {{-1, 0, 1}, {0, 1, -1}, {1, 1, 0}, {1, 1, 1}}}], 2], ImageSize → 300]
```

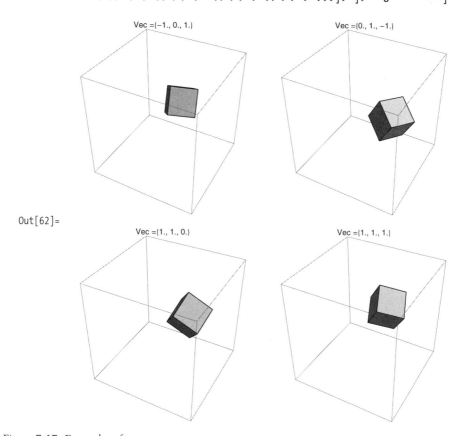

Out[62]=

Figure 7-17. Examples of Rotate

Discussion

In addition to the primitive transformations shown in the solution, Mathematica
provides support for transformation matrices and symbolic transformation functions.
Matrices include RotationMatrix, ScalingMatrix, ShearingMatrix, and Reflection-
Matrix. The transformation functions are RotationTransform, TranslationTransform,
ScalingTransform, ShearingTransform, ReflectionTransform, RescalingTransform,
AffineTransform, and LinearFractionalTransform. A smattering of examples is given here.

Transformations work in conjunction with the function GeometricTransformation, which takes a graphic and either a transformation or a matrix.

ShearingTransform[θ,v,n] is an area or volume preserving transformation that adds a slant, also known as a shear, to a graphic. Shear is specified in terms of an angle θ along a vector v and normal to a second vector n. Figure 7-18 shows a polyhedron in its original state followed by a shear transform. A translucent cube is also transformed to give a sense of the angles.

```
In[63]:= Module[{poly}, poly = PolyhedronData["DisdyakisDodecahedron"][[1]];
         GraphicsRow[{
           Graphics3D[{Green, poly}, Boxed → False, ViewPoint → Front],
           Graphics3D[{Green,
             GeometricTransformation[poly,
               ShearingTransform[Pi / 6, {1, 0, 0}, {0, 0, 1}]], Opacity[0.1],
             GeometricTransformation[Cuboid[{-1.5, -1.5, -1.5}, {1.5, 1.5, 1.5}],
               ShearingTransform[Pi / 6, {1, 0, 0}, {0, 0, 1}]]},
             Boxed → False, ViewPoint → Front]}
         ]]
```

Out[63]=

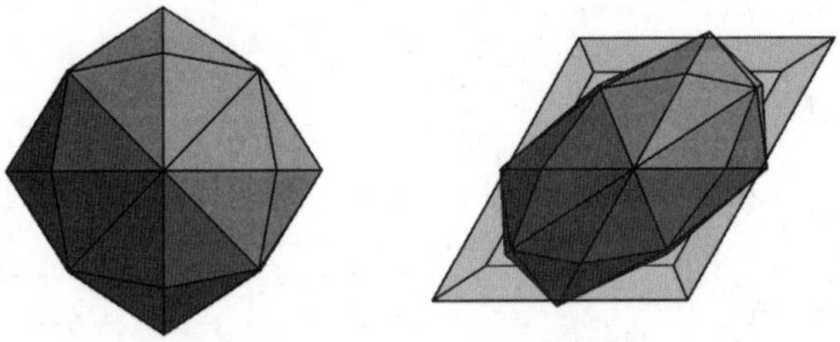

Figure 7-18. Example of ShearingTransform

7.15 Exploring Polyhedra

Problem

You want to investigate the characteristics of various polyhedra.

Solution

Mathematica 6 includes `PolyhedronData`, which is effectively an embedded database of polyhedra attributes. Apropos to this chapter, `PolyhedronData` contains the 3D graphics data for a variety of common and exotic polyhedra. If you call `PolyhedronData[]` with no arguments, it returns a list of all polyhedra it has information about.

```
In[64]:= Partition[
             PolyhedronData["Properties"],
             4, 4, {1, 1}, {}] // TableForm
```

```
Out[64]//TableForm=
```

AdjacentFaceIndices	AlternateNames	AlternateStandardNames	Amphichiral
Antiprism	Archimedean	ArchimedeanDual	Centroid
Chiral	Circumcenter	Circumradius	Circumsphere
Classes	Compound	Concave	Convex
Cuboid	DefaultOrientation	Deltahedron	DihedralAngleRules
DihedralAngles	Dipyramid	DualCompound	DualName
DualScale	EdgeCount	EdgeIndices	EdgeLengths
Edges	Equilateral	FaceCount	FaceCountRules
FaceIndices	Faces	GeneralizedDiameter	Hypercube
Image	Incenter	InertiaTensor	Information
Inradius	Insphere	Johnson	KeplerPoinsot
Midcenter	Midradius	Midsphere	Name
NetCoordinates	NetCount	NetEdgeIndices	NetEdges
NetFaceIndices	NetFaces	NetImage	NotationRules
Orientations	Orthotope	Platonic	PolyhedronIndices
Prism	Pyramid	Quasiregular	RectangularParallelepiped
RegionFunction	Rhombohedron	Rigid	SchlaefliSymbol
SelfDual	Shaky	Simplex	SkeletonCoordinates
SkeletonGraphName	SkeletonImage	SkeletonRules	SpaceFilling
StandardName	StandardNames	Stellation	StellationCount
SurfaceArea	SymmetryGroupString	Uniform	UniformDual
VertexCoordinates	VertexCount	VertexIndices	Volume
WythoffSymbol	Zonohedron		

If you call `PolyhedronData[poly]`, where poly is the name of the polyhedron, it will return the graphic. The code given here creates a labeled grid of a random selection of 24 polyhedra known to Mathematica 7. Here `StringSplit` uses a regular expression to parse the names on CamelCase boundaries and inserts a new line so the names fit inside the grid cells.

```
In[65]:= BlockRandom[
    SeedRandom[4]; Block[{p = Append[PolyhedronData[#],
        {PlotLabel → Text[Style[StringJoin[StringSplit[ToString[#],
            RegularExpression["([a-z])([A-Z])"] → "$1\n$2"]],
        FontSize → 10, TextAlignment → Center]], Boxed → False,
        ImageSize → Large]} & /@ RandomChoice[PolyhedronData[], 20]},
    Grid[Partition[Show[#, ImageSize → 95] & /@ p, 5], Spacings → {0, 0}]
    ]
]
```

Out[65]=

Gyroelongated Pentagonal Bicupola

Truncated Cube

Gyroelongated Square Pyramid

Gyroelongated Triangular Cupola

Dodecahedron Small Triambic Icosahedron Compound

Gyroelongated Pentagonal Cupola

Gyroelongated Triangular Bicupola

Augmented Truncated Dodecahedron

Gyroelongated Triangular Cupola

Elongated Pentagonal Gyrobirotunda

Parabidiminished Rhombicosidodecahedron

Tetrahedron

Rhombic Icosahedron

Elongated Triangular Cupola

Triaugmented Hexagonal Prism

Augmented Truncated Dodecahedron

Elongated Triangular Gyrobicupola

Biaugmented Triangular Prism

Triakis Icosahedron

Tetrahedron Three Compound

Discussion

PolyhedraData contains a treasure trove of polyhedra information. In the solution we demonstrate how to extract graphics by name. Here we show the input form of a cube.

```
In[66]:= PolyhedronData["Cube"] // InputForm
Out[66]//InputForm=
         Graphics3D[GraphicsComplex[{{-1/2, -1/2, -1/2}, {-1/2, -1/2, 1/2}, {-1/2,
         1/2, -1/2}, {-1/2, 1/2, 1/2}, {1/2, -1/2, -1/2},
            {1/2, -1/2, 1/2}, {1/2, 1/2, -1/2}, {1/2, 1/2, 1/2}}, Polygon[{{8, 4, 2,
         6}, {8, 6, 5, 7}, {8, 7, 3, 4}, {4, 3, 1, 2},
               {1, 3, 7, 5}, {2, 1, 5, 6}}]]]
```

The solution also exploits the ability to list all the polyhedra by providing no arguments. The solution used the first 20, but there are many more, as you can see.

```
In[67]:= Length[PolyhedronData[]]
Out[67]= 187
```

You can explore all of them with this little dynamic widget.

```
In[68]:= DynamicModule[{poly = "DodecahedronSixCompound"},
            Row[{PopupMenu[Dynamic[poly], PolyhedronData[]],
               Dynamic[PolyhedronData[poly]]}, " "]]
```

Out[68]=   DodecahedronSixCompound

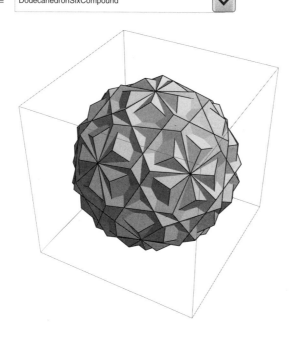

The polyhedra are grouped into classes. You can get a list of these classes or a list of the members of a particular class.

```
In[69]:= PolyhedronData["Classes"]
Out[69]= {Amphichiral, Antiprism, Archimedean, ArchimedeanDual, Chiral, Compound,
          Concave, Convex, Cuboid, Deltahedron, Dipyramid, Equilateral, Hypercube,
          Johnson, KeplerPoinsot, Orthotope, Platonic, Prism, Pyramid, Quasiregular,
          RectangularParallelepiped, Rhombohedron, Rigid, SelfDual, Shaky,
          Simplex, SpaceFilling, Stellation, Uniform, UniformDual, Zonohedron}
```

```
In[70]:= PolyhedronData["Chiral"]
Out[70]= {GyroelongatedPentagonalBicupola, GyroelongatedPentagonalBirotunda,
          GyroelongatedPentagonalCupolarotunda, GyroelongatedSquareBicupola,
          GyroelongatedTriangularBicupola, PentagonalHexecontahedron,
          PentagonalIcositetrahedron, SnubCube, SnubDodecahedron}
```

Polyhedra also have various properties, which you can list or use with a polyhedron to retrieve the value.

```
In[71]:= PolyhedronData["Properties"]
Out[71]= {AdjacentFaceIndices, AlternateNames, AlternateStandardNames, Amphichiral,
          Antiprism, Archimedean, ArchimedeanDual, Centroid, Chiral, Circumcenter,
          Circumradius, Circumsphere, Classes, Compound, Concave, Convex, Cuboid,
          DefaultOrientation, Deltahedron, DihedralAngleRules, DihedralAngles,
          Dipyramid, DualCompound, DualName, DualScale, EdgeCount, EdgeIndices,
          EdgeLengths, Edges, Equilateral, FaceCount, FaceCountRules, FaceIndices,
          Faces, GeneralizedDiameter, Hypercube, Image, Incenter, InertiaTensor,
          Information, Inradius, Insphere, Johnson, KeplerPoinsot, Midcenter,
          Midradius, Midsphere, Name, NetCoordinates, NetCount, NetEdgeIndices,
          NetEdges, NetFaceIndices, NetFaces, NetImage, NotationRules,
          Orientations, Orthotope, Platonic, PolyhedronIndices, Prism, Pyramid,
          Quasiregular, RectangularParallelepiped, RegionFunction, Rhombohedron,
          Rigid, SchlaefliSymbol, SelfDual, Shaky, Simplex, SkeletonCoordinates,
          SkeletonGraphName, SkeletonImage, SkeletonRules, SpaceFilling,
          StandardName, StandardNames, Stellation, StellationCount, SurfaceArea,
          SymmetryGroupString, Uniform, UniformDual, VertexCoordinates,
          VertexCount, VertexIndices, Volume, WythoffSymbol, Zonohedron}
```

```
In[72]:= PolyhedronData["GyroelongatedPentagonalBicupola", "VertexCount"]
Out[72]= 30
```

```
In[73]:= PolyhedronData["Cube", "Faces"]
```

$$Out[73]= \text{GraphicsComplex}\Big[\Big\{\Big\{-\frac{1}{2}, -\frac{1}{2}, -\frac{1}{2}\Big\}, \Big\{-\frac{1}{2}, -\frac{1}{2}, \frac{1}{2}\Big\}, \Big\{-\frac{1}{2}, \frac{1}{2}, -\frac{1}{2}\Big\},$$
$$\Big\{-\frac{1}{2}, \frac{1}{2}, \frac{1}{2}\Big\}, \Big\{\frac{1}{2}, -\frac{1}{2}, -\frac{1}{2}\Big\}, \Big\{\frac{1}{2}, -\frac{1}{2}, \frac{1}{2}\Big\}, \Big\{\frac{1}{2}, \frac{1}{2}, -\frac{1}{2}\Big\}, \Big\{\frac{1}{2}, \frac{1}{2}, \frac{1}{2}\Big\}\Big\},$$
$$\text{Polygon}\big[\{\{8, 4, 2, 6\}, \{8, 6, 5, 7\}, \{8, 7, 3, 4\},$$
$$\{4, 3, 1, 2\}, \{1, 3, 7, 5\}, \{2, 1, 5, 6\}\}\big]\Big]$$

Skeletal images show the polygons in terms of connected graphs.

```
In[74]:= GraphicsRow[{PolyhedronData["Cube", "SkeletonImage"], PolyhedronData[
        "GyroelongatedPentagonalBicupola", "SkeletonImage"]}, ImageSize → Medium]
```

Out[74]=

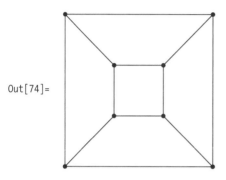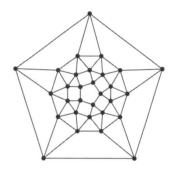

NetImage is my favorite aspect of PolyhedronData because it shows how to make a cutout that can be folded into an actual 3D model of the named polyhedron. My kids like this one, too, although I have to do all the tedious parts!

```
In[75]:= GraphicsRow[{PolyhedronData["GyroelongatedPentagonalBicupola", "NetImage"],
        Import[FileNameJoin[{NotebookDirectory[], "..", "images",
        "GyroelongatedPentagonalBicupolaConstr.PNG"}]]}]
```

Out[75]=

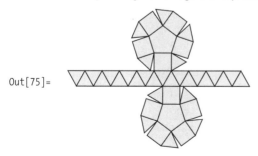

See Also

GraphData, KnotData, and LatticeData are equally cool graphical data sources that you can explore on your own. Refer to the Mathematica documentation.

7.16 Importing 3D Graphics from CAD and Other 3D Software

Problem

You have 3D data from another application that you would like to view or manipulate within Mathematica.

Solution

Mathematica 6 can import several popular 3D graphics formats, including Drawing Exchange Format (DXF) produced by AutoCAD and other CAD packages.

```
In[76]:= dxf = Import["ExampleData/helicopter.dxf.gz", ImageSize → Small]
```

Out[76]=

Discussion

Mathematica's symbolic representation makes it possible to manipulate imported graphics via pattern matching.

You can change colors and directives.

```
In[77]:= GraphicsRow[{dxf /. RGBColor[1., 0., 0.] → RGBColor[0, 1., 1.],
            dxf /. {RGBColor[__], Polygon[x_]} :> {EdgeForm[Dashed], Polygon[x]}},
          ImageSize → 400]
```

Out[77]=

You can extract elements based on properties. Here we delete all nonyellow polygons (i.e., all but the rotor).

```
In[78]:= DeleteCases[dxf, Except[{RGBColor[1., 1., 0.], Polygon[__]}], {5}]
```

Out[78]=

You can emphasize the component polygons by shrinking each toward its center and changing all colors to dark gray.

```
In[79]:= shrink[t_, Polygon[x_List, opts___]] := Module[
          {c = Plus @@ x / Length[x]}, Polygon[Map[(c + (1 - t) (# - c)) &, x], opts]]
```

```
In[80]:= dxf /. {x_Polygon :> shrink[0.4, x],
          RGBColor[_, _, _] :> GrayLevel[0.3], Small :> 600}
```

Out[80]=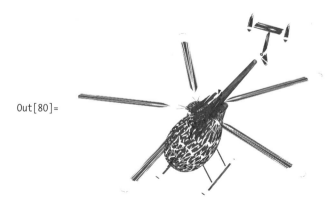

CHAPTER 8

Image Processing

I have a picture
Pinned to my wall
An image of you and of me and we're laughing
We're loving it all

...

You say I'm a dreamer
We're two of a kind
Both of us searching for some perfect world
We know we'll never find

Thompson Twins, "Hold Me Now"

8.0 Introduction

Image processing is a field with many challenges. The first challenge is the magnitude of the data. Consider that a simple 256×256 pixel grayscale image will contain 65,536 bytes of data for the pixel values alone. Larger color images can contain many times this amount. The second challenge is the raster form of the image data, which is optimized for display, not for detecting distinct visual elements. A third challenge is the noise and other artifacts of the image-capture process. A final challenge is the lack of contextual information; most images do not encode where they were taken, the lighting conditions, the device used, and so on (although this is beginning to change). In my opinion, these challenges make working on image processing very rewarding, especially when one considers that significant portions of our brains are dedicated to visual perception. Finding algorithms that achieve the kinds of visual-processing tasks that the brain performs is one way to begin to peel away the veil obscuring the workings of our most mysterious organ.

The field of image processing is very broad; this chapter only samples a small fraction of the relevant problems. The choice of topics is largely a function of the author's interests and experience. The full scope of image-processing research includes efficient encoding of images and video, image enhancement and restoration, image segmentation, recovering spatial shape from shading and pattern distortions, learning about 3D from multiple 2D images, as well as image recognition. Researchers in this field rely on a wide variety of mathematical techniques; hence, Mathematica is an ideal platform to get one's feet wet.

Image Representation

Mathematica uses the function Import to load images into a format suitable for processing and display within the frontend. When you use Import on an image file in versions of Mathematica prior to 7, you get a Graphics object that typically contains a single Mathematica graphics primitive called Raster. A Raster represents a 2D array of grayscale or color cells. A gray cell value will be a single number; a color cell value will be three or four numbers. An option called ColorFunction tells Mathematica how to map the cell values to display colors. Typical encodings are RGBColor, GrayLevel, and Hue. Most of the recipes in this chapter deal with grayscale images; however, the first recipe shows you how to transform red-green-blue (RGB) images to other encodings that are appropriate for the kinds of algorithms in these recipes.

As of version 7, Mathematica images have their own representation, called Image, which is distinct from Graphics (although you can request the older format for backward compatibility using "Graphic" with Import). To make these recipes compatible to both versions 6 and 7, I use the following functions throughout this chapter. However, in some recipes these are not sufficient because the code assumed Graphics form when recreating the image for display, and hence, expected Graphics options to be present in the imported version.

```
In[18]:= Clear[getImgData, getImgRange, getImgDim, rasterReplace]

        getImgData[img_Graphics] := img[[1, 1]]
        getImgData[img_Image]    := Reverse[ImageData[img, "Byte"]]

        getImgRange[img_Graphics] := img[[1, 3]]
        getImgRange[img_Image] := Module[{},
          Switch[ImageType[img], "Bit", {0, 1}, "Byte",
            {0, 255}, "Bit16", {0, 65 535}, "Real", {0.0, 1.0}]]

        getImgDim[img_Graphics] := img[[1, 2, 2]] - img[[1, 2, 1]]
        getImgDim[img_Image] := ImageDimensions[img]
```

```
getImgCoord[img_Graphics] := img[[1, 2]]
getImgCoord[img_Image]    := {{0, 0}, getImgDim[img]}

rasterReplace[img_Graphics, raster_List, opts___] :=
  Graphics[Raster[raster, img[[1, 2]]], opts, Sequence @@ Options[img[[1]]]],
    Sequence @@ Options[img]]

rasterReplace[img_Image, raster_List, opts___] :=
  Image[raster, img[[2]]], opts, Sequence @@ Options[img]]
```

Image Processing in Mathematica 7

Most of this chapter was originally written prior to the release of Mathematica 7, which introduced many native functions for image processing. After the release of version 7, I added content and augmented some of the recipes. However, I still left most of the custom algorithms intact, rather than just rewrite everything in terms of the built-in constructs. As I stated previously, I believe image-processing algorithms are interesting in their own right. The Mathematica 7 functions are very easy to use; if you want to sharpen an image, for example, use Sharpen and you are done. However, if you want to understand the mathematics, see Recipe 8.5 or 8.6. In some recipes, I simply refer you to the appropriate Mathematica function in the "See Also" section. There are some common image transformations that are not covered in this chapter, but most are easily implemented and are native to Mathematica 7. If you need to crop, pad, rotate, and so on, you will want to upgrade to version 7, which has ImageCrop, ImagePad, ImageResize, ImageTake, and ImageRotate.

See Also

The recipes in this chapter draw heavily on Rafael C. Gonzalez and Richard E. Woods's *Digital Image Processing,* Second Edition (Addison-Wesley). This is one of the classic texts in the field, and any individual who has a serious interest in image processing should own this text. Although I relied on the second edition, I would recommend buying the latest (third) edition, published by Prentice Hall in 2008.

If you have never worked with images in Mathematica, consult the documentation and experiment with the functions Import, Graphics, and Raster before diving into these recipes.

8.1 Extracting Image Information

Problem

You want to extract information from one or more image files for manipulation by Mathematica or for combining into a new image.

Solution

Use the two-argument version of the Import function to selectively import data from an image file. Using Import with a PNG, GIF, TIFF, BMP, or other supported image format will import the image and display it in the Mathematica frontend. However, sometimes you might want to extract a subset of the image data for manipulation rather than display. What information can you extract? This is answered using a second argument of "Elements".

```
In[200]:=  Import[FileNameJoin[
              {NotebookDirectory[], "..", "images", "truck.jpg"}], "Elements"]

Out[200]= {Aperture, BitDepth, CameraTopOrientation, ColorMap, ColorSpace, Data,
            DataType, Date, Exposure, FocalLength, Graphics, GrayLevels, Image,
            ImageSize, ISOSpeed, Manufacturer, Model, RawData, RGBColorArray}
```

Note that not every image will provide the same level of information. The image format and the device that produced the image determine which elements are available.

```
In[201]:=  Import[FileNameJoin[
              {NotebookDirectory[], "..", "images", "mechanism1.png"}], "Elements"]

Out[201]= {BitDepth, ColorSpace, Data, DataType,
            Graphics, GrayLevels, Image, ImageSize, RGBColorArray}
```

Once you know which elements are available, you can extract them by name.

```
In[202]:=  Import[FileNameJoin[
              {NotebookDirectory[], "..", "images", "truck.jpg"}], "BitDepth"]

Out[202]= 8
```

Note that an image element might be supported but not available, in which case Import will return None.

```
In[203]:=  Import[
              FileNameJoin[{NotebookDirectory[], "..", "images", "truck.jpg"}], "Model"]

Out[203]= None
```

However, if you ask for the value of an element that is not supported, Import will fail.

```
In[204]:= Import[FileNameJoin[{NotebookDirectory[], "..", "images", "truck.jpg"}],
          "Copyright"]
```

> Import::noelem :
> The Import element "Copyright" is not present when
>   importing as JPEG. >>

```
Out[204]= $Failed
```

Discussion

From an image processing point of view, the elements you will most likely extract are "Graphics", "GrayLevels", "Data", and "RGBColorArray". The "Graphics" element is the default element for an image file. It extracts the image in a format suitable for immediate display in the frontend.

```
In[205]:= Import[FileNameJoin[{NotebookDirectory[], "..", "images", "truck.jpg"}],
          "Graphics"]
```

Out[205]=

Note, if you want to extract the "Graphics" format without displaying it, terminate the expression with a semicolon.

```
In[206]:= image = Import[FileNameJoin[
             {NotebookDirectory[], "..", "images", "truck.jpg"}], "Graphics"];
```

The "GrayLevels" element will convert color image data to gray level data. That is, it will return a 2D array of pixel gray values in the range 0 (black) to 1 (white). Here I use Short to only show a few of the gray level values.

```
In[207]:= Short[Import[FileNameJoin[
              {NotebookDirectory[], "..", "images", "truck.jpg"}], "GrayLevels"], 6]
Out[207]//Short=
            {{0.283235, 0.330294, 0.270298, 0.242804, 0.227118, 0.190608,
             0.190608, 0.161494, 0.181102, 0.156357, 0.21518, 0.322149, 0.388816,
             0.446467, 0.524855, 0.576922, 0.620016, 0.646208, ≪125≫,
             0.980071, 0.988663, 0.980373, 0.981588, 0.98551, 0.984592, 0.984592,
             0.984122, 0.972357, 0.985016, 0.985016, 0.984973, 0.984078,
             0.984078, 0.984592, 0.984592, 0.983698}, ≪118≫, {≪1≫}}
```

The "Data" element will extract the image pixel data as it is stored in the image file. The format of the data will vary depending on the image type, but typically it will be a matrix of RGB triplets for a color image and gray values for a grayscale image both in the range [0,255].

```
In[208]:= Short[Import[FileNameJoin[
              {NotebookDirectory[], "..", "images", "truck.jpg"}], "Data"], 6]
Out[208]//Short=
            {{{86, 67, 63}, {98, 79, 75}, {82, 64, 60}, {73, 58, 53}, {69, 54, 49},
             {57, 46, 40}, {57, 46, 40}, {47, 40, 32}, {52, 45, 37}, {43, 40, 31},
             {58, 55, 46}, {82, 84, 73}, {99, 101, 90}, {113, 116, 105}, {131, 137, 125},
             {141, 152, 138}, {150, 164, 149}, {152, 173, 156}, {150, 175, 156},
             {141, 168, 149}, {136, 160, 144}, {142, 165, 149}, {149, 169, 157},
             {155, 173, 161}, {146, 163, 153}, {145, 165, 154}, {146, 167, 158},
             ≪107≫, {246, 245, 241}, {250, 249, 245}, {255, 255, 251},
             {255, 255, 251}, {249, 251, 248}, {248, 250, 247}, {247, 251, 252},
             {249, 253, 254}, {248, 252, 255}, {247, 251, 252}, {248, 255, 248},
             {246, 253, 245}, {249, 252, 245}, {250, 253, 246}, {252, 251, 249},
             {252, 251, 249}, {254, 249, 253}, {251, 246, 250}, {254, 249, 255},
             {254, 249, 255}, {252, 250, 255}, {252, 250, 253}, {252, 250, 253},
             {252, 251, 249}, {252, 251, 249}, {252, 251, 247}}, ≪118≫, {≪1≫}}
```

```
In[209]:=  Short[Import[FileNameJoin[
              {NotebookDirectory[], "..", "images", "truck.jpg"}], "RGBColorArray"], 6]
Out[209]//Short=
              {{RGBColor[0.337255, 0.262745, 0.247059],
                RGBColor[0.384314, 0.309804, 0.294118],
                RGBColor[0.321569, 0.25098, 0.235294],
                RGBColor[0.286275, 0.227451, 0.207843],
                RGBColor[0.270588, 0.211765, 0.192157],
                ≪150≫, RGBColor[0.988235, 0.980392, 0.992157],
                RGBColor[0.988235, 0.980392, 0.992157],
                RGBColor[0.988235, 0.984314, 0.976471],
                RGBColor[0.988235, 0.984314, 0.976471],
                RGBColor[0.988235, 0.984314, 0.968627]}, ≪119≫}
```

See Also

More details can be found in the Mathematica documentation for Import and the formats JPEG, TIFF, BMP, PNG, and GIF.

8.2 Converting Images from RGB Color Space to HSV Color Space

Problem

You have an image that is represented in RGB but most image-processing algorithms demand the hue-saturation-value (HSV) color space model.

Solution

The solution starts with defining some primitives to compute Hue, Saturation, and Value from Red, Green, and Blue intensities.

The HSV color model is often depicted geometrically as a cone (see *http://en. wikipedia.org/wiki/Image:HSV_cone.png*). The hue can be thought of as the angle of a vector rotating around the center, with angles close to 0 degrees corresponding to red and increasing angles moving through the rainbow out to violet and returning again to red. To simplify the math, we first scale the standard RGB values that range from 0 to 255 to values that range between 0 and 1. Mathematically speaking, you compute hue by finding which two of the three scaled RGB color intensities dominate and then using their difference to compute an angular offset from a starting angle determined by the third (least dominant) color. Here you divide the circle into six regions (red, orange, yellow, green, blue, violet) with i specifying the start region and f acting as a factor determining the offset from i. This value is scaled by the difference between the most dominant (rgbMax) and least dominant (rgbMin) color to yield a value between 0 and 6. Finally you divide by 6 to get a value for hue in the range [0,1].

```
In[210]:= HueValue[r_Integer, g_Integer, b_Integer] :=
            HueValue2[r / 255.0, g / 255.0, b / 255.0]
          HueValue2[r_ /; r ≤ 1, g_ /; g ≤ 1, b_ /; b ≤ 1] :=
            Module[{minRGB = Min[r, g, b], maxRGB = Max[r, g, b], f, i},
              Which[maxRGB == minRGB, Return[0],
                minRGB == r , f  = g - b; i = 3,
                minRGB == g, f = b - r; i = 5,
                minRGB == b, f = r - g; i = 1];
              (i - f / (maxRGB - minRGB)) / 6]
```

Saturation is a measure of the purity of the hue. Highly saturated colors are dominated by a single color, whereas low saturation yields colors that are more muted. Geometrically, saturation is depicted as the distance from the center to the edge of the HSV cone. Mathematically, saturation is the difference between the most dominant and least dominant color scaled by the most dominant. Again, you scale RGB integer values to the range [0,1].

```
In[212]:= SatValue[r_Integer, g_Integer, b_Integer] :=
            SatValue2[r / 255.0, g / 255.0, b / 255.0]
          SatValue2[r_ /; r ≤ 1, g_ /; g ≤ 1, b_ /; b ≤ 1] :=
            Module[{minRGB = Min[r, g, b], maxRGB = Max[r, g, b]},
              If[maxRGB > 0, (maxRGB - minRGB) / maxRGB, 0]]
```

The third component of the HSV triplet is the value, which is also known as brightness (HSV is sometimes referred to as HSB). The brightness is the simplest to compute since it is simply the value of the most dominant RGB value scaled to the range [0,1]. Geometrically, the value is the distance from the apex (dark) of the HSV cone to the base (bright).

```
In[214]:= BrightValue[r_Integer, g_Integer, b_Integer] := Max[r, g, b] / 255.0
```

Given these primitives, it becomes a relatively simple matter to translate an image from RGB space to HSV space. But before you can do this, you need to understand how Mathematica represents imported images. The applicable function is called Raster, and it depicts a rectangular region of color or gray level cells. See the "Discussion" section on page 338 for more information on Raster. The goal is to transform the RGB color cells to HSV color cells. An easy way to do that is to linearize the 2D grid into a linear array and then use the techniques from Recipe 2.1 to transform this RGB array into an HSV array. To get everything back to a 2D grid, we use the Partition function with information from the original image to get the proper width and height. To get HSV images to display properly, we tell Mathematica to use Hue as the ColorFunction. Finally, we copy options from the original graphic to the new graphic, which requires a sequence rather than a list.

```
In[215]:=  (*RGB2HSV[image_Graphics] :=
             Module[{rgb =Flatten[getImgData[image],1],hsv,width,height},
               {width,height} = getImgDim[image];
               hsv =
                 {Apply[HueValue,#], Apply[SatValue,#],Apply[BrightValue,#]}& /@ rgb;
               Graphics[Raster[Partition[hsv,width], {{0,0},getImgDim[image]},
                 ColorFunction→Hue],Sequence @@ Options[image]]]*)


           RGB2HSV[image_Graphics] :=
             Module[{rgb = Flatten[getImgData[image], 1], hsv, width, height},
               {width, height} = getImgDim[image];
               hsv = {Apply[HueValue, #],
                    Apply[SatValue, #], Apply[BrightValue, #]} & /@ rgb;
               rasterReplace[image, Partition[hsv, width], ColorFunction → Hue]]

In[216]:=  image = Import[FileNameJoin[
             {NotebookDirectory[], "..", "images", "truck.jpg"}], "Graphics"]
```

Out[216]=

```
In[217]:=  imageHSV = RGB2HSV[image]
```

Out[217]=

These two images of the red truck look identical, but we can see they have a very different internal representation by inspecting a portion of each Raster.

```
In[218]:= Short[getImgData[image][[1]], 3]
Out[218]//Short=
        {{104, 122, 142}, {99, 117, 137}, {94, 112, 132},
         {94, 112, 132}, {98, 119, 138}, {104, 125, 144}, {106, 127, 146},
         {106, 127, 146}, {101, 124, 142}, {101, 124, 142}, {100, 123, 141},
         {99, 122, 140}, {95, 121, 138}, ≪134≫, {94, 116, 130},
         {92, 114, 128}, {92, 114, 128}, {93, 115, 129}, {95, 117, 131},
         {99, 121, 135}, {98, 120, 134}, {98, 120, 134}, {98, 120, 134},
         {99, 121, 135}, {101, 123, 137}, {103, 125, 139}, {104, 126, 140}}

In[219]:= Short[getImgData[imageHSV][[1]], 3]
Out[219]//Short=
        {{0.587719, 0.267606, 0.556863}, {0.587719, 0.277372, 0.537255},
         {0.587719, 0.287879, 0.517647}, ≪155≫,
         {0.564815, 0.258993, 0.545098}, {0.564815, 0.257143, 0.54902}}
```

Discussion

The major color spaces in popular use are RGB, HSV, and cyan-magenta-yellow-black (CMYK). RGB is the most common format because it maps directly onto display technology. The problem with RGB is that it is not very good for image analysis because colors that are close in perceptual space are not grouped together in RGB space. CMYK is most often used in printing. HSV is popular in image processing applications because the mathematical distance between the colors is more closely aligned with human judgments, yielding a closer approximation to human perception of color. Another advantage of HSV is that one can immediately convert from color to grayscale by discarding the hue and saturation components and retaining the value component.

```
In[220]:= imageHSV /. {{_Real, _Real, v_Real} → v, Hue → GrayLevel}
```

Out[220]=

Doing image processing in Mathematica requires familiarity with the Raster graphics primitive. When an image is imported from a JPEG, BMP, or GIF file, it will be represented as an RGB or grayscale Raster with cell values ranging from 0 through 255. The ColorFunction will be RGBColor for color image and GrayLevel for grayscale images. There are several forms of the Raster function, but the form you will typically encounter in image processing is Raster[array, dimensions, scale, ColorFunction → function], where array is a 2D array of integers or RGB triplets, dimensions defines a rectangle of the form {{xmin,ymin}, {xmax,ymax}}, scale specifies the minimum and maximum values in the array (typically {0,255}), and function is either GrayLevel or RGBColor. A good way to test algorithms is to mathematically create rasters so you have controlled test cases.

For example, the following is a green gradient in RGB space that varies from black in the lower left corner to bright green in the upper right. (Of course, you'll need to try the code yourself to view the color effects.)

```
In[221]:= greenGradientRGB = Graphics[
            Raster[Table[{0, Min[g*16 + x, 255], 0}, {g, 0, 15}, {x, 0, 15}],
            {{0, 0}, {16, 16}}, {0, 255}], ImageSize → {160, 160}]
```

Out[221]=

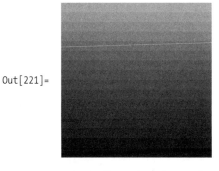

```
In[222]:= greenGradientHSV = RGB2HSV[greenGradientRGB]
```

Out[222]=

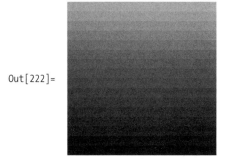

```
In[223]:= greenGradientHSV[[1, 2]]
Out[223]= {{0, 0}, {16, 16}}
```

In HSV space, we expect the hue coordinate to be a constant (1/3) with the exception of the black corner element. The saturation should also be constant and the brightness values should form a straight line when plotted. This is easy to check.

```
In[224]:= Union[Flatten[getImgData[greenGradientHSV] /. {h_, _, _} :> h]]
Out[224]= {0, 0.333333}
```

```
In[225]:= Count[Flatten[getImgData[greenGradientHSV] /. {h_, _, _} :> h], 0]
Out[225]= 1
```

```
In[226]:= Count[Flatten[getImgData[greenGradientHSV] /. {h_, _, _} :> h],
              0.3333333333333333`]
Out[226]= 255
```

```
In[227]:= ListPlot[Flatten[getImgData[greenGradientHSV] /. {_, _, v_} :> v],
              ImageSize -> Small]
```

Out[227]=

See Also

In Mathematica 7, use ColorConvert (see the documentation center: *http://bit.ly/irShF*).

Wikipedia has several very approachable articles on color models. See *http://bit.ly/lWvVW*, *http://bit.ly/2DZAhY*, *http://bit.ly/3jawwr*, and *http://bit.ly/2qHxrI*.

Color renderings of the images in this chapter can be found at *http://bit.ly/xIgx7* or *http://www.mathematicacookbook.com*.

8.3 Enhancing Images Using Histogram Equalization

Problem

You have an image that is too dark or too light and you would like to increase contrast.

Solution

You obtain the histogram of a grayscale image using BinCounts on the flattened raster matrix. If an image has poor contrast, you will see that the histogram is skewed when you plot the histogram using BarChart.

```
In[228]:= overexposed = Import[FileNameJoin[{NotebookDirectory[],
              "..", "images", "truckOverExposed.jpg"}], "Graphics"]
```

Out[228]=

```
In[229]:= Quiet[Needs["BarCharts`"]]
```

```
In[230]:= histogramPlot[image_Graphics] :=
            Module[{pixels = Flatten[getImgData[image]], min, max, dx, width, height},
              {min, max} = If[MatchQ[getImgRange[image], {_, _}],
                getImgRange[image], {0, 1}];
              dx = (max - min) / 255.0;
              BarChart[BinCounts[pixels, {min, max + dx, dx}], BarLabels → None,
                BarStyle → Black, BarSpacing → 0.25, BarEdges → False]]
```

In[231]:= **histogramPlot[overexposed]**

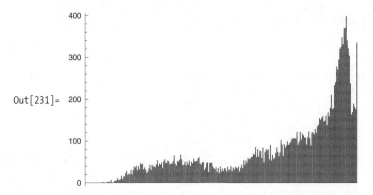

Out[231]=

Histogram equalization works by using the image distribution to derive a transformation function that will always yield a more uniform distribution of gray levels despite the shape of the input image's distribution. The solution below will work on any grayscale image but is not very efficient. I'll implement a more efficient solution in the "Discussion" section on page 343 and also cover theory that explains why this transformation works.

```
In[232]:= histCDF[x_, histogram_, n_] :=
            N[Sum[histogram[[i]], {i, 1, x + 1, 1}] * 255 / n]

In[233]:= histogramCorrect[image_Graphics] :=
            Module[{pixels = Flatten[getImgData[image]],
               min, max, histogram, width, height, nPixels, outpix},
              (*Extract the image's dimensions.*)
              {width, height} = getImgDim[image] ;
              (*Extract the image's range, which if unspecified implies [0,1].*)
              {min, max} =
               If[MatchQ[getImgRange[image], {_, _}], getImgRange[image], {0, 1}];
              (*Normalize the data to the range [0,255] if necessary.*)
              pixels = If[{min, max} == {0, 255},
                pixels, Round[Rescale[pixels, {min, max}, {0, 255}]]];
              (*Compute histogram. Use 256 as the upper limit because
                the BinCount range is of the form [min,max].*)
              histogram = BinCounts[pixels, {0, 256, 1}];
              (*Transform by treating the
                histogram as a cumulative distribution function.*)
              nPixels = width * height;
              outpix = histCDF[#, histogram, nPixels] & /@ pixels;
              Graphics[Raster[Partition[outpix, width], image[[1, 2]], {0, 255},
                ColorFunction → GrayLevel], Sequence @@ Options[image]]]
```

In[234]:= **corrected = histogramCorrect[overexposed]**

Out[234]=

Note how the histogram of the corrected image is more spread out than the input.

In[235]:= **histogramPlot[corrected]**

Out[235]=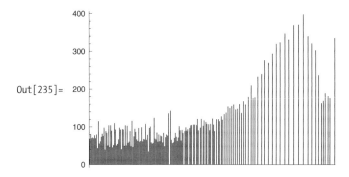

Discussion

The theory behind automatic histogram equalization is based on probability theory. View the gray levels of an image as a random variable in the interval [0,1]. It is clear that grayscale ranges in the [0,255] range can be scaled to [0,1] simply by dividing by 255. Let pr[r] denote the *probability density function* (PDF) of the input image. Let ps[s] denote the desired PDF of the output image. In this case, we want ps[s] to be uniform. Let T[r] denote the transformation function applied to the input r to produce output s with PDF ps[s]. We want T[r] to be a single-valued monotonically increasing function. Single valued is necessary so that the inverse exists; monotonic prevents the transformation from inverting gray levels. We also want T[r] to have range [0,1]. Given these conditions, we know from probability that the transformed PDF is related to the original PDF by:

$$ps[s] = pr[r] \left| \frac{dr}{ds} \right|$$

In the solution, we used the discrete form of the cumulative density function (CDF) as $T[r]$. The continuous form of the CDF is

$$s = T[r] = \int_0^r pr[w]\, dw$$

By substitution, we obtain

$$\frac{d\ s}{d\ r} = \frac{d\ T[r]}{d\ r} = \frac{d}{d\ r}\left(\int_0^r pr[w]\, dw\right)$$

We can ask Mathematica to evaluate this derivative for us by entering it in Mathematica syntax.

```
In[236]:= D[∫₀ʳ pr[w] dw, r]
Out[236]= pr[r]
```

By substitution into the original equation, we get

$$s[s] = pr[r]\left|\frac{1}{pr[r]}\right|$$

Since the probabilities are always positive, we can remove the absolute value to prove that

$$s[s] = 1$$

This means that the PDF of s is 1; hence, we have a uniform distribution. This demonstrates that in the continuous case, using the CDF as a transformation always yields a uniform distribution regardless of the characteristics of the input PDF. Of course, these results for the continuous domain do not translate exactly to the discrete domain, but it suggests that the discrete CDF will tend to shift gray levels to a more uniform range. To gain some deeper insight, you can plot the transformation function obtained from the histogram of the overexposed image.

```
In[237]:= ClearAll[T, i, k, histogram, nPixels];
          histogram = BinCounts[Flatten[getImgData[overexposed]], {0, 256, 1}];
          nSum = Total[histogram];
          nPixels = Times @@ (getImgDim[overexposed]);
          T[k_] := N[Sum[histogram[[i]], {i, 1, k + 1, 1}]/nPixels] * 255
          Plot[T[x], {x, 0, 255}, PlotRange → Automatic]
```

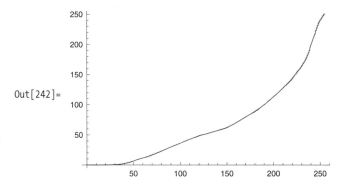

Out[242]=

This shows that all but the brightest levels will be mapped to darker levels; thus an overly bright image will tend to be darkened. The opposite will occur for an overly dark (underexposed) input image.

The nature of the transformation function leads to an obvious optimization: a precomputed lookup table computed in a single pass using FoldList. This lookup table can be used as the transformation function. This produces an O(nPixels) algorithm from our original O(nLevels * nPixels).

```
In[243]:= histogramCorrect2[image_Graphics] :=
            Module[{pixels = Flatten[getImgData[image]], min, max,
              histogram, transform, width, height, nPixels, outpix},
              (*Extract the image's dimensions.*)
              {width, height} = getImgDim[image];
              (*Extract the image's range, which if unspecified implies [0,1].*)
              {min, max} =
               If[MatchQ[getImgRange[image], {_, _}], getImgRange[image], {0, 1}];
              (*Normalize the data to the range [0,255] if necessary.*)
              pixels = If[{min, max} == {0, 255},
                pixels, Round[Rescale[pixels, {min, max}, {0, 255}]]];
              (*Compute histogram. Use 256 as the upper limit because
                 the BinCount range is of the form [min,max).*)
              histogram = BinCounts[pixels, {0, 256, 1}];
              (*Transform by treating the
               histogram as a cumulative distribution function.*)
              nPixels = width * height;
              transform = N[Rest[FoldList[Plus, 0, histogram]] * 255 / nPixels];
              outpix = transform[[#+1]] & /@ pixels;
              Graphics[Raster[Partition[outpix, width], image[[1, 2]], {0, 255},
                ColorFunction → GrayLevel], Sequence @@ Options[image]]]
```

As you can see, there is a two-orders-of-magnitude performance improvement for histogramCorrect2.

```
In[244]:= timingOrig = Timing[histogramCorrect[overexposed]][[1]];
          timingNew = Timing[histogramCorrect2[overexposed]][[1]];
          Grid[{{"original", "new"}, {timingOrig, timingNew}}]
```
```
          original   new
Out[246]=   2.356    0.015
```

Here are the histograms from each for comparison.

```
In[247]:= GraphicsRow[{histogramPlot[histogramCorrect2[overexposed]],
              histogramPlot[histogramCorrect[overexposed]]}]
```

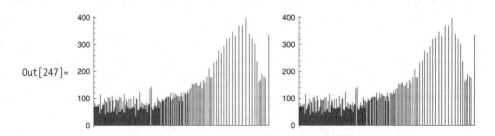

Mathematica 7 has the native function ImageHistogram for plotting an image's histogram.

```
In[248]:= GraphicsRow[{ImageHistogram[histogramCorrect2[overexposed]],
              ImageHistogram[histogramCorrect[overexposed]]}]
```

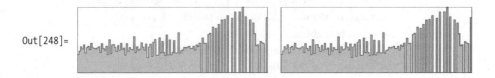

See Also

Recipe 8.3 shows how histograms can be used to match one image's contrast to that of a reference image.

8.4 Correcting Images Using Histogram Specification

Problem

You need to transform the gray levels of an image to match another image's histogram.

Solution

To match a histogram of one image to another, you produce the equalization transform of the input image as in Recipe 8.1. You then produce the equalization transform of the target image, and from that and the input transform, derive the final specification transform. Next, map the input through the specification transform to yield an image that approaches the target image's histogram. Since you need to build the equalization transform for each image, it makes sense to factor that logic into a separate function. Here I call it buildEqualizationMap. You will recognize the basic logic from Recipe 8.2.

```
In[249]:= buildEqualizationMap[image_Graphics] :=
            Module[{pixels , min, max, histogram, width, height, nPixels},
              pixels = Flatten[getImgData[image]];
              {min, max} = If[MatchQ[getImgRange[image], {_, _}],
                getImgRange[image], {0, 1}];
              pixels = If[{min, max} == {0, 255}, pixels,
                Rescale[pixels, {min, max}, {0, 255}]];
              nPixels = Length[pixels] ;
              histogram = BinCounts[pixels, {0, 256, 1}];
              N[Rest[FoldList[Plus, 0, histogram]] * 255 / nPixels]]
```

The main function must build the map for each image and use those maps to derive the final transformation (here it is called specMap). The logic underlying the derivation of specMap is explained in the "Discussion" section on page 349 and was adapted from work by Nikos Drakos and Ross Moore (refer to the "See Also" section on page 351). Here we take advantage of Reap and Sow to build up specMap incrementally without the overhead of Append.

```
In[250]:= specificationMap[inputMap_List, targetMap_List] :=
          Module[{i, j = 0}, Reap[Do[
                If[(inputMap[[i + 1]] <= targetMap[[j + 1]]),
                   Sow[j],
                     While[inputMap[[i + 1]] > targetMap[[j + 1]], j++];
                       Sow[If[(targetMap[[j + 1]] - inputMap[[i + 1]]) >
                   (inputMap[[i + 1]] - targetMap[[j]]), j--, j]]
                   ], {i, 0, 255}]][[2, 1]]]

In[251]:= histogramSpecification[input_Graphics, target_Graphics] :=
          Module[{pixels, min, max, histogram, width,
             height, nPixels, inputMap, targetMap, specMap, outpix},
            (*Compute histogram mapping of target.*)
            targetMap = buildEqualizationMap[target];
            (*Compute histogram mapping of input.*)
            inputMap = buildEqualizationMap[input];
          (*Compute inverse of targetMap.*)
            specMap = specificationMap[inputMap, targetMap];
            (*Use inverse to transform input.*)
            outpix = Flatten[getImgData[input]];
            (*outpix = inputMap[[Round[#]+1]]&/@ outpix;*)
            outpix = specMap[[Round[#] + 1]] & /@ outpix ;
            {width, height} = getImgDim[input] ;
            Graphics[Raster[Partition[outpix, width], input[[1, 2]], {0, 255},
               ColorFunction → GrayLevel], Sequence @@ Options[input]]]
```

To demonstrate histogramSpecification, I'll synthesize two raster images with different grayscale levels, using one as the input and the other as the target. In Recipe 8.4 there is a much less contrived example of this algorithm's application.

```
In[252]:= test = Graphics[Raster[Table[i * j / 2, {i, 1, 16}, {j, 1, 16}],
             {{0, 0}, {16, 16}}, {0, 255}], ImageSize → {64, 64}]
```

Out[252]=

```
In[253]:= target = Graphics[Raster[Table[i * j - 1, {i, 1, 16}, {j, 1, 16}],
            {{0, 0}, {16, 16}}, {0, 255}], ImageSize → {64, 64}]
```

Out[253]=

Here you can see the darker test image has been shifted toward the lighter target image.

```
In[254]:= histogramSpecification[test, target]
```

Out[254]=

Discussion

In Recipe 8.2 we saw how histograms can be used to automatically equalize an image's contrast. However, sometimes it is preferable to equalize based on a reference histogram rather than a uniform distribution. This often arises when transformations are applied to an image and have side effects that reduce contrast—side effects we wish to undo by shifting the image back to the grayscale distribution of the original image (see Recipe 8.4).

To appreciate the theory behind the solution, imagine an image that has a uniform grayscale distribution. Suppose you want to transform this hypothetical image to the distribution of the target image. How could you produce such a transformation? You already know how to transform the target image to a uniform distribution (Recipe 8.2); it follows that the inverse of this transformation will take the uniform distribution back to the target distribution. If we had this inverse distribution, we could proceed as follows:

1. Transform the input image to a uniform distribution using Recipe 8.2.
2. Use the inverse of the target equalization transformation to transform the output of (1) to the distribution of the target.

The key to the solution is finding the inverse. Since you are working in a discrete domain, you cannot hope to find the exact inverse, but you can approximate the inverse by flipping the targetMap, taking the minimal unique values, and filling in missing values with the next closest higher entry. The function inverseEqualization-Map shown here will build such an inverse from an image. However, if you inspect the code in histogramSpecification, you'll see that for efficiency the inverse is never built, but rather it computes the specification map directly using specificationMap from the input and target equalization transformations (inputMap and targetMap).

```
In[255]:=  expand[p1_List, p2_List] := Reap[Sow[p1];
              Do[Sow[{i, p2[[2]]}], {i, p1[[1]] + 1, p2[[1]] - 1}]][[2, 1]]
           buildPartialInverseEqualizationMap[image_Graphics] :=
           Module[{map = buildEqualizationMap[image]},
             Union[{{0, 0}}, Table[{Round[map[[i + 1]]], i}, {i, 0, 255}],
               {{256, 255}}, SameTest → (#1[[1]] == #2[[1]] &)]]
           inverseEqualizationMap[image_Graphics] := Flatten[
             expand @@@ Partition[buildPartialInverseEqualizationMap[image], 2, 1],
             1][[All, 2]]
```

We can gain some insight into this process by creating a function histogram-SpecificationPlot, which plots the input transform, target transform, target inverse, and the resulting histogram specification transform. These plots show how input gray levels are mapped to output gray levels. If you are not convinced that specificationMap gives the desired transformation, replace the plot of specMap with inverseMap[#]& /@ inputMap to see that it yields the same plot.

```
In[258]:=  Needs["PlotLegends`"]
           histogramSpecificationPlot[input_Graphics, target_Graphics] :=
           Module[{inputMap, targetMap, inverseMap, specMap},
             (*Compute histogram mapping of target.*)
             targetMap = buildEqualizationMap[target];
             (*Compute histogram mapping of input.*)
             inputMap = buildEqualizationMap[input];
             inverseMap = inverseEqualizationMap[target];
             (*Compute inverse of targetMap.*)
             specMap = specificationMap[inputMap, targetMap];
             ListPlot[{inputMap, targetMap, inverseMap, specMap},
               PlotMarkers → Automatic, Joined → True, MaxPlotPoints → 50,
               PlotLegend → {"inputEq", "targetEq", "inverseTarget", "spec"},
               LegendPosition → {0.7, -0.5}, LegendSize → 0.4,
               LegendShadow → None, ImageSize → Large]]
```

`In[260]:=` `histogramSpecificationPlot[test, target]`

`Out[260]=`

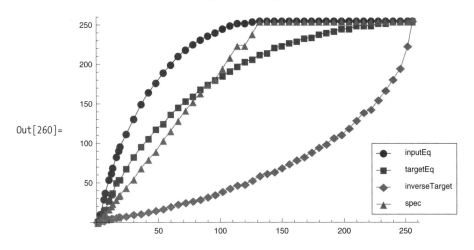

See Also

The theory behind histogram specification can be found in Gonzalez and Woods, but for the implementation, I am indebted to Professor Ruye Wang's lecture notes, available at *http://bit.ly/4oSglp*. Wang's lecture contains information originally published by Nikos Drakos (University of Leeds) and Ross Moore (Macquarie University, Sydney).

8.5 Sharpening Images Using Laplacian Transforms

Problem

You want to emphasize edges in the image and make them easier for the eye to pick out. You want to work in the spatial domain.

Solution

This transformation is performed as a convolution of the image with one of the Laplacian kernels in Figure 8-1.

Transforms	Subtract transform from image	Add transform to image
Sharpens in vertical and horizontal	$\begin{pmatrix} 0 & 1 & 0 \\ 1 & -4 & 1 \\ 0 & 1 & 01 \end{pmatrix}$	$\begin{pmatrix} 0 & -1 & 0 \\ -1 & 4 & -1 \\ 0 & -1 & 0 \end{pmatrix}$
Also sharpens in diagonal	$\begin{pmatrix} 1 & 1 & 1 \\ 1 & -8 & 1 \\ 1 & 1 & 1 \end{pmatrix}$	$\begin{pmatrix} -1 & -1 & -1 \\ -1 & 8 & -1 \\ -1 & -1 & -1 \end{pmatrix}$

Figure 8-1. Laplacian kernels

The built-in function ListConvolve makes it easy to implement image convolution in Mathematica. The only caveat is that by default, ListConvolve returns a matrix that is smaller than the input. However, you can specify a cyclic convolution by passing a third parameter of 1 to ListConvolve to make the output size match the input size. Refer to the ListConvolve Mathematica documentation for clarification.

```
In[261]:= sharpenWithLaplacian[image_Graphics,
             kernel_List : {{-1, -1, -1}, {-1, 8, -1}, {-1, -1, -1}}] :=
           Module[{transformed, sharpened},
             transformed = ListConvolve[kernel, getImgData[image], 1];
             sharpened = N[getImgData[image] + Sign[kernel[[2, 2]]] * transformed];
             Graphics[
               Raster[Rescale[sharpened, {Min[##], Max[##]} & @@ Flatten[sharpened],
                 {0, 255}], image[[1, 2]], {0, 255},
               ColorFunction → GrayLevel], Sequence @@ Options[image]]]
```

Here we want to see more fine detail of the craters in an image of the moon. The transform achieves this but we lose contrast. We can readjust contrast using the histogramSpecification algorithm from Recipe 8.3.

```
In[262]:=  image = Import[FileNameJoin[
             {NotebookDirectory[], "..", "images", "moon.jpg"}], "Graphics"]
```

Out[262]=

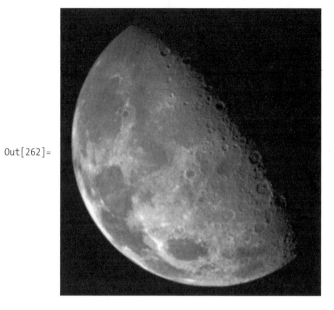

```
In[263]:=  sharpenWithLaplacian[image]
```

Out[263]=

In[264]:= histogramSpecification[sharpenWithLaplacian[image], image]

Out[264]=

Discussion

The Laplacian of a continuous 2D function is given as

$$\nabla^2 f = \frac{\partial^2 f}{\partial^2 x^2} + \frac{\partial^2 f}{\partial^2 y^2}$$

This equation is not useful for image processing and must be converted to discrete form. A common way to do this is to express each component in finite difference form and sum the result.

$$\frac{\partial^2 f}{\partial^2 x^2} = f(x+1,y) + f(x-1,y) - 2f(x,y)$$

$$\frac{\partial^2 f}{\partial^2 y^2} = f(x,y+1) + f(x,y-1) - 2f(x,y)$$

$$\nabla^2 f = f(x+1,y) + f(x-1,y) + f(x,y+1) + f(x,y-1) - 4 f(x,y)$$

This leads to the convolution kernel shown in Figure 8-2a. To improve results in the diagonal directions, one can add terms for each of the four diagonal components— for example, f(x+1,y+1)—each which contributes a negative f(x,y) term leading to the kernel in Figure 8-2b. Equivalently, one can multiply each of these kernels by -1, with the sign of the center value determining whether you add or subtract the transformation from the input image to get the sharpened version. Since the operation is based on second derivatives, it creates a sharp response in areas of discontinuities and a shallow response around more slowly varying gray levels. This can be seen by viewing the output of the transformation directly (i.e., before it is added to the input image).

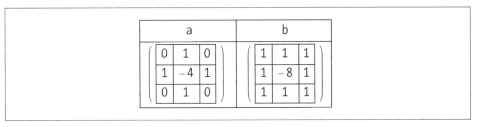

a			b		
0	1	0	1	1	1
1	-4	1	1	-8	1
0	1	0	1	1	1

Figure 8-2. Convolution kernels

```
In[265]:= laplacianImage[image_Graphics,
            kernel_List : {{-1, -1, -1}, {-1, 8, -1}, {-1, -1, -1}}] :=
          Module[{transformed}, transformed =
            ListConvolve[kernel, getImgData[image], 1];
          Graphics[Raster[Rescale[transformed, {Min[##], Max[##]} & @@
              Flatten[transformed], {0, 255}], image[[1, 2]], {0, 255},
            ColorFunction → GrayLevel], Sequence @@ Options[image]]]]

In[266]:= laplacianImage[image]
```

Out[266]=

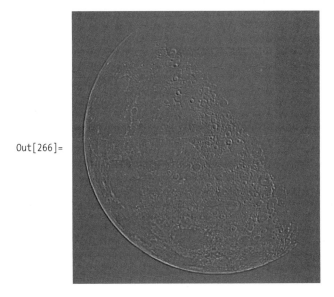

See Also

In Mathematica 7, you can use Sharpen (*http://bit.ly/2rutpn*).

8.6 Sharpening and Smoothing with Fourier Transforms

Problem

You want to emphasize either the low or high frequency characteristics of an image.

Solution

Fourier-based image processing in Mathematica is particularly easy to implement since it has the native function Fourier, which implements a high-quality version of the *Fast Fourier Transform* (FFT). The basic steps of Fourier image processing are

1. Obtain the Fourier transform of the image.

2. Center the Fourier transform using one of the techniques explained in the discussion here.

3. Apply a filtering function to the transformed result.

4. Undo the centering.

5. Apply the inverse Fourier transform, discarding any residual imaginary components.

```
In[95]:= Clear[fourierFilter];
         fourierFilter[image_, filter_] :=
           Module[{four , trans, cols = Length[getImgData[image][[1]]],
             rows = Length[getImgData[image]]},
            trans = Table[(-1)^(x+y), {x, 1, rows}, {y, 1, cols}];
            (*Centering transforms*)
            four = Fourier[getImgData[image] *trans, FourierParameters -> {1, -1}];
            four =
             Table[filter[x, y, rows, cols], {x, 1, rows}, {y, 1, cols}] * four;
            four = Abs[InverseFourier[four, FourierParameters -> {1, -1}] * trans];
            Graphics[Raster[four, getImgCoord[image], {Min[##], Max[##]}] & @@
                Flatten[four], ColorFunction → (GrayLevel[#1, 1] &)]]]
```

The fourierFilter function is designed to work with a custom filter function. Here are some common functions found in the literature. See the "Discussion" section on page 358 for more details.

```
In[11]:= dist[u_, v_, rows_, cols_] := Sqrt[(u - rows / 2.)^2 + (v - cols / 2.)^2]
```

```
In[12]:= idealLowPass[u_, v_, rows_, cols_, d0_] :=
          If[dist[u, v, rows, cols] ≤ d0, 1, 0]
```

```
In[13]:= idealHighPass[u_, v_, rows_, cols_, d0_] :=
          If[dist[u, v, rows, cols] ≤ d0, 0, 1]
```

```
In[14]:= butterWorthLowPass[u_, v_, rows_, cols_, d0_, n_] :=
          1.0 / (1.0 + (dist[u, v, rows, cols] / d0)^2 n)
```

One can use a low-pass filter for blurring an image. This might be done as a single stage of a multistage process applied to text that will be processed by OCR software. For example, blurring can diminish gaps in letters. This might be followed by a threshold transformation and other adjustments.

```
In[100]:= image = ColorConvert[
            Import[FileNameJoin[{NotebookDirectory[], "..", "images", "text2.png"}]],
            "Graphics", ImageSize → Medium], "GrayScale"]
```

Out[100]=

"Upon receiving the notification from OFTA, FTNS and PMRS Operators will provide test numbers to HKTI within one week, HKTI will notify all its major direct international carriers about the numbering change and the implementation schedules and secure seek their positive acknowledgment within two weeks' one month time. Before the actual implementation, HKTI should make preparations and carry out co-ordinate testing with the direct international carriers to ascertain the accessibility and usability of the new numbers. In case of difficulties, HKTI should report immediately to OFTA so that appropriate contingency plan may be worked out by OFTA in consultation with the FTNS and the PMRS operators."

```
In[103]:= image2 = fourierFilter[image, butterWorthLowPass[#1, #2, #3, #4, 90, 1] &]
```

Out[103]=

"Upon receiving the notification from OFTA, FINS and PMRS Operators will provide test numbers to HKTI within one week, HKTI will notify all its major direct international carriers about the numbering change and the implementation schedules and ~~secure~~ seek their positive acknowledgment within ~~two weeks'~~ one month time. Before the actual implementation, HKTI should make preparations and ~~carry out~~ co-ordinate testing with the direct international carriers to ascertain the accessibility and usability of the new numbers. In case of difficulties, HKTI should report immediately to OFTA so that appropriate contingency plan may be worked out by OFTA in consultation with the FINS and the PMRS operators."

Discussion

An important step in this algorithm is centering the zero frequency component of the transform. This allows filter functions to use the distance from the center as a function of increasing frequency. There are two ways to achieve centering. One way is to preprocess the image before it is transformed by multiplying it by the function $(-1)^{x+y}$. This function produces a matrix of alternating values 1 and -1. This is the technique used in the solution.

```
In[274]:= Table[(-1)^{x+y}, {x, 1, 10}, {y, 1, 10}] // MatrixForm
Out[274]//MatrixForm=
```

$$\begin{pmatrix}
1 & -1 & 1 & -1 & 1 & -1 & 1 & -1 & 1 & -1 \\
-1 & 1 & -1 & 1 & -1 & 1 & -1 & 1 & -1 & 1 \\
1 & -1 & 1 & -1 & 1 & -1 & 1 & -1 & 1 & -1 \\
-1 & 1 & -1 & 1 & -1 & 1 & -1 & 1 & -1 & 1 \\
1 & -1 & 1 & -1 & 1 & -1 & 1 & -1 & 1 & -1 \\
-1 & 1 & -1 & 1 & -1 & 1 & -1 & 1 & -1 & 1 \\
1 & -1 & 1 & -1 & 1 & -1 & 1 & -1 & 1 & -1 \\
-1 & 1 & -1 & 1 & -1 & 1 & -1 & 1 & -1 & 1 \\
1 & -1 & 1 & -1 & 1 & -1 & 1 & -1 & 1 & -1 \\
-1 & 1 & -1 & 1 & -1 & 1 & -1 & 1 & -1 & 1
\end{pmatrix}$$

Alternatively, one can postprocess the Fourier output by swapping quadrants using the quadSwap function.

```
In[275]:= quadSwap[matrix_List] := Module[{width, height, q1, q2, q3, q4},
            {width, height} = {Length[matrix[[1]]], Length[matrix]};
            q1 = matrix[[1 ;; Floor[height/2], 1 ;; Floor[width/2]]];
            q2 = matrix[[1 ;; Floor[height/2], Floor[width/2] + 1 ;; width]];
            q3 =
             matrix[[Floor[height/2] + 1 ;; height, Floor[width/2] + 1 ;; width]];
            q4 = matrix[[Floor[height/2] + 1 ;; height, 1 ;; Floor[width/2]]];
            Join[Join[q3, q4, 2], Join[q2, q1, 2]]]
```

```
In[276]:= (testQuadSwap = Table[
            If[x <= 5 && y <= 5, 1, If[x > 5 && y <= 5, 4, If[x ≤ 5 && y > 5, 2, 3]]],
            {x, 1, 10}, {y, 1, 10}]) // MatrixForm
```

Out[276]//MatrixForm=

$$
\begin{pmatrix}
1 & 1 & 1 & 1 & 1 & 2 & 2 & 2 & 2 & 2 \\
1 & 1 & 1 & 1 & 1 & 2 & 2 & 2 & 2 & 2 \\
1 & 1 & 1 & 1 & 1 & 2 & 2 & 2 & 2 & 2 \\
1 & 1 & 1 & 1 & 1 & 2 & 2 & 2 & 2 & 2 \\
1 & 1 & 1 & 1 & 1 & 2 & 2 & 2 & 2 & 2 \\
4 & 4 & 4 & 4 & 4 & 3 & 3 & 3 & 3 & 3 \\
4 & 4 & 4 & 4 & 4 & 3 & 3 & 3 & 3 & 3 \\
4 & 4 & 4 & 4 & 4 & 3 & 3 & 3 & 3 & 3 \\
4 & 4 & 4 & 4 & 4 & 3 & 3 & 3 & 3 & 3 \\
4 & 4 & 4 & 4 & 4 & 3 & 3 & 3 & 3 & 3
\end{pmatrix}
$$

```
In[277]:= quadSwap[testQuadSwap] // MatrixForm
```

Out[277]//MatrixForm=

$$
\begin{pmatrix}
3 & 3 & 3 & 3 & 3 & 4 & 4 & 4 & 4 & 4 \\
3 & 3 & 3 & 3 & 3 & 4 & 4 & 4 & 4 & 4 \\
3 & 3 & 3 & 3 & 3 & 4 & 4 & 4 & 4 & 4 \\
3 & 3 & 3 & 3 & 3 & 4 & 4 & 4 & 4 & 4 \\
3 & 3 & 3 & 3 & 3 & 4 & 4 & 4 & 4 & 4 \\
2 & 2 & 2 & 2 & 2 & 1 & 1 & 1 & 1 & 1 \\
2 & 2 & 2 & 2 & 2 & 1 & 1 & 1 & 1 & 1 \\
2 & 2 & 2 & 2 & 2 & 1 & 1 & 1 & 1 & 1 \\
2 & 2 & 2 & 2 & 2 & 1 & 1 & 1 & 1 & 1 \\
2 & 2 & 2 & 2 & 2 & 1 & 1 & 1 & 1 & 1
\end{pmatrix}
$$

I include both methods because you may encounter either of them in the literature. Gonzalez and Woods use the preprocessing technique, although I find the post-processing technique easier to understand conceptually.

It is difficult to appreciate the meaning of complex images after they are mapped into the frequency domain. However, almost every image-processing text that discusses the Fourier transform will provide images of the transformation after centering. The fourierImage function below does this using quadSwap, whereas fourier-Image2 uses $(-1)^{x+y}$. You can see that they produce equivalent results. You'll notice that each function maps Log[#+1] over the pixel values because Fourier transforms produce images with a much too large dynamic range.

```
In[278]:= fourierImage[image_Graphics] :=
             Module[{four = Map[Log[# + 1] &, quadSwap[Abs[
                    Fourier[getImgData[image], FourierParameters → {1, -1}]]], 2]},
                Graphics[Raster[four, image[[1, 2]], {Min[##], Max[##]} & @@
                    Flatten[four], ColorFunction → GrayLevel], Options[image]]]
In[279]:= fourierImage2[image_Graphics] := Module[{width, height, trans, four},
             {cols, rows} = getImgDim[image];
             trans = Table[(-1)^(x+y), {x, 1, rows}, {y, 1, cols}];
             four = Map[Log[# + 1] &, Abs[
                    Fourier[getImgData[image] * trans, FourierParameters → {1, -1}]], 2];
                Graphics[Raster[four, image[[1, 2]], {Min[##], Max[##]} & @@
                    Flatten[four], ColorFunction → GrayLevel], Options[image]]]
In[280]:= fourierImage[image]
```

Out[280]=

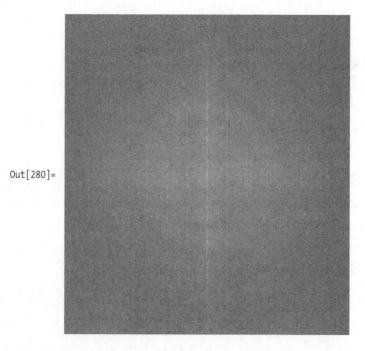

In[281]:= **fourierImage2[image]**

Out[281]=

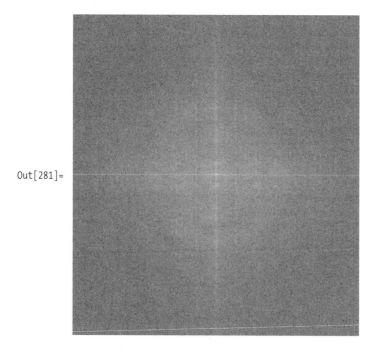

8.7 Detecting Edges in Images

Problem

You want to detect boundaries between distinct objects in an image possibly as a preprocessing step to object recognition.

Solution

Two popular methods of edge detection are the *Sobel* and *Laplacian of the Gaussian* (LoG) algorithms. The Sobel is based on first-order derivatives that approximate the gradient. The LoG algorithm combines the second-order Laplacian that we used in

Recipe 3.3 with a Gaussian smoothing to reduce the sensitivity of the Laplacian to noise. See the "Discussion" section on page 364 for further details. This implementation uses transformation rules that map intermediate gray levels to either white or black to emphasize the edges.

The edgeDetectSobel function provides the orientation optional parameter for extracting just the *x* edges {1,0}, just the *y* edges {0,1}, or both {1,1} (the default).

```
In[282]:= edgeDetectSobel[image_Graphics, orientation_List : {1, 1}] :=
            Module[{yKernel = orientation[[2]] * {{1, 0, -1}, {2, 0, -2}, {1, 0, -1}},
              xKernel = orientation[[1]] * {{1, 2, 1}, {0, 0, 0}, {-2, -1, -1}},
              transformed},
              transformed = Abs[ListConvolve[xKernel, getImgData[image], 1]] +
                Abs[ListConvolve[yKernel, getImgData[image], 1]];
              Graphics[Raster[transformed /. {x_ /; x < 127 -> 0, x_ /; x >= 127 -> 255},
                image[[1, 2]], {0, 255}, ColorFunction -> GrayLevel],
              Sequence @@ Options[image]]]
```

The edgeDetectLOG function provides a way to customize the kernel. See the "Discussion" section on page 364 for criteria of appropriate kernels.

```
In[283]:= edgeDetectLOG[image_Graphics,
            kernel_List : {{0, 0, -1, 0, 0}, {0, -1, -2, -1, 0},
              {-1, -2, 16, -2, -1}, {0, -1, -2, -1, 0}, {0, 0, -1, 0, 0}}] :=
            Module[{transformed}, transformed =
              ListConvolve[kernel, getImgData[image], 1];
              Graphics[Raster[transformed /. {x_ /; x < 127 -> 0, x_ /; x >= 127 -> 255},
                image[[1, 2]], {0, 255}, ColorFunction -> GrayLevel],
              Sequence @@ Options[image]]]

In[284]:= mech = Import[FileNameJoin[
              {NotebookDirectory[], "..", "images", "mechanism.png"}], "Graphics"];
```

```
In[285]:= GraphicsGrid[{{mech, edgeDetectSobel[mech]},
         {edgeDetectSobel[mech, {0, 1}], edgeDetectSobel[mech, {1, 0}]},
         {edgeDetectLOG[mech] , edgeDetectLOG[mech,
           2 * {{0, 0, -1, 0, 0}, {0, -1, -2, -1, 0}, {-1, -2, 16, -2, -1},
             {0, -1, -2, -1, 0}, {0, 0, -1, 0, 0}}]}},
       ImageSize → Medium, Dividers → All]
```

Out[285]=

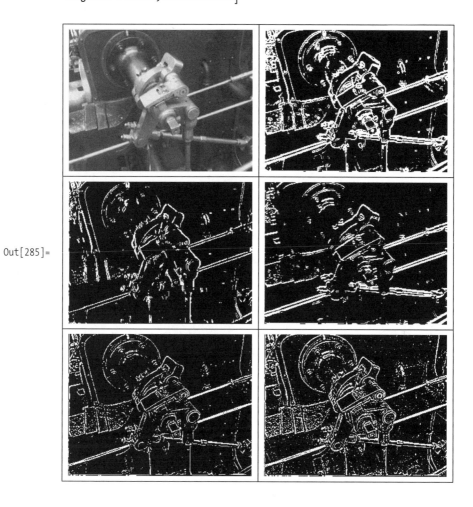

Discussion

An edge is a set of connected pixels that lie on the boundary of two regions. Edges are local areas of discontinuity rather than more global regions. An ideal edge would have a sharp transition between two very different grayscale values; however, few realistic images will have edges that are so sharply defined. Typically an edge transition will be in the form of a ramp from one level to the next, possibly with some noise superimposed on the transition. See Gonzalez and Woods for some nice visualizations of these concepts.

Since edges are transitions, it is not surprising that methods of edge detection are based on mathematical derivatives. First derivatives of a noisy ramp will produce an approximate square wave transition along the length of the ramp. Second derivatives will form a spike at the start of the edge transition and one of opposite sign at the end.

The Sobel masks and Laplacian masks approximate first and second derivatives in the discrete domain. There are two masks in the first-derivative Sobel method. The first finds horizontal edges; the second finds vertical edges. The function edge-DetectSobel is written so that you can use the second parameter to emphasize both edges {1,1}, horizontal edges {1,0}, or vertical edges {0,1}.

The edgeDetectLOG functions uses a larger 5 × 5 mask to better approximate the Mexican hat response function sought by that transformation (large central peak, with rapid tapering off, followed by a gentle increase). This transformation creates finer lines but is more sensitive to image noise.

Mathematica 7 has ImageConvolve. Here is an example using a Sobel mask.

```
In[286]:= ImageResize[ImageConvolve[Import[
              FileNameJoin[{NotebookDirectory[], "..", "images", "mechanism.png"}]],
              {{-1, 0, 1}, {-2, 0, 2}, {-1, 0, 1}}], 250]
```

Out[286]=

8.8 Image Recognition Using Eigenvectors (Eigenimages)

Problem

Given an initial training set of images, you want to find the best match of an input image to an image in the training set.

Solution

Here we show a solution that uses concepts from *principal component analysis* (PCA) and information theory to map a high-dimensional training set of images into a lower dimension such that the most significant features of the data are preserved. This allows new images to be classified in terms of the training set.

```
In[287]:=  (*Helper for vectorizing and scaling image data*)
           imageVector[image : (_Graphics | _Image)] :=
           N[Rescale[Flatten[getImgData[image]]]]


           (*Computes eigenimage vectors, avg image vector,
           and eigenvectors of reduced M x M system
           where M is the number of training images*)
           eigenImageElements[images_List, frac_ : 0.5] :=
           Module[{imgMatrix = imageVector /@ images,
              imgMatrixAdj, imgAverage, eigenVecs},
             imgAverage = N[Total[imgMatrix] / Length[imgMatrix]];
             imgMatrixAdj = (# - imgAverage) & /@ imgMatrix;
             eigenVecs = Eigenvectors[Dot[imgMatrixAdj, Transpose[imgMatrixAdj]]] ;
             imgMatrixAdj =
               Dot[Take[eigenVecs, Ceiling[frac * Length[eigenVecs]]], imgMatrix];
             {imgMatrixAdj, imgAverage, eigenVecs}]


           (*Computes the eigenimages and
            average image from a set of training images*)
           eigenImages[images_List, frac_ : 0.5] :=
           Module[{eigenImages, imgAvg, dummy, img1 = images[[1]], width},
             {eigenImages, imgAvg, dummy} = eigenImageElements[images, frac];
             width = getImgDim[img1][[1]];
             Graphics[Raster[Partition[Rescale[#], width], img1[[1, 2]], {0.0, 1.0}],
                Options[img1]] & /@ Append[eigenImages , imgAvg]
             ]
```

```
(*Computes a set of weight vectors for each input image,
and acceptance threshold for matching new
 images based on the results from eigenImageElements*)
eigenImageRecognitionElements[images_List, frac_ : 0.5] :=
 Module[
  {eigenImages, imgAvg, dummy, weightVecs, thresholdVec, threshold},
  {eigenImages, imgAvg, dummy} = eigenImageElements[images, frac];
  weightVecs =
   Table[Dot[imageVector[images[[i]]] - imgAvg, eigenImages[[j]]],
    {i, 1, Length[images]}, {j, 1, Length[eigenImages]}];
  thresholdVec = Table[Dot[imgAvg, eigenImages[[i]]],
    {i, 1, Length[eigenImages]}];
  threshold = Min[EuclideanDistance[thresholdVec, #] & /@ weightVecs]/2;
  EigenImageElements[{weightVecs, threshold, eigenImages, imgAvg}]]

(*Given a training set, determines if a test image matches any image in
 the set and also returns the possible matches ranked best to worst*)
eigenImageRecognition[images_List,
  testImage : (_Graphics | _Image), frac_ : 0.5] :=
 Module[{eigenImages, imgAvg, dummy, weightVecs, testVec,
   matchDistances, matchOrdering, match, thresholdVec, threshold},
  {weightVecs, threshold, eigenImages, imgAvg} =
   eigenImageRecognitionElements[images, frac][[1]];
  testVec = Table[Dot[imageVector[testImage] - imgAvg, eigenImages[[i]]],
    {i, 1, Length[eigenImages]}];
  matchDistances = EuclideanDistance[testVec, #] & /@ weightVecs;
  matchOrdering = Ordering[matchDistances];
  matchDistances = matchDistances[[matchOrdering]];
  {matchDistances[[1]] ≤ threshold,
   Inner[List, matchOrdering, matchDistances, List]}
 ]
```

```
(*This function is more efficient when many test images need to
  be matched since it allows you to compute the eigenImageElements
  once for the training set and reuse it for each test image.*)
eigenImageRecognition[eigenImageElements_EigenImageElements,
  testImage : (_Graphics | _Image), frac_ : 0.5] :=
Module[{eigenImages, imgAvg, dummy, weightVecs, testVec,
  matchDistances, matchOrdering, match, thresholdVec, threshold},
  {weightVecs, threshold, eigenImages, imgAvg} = eigenImageElements[[1]] ;
  testVec = Table[Dot[imageVector[testImage] - imgAvg, eigenImages[[i]]],
    {i, 1, Length[eigenImages]}];
  matchDistances = EuclideanDistance[testVec, #] & /@ weightVecs;
  matchOrdering = Ordering[matchDistances];
  matchDistances = matchDistances[[matchOrdering]];
  {matchDistances[[1]] ≤ threshold,
    Inner[List, matchOrdering, matchDistances, List]}
  ]
```

I use a training set of faces obtained from the Yale Faces Database. These images
were labeled "normal" in the database and were normalized manually in Photoshop
to center the faces and equalize image dimensions.

```
In[293]:= faces = Import[#, "Graphics"] & /@ FileNames[FileNameJoin[
            {NotebookDirectory[], "..", "images", "faces", "subject*.png"}]];
```

Discussion

The solution is based on work performed by Matthew Turk and Alex Pentland at
the MIT Media Laboratory. They were inspired by earlier work by L. Sirovich and
M. Kirby for representing faces using PCA to efficiently encode face images. PCA is a
technique for identifying patterns in data by highlighting similarities and differences.
PCA is used to reduce high-dimensional data sets. It uses the most significant eigenvectors (those with the greatest eigenvalues) of a covariance matrix to project
the high-dimensional data on a smaller dimensional subspace in terms of the
eigenvectors.

In the case of image recognition, you start with a training set of images normalized
to the same dimensions. For this example I used images from the Yale Face
Database that I normalized to 180×240 pixels with the face centered.

```
In[294]:= GraphicsGrid[Partition[faces, 5], ImageSize → Medium]
```

Out[294]=

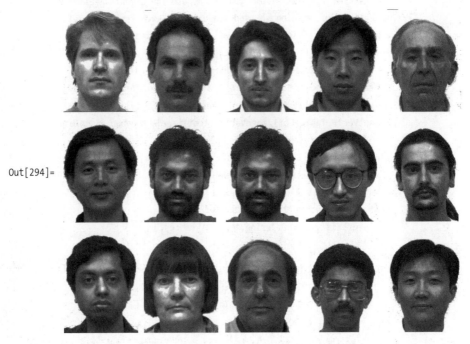

The first step is to represent the images as vectors by flattening and normalizing the raster data. The helper function imageVector is used for that purpose. The vectors are then grouped into a matrix of 15 rows and 43,200 (180 × 240) columns and normalized by subtracting the average of all images from each image. If the solution used PCA directly, it would then need to generate a 43,200 × 43,200 covariance matrix and solve for the 43,200 eigensystem. Clearly this brute force attack is intractable. Rather, the solution takes advantage of the fact that in a system where the number of images (15) is much less than the number of data points (43,200), most eigenvalues will be zero. Hence, it takes an indirect approach of computing the eigenvectors of a smaller 15 × 15 matrix obtained from multiplying the image matrix by its transpose as explained in Turk and Pentland. A fraction (half by default) of these eigenvectors are then used to compute the eigenimages from the original image data. This work is encapsulated in the function eigenImageElements, which returns the eigenimages, the average image, and the computed eigenvectors of the smaller matrix. This prevents the need to recompute these values in other functions.

The function eigenImages is used to visualize the results. It returns a list of graphics containing each of the eigenimages plus the average image. Here we show all 16 (15 eigen + 1 average) images by setting frac to 1. The ghostlike quality is a standard feature of eigenimages of faces. Recalling that the lightest areas of a grayscale image represent the largest magnitudes, you can see the elements of each image that are emphasized. For example, the area around the cheek bones of the first image are the most significant.

```
In[295]:= GraphicsGrid[Partition[eigenImages[faces, 0.95], 5, 5, {1, 1}, Graphics[]],
          ImageSize → Medium]
```

Out[295]=

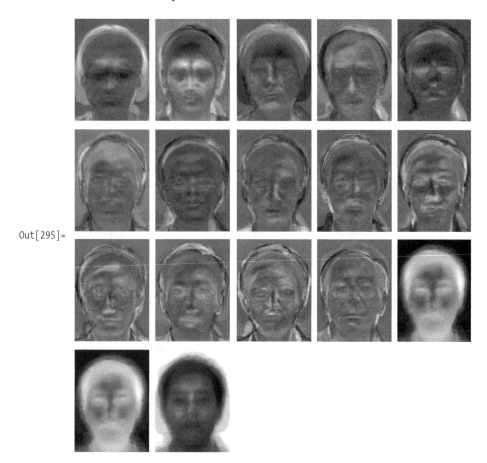

The eigenimages can be used as a basis for image recognition by using the product of the eigenimages and the original images to form a vector of weights for each test image. The weights represent the contribution of eigenimage to the original image. Given these weight vectors, you can compute similar weights for an unknown image and use the Euclidean distance as a classification metric. If the distance is below a certain threshold, then a match is declared.

The test images are derived from some non-face images, some distortions of facial images, and other poses of the faces in the training set. The function eigenImage-Recognition returns a Boolean and a ranking list. The Boolean determines if the test image fell in the threshold of the training set. The threshold is computed using the av erage image distance. The ranking set ties the index to the image in the training set and the distance in order of increasing distance. This means the first entry is the best match to the training image.

```
In[296]:= testFaces = Import[#, "Graphics"] & /@ FileNames[FileNameJoin[
            {NotebookDirectory[], "..", "images", "faces", "test", "*.png"}]];
```

```
In[297]:= GraphicsGrid[
            Partition[testFaces, 6, 6, {1, 1}, Graphics[]], ImageSize → Medium]
```

Out[297]=

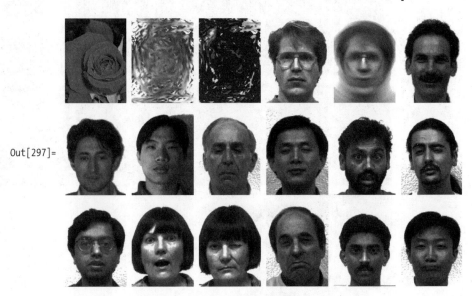

```
In[298]:= eir = eigenImageRecognitionElements[faces];
        results = eigenImageRecognition[eir, #] & /@ testFaces ;
```

The code that follows displays the best match in the training set that corresponds to the test image. If the threshold was not met, an X is superimposed on the image.

```
In[300]:= GraphicsGrid[Partition[If[#[[1]], faces[[#[[2, 1, 1]]]],
              Graphics[{faces[[#[[2, 1, 1]]]][[1]], Red, Thick,
                Line[{{180, 1}, {1, 240}}], Line[{{1, 1}, {180, 240}}]}]] & /@
            results, 6, 6, {1, 1}, Graphics[]], ImageSize → Medium]
```

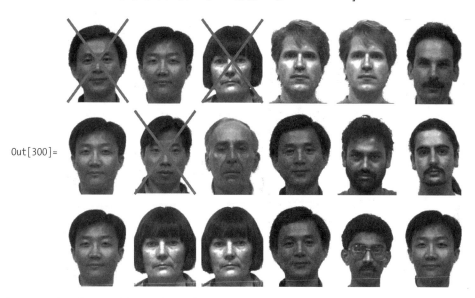

Out[300]=

These results show a false positive for the second image in the first row, the first images in the second and third rows, and the fourth image in the third row. There is a false negative for the second image in the second row, meaning there was a correct match but it fell below the threshold. All other results are correct. This is pretty good considering the small size of the training set.

See Also

The images used here can be found at *http://bit.ly/xlgx7* or *http://www.mathematica cookbook.com*. The original Yale Face Database can be found at *http://bit.ly/52lgvb*.

The original research of paper *Eigenfaces for Recognition* by Matthew Turk and Alex Pentland from the *Journal of Cognitive Neuroscience* (Volume 3, Number 1) can be found at *http://bit.ly/7OSSBw*.

An excellent tutorial by Lindsay I. Smith on PCA can be found at *http://bit.ly/6CJTWn*.

CHAPTER 9

Audio and Music Processing

Deep in the back of my mind is an unrealized sound
Every feeling I get from the street says it soon
could be found
When I hear the cold lies of the pusher,
I know it exists
It's confirmed in the eyes of the kids, emphasized
with their fists

...

The music must change
For we're chewing a bone
We soared like the sparrow hawk flied
Then we dropped like a stone
Like the tide and the waves
Growing slowly in range
Crushing mountains as old as the Earth
So the music must change

The Who, "Music Must Change"

9.0 Introduction

Audio and music can be approached in three different ways with Mathematica: (1) as traditional musical notes with associated pitch names and other specifications, such as duration, timbre, loudness, etc.; (2) as abstract mathematical waveforms that represent vibrating systems; and (3) as digitally represented sound—just think of .wav and .aiff files. If nothing else, this chapter should hint at the ease with which Mathematica can be put in the service of the arts. Let's make some music!

Mathematica allows you to approach music and sound in at least three different ways. You can talk to Mathematica about musical notes such as "C" or "Fsharp". You can directly specify other traditional concepts, such as timbre and loudness, with Mathematica's Sound, SoundNote, and PlayList functions. You can ask Mathematica to play analog waveforms. And you can ask Mathematica to interpret digital sound samples.

9.1 Creating Musical Notes

Problem

You want to create musical notes corresponding to traditional musical notation.

Solution

The Mathematica function SoundNote represents a musical sound. SoundNote uses either a numerical convention, for which middle C is represented as zero, or it accepts strings like "C", "C3", or "Aflat4", where "A0" represents the lowest note on a piano keyboard.

In[691]:= **Sound[SoundNote[0]]**

Out[691]=

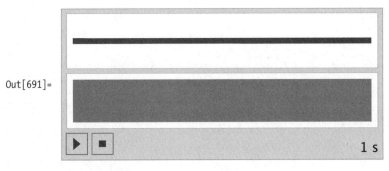

In[692]:= **Sound[SoundNote["C"]]**

Out[692]=

Discussion

SoundNote assumes you want to play a piano sound, for exactly one second, at a medium volume. You can override these presets. Here's a loud (SoundVolume→1), short (0.125 second), guitar blast ("GuitarOverdriven").

```
In[693]:= Sound[SoundNote[0, 0.125, "GuitarOverdriven", SoundVolume → 1]]
```

Out[693]=

0.13 s

9.2 Creating a Scale or a Melody

Problem

You want to create a sequence of notes, like a scale or single-note melody.

Solution

Sound can accept a list of notes, which it will play sequentially. Here is a whole-tone scale specified to take exactly 1.5 seconds to play in its entirety.

```
In[694]:= Sound[{SoundNote[0], SoundNote[2], SoundNote[4],
          SoundNote[6], SoundNote[8], SoundNote[10], SoundNote[12]}, 1.5]
```

Out[694]=

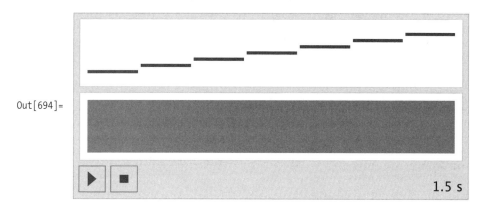

1.5 s

Here's an alternative syntax using Map (/@), which requires less typing and collects the note specifications into a list.

In[695]:= **Sound[SoundNote[#] & /@ {0, 2, 4, 6, 8, 10, 12, 14, 16, 18, 20, 24}, 1.0]**

Out[695]=

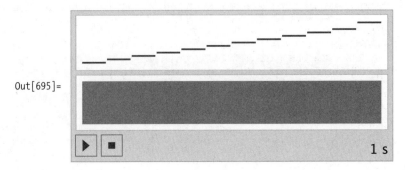

1 s

Here's a randomly generated melody composed of notes from an A♭ major scale. The duration of each note is specified as 0.125 second. The duration specification, now a parameter of SoundNote rather than an overall specification of the entire melody as in the previous examples, sets the stage for the next example.

In[696]:= **Sound[SoundNote[#, 0.125] & /@ RandomChoice[**
{"Aflat2", "Bflat2", "C3", "Dflat3", "Eflat3", "F3", "G3", "Aflat3"}, 10]]

Out[696]=

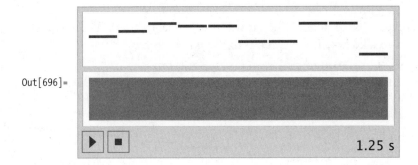

1.25 s

9.3 Adding Rhythm to a Melody

Problem

You need to specify a melody for which the notes have different rhythm values.

Solution

Replace the 0.125 specification in the previous example with other values. Since you're generating a random melody, why not generate random durations?

```
In[697]:= Sound[
            SoundNote[#, RandomChoice[{0.125, 0.5, 0.75, 1.0}]] & /@ RandomChoice[
                {"Aflat2", "Bflat2", "C3", "Dflat3", "Eflat3", "F3", "G3", "Aflat3"}, 10]]
```

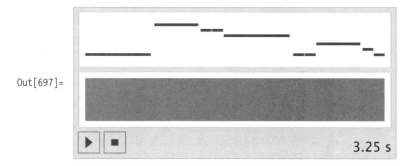

Out[697]=

Here, the weighting feature of RandomChoice is used to guarantee a preponderance of short notes.

```
In[698]:= Sound[
            SoundNote[#, RandomChoice[{10, 1, 1, 1} → {0.125, 0.5, 0.75, 1.0}]] & /@
                RandomChoice[{"Aflat2", "Bflat2", "C3",
                    "Dflat3", "Eflat3", "F3", "G3", "Aflat3"}, 10]]
```

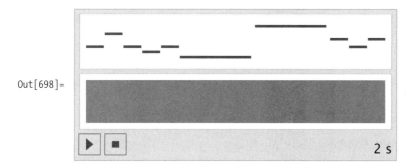

Out[698]=

9.4 Controlling the Volume

Problem

You would like to add some phrasing to your melody by controlling the volume.

Solution

Unlike duration, which is specified as a parameter to SoundNote, you control the volume with an option setting. Pulling everything together from the examples above and adding a randomized volume yields this funky guitar pattern. Anyone for a cup of Maxwell House coffee?

```
In[699]:= Sound[SoundNote[#, 0.125, "GuitarMuted", SoundVolume → RandomReal[]] & /@
            RandomChoice[{20, 1, 1, 1, 1, 1} → {0, 2, 4, 7, 9, 12}, 56]]
```

Out[699]=

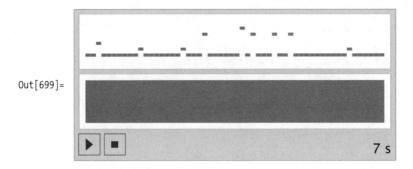

7 s

9.5 Creating Chords

Problem

You want to move beyond simple sequences of single notes to chord patterns.

Solution

To make a chord, give SoundNote a list of notes. For example, you can specify the C major triad using the pitches C, E, and G specified as a list of numbers {0,4,7}. Don't confuse making chords by giving SoundNote a list of notes with making melodies by giving Sound a list of SoundNotes.

```
In[700]:= Sound[SoundNote[{0, 4, 7}]]
```

Out[700]=

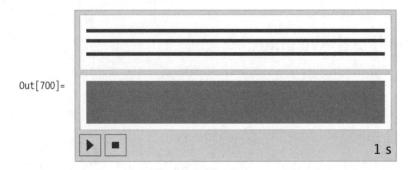

1 s

9.6 Playing a Chord Progression

Problem

You want to make a chord progression.

Solution

This is the same as making melodies. Spell out the chords in your chord progression as lists inside a list. Feed them into SoundNote using Map.

```
In[701]:= Sound[SoundNote[#, 0.5] & /@
            {{"C3", "E3", "G3"}, {"F3", "A3", "C4"}, {"G3", "B3", "D4"}}]
```

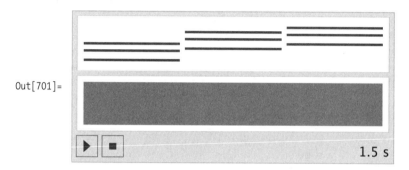

Out[701]=

Here's a popular pop song progression.

```
In[702]:= Sound[SoundNote[#, 1] & /@ {{"C3", "E3", "G3"},
            {"B2", "E3", "G3"}, {"Bb2", "E3", "G3"}, {"A2", "E3", "G3"},
            {"Aflat2", "Eflat3", "G3"}, {"G2", "C3", "D3", "G3"}, {"C3", "E3", "G3"}}]
```

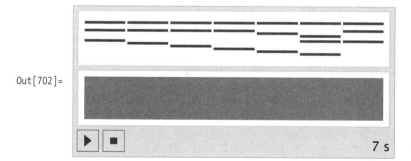

Out[702]=

9.7 Writing Music with Traditional Chord Notation

Problem

You want to specify a chord progression using traditional notation. For example, you would like to write something like:

```
In[703]:=  myProg = "C A7 d-7 F/G C";
```

or, using roman numerals as is common in jazz notation,

```
In[704]:=  myJazzProgression = "<Eb>   I vi-9 II7/#9b13 ii-9 V7sus I";
```

Solution

Mathematica can deftly handle this task with its String manipulation routines and its pattern recognition functions. First, decide which chord symbols will be allowed. Here's a list of jazz chords: Maj7/9, Majadd9, add9, Maj7#11, Maj7/13, Maj7/#5, Maj7, Maj, -7b5, -7, -9, -11, min, 7/b913, 7/#9b13, 7/b9b13, 7/b9#11, 7/b5, 7/b9, 7/#9, 7/#11, 7/13, 7, 7/9, 7sus, and sus.

The rules below turn the chord names into the appropriate scale degree numbers in the key of C. Later, as a second step, you'll transpose these voicings to other keys.

```
In[705]:=  chordSpellingRules = {"Maj7/9" :> {0, 4, 7, 11, 14}, "Majadd9" :> {0, 2, 4, 7},
               "add9" :> {0, 2, 4, 7}, "Maj7/#11" :> {0, 4, 7, 11, 14, 18},
               "Maj7/13" :> {2, 6, 9}, "Maj7/#5" :> {4, 8, 11}, "Maj7" :> {0, 4, 7, 11},
               "Maj" :> {0, 4, 7},
               (*lstead - added rule so "F" works*)
               "" :> {0, 4, 7},
               "-7b5" :> {0, 3, 6, 10}, "-7" :> {0, 3, 7, 10},
               "-9" :> {0, 3, 7, 10, 14}, "-11" :> {0, 3, 7, 10, 14, 17},
               "min" :> {0, 3, 7},
               (*lstead - added rule so "D-" works*)
               "-" :> {0, 3, 7},
               "7/b913" :> {1, 4, 9, 10}, "7/#9b13" :> {0, 3, 8}, "7/b9b13" :> {1, 4, 8, 10},
               "7/b9#11" :> {1, 4, 6, 10}, "7/b5" :> {0, 4, 6, 10},
               "7/b9" :> {1, 4, 7, 10}, "7/#9" :> {4, 10, 15},
               "7/#11" :> {0, 4, 7, 10, 14, 18}, "7/13" :> {4, 9, 10, 14}, "7" :> {0, 4, 7, 10},
               "7/9" :> {0, 4, 7, 10, 14}, "7sus" :> {0, 5, 7, 10}, "sus" :> {0, 5, 7, 12}};
```

```
romanRoots = {"bIII" :> 3, "III" :> 4, "bII" :> 1, "II" :> 2, "#II" :> 3,
    "IV" :> 5, "#IV" :> 6, "bVII" :> 10, "VII" :> 11, "bVI" :> 8, "VI" :> 9,
    "#VI" :> 10, "bV" :> 6, "V" :> 7, "#V" :> 8, "I" :> 0, "#I" :> 1};
letterRoots = {"C" :> 0, "C#" :> 1, "Db" :> 1, "D" :> 2, "D#" :> 3,
    "Eb" :> 3, "E" :> 4, "F" :> 5, "F#" :> 6, "Gb" :> 6, "G" :> 7,
    "G#" :> 8, "Ab" :> 8, "A" :> 9, "Bb" :> 10, "B" :> 11};
roots = Join[romanRoots, letterRoots]
```

```
Out[708]= {bIII :> 3, III :> 4, bII :> 1, II :> 2, #II :> 3, IV :> 5, #IV :> 6,
    bVII :> 10, VII :> 11, bVI :> 8, VI :> 9, #VI :> 10, bV :> 6, V :> 7, #V :> 8,
    I :> 0, #I :> 1, C :> 0, C# :> 1, Db :> 1, D :> 2, D# :> 3, Eb :> 3, E :> 4,
    F :> 5, F# :> 6, Gb :> 6, G :> 7, G# :> 8, Ab :> 8, A :> 9, Bb :> 10, B :> 11}
```

Make a table by concatenating together each possible root and type. Then /. can be used to decode chord.

```
In[709]:= compoundRules = Table[ToUpperCase[l[[1, 1]] ~~ l[[2, 1]]] ->
            {l[[1, 2]], l[[2, 2]]}, {l, Tuples[{roots, chordSpellingRules}]}];
        drules = Dispatch[compoundRules];
```

Now create a function for converting the chord string into a progression representation.

```
In[711]:= progressionFromString[s_] :=
        Block[{su, ss},
          ss = StringSplit[s, Whitespace];
          progression[First[ss], ToUpperCase[Rest[ss]]]]


        progression[key_, chords_] :=
        Block[{keyCenter, lh, rh},
          keyCenter = StringCases[key,
              RegularExpression["(?i)[a-z]+"]][[1]] /. letterRoots;
          progression[key, chords, keyCenter,
            Table[
              {lh, rh} = (chord /. drules);
              lh = lh + keyCenter - 24;
              rh = rh + lh + 24;
              Flatten[{lh, rh}],
              {chord, chords}]]]
```

And a function to play the progression.

```
In[713]:= playProgression[progression[k_, csyms_, kn_, chords_]] :=
        Sound[SoundNote[#, 1] & /@ chords, 5]
```

Let's test it on a jazz progression.

```
In[714]:= jazzS = "<Eb>    I vi-9 II7/#9b13 ii-9 V7sus I";
```

```
In[715]:= jazzP = progressionFromString[jazzS]
```

```
Out[715]= progression[<Eb>, {I, VI-9, II7/#9B13, II-9, V7SUS, I},
            3, {{-21, 3, 7, 10}, {-12, 12, 15, 19, 22, 26}, {-19, 5, 8, 13},
            {-19, 5, 8, 12, 15, 19}, {-14, 10, 15, 17, 20}, {-21, 3, 7, 10}}]
```

```
In[716]:= playProgression[jazzP]
```

Out[716]=
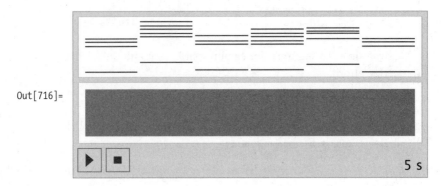

Let's add some rhythm and volume.

```
In[717]:= buffer = progressionFromString[jazzS][[4]]
           Sound[MapIndexed[SoundNote[#, {1, 0.5, 0.5, 0.75, 0.25, 1}[[Sequence @@ #2]],
               SoundVolume → RandomReal[0.5, 1]] &, buffer]]
```

```
Out[717]= {{-21, 3, 7, 10}, {-12, 12, 15, 19, 22, 26}, {-19, 5, 8, 13},
           {-19, 5, 8, 12, 15, 19}, {-14, 10, 15, 17, 20}, {-21, 3, 7, 10}}
```

Out[718]=
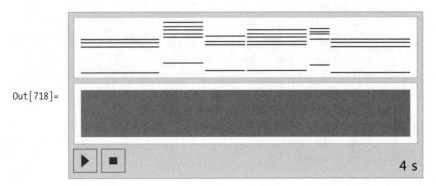

Discussion

There's a very unsatisfying feature to the result: the chords jump around in an unmusical way. A piano player would typically invert the chords to keep the voicings centered around middle C. So for example, when playing a CMaj7 chord, which is defined as {0,4,7,11} or {"C3","E3","G3","B3"}, a piano player might drop the top two notes down an octave and play {-5,-1,0,4} or {"G2","B2","C3","E3"}. You can use Mathematica's Mod function to achieve the same result. Here the notes greater than 6 {"F#3"} are transposed down an octave simply by subtracting 12 from them.

```
In[719]:= buffer
Out[719]= {{-21, 3, 7, 10}, {-12, 12, 15, 19, 22, 26}, {-19, 5, 8, 13},
          {-19, 5, 8, 12, 15, 19}, {-14, 10, 15, 17, 20}, {-21, 3, 7, 10}}
```

Currently in the buffer, the nonbass notes are all positive, so this rule, which uses /; n>0 as a condition, leaves the (negative) bass notes untouched while processing the rest of the voicing.

```
In[720]:= buffer /. {n_Integer /; n > 0 :> Mod[n, 12, -5]}
Out[720]= {{-21, 3, -5, -2}, {-12, 0, 3, -5, -2, 2}, {-19, 5, -4, 1},
          {-19, 5, -4, 0, 3, -5}, {-14, -2, 3, 5, -4}, {-21, 3, -5, -2}}
```

```
In[721]:=
          Sound[SoundNote[#, 1] & /@ ( buffer /. {n_Integer /; n > 0 :> Mod[n, 12, -5]})]
```

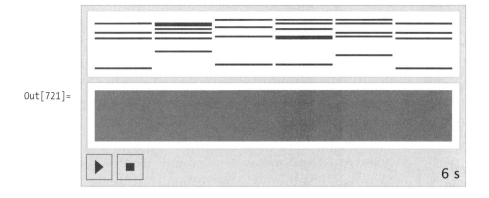

```
Out[721]=
```

6 s

Here's another progression showing all the steps in one place.

```
In[722]:= buffer = progressionFromString["<F> F Eb7 F C7 d- Bb7 C7 F"][[4]];
          Sound[
           SoundNote[#, 1] & /@ ( buffer /. {n_Integer /; n > 0 :> Mod[n, 12, -5]})]
```

Out[723]=

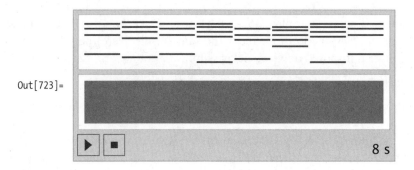

9.8 Creating Percussion Grooves

Problem

You want to make percussion sounds.

Solution

Mathematica has implemented 60 percussion instruments as specified in the General MIDI (musical instrument digital interface) specification.

Here the percussion instruments are listed in alphabetical order. Some of the names are not obvious. For example, there is no triangle or conga, instead there's "MuteTriangle", "OpenTriangle", "HighCongaMute", "HighCongaOpen", and "LowConga".

```
In[724]:= allPerc = {"BassDrum", "BassDrum2", "BellTree", "Cabasa", "Castanets",
           "ChineseCymbal", "Clap", "Claves", "Cowbell", "CrashCymbal",
           "CrashCymbal2", "ElectricSnare", "GuiroLong", "GuiroShort", "HighAgogo",
           "HighBongo", "HighCongaMute", "HighCongaOpen", "HighFloorTom",
           "HighTimbale", "HighTom", "HighWoodblock", "HiHatClosed", "HiHatOpen",
           "HiHatPedal", "JingleBell", "LowAgogo", "LowBongo", "LowConga",
           "LowFloorTom", "LowTimbale", "LowTom", "LowWoodblock", "Maracas",
           "MetronomeBell", "MetronomeClick", "MidTom", "MidTom2", "MuteCuica",
           "MuteSurdo", "MuteTriangle", "OpenCuica", "OpenSurdo", "OpenTriangle",
           "RideBell", "RideCymbal", "RideCymbal2", "ScratchPull", "ScratchPush",
           "Shaker", "SideStick", "Slap", "Snare", "SplashCymbal", "SquareClick",
           "Sticks", "Tambourine", "Vibraslap", "WhistleLong", "WhistleShort"};
```

Here's what each instrument sounds like. The instrument name is fed into `SoundNote` where, more typically, the note specification should be. In fact, in the Standard MIDI specification, each percussion instrument is represented as a single pitch in a "drum" patch. So for example, "BassDrum" is C0, "BassDrum2" is C#0, "Snare" is D0, and so on. Therefore, it makes sense for Mathematica to treat these instruments as notes, not as "instruments" as was done above for "Piano", "GuitarMuted", and "GuitarOverDriven".

In[725]:= `Sound[SoundNote[#, 0.125] & /@ allPerc]`

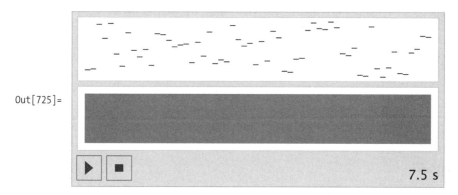

Out[725]=

7.5 s

Here's a measure's worth of closed hi-hat:

In[726]:= `Sound[SoundNote[#, 0.125] & /@ Table["HiHatClosed", {8}]]`

Out[726]=

1 s

And here's something with a little more pizzazz. Both the choice of instrument and volume are randomized.

```
In[727]:= Sound[SoundNote[#, 0.125, SoundVolume → RandomReal[{0.25, 1}]] & /@
            Table[RandomChoice[{"HiHatOpen", "HiHatClosed", "HiHatPedal"}], {16}]]
```

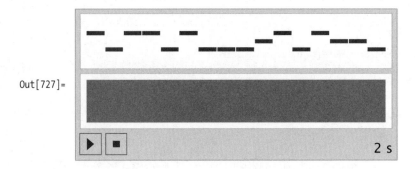

Out[727]=

9.9 Creating More Complex Percussion Grooves

Problem

You want to create a drum kit groove for a pop song using kick, snare, and hi-hat.

Solution

This task is the percussion equivalent of making chords, because on certain beats all three instruments could be playing, on other beats only one instrument or possibly none. Here's the previous hi-hat pattern, played at a slower tempo.

```
In[728]:= Sound[SoundNote[#, 0.25] & /@ Table["HiHatClosed", {8}]]
```

Out[728]=

Here's a kick drum pattern. Use None as a rest indication.

```
In[729]:= Sound[SoundNote[#, 0.25] & /@
            {"BassDrum", None, None, "BassDrum", "BassDrum", None, None, None}]
```

Out[729]=

1.25 s

Here's the snare drum backbeat. The display omits the leading rests, so the picture is a little misleading. As soon as we integrate this with the hi-hat and kick drum, everything will look correct.

```
In[730]:= Sound[SoundNote[#, 0.25] & /@
            {None, None, "Snare", None, None, None, "Snare", None}]
```

Out[730]=

1.75 s

Each list has exactly eight elements, so we can use Transpose to interlace the elements.

```
In[731]:= groove = Transpose[{Table["HiHatClosed", {8}],
            {"BassDrum", None, None, "BassDrum", "BassDrum", None, None, None},
            {None, None, "Snare", None, None, None, "Snare", None}}]
Out[731]= {{HiHatClosed, BassDrum, None}, {HiHatClosed, None, None},
            {HiHatClosed, None, Snare}, {HiHatClosed, BassDrum, None},
            {HiHatClosed, BassDrum, None}, {HiHatClosed, None, None},
            {HiHatClosed, None, Snare}, {HiHatClosed, None, None}}
```

In[732]:= Sound[SoundNote[#, 0.25] & /@ groove]

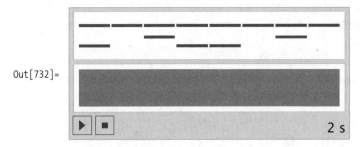

Out[732]=

2 s

An entire tune can now be made by repeating this one-measure groove as many times as desired.

In[733]:= Sound[SoundNote[#, 0.25] & /@ Flatten[Table[groove, {4}], 1]]

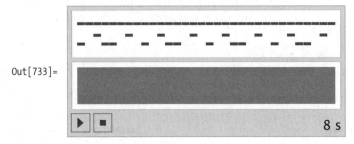

Out[733]=

8 s

Discussion

Getting the curly braces just right in Mathematica's syntax can be a little frustrating. Without Flatten in the example above, the SoundNote function is confused by the List-within-List results of the Table function. Consequently, you get no output.

In[734]:= Sound[SoundNote[#, 0.25] & /@ Table[groove, {4}]]

```
Out[734]= Sound[
            {SoundNote[{{"HiHatClosed", "BassDrum", None}, {"HiHatClosed", None, None},
                {"HiHatClosed", None, "Snare"}, {"HiHatClosed", "BassDrum", None},
                {"HiHatClosed", "BassDrum", None}, {"HiHatClosed", None, None},
                {"HiHatClosed", None, "Snare"}, {"HiHatClosed", None, None}}, 0.25`],
             SoundNote[{{"HiHatClosed", "BassDrum", None}, {"HiHatClosed", None, None},
                {"HiHatClosed", None, "Snare"}, {"HiHatClosed", "BassDrum", None},
                {"HiHatClosed", "BassDrum", None}, {"HiHatClosed", None, None},
                {"HiHatClosed", None, "Snare"}, {"HiHatClosed", None, None}}, 0.25`],
```

```
SoundNote[{{"HiHatClosed", "BassDrum", None}, {"HiHatClosed", None, None},
    {"HiHatClosed", None, "Snare"}, {"HiHatClosed", "BassDrum", None},
    {"HiHatClosed", "BassDrum", None}, {"HiHatClosed", None, None},
    {"HiHatClosed", None, "Snare"}, {"HiHatClosed", None, None}}, 0.25`],
  SoundNote[{{"HiHatClosed", "BassDrum", None}, {"HiHatClosed", None, None},
    {"HiHatClosed", None, "Snare"}, {"HiHatClosed", "BassDrum", None},
    {"HiHatClosed", "BassDrum", None}, {"HiHatClosed", None, None},
    {"HiHatClosed", None, "Snare"}, {"HiHatClosed", None, None}}, 0.25`]}]
```

Furthermore, with a simple Flatten wrapped around the Table function, each hit is treated individually; we lose the chordal quality of the drums hitting simultaneously. Go back and notice that the correct idea is to remove just one layer of braces by using Flatten[... , 1].

In[735]:= Sound[SoundNote[#, 0.25] & /@ Flatten[Table[groove, {4}]]]

Out[735]=

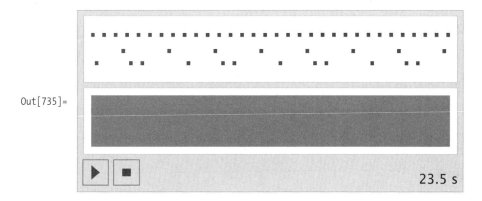

23.5 s

9.10 Exporting MIDI files

Problem

You want to save your Mathematica expression as a standard MIDI file.

Solution

Mathematica can export any expression composed of Sound and SoundNote expressions as a standard MIDI file. The rub, however, is that Mathematica does not import MIDI files. So let's create some utilities that at the very least let you look at the guts of standard MIDI files.

Here's a simple phrase that gets exported as the file *myPhrase.mid*.

```
In[736]:= myPhrase = Sound[
            {SoundNote[0], SoundNote[4], SoundNote[7], SoundNote[{0, 4, 7, 12}]}]
```

Out[736]=

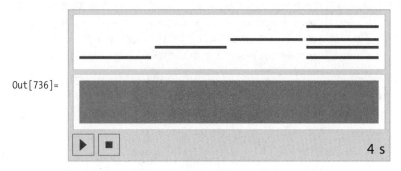

```
In[737]:= Export["myPhrase.mid", myPhrase]
Out[737]= myPhrase.mid
```

9.11 Playing Functions As Sound

Problem

You want to listen to the waveform generated by a mathematical function.

Solution

If you know how to plot a function in Mathematica:

```
In[738]:= Plot[Sin[1000 * 2 π * t], {t, 0, 0.001}, ImageSize → 300]
```

Out[738]=

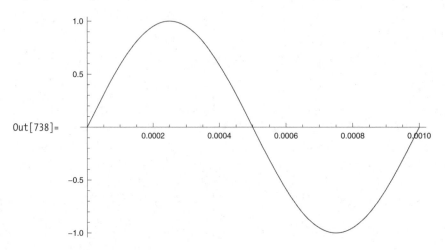

You can play a function. Play uses the same syntax as Plot. However, you don't want to listen to 1/1000th of a second, which is what was plotted above, so specify something like {t, 0, 1}.

In[739]:= **Play[Sin[1000 * 2 π * t], {t, 0, 1}]**

Out[739]=

Discussion

Here are other crazy-sounding functions.

In[740]:= **Play[Sin[300 2 π t Exp[t]], {t, 0, 8}]**

Out[740]=

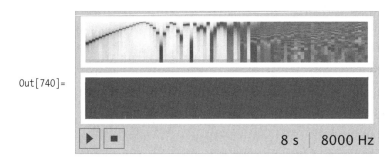

In[741]:= **Play[(2 + Cos[40 t^2]) Sin[700 t^2], {t, 0, 10}]**

Out[741]=

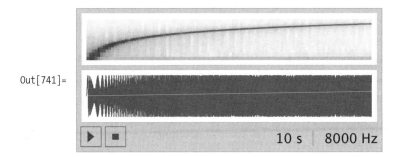

9.12 Adding Tremolo

Problem

You want to add tremolo.

Solution

"Tremolo" is the musical term for amplitude modulation. Here a 20 Hz signal modifies the amplitude of a 1,000 Hz signal.

In[742]:= `Plot[ (2 + Sin[20*2 π*t]) *Sin[1000*2 π*t], {t, 0, 0.1}, ImageSize -> 300]`

Out[742]=

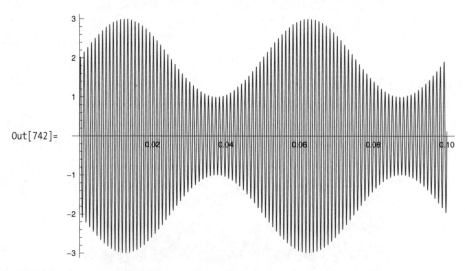

And here, a 5 Hz signal modifies a 1,000 Hz signal.

In[743]:= `Play[ (2 + Sin[5*2 π*t]) *Sin[1000*2 π*t], {t, 0, 1}]`

Out[743]=

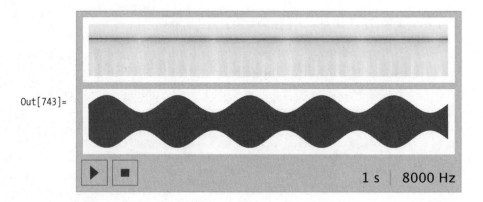

9.13 Adding Vibrato

Problem

You want to add vibrato.

Solution

Vibrato is frequency modulation. Notice that the sine wave alternates between regions of compression and expansion.

```
In[744]:= Plot[(Sin[(1 + Sin[250 * 2 π * t]) * 1000 * 2 π * t]),
            {t, 0, 0.010}, ImageSize → 400, AspectRatio → 0.5]
```

Out[744]=

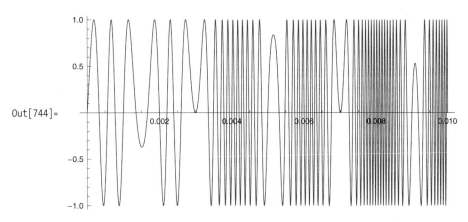

Here the parameters are adjusted for listening.

```
In[745]:= Play[(Sin[(1 + 0.002 Sin[5 * 2 π * t]) * 1000 * 2 π * t]), {t, 0, 1}]
```

Out[745]=

Why not put the two modulations together: tremolo and vibrato?

```
In[746]:= Play[(2 + Sin[5 * 2 π * t]) *
            Sin[(1 + 0.002 Sin[5 * 2 π * t]) * 1000 * 2 π * t], {t, 0, 1}]
```

Out[746]=

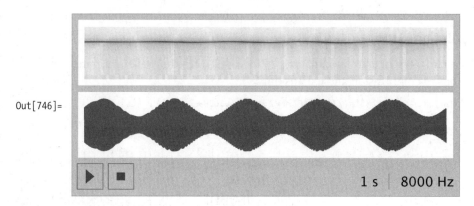

9.14 Applying an Envelope to a Signal

Problem

You want to apply an envelope to your signal.

Solution

The Mathematica function Piecewise is the perfect tool for creating an envelope. Here is the popular attack-decay-sustain-release (ADSR) envelope.

```
In[747]:= Plot[Piecewise[{
            {6 t, t < 1},
            {6 - 5 (t - 1), t < 2},
            {1, t < 4},
            {1 - 0.5 (t - 4), t < 6}
            }],
          {t, 0, 6},
          PlotStyle → AbsoluteThickness[2],
          ImageSize → {300, 150}, AspectRatio → 0.5
          ]
```

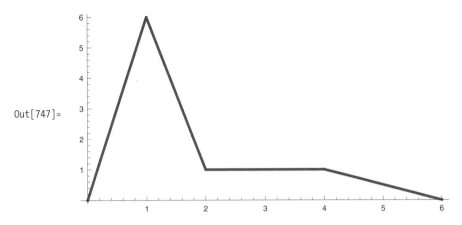

Out[747]=

Sine waves are typically represented as amplitude * sine (ωt). You can simply substitute the entire Piecewise[] envelope for amplitude.

```
In[748]:= Plot[
           Piecewise[{
               {6 t, t < 1},
               {-5 (t - 1) + 6, t < 2},
               {1, t < 4},
               {-0.5 (t - 4) + 1, t < 6}}
             ] * Sin[6 * 2 π * t],
           {t, 0, 6},
           PlotRange → All
           ]
```

Out[748]=

Listen!

```
In[749]:= Play[
            Piecewise[{
                {(6 t), t < 1},
                {(-5 (t - 1) + 6), t < 2},
                {(1), t < 4},
                {(-0.5 (t - 4) + 1), t < 6}
              }] * Sin[1000 * 2 π * t],
            {t, 0, 6}
          ]
```

Out[749]=

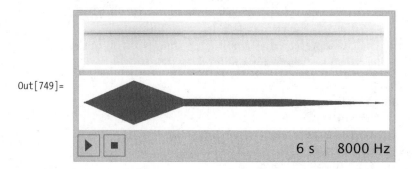

6 s | 8000 Hz

Discussion

Calculating the envelope functions for the four regions is not as hard as you might expect. Perhaps you remember the equation for a straight line: $y = m\,x + b$, where m is the slope of the line and b is the y-intercept. Here is a line with a slope of -2 that intercepts the y-axis at $y = 4$, so its equation is $y = -2x + 4$.

```
In[750]:= Plot[-2 x + 4, {x, 0, 2}, PlotRange → {{0, 4}, {-1, 4}},
            PlotStyle → {AbsoluteDashing[{4, 4}], {Thick, Black}}]
```

Out[750]=

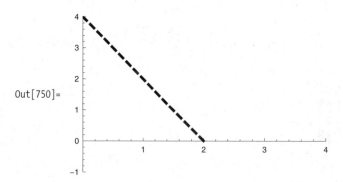

If this were the function for the second portion of the envelope, the decay portion, you would need to shift this line to the right. You can shift the line to the right simply by replacing x with (x - displacement). In general, the template for creating the equations for the Piecewise functions will be: y = m (x - displacement) + initial value of segment. Notice that what was at first the y-intercept is now the "initial value of the segment." The line here is shifted two units to the right, and the new equation is y = -2 (x - 2) + 4. If we simplify the right side, the equation becomes y = $-2x$ + 8. This line has the same -2 slope but would intercept the y-axis at y = 8 if we were to extend the line to the left.

```
In[751]:= Plot[-2 (x - 2) + 4, {x, 0, 4}, PlotRange → {{0, 4}, {-1, 4}},
            PlotStyle → {AbsoluteDashing[{4, 4}], {Thick, Black}}]
```

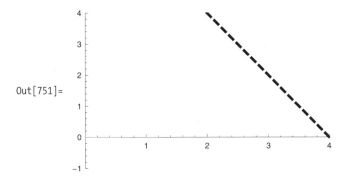

Out[751]=

9.15 Exploring Alternate Tunings

Problem

You want to explore different partitions of the musical scale and alternate instrument tunings.

Solution

Modern Western music uses *tempered tuning*, which is a slight compromise to the vibrations of the natural world, or at least the perfection of the natural world as the Greeks described it 3,000 years ago. The ancient Greeks (and even earlier, the Babylonians) noticed that when objects vibrate in simple, integer ratios to each other, the resulting sound is pleasant. The simple ratio of 2:1 is so pleasant that we perceive it as an equivalence. When two notes vibrate in a ratio of 2:1, we say they have the same pitch but are in different octaves. The history of music has been the history of partitioning the octave.

The first obvious division of the octave is created by the next simplest ratio, a 3:1 ratio. Consider the following schematic of a vibrating string. The only requirement on the string is that its endpoints remain fixed. The string can vibrate in many different modes, as shown in the first column. Each mode has a characteristic number of still points, called "nodes," that appear symmetrically along the length of the string. Each mode also has a characteristic rate of vibration, which is a simple integer multiple to the lowest fundamental frequency. Notice that three out of the first four harmonics are octave equivalences. The third harmonic, situated between the second and fourth harmonics, has a ratio of 3:2 to the second harmonic and 3:4 to the fourth. These were the kinds of simple ratios that appealed to the Greeks.

```
In[752]:= SetOptions[Plot, ImageSize → {150, 30}, AspectRatio → 0.2,
            Ticks → None, PlotStyle → AbsoluteThickness[2]];
        Style[Grid[{
            {"mode", "harmonic", "musical interpretation", "ratio to fundamental"},

            {Plot[Sin[400 × 2 π * t], {t, 0, 0.005}], "4th", "octave", "4/1"},

            {Plot[Sin[300 × 2 π * t], {t, 0, 0.005}], "3rd", "fifth", "3/1"},

            {Plot[Sin[200 × 2 π * t], {t, 0, 0.005}], "2nd", "octave", "2/1"},

            {Plot[Sin[100 × 2 π * t], {t, 0, 0.005}, PlotRange → {-1, 1}],
             "1st", "tonic", "1"}
            },
            Frame → All,
            Background → {White, {White, White, White, White, White}}
            ], 14, "Label"]
        ]
```

Out[753]=

mode	harmonic	musical interpretation	ratio to fundamental
	4th	octave	$\frac{4}{1}$
	3rd	fifth	$\frac{3}{1}$
	2nd	octave	$\frac{2}{1}$
	1st	tonic	1

mode	harmonic	musical interpretation	ratio to fundamental
	4th	octave	$\frac{4}{1}$
	3rd	fifth	$\frac{3}{1}$
	2nd	octave	$\frac{2}{1}$
	1st	tonic	1

Out[90]=

mode	harmonic	musical interpretation	ratio to fundamental
	4th	octave	$\frac{4}{1}$
	3rd	fifth	$\frac{3}{1}$
	2nd	octave	$\frac{2}{1}$
	1st	tonic	1

The following keyboard shows how a successive application of the 3:2 ratio can be used to build the entire chromatic scale. After 12 applications of this 3:2 ratio, every note of the modern chromatic scale has been visited once and we are returned to starting pitch—sort of!

```
In[754]:=  With[{y1 = -1.6, y2 = 6.5},
              whiteKeys = Table[Rectangle[{x, 0}, {x + 1, 5}], {x, 0, 49}];
              blackKeys = Table[Rectangle[{octave + x + 0.65, 2}, {octave + x + 1.3, 5}],
                 {x, {0, 1, 3, 4, 5}}, {octave, 0, 42, 7}];
              sequential = Sort[Flatten@Join[whiteKeys, blackKeys]];
              highlights = sequential[[Table[n, {n, 1, 85, 7}]]];
              keyboard = {White, EdgeForm[{Black, AbsoluteThickness[1]}], whiteKeys,
                 Gray, highlights, Black, blackKeys, Gray, highlights[[7 ;; 11]]};
              Graphics[{keyboard,
                 Style[{Text["1", {0.5, y1}], Text[3/2, {4.5, y1}], Text[(3/2)^2,
                     {8.5, y1}], Text[(3/2)^3, {12.5, y1}], Text[(3/2)^4, {16.5, y1}],
                    Text[(3/2)^5, {20.5, y1}], Text[(3/2)^6, {25, y2}],
                    Text[(3/2)^7, {29, y2}], Text[(3/2)^8, {33, y2}],
                    Text[(3/2)^9, {37, y2}], Text[(3/2)^10, {41, y2}],
                    Text[(3/2)^11, {45.5, y1}], Text[(3/2)^12, {49.5, y1}]}, 9]
                 }, ImageSize -> {550, 200}]]
```

Out[754]=

729 / 2187 / 6561 / 19 683 / 59 049 /
64　128　256　512　1024

1　3/　9/　27/　81/　243/　　　　　　　177 147 / 531 441 /
　　2　4　8　16　32　　　　　　　　　　2048　　4096

There's a problem: $(3/2)^{12}$ represents the C seven octaves above the starting C and should equal a C with a frequency ratio of $2^7 = 128$, but $(3/2)^{12}$ equals 129.75. The equal temperament solution to this problem is to distribute this discrepancy equally over all the intervals. In other words, in equal temperament, every interval is made slightly, and equally, "out of tune." Johann Sebastian Bach composed a series of keyboard pieces in 1722 called "The Well-Tempered Clavier" to demonstrate that this compromise was basically imperceptible and had no negative impact on the beauty of the music.

Mathematically, equal temperament means that the frequency of each pitch should have the same ratio to its immediate lower neighbor's frequency. Call this ratio α. Then it must be the case that if a chromatic scale, which contains 12 pitches, takes you from some frequency to twice that frequency, then $\alpha^{12} = 2$. So the ratio of a semitone in equal temperament is 1.0596.

In[755]:= $\alpha = \sqrt[12]{2.0}$
Out[755]= 1.05946

Out[92]= 1.05946

1.05946

However, now that we have the octave in perfect shape, every other interval is slightly "wrong"—or at least wrong according to the manner in which the Greeks were trying to make their intervals. So for example, a Pythagorean fifth, which is 3/2 = 1.5, is slightly flat in equal temperament (the musical interval of a fifth is composed of seven half-steps).

In[756]:= α^7
Out[756]= 1.49831 [7]

In[757]:= **1.498307**
Out[757]= 1.49831

Now that we've gone through the basics of tuning, how do you use Mathematica to explore alternate tunings?

Discussion

As explained above, tuning instruments in the modern Western world is based on dividing the octave into 12 equal segments. If the ratio of the semitone C to C# is called α, then the ratio of the octave from C3 to C4 is α^{12} and should equal 2.0. Therefore you can calculate α to be the 12th root of 20.

```
In[758]:=  α = ¹²√2.0
Out[758]=  1.05946

  Out[95]=  1.05946

           1.05946
```

Here's the equal-tempered chromatic scale, sometimes referred to as 12-TET (twelve-tone equal temperament):

```
In[759]:=  TET = Table[Sin[440.0 * αⁿ * 2 π * t], {n, 0, 12}]
Out[759]=  {Sin[2764.6 t], Sin[2928.99 t], Sin[3103.16 t],
            Sin[3287.68 t], Sin[3483.18 t], Sin[3690.3 t],
            Sin[3909.74 t], Sin[4142.22 t], Sin[4388.53 t],
            Sin[4649.49 t], Sin[4925.96 t], Sin[5218.87 t], Sin[5529.2 t]}

  Out[96]=  {Sin[2764.6 t], Sin[2928.99 t], Sin[3103.16 t],
            Sin[3287.68 t], Sin[3483.18 t], Sin[3690.3 t],
            Sin[3909.74 t], Sin[4142.22 t], Sin[4388.53 t],
            Sin[4649.49 t], Sin[4925.96 t], Sin[5218.87 t], Sin[5529.2 t]}

           {Sin[2764.6 t], Sin[2928.99 t], Sin[3103.16 t],
            Sin[3287.68 t], Sin[3483.18 t], Sin[3690.3 t],
            Sin[3909.74 t], Sin[4142.22 t], Sin[4388.53 t],
            Sin[4649.49 t], Sin[4925.96 t], Sin[5218.87 t], Sin[5529.2 t]}
```

In[760]:= Show[Play[#, {t, 0, 0.25}] & /@ TET]

Out[760]=

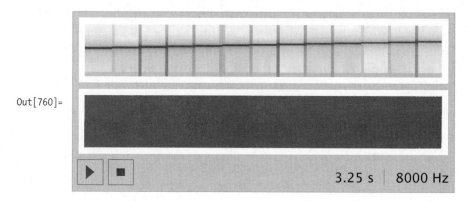

3.25 s | 8000 Hz

The equal-tempered major scale is

In[761]:= Show[Play[#, {t, 0, 0.25}] & /@ TET[[1 + {0, 2, 4, 5, 7, 9, 11, 12}]]]

Out[761]=

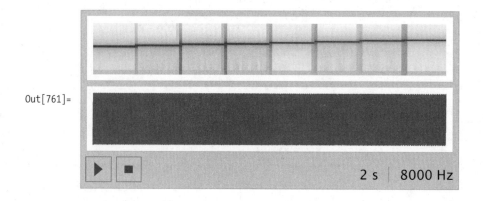

2 s | 8000 Hz

9.16 Importing Digital Sound Files

Problem

You want to import a digital sound file, for example, a WAV or AIFF file.

Solution

Mathematica imports many standard file formats. Both AIFF and WAV are in the list.

```
In[762]:= $ImportFormats
Out[762]= {3DS, ACO, AIFF, ApacheLog, AU, AVI, Base64, Binary, Bit, BMP, Byte, BYU,
            BZIP2, CDED, CDF, Character16, Character8, Complex128, Complex256,
            Complex64, CSV, CUR, DBF, DICOM, DIF, Directory, DXF, EDF, ExpressionML,
            FASTA, FITS, FLAC, GenBank, GeoTIFF, GIF, Graph6, GTOPO30, GZIP,
            HarwellBoeing, HDF, HDF5, HTML, ICO, Integer128, Integer16, Integer24,
            Integer32, Integer64, Integer8, JPEG, JPEG2000, JVX, LaTeX, List, LWO,
            MAT, MathML, MBOX, MDB, MGF, MMCIF, MOL, MOL2, MPS, MTP, MTX, MX, NB,
            NetCDF, NOFF, OBJ, ODS, OFF, Package, PBM, PCX, PDB, PDF, PGM, PLY, PNG,
            PNM, PPM, PXR, QuickTime, RawBitmap, Real128, Real32, Real64, RIB,
            RSS, RTF, SCT, SDF, SDTS, SDTSDEM, SHP, SMILES, SND, SP3, Sparse6, STL,
            String, SXC, Table, TAR, TerminatedString, Text, TGA, TIFF, TIGER,
            TSV, UnsignedInteger128, UnsignedInteger16, UnsignedInteger24,
            UnsignedInteger32, UnsignedInteger64, UnsignedInteger8, USGSDEM, UUE,
            VCF, WAV, Wave64, WDX, XBM, XHTML, XHTMLMathML, XLS, XML, XPORT, XYZ, ZIP}
```

Using the "Data" specification will save you the aggravation of decoding the syntax of the imported data. Don't forget the semicolon, which prevents Mathematica from listing all the sample points. The easiest way to access a file is to type Import[ ], place your cursor between the empty brackets, choose File... from the Insert Menu, navigate in the dialog box to the file you want to open.

```
In[763]:= file = FileNameJoin[{NotebookDirectory[], "..", "data", "JCK_01.aif"}];
          data = Flatten@Import[file, "Data"];
```

You'll need to know the sample rate and whether this file is a mono or stereo, so do a second Import on the same file but specify "Options".

```
In[765]:= Import[file, "Options"]
Out[765]= {AudioChannels → 1, AudioEncoding → Integer16, SampleRate → 48 000}
```

If you simply wanted to play the file, specify "Sound" as the second parameter.

```
In[766]:= snd = Import[file, "Sound"];
```

This returns a Sound object.

```
In[767]:= snd // Head
Out[767]= Sound
```

And can be played like so:

```
In[768]:= snd
```

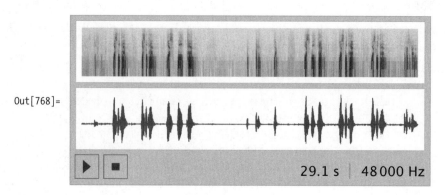

Out[768]=

29.1 s | 48 000 Hz

Discussion

Sound files can be huge, and as such, become difficult to work with.

```
In[769]:= Length[data]
Out[769]= 1 396 853
```

Here's a quick way to get an overview of a sound file. Mathematica is being asked to display every thousandth sample point. You can easily see there are a handful of bursts of energy.

```
In[770]:= SetOptions[ListLinePlot,
            ImageSize → {500, 150}, AspectRatio → 0.25, PlotRange → All];

In[771]:= SetOptions[ListPlot, ImageSize → {500, 150},
            AspectRatio → 0.25, PlotRange → All];

In[772]:= ListLinePlot[data[[1 ;; 1 396 000 ;; 1000]]]
```

Out[772]=

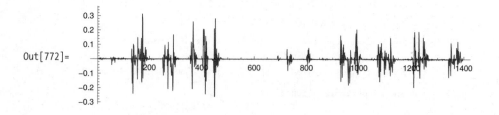

Focus on the three wavelets between 900 and 1,300.

In[773]:= **ListLinePlot[data[[900000 ;; 1300000]]]**

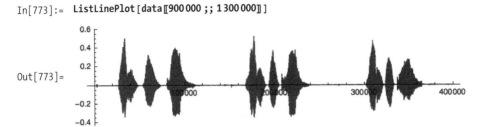

Out[773]=

"Yes we can; yes we can; yes we can!"

In[774]:= **Sound[SampledSoundList[data[[900000 ;; 1300000]], 48000]]**

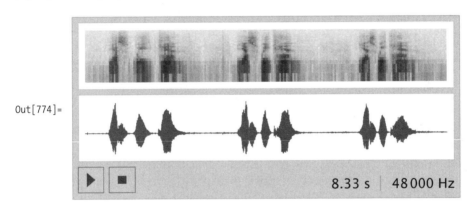

Out[774]=

8.33 s │ 48000 Hz

9.17 Analyzing Digital Sound Files

Problem

You want to do a Fourier analysis on a sound file. Fourier analysis is a means of investigating the energy in a signal. Specifically, Fourier analysis will report on the energy spectrum of a signal versus frequency. The mathematics behind Fourier analysis is quite sophisticated, but armed with just a few principles, you can put Mathematica's Fourier tools to work for you.

Solution

Typically you'll start with a digitized signal. The sampling rate will determine the highest frequency that can be investigated. This highest frequency is called the Nyquist frequency and is always exactly one half the sampling rate. For this "Yes we can!" sample, which was digitized at 48 KHz, the highest frequency is 24 KHz. (It's not coincidental that this frequency is slightly greater than the limits of human hearing.) Notice the plot is symmetric about the Nyquist frequency.

The number of sample points used in any analysis is also critical. Here exactly one second of audio, that is, 48,000 sample points, is being analyzed. The 48,000 points from the time domain yield 48,000 points in the frequency domain, but as you can see, the right side of the plot, between points 24,000 and 48,000, is just a mirror duplication of the points between 0 and 24,000. This is an artifact of the underlying mathematics, and there is no additional information in this half of the plot.

In[775]:= `ListLinePlot[Abs[Fourier[data⟦900 000 ;; 900 000 + 48 000⟧]]]`

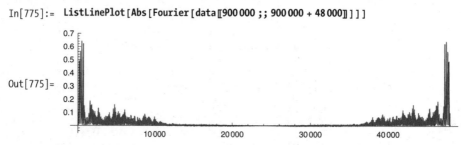

Since this is speech, you can focus on the first 2,000 points, which correspond to frequencies 0 to 2,000 Hz. Later you'll see that 2,000 points of a Fourier analysis doesn't always mean frequencies 0 through 2,000 Hz. It does in this case because you started with 48,000 sample points in the time domain that equals the sampling rate and created a one-to-one relationship between data points and frequencies in the frequency domain. You can see that this speaker has four significant frequency resonances to his voice at approximately 150 Hz, 300 Hz, 490 Hz, and 700 Hz. These resonances are known as *formants*. Notice, the `Ticks` option customized the labeling of the x-axis.

In[776]:= `ListLinePlot[Abs[Fourier[data⟦900 000 ;; 900 000 + 48 000⟧]]]⟦1 ;; 2000⟧,`
`Ticks → {{150, 300, 490, 700, 1000, 1500, 2000}, Automatic}]`

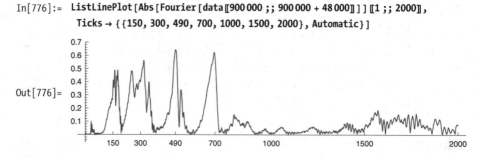

Typically, when analyzing voice, one second is too long of a sample. Just think how many syllables you utter in one second of normal speech. A much more appropriate length would be 1/10 or 1/20 or even 1/30 of a second. You can easily identify various phonemes of "yes we can" in the plot below: the "yeh" and "sss" of the "yes," the singular vowel sound of "we," and the hard "c" and "an" of "can."

```
In[777]:= ListLinePlot[data[[925000 ;; 925000 + 96000]],
            PlotRange -> All, AxesOrigin → {0, -0.4}]
```

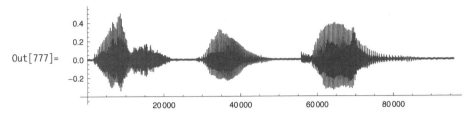

Out[777]=

Here's the "we," which is very homogeneous.

```
In[778]:= ListLinePlot[data[[955000 ;; 955000 + 9600]], PlotRange -> All]
```

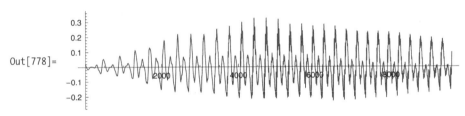

Out[778]=

You're now looking at 9,600 sample points (9,600/48,000 = 1/5 sec) in the time domain, so each point in the frequency domain represents 48,000/9,600 = 5 Hz. There's a direct trade-off between using as few sample points as possible to narrow the analysis to a single phoneme, versus sampling enough points to ascertain a desired precision in the frequency domain.

```
In[779]:= pts = Abs[Fourier[data[[955000 ;; 955000 + 9600]]]][[1 ;; 100]];
            ListPlot[pts, Joined → True,
              Epilog → {MapIndexed[Point[{Sequence @@ #2, #}] &, pts]},
              Ticks → {Table[{n, 5 * n}, {n, 0, 100, 10}], Automatic},
              PlotRange → All, Filling → Axis]
```

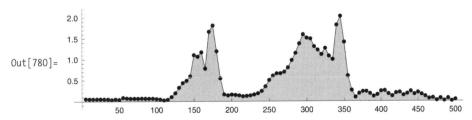

Out[780]=

Here, half as many points (4,800) sampled from the same region focuses our analysis in the time domain, but each sample point now represents 10 Hz. Perhaps we're losing some detail in the 150-200 Hz range, as well as the 300-350 Hz range?

```
In[781]:= pts = Abs[Fourier[data[[955000 ;; 955000 + 4800]]]][[1 ;; 100]];
          ListPlot[pts, Joined → True,
            Epilog → {MapIndexed[Point[{Sequence @@ #2, #}] &, pts]},
            Ticks → {Table[{n, 10 * n}, {n, 0, 100, 10}], Automatic},
            PlotRange → All, Filling → Axis]
```

Out[782]=

9.18 Slicing a Sample

Problem

You want a Fourier analysis over time.

Solution

You can partition the data into 1/30 of a second slices and do an analysis on each slice. Each sample point in the frequency domain will be 30 Hz, which is "wider" than the previous examples, but the precision in the time domain will more than make up for it.

```
In[783]:= ffts = Table[Fourier[data[[t ;; t + 1600 - 1]]],
              {t, 900000, 900000 + 1600 * 250, 1600}];
```

Take just the lowest 100 frequency bands, frequencies 0-3,000 Hz.

```
In[784]:= lines = Abs[ffts[[All, 1 ;; 100]]];
```

With Mathematica's Graphics3D primitives, you can make this waterfall-style chart, where time is left to right across the front, and frequency is front to back.

```
In[785]:= Graphics3D[
            Line[#] & /@ MapIndexed[List[Sequence @@ #2, #] &, lines, {-1}],
            PlotRange → {{0, 250}, {0, 60}, {0, 4}}, BoxRatios → {4, 2, 1},
            ImageSize → 500, SphericalRegion → True,
            ViewPoint → {1, -1, 0.75}, Boxed → True]
```

Out[785]=

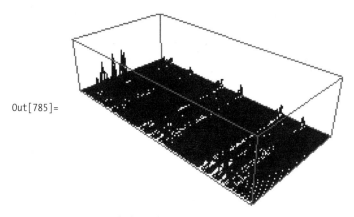

ListLinePlot accomplishes the same thing but interpolates the individual lines into surfaces.

```
In[786]:= ListPlot3D[lines,
            Mesh → None, PlotRange → All, ImageSize → 500,
            SphericalRegion → True, ViewPoint → {-1, 1, 0.75},
            Boxed → False, ColorFunction → (GrayLevel[1 - #3] &),
            Ticks → {Function[{min, max}, Table[{i, i*30}, {i, 0, Floor[max], 10}]],
              Function[{min, max},
                Table[{i, i*0.033 // Round}, {i, 0, Floor[max], 30}]], Automatic}
          ]
```

Out[786]=

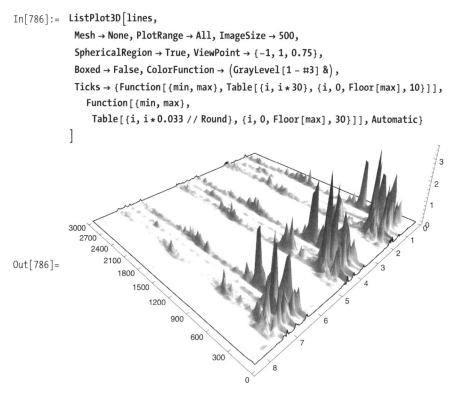

Discussion

Now that you've seen the previous 3D displays, perhaps these contour plots will make immediate sense to you. These are bird's-eye views of the 3D plots. You can really finesse these plots to bring out the details. Look at the color versions provided in the online version of this book.

```
In[787]:= ListContourPlot[
            Transpose@Table[Abs[Fourier[data[[n ;; n + 1600 - 1]]]][[1 ;; 120]],
              {n, 900 000, 900 000 + 1600 * 250, 1600}],
            Contours → 20, ContourShading → None, ImageSize → {500, 300},
            AspectRatio → 0.5, Ticks → {None, None},
            FrameTicks → {Automatic,
              Function[{min, max}, Table[{i, i * 15}, {i, 0, max, 20}]]}]
```

Out[787]=
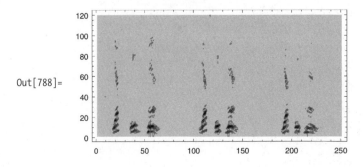

Tweaking the Contours and ContourShading options prevent the white-outs in the peak regions.

```
In[788]:= ListContourPlot[
            Transpose@Table[Abs[Fourier[data[[n ;; n + 1600 - 1]]]][[1 ;; 120]],
              {n, 900 000, 900 000 + 1600 * 250, 1600}],
            Contours → Function[{min, max}, Range[0, max, 0.25]],
            ContourShading → Table[GrayLevel[1 - n / 16.], {n, 16}], PlotRange → All,
            ImageSize → {800, 400}, AspectRatio → 0.5]
```

Out[788]=

A Spectrograph

ArrayPlot is another perfect tool to display the results. ArrayPlot will automatically scale the results such that the greater the energy content in the frequency domain, the darker the plot. Frequency runs across the page, as shown previously in Recipe 9.17, whereas the individual slices run down the page.

```
In[789]:= SetOptions[ArrayPlot, ImageSize → {600, 200}, AspectRatio → 0.25];
```

```
In[790]:= ArrayPlot[Table[Abs[Fourier[data[[n ;; n + 1600 - 1]]]][[1 ;; 100]],
            {n, 900 000, 900 000 + 1600 * 250, 1600}],
          FrameTicks → {Automatic, Table[{n, 30 * n}, {n, 0, 100, 5}]}]
```

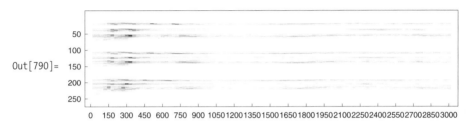

Out[790]=

You can improve on ArrayPlot's formatting. Convention wants time to run left to right across the page and frequency to run bottom to top. Transpose will reverse the axes, but you'll also need DataReversed→True to make time run left to right.

```
In[791]:= ArrayPlot[Transpose@Table[Abs[Fourier[data[[n ;; n + 1600 - 1]]]][[1 ;; 120]],
            {n, 900 000, 900 000 + 1600 * 250, 1600}],
          FrameTicks → {Table[{n, 30 * n}, {n, 0, 100, 10}],
            Table[{n, 0.03333 * n // Round}, {n, 0, 250, 30}]}, DataReversed → True]
```

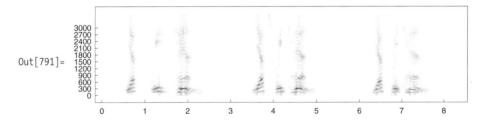

Out[791]=

You could set a threshold and display in black and white.

```
In[792]:= ArrayPlot[Transpose@Table[Abs[Fourier[data[[n ;; n + 1600 - 1]]]][[1 ;; 120]],
            {n, 900 000, 900 000 + 1600 * 250, 1600}] /.
          {_Real? (# >= 0.3 &) :> 1, _Real? (# < 0.3 &) :> 0},
```

```
In[792]:=  FrameTicks → {Table[{n, 30 * n}, {n, 0, 100, 10}],
              Table[{n, 0.03333 * n // Round}, {n, 0, 250, 30}]}, DataReversed → True]
```

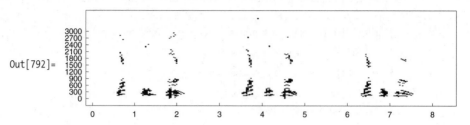

Or, you could zoom in and look more closely at the lower frequencies.

```
In[793]:=  ArrayPlot[Transpose@Table[Abs[Fourier[data[[n ;; n + 1600 - 1]]]][[1 ;; 30]],
              {n, 900 000, 900 000 + 1600 * 250, 1600}],
              FrameTicks → {Table[{n, 30 * n}, {n, 0, 30, 5}],
              Table[{n, 0.03333 * n // Round}, {n, 0, 250, 30}]}, DataReversed → True]
```

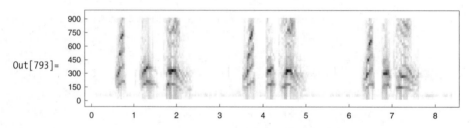

CHAPTER 10

Algebra

When a problem comes along
You must whip it
Before the cream sits out too long
You must whip it
When something's going wrong
You must whip it

Now whip it
Into shape
Shape it up
Get straight
Go forward
Move ahead
Try to detect it
It's not too late
To whip it
Whip it good

Devo, "Whip It"

10.0 Introduction

Algebra can be divided into elementary algebra and abstract algebra. Elementary algebra is the kind we all learned in high school. Mathematica is well equipped to solve problems in elementary algebra, and many of the recipes in this chapter show you how to leverage these features. Mathematica does not presently have deep support for abstract algebra, which is concerned with constructs such as groups, rings, and fields. However, there are third-party packages available for exploring abstract algebra, and I provide references for those.

Mathematica's ability to do algebraic manipulation is important for two reasons. First, many problems, although conceptually easy to solve by hand, are tedious, and it makes sense to have Mathematica relieve you of this drudgery. Recipe 10.1 shows you how to solve algebraic equations; Recipe 10.2 shows how to work backward from a root to a polynomial. However, helping you solve algebraic equations is not the most important part of this chapter. Rather, you will often find that Mathematica will not automatically give you an answer in the form you desire. Knowing how to coax expressions into the desired form is an important skill in your day-to-day use of Mathematica. Recipe 10.3 is geared to helping you gain proficiency in this area. It is easy enough to create a polynomial by typing input into Mathematica, but if you want to generate a polynomial of a specific form, Recipe 10.4 will show you how. On the other hand, if you need to break up a polynomial into parts to perform some low-level manipulations, you will want to look at Recipe 10.5. Diving a bit deeper into abstraction, Recipe 10.6 investigates division and related operations on polynomials.

See Also

Allen C. Hibbard and Kenneth M. Levasseur have developed "Exploring Abstract Algebra with Mathematica" (*http://bit.ly/CHT9O*), which can be freely downloaded after registering.

10.1 Solving Algebraic Equations

Problem

You want to solve an algebraic equation for its unknowns.

Solution

Use Solve with expressions of the form **left-hand-side == right-hand-side** and the unknown variable (or variables) provided as the second argument. Results are returned as rules.

```
In[2]:= Solve[x^2 - 2 x - 3 == 0, x]
Out[2]:= {{x → -1}, {x → 3}}
```

Solve takes either a single expression, as above, or a list of expressions or several expressions linked with &&. As you would expect, solutions can be found in symbolic form.

$$In[3]:= \text{Solve}\left[\{a\,x + 2\,y == 7, 3\,b\,x - y == 1\}, \{x, y\}\right]$$

$$Out[3]= \left\{\left\{x \to \frac{9}{a + 6\,b}, y \to -\frac{a - 21\,b}{a + 6\,b}\right\}\right\}$$

$$In[4]:= \text{Solve}\left[a\,x - 2\,y == 7\ \&\&\ 2\,b\,x + y == 0, \{x, y\}\right]$$

$$Out[4]= \left\{\left\{x \to \frac{7}{a + 4\,b}, y \to -\frac{14\,b}{a + 4\,b}\right\}\right\}$$

Discussion

Solve works best with linear and polynomial equations. For expressions involving constraints, inequalities, or non-algebraic expressions, you should use Reduce. (In Mathematica 8.0, Solve will be enhanced to cover a much larger class of problems, thus reducing the need to Reduce!)

```
In[5]:= Reduce[x > 0 && x^2 - 2 x - 3 == 0, x]
Out[5]= x == 3
```

Reduce does not use rules because it may need to express solutions in terms of intervals.

```
In[6]:= Reduce[x > 0 && x^2 < 2, x]
```
$$Out[6]= 0 < x < \sqrt{2}$$

FindRoot is appropriate when you are looking for numerical solutions and have provided a starting point where you want Mathematica to search. FindRoot is a numerical method, so it can solve a larger class of expressions then Solve, although it is not guaranteed to converge.

```
In[7]:= FindRoot[x^2 - 2 x - 3 == 0, {x, -3}]
Out[7]= {x → -1.}
```

```
In[8]:= FindRoot[x^2 - Exp[2 x] - 3 == x, {x, 0}]
Out[8]= {x → -1.32237}
```

10.2 Finding a Polynomial from a Given Root

Problem

You have an *algebraic number* and you want a polynomial that has the number among its roots. This is the opposite of Solve, which finds the roots given a polynomial.

Solution

Use MinimalPolynomial to find the minimal polynomial (least degree) with the given value as a root.

```
In[9]:= poly = MinimalPolynomial[Sqrt[2] + Sqrt[5], x]
```
$$Out[9]= 9 - 14 x^2 + x^4$$

```
In[10]:= Last[Solve[poly == 0, x]] // FullSimplify
```
$$Out[10]= \left\{ x → \sqrt{2} + \sqrt{5} \right\}$$

Discussion

As you would expect, complex numbers are allowed.

```
In[11]:= MinimalPolynomial[2 + I, x]
Out[11]= 5 - 4 x + x²
```

Numbers must be *explicitly* algebraic or you will get an error. Trying to use Minimal-Polynomial with Pi is doomed, since Pi is a transcendental number, but a rational approximation of Pi fails as well because it is not explicitly algebraic.

```
In[12]:= MinimalPolynomial[Pi, x]
```

```
MinimalPolynomial::nalg :
    π is not an explicit algebraic number. >>
```

```
Out[12]= MinimalPolynomial[π, x]
```

```
In[13]:= MinimalPolynomial[3.14, x]
```

```
MinimalPolynomial::nalg :
    3.14` is not an explicit algebraic number. >>
```

```
Out[13]= MinimalPolynomial[3.14, x]
```

Use Rationalize to work around this limitation.

```
Out[14]= MinimalPolynomial[Rationalize[3.14], x]
Out[14]= -157 + 50 x
```

10.3 Transforming Expressions to Other Forms

Problem

You have a symbolic expression that you would like to transform to a different form. This problem often arises when you get a result from a Mathematica computation that is in a form you don't want. One common requirement is to simplify the expression.

Solution

The two most important symbolic transformations are Simplify and FullSimplify. These functions attempt to apply algebraic and other transformations to an expression that will convert it to an equivalent form that contains fewer symbols. The main difference between Simplify and FullSimplify is that FullSimplify will consider a much larger set of transformations, including special functions. As a result, FullSimplify is often more effective but also slower.

Here Simplify and FullSimplify ultimately arrive at the same answer, but FullSimplify takes well over a minute, whereas Simplify completes in just over a second.

In[15]:= Timing[Simplify[Sin[(x + y + z)^2] Cos[(z + y + x)^2]]]

Out[15]= $\left\{0.764, \frac{1}{2} Sin[2 (x + y + z)^2]\right\}$

In[16]:= Timing[FullSimplify[Sin[(x + y + z)^2] Cos[(z + y + x)^2]]]

In[16]:= $\left\{38.626, \frac{1}{2} Sin[2 (x + y + z)^2]\right\}$

Discussion

Simplify and FullSimplify perform fully automated simplification. However, you sometimes want to apply more targeted transformations. For example, a common transformation is to bring together a sum over a common denominator.

In[17]:= Together[
        a / (a^2 + b^2 + c^2) + b / (a^2 + b^2 + c^2) + c / (a^2 + b^2 + c^2)]

In[17]:= $\dfrac{a + b + c}{a^2 + b^2 + c^2}$

Apart is another useful transformation that represents an expression as sums of partial fractions.

In[18]:= Apart[4 / ((1 + x) (5 + x))]

In[18]:= $\dfrac{1}{1 + x} - \dfrac{1}{5 + x}$

Polynomial transformations are a very important class, exemplified by functions like Factor, FactorTerms, FactorSquareFree, Expand, and ExpandAll.

In[19]:= Factor[$21 - 4 x - x^2$]

In[19]:= $-(-3 + x) (7 + x)$

Expand is the opposite of Factor and expands out sums of products and positive powers.

```
In[20]:=  Expand[%]
Out[20]=  21 - 4 x - x²
```

```
In[21]:=  Expand[(1 + x)^5]
Out[21]=  1 + 5 x + 10 x² + 10 x³ + 5 x⁴ + x⁵
```

```
In[22]:=  Factor[%]
Out[22]=  (1 + x)⁵
```

ExpandAll is similar to Expand but reaches in deeper into the expression, for example, into arguments of functions like Sin or Exp. Notice how Expand has no effect on a nested polynomial but ExpandAll does.

```
In[23]:=  Expand[Sin[(1 + x)⁵]]
Out[23]=  Sin[(1 + x)⁵]
```

```
In[24]:=  ExpandAll[Sin[(1 + x)⁵]]
Out[24]=  Sin[1 + 5 x + 10 x² + 10 x³ + 5 x⁴ + x⁵]
```

You can also narrow the scope of Expand to the numerator or denominator of a rational expression using ExpandNumerator and ExpandDenominator, respectively.

```
In[25]:=  With[{expr = (1 + x)^3 / (3 + x)^4},
            Row[{ExpandNumerator[expr], ExpandDenominator[expr]}, Invisible[expr]]]
```

$$Out[25]= \quad \frac{1 + 3 x + 3 x^2 + x^3}{(3 + x)^4} \qquad \frac{(1 + x)^3}{81 + 108 x + 54 x^2 + 12 x^3 + x^4}$$

Collect does the job of Expand but also collects terms of matching powers of some variable. Compare the results of Expand and Collect given here.

```
In[26]:=  Expand[(a + x)^2 (b + x)^3]
Out[26]=  a² b³ + 3 a² b² x + 2 a b³ x + 3 a² b x² + 6 a b² x² +
          b³ x² + a² x³ + 6 a b x³ + 3 b² x³ + 2 a x⁴ + 3 b x⁴ + x⁵
```

```
In[27]:=  Collect[(a + x)^2 (b + x)^3, x]
In[27]:=  a² b³ + (3 a² b² + 2 a b³) x + (3 a² b + 6 a b² + b³) x² +
          (a² + 6 a b + 3 b²) x³ + (2 a + 3 b) x⁴ + x⁵
```

FactorTerms factors out numerical terms or terms that do not depend on particular variables.

```
In[28]:=  FactorTerms[Expand[(3 + 3 x)^5]]
Out[28]=  243 (1 + 5 x + 10 x² + 10 x³ + 5 x⁴ + x⁵)
```

```
In[29]:= Expand[(y + y x)^5]
Out[29]= y^5 + 5 x y^5 + 10 x^2 y^5 + 10 x^3 y^5 + 5 x^4 y^5 + x^5 y^5

In[30]:= FactorTerms[%, y]
Out[30]= (1 + 5 x + 10 x^2 + 10 x^3 + 5 x^4 + x^5) y^5
```

Another important class of transformations are trigonometric transformations. These include TrigFactor, TrigExpand, TrigExpandAll, and TrigReduce.

```
In[31]:= TrigFactor[Sin[3 x]]
Out[31]= (1 + 2 Cos[2 x]) Sin[x]
```

TrigExpand removes sums and products inside arguments by expanding the expression using trigonometric identities.

```
In[32]:= TrigExpand[Sin[3 x + 1]]
Out[32]= Cos[x]^3 Sin[1] + 3 Cos[1] Cos[x]^2 Sin[x] -
             3 Cos[x] Sin[1] Sin[x]^2 - Cos[1] Sin[x]^3

          Cos[x]^3 Sin[1] + 3 Cos[1] Cos[x]^2 Sin[x] -
             3 Cos[x] Sin[1] Sin[x]^2 - Cos[1] Sin[x]^3

          Cos[x]^3 Sin[1] + 3 Cos[1] Cos[x]^2 Sin[x] -
             3 Cos[x] Sin[1] Sin[x]^2 - Cos[1] Sin[x]^3
```

TrigReduce transforms an expression so that it is linear in the trigonometric terms (no powers or multiplications of two different trig functions).

```
In[33]:= TrigReduce[Sin[3 x]^2 Cos[2 x]]
              1
Out[33]=  -  (2 Cos[2 x] - Cos[4 x] - Cos[8 x])
              4
```

See Also

Mathematica has quite a few specialized functions for manipulating polynomials and extracting portions of their structure. See *tutorial/AlgebraicOperationsOnPolynomials* in the documentation.

A complete overview of algebraic manipulations can be found at *tutorial/Algebraic ManipulationOverview*.

10.4 Generating Polynomials

Problem

You want to generate a polynomial of a specific degree.

Solution

A simple solution uses Sum and Subscript. Here I generate a fourth-degree polynomial.

```
In[34]:= Sum[Subscript[a, i] x^i, {i, 0, 4}]
```

$$Out[34]= a_0 + x\,a_1 + x^2\,a_2 + x^3\,a_3 + x^4\,a_4$$

Discussion

If, other than the degree, you don't care about the particular form of the polynomial, then the solution is fine. However, if you want to specify the coefficients, you can generate a polynomial with Dot.

```
In[35]:= ClearAll[makePoly]
         SetAttributes[makePoly, HoldRest]; makePoly[coef_List, var_: x] :=
         Dot[Table[var^i, {i, 0, Length[coef] - 1}], coef]
```

```
In[37]:= makePoly[{a, b, c, d, e}]
```

$$Out[37]= a + b\,x + c\,x^2 + d\,x^3 + e\,x^4$$

Here I specify a variable other than *x*.

```
In[38]:= makePoly[{a, b, c, d, e}, z]
```

$$Out[38]= a + b\,z + c\,z^2 + d\,z^3 + e\,z^4$$

Many mathematics textbooks show polynomials from highest to lowest degree, and you may want to generate and display your polynomials in this order as well. Replace Dot with Inner and use HoldForm so the sum is not reordered by Mathematica. Note how I changed Table to generate terms from highest degree to lowest.

```
In[39]:= ClearAll[makePoly2]
         SetAttributes[makePoly2, HoldRest];
         makePoly2[coef_List, var_: x] := Inner[Times,
             Table[var^i, {i, Length[coef] - 1, 0, -1}], coef, HoldForm[Plus[##]] &]
```

```
In[41]:= makePoly2[{a, b, c, d, e}, z]
```

$$Out[41]= a\,z^4 + b\,z^3 + c\,z^2 + d\,z + e$$

10.5 Decomposing Polynomials into Their Constituent Parts

Problem

You want to extract a list of coefficients, monomials, or variables from a given polynomial.

Solution

Two useful primitives for decomposing polynomials are `CoefficientList` and `MonomialList`. First I generate a polynomial, per Recipe 10.4.

```
In[42]:= poly = Sum[Subscript[a, i] x^i, {i, 0, 6}]
Out[42]= a_0 + x a_1 + x^2 a_2 + x^3 a_3 + x^4 a_4 + x^5 a_5 + x^6 a_6
```

Use `CoefficientList` to extract a list of coefficients of poly.

```
In[43]:= CoefficientList[poly, x]
In[43]:= {a_0, a_1, a_2, a_3, a_4, a_5, a_6}
```

Use `MonomialList` to extract a list of the individual monomial terms of poly.

```
In[44]:= MonomialList[poly]
Out[44]= {a_0, x^6 a_6, x^5 a_5, x^4 a_4, x^3 a_3, x^2 a_2, x a_1}
```

If you only want the variables of the polynomial, use `Variables`.

```
In[45]:= Variables[(x + 1)^2 (y + 3)^3]
Out[45]= {x, y}
```

Discussion

In addition to `CoefficientList`, you can pick coefficients that match a specific form using `Coefficient`.

```
In[46]:= Coefficient[8 + 12 x + 6 x^2 + x^3, x^2]
Out[46]= 6
```

`Coefficient` also takes a third argument, which specifies the power of the second argument. So the same extraction can be done as shown here.

```
In[47]:= Coefficient[8 + 12 x + 6 x^2 + x^3, x, 2]
In[47]:= 6
```

Conveniently, this also allows you to extract the constant term.

```
In[48]:= Coefficient[8 + 12 x + 6 x^2 + x^3, x, 0]
Out[48]= 8
```

Returning to `MonomialList`, there is a third argument that allows you to change the order of the monomials returned. The available orderings are `"Lexicographic"`, `"DegreeLexicographic"`, `"DegreeReverseLexicographic"`, `"NegativeLexicographic"`, `"NegativeDegreeLexicographic"`, and `"NegativeDegreeReverseLexicographic"`. Refer to the documentation of `MonomialList` for definitions.

```
In[49]:= poly = Expand[(x + 2)^2 (y + 3)^3]

Out[49]= 108 + 108 x + 27 x² + 108 y + 108 x y +
         27 x² y + 36 y² + 36 x y² + 9 x² y² + 4 y³ + 4 x y³ + x² y³
```

```
In[50]:= MonomialList[poly, {x, y}, "DegreeLexicographic"]

Out[50]= {x² y³, 9 x² y², 4 x y³, 27 x² y, 36 x y², 4 y³, 27 x², 108 x y, 36 y², 108 x, 108 y, 108}
```

```
In[51]:= MonomialList[poly, {x, y}, "Lexicographic"]

Out[51]= {x² y³, 9 x² y², 27 x² y, 27 x², 4 x y³, 36 x y², 108 x y, 108 x, 4 y³, 36 y², 108 y, 108}
```

```
In[52]:= MonomialList[poly, {x, y}, "NegativeDegreeLexicographic"]

Out[52]= {108, 108 x, 108 y, 27 x², 108 x y, 36 y², 27 x² y, 36 x y², 4 y³, 9 x² y², 4 x y³, x² y³}
```

After using MonomialList to get the monomials in the desired order, you can display the polynomial in that order using HoldForm.

```
In[53]:= HoldForm[Plus[##]] & @@ MonomialList[poly, {x, y}, "Lexicographic"]

Out[53]= x² y³ + 9 x² y² + 27 x² y + 27 x² + 4 x y³ +
         36 x y² + 108 x y + 108 x + 4 y³ + 36 y² + 108 y + 108
```

See Also

You may also want to consider CoefficientArrays and CoefficientRules. See the Mathematica documentation for these functions.

10.6 Dividing Polynomials by Other Polynomials

Problem

You want to divide polynomials, find remainders, greatest common divisor (GCD), or least common multiple (LCM).

Solution

Use PolynomialQuotient or PolynomialRemainder. If you need both, use Polynomial-QuotientRemainder.

```
In[54]:= PolynomialQuotient[x^3 + x^2 - x + 1, x + 1, x]

Out[54]:= -1 + x²
```

```
In[55]:= PolynomialRemainder[x^3 + x^2 - x + 1, x + 1, x]

Out[55]= 2
```

```
In[56]:= PolynomialQuotientRemainder[x^3 + x^2 - x + 1, x + 1, x]

Out[56]= {-1 + x², 2}
```

Discussion

Mathematica also provides PolynomialMod, which uses an algorithm based on repeated subtraction and, hence, never performs a division. In contrast, Polynomial-Remainder is implemented in terms of PolynomialQuotient.

```
In[57]:= With[{poly = x^3 + x^2 - x + 1, divisor = x^2},
           Simplify[poly - (divisor * PolynomialQuotient[poly, divisor, x])] ===
             PolynomialRemainder[poly, divisor, x]]
Out[57]= True
```

In many cases, PolynomialMod and PolynomialRemainder will return the same result. In particular, for univariate rational polynomials, PolynomialRemainder is the same as PolynomialMod.

```
In[58]:= PolynomialMod[x^3 + x^2 - x + 1, x^2] ===
           PolynomialRemainder[x^3 + x^2 - x + 1, x^2, x]
Out[58]= True
```

```
In[59]:= PolynomialMod[x^3 + x^2 - x + 1, x] ===
           PolynomialRemainder[x^3 + x^2 - x + 1, x, x]
Out[59]= True
```

If the divisor is a constant or multivariate, the functions work differently. In the case of PolynomialMod, a constant m reduces the coefficients module m whereas PolynomialRemainder will always give 0.

```
In[60]:= PolynomialMod[13 x^3 + 15 x^2 - 5 x + 7, 7]
Out[60]= 2 x + x^2 + 6 x^3
```

```
In[61]:= PolynomialRemainder[x^3 + x^2 - x + 1, 7, x]
Out[61]= 0
```

In the multivariate case, PolynomialMod determines variable order based on OrderedQ.

```
In[62]:= PolynomialMod[a x^3 + 2 a x^2 - 5 ax + 1, x + a]
Out[62]:= 1 - 5 ax - 2 x^3 - x^4
```

```
In[63]:= PolynomialRemainder[a x^3 + 2 a x^2 - 5 ax + 1, x + a, x]
Out[63]= 1 + 2 a^3 - a^4 - 5 ax
```

Both PolynomialMod and PolynomialRemainder allow you to compute the result module to a specific integer n by specifying the option Modulus→n. This means the computation is over the finite ring of integers Z_n. The default is Modulus→0, meaning the
infinite set of integers.

```
In[64]:= PolynomialRemainder[x^2 + 2 x + 2, x, x]
Out[64]= 2
```

Given these polynomial generalizations of division, it makes sense to discuss GCD
and LCM.

```
In[65]:= PolynomialGCD[10 x^3 + 2, 30 x^3 + 6]
Out[65]= 2 + 10 x^3
```

Here we show that polynomials with coefficients with LCM less than the product
will result in polynomials with LCM different than their product.

```
In[66]:= With[{p1 = 12 x + 18, p2 = 18 x + 24},
            Grid[{Expand /@ { PolynomialLCM[p1, p2], p1 * p2}}, Dividers → All ]]
```
Out[66]=
| $72 + 102 x + 36 x^2$ | $432 + 612 x + 216 x^2$ |

Observe that

```
In[67]:= {LCM[18, 24], LCM[12, 18]}
Out[67]= {72, 36}
```

```
In[68]:= 612 / 102 == 432 / 72 == 216 / 36 == GCD[18, 24, 12]
Out[68]= True
```

CHAPTER 11

Calculus: Continuous and Discrete

Time may change me
But I can't trace time
I said that time may change me
But I can't trace time
David Bowie, "Changes"

11.0 Introduction

This chapter primarily focuses on the types of problems students and teachers will cover in college-level mathematics courses and how Mathematica can be used as a calculator (tool for getting an answer) and a teacher (tool for gaining insight into a mathematical problem). However, this focus was largely pragmatic and does not imply that Mathematica is limited to introductory calculus. Quite the contrary. Mathematica has been leading the charge among computer algebra systems since its inception, and with each new release the depth and breadth of its abilities in symbolic calculus improve. My goal in most of these recipes is to provide a starting point for the inexperienced user. Experts will probably find little that is new or highly original. This was a conscious choice based on space limitations. I am quite certain one could write a small cookbook by turning each recipe here into an entire chapter! Such is the depth of Mathematica's abilities.

Most of the recipes in this chapter address what is commonly known as infinitesimal or continuous calculus. These problems deal with limits (Recipe 11.1), series (Recipe 11.3), derivatives (Recipe 11.4), integrals (Recipe 11.5), and differential equations (Recipe 11.6). A common application of calculus is finding minimums and maximums. Mathematica packages these techniques into `Minimize`, `Maximize`, and related functions (Recipe 11.7). When you use your calculus skills to solve real engineering and physics problems, you are bound to run smack into applications that involve vector calculus. Mathematica has a package of functions specifically dedicated to vector calculus, and we touch on some of this functionality in Recipe 11.8.

Although the calculus of continuous functions still plays a dominant role, discrete calculus is extremely important and has been garnering increasing attention lately due to research in such varied domains as string theory, probability theory, theory of algorithms, and combinatorics, to name a few. Mathematica 7 has enhanced its discrete calculus abilities. Recipes 11.9 through 11.11 help you start using these capabilities.

See Also

A guide to all functions related to infinitesimal calculus can be found in the Mathematica documentation at *guide/Calculus*.

A guide to all functions related to discrete calculus can be found in the Mathematica documentation at *guide/DiscreteCalculus*.

11.1 Computing Limits

Problem

You want to determine the value of a function as a variable approaches a specific value, even if evaluating the function at that limit may give an indeterminate result.

Solution

The functions Sin[x]/x, Sin[x^2]/x, and Sin[x]/x^2 each evaluate to the indeterminate value 0/0 at x = 0; however, their limits as x approaches zero are quite definite and different.

```
In[1]:= Limit[Sin[x] /x, x → 0]
Out[1]= 1

In[2]:= Limit[Sin[x^2] /x, x → 0]
Out[2]= 0

In[3]:= Limit[Sin[x] /x^2, x → 0]
Out[3]= ∞
```

Discussion

Plotting functions around the limiting value is often a good way to provide visual insight into the limiting value.

```
In[4]:= GraphicsRow[{Plot[Sin[x] /x, {x, -1, 1}],
          Plot[Sin[x^2] /x, {x, -1, 1}], Plot[Sin[x] /x^2, {x, -1, 1}]}]
```

Out[4]=

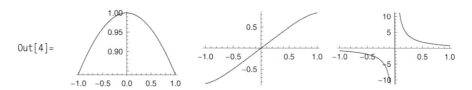

Here you can see that the last function has different limits depending on whether one approaches the limit from the left or the right. You can specify which limit you want using the option Direction.

```
In[5]:= (*From the left*) Limit[Sin[x] /x^2, x -> 0, Direction → 1]
Out[5]= -∞
```

```
In[6]:= (*From the right*) Limit[Sin[x] /x^2, x -> 0, Direction → -1]
Out[6]= ∞
```

11.2 Working with Piecewise Functions

Problem

You want to express a function in terms of two or more functions over different intervals.

Solution

Mathematica supports a function Piecewise for composing a complex function out of simpler functions using predicates to determine which of the simpler functions apply.

```
In[7]:= f[x_] =
          Piecewise[{{Sqrt[1/x^2], x < -0.3}, {1/x, x > 0.3 }, {3.33, True}}]
```

$$Out[7]= \begin{cases} \sqrt{\dfrac{1}{x^2}} & x < -0.3 \\ \dfrac{1}{x} & x > 0.3 \\ 3.33 & \text{True} \end{cases}$$

In[8]:= `Plot[f[x], {x, -3, 3}]`

Out[8]=

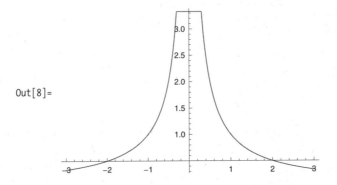

Discussion

`Clip`, `Sign`, and `UnitStep` are special cases of built-in piecewise functions. `Clip` constrains its input to a minimum and maximum value (default -1 and +1). `Sign` gives -1 or 1 depending on whether the input is negative or positive, and `UnitStep` is 0 for negative values and 1 for values greater than or equal to zero.

In[9]:= `GraphicsRow[{Plot[Clip[2 Sin[x]], {x, -Pi, Pi}, PlotLabel -> "Clip"],`
        `Plot[Sign[2 Sin[x]], {x, -Pi, Pi}, PlotLabel -> "Sign"],`
        `Plot[UnitStep[2 Sin[x]], {x, -Pi, Pi}, PlotLabel -> "UnitStep"]},`
        `ImageSize → {500, 150}]`

Out[9]=

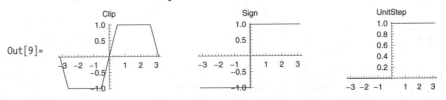

You can differentiate and integrate piecewise functions, and you'll get a piecewise function.

In[10]:= `D[Clip[2 Sin[x]], x]`

Out[10]= $\begin{cases} 0 & \text{Sin}[x] < -\frac{1}{2} \ || \ \text{Sin}[x] > \frac{1}{2} \\ 2\,\text{Cos}[x] & \text{True} \end{cases}$

In[11]:= `Integrate[Clip[2 Sin[x]], x]`

Out[11]= $\begin{cases} -x & \text{Sin}[x] < -\frac{1}{2} \\ x & \text{Sin}[x] > \frac{1}{2} \\ -2\,\text{Cos}[x] & \text{True} \end{cases}$

PiecewiseExpand can take a nested piecewise function and return a single function. You can use this to show that Min, Max, and Abs are also special cases of piecewise functions.

In[12]:= **PiecewiseExpand[Max[w, x, y, z]]**

$$\text{Out[12]=} \begin{cases} w & w - x \geq 0 \,\&\&\, w - y \geq 0 \,\&\&\, w - z \geq 0 \\ x & w - x < 0 \,\&\&\, x - y \geq 0 \,\&\&\, x - z \geq 0 \\ y & w - y < 0 \,\&\&\, x - y < 0 \,\&\&\, y - z \geq 0 \\ z & \text{True} \end{cases}$$

In[13]:= **PiecewiseExpand[Clip[Min[x, y]]]**

$$\text{Out[13]=} \begin{cases} -1 & \left(x < -1 \,\&\&\, x - y \leq 0\right) \,||\, \left(x - y > 0 \,\&\&\, y < -1\right) \\ 1 & \left(x > 1 \,\&\&\, x - y \leq 0\right) \,||\, \left(x - y > 0 \,\&\&\, y > 1\right) \\ x & -1 \leq x \leq 1 \,\&\&\, x - y \leq 0 \\ y & \text{True} \end{cases}$$

11.3 Using Power Series Representations

Problem

You want to find the series expansion of a function.

Solution

The Mathematica function Series will generate the series expansion of a function about a point to a specified order. It produces a SeriesObject, which Mathematica will display as a traditional series expansion.

In[14]:= **Series[Sin[x], {x, 0, 10}]**

$$\text{Out[14]=} \; x - \frac{x^3}{6} + \frac{x^5}{120} - \frac{x^7}{5040} + \frac{x^9}{362\,880} + O[x]^{11}$$

In[15]:= **% // InputForm**
Out[15]//InputForm=
            SeriesData[x, 0, {1, 0, -1/6, 0, 1/120, 0, -1/5040, 0, 1/362880}, 1, 11, 1]

You use Normal to create a regular Mathematica expression. Here I also use Evaluate because I am defining a function and want Normal to evaluate immediately even though the function is defined using SetDelayed (:=). Equivalently, you can use Set (=) to define the function without Evaluate.

In[16]:= **f[x_] := Evaluate[Normal[Series[Sin[x], {x, 0, 10}]]]**

You visualize the accuracy of the series approximation by plotting over successively larger intervals. As expected, this series approximation begins to diverge as you move away from the origin.

In[17]:= GraphicsColumn[Table[Plot[{Sin[x], f[x]}, {x, -n Pi, n Pi}], {n, 1, 3}]]

Out[17]=

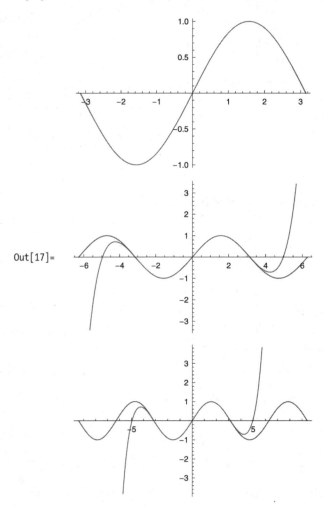

Discussion

You can compute the inverse of a series using InverseSeries.

In[18]:= fInv[x_] = Normal[InverseSeries[Series[Sin[x], {x, 0, 10}]]]

Out[18]= $x + \dfrac{x^3}{6} + \dfrac{3 x^5}{40} + \dfrac{5 x^7}{112} + \dfrac{35 x^9}{1152}$

In[19]:= `Plot[{ArcSin[x] , fInv[x]}, {x, -1, 1}, ImageSize → Small]`

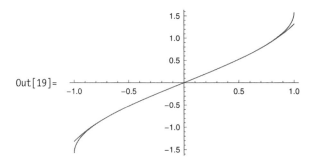

Out[19]=

11.4 Differentiating Functions

Problem

You want to compute derivatives or partial derivatives of functions in symbolic form. You may do this as a means of creating new functions or as a means of teaching the concepts that underlie differentiation.

Solution

Mathematica allows you to enter derivatives in input form as `D[f[x], x]` or in standard form as $\partial_x f[x]$.

In[20]:= `D[Sin[x], x]`
Out[20]= `Cos[x]`

In[21]:= ∂_x `Sin[x]`
Out[21]= `Cos[x]`

Higher-order derivatives are specified as `D[f[x],{x,n}]` where *n* is 2 for the second derivative, 3 for the third, and so on. In standard form, the second derivative can be entered as $\partial_{\{x,2\}} f[x]$.

In[22]:= `D[Sin[x], {x, 2}]`
Out[22]= `-Sin[x]`

Partial derivatives are easily accommodated as well using several equivalent notations.

In[23]:= `D[Sin[x] Sin[y], {x, 1}]`
Out[23]= `Cos[x] Sin[y]`

```
In[24]:=  D[Sin[x] Sin[y], x, x, y]
Out[24]=  -Cos[y] Sin[x]

In[25]:=  D[Sin[x] Sin[y], {x, 2}, {y, 1}]
Out[25]=  -Cos[y] Sin[x]
```

Discussion

Mathematica also recognizes prime notation, but this notation is more commonly used in Mathematica when entering a differential equation. See the sidebar "Mathematica's Representation of Differentiation" on page 433 for some important subtleties.

```
In[26]:=  {Sin'[x], Sin''[x]}
Out[26]=  {Cos[x], -Sin[x]}
```

You can use D along with Solve to differentiate implicit functions. Simply use D as usual and use Solve to find the solution in terms of y'[x].

```
In[35]:=  implicitFunction = x^4 + 2 y[x]^2 == 8;
          Solve[D[implicitFunction, x], y'[x]]
```

$$Out[36]= \left\{\left\{y'[x] \to -\frac{x^3}{y[x]}\right\}\right\}$$

There are cases where you may want to use the D to synthesize a function on the fly. In this case, use Set (=) to perform the differentiation operation immediately or use Evaluate with SetDelayed (:=).

```
In[37]:=  f1[x_] = D[Sin[Pi x Cos[x ^ 2]], x];

In[38]:=  f2[x_] := Evaluate[D[Sin[Pi x Cos[x ^ 2]], x]]

In[39]:=  {f1[2.], f2[2.]}
Out[39]=  {-9.65614, -9.65614}
```

If you forget to do so, you will get an error when you call the function with a literal value.

```
In[40]:=  f3[x_] := D[Sin[Pi x Cos[x ^ 2]], x]

In[41]:=  f3[2.]
```

┌───┐
│ General::ivar : 2.` is not a valid variable. ≫   │
└───┘

$$Out[41]= \partial_{2.} 0.82226$$

Mathematica's Representation of Differentiation

More importantly, the prime notation is not synonymous with D[] but rather with a differential operator of the form Derivative[n]. The operator form clarifies ambiguities that would result from using it with functions of more than one variable. Think of Derivative[n1, n2, ...] as an operator that acts on a function to produce the specific derivative. The number of *n*'s should not exceed the number of variables of the function since each *n* is associated with the *n*th derivative of the corresponding variable. Some examples should help clarify.

First derivative with respect to *x*:

```
Derivative[1][f][x, y]
```
$$1 - \frac{x^2}{2} + \frac{x^4}{24} - \frac{x^6}{720} + \frac{x^8}{40320}$$

```
f'[x, y]
```
$$1 - \frac{x^2}{2} + \frac{x^4}{24} - \frac{x^6}{720} + \frac{x^8}{40320}$$

First derivative with respect to *x*, then *y*:

```
Derivative[1, 1][f][x, y]
```
$$f^{(1,1)}[x, y]$$

```
f^{(1,1)}[x, y]
```
$$f^{(1,1)}[x, y]$$

First derivative with respect to *x*, then second derivative with respect to *y*:

```
Derivative[1, 2][f][x, y]
```
$$f^{(1,2)}[x, y]$$

```
f^{(1,2)}[x, y]
```
$$f^{(1,2)}[x, y]$$

For the most part, you should work with D[] directly, but keep the operator notation in the back of your mind because it is how Mathematica represents derivatives internally.

```
D[f[x, y], x, y] // FullForm
```
$$\text{Derivative}[1, 1][f][x, y]$$

```
Derivative[1, 1][f][x, y]
```
$$f^{(1,1)}[x, y]$$

Many students will use Mathematica to check the answers to their calculus homework, but Mathematica is also useful for generating demonstrations of the fundamental concepts underlying differentiation. For example, the derivative of a function at a point is the slope of the tangent to the function at that point. Further, given two points, the slope of the secant drawn between these points approaches the derivative as the points approach each other along the curve. The following function uses Mathematica's dynamic features to generate presentations of this fact using any function and starting points as input.

```
In[42]:= makeDerivativeDemo[f_, x1_, x2_, opts : OptionsPattern[]] :=
          DynamicModule[{fp, f2, p1, p2, g, slope, slopeText, buildPlot, minX, maxX},
           p1 = {x1, f[x1]};
           p2 = {x2, f[x2]};
           g = buildPlot[f, fp, f2, p1, p2];
           With[{plotRange = Inner[{Min[## - 3], Max[## + 3]} &, p1, p2, List]},
            minX = plotRange[[1, 1]];
            maxX = plotRange[[1, 2]];
            Dynamic[
             Graphics[{g[[1]], Line[{p1, p2}],
               Locator[Dynamic[p1, {(p1 = {#[[1]], f[#[[1]]]}) &,
                  (g = buildPlot[f, fp, f2, p1, p2]) &}], Appearance -> Small],
               Locator[Dynamic[p2, {(p2 = {#[[1]], f[#[[1]]]}) &,
                  (g = buildPlot[f, fp, f2, p1, p2]) &}], Appearance -> Small]},
              FilterRules[{opts}, Options[g]], PlotRange -> plotRange,
              Options[g]]]
            ],
           Initialization :> (
            (*The actual derivative*)
            fp[x_] := Evaluate[D[f[x], x]];
            (*Function for tangent line at x0*)
            f2[x0_, x_] := Module[{}, f[x0] + fp[x0] (x - x0)];
            (*Text for slope of line from p1 to p2*)
            slopeText[p1_, p2_] :=
             Module[{s}, s = Divide @@ (1.0 / (p2 - p1)); ToString[s]];
            (*Plot function, tangent line, and text label*)
            buildPlot[ff_, fp_, f2_, p1_, p2_] := Module[{},
             Normal[
              Plot[{ff[x], f2[p1[[1]], x]}, {x, p1[[1]] - 3, p2[[1]] + 3},
               Epilog -> {Inset[Panel["Secant slope = " <>
                     slopeText[p1, p2] <>
                     "\nDerivative = " <>
                     ToString[N[fp[p1[[1]]]]]], {Left, Top}, {Left, Top}]}
              ]]
             ]
            )]]
```

```
In[43]:=  makeDerivativeDemo[Sin[Pi Cos[#]] &, 1.25, 1.75]
```

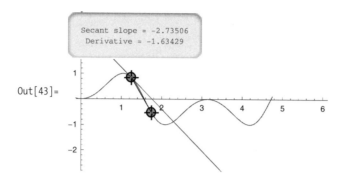

Out[43]=

11.5 Integration

Problem

You want to solve problems that involve indefinite or definite integrals using symbolic integration.

Solution

Use Integrate or ∫ to compute single, double, or higher-order integrations. Indefinite integrals specify an expression and the variables of integration.

```
In[44]:=  Integrate[1/x, x]
Out[44]=  Log[x]
```

Definite integrals provide the minimum and maximum limits, which can be constants or expressions.

```
In[45]:=  Integrate[1/x, {x, 1, 10.0}]
Out[45]=  2.30259
```

```
In[46]:=  Clear[a, b];
          Integrate[x^2, {x, a, b}]
                   a³   b³
Out[47]=       -  ── + ──
                   3    3
```

The minimum and maximum limits can be -Infinity or Infinity.

```
In[48]:=  Integrate[1/ (x^3 + x^2), {x, 1, Infinity}]
Out[48]=  1 - Log[2]
```

Discussion

Integrate will easily handle most integration problems you are likely to encounter in school, engineering, and science.

$$\text{In[49]:=} \quad \int \frac{z^2}{(z^2 - 1)\sqrt{z^2 + 1}} \, dz$$

$$\text{Out[49]=} \quad \frac{1}{4}\left(4\,\text{ArcSinh}[z] + \sqrt{2}\left(\text{Log}[-1+z] - \text{Log}[1+z] + \right.\right.$$
$$\left.\left.\text{Log}\left[-1+z-\sqrt{2}\,\sqrt{1+z^2}\right] - \text{Log}\left[1+z+\sqrt{2}\,\sqrt{1+z^2}\right]\right)\right)$$

Double and higher-order integrals are computed with a single Integrate function by adding multiple integration variables. However, if you use the traditional integration notation, you will use multiple integral symbols.

$$\text{In[50]:=} \quad \text{Integrate}\left[\text{Sin}[2\,\text{Pi}\,z\,y/x]\,x\,y\,z,\,x,\,y,\,z\right]$$

$$\text{Out[50]=} \quad \frac{1}{64\,\pi^2}\left(x\left(\left(-2\,\pi\,x^2\,y\,z + 4\,\pi^3\,y^3\,z^3\right)\text{Cos}\left[\frac{2\,\pi\,y\,z}{x}\right] + \right.\right.$$
$$x\left(-3\,x^2 + 2\,\pi^2\,y^2\,z^2\right)\text{Sin}\left[\frac{2\,\pi\,y\,z}{x}\right]\right) +$$
$$\left.4\left(x^4 + 2\,\pi^4\,y^4\,z^4\right)\text{SinIntegral}\left[\frac{2\,\pi\,y\,z}{x}\right]\right)$$

$$\text{In[51]:=} \quad \int\!\!\int\!\!\int x\,y\,z\,dx\,dy\,dz$$

$$\text{Out[51]=} \quad \frac{1}{8}\,x^2\,y^2\,z^2$$

Some integrations may return with conditionals and assumptions due to convergence issues. You can eliminate these by providing your own assumptions.

$$\text{In[52]:=} \quad \text{Integrate}\left[\text{Exp}\left[-c\,x^2\right],\,\{x,\,-\infty,\,\infty\}\right]$$

$$\text{Out[52]=} \quad \text{If}\left[\text{Re}[c] > 0,\,\frac{\sqrt{\pi}}{\sqrt{c}},\,\text{Integrate}\left[e^{-c\,x^2},\,\{x,\,-\infty,\,\infty\},\,\text{Assumptions} \to \text{Re}[c] \le 0\right]\right]$$

$$\text{In[53]:=} \quad \text{Integrate}\left[\text{Exp}\left[-c\,x^2\right],\,\{x,\,-\infty,\,\infty\},\,\text{Assumptions} \to c > 0\right]$$

$$\text{Out[53]=} \quad \frac{\sqrt{\pi}}{\sqrt{c}}$$

You also do this using GenerateConditions → False.

```
In[54]:= Integrate[Exp[-c x^2], {x, -∞, ∞}, GenerateConditions → False]
```

$$Out[54]= \frac{\sqrt{\pi}}{\sqrt{c}}$$

You can also get piecewise functions as a result of Integrate.

```
In[55]:= Integrate[Abs[x + Abs[x]^2], x, Assumptions → x ∈ Reals]
```

$$Out[55]= \begin{cases} \frac{x^2}{2} + \frac{x^3}{3} & x \le -1 \\ \frac{1}{3} - \frac{x^2}{2} - \frac{x^3}{3} & -1 < x \le 0 \\ \frac{1}{3} + \frac{x^2}{2} + \frac{x^3}{3} & True \end{cases}$$

When Integrate is unable to solve the integration, it will return the unevaluated integral in symbolic form.

```
In[56]:= Integrate[Exp[1/(Log[x] + 1)], {x, 2, 3}]
```

$$Out[56]= \int_{2}^{3} e^{\frac{1}{1+Log[x]}} \, dx$$

Applications of integration are numerous, and it would be impossible to provide even a small representative set of examples here. Rather, I will provide examples that emphasize how Integrate can be combined with other Mathematica functions in non-obvious ways.

A simple application is a function to compute the area between two arbitrary curves given two points. When you create functions that embed Integrate, you often want to allow options to pass through to increase generality.

```
In[57]:= areaBetweenTwoCurves[expr1_, expr2_, var_, a_,
            b_, opts : OptionsPattern[]] := Integrate[expr1 - expr2,
            {var, a, b}, Sequence @@ FilterRules[{opts}, Options[Integrate]]]

In[58]:= areaBetweenTwoCurves[x, x^2, x, 0, 1]
```

$$Out[58]= \frac{1}{6}$$

This would generate a huge messy conditional if not for the ability to pass assumptions about the arbitrary bounds a and b.

```
In[59]:= areaBetweenTwoCurves[Log[x], Sin[x], x, a, b, Assumptions → a > 0 && b > 0]
Out[59]= a - b - Cos[a] + Cos[b] - a Log[a] + b Log[b]
```

Create a table of volumes of hyperspheres. Here Boole maps True to 1 and False to 0. Note that the list of integration limits must be converted to a sequence using

Apply (@@). By the way, this is a very expensive way to calculate volume of a hypersphere, but it does illustrates how to parameterize the order of integration. Search for hyperspheres on Wikipedia or Wolfram's MathWorld to find a more practical formula.

```
In[60]:= Table[Integrate[Boole[Sum[x[i]^2, {i, 1, n}] ≤ 1],
            Sequence @@ Table[{x[j], -Infinity, Infinity}, {j, 1, n}],
            GenerateConditions → True], {n, 1, 5}]
```
$$Out[60]= \left\{2, \pi, \frac{4\pi}{3}, \frac{\pi^2}{2}, \frac{8\pi^2}{15}\right\}$$

You can combine Integrate with differentiation to create a general function to compute the length of a curve between two points.

```
In[61]:= Clear[lengthOfCurve]
```

```
In[62]:= lengthOfCurve[expr_, var_, a_, b_, opts : OptionsPattern[]] :=
            Integrate[Sqrt[1 + D[expr, var]^2], {var, a, b},
            Sequence @@ FilterRules[{opts}, Options[Integrate]]]
```

Or, you can compute the length of the hypotenuse of a right triangle.

```
In[63]:= lengthOfCurve[x, x, 0, 1]
```
$$Out[63]= \sqrt{2}$$

Verify the formula for the circumference of a circle given its radius by taking twice the arc length of a semicircle.

```
In[64]:= 2 lengthOfCurve[Sqrt[r^2 - x^2], x, -r, r, Assumptions → r > 0]
```
$$Out[64]= 2\pi r$$

Here is a purely symbolic solution with assumptions to simplify results.

```
In[65]:= lengthOfCurve[Exp[x], x, a, b, Assumptions → (a > 0 && b > 0)]
```
$$Out[65]= -\sqrt{1 + e^{2a}} + \sqrt{1 + e^{2b}} + \frac{1}{2} Log\left[\frac{\left(1 + \sqrt{1 + e^{2a}}\right)\left(-1 + \sqrt{1 + e^{2b}}\right)}{\left(-1 + \sqrt{1 + e^{2a}}\right)\left(1 + \sqrt{1 + e^{2b}}\right)}\right]$$

11.6 Solving Differential Equations

Problem

You have a model of a system described by a differential equation and you want to solve that equation symbolically. Two related problems are getting the equation in a form Mathematica expects and getting the solution in the form you expect.

Solution

An undergraduate student of engineering or physics will commonly need to solve differential equations that model simple systems. A common problem is an undamped oscillator composed of a mass hanging from a spring. The problem may appear in a textbook as

```
In[66]:= m y'' + k y = 0
```

This says that the force (mass × acceleration) is balanced by the force of the spring, as given by Hooke's law, where k is the spring constant. The key to solving this equation in Mathematica using DSolve is to make the equation more explicit. Specifically, the equation omits the time variable. You must also replace the = symbol with == and tell Mathematica what equation we are solving for and what are the variables.

```
In[67]:= DSolve[m y''[t] + k y[t] == 0, y[t], t]
```

$$\text{Out[67]= } \left\{\left\{y[t] \to C[1] \, \text{Cos}\left[\frac{\sqrt{k} \, t}{\sqrt{m}}\right] + C[2] \, \text{Sin}\left[\frac{\sqrt{k} \, t}{\sqrt{m}}\right]\right\}\right\}$$

The solution is given as a replacement rule, and since the equation is a second order, two constants, C[1] and C[2], are introduced. You can provide initial conditions to eliminate the constants. In this case, you can also render the solution in its customary form by replacing Sqrt[k]/Sqrt[m] by the angular frequency ω.

```
In[68]:= DSolve[{m y''[t] + k y[t] == 0, y[0] == 1, y'[0] == 1}, y[t], t] /.
         {Sqrt[k] / Sqrt[m] → ω}
```

$$\text{Out[68]= } \left\{\left\{y[t] \to \frac{\sqrt{k} \, \text{Cos}[t \, \omega] + \sqrt{m} \, \text{Sin}[t \, \omega]}{\sqrt{k}}\right\}\right\}$$

Discussion

The solutions provided by DSolve are not automatically simplified, and you often will want to use Simplify or FullSimplify to postprocess them into a more mathematically friendly form. This is especially relevant when comparing the answer DSolve finds with answers provided in a typical textbook. Consider this problem adapted from *Advanced Engineering Mathematics* by Erwin Kreyszig (John Wiley). Here you want to find the solution to a differential equation describing the speed of a fluid flowing out of an opening in a container.

```
In[69]:= k = 0.00266 ;
         eq = {h'[t] == -k Sqrt[h[t]], h[0] == 150};
         sol = DSolve[eq, h[t], t]
```

$$\text{Out[71]}= \left\{\left\{h[t] \to 150. - 0.0325782\, t + 1.7689 \times 10^{-6}\, t^2\right\},\right.$$
$$\left.\left\{h[t] \to 150. + 0.0325782\, t + 1.7689 \times 10^{-6}\, t^2\right\}\right\}$$

Given the physics of the problem, it should be clear we want the first solution (the second solution has the height increasing with time).

```
In[72]:= FullSimplify[sol[[1]]]
```

$$\text{Out[72]}= \left\{h[t] \to 1.7689 \times 10^{-6}\ (-9208.61 + t)\ (-9208.61 + t)\right\}$$

Although this has simplified the result somewhat, it is a much more complicated solution than the one provided by Kreyszig, which is

```
In[73]:= ( Sqrt[150] -0.00133` t)^2
```

$$\text{Out[73]}= \left(5\sqrt{6} - 0.00133\, t\right)^2$$

Did DSolve give the wrong result? A common mistake when using Mathematica is to prematurely substitute specific constants as I did above. It is often advisable to solve equations entirely in symbolic form and substitute constants later.

```
In[74]:= eq = {h'[t] == -k1 Sqrt[h[t]], h[0] == h0};
         sol = FullSimplify[DSolve[eq, h[t], t][[1]]]
```

$$\text{Out[75]}= \left\{h[t] \to \frac{1}{4} \left(-2\sqrt{h0} + k1\, t\right)^2\right\}$$

Although this did not get us all the way to the form of the book's solution, you are more likely to see the final transformation that will demonstrate that DSolve was correct. It hinges on noticing that 1/4 is the same as (-1/2)*(-1/2).

$$\frac{1}{4}\left(-2\sqrt{h0} + k1\, t\right)^2 ==$$

$$\frac{1}{4}\left(-2\sqrt{h0} + k1\, t\right)\left(-2\sqrt{h0} + k1\, t\right) ==$$

$$-\frac{1}{2}\left(-2\sqrt{h0} + k1\, t\right) -\frac{1}{2}\left(-2\sqrt{h0} + k1\, t\right) ==$$

$$\left(\sqrt{h0} - \frac{k1}{2}\, t\right)\left(\sqrt{h0} - \frac{k1}{2}\, t\right) ==$$

$$\left(\sqrt{h0} - \frac{k1}{2}\, t\right)^2$$

Substituting h0 and k1 with the constants shows that Mathematica did get the correct solution. Alternatively, you can ask Mathematica to prove its solution is equal to the book's solution by using Resolve and ForAll. The only problem here is that Mathematica does not show its work!

$$\text{In[76]:= } \mathtt{Resolve}\Big[\mathtt{ForAll}\Big[\{\mathtt{h0, k1, t}\}, \frac{1}{4}\Big(-2\sqrt{\mathtt{h0}} + \mathtt{k1\,t}\Big)^{2} == \Big(\sqrt{\mathtt{h0}} - \frac{\mathtt{k1}}{2}\mathtt{t}\Big)^{2}\Big]\Big]$$

Out[76]= True

11.7 Solving Minima and Maxima Problems

Problem

You want to find the minimum or maximum values of a function. You may need to find these extremes subject to constraints or for numbers in a specific domain (e.g., integers).

Solution

Although there are standard techniques used in calculus for finding extrema, Mathematica provides the specific functions Minimize and Maximize, which provide a great deal of power.

```
In[77]:= Maximize[1 - (-2 + x)^2 - (-1 + x)^4, x] // N
Out[77]= {0.710727, {x → 1.58975}}

In[78]:= Minimize[2 x^4 - 3 x^2 + x, x] // N
Out[78]= {-2.0293, {x → -0.939693}}
```

Discussion

For many applications of minimization or maximization, you are interested in the extreme value within a specific interval.

```
In[79]:= Maximize[{((x - 3)^3 - 2 x^2 - x), -1 < x < 4}, x] // N
Out[79]= {-9.3726, {x → 1.48085}}
```

I restrict this discussion to Maximize for simplicity, but everything here applies to Minimize as well. If you are interested in displaying the result of Maximize, you will want to force the result to numerical form, as we did in the solution. Maximize will keep the result in exact form if it is given input in exact form. For polynomials, this typically means the result will be expressed in terms of radicals or Root objects. A Root[f,k] object represents the kth solution to a polynomial equation f[x] == 0.

In[80]:= **Maximize[{((x - 3)^3 - 2 x^2 - x), -1 < x < 4}, x]**

Out[80]= $\left\{-27 + \dfrac{26}{3} \left(11 - \sqrt{43}\right) - \dfrac{11}{9} \left(11 - \sqrt{43}\right)^2 + \dfrac{1}{27} \left(11 - \sqrt{43}\right)^3,\right.$

$\left\{x \to \dfrac{1}{3} \left(11 - \sqrt{43}\right)\right\}\right\}$

In[81]:= **Maximize$\left[1 - (-2 + x)^2 - (-1 + x)^4, x\right]$**

Out[81]= $\left\{-4 + 8\,\text{Root}\left[-4 + 7\,\#1 - 6\,\#1^2 + 2\,\#1^3\,\&,\ 1\right] - \right.$

$7\,\text{Root}\left[-4 + 7\,\#1 - 6\,\#1^2 + 2\,\#1^3\,\&,\ 1\right]^2 + 4\,\text{Root}\left[-4 + 7\,\#1 - 6\,\#1^2 + 2\,\#1^3\,\&,\ 1\right]^3 -$

$\left.\text{Root}\left[-4 + 7\,\#1 - 6\,\#1^2 + 2\,\#1^3\,\&,\ 1\right]^4,\ \left\{x \to \text{Root}\left[-4 + 7\,\#1 - 6\,\#1^2 + 2\,\#1^3\,\&,\ 1\right]\right\}\right\}$

Sometimes you want to find solutions for integer values only. You can constrain Maximize to the integers in one of two ways. You might recognize this problem as an instance of a knapsack problem where you are optimizing the value of the knapsack (item1 has value 8, item2 11, and so on) subject to size constraint of 14 where item1 has size 5 and so on.

In[82]:= **Maximize$\left[\{8\,x1 + 11\,x2 + 6\,x3 + 4\,x4,\right.$**

$5\,x1 + 7\,x2 + 4\,x3 + 3\,x4 \le 14\ \&\&\ x1 < 2\ \&\&\ x2 < 2\ \&\&\ x3 < 2\ \&\&$

$x4 < 2\ \&\&\ \text{Element}\left[x1 \mid x2 \mid x3 \mid x4,\ \text{Integers}\right]\},\ \{x1, x2, x3, x4\}\right]$

Out[82]= $\{21,\ \{x1 \to 0,\ x2 \to 1,\ x3 \to 1,\ x4 \to 1\}\}$

A more convenient notation when all variables are integer is to specify the domain as the third argument to Maximize.

In[83]:= **Maximize$\left[\{8\,x1 + 11\,x2 + 6\,x3 + 4\,x4,\ 5\,x1 + 7\,x2 + 4\,x3 + 3\,x4 \le 14\ \&\&\right.$**

$x1 < 2\ \&\&\ x2 < 2\ \&\&\ x3 < 2\ \&\&\ x4 < 2\},\ \{x1, x2, x3, x4\},\ \text{Integers}\right]$

Out[83]= $\{21,\ \{x1 \to 0,\ x2 \to 1,\ x3 \to 1,\ x4 \to 1\}\}$

Maximize seeks a global maximum, whereas an alternative function, FindMaximum, seeks a local maximum (there is also FindMinimum for local minimums). FindMaximum allows you to specify a starting point for the search, but otherwise has a very similar form to Maximize. The following program demonstrates the difference between Maximize and FindMaximum. The advantage of FindMaximum is that it does not require the objective function to be differentiable.

```
In[84]:=  Clear["Global`*"];
          f[x_] := x Cos[0.1 Exp[x]] Sin[0.1 Pi Exp[x]] ;
          globalMax = Maximize[{f[x], 0 < x < 5}, x];
          localMax = FindMaximum[f[x], {x, 0}];
          Plot[f[x], {x, 0, 5}, Epilog → {PointSize[0.02],
            Red, Point[{x, f[x]}] /. Last[globalMax] ,
            Blue, Point[{x, f[x]}] /. Last[localMax] }]
```

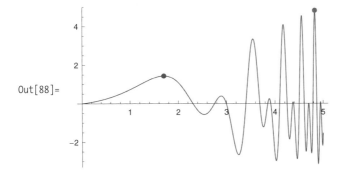

Out[88]=

11.8 Solving Vector Calculus Problems

Problem

You want to find solutions to problems within vector fields. Such problems arise in mechanics, electromagnetic theory, and fluid dynamics.

Solution

Simple vector calculus problems can be solved in terms of the calculus primitives discussed in this chapter's recipes along with vector functions like Dot and Cross. For example, line integrals are commonly used to calculate work performed when moving a particle along a path in a vector field. Here F is the vector equation of the field, f is the equation of the path through the field, var is the parameter of f, and a and b are the start and end points of the path.

```
In[89]:=  lineIntegral[F_, f_, var_, a_, b_] :=
            Integrate[Dot[F[f[var]], D[f[var], var]], {var, a, b}]
          F[{x_, y_, z_}] := {x + y, y^2, x - z}
          f[t_] := {-t + 1, t + 2, -6 t + 1}
          lineIntegral[F, f, t, 0, 1]
                35
Out[92]=  - ──
                3
```

Another common operation in vector calculus is the surface integral over scalar functions and vector fields. Surface integrals are the 2D analog of line integrals. One way to think of the scalar surface integral is to imagine a surface f made of a material whose density varies as described by a second function g. The surface integral of f over g is then the mass per unit thickness.

```
In[93]:= surfaceIntegralScalar[g_, f_, {v1_, v1a_, v1b_}, {v2_, v2a_, v2b_}] :=
           Integrate[g[f[v1, v2]] Norm[Cross[D[f[v1, v2], v1], D[f[v1, v2], v2]]],
             {v1, v1a, v1b}, {v2, v2a, v2b}]
```

For example, consider the surface f1, which is a half sphere over the interval $\{\phi, 0, Pi/2\}$ and $\{\theta, 0, 2 Pi\}$, and compute the surface integral given a density function given by $(x^2 + y^2) z$.

```
In[94]:= f1[φ_, θ_] := {Sin[φ] Cos[θ], Sin[φ] Sin[θ], Cos[φ]}
          g1[{x_, y_, z_}] := (x^2 + y^2) z

          surfaceIntegralScalar[g1, f1, {φ, 0, Pi/2}, {θ, 0, 2 Pi}]

Out[96]= π
         ─
         2
```

If we use a constant function (uniform density), we get the surface area of the half sphere as expected (surface area of an entire sphere is $4 \pi r^2$).

```
In[97]:= g2[{x_, y_, z_}] := 1
          surfaceIntegralScalar[g2, f1, {φ, 0, Pi/2}, {θ, 0, 2 Pi}]

Out[98]= 2 π
```

For a vector field, there is a similar equation using Dot in place of scalar multiplication by the norm. The traditional way to visualize the vector surface interval is to consider a fluid flowing through a surface where there is a vector function F describing the velocity of the fluid at various points on the surface. The surface integral is then the *flux*, or the quantity of fluid flowing through the surface in unit time.

```
In[99]:= surfaceIntegralVector[F_, f_, {v1_, v1a_, v1b_}, {v2_, v2a_, v2b_}] :=
           Integrate[Dot[F[f[v1, v2]], Cross[D[f[v1, v2], v1], D[f[v1, v2], v2]]],
             {v1, v1a, v1b}, {v2, v2a, v2b}]
```

Here is the solution to the flux described by $\{3 y, -z, x^2\}$ through a surface described parametrically as $\{s t, s + t, (s^2 - t^2)/2\}$.

```
In[100]:= f[s_, t_] := {s t, s + t, (s^2 - t^2)/2}
           F[{x_, y_, z_}] := {3 y, -z, x^2}
           surfaceIntegralVector[F, f, {s, 0, 1}, {t, 0, 3}]

Out[102]= -15
```

A standard result from electrostatics is that the net flux out of a unit sphere, for a field that is everywhere normal, is zero. We can verify this as follows:

```
In[103]:= F2[{x_, y_, z_}] := {1, 1, 1} / (x^2 + y^2 + z^2)

In[104]:= f2[θ_, φ_] := {Sin[φ] Cos[θ], Sin[φ] Sin[θ], Cos[φ]}

In[105]:= surfaceIntegralVector[F2, f2, {θ, 0, 2 Pi}, {φ, 0, Pi}]
Out[105]= 0
```

Discussion

The solution shows how the calculus primitives and other Mathematica functions can be used to build up higher-order vector calculus solutions. However, if you are interested in solving problems in vector calculus, the package VectorAnalysis` is definitely worth a look. Be forewarned that you might be in for a bit of a learning curve with this particular package, but it offers a lot of functionality. An important feature of the package is that it simplifies working in different coordinate systems. Before you can make effective use of VectorAnalysis`, you need to understand how coordinate systems are used and which coordinate system is appropriate to your problem.

```
In[106]:= Needs["VectorAnalysis`"]

In[107]:= CoordinateSystem
Out[107]= Cartesian

In[108]:= SetCoordinates[Spherical]
Out[108]= Spherical[Rr, Ttheta, Pphi]

In[109]:= CoordinateSystem
Out[109]= Spherical
```

When you use VectorAnalysis`, you will typically want to use functions in that package in place of some standard Mathematica functions such as Dot and Cross. This is because the alternatives DotProduct and CrossProduct respect the current coordinate system. For example, if the current coordinate system is Spherical, you expect the following DotProduct to be zero because the vectors are orthogonal in spherical coordinates.

```
In[110]:= DotProduct[{1, Pi / 2, 0}, {1, Pi / 2, Pi / 2}]
Out[110]= 0
```

In contrast, Dot and Cross always assume Cartesian coordinates.

In[111]:= `Dot[{1, Pi / 2, 0}, {1, Pi / 2, Pi / 2}]`

Out[111]= $1 + \dfrac{\pi^2}{4}$

Some of the most important vector calculus operations are Div (divergence), Grad (gradient), Curl, and the Laplacian. Although it would make a nice exercise to implement these from the calculus primitives, as I did for line and surface integrals, there is no need if you use the VectorAnalysis` package. These operations use the default coordinate system, or you can specify a specific coordinate system as a separate argument.

The divergence represents the instantaneous outflow of a vector field at each point.

In[112]:= `Together[Div[{1, 1, 1} / (x^2 + y^2 + z^2), Cartesian[x, y, z]]]`

Out[112]= $-\dfrac{2\,(x + y + z)}{\left(x^2 + y^2 + z^2\right)^2}$

The curl of a vector field represents the amount of rotation.

In[113]:= `Together[Curl[{1, 1, 1} / (x^2 + y^2 + z^2), Cartesian[x, y, z]]]`

Out[113]= $\left\{-\dfrac{2\,(y - z)}{\left(x^2 + y^2 + z^2\right)^2},\ \dfrac{2\,(x - z)}{\left(x^2 + y^2 + z^2\right)^2},\ -\dfrac{2\,(x - y)}{\left(x^2 + y^2 + z^2\right)^2}\right\}$

By definition, the divergence of the curl must be zero since the curl has no net outflow.

In[114]:= `SetCoordinates[Cartesian[x, y, z]];`
`Div[Curl[{1, 1, 1} / (x^2 + y^2 + z^2)]]`

Out[115]= `0`

The gradient of a function f is a vector-valued function that indicates the direction in which f is increasing most rapidly. If you were climbing a hill, you would move in the direction of the gradient at each point to reach the top (strictly speaking the gradient would only be guaranteed to be directing you to a local peak). You can visualize the meaning of the gradient by using VectorPlot. I restrict the result to 2D for easier visualization.

```
In[116]:= GraphicsRow[{Plot3D[x² y³, {x, -1, 1}, {y, -1, 1}, PlotRange → Full],
              VectorPlot[Evaluate[Drop[Grad[ x² y³ 1, Cartesian[x, y, z]], -1]],
              {x, -1, 1}, {y, -1, 1}]}, ImageSize → 500]
```

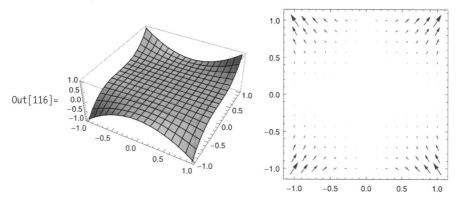

Out[116]=

See Also

The Mathematica tutorial to the VectorAnalysis package is essential reading for using those functions.

Div, Grad, Curl, and All That by H. M. Schey (W.W. Norton) and *Vector Calculus* by Paul C. Matthews (Springer) are two of my favorite informal introductions to vector calculus.

11.9 Solving Problems Involving Sums and Products

Problem

You want to solve problems in discrete calculus that are expressed in terms of sums or products.

Solution

Mathematica can handle infinite sums and products with ease, provided, of course, they converge.

$$In[117]:= \sum_{n=1}^{\infty} \frac{1}{n^2}$$

$$Out[117]= \frac{\pi^2}{6}$$

$$\text{In[118]:= } \prod_{i=2}^{\infty} \left(1 - \frac{1}{i^3}\right)$$

$$\text{Out[118]= } \frac{\text{Cosh}\left[\frac{\sqrt{3}\,\pi}{2}\right]}{3\,\pi}$$

Discussion

If sums or products don't converge, Mathematica will let you know by emitting an error. You can test for convergence without evaluating the sum using Sum-Convergence.

$$\text{In[119]:= } \sum_{n=1}^{\infty} \frac{1}{n}$$

Sum::div : Sum does not converge. >>

$$\text{Out[119]= } \sum_{n=1}^{\infty} \frac{1}{n}$$

$$\text{In[120]:= } \text{Table}\left[\left\{\frac{1}{n^k}, \text{SumConvergence}\left[\frac{1}{n^k}, n\right]\right\}, \{k, 1, 4\}\right] \text{ // TableForm}$$

Out[120]//TableForm=

$$\frac{1}{n} \quad \text{False}$$

$$\frac{1}{n^2} \quad \text{True}$$

$$\frac{1}{n^3} \quad \text{True}$$

$$\frac{1}{n^4} \quad \text{True}$$

As with Integrate, Sum can specify multiple summation variables. In traditional form these sums are rendered as a multiple summation, but keep in mind that these are entered as Sum[expr,{n,nmin,nmax},{m,mmin,mmaz}] rather than Sum[Sum[expr, {n,nmin,nmax}],{m,mmin,mmaz}].

This double summation has a surprisingly simply solution.

$$\text{In[121]:= } \sum_{m=1}^{\infty}\sum_{n=1}^{\infty} \frac{m^2\,n}{2^m\,(m\,2^n + 2^m\,n)}$$

$$\text{Out[121]= } 2$$

This is a very famous sum attributed to Srinivasa Ramanujan, one of India's greatest mathematical geniuses. You might think that Mathematica is just doing some simple pattern matching to recognize this result; however, substitute for any of the magic constants in this formula, and Mathematica will handle it just as well (but don't expect the answer to be as pretty).

$$\text{In[122]:= } \frac{2 \sqrt{2}}{9801} \sum_{k=0}^{\infty} \frac{(4 k) ! \ (1103 + 26\,390\,k)}{(k!)^4 \ 396^{4 k}}$$

$$\text{Out[122]= } \frac{1}{\pi}$$

$$\text{In[123]:= } \sum_{k=0}^{\infty} \frac{(3 k) ! \ (5 + 10 k)}{(k!)^4 \ 300^{4 k}}$$

$$\text{Out[123]= } \frac{1}{135\,000\,000} \left(675\,000\,000 \ \text{HypergeometricPFQ} \left[\left\{ \frac{1}{3}, \frac{2}{3} \right\}, \{1, 1\}, \frac{1}{300\,000\,000} \right] + \text{HypergeometricPFQ} \left[\left\{ \frac{4}{3}, \frac{5}{3} \right\}, \{2, 2\}, \frac{1}{300\,000\,000} \right] \right)$$

Here is a very pretty formula for π that combines an infinite sum and an infinite product.

$$\text{In[124]:= } \frac{\prod_{n=1}^{\infty} \left(1 + \frac{1}{4 n^2 - 1} \right)}{\sum_{n=1}^{\infty} \frac{1}{4 n^2 - 1}}$$

$$\text{Out[124]= } \pi$$

As of version 7, Mathematica can handle indefinite sums and products. Mathematica will seek to eliminate the sum if possible. For example, the sum over k of a polynomial is another polynomial that can be expressed in terms of k, and products over polynomials will invariably reduce to some expression involving Gamma.

$$\text{In[125]:= } \sum_{k} \left(3 k^3 - k^2 + 3 k + 5 \right)$$

$$\text{Out[125]= } \frac{1}{12} k \left(40 + 33 k - 22 k^2 + 9 k^3 \right)$$

$$\text{In[126]:= } \prod_{k} \left(k^2 - 3 k + 5 \right)$$

$$\text{Out[126]= } \frac{3 \cosh \left[\frac{\sqrt{11} \ \pi}{2} \right] \text{Gamma} \left[-\frac{3}{2} - \frac{i \sqrt{11}}{2} + k \right] \text{Gamma} \left[-\frac{3}{2} + \frac{i \sqrt{11}}{2} + k \right]}{\pi}$$

The Z-transform is an important infinite sum used in signal processing. It is defined as $\text{Sum[f[n] z^-n,\{n,0,Infinity\}]}$, but is directly supported using ZTransform.

$$\text{In[127]:= ZTransform[n^2, n, z]}$$

$$\text{Out[127]= } \frac{z \ (1 + z)}{(-1 + z)^3}$$

Here is an unconventional application for Sum, but one that is sometimes used in discrete math to introduce the idea of a generating function. You can use Sum to construct a generating function for solutions to problems like x1+x2+x3 == 12 subject to x1 >= 4, x2 >= 2, and 5 >= x3 >= 2. Each Sum is constructed from the smallest number the associated variable can take to the largest, by considering the smallest the other variables can take. For example, x1 must be at least 4 but can't be greater than 12-2-2 = 8, since x2 and x3 must each be at least 2. Here we use Expand to generate the polynomial and Cases to find the exponents that sum to 12, thus giving all solutions.

$$\text{In[128]:= Cases}\left[\text{ Expand}\left[\sum_{n=4}^{8} x1^n \sum_{n=2}^{6} x2^n \sum_{n=2}^{5} x3^n\right],\right.$$
$$\left. x1^{n1\_} x2^{n2\_} x3^{n3\_} \text{ /; n1 + n2 + n3 == 12} \mapsto \{n1, n2, n3\}\right]$$
Out[128]= {{8, 2, 2}, {7, 3, 2}, {6, 4, 2}, {5, 5, 2}, {4, 6, 2}, {7, 2, 3}, {6, 3, 3},
{5, 4, 3}, {4, 5, 3}, {6, 2, 4}, {5, 3, 4}, {4, 4, 4}, {5, 2, 5}, {4, 3, 5}}

If you only care about the number of solutions, it would fall out of the coefficient of x^{12} in the expansion of this polynomial.

$$\text{In[129]:= Cases}\left[\text{ Expand}\left[\sum_{n=4}^{8} x^n \sum_{n=2}^{6} x^n \sum_{n=2}^{5} x^n\right], a\_ x^{12} \mapsto a\right]$$
Out[129]= {14}

See Also

See Recipe 11.11 for more information on generating functions in Mathematica.

Readers who are interested in gaining insight into the algorithms that underlie Mathematica's amazing feats with infinite sums should read *A=B* by Marko Petkovsek, Herbert S. Wilf, and Doron Zeilberger (A K Peters), which is available online at *http://bit.ly/1LJiwe*.

11.10 Solving Difference Equations

Problem

You want to solve problems that arise in discrete systems such as finance, actuarial science, dynamical systems, and numerical analysis. Many such problems can be modeled as recurrence relations, also known as difference equations.

Solution

RSolve is used to solve difference equations. A simple problem where RSolve applies is in mortgage calculations. Suppose you want to derive a function for the outstanding principal over the life of a loan. Let's say the yearly interest rate is 5.75%, the monthly payment is $1,000.00, and the term is 30 years. This loan can be described as the following difference equation. Here the constraint y[360] == 0 arises from the condition that the last payment is zero (I am using y[0] as the origin).

```
In[130]:=  i = 0.0575;
           payment = 1000.00;
           sol = RSolve[{y[n + 1] == (1 + i / 12) y[n] - payment, y[360] == 0}, y, n]
Out[132]=  {{y → Function[{n}, 0.995231 × 2.71828^{-0.00478022 n}
              (209696. × 1.00479^n - 37516.4 × 1.00479^n 2.71828^{0.00478022 n})]}}
```

From this we can figure out the initial principal or the payoff at any given month:

```
In[133]:=  y[0] /. sol[[1]]
Out[133]=  171358.
```

After 60 months, or 5 years, very little has been paid off, which is quite depressing but a fact of life.

```
In[134]:=  y[0] - y[60] /. sol[[1]]
Out[134]=  12402.6
```

Discussion

Setting up a difference equation is often a matter of solving the problem by hand for small values of *n* and then detecting the relationship between successive values. Consider the Towers of Hanoi puzzle. A one-disk problem is solved in one move (T[1] = 1), a two-disk problem is solved in three moves (T[2] = 3), and three-disk problem is solved in seven moves (T[3] = 7). It follows then that T[n] = 2 T[n-1] + 1.

```
In[135]:=  RSolve[{T[n] == 2 T[n - 1] + 1, T[1] == 1}, T, n]
Out[135]=  {{T → Function[{n}, -1 + 2^n]}}
```

A seemingly innocent difference equation can result in a solution involving complex numbers. This is a second-order equation, so two initial values are required to get an exact solution with no arbitrary constants.

```
In[136]:=  sol = RSolve[{a[n] == 2 (a[n - 1] - a[n - 2]), a[0] == 1, a[1] == 2}, a, n]
Out[136]=  {{a → Function[{n}, ($\frac{1}{2}$ + $\frac{i}{2}$) ((1 - i)^n - i (1 + i)^n)]}}
```

Note that like DSolve, RSolve does not try to simplify the result. It is advisable to try to simplify it; in this case, you see that complex numbers disappear, and the result is in terms of trigonometric functions, which you may not have expected.

```
In[137]:= FullSimplify[a[n] /. sol[[1]]]
Out[137]= (1 - i)^{-1+n} + (1 + i)^{-1+n}
```

As with DSolve, if you do not provide initial conditions, you will get solutions involving arbitrary constants of the form C[N].

```
In[138]:= RSolve[{a[n] - 3 a[n - 1] == 5 (3^n)}, a, n]
Out[138]= {{a → Function[{n}, 5 × 3^n n + 3^{-1+n} C[1]]}}
```

These solutions were found in terms of pure functions because we asked for the solution in terms of a, but you can change the form of the second argument to a[n] to get the solution in that form.

```
In[139]:= sol = RSolve[{a[n] - 3 a[n - 1] == 5 (3^n)}, a[n], n]
Out[139]= {{a[n] → 5 × 3^n n + 3^{-1+n} C[1]}}
```

You can evaluate this solution for specific n and C[1] using ReplaceAll (//.).

```
In[140]:= a[n] //. Flatten[{sol, n → 3, C[1] → 2}]
Out[140]= 423
```

See Also

One of the best introductions to the subject of difference equations is *An Introduction to Difference Equations* by Saber Elaydi (Springer).

11.11 Generating Functions and Sequence Recognition

Problem

You want Mathematica to generate a function associated with a particular sequence or to infer a function that will produce the sequence for successive integers.

Solution

Use FindGeneratingFunction to derive the generating function for a sequence. Recall that the power series of a generating function encodes the sequence in its coefficients.

```
In[141]:= g = FindGeneratingFunction[{1, 4, 9, 16, 25, 36, 49, 64, 81, 100}, x]
```

$$Out[141]= \frac{-1 - x}{(-1 + x)^3}$$

```
In[142]:= Series[g, {x, 0, 12}]
```

$$Out[142]= 1 + 4 x + 9 x^2 + 16 x^3 + 25 x^4 + 36 x^5 + 49 x^6 +$$
$$64 x^7 + 81 x^8 + 100 x^9 + 121 x^{10} + 144 x^{11} + 169 x^{12} + O[x]^{13}$$

Use FindSequenceFunction to find an expression that maps the integers to the specified sequence.

```
In[143]:= s = FindSequenceFunction[{1, 4, 9, 16, 25, 36, 49, 64, 81, 100}, n]
```

$$Out[143]= n^2$$

```
In[144]:= Table[s, {n, 1, 12}]
```

$$Out[144]= \{1, 4, 9, 16, 25, 36, 49, 64, 81, 100, 121, 144\}$$

Discussion

FindSequenceFunction can deal with sequences that are not strictly increasing and with noninteger sequences.

```
In[145]:= FindSequenceFunction[{-1, 3, -11, 13, -29, 31, -55,
            57, -89, 91, -131, 133, -181, 183, -239}, n] // FullSimplify
```

$$Out[145]= (-1)^n \left(-(-1)^n (-1 + n) + n^2\right)$$

$$In[146]:= FindSequenceFunction\left[\left\{0, \frac{2}{9}, \frac{3}{8}, \frac{12}{25}, \frac{5}{9}, \frac{30}{49}, \frac{21}{32}, \frac{56}{81}, \frac{18}{25}, \frac{90}{121}\right\}, x\right]$$

$$Out[146]= \frac{-x + x^2}{(1 + x)^2}$$

You can synthesize a generating function from an expression using GeneratingFunction.

$$In[147]:= g = GeneratingFunction\left[\frac{1}{(n + 1)!}, n, x\right]$$

$$Out[147]= \frac{-1 + e^x}{x}$$

And recover the sequence to the Nth term using the following expression:

```
In[148]:=  With[{N = 12},
              1/Table[SeriesCoefficient[Simplify[Series[g, {x, 0, N}]], n], {n, 1, N}]]
Out[148]=  {2, 6, 24, 120, 720, 5040, 40320, 362880,
              3628800, 39916800, 479001600, 6227020800}
```

See Also

For the nonexpert, a very approachable book on generating functions is *Generating-functionology* by Herbert S. Wilf (A K Peters). An online version can be found at *http://bit.ly/3bkssK*.

CHAPTER 12

Statistics and Data Analysis

Watching in a trance
The crew is certain
Nothing left to chance

...

Starting to collect
Requested data
"What will it affect
When all is done?"
Thinks Major Tom

Peter Schilling, "Major Tom (Coming Home)"

12.0 Introduction

Ask statisticians what software they use, and chances are (no pun intended), they will mention SAS, SPSS, or maybe even R. Those systems are quite good, but most are highly specialized for statistical work. With the release of version 7, Wolfram has substantially beefed up the statistical capabilities of Mathematica. Given everything else Mathematica can do, it is now a compelling alternative for statistics and data analysis. An entire Mathematica statistical cookbook could be written; therefore, this chapter is necessarily incomplete. I have selected these recipes for this chapter to provide jumping-off points for further exploration. You should consult the Mathematica documentation for more depth, and nonexperts should consider Sarah Boslaugh and Paul Andrew Watters' *Statistics in a Nutshell* (O'Reilly) for a broad overview of the relevant concepts.

Even readers without much interest in statistics are encouraged to skim these recipes because there are demonstrations here that have application outside statistics proper. Most users of Mathematica are comfortable with basic statistical metrics, such as mean and variance, but perhaps you are rusty on quantiles. All are covered in Recipe 12.1. Every programmer needs to generate random numbers from time to time, and it is useful to know how to use different distributions beside the standard uniform distribution (Recipe 12.2). Students and teachers of probability will appreciate Mathematica's ability to manipulate and plot a variety of common (and not so common) distributions (Recipe 12.3) as well as the ability to illustrate statistical theorems and puzzles (Recipes 12.4 and 12.16). Advanced statisticians and researchers will get a lot of use out of Mathematica's data analysis features, covered in Recipes 12.5 through 12.13. Finally, Recipe 12.14 demonstrates plots that are specific to statistical analysis.

This chapter often synthesizes data using random generation. In these cases, I seed the random number generator with a specific seed so the results are repeatable. There is no magic behind the seeds specified other than they provided a reasonable result. When I use specific data in these recipes, it is plausible but entirely fabricated and should not be construed as coming from an actual experiment.

12.1 Computing Common Statistical Metrics of Numerical and Symbolic Data

Problem

You want to perform common statistical analysis of data sets. These metrics represent the entry-level statistical functions that all users of Mathematica should have under their belts.

Solution

It should come as little surprise that Mathematica is equipped with the standard statistical functions. Here I use the byte count of Mathematica files on my folder as a source of data.

```
In[1]:= data = N[ FileByteCount /@
          FileNames[FileNameJoin[{NotebookDirectory[], "*.nb"}]]];
       (*Compute the mean.*)
       Mean[data]
Out[2]= 2.45023 × 10^6
```

The statistical functions you will use most in Mathematica (Mean, Median, Max, Min, Variance, and StandardDeviation) have obvious names and obvious uses. Here I get a bit fancy by computing a table in one step by using Through with the list of functions.

```
In[3]:= Module[{statFuncs},
           statFuncs = {Mean, Median, Max, Min, Variance, StandardDeviation};
           TableForm[{Through[statFuncs[data]]},
             TableHeadings → {None, ToString /@ statFuncs}]]
Out[3]//TableForm=
```

Mean	Median	Max	Min	Variance	StandardDeviation
2.45023×10^6	114698.	3.62386×10^7	1019.	3.94825×10^{13}	6.28351×10^6

Not quite as pedestrian, quantiles are a common concept in statistics that generalizes the concept of median to other subdivisions.

```
In[4]:= (*Find the lower quantile.*)
        Quantile[data, 1/4]
Out[4]= 14412.
```

```
In[5]:= (*Find the 1/2, 1/3, 1/4, ... 1/10.*)
        Quantile[data, #] & /@ Table[1/n, {n, 2, 10}]
Out[5]= {114698., 26623., 14412., 7712., 6102., 5456., 4775., 3865., 3514.}
```

```
In[6]:= Quantile[data, 1/2]
Out[6]= 114698.
```

When used with default parameters Quantile always returns some element in the actual list. Thus, Quantile[data, 1/2] may not be the same as Median.

```
In[7]:= Quantile[data, 1/2] == Median[data]
Out[7]= True
```

With the following parameters, Quantile and Median are identical. See Quantile documentation for the meaning of these parameters.

```
In[8]:= Quantile[data, 1/2, {{1/2, 0}, {0, 1}}] == Median[data]
Out[8]= True
```

Discussion

The basic functions covered in the solution are no doubt familiar and hardly warrant further elaboration except to note their generality.

All of the statistics functions in Mathematica work with SparseArray, which is very convenient when you have a very large but sparse data set.

```
In[9]:= N[Mean[SparseArray[{1 → 10, 2 → 11, 3 → 12, 4 → 11}, {10000}, 7]]]
Out[9]= 7.0016
```

Further, given Mathematica's symbolic nature, you should not be too surprised that it can do more than other common data analysis applications, such as MS Excel.

```
In[10]:= Clear[a, b, c, d];
         Variance[{a, a, a, c, c, b, d, d}]
```

$$Out[11]= \frac{1}{56} \left(3 \, (5\,a - b - 2\,c - 2\,d)\, \mathrm{Conjugate}[a] + (-3\,a + 7\,b - 2\,c - 2\,d)\, \mathrm{Conjugate}[b] + \right.$$
$$\left. 2\,(-3\,a - b + 6\,c - 2\,d)\, \mathrm{Conjugate}[c] + 2\,(-3\,a - b - 2\,c + 6\,d)\, \mathrm{Conjugate}[d]\right)$$

What does this result mean? It is the formula for computing the variance of a set of data with 3 *a*'s, 1 *b*, 2 *c*'s and 2 *d*'s. You can use this formula using ReplaceAll.

```
In[12]:= Variance[{a, a, a, c, c, b, d, d}]  /.  {a → 1, b → 2, c → 3, d → 4}
```

$$Out[12]= \frac{95}{56}$$

This is exactly the result you would get if you took the direct route.

```
In[13]:= Variance[{1, 1, 1, 3, 3, 2, 4, 4}]
```

$$Out[13]= \frac{95}{56}$$

This may seem completely academic; for many of you, it will be so. Yet consider that symbolic form allows you to perform further symbolic manipulations that account for properties you may know about the symbolic data. For example, imagine the items were all angles in radians in a given relationship and you wanted to know the formula for the variance of their sine. Such examples are contrived only until you need to do a similar transformation.

```
In[14]:= TrigFactor[FullSimplify[
            Variance[{a, a, a, c, c, b, d, d}]  /.  {a → Sin[x], b → Sin[2 x],
              c → Sin[3 x], d → Sin[4 x]}, Assumptions → x ∈ Reals ]]
```

$$Out[14]= \frac{1}{14} \mathrm{Cos}\left[\frac{x}{2}\right]^2 \, (93 - 100\,\mathrm{Cos}[x] + 94\,\mathrm{Cos}[2\,x] -$$
$$64\,\mathrm{Cos}[3\,x] + 64\,\mathrm{Cos}[4\,x] - 16\,\mathrm{Cos}[5\,x] + 24\,\mathrm{Cos}[6\,x])\,\mathrm{Sin}\left[\frac{x}{2}\right]^2$$

These symbolic capabilities also imply you can use these functions with common distributions rather than on individual values.

```
In[15]:= {Mean[LogNormalDistribution[0, 1]], Variance[HalfNormalDistribution[1]],
          StandardDeviation[InverseGaussianDistribution[1, 2]]}
```

$$Out[15]= \left\{\sqrt{e}\, , \, \frac{1}{2}\,(-2 + \pi)\, , \, \frac{1}{\sqrt{2}}\right\}$$

Another common statistical metric is the mode. This function is called Commonest in Mathematica and can be used to find the commonest or the *n* commonest. Related to this is a new function in version 7, Tally, that gives the individual counts.

```
In[16]:= list = First[RealDigits[Pi, 10, 50]];
```

```
In[17]:= {Commonest[list], Commonest[list, 3]}
Out[17]= {{3}, {3, 1, 9}}
```

```
In[18]:= Tally[list]
Out[18]= {{3, 9}, {1, 5}, {4, 4}, {5, 5}, {9, 8}, {2, 5}, {6, 4}, {8, 5}, {7, 4}, {0, 1}}
```

See Also

There is a multivariate statistics package (see *MultivariateStatistics/guide/Multivariate StatisticsPackage*) that generalizes notions of mean, median, and so on, to multiple dimensions. Here you will find functions such as SpatialMedian, SimplexMedian, and PolytopeQuantile, which clearly are targeted at specialists.

12.2 Generating Pseudorandom Numbers with a Given Distribution

Problem

You want to generate random numbers that have nonuniform distributions. Many recipes in this book use RandomReal and RandomInteger, but these functions give uniform distributions unless you specify otherwise.

Solution

Both RandomReal and RandomInteger can take a distribution as their first argument. RandomReal uses continuous distributions, including NormalDistribution, HalfNormal-Distribution, LogNormalDistribution, InverseGaussianDistribution, GammaDistribution, ChiSquareDistribution, and others. RandomInteger uses discrete distributions, such as BernoulliDistribution, GeometricDistribution, HypergeometricDistribution, PoissonDistribution, and others.

```
In[19]:= RandomReal[NormalDistribution[], 10]
Out[19]= {-0.96524, 1.19926, 0.989088, 0.156427, -0.336326,
          -1.66671, 0.149802, -0.464219, -0.998164, 0.948215}
```

```
In[20]:= RandomInteger[PoissonDistribution[5], 10]
Out[20]= {5, 2, 6, 5, 6, 4, 3, 4, 4, 5}
```

Discussion

You can visualize distributions using BinCounts and BarChar.

```
In[21]:= GraphicsRow[
            {BarChart[BinCounts[RandomInteger[GeometricDistribution[0.3], 5000]]],
             BarChart[BinCounts[RandomInteger[PoissonDistribution[5], 5000]]]}]
```

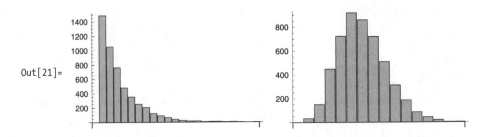

Out[21]=

Another way to visualize the various continuous distributions is to generate a random raster using each distribution. How would you rewrite this to remove the redundancy? (Hint: functional programming!)

```
In[22]:= GraphicsGrid[{{Graphics[Point[RandomReal[{0, 1}, {500, 2}]]],
            Graphics[Point[RandomReal[NormalDistribution[], {500, 2}]]],
            Graphics[Point[RandomReal[HalfNormalDistribution[1], {500, 2}]]],
            Graphics[Point[RandomReal[LogNormalDistribution[0, 1], {500, 2}]]],
            Graphics[
              Point[RandomReal[InverseGaussianDistribution[1, 1], {500, 2}]]]},
            {"Uniform", "Normal", "HalfNormal", "LogNormal", "InverseGaussian"}}]
```

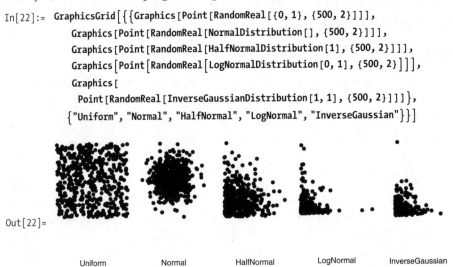

Out[22]=

See Also

Other useful functions to explore in the Mathematica documentation are Seed-Random, BlockRandom, and RandomComplex.

See Recipe 12.12 for a common method for testing random generators based on the chi-square distribution.

12.3 Working with Probability Distributions

Problem

You want to compute the probability density function (PDF) and cumulative density function (CDF) of various distributions. You may also want to determine the characteristic function of the associated distribution.

Solution

Use PDF to compute the probability density function and CDF to compute the cumulative density function. I illustrate the use of these functions using the standardized normal distribution (mean 0 and variance 1).

```
In[23]:=  Plot[PDF[NormalDistribution[0, 1], x], {x, -3, 3}]
```

Out[23]=
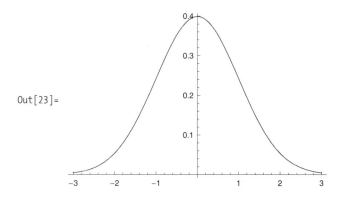

`In[24]:=` `Plot[CDF[NormalDistribution[0, 1], x], {x, -3, 3}]`

`Out[24]=`

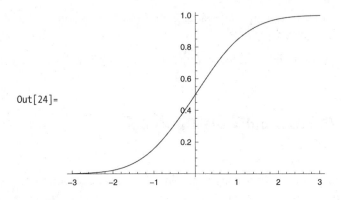

Discussion

The CDF is obtained from the PDF by integrating the PDF from $-\infty$ to x, which you can illustrate in Mathematica very easily. The implementation given here is designed to execute the integration only once and then store it as a new function for subsequent evaluation, so it is almost as fast as the built-in CDF. There is no compelling reason to use this over the built-in CDF implementation. It is here strictly as an illustration of the relationship. If you use Mathematica to teach statistics, it is a good idea to peek under the covers of black box functions like CDF whenever possible.

```
In[25]:= cdf[dist_] := cdf[dist] =
             Function[{x}, Evaluate[Integrate[PDF[dist, x1], {x1, -Infinity, x}]]]
         Plot[cdf[NormalDistribution[0, 1]][x], {x, -3, 3}]
```

`Out[26]=`

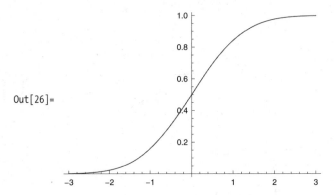

Clearly, you can also obtain the closed-form formula for the CDF of any particular distribution.

```
In[27]:= Integrate[PDF[NormalDistribution[0, 1], x], x]

Out[27]= 1/2 Erf[ x/√2 ]
```

Find the value at -∞.

```
In[28]:= % //. x → -Infinity

Out[28]= - 1/2
```

So the closed-form value for the CDF of the normal distribution is

```
In[29]:= cumNormDist[x_] := Erf[x / Sqrt[2]] / 2 + 0.5
```

The classic application of a PDF is in computing the probability that a particular value falls within some range. For example, consider the probability of a value falling between 0 and 0.25 for various distributions.

```
In[30]:= Integrate[PDF[#, x], {x, 0, 0.25}] & /@
            {UniformDistribution[{0, 1}], NormalDistribution[0, 1],
             HalfNormalDistribution[1], ChiSquareDistribution[2]}

Out[30]= {0.25, 0.0987063, 0.158106, 0.117503}
```

Based on the definition of the CDF, it is easy to see that it computes the probability that a value will be less than or equal to a specific value. Subtracting the CDF from 1 will give the probability of a value being greater than a specified limit.

```
In[31]:= (*Probability that a normally distributed random variable will
            be less than or equal to 0.5*)CDF[NormalDistribution[0, 1], 0.5]

Out[31]= 0.691462
```

```
In[32]:= (*Probability that a normally distributed random variable will
            be greater than 0.8*)1 - CDF[NormalDistribution[0, 1], 0.8]

Out[32]= 0.211855
```

```
In[33]:= (*Probability that a normally distributed random
            variable will be less than -1 or greater than 1*)
         CDF[NormalDistribution[0, 1], -1.] +
            (1 - CDF[NormalDistribution[0, 1], 1.])

Out[33]= 0.317311
```

When you plot a PDF, you can use ColorFunction to highlight regions of interest, but make sure you also set Filling → Axis and ColorFunctionScaling → False. Here I plot the regions of interest whose total area (and hence probability) is approximately 0.317311.

```
In[34]:= Plot[PDF[NormalDistribution[0, 1], x], {x, -3, 3},
          ColorFunction -> Function[{x, y}, If[x < -1 || x > 1, LightGray, White]],
          Filling -> Axis, FillingStyle → Automatic, ColorFunctionScaling → False,
          ImageSize -> Small, Axes → {True, False}, Mesh → Full]
```

Out[34]=

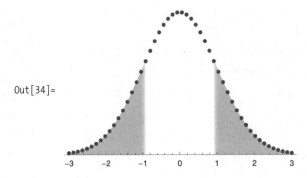

Use CharacteristicFunction[dist,var] to extract the characteristic function of a distribution in terms of a variable var. Here are the functions for five common distributions.

```
In[35]:= Row[CharacteristicFunction[#, t] & /@ {UniformDistribution[{0, 1}],
          NormalDistribution[0, 1], HalfNormalDistribution[1],
          ChiSquareDistribution[2], PoissonDistribution[3]}, ", "]
```

$$\text{Out[35]= } -\frac{i\left(-1+e^{i\,t}\right)}{t}\text{ , } e^{-\frac{t^2}{2}}\text{ , } e^{-\frac{\pi t^2}{4}}\left(1+i\,\text{Erfi}\left[\frac{\sqrt{\pi}\,t}{2}\right]\right)\text{ , } \frac{1}{1-2\,i\,t}\text{ , } e^{3\left(-1+e^{i\,t}\right)}$$

See Also

Recipe 12.12 demonstrates an application of the chi-square distribution.

Recipe 12.6 demonstrates metrics for capturing the shapes of various distributions.

12.4 Demonstrating the Central Limit Theorem

Problem

You want to illustrate the central limit theorem (CLT) to yourself or your students.

Solution

The CLT states that the mean of sufficiently large samples from any distribution will approximate a normal distribution. You can illustrate this by averaging suitably large random samples from a nonnormal distribution, such as the uniform distribution.

```
In[36]:= BarChart[BinCounts[Mean /@ Table[RandomReal[{-100, 100}, 30], {200}]]]
```

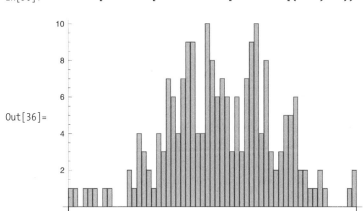

Out[36]=

Discussion

The CLT is often stated in a very technical way. In *Statistics in a Nutshell*, Boslaugh and Watters explain that the CLT "states that the sampling distribution of the sample mean approximates the normal distribution, regardless of the distribution of the population from which samples are drawn, if the sample size is sufficiently large" (137). Other references define it in an equally technical way. The solution shows that the concept is not difficult, although the result is certainly not obvious. The solution demonstrates 200 samples of uniformly generated lists of random numbers, each of length 30, being averaged and then the counts of each integer-valued range being organized into bins and plotted. The shape looks roughly normal, which is the prediction of the CLT. BinCounts, Mean, and RandomReal are relatively easy to understand (see prior recipes), so this makes the idea behind the CLT rather concrete.

To further emphasize that this is not a property of the uniform distribution, you can substitute other distributions. These use finer grained bins due to the tighter range of numbers generated, but the result is similar. As an exercise, wrap a Manipulate around the code in the "Solution" section above and adjust both the sample size and the number of samples. This will illustrate that the validity of the CLT is predicated on a sufficiently large number of samples of sufficiently large size.

```
In[37]:= BarChart[BinCounts[Mean /@
            Table[RandomReal[HalfNormalDistribution[0.5], 40], {1000}], 0.05]]
```

Out[37]=

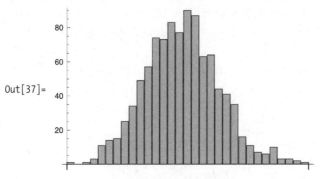

```
In[38]:= BarChart[BinCounts[Mean /@
            Table[RandomReal[ExponentialDistribution[1], 25], {1000}], 0.05]]
```

Out[38]=

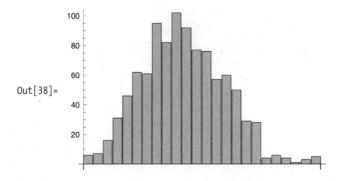

See Also

A proof of the CLT can be found at Wolfram MathWorld: *http://bit.ly/S00Y1*.

12.5 Computing Covariance and Correlation of Vectors and Matrices

Problem

You want to measure the relationship between data sets to see if they vary about the mean in a similar way (covariance) or if there is a linear relationship (correlation).

Solution

```
In[39]:= Module[{data1, data2, data3},
             data1 = {1, 3, 5, 7, 9, 11, 13};
             data2 = {2, 4, 6, 8, 10, 12, 14};
             data3 = {100, 99, 98, 97, 96, 95, 94};
             TableForm[{
             {Covariance[data1, data2],
                 Covariance[data1, data3], Covariance[data2, data3]},
                 {Correlation[data1, data2], Correlation[data1, data3],
                 Correlation[data2, data3]}
                 } // N, TableHeadings → {{"Covariance", "Correlation"},
                 {"1 vs 2", "1 vs 3", "2 vs 3"}}]]
```
Out[39]//TableForm=

	1 vs 2	1 vs 3	2 vs 3
Covariance	18.6667	−9.33333	−9.33333
Correlation	1.	−1.	−1.

Discussion

Covariance and Correlation both operate on matrices. If you pass a single matrix, it will return a covariance (or correlation) matrix resulting from computing the covariance between each column. To demonstrate this clearly, I'll engineer a matrix with an obvious relationship between the first and second column and a weak correlation of these in a third column. The output matrix will always be symmetrical. The correlation matrix will always have ones on the diagonal, since these entries represent correlations of columns with themselves. You can also pass two matrices, in which case you get the covariance (or correlation) with respective columns.

```
In[40]:= SeedRandom[2];
         (data = Transpose[{{0, 1, 2, 3, 4, 5, 6, 7, 8, 9},
             {0, 10, 20, 30, 40, 50, 60, 70, 80, 90},
             RandomReal[{-1, 1}, 10]}]) // TableForm
```
Out[41]//TableForm=

```
        0  0   0.44448
        1  10  −0.781103
        2  20  −0.0585946
        3  30  0.0711637
        4  40  0.166355
        5  50  −0.412115
        6  60  −0.669691
        7  70  0.202516
        8  80  0.508435
        9  90  0.542246
```

```
In[42]:=  Covariance[data] // TableForm
Out[42]//TableForm=
          9.16667   91.6667   0.467288
          91.6667   916.667   4.67288
          0.467288  4.67288   0.228412

In[43]:=  Correlation[data] // TableForm
Out[43]//TableForm=
          1.         1.         0.322938
          1.         1.         0.322938
          0.322938   0.322938   1.

In[44]:=  Correlation[data, data^2] // TableForm
Out[44]//TableForm=
          0.962691   0.962691   0.00604923
          0.962691   0.962691   0.00604923
          0.442467   0.442467   -0.522003
```

12.6 Measuring the Shape of Data

Problem

You want to summarize the shape of your data using some common statistical measures.

Solution

Use Skewness to measure the asymmetry of a distribution. A symmetrical distribution like the NormalDistribution will have skewness of zero. A positive skewness indicates the right tail is longer, while a negative skewness indicates the left tail is longer.

```
In[45]:=  dist1 = NormalDistribution[0, 1];
          dist2 = ChiSquareDistribution[1]; dist3 = BetaDistribution[8, 2];
          Grid[{{Text[Style["Skewness", Bold, 14]], Text[Style["Plot", Bold, 14]]},
            {Skewness[dist1], Plot[PDF[dist1, x], {x, -5, 5}]},
            {Skewness[dist2], Plot[PDF[dist2, x], {x, 0, 5}]},
            {Skewness[dist3], Plot[PDF[dist3, x], {x, 0, 1}]}}, Frame → All]
```

Skewness	Plot
Out[46]= 0	
$2\sqrt{2}$	
$-\dfrac{\sqrt{11}}{4}$	

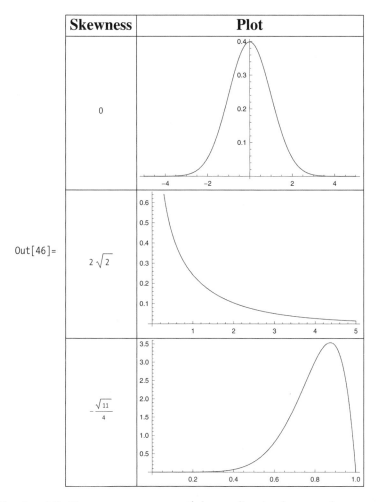

Use QuartileSkewness to measure if the median is closer to the upper or lower quartile. QuartileSkewness is a more robust measure of skewness in the presence of extreme values.

```
In[47]:= data = {0.1, 0.3, 0.7, 1, 0.6, 99, 0.8, 2, 2.1, 0.95, 1.7, 0.69};
         {QuartileSkewness[data], Skewness[data]}
Out[48]= {0.618257, 3.01242}
```

Use Kurtosis to measure the sharpness of the peak of a distribution. A high kurtosis distribution has a sharper peak and longer, fatter tails, whereas a low kurtosis distribution has a more rounded peak and shorter, thinner tails.

```
In[49]:= dist1 = LogNormalDistribution[0, 1];
         dist2 = NormalDistribution[0, 1]; dist3 = BetaDistribution[1, 1];
         Grid[
          {{Text[Style["Kurtosis", Bold, 14]], Text[Style["Plot", Bold, 14]]},
           {Kurtosis[dist1] // N, Plot[PDF[dist1, x], {x, 0, 6}]},
           {Kurtosis[dist2] // N, Plot[PDF[dist2, x], {x, 0, 6}]},
           {Kurtosis[dist3] // N, Plot[PDF[dist3, x], {x, 0, 6}]}}, Frame → All]
```

Out[49]=

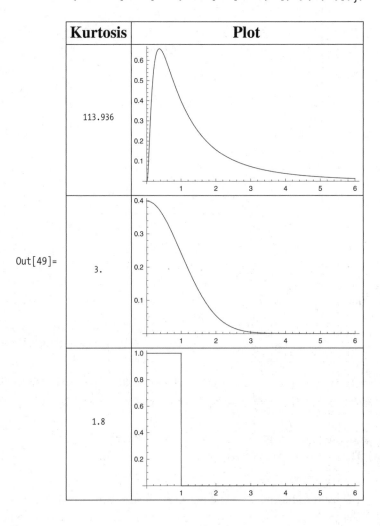

Discussion

CentralMoment is a fundamental measure that underlies statistical measures of shape. It is computed as

$$\frac{1}{n} \sum_i (x_i - \overline{x})^r$$

The second central moment of a data set is called the population variance (which is not as commonly used as sample variance as computed by the Variance function).

```
In[50]:= data = {0.1, 0.3, 0.7, 1, 0.6, 99, 0.8, 2, 2.1, 0.95, 1.7, 0.69};

In[51]:= Table[CentralMoment[data, i], {i, 1, 3}]
Out[51]= {1.77636×10⁻¹⁵, 734.086, 59915.}
```

Skewness is equivalent to CentralMoment[list,3]/CentralMoment[list,2]^(3/2); Kurtosis is CentralMoment[list,4]/CentralMoment[list,2]^2.

12.7 Finding and Adjusting for Outliers

Problem

You have a large data set and you want to identify outliers and possibly adjust the statistics to compensate.

Solution

A simple way to identify outliers is to use Sort and inspect the beginning and end of the list. You can also look at a certain number of elements near the minimum and maximum using Nearest.

```
In[52]:= data = Join[{0.0001, 0.0005}, RandomReal[{10, 30}, 500], {1000, 1007}];
         {min, max} = {Min[data], Max[data]};
         {Nearest[data, min, 5], Nearest[data, max, 5]}
Out[54]= {{0.0001, 0.0005, 10.0021, 10.1101, 10.1403},
          {1007, 1000, 29.9915, 29.9773, 29.975}}
```

You can also compute the trimmed mean, which is the mean after dropping a fraction of the smallest and largest elements.

```
In[55]:= {Mean[data], TrimmedMean[data, 0.2]}
Out[55]= {24.0623, 20.173}
```

Discussion

Here I take advantage of a feature of Tally that allows you to provide custom equivalence function. The idea here is to treat values within a specified distance of each other as equal. In this case, I use distance 5. This shows that there are 3 clusters of values in the data and some outliers with low frequency of occurrence.

```
In[56]:= Tally[data, (Abs[#1 - #2] < 5) &] // TableForm
Out[56]//TableForm=
         0.0001    2
         25.5715   235
         10.4722   135
         17.0082   130
         1000      1
         1007      1
```

12.8 Fitting Data Using a Linear Model

Problem

You have a data set and would like to find a linear model of the data. A linear model is commonly called a "linear regression." A linear model has various statistics that define its accuracy, and you typically want to obtain these as well.

Solution

```
In[57]:= data = Table[{x, x + RandomReal[{-2, 3}]}, {x, 1, 20}];
```

Use Fit in versions prior to Mathematica 7.

```
In[58]:= linFit[x_] := Evaluate[Fit[data, {1, x}, x]]

In[59]:= Show[ListPlot[data], Plot[linFit[x], {x, 1, 20}], ImageSize → Small]
```

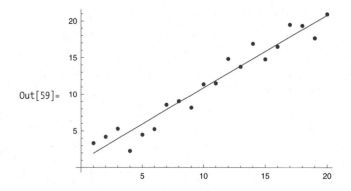

Use LinearModelFit in version 7 and above to build a linear model that you can then use to plot or extract statistics.

```
In[60]:= lm = LinearModelFit[data, x, x];
         Show[ListPlot[data], Plot[lm[x], {x, 1, 20}], ImageSize → Small]
```

Out[60]=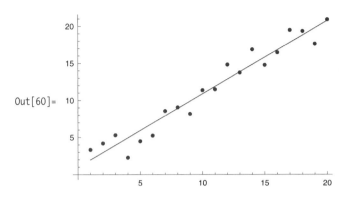

Discussion

LinearModelFit is a vast improvement over Fit since it is not just a way to synthesize a function. Once you have constructed a linear model, you can query its various properties, of which there are quite a few. To find out what is available, simply ask the model. Ask for a specific property by name.

```
In[62]:= lm["Properties"]
Out[62]= {AdjustedRSquared, AIC, ANOVATable, ANOVATableDegreesOfFreedom,
         ANOVATableEntries, ANOVATableFStatistics, ANOVATableMeanSquares,
         ANOVATablePValues, ANOVATableSumsOfSquares, BetaDifferences, BestFit,
         BestFitParameters, BIC, CatcherMatrix, CoefficientOfVariation,
         CookDistances, CorrelationMatrix, CovarianceMatrix, CovarianceRatios,
         Data, DesignMatrix, DurbinWatsonD, EigenstructureTable,
         EigenstructureTableEigenvalues, EigenstructureTableEntries,
         EigenstructureTableIndexes, EigenstructureTablePartitions,
         EstimatedVariance, FitDifferences, FitResiduals, Function,
         FVarianceRatios, HatDiagonal, MeanPredictionBands,
```

MeanPredictionConfidenceIntervals, MeanPredictionConfidenceIntervalTable,
MeanPredictionConfidenceIntervalTableEntries, MeanPredictionErrors,
ParameterConfidenceIntervals, ParameterConfidenceIntervalTable,
ParameterConfidenceIntervalTableEntries, ParameterConfidenceRegion,
ParameterErrors, ParameterPValues, ParameterTable, ParameterTableEntries,
ParameterTStatistics, PartialSumOfSquares, PredictedResponse, Properties,
Response, RSquared, SequentialSumOfSquares, SingleDeletionVariances,
SinglePredictionBands, SinglePredictionConfidenceIntervals,
SinglePredictionConfidenceIntervalTable,
SinglePredictionConfidenceIntervalTableEntries, SinglePredictionErrors,
StandardizedResiduals, StudentizedResiduals, VarianceInflationFactors}

```
In[63]:= lm["RSquared"]
Out[63]= 0.944788
```

```
In[64]:= lm["MeanPredictionErrors"]
Out[64]= {0.627101, 0.579603, 0.533846, 0.490318, 0.449667, 0.412744,
          0.380636, 0.354652, 0.336216, 0.326608, 0.326608, 0.336216, 0.354652,
          0.380636, 0.412744, 0.449667, 0.490318, 0.533846, 0.579603, 0.627101}
```

```
In[65]:= lm["BestFit"]
Out[65]= 0.981879 + 0.990357 x
```

You can also get the best Fit function by using Normal.

```
In[66]:= Normal[lm]
Out[66]= 0.981879 + 0.990357 x
```

See Also

FindFit and LeastSquares are other related functions you can explore in the Math-ematica documentation.

GeneralizedLinearModelFit and DesignMatrix are Mathematica 7 functions that are also worth exploring in the documentation and tutorials.

12.9 Fitting Data Using a Nonlinear Model

Problem

You want to fit data to a function for which you have knowledge of the mathematical model. Specifically, you know the model is nonlinear and, hence, neither Fit nor LinearModelFit is appropriate.

Solution

Use FindFit in versions prior to Mathematica 7.

```
In[67]:=  SeedRandom[3];
          (*Randomly generate data that is not linear.*)
          data = Sort[RandomSample[Table[{x, 3 Exp[x - 8 ]}, {x, 0, 10, 0.1}], 22]]
Out[68]=  {{0.9, 0.00247531}, {1.3, 0.00369274}, {1.7, 0.00550891},
           {2.7, 0.0149748}, {2.9, 0.0182902}, {3.2, 0.0246892},
           {3.5, 0.033327}, {3.6, 0.036832}, {3.9, 0.049718}, {4.6, 0.10012},
           {5.4, 0.222821}, {5.8, 0.332409}, {5.9, 0.367369}, {6.1, 0.448706},
           {6.2, 0.495897}, {6.8, 0.903583}, {7.5, 1.81959}, {8., 3.},
           {8.7, 6.04126}, {8.8, 6.67662}, {8.9, 7.37881}, {9.6, 14.8591}}
```

```
In[69]:=  FindFit[data , a Exp[b + c x] + d, {a, b, c, d}, x]
Out[69]=  {a → 0.0608805, b → -4.10255, c → 1., d → 3.33224 × 10^{-17}}
```

Use NonLinearModel fit in Mathematica 7 as a more complete solution.

```
In[70]:=  nlm = NonlinearModelFit[data, a Exp[b + c x] + d, {a, b, c, d}, x];
```

```
In[71]:=  Normal[nlm]
Out[71]=  3.33224 × 10^{-17} + 0.0608805 e^{-4.10255+1. x}
```

```
In[72]:=  Show[ListPlot[data], Plot[nlm[x], {x, 0, 10}], Frame → True]
```

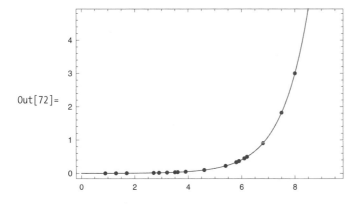

Out[72]=

Discussion

As with LinearModelFit, NonlinearModelFit encapsulates a wealth of information.

```
In[73]:= nlm["Properties"]
Out[73]= {AdjustedRSquared, AIC, ANOVATable, ANOVATableDegreesOfFreedom,
          ANOVATableEntries, ANOVATableMeanSquares, ANOVATableSumsOfSquares,
          BestFit, BestFitParameters, BIC, CorrelationMatrix, CovarianceMatrix,
          CurvatureConfidenceRegion, Data, EstimatedVariance, FitCurvatureTable,
          FitCurvatureTableEntries, FitResiduals, Function, HatDiagonal,
          MaxIntrinsicCurvature, MaxParameterEffectsCurvature, MeanPredictionBands,
          MeanPredictionConfidenceIntervals, MeanPredictionConfidenceIntervalTable,
          MeanPredictionConfidenceIntervalTableEntries,
          MeanPredictionErrors, ParameterBias, ParameterConfidenceIntervals,
          ParameterConfidenceIntervalTable, ParameterConfidenceIntervalTableEntries,
          ParameterConfidenceRegion, ParameterErrors, ParameterPValues,
          ParameterTable, ParameterTableEntries, ParameterTStatistics,
          PredictedResponse, Properties, Response, RSquared, SingleDeletionVariances,
          SinglePredictionBands, SinglePredictionConfidenceIntervals,
          SinglePredictionConfidenceIntervalTable,
          SinglePredictionConfidenceIntervalTableEntries,
          SinglePredictionErrors, StandardizedResiduals, StudentizedResiduals}
```

For example, you can extract and plot confidence bands for various confidence levels.

```
In[74]:= SeedRandom[30];
         data = Sort[
            RandomSample[Table[{x, Exp[x + 1.3 Sin[x]]}, {x, 0, 10, 0.1}], 15]];
         nlm = NonlinearModelFit[data, a x Exp[b + c x] + d, {a, b, c, d}, x];
         {bands90[x_], bands95[x_], bands99[x_], bands999[x_]} =
            Table[nlm["MeanPredictionBands", ConfidenceLevel → cl],
            {cl, {.9, .95, .99, .999}}];
         Show[ListPlot[data], Plot[{nlm[x], bands90[x], bands95[x], bands99[x],
            bands999[x]}, {x, 1, 10}, Filling → {2 → {1}, 3 → {2}, 4 → {3}, 5 → {4}}]]
```

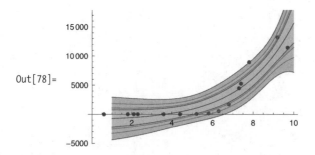

Out[78]=

Or you can extract a variety of statistics.

```
In[79]:=  nlm["MeanPredictionErrors"]
Out[79]=  {854.599, 758.348, 729.776, 709.976, 580.188, 526.565, 526.883,
          567.372, 617.731, 669.962, 711.146, 717.15, 732.972, 968.248, 1442.15}
```

```
In[80]:=  nlm["ANOVATable"]
```

	DF	SS	MS
Model	4	4.04209×10^8	1.01052×10^8
Error	11	3.28552×10^7	2.98683×10^6
Uncorrected Total	15	4.37064×10^8	
Corrected Total	14	2.96124×10^8	

Out[80]=

```
In[81]:=  nlm["CorrelationMatrix"] // TableForm
Out[81]//TableForm=
          1.         1.         -0.993792  -0.777438
          1.         1.         -0.993792  -0.777438
          -0.993792  -0.993792  1.         0.730294
          -0.777438  -0.777438  0.730294   1.
```

See Also

The statistical model analysis guide (*guide/StatisticalModelAnalysis*) is a good starting point for exploring all the new modeling capabilities in Mathematica 7.

12.10 Creating Interpolation Functions from Data

Problem

You have a set of data points and want to construct a function you can use to predict values at other points.

Solution

Normally, you would interpolate data that was obtained in the wild without any a priori notion of the underlying function. However, as a simple illustration, I'll sample data from a known function.

```
In[82]:=  xvalues = Sort[RandomReal[{-4 Pi, 4 Pi}, 18]];
          data = Table[{x, Sin[x]}, {x, xvalues}];
          fData = Interpolation[data]
Out[84]=  InterpolatingFunction[{{-11.3374, 12.5436}}, <>]
```

In[85]:= `Plot[{fData[x], Sin[x]}, {x, -2 Pi, 2 Pi}, PlotStyle → {Thin, Dashed}]`

Out[85]=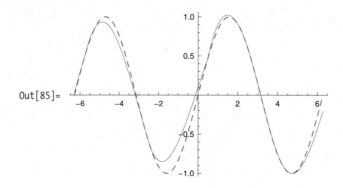

Discussion

Interpolation returns an `InterpolationFunctionObject`, which can be used just like a normal function. The default order for Interpolation is 3 but this can be varied using the option `InterpolationOrder`.

In[86]:= `fData1 = Interpolation[data, InterpolationOrder → 1];`
`fData2 = Interpolation[data, InterpolationOrder → 2];`
`fData3 = Interpolation[data, InterpolationOrder → 3];`

In[89]:= `Plot[{fData1[x], fData2[x], fData3[x]},`
`{x, -2 Pi, 2 Pi}, PlotStyle → {Dashed, Thin, Thick}]`

Out[89]=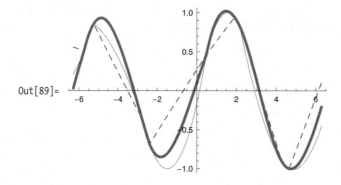

12.11 Testing for Statistically Significant Difference Between Groups Using ANOVA

Problem

You have experimental data suggesting a linear relationship between an independent and dependent variables; however, you are unsure if the relationship is causal. You run an experiment using an experimental group and a control group. You want to know if the results of the experiment are statistically significant.

Solution

Analysis of variance (ANOVA) is a popular statistical technique that is very important in the analysis of experimental results. Mathematica provides this functionality in a package aptly named ANOVA`. To illustrate the use of this package, I borrow a toy example from Boslaugh and Watters' *Statistics in a Nutshell*. Imagine you collected the data in table coffeeIQ suggesting a relationship between coffee consumption in cups and IQ as measured by some standardized IQ test.

```
In[90]:=  coffeeIQ = {{2, 123}, {1, 112}, {1, 102}, {1, 98},
             {0, 79}, {0, 87}, {1, 102}, {2, 120}, {2, 120}, {3, 145}};
```

```
In[91]:=  lm = LinearModelFit[coffeeIQ, x, x];
          Show[ListPlot[coffeeIQ], Plot[lm[x], {x, 0, 4}], ImageSize → Small]
```

Out[92]=
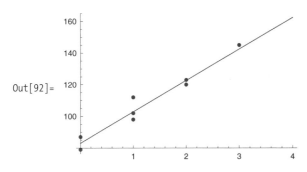

```
In[93]:=  Normal[lm]
Out[93]=  83.0247 + 19.8272 x
```

The question that remains is whether there is a causal relationship between caffeine and IQ, since one could equally suppose smart people just like to drink coffee. To investigate further, you design an experiment with two randomly selected groups: everyone in the first group receives a caffeine pill, and those in the second group receive a placebo. The pills are administered in a double-blind method, at the same time, under the exact same conditions, and each group is administered an IQ test at a specific time after the pills were taken. From these experiments you obtain the following data, where the first entry is 1 for those who received the caffeine and 0 for those who received the placebo. The second entry is the measured IQ.

```
In[94]:= experiments = {{1, 110}, {1, 100}, {1, 120}, {1, 125}, {1, 120}, {1, 120},
           {1, 115}, {1, 98}, {1, 95}, {1, 91}, {0, 100}, {0, 95}, {0, 100},
           {0, 122}, {0, 115}, {0, 88}, {0, 97}, {0, 87}, {0, 92}, {0, 76}};
```

Using ANOVA you see

```
In[95]:= Needs["ANOVA`"]
```

```
In[96]:= ANOVA[experiments]
```

Out[96]= $\left\{ \text{ANOVA} \rightarrow \begin{array}{lccccc} & \text{DF} & \text{SumOfSq} & \text{MeanSq} & \text{FRatio} & \text{PValue} \\ \text{Model} & 1 & 744.2 & 744.2 & 4.47415 & 0.0486171 \\ \text{Error} & 18 & 2994. & 166.333 & & \\ \text{Total} & 19 & 3738.2 & & & \end{array}, \text{CellMeans} \rightarrow \begin{array}{ll} \text{All} & 103.3 \\ \text{Model[0]} & 97.2 \\ \text{Model[1]} & 109.4 \end{array} \right\}$

Here the important results are the FRatio (higher is better) and PValue (smaller is better). The PValue is the probability of obtaining the result at least as extreme as the one that was actually observed, given that the null hypothesis is true. Typically one will reject the null hypothesis when the PValue is less than 0.05.

Discussion

You may wonder why the output of ANOVA is formatted as it is. Here Mathematica is emulating a popular statistics package called Minitab. You can drill down to the raw values easily enough.

```
In[97]:= (ANOVA /. ANOVA[experiments])[[1]]
Out[97]= {{1, 744.2, 744.2, 4.47415, 0.0486171}, {18, 2994., 166.333}, {19, 3738.2}}
```

The solution shows a one-way ANOVA. It is frequently the case that there are multiple independent variables. In this case, you must describe the model and variables more precisely. For example, suppose you were measuring height and age of men as a predictor of income. For the purpose of this experiment, we will designate men under 5'10" as "short," assigning them height classification 1 and "tall" men classification 2. Similarly, we will define "young" men as under 40 with age classification 1 and "mature" men with age classification 2.

```
In[98]:= twowaydata = {{1, 1, 30 000}, {1, 1, 65 000}, {1, 1, 57 000}, {1, 1, 45 000},
            {1, 2, 49 000}, {1, 2, 87 000}, {1, 2, 56 000}, {1, 2, 90 000},
            {2, 1, 55 000}, {2, 1, 88 000}, {2, 1, 104 000}, {2, 1, 88 000},
            {2, 2, 75 000}, {2, 2, 101 000}, {2, 2, 150 000}, {2, 2, 125 000}};
```

```
In[99]:= ANOVA[twowaydata, {height, age, All}, {height, age}] //
            Style[#, FontTracking → "Condensed"] &
```

Out[99]= {ANOVA →

	DF	SumOfSq	MeanSq	FRatio	PValue
height	1	5.89056×10^9	5.89056×10^9	11.053	0.00605829
age	1	2.52506×10^9	2.52506×10^9	4.73801	0.0501898
age height	1	6.00625×10^7	6.00625×10^7	0.112701	0.742887
Error	12	6.39525×10^9	5.32938×10^8		
Total	15	1.48709×10^{10}			

$$
\text{CellMeans} \rightarrow
\begin{array}{ll}
\text{All} & 79062.5 \\
\text{height}[1] & 59875. \\
\text{height}[2] & 98250. \\
\text{age}[1] & 66500. \\
\text{age}[2] & 91625. \\
\text{age}[1]\,\text{height}[1] & 49250. \\
\text{age}[1]\,\text{height}[2] & 83750. \\
\text{age}[2]\,\text{height}[1] & 70500. \\
\text{age}[2]\,\text{height}[2] & 112750.
\end{array}
$$

Here I use All in the model input to indicate I want to analyze all products of the main effects. You can also specify the products individually. For example, if you want to analyze the significance of height and height and age together, you can specify the model parameter as {height, age height}.

```
In[100]:= ANOVA[twowaydata, {height, age height }, {height, age}] //
          Style[#, FontTracking → "Condensed"] &
```

Out[100]= {ANOVA →

	DF	SumOfSq	MeanSq	FRatio	PValue
height	1	5.89056×10^9	5.89056×10^9	11.053	0.00605829
age height	2	2.58513×10^9	1.29256×10^9	2.42535	0.13043
Error	12	6.39525×10^9	5.32938×10^8		
Total	15	1.48709×10^{10}			

All	79062.5
height[1]	59875.
height[2]	98250.
CellMeans → age[1] height[1]	49250.
age[1] height[2]	83750.
age[2] height[1]	70500.
age[2] height[2]	112750.

There are a few standard post hoc tests you can run to determine which group's means were significantly different given SignificanceLevel (default is 0.05). I will not delve into the statistics behind these tests. You should refer to one of the resources in the "See Also" section on page 483. The output is fairly self-explanatory. Here we see that using the Bonferroni and Tukey tests, variation in income due to height was statistically significant between groups 1 and 2, but age did not show up as significant for either test.

```
In[101]:= ANOVA[twowaydata, {height, age , All }, {height, age},
          SignificanceLevel → 0.05, PostTests → {Tukey, Bonferroni},
          CellMeans → False] // Style[#, FontTracking → "Condensed"] &
```

Out[101]= {ANOVA →

	DF	SumOfSq	MeanSq	FRatio	PValue
height	1	5.89056×10^9	5.89056×10^9	11.053	0.00605829
age	1	2.52506×10^9	2.52506×10^9	4.73801	0.0501898
age height	1	6.00625×10^7	6.00625×10^7	0.112701	0.742887
Error	12	6.39525×10^9	5.32938×10^8		
Total	15	1.48709×10^{10}			

	Bonferroni {1, 2}		Bonferroni {}	
PostTests → {height →		, age →		}}
	Tukey {1, 2}		Tukey {}	

Returning to the data from the "Solution" section on page 479, we can see how the tests can pass at one significance level but fail at a tighter tolerance. Note also how I use the output as a replacement rule to extract only the test results.

```
In[102]:= PostTests /. ANOVA[experiments , SignificanceLevel → 0.05,
             PostTests → {Tukey, Bonferroni}, CellMeans → False]

                          Bonferroni  {0, 1}
Out[102]= {Model →                          }
                          Tukey       {0, 1}
```

```
In[103]:= PostTests /. ANOVA[experiments , SignificanceLevel → 0.01,
             PostTests → {Tukey, Bonferroni}, CellMeans → False]

                          Bonferroni  {}
Out[103]= {Model →                        }
                          Tukey       {}
```

In the examples given here, I have also used the option CellMeans → False, which suppresses the display of the means.

See Also

Basic information on ANOVA can be found on Wikipedia at *http:/bit.ly/bf8PrO*, and in Boslaugh and Watters, *Statistics in a Nutshell*.

12.12 Hypothesis Testing with Categorical Data

Problem

You want to determine if there are statistically significant relationships within categorical data.

Solution

The chi-square test is a standard computation on categorical data. Categorical data is that for which the response is a choice among a set of discrete categories rather than a measurement on a continuous scale. Common examples are sex {male, female}, party {Democrat, Republican}, or sometimes data that could be placed on a scale but for simplicity is lumped into discrete groups, for example, blood pressure {low, normal, prehypertensive, hypertensive}. Experiments using categorical data often result in tables; hence, the data is called row-column (RC) data.

Here is a simplest possible example (borrowed from *Statistics in a Nutshell*) showing a two-by-two table relating smoking to lung cancer.

	Lung Cancer Diagnosis	No Lung Cancer Diagnosis
Currently smoke	60	300
Do not currently smoke	10	390

The chi-square test is a test for independence. If the RC data is independent, there is no demonstrated relationship between smoking and cancer (the null hypothesis); otherwise, there is evidence for the alternate hypothesis. The chi-square statistic starts with the computation of expected, values for each cell. The formula is

$$E_{ij} = \frac{i \text{ th row total} * j \text{ th row total}}{\text{grand total}}$$

This is easily computed for the entire table using Outer.

```
In[104]:= data := {{60, 300}, {10, 390}};
```

```
Out[105]= expectedValues[rc_List] := Module[{rowTotals, colTotals, grandTotal},
            colTotals := Total[rc] ;
            rowTotals := Total[Transpose[rc]];
            grandTotal := Total[rowTotals] ;
            Outer[Times, rowTotals, colTotals] / grandTotal]
```

The chi-square value is computed by taking the differences between expected and observed, squaring the result, dividing it by expected, and summing all the ratios.

```
In[106]:= chiSquare[data_List] := Module[{ev}, ev = expectedValues[data];
            Total[((data - ev) ^ 2 ) / ev, 2]]
```

```
In[107]:= expectedValues[data] // N // TableForm
Out[107]//TableForm=
            33.1579   326.842
            36.8421   363.158
```

```
In[108]:= chiSquare[data] // N
Out[108]= 45.4741
```

To interpret this result, you need to compute PValue. The smaller the p-value, the more confident you can be in rejecting the null hypothesis.

```
In[109]:= Needs["HypothesisTesting`"]
            ChiSquarePValue[45.4741, 1]
Out[110]= OneSidedPValue → 1.54671×10^{-11}
```

Discussion

The second argument to ChiSquarePValue specifies the degrees of freedom of the distribution. In the solution example, we use 1 without explanation. The rule for computing the degrees of freedom for RC data is (numRows -1)(numCols -1).

```
In[111]:= degreesOfFreedom[rc_List] := Times @@ (Dimensions[rc] - 1)
```

```
In[112]:= degreesOfFreedom[data]
Out[112]= 1
```

In the literature you will often find tables of critical values for various distributions relative to a significance level called alpha (α). For example, a common value for alpha is 0.05, which represents 95% confidence or (1 - α) * 100%. The critical value for a specified degree of freedom is the lower (or upper) bound for chiSquare in the solution that would give you the required confidence. Computing the critical value is the problem of finding a limit that gives the specified alpha as the area under the PDF for the distribution. We can compute these values efficiently using FindRoot and NIntegrate.

```
In[113]:= chiSqUpperP[criticalValue_, df_] := With[{infinity = 1000}, NIntegrate[
            PDF[ChiSquareDistribution[df], x], {x, criticalValue, infinity}]]
          chiSqLowerP[criticalValue_, df_] := NIntegrate[
            PDF[ChiSquareDistribution[df], x], {x, 0, criticalValue}]
          criticalValueUpper[alpha_, df_] :=
           FindRoot[chiSqUpperP[c, df] == alpha, {c, 0.1}]
          criticalValueLower[alpha_, df_] :=
           FindRoot[chiSqLowerP[c, df] == alpha, {c, 0.1}]
```

The critical value for the experiment in the solution is

```
In[117]:= criticalValueUpper[0.05, 1] // Quiet
Out[117]= {c → 3.84146}
```

Our result was 45.47, so the result was well over the critical value. A result below the lower critical value is also acceptable, but clearly that does not apply to this experiment.

```
In[118]:= criticalValueLower[0.05, 1] // Quiet
Out[118]= {c → 0.00393214}
```

Given these functions, you can create your own tables of critical values like those in the *NIST/SEMATECH e-Handbook of Statistical Methods* website (*http://bit.ly/AbGvb*).

```
In[119]:= chiSqCritValues[dfFrom_, dfTo_] := With[{alphas = {0.10, 0.05, 0.01, 0.001}},
            TableForm[Table[c /. criticalValueUpper[alpha, df], {df, dfFrom, dfTo},
              {alpha, alphas}], TableHeadings → {Range[dfFrom, dfTo], alphas}]]
```

```
In[120]:=  chiSqCritValues[1, 10] // Quiet
Out[120]//TableForm=
```

	0.1	0.05	0.01	0.001
1	2.70554	3.84146	6.6349	10.8276
2	4.60517	5.99146	9.21034	13.8155
3	6.25139	7.81473	11.3449	16.2662
4	7.77944	9.48773	13.2767	18.4668
5	9.23636	11.0705	15.0863	20.515
6	10.6446	12.5916	16.8119	22.4577
7	12.017	14.0671	18.4753	24.3219
8	13.3616	15.5073	20.0902	26.1245
9	14.6837	16.919	21.666	27.8772
10	15.9872	18.307	23.2093	29.5883

See Also

More information on using ChiSquare can be found in the *NIST/SEMATECH e-Handbook of Statistical Methods* website (*http://bit.ly/AbGvb*).

A tutorial on the complete HypothesisTesting` package in Mathematica can be found in the documentation (*HypothesisTesting/tutorial/HypothesisTesting*).

12.13 Grouping Data into Clusters

Problem

You want to group data in separate lists based on a metric like Euclidean distance or Hamming distance. This problem arises in a wide variety of contexts, including market research, demographics, informatics, risk analysis, and so forth.

Solution

Use FindClusters with the default Euclidean distance function for numbers and vectors.

```
In[121]:=  FindClusters[{1, 100, 2, 101, 3, 102, 1000, 1010, 4, 1020, 7}]
Out[121]=  {{1, 2, 3, 4, 7}, {100, 101, 102}, {1000, 1010, 1020}}
```

When you use FindClusters with strings, this distance function is "edit distance" or the number of character changes to get from one string to another.

```
In[122]:=  FindClusters[DictionaryLookup[_ ~~ "ead" ~~ _]]
Out[122]=  {{beads, heads, leads, reads}, {beady, heady, Meade, Reade, ready}}
```

You can insist on a specific number of clusters.

```
In[123]:= FindClusters[{1, 100, 2, 101, 3, 102, 1000, 1010, 4, 1020, 7}, 4]
Out[123]= {{1, 2, 3, 4}, {100, 101, 102}, {1000, 1010, 1020}, {7}}
```

Discussion

If you need to cluster data by a key or criterion that is not part of the data, transform the data into the form {key1→data1, key2→data2, ...}. When FindClusters sees this format, it will cluster that data using the keys. For example, say you retrieve some data from a database with names and ages and you want to cluster names by age.

```
In[124]:= data = {{"Wanda", 41}, {"Sal", 44}, {"Leo", 9},
              {"Salvatore", 6}, {"Steven", 37}, {"Adrian", 3}};
          (*Use ReplaceAll (/.) to transform data into the right format.*)
          FindClusters[data /. {name_, age_} :> age → name]
Out[125]= {{Wanda, Sal, Steven}, {Leo, Salvatore, Adrian}}
```

If you don't want to lose the ages, you can use the following variation:

```
In[126]:= FindClusters[data /. {name_, age_} :> age → {name, age}]
Out[126]= {{{Wanda, 41}, {Sal, 44}, {Steven, 37}},
           {{Leo, 9}, {Salvatore, 6}, {Adrian, 3}}}
```

There is also a variation that is more convenient when the keys and values are in separate lists.

```
In[127]:= keys = {41, 44, 9, 6, 37, 3} ;
          values = {"Wanda", "Sal", "Leo", "Salvatore", "Steven", "Adrian"};
          FindClusters[keys → values]
Out[129]= {{Wanda, Sal, Steven}, {Leo, Salvatore, Adrian}}
```

You can also handle the situation via a custom distance function, which is a more general solution since the function can use other metrics besides Euclidean distance.

```
In[130]:= FindClusters[data,
          DistanceFunction → Function[{x, y}, Abs[x[[2]] - y[[2]]]]]
Out[130]= {{{Wanda, 41}, {Sal, 44}, {Steven, 37}},
           {{Leo, 9}, {Salvatore, 6}, {Adrian, 3}}}
```

Mathematica provides a variety of built-in distance functions that cater to different conceptions of closeness as well as different data types. For numbers, vectors, and higher-order tensors, you can use EuclideanDistance, SquaredEuclideanDistance, ManhattanDistance, ChessboardDistance, CanberraDistance, CosineDistance, Correlation-Distance, or BrayCurtisDistance. For example, CosineDistance (also known as angular distance) is often used with highly dimensional data. Here we generate a data set of 800 vectors of length 50. By design, the vectors are clumped into four groups by magnitude, so it should be of little surprise that FindClusters using default Euclidean-Distance discovers four clusters.

```
In[131]:= data =
          Join[RandomReal[{-10, -5}, {200, 50}], RandomReal[{-5, 0}, {200, 50}],
            RandomReal[{0, 1}, {200, 50}], RandomReal[{5, 10}, {200, 50}]];
In[132]:= Length[FindClusters[data]]
Out[132]= 4
```

However, using CosineDistance, which is insensitive to vector length, only two clusters are found.

```
In[133]:= Length[FindClusters[data, DistanceFunction -> CosineDistance]]
In[133]:= 2
```

For Boolean vectors, you can use MatchingDissimilarity, JaccardDissimilarity, RussellRaoDissimilarity, SokalSneathDissimilarity, RogersTanimotoDissimilarity, DiceDissimilarity, and YuleDissimilarity. Consider a problem that turns the game of 20 Questions on its head. I devised 20 questions in a somewhat haphazard fashion and then selected a bunch of nouns as they came into my head (Table 12-1). The idea here is to associate a Boolean vector with each noun based on how one might answer the questions in relation to the noun. Some of the questions are very subjective, and some don't really apply to all nouns, but to stay in the domain of Boolean, I forced myself to choose either true or false.

Table 12-1. Twenty Questions

Number	Question
1	Is it living?
2	Is it bigger than a bread box?
3	Is it soft?
4	Is it visible?
5	Is it man – made?
6	Is it flammable?
7	Is it famous?
8	Does it run on electricity?
9	Does it have hair or fur?
10	Does it process information?
11	Does it usually cost more than $1000?
12	Is it mostly one color?
13	Can you sell it legally?
14	Does it conduct electricity?
15	Can you bend it without breaking and it retains its new shape?
16	Can an average human lift it?
17	Can it been seen with the unaided eye?
18	Can you transfer it over the Internet?
19	Is it scary?
20	Does its English name come before Lizard in the dictionary?

The nouns I applied these questions to are

```
In[135]:= words = {"cat", "PC", "Java", "bird", "airplane", "Obama", "Mathematica",
            "Hillary Clinton", "weather", "time", "wind", "tunnel",
            "carpenter", "house", "red", "beer", "LSD", "Nintendo Wii",
            "John Lennon", "Paul McCartney", "Howard Stern", "mother", "Linux",
            "candle", "paper", "rock", "scissors", "steak", "broccoli"};
```

I'll only show part of the data set (you can find it in the file *20Q.nb* in the downloads from the book's website) .

```
In[136]:= {{True, True, True, True, False, True, False, False, True, True, False,
            False, True, True, False, True, True, False, False, True} → "cat",
          {False, True, False, True, True, False, False, True, False, True, True,
            False, True, False, False, True, True, False, False, False} → "PC",
          {False, False, False, True, True, True, False, False, False, True,
            False, False, True, False, False, False, True, True, False, True} →
            "Java", {True, False, True, True, False, True, False,
            False, False, True, False, True, True, True, False,
            True, True, False, False, True} → "bird"} // TableForm
Out[136]//TableForm=
        {True, True, True, True, False, True, False, False, True, True, False, False, True, True, False, True, True, False, False, True} → cat
        {False, True, False, True, True, False, False, True, False, True, True, False, True, False, False, True, True, False, False, False} → PC
        {False, False, False, True, True, True, False, False, False, True, False, False, True, False, False, False, True, True, False, True} → Java
        {True, False, True, True, False, True, False, False, False, True, False, True, True, True, False, True, True, False, False, True} → bird
```

Assuming the full data set is stored in the variable data, we can see how Find-Clusters partitions the data using the various Boolean distance functions.

```
In[137]:= Column[FindClusters [ Flatten[data, 2],
            DistanceFunction -> MatchingDissimilarity]]
          {Cat, bird, airplane, Obama, Hillary Clinton, carpenter,
Out[137]=   John Lennon, Paul McCartney, Howard Stern, mother, broccoli}
          {PC, Java, Mathematica, weather, time, wind, tunnel, house, red,
            beer, LSD, Nintendo Wii, Linux, candle, paper, rock, scissors, steak}
```

```
In[138]:= Column[FindClusters [ Flatten[data, 2],
            DistanceFunction -> JaccardDissimilarity]]
          {Cat, Obama, Hillary Clinton, carpenter,
            John Lennon, Paul McCartney, Howard Stern, mother}
Out[138]=  {PC, Java, Mathematica, weather, time,
            wind, tunnel, house, Nintendo Wii, Linux, rock}
          {bird, airplane, red, beer, LSD, candle, paper, scissors, steak, broccoli}
```

By transforming Boolean value to 0 and 1, you can see how EuclideanDistance and ManhattanDistance tend to create a larger number of clusters.

```
In[139]:= Column[FindClusters [ Flatten[data, 2] /. {False → 0., True → 1.},
            DistanceFunction → EuclideanDistance]]

Out[139]=  {Cat, bird, airplane, beer, steak, broccoli}
           {PC, Java, Mathematica, house, LSD,
            Nintendo Wii, Linux, candle, paper, rock, scissors}
           {Obama, Hillary Clinton, carpenter,
            John Lennon, Paul McCartney, Howard Stern, mother}
           {weather, time, wind, tunnel, red}
```

```
In[140]:= Column[FindClusters [ Flatten[data, 2] /. {False → 0., True → 1.},
            DistanceFunction → ManhattanDistance]]

Out[140]=  {Cat, bird, beer, steak, broccoli}
           {PC, Mathematica, tunnel, red, LSD,
            Nintendo Wii, candle, paper, rock, scissors}
           {Java, Linux}
           {airplane, house}
           {Obama, Hillary Clinton, carpenter,
            John Lennon, Paul McCartney, Howard Stern, mother}
           {weather, time, wind}
```

For strings, you can choose from EditDistance, DamerauLevenshteinDistance, and HammingDistance.

```
In[141]:= FindClusters[Prepend[DictionaryLookup["b" ~~ __ ~~ "i"], "brocolli"],
            DistanceFunction → EditDistance]

Out[141]= {{brocolli, bacilli, beriberi, bouzouki, broccoli, bronchi},
           {bani, banzai, bhaji, bikini, blini, bonsai, borzoi}}
```

HammingDistance requires equal length strings, otherwise it will report an error. I added a preprocessing function that pads each string at the end with blanks to make each as long as the longest string in the list.

```
In[142]:= lengthNormalize[words_List] := Module[{maxLen},
            maxLen = Max[StringLength /@ words];
            StringInsert[#,
              StringJoin[Table[" ", {maxLen - StringLength[#]}]], -1] & /@ words]
```

```
In[143]:= FindClusters[
            lengthNormalize[Prepend[DictionaryLookup["b" ~~ _ ~~ "i"], "brocolli"]],
            DistanceFunction → HammingDistance]
Out[143]= {{brocolli, beriberi, bouzouki, broccoli, bronchi }, {bacilli ,
            bani    , banzai , bhaji   , bikini  , blini   , bonsai  , borzoi  }}
```

For advanced applications of FindCluster, you can tweak fine-grained aspects of the clustering algorithm via the Method option. Consult the FindClusters tutorial for detailed specifications of Method that provide for custom significance tests and linkage tests.

See Also

The tutorial for partitioning data into clusters (*tutorial/PartitioningDataIntoClusters*) is the essential resource for advanced features of FindClusters.

The Mathematica 7 function Gather is a special case of FindClusters: it groups identical elements, which is akin to clustering only when the distance is zero.

12.14 Creating Common Statistical Plots

Problem

You want to visualize experimental data in a manner that effectively summarizes all the standard statistical measures.

Solution

The BoxWhiskerPlot is an excellent way to visually convey the essential statistics of one or more data sets.

```
In[144]:=  Needs["StatisticalPlots`"]
           dataSet1 = {100, 95, 100, 122, 115, 88, 97, 87, 92, 76}
           dataSet2 = {110, 100, 120, 125, 120, 120, 115, 98, 95, 91}
           BoxWhiskerPlot[dataSet1, dataSet2, BoxLabels → {"Control", "Treatment"}]
Out[145]=  {100, 95, 100, 122, 115, 88, 97, 87, 92, 76}

In[146]:=  {110, 100, 120, 125, 120, 120, 115, 98, 95, 91}
```

Out[147]=
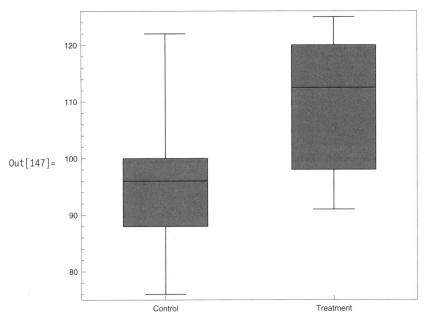

Discussion

A box plot shows the minimum, maximum, median (black line), and middle quantile (box). There are options to change orientation (BoxOrientation), spacing (BoxExtraSpacing), styles (BoxLineStyle, BoxMedianStyle, BoxFillingStyle), and display of outliers (BoxOutliers, BoxOutlierMarkers). You can also show other quantiles using BoxQuantile.

```
In[148]:= BoxWhiskerPlot[dataSet1, dataSet2, BoxLabels → {"Control", "Treatment"},
           BoxOrientation → Horizontal, BoxMedianStyle → Dashed, BoxQuantile → 1/3]
```

Out[148]=

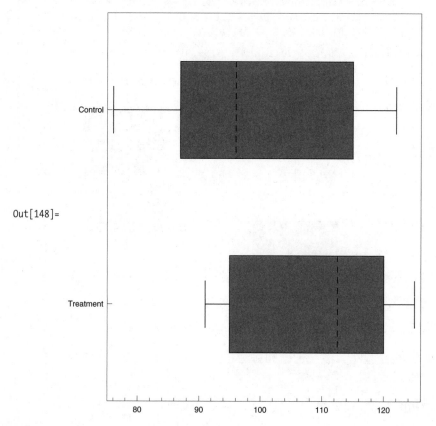

Other common statistical chart types include StemLeafPlot, ParetoPlot, QuantilePlot, and PairwiseScatterPlot.

```
In[149]:= StemLeafPlot[dataSet1]
```

Out[149]=

Stem	Leaves
7	6
8	78
9	257
10	00
11	5
12	2

Stem units: 10

A Pareto plot combines a bar chart of percentages of categories with a plot of cumulative percentages. It is often used in quality control applications for which the data might be defects for various products.

```
In[150]:= RandomSeed[666];
          ParetoPlot[Flatten[Table[i, {i, 1, 7}, {RandomInteger[{1, 12}]}]]]
```

Out[151]=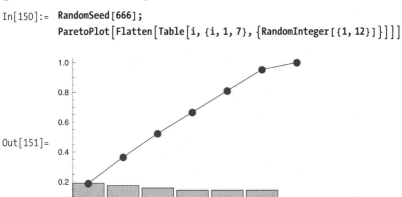

Quantile plots are used to visualize whether two data sets come from the same population. If so, the data lies along a straight line reference line.

```
In[152]:= GraphicsRow[
          {QuantilePlot[RandomReal[{-1, 1}, 100], RandomReal[{-1, 1}, 100]],
           QuantilePlot[RandomReal[{-1, 1}, 100],
            RandomReal[NormalDistribution[0, 1], 100]]}]
```

Out[152]=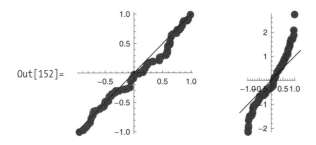

PairwiseScatterPlot plots each column of a matrix against each of the other columns. The diagonals will always be straight lines. The following plot of 2006, 2007, and 2008 Dow Jones Industrial Average (DJIA) data shows how 2006 and 2008 had nearly inverse trends, whereas 2007 deviated in the middle of the year from the 2008 data.

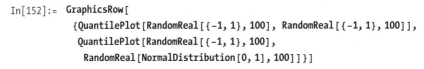

```
In[153]:=  PairwiseScatterPlot[Transpose[{Rescale[
              FinancialData["^DJI", {{2006, 1, 1}, {2006, 12, 31}}]][[All, 2]]],
          Rescale[FinancialData["^DJI", {{2007, 1, 1}, {2007, 12, 31}}]][[All, 2]]],
          Drop[Rescale[FinancialData["^DJI", {{2008, 1, 1}, {2008, 12, 31}}]][[
              All, 2]]], 2]}], DataLabels → {"2006", "2007", "2008"}]
```

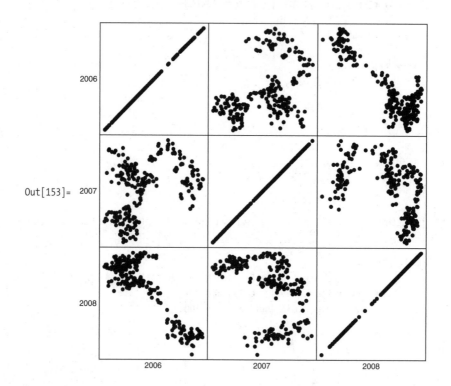

Out[153]=

See Also

The tutorial *StatisticalPlots/tutorial/StatisticalPlots* in the documentation provides many examples for customizing these plots to your needs.

12.15 Quasi-Random Number Generation

Problem

You need to generate random numbers, but you want to avoid the inevitable clustering that occurs using pseudorandom generators. This type of generator is sometimes called quasirandom.

Solution

Notice the clumping in this randomly generated list plot of 500 points.

```
In[154]:= With[{N = 500},
            ListPlot[ RandomReal[{0, 1}, {N, 2}],
              PlotStyle → Black, Frame → True, AspectRatio → 1, ImageSize → Small]]
```

Out[154]=

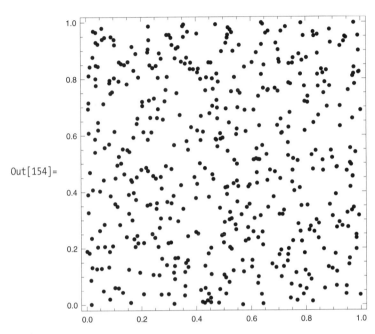

The van der Corput sequence takes the digits of an integer in a given base b, and then reflects them about the decimal point. This maps the numbers from 1 to n into a set of numbers [0,1] in an even distribution, provided n is one less than a power of the base.

```
In[155]:= corput[n_, b_] :=
            IntegerDigits[n, b].(b ^ Range[-Floor[Log[b, n] + 1], -1]);
          SetAttributes[corput, Listable]
```

The Halton sequence shows that a good way to distribute the values in *n* dimensions is to use the first *n* primes as the bases used with van der Corput.

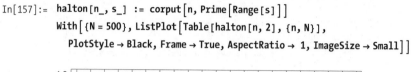

```
In[157]:= halton[n_, s_] := corput[n, Prime[Range[s]]]
          With[{N = 500}, ListPlot[Table[halton[n, 2], {n, N}],
             PlotStyle → Black, Frame → True, AspectRatio → 1, ImageSize → Small]]
```

Out[158]=

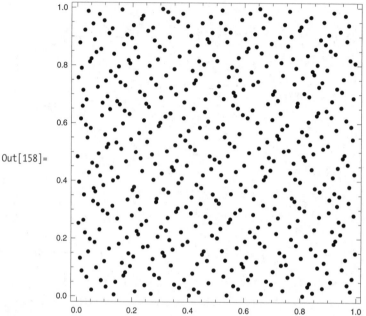

As you can see, this gives far less clumpy distribution of points than RandomReal gives.

Discussion

These quasirandom numbers are often used in simulations and Monte Carlo methods. One problem with these sequences is that they always give you the same set of numbers. One possibility is to perturb each number by a small random epsilon (e). This more or less preserves the even distribution provided the random perturbation is small.

```
In[159]:= halton[n_, s_, e_] :=
            Clip[corput[n, Prime[Range[s]]] + RandomReal[{-e, e}], {0, 1}]

In[160]:= With[{N = 500},
            GraphicsRow[{
              ListPlot[Table[halton[n, 2, 0.01], {n, N}],
                PlotStyle → Black, Frame → True, AspectRatio → 1, ImageSize → Small],
              ListPlot[Table[Halton[n, 2, 0.05], {n, N}],
                PlotStyle → Black, Frame → True, AspectRatio → 1, ImageSize → Small]}]]
```

Out[160]=

See Also

An excellent reference is this *Quasi-Monte Carlo Simulation* website found at *http://bit.ly/2vdGQs*.

Interesting papers and Mathematica notebooks that explore quasirandomness can be found at James Propp's University of Massachusetts Lowell website (*http://bit.ly/7kC32*).

12.16 Creating Stochastic Simulations

Problem

You want to create a simulation as a means of developing a better understanding of the long-term behavior of a system governed by randomness.

Solution

One of the most well-known types of stochastic processes is the random walk. A random walk can occur in one-, two-, three-, or even higher dimensional space, but it is easiest to visualize in one or two dimensions. Here I show a random walk on a 2D lattice. A particle (or drunkard, if you prefer) starts at the origin {0,0} and can take a step east {0,1}, west {0,-1}, north {1,0} or south {-1,0}.

```
In[161]:= latticeWalk2D[n_] := Module[{start = {0, 0},
              east = {1, 0}, west = {-1, 0}, north = {0, 1}, south = {0, -1}},
            NestList[# + RandomChoice[{east, west, north, south}] &, start, n]]
```

The walk is generated by specifying a number of steps and can be visualized using ListLinePlot or using arrows for each step, as I show in Out[163] below. Here I use SeedRandom only to make sure I always get the same walk no matter how many times this notebook is evaluated before going to press!

```
In[162]:= SeedRandom[1004]; walk = latticeWalk2D[50]
Out[162]= {{0, 0}, {-1, 0}, {0, 0}, {0, 1}, {0, 0}, {0, 1}, {-1, 1}, {-1, 2},
           {0, 2}, {-1, 2}, {-1, 1}, {-2, 1}, {-1, 1}, {-1, 2}, {0, 2}, {0, 1},
           {0, 2}, {-1, 2}, {-1, 1}, {-1, 0}, {-1, 1}, {-2, 1}, {-3, 1}, {-4, 1},
           {-4, 2}, {-5, 2}, {-5, 3}, {-6, 3}, {-6, 2}, {-5, 2}, {-6, 2}, {-6, 1},
           {-5, 1}, {-5, 0}, {-5, -1}, {-5, -2}, {-6, -2}, {-7, -2}, {-8, -2},
           {-9, -2}, {-10, -2}, {-10, -3}, {-10, -4}, {-11, -4}, {-10, -4},
           {-11, -4}, {-10, -4}, {-11, -4}, {-12, -4}, {-11, -4}, {-10, -4}}
```

```
In[163]:= Graphics[{Arrowheads[Small], Arrow /@ Partition[walk, 2, 1],
            PointSize[0.03], Green, Point[First[walk]], Red,
            Point[Last[walk]]}, ImageSize → All, Axes → True]
```

Out[163]=

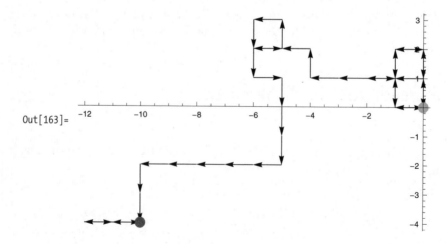

Discussion

Some simulations contain constraints on what can happen at each step. For example, if you wanted a walk for which a back-step is disallowed, you could remember the previous step and remove its inverse from the population on the generation.

```
In[164]:= latticeWalk2DNoBackStep[n_] :=
            Module[{start = {0, 0}, east = {1, 0}, west = {-1, 0},
              north = {0, 1}, south = {0, -1}, steps, last},
              steps = {east, west, north, south};
              (*Initialize last to a step not in the
                population so not to remove anything the first time.*)
              last = {1, 1};
              (*At each step the inverse (-last)
                is removed from possible steps using Complement.*)
              NestList[# + (last = RandomChoice[Complement[steps, {-last}]]) &,
                start, n]]
```

```
In[165]:= SeedRandom[778]; walk = latticeWalk2DNoBackStep[25]
Out[165]= {{0, 0}, {1, 0}, {2, 0}, {2, -1}, {3, -1}, {4, -1}, {5, -1}, {5, -2},
          {6, -2}, {6, -1}, {6, 0}, {5, 0}, {4, 0}, {4, 1}, {5, 1}, {5, 2}, {6, 2},
          {7, 2}, {7, 1}, {7, 0}, {8, 0}, {9, 0}, {9, 1}, {8, 1}, {8, 2}, {8, 3}}
```

```
In[166]:= Graphics[{Arrowheads[Small], Arrow /@ Partition[walk, 2, 1],
            PointSize[0.02], Green, Point[First[walk]], Red,
            Point[Last[walk]]}, ImageSize → Medium, Axes → True]
```

Out[166]=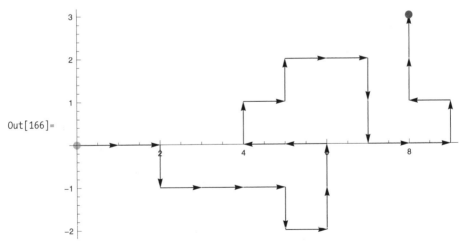

Given a simulation, you will usually want to understand its behavior over many runs. One obvious metric is the distance from the origin. You might postulate, for example, that the average distance from the origin for latticeWalk2D will be less than `latticeWalk2DNoBackStep`. By running the simulation 500 times for each case and computing the mean, median, and other statistics, you can be more confident this intuition is correct. You can also see that the advantage seems to be only about two steps.

```
In[167]:= Module[{distL2D, distL2DNoBack, walkDistance,
            statFuncs = {Mean, Median, Max, Min, Variance, StandardDeviation}},
          walkDistance[walk_] := ManhattanDistance[First[walk], Last[walk]];
          distL2D = Table[walkDistance[latticeWalk2D[25]], {500}];
          distL2DNoBack =
           Table[walkDistance[latticeWalk2DNoBackStep[25]], {500}];
          TableForm[{Through[statFuncs[distL2D]],
            Through[statFuncs[distL2DNoBack]]} // N, TableHeadings →
           {{"Unconstrained", "No Back Step"}, ToString /@ statFuncs}]]
```
Out[167]//TableForm=

	Mean	Median	Max	Min	Variance	StandardDeviation
Unconstrained	5.616	5.	15.	1.	8.69393	2.94855
No Back Step	7.78	7.	21.	1.	13.8754	3.72496

Simulation is also powerful as a tool for persuading someone of a truth that seems to defy intuition. A famous example is the Monty Hall problem. This problem is named after a U.S. game show called "Let's Make a Deal," which was popular in the 1960s and '70s and hosted by Monty Hall. A well-known statement of the problem was published in *Parade* magazine ("Ask Marilyn," Sept. 1990, 16):

> Suppose you're on a game show, and you're given the choice of three doors: Behind one door is a car; behind the others, goats. You pick a door, say No. 1, and the host, who knows what's behind the doors, opens another door, say No. 3, which has a goat. He then says to you, "Do you want to pick door No. 2?" Is it to your advantage to switch your choice?

For many people, the intuitive answer is that there is no advantage in switching because there is a 50/50 chance you have the car either way you go. There even seems to be a bias for not switching, based on the platitude "go with your first instincts." However, if you analyze the problem correctly (see the following analysis) there is a 2/3 probability of getting the car if you switch. But the analysis is subtle and apparently fails to convince even some very intelligent people, so perhaps a simulation is helpful. An advantage of creating the simulation is that it makes it clear just what you mean by this problem. Specifically, we are talking about the best decision over many trials for a problem where the initial choice of door is random, the placement of the car is random, and Monty always shows the door that contains a goat. In this simulation, we call sticking with your first choice `strategy1` and switching to the remaining door `strategy2`. The simulation is purposefully without any cute functional programming tricks so it is clear that at each step we are accurately following the rules of the game.

```
In[168]:=  (*randomPick is similar to RandomChoice except we want
             the position of the choice rather than the choice itself.*)
           randomPick[choices_List] :=
           Module[{}, RandomInteger[{1, Length[choices]}]]
           (*simulateStrat1VSStrat2 computes the winnings over a number
           of trials for strategy1 (stick) and strategy2 (switch).*)
           simulateStrat1VSStrat2[trials_Integer] :=
           Module[{GOAT = 0, CAR = 1, doors, firstPick, secondPick,
             winnings1 = 0, winnings2 = 0, doorsTemp, makePrizes},
             (*There are 3 possible initial game configurations. These
             can be generated using Permutations.*)
             SeedRandom[];
             Do[
               (*Randomly pick one of the
                three possible initial game configurations.*)
               doors = RandomSample[{GOAT, GOAT, CAR}];
               (*Contestant picks a door at random. Recall this
                is the position of the prize, not the prize itself.*)
               firstPick = randomPick[doors];
               (*Winnings of contestant who keeps first pick always*)
               winnings1 += doors[[firstPick]];
               (*Delete first pick from choices.*)
               doorsTemp = Drop[doors, {firstPick}];
               (*Delete goat from remaining; this is where Monty shows the goat.
                  Here I use position to find a goat and, since there could be two,
                  I arbitrarily remove the first.*)
               doorsTemp = Drop[doorsTemp, Position[doorsTemp, GOAT][[1]]];
               (*Contestant following second
                strategy always switches to remaining prize.*)
               secondPick = doorsTemp[[1]];
               (*Winnings of contestant who switches*)
               winnings2 += secondPick,
               {trials}];
             {winnings1, winnings2}]
```

You can now simulate any number of games and compare the accumulated winnings over that many games. Here I show the results where the number of games varies from 10 to 100,000 in increments of powers of 10. Clearly strategy2, always switching, is the way to play the Monty Hall game.

```
In[170]:= Table[simulateStrat1VSStrat2[10^i], {i, 1, 5}] // TableForm
Out[170]//TableForm=
        4      6
        34     66
        304    696
        3345   6655
        33321  66679
```

The Monty Hall game analysis that leads to the correct conclusion is as follows: Consider the probability of *not* picking the car at the start of the game. Since there are 2 goats and 1 car, the probability of not picking a car is 2/3. Now consider what happens when Monty shows you a goat. In effect he tells you that IF you did not pick a car initially, THEN there is definitely a car behind the remaining door. We agreed that the probability of not having picked the car initially was 2/3, so now the probability of the car being behind the remaining door must be 2/3. The simulation we're given shows this to be the case.

See Also

Computer Simulations with Mathematica: Explorations in Complex Physical and Biological by Richard J. Gaylord and Paul R. Wellin (Springer-Verlag TELOS) demonstrates a variety of simple simulations, but some of the examples need to be updated to Mathematica 6 and 7.

Chapter 14, "Financial Engineering," contains an example of Monte Carlo simulation that is a very popular technique in finance and the physical sciences.

The Wolfram Demonstration Project (*http://bit.ly/40hsJD*) contains many small simulation problems that exploit Mathematica's dynamic capabilities.

CHAPTER 13

Science and Engineering

Mmm—but it's poetry in motion
And when she turned her eyes to me
As deep as any ocean
As sweet as any harmony
Mmm—but she blinded me with science
And failed me in geometry

When she's dancing next to me
"Blinding me with science—science!"
"Science!"
I can hear machinery
"Blinding me with science—science!"
"Science!"

Thomas Dolby, "She Blinded Me With Science"

13.0 Introduction

Scientists and engineers make up a large part of the Mathematica user base, and it is hard to think of any scientific or engineering practitioner, no matter how specialized, who could not benefit from Mathematica. I am neither a scientist nor an engineer by profession, but just fiddling around with Mathematica has given me insights into scientific and engineering ideas that otherwise would have taken many years of study.

The goals of this chapter are threefold. First, I want to illustrate techniques for organizing solutions to problems. Many science and engineering problems require numerous variables, and organization becomes paramount. There is not one correct way to organize complex solutions, but I provide two different approaches in Recipes 13.6 and 13.11. The second goal is to take some of the theoretical recipes covered in earlier chapters and apply them to real-world problems. I often see posts on Mathematica's primary mailing list questioning the usefulness of function or pattern-based programming on real-world problems. Other posters express a wish to use these techniques but can't get themselves on the right track. This chapter contains recipes to which most scientists and engineers can relate, and all use a mixture of functional and pattern-based ideas. An auxiliary goal is to take some of the functions introduced in Chapter 11 and make each the focus of a recipe. The third goal of the chapter is to introduce some special features of Mathematica that we did not have occasion to discuss in earlier recipes.

One important feature introduced in Mathematica 6 that gained momentum in version 7 is curated data sources. These high-quality data sources alone are worth the cost of admission to Mathematica's user base. Recipes 13.1 through 13.4 discuss some sources pertinent to the sciences. Chapter 14 includes recipes related to financial data sources. All these sources have a uniform, self-describing structure. You can query any data source for the kinds of data it provides using syntax `DataSource["Properties"]`. This will give you a list of properties. Each property describes an important subset of the data held by the source. You use the properties along with keys to retrieve particular values. For example, `ElementData[1, "AtomicWeight"]` gives 1.00794, the atomic weight of hydrogen. Once you master the data source concept, you will quickly be able to leverage new data sources as they become available.

Recipe 13.5 applies the discrete calculus function `RSolve` from Recipe 11.10 to solve a standard predator-prey problem. Here I also demonstrate how Mathematica's interactive features can be used to explore the solution space and gain insight into the dynamics of the problem.

In Recipe 13.6, I solve a relatively straightforward problem in rigid body dynamics. The primary purpose of this recipe is to illustrate one way you might organize a problem with many objects and many parameters per object. This recipe highlights Mathematica's flexible ways of creating names of things, an ability you should exploit when modeling complex problems. Recipe 13.11 uses the topic of finite element method (FEM) to illustrate an alternate way to organize a problem that uses a lot of data and a variety of related functions. The interface developed here follows a trend that is becoming more popular in new Mathematica features (e.g., `LinearModelFit`).

Recipes 13.7 through 13.10 focus on applied differential equations. Here I solve some problems symbolically using `DSolve` and some problems numerically using `NDSolve`. These recipes show how to set up initial and boundary conditions, how to leverage Fourier series in obtaining solutions, and how to visualize solutions.

13.1 Working with Element Data

Problem

You want to perform computations that take as input information about the chemical elements. You may also want to create visual displays of this information for reference or classroom use.

Solution

You can list the names of all the elements using `ElementData[]` or the name of the *n*th element using `ElementData[n]`.

```
In[1]:= ElementData[]
Out[1]= {Hydrogen, Helium, Lithium, Beryllium, Boron, Carbon, Nitrogen, Oxygen,
          Fluorine, Neon, Sodium, Magnesium, Aluminum, Silicon, Phosphorus, Sulfur,
          Chlorine, Argon, Potassium, Calcium, Scandium, Titanium, Vanadium,
          Chromium, Manganese, Iron, Cobalt, Nickel, Copper, Zinc, Gallium,
          Germanium, Arsenic, Selenium, Bromine, Krypton, Rubidium, Strontium,
          Yttrium, Zirconium, Niobium, Molybdenum, Technetium, Ruthenium, Rhodium,
          Palladium, Silver, Cadmium, Indium, Tin, Antimony, Tellurium, Iodine,
          Xenon, Cesium, Barium, Lanthanum, Cerium, Praseodymium, Neodymium,
          Promethium, Samarium, Europium, Gadolinium, Terbium, Dysprosium,
          Holmium, Erbium, Thulium, Ytterbium, Lutetium, Hafnium, Tantalum,
          Tungsten, Rhenium, Osmium, Iridium, Platinum, Gold, Mercury, Thallium,
          Lead, Bismuth, Polonium, Astatine, Radon, Francium, Radium, Actinium,
          Thorium, Protactinium, Uranium, Neptunium, Plutonium, Americium,
          Curium, Berkelium, Californium, Einsteinium, Fermium, Mendelevium,
          Nobelium, Lawrencium, Rutherfordium, Dubnium, Seaborgium, Bohrium,
          Hassium, Meitnerium, Darmstadtium, Roentgenium, Ununbium, Ununtrium,
          Ununquadium, Ununpentium, Ununhexium, Ununseptium, Ununoctium}

In[2]:= ElementData[1]
Out[2]= Hydrogen
```

Mathematica will return properties of an element if given its number and the name of the property.

```
In[3]:= Row[{ElementData[1], ElementData[1, "AtomicNumber"],
          ElementData[1, "AtomicWeight"], ElementData[1, "Phase"]}, "\t"]
Out[3]= Hydrogen    1    1.00794    Gas
```

Discussion

You can see from the list of all properties that Mathematica has a comprehensive database of elemental data. Be aware that CommonCompoundNames will pull in a lot of data if you use it with a common element like hydrogen.

```
In[4]:=  Partition[ElementData["Properties"], 3, 3, 1, ""] // TableForm
Out[4]//TableForm=
```

Abbreviation	AbsoluteBoilingPoint	AbsoluteMeltingPoint
AdiabaticIndex	AllotropeNames	AllotropicMultiplicities
AlternateNames	AlternateStandardNames	AtomicNumber
AtomicRadius	AtomicWeight	Block
BoilingPoint	BrinellHardness	BulkModulus
CASNumber	Color	CommonCompoundNames
CovalentRadius	CriticalPressure	CriticalTemperature
CrustAbundance	CrystalStructure	CuriePoint
DecayMode	Density	DiscoveryCountries
DiscoveryYear	ElectricalConductivity	ElectricalType
ElectronAffinity	ElectronConfiguration	ElectronConfigurationString
Electronegativity	ElectronShellConfiguration	FusionHeat
GasAtomicMultiplicities	Group	HalfLife
HumanAbundance	IconColor	IonizationEnergies
IsotopeAbundances	KnownIsotopes	LatticeAngles
LatticeConstants	Lifetime	LiquidDensity
MagneticType	MassMagneticSusceptibility	MeltingPoint
Memberships	MeteoriteAbundance	MohsHardness
MolarMagneticSusceptibility	MolarVolume	Name
NeelPoint	NeutronCrossSection	NeutronMassAbsorption
OceanAbundance	Period	Phase
PoissonRatio	QuantumNumbers	Radioactive
RefractiveIndex	Resistivity	ShearModulus
SolarAbundance	SoundSpeed	SpaceGroupName
SpaceGroupNumber	SpecificHeat	StableIsotopes
StandardName	SuperconductingPoint	ThermalConductivity
ThermalExpansion	UniverseAbundance	Valence
VanDerWaalsRadius	VaporizationHeat	VickersHardness
VolumeMagneticSusceptibility	YoungModulus	

The most obvious application of ElementData is to create a periodic table. The ElementData documentation shows code for a simple table. Here I show a more ambitious one, complete with Tooltip.

```
In[5]:= makeElemDetail[a_] :=
        Module[{abr, name, atomicWeight, density, melting, boiling, color, phase},
          {abr, name, atomicWeight, density, melting, boiling, color, phase} = Table[
            ElementData[a, p], {p, {"Abbreviation", "StandardName", "AtomicWeight",
              "Density", "MeltingPoint", "BoilingPoint", "Color", "Phase"}}]];
          Grid[{{name, SpanFromLeft, a}, {abr, atomicWeight, "amu"},
            {"Density", density, "Kg/m³"}, {"Melting Pt", melting, "C"},
            {"Boiling Pt.", boiling, "C"}, {"Phase", color, phase}}, Frame → All,
           Alignment → {{Left, Right, Right}, {Center, Center, Center}}]
        ]

      makeElem[a_, size_] :=
        Module[{abr, name, atomicWeight}, abr = ElementData[a, "Abbreviation"];
          atomicWeight = ElementData[a, "AtomicWeight"];
          Graphics[{Text[Style[ToString[a], 9, Bold,
              FontFamily -> "Helvetica", TextAlignment → Center], {0, 20}],
            Text[Style[abr, 20, FontWeight → "Bold", FontFamily -> "Helvetica"],
              {0, 0}], Text[Style[ToString[atomicWeight], 8,
              FontFamily -> "Helvetica", TextAlignment → Center], {0, -20}]},
           ImageSize → {size, size}]]

      makePeriodicTable[w_, h_] :=
        Module[{elemData, frame, background, re1 = 57, re2 = 71, re3 = 89,
          re4 = 103, gsz = 42}, elemData = Table[ElementData[e, p],
           {e, 1, 118}, {p, {"AtomicNumber", "Period", "Group"}}];
          frame = {None, None, Cases[elemData,
             {a_Integer, p_, g_Integer} :> ({p, g} → True)]};
          background = {None, None, Cases[elemData, {a_Integer, p_, g_Integer} :>
               ({p, g} → ElementData[a, "IconColor"])]};
          Column[{
            GraphicsGrid[Normal[SparseArray[
                Cases[elemData, {a_Integer, p_, g_Integer} :> ({p, g} → a)]]] /.
              {a_Integer /; a > 0 :> Tooltip[makeElem[a, gsz], makeElemDetail[a]],
                0 → Graphics[{}]}, Frame → frame, Background -> background,
             ImageSize → {w, h}],
            GraphicsGrid[{Table[Tooltip[makeElem[a, gsz], makeElemDetail[a]],
               {a, re1, re2}], Table[makeElem[a, gsz], {a, re3, re4}]},
             ImageSize → {w - 100, 100}, Background → {None, None,
               Flatten[Table[{{1, a - re1 + 1} -> ElementData[a, "IconColor"],
                  {2, a - re1 + 1} -> ElementData[a + re3 - re1, "IconColor"]},
                 {a, re1, re2}]]}], Alignment → {Center, Automatic}]]
```

```
In[8]:= makePeriodicTable[650, 300]
```

Out[8]=

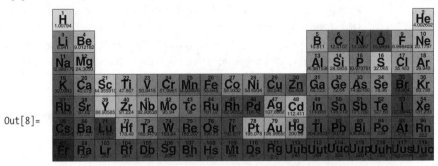

13.2 Working with Chemical Data

Problem

You want to perform computations that take as input information about the chemical compounds. You may also want to create visual displays of this information for reference or classroom use.

Solution

ChemicalData is a curated data source. You can request chemical information by common names, registry numbers, IUPAC-like names, or structure strings.

```
In[9]:= ChemicalData["Water"]
```

Out[9]=   H   H
            \   /
             O

```
In[10]:= ChemicalData["CO2", "IUPACName"]
Out[10]= carbon dioxide
```

```
In[11]:= ChemicalData["CID5234", "Name"]
Out[11]= {sodium chloride, sodium chloride-35 Cl}
```

```
In[12]:= ChemicalData["Glucose", "CompoundFormulaDisplay"]
Out[12]= {C_6H_{12}O_6, C_6H_{12}O_6, C_6H_{12}O_6, C_6H_{12}O_6}
```

In[13]:= `GraphicsRow[ChemicalData["Glucose", "MoleculePlot"], ImageSize → Large]`

Out[13]=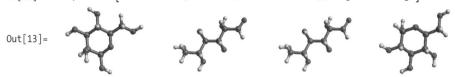

Discussion

The list of properties of chemical compounds is quite impressive. The table below lists a random subset of the full list of 101 properties.

In[14]:= `Partition[Sort[RandomSample[ChemicalData["Properties"], 30]], 3] //`
         `TableForm`

Out[14]//TableForm=

AcidityConstant	BoilingPoint	CHStructureDiagram
CIDNumber	CompoundFormulaDisplay	CriticalPressure
CriticalTemperature	FlashPointFahrenheit	FormattedName
HildebrandSolubility	IUPACName	MDLNumber
MeltingPoint	NFPAHazards	NFPAHealthRating
NFPALabel	NonStandardIsotopeCount	NonStandardIsotopeNumbers
PartitionCoefficient	Phase	Resistivity
RotatableBondCount	SideChainAcidityConstant	SpaceFillingMoleculePlot
StructureDiagram	TautomerCount	TopologicalPolarSurfaceArea
VaporPressureTorr	VertexTypes	Viscosity

At the time of this writing, Mathematica has curated data on over 34,300 compounds, subdivided into 67 classes.

In[15]:= `Length[ChemicalData[]]`
Out[15]= 34336

In[16]:= `ChemicalData["Classes"]`
Out[16]= {AcidAnhydrides, AcidHalides, Acids, Alcohols, Aldehydes, Alkanes,
         Alkenes, Alkynes, Alloys, Amides, Amines, AminoAcidDerivatives,
         AminoAcids, Arenes, Aromatic, Bases, Brominated, Carbohydrates,
         CarboxylicAcids, Catalysts, Cations, Ceramics, Chiral, Chlorinated,
         Dendrimers, Esters, Ethers, Fluorinated, Furans, Gases, Halogenated,
         HeavyMolecules, Heterocyclic, Hydrides, Hydrocarbons, Imidazoles,
         Indoles, Inorganic, Iodinated, IonicLiquids, Ketones, Ligands,
         Lipids, Liquids, MetalCarbonyls, Monomers, Nanomaterials, Nitriles,
         Organic, Organometallic, Oxides, Phenols, Piperazines, Piperidines,
         Polymers, Pyrazoles, Pyridines, Pyrimidines, Quinolines, Salts, Solids,
         Solvents, Sulfides, SyntheticElements, Thiazoles, Thiols, Thiophenes}

There are six kinds of structural diagrams that can be used to visualize these compounds. Here, for example, are representations for what may be one of your favorites, for better or worse—caffeine.

```
In[17]:= GraphicsGrid[Partition[
            Table[ChemicalData["Caffeine", p], {p, {"CHColorStructureDiagram",
            "CHStructureDiagram", "ColorStructureDiagram", "StructureDiagram",
                "MoleculePlot", "SpaceFillingMoleculePlot"}}], 3], ImageSize → Large]
```

Out[17]=

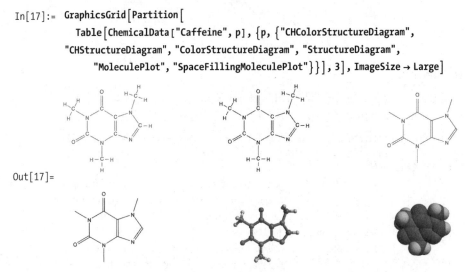

You can use the data to analyze relationships between properties. Here I show a plot of inverse vapor pressure to boiling point for all liquids with a Tooltip around each point so outliers are easy to identify. Cases is used to filter out any MissingData entries.

```
In[18]:=
        ListLogLogPlot[Cases[Table[{ChemicalData[c, "VaporPressure"],
            ChemicalData[c, "BoilingPoint"], c}, {c, ChemicalData["Liquids"]}],
            {vp_Real, bp_Real, c_String} :→ Tooltip[{1 / vp, bp}, c]]]
```

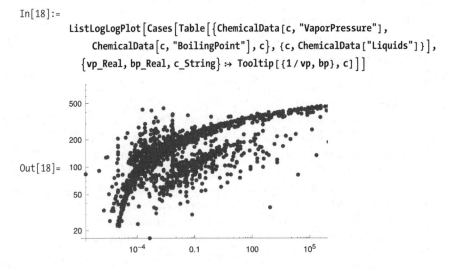

Out[18]=

13.3 Working with Particle Data

Problem

You want to perform computations that take as input information about the elementary particles. You may also want to create visual displays of this information for reference or classroom use.

Solution

```
In[19]:=  ParticleData["Classes"]

Out[19]=  {Baryon, BBBarMeson, Boson, BottomBaryon, BottomMeson,
           CCBarMeson, CharmedBaryon, CharmedMeson, Fermion, GaugeBoson,
           Hadron, Lepton, LongLived, Meson, Neutrino, Pentaquark, Quark,
           Stable, StrangeBaryon, StrangeCharmedBaryon, StrangeCharmedMeson,
           StrangeMeson, UnflavoredBaryon, UnflavoredMeson}
```

It is easy to create functions that generate tables of particle information. The function particleTable accepts a list of one or more class memberships (e.g., Baryon, LongLived, and others from ParticleData["Classes"]) and a list of properties to use as columns. The helper function particleData reformats "QuarkContent" into a more concise representation. You will often want to filter out entries that are missing since there is only partial data available for exotic particles.

```
In[20]:=  particleData[p_, "QuarkContent"] :=
            Flatten[ ParticleData[p, "QuarkContent"] /.
              q_String :> ParticleData[q, "Symbol"]]
          particleData[p_, prop_] := ParticleData[p, prop]
          particleTable[memberships_List, properties_List] := Module[{},
          Grid[Prepend[
              Table[particleData[particle, #] & /@ properties,
                {particle, Select[ParticleData[],
                  (Intersection[ParticleData[#, "Memberships"], memberships] ==
                    memberships ) &]}], properties] /.
              {Missing["Unknown"] -> "?", Missing["NotAvailable"] -> "N/A"},
            Frame -> All,
            ItemStyle ->
            {Automatic, Automatic, {{{1, 1}, {1, Length[properties]}} -> Bold}}]
          ]
```

Create a table of long-lived baryons. A *baryon* is a particle made of three quarks, and *long-lived* refers to particles whose lifetime is greater than 10^{-20} seconds.

In[23]:= `particleTable[{"Baryon", "LongLived"}, {"StandardName",`
`    "Symbol", "Mass", "Charge", "Lifetime", "Isospin", "QuarkContent"}]`

Out[23]=

StandardName	Symbol	Mass	Charge	Lifetime	Isospin	QuarkContent
Lambda	Λ	1115.683	0	2.632×10^{-10}	0	$\{s, d, u\}$
LambdaBar	$\overline{\Lambda}$	1115.683	0	2.632×10^{-10}	0	$\{\overline{s}, \overline{d}, \overline{u}\}$
Neutron	n	939.56536	0	885.6	$\frac{1}{2}$	$\{d, d, u\}$
NeutronBar	$\overline{n}$	939.56536	0	885.6	$\frac{1}{2}$	$\{\overline{d}, \overline{d}, \overline{u}\}$
Omega	Ω	1672.45	-1	8.21×10^{-11}	0	$\{s, s, s\}$
OmegaBar	$\overline{\Omega}$	1672.45	1	8.21×10^{-11}	0	$\{\overline{s}, \overline{s}, \overline{s}\}$
Proton	p	938.27203	1	∞	$\frac{1}{2}$	$\{d, u, u\}$
ProtonBar	$\overline{p}$	938.27203	-1	∞	$\frac{1}{2}$	$\{\overline{d}, \overline{u}, \overline{u}\}$
SigmaBarMinus	$\overline{\Sigma}^-$	1189.37	-1	8.018×10^{-11}	1	$\{\overline{s}, \overline{u}, \overline{u}\}$
SigmaBarPlus	$\overline{\Sigma}^+$	1197.449	1	1.48×10^{-10}	1	$\{\overline{s}, \overline{d}, \overline{d}\}$
SigmaBarZero	$\overline{\Sigma}^0$	1192.642	0	7.4×10^{-20}	1	$\{\overline{s}, \overline{d}, \overline{u}\}$
SigmaMinus	Σ^-	1197.449	-1	1.48×10^{-10}	1	$\{s, d, d\}$
SigmaPlus	Σ^+	1189.37	1	8.018×10^{-11}	1	$\{s, u, u\}$
SigmaZero	Σ^0	1192.642	0	7.4×10^{-20}	1	$\{s, d, u\}$
XiBarPlus	$\overline{\Xi}^+$	1321.31	1	1.64×10^{-10}	$\frac{1}{2}$	$\{\overline{s}, \overline{s}, \overline{d}\}$
XiBarZero	$\overline{\Xi}^0$	1314.83	0	2.90×10^{-10}	$\frac{1}{2}$	$\{\overline{s}, \overline{s}, \overline{u}\}$
XiMinus	Ξ^-	1321.31	-1	1.64×10^{-10}	$\frac{1}{2}$	$\{s, s, d\}$
XiZero	Ξ^0	1314.83	0	2.90×10^{-10}	$\frac{1}{2}$	$\{s, s, u\}$
{LambdaB, 0}	Λ_b	5624.	0	1.23×10^{-12}	0	$\{b, d, u\}$
{LambdaBBar, 0}	$\overline{\Lambda}_b$	5624.	0	1.23×10^{-12}	0	$\{\overline{b}, \overline{d}, \overline{u}\}$
{LambdaC, 1}	Λ_c	2286.46	1	2.0×10^{-13}	0	$\{c, d, u\}$
{LambdaCBar, -1}	$\overline{\Lambda}_c$	2286.46	-1	2.0×10^{-13}	0	$\{\overline{c}, \overline{d}, \overline{u}\}$
{OmegaC, 0}	Ω_c	2697.5	0	6.9×10^{-14}	0	$\{c, s, s\}$
{OmegaCBar, 0}	$\overline{\Omega}_c$	2697.5	0	6.9×10^{-14}	0	$\{\overline{c}, \overline{s}, \overline{s}\}$
{XiC, 0}	Ξ_c^0	2471.	0	1.1×10^{-13}	$\frac{1}{2}$	$\{c, s, d\}$
{XiC, 1}	Ξ_c^+	2467.9	1	4.42×10^{-13}	$\frac{1}{2}$	$\{c, s, u\}$
{XiCBar, -1}	$\overline{\Xi}_c^-$	2467.9	-1	4.42×10^{-13}	$\frac{1}{2}$	$\{\overline{c}, \overline{s}, \overline{u}\}$
{XiCBar, 0}	$\overline{\Xi}_c^0$	2471.	0	1.1×10^{-13}	$\frac{1}{2}$	$\{\overline{c}, \overline{s}, \overline{d}\}$
{XiCC, 1}	Ξ_{cc}	3518.9	1	3.3000×10^{-14}	?	$\{c, c, d\}$
{XiCCBar, -1}	$\overline{\Xi}_{cc}$	3518.9	-1	3.3000×10^{-14}	?	$\{\overline{c}, \overline{c}, \overline{d}\}$

Discussion

The list of properties available in particle data are as follows:

```
In[24]:= Transpose[Partition[ParticleData["Properties"], 9, 9, 1, ""]] // TableForm
Out[24]//TableForm=
        Antiparticle  Excitations     Isospin               PDGNumber
        BaryonNumber  FullDecayModes  IsospinMultiplet      QuarkContent
        Bottomness    FullSymbol      IsospinProjection     Spin
        Charge        GenericFullSymbol LeptonNumber        Strangeness
        ChargeStates  GenericSymbol   Lifetime              Symbol
        Charm         GFactor         Mass                  Topness
        CParity       GParity         MeanSquareChargeRadius UnobservedDecayModes
        DecayModes    HalfLife        Memberships           Width
        DecayType     Hypercharge     Parity
```

```
In[25]:= ParticleData["Classes"]
Out[25]= {Baryon, BBBarMeson, Boson, BottomBaryon, BottomMeson,
        CCBarMeson, CharmedBaryon, CharmedMeson, Fermion, GaugeBoson,
        Hadron, Lepton, LongLived, Meson, Neutrino, Pentaquark, Quark,
        Stable, StrangeBaryon, StrangeCharmedBaryon, StrangeCharmedMeson,
        StrangeMeson, UnflavoredBaryon, UnflavoredMeson}
```

A scatter plot of mass versus spin versus charge shows large voids where there are no known particles (or where the values are unknown).

```
In[26]:= ListPointPlot3D[
        Cases[Sort[{ParticleData[#, "Mass"], ParticleData[#, "Spin"],
            ParticleData[#, "Charge"]} & /@ ParticleData["Hadron"]],
        {_?NumberQ, _?NumberQ, _?NumberQ}], AxesLabel →
        {"mass", "spin", "charge"}]
```

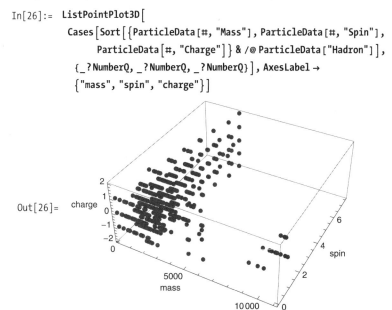

Out[26]=

DecayModes and FullDecayModes list the ways the particle can decay; FullDecayModes also lists those predicted by theory but not observed in detectors. The number (or interval) display with the decay mode is the branch ratio.

```
In[27]:= Flatten[Table[p → #& /@ ParticleData[p, "DecayModes"],
            {p, {"DeltaMinus", "DeltaZero", "DeltaPlus", "Lambda"}}], 1] // TableForm
Out[27]//TableForm=
            DeltaMinus → {{Neutron, PiMinus}, 1.00}
            DeltaZero → {{Neutron, Photon}, Interval[{0.0051, 0.008}]}
            DeltaPlus → {{Proton, Photon}, Interval[{0.0051, 0.008}]}
            Lambda → {{Proton, PiMinus}, 0.639}
            Lambda → {{Neutron, PiZero}, 0.358}
            Lambda → {{Neutron, Photon}, 0.00175}
            Lambda → {{Proton, PiMinus, Photon}, 0.00084}
            Lambda → {{Proton, Electron, ElectronNeutrinoBar}, 0.000832}
            Lambda → {{Proton, Muon, MuonNeutrinoBar}, 0.000157}
```

13.4 Working with Genetic Data and Protein Data

Problem

You want to use Mathematica's pattern matching and computational capabilities to develop bioinformatics applications. GenomeData and ProteinData provide the raw materials for this application.

Solution

Get the first 100 nucleobases (or, simply, bases) on the male X chromosome.

```
In[28]:= GenomeData[{"ChromosomeX", {1, 100}}]
Out[28]= CTAACCCTAACCCTAACCCTAACCCTAACCCTAACCCTCTGAAAGTGGACCTATCAGCAGGATGTGGGTGGGAG·
            CAGATTAGAGAATAAAAGCAGACTGC
```

Get the first 10 proteins known to Mathematica and show number of amino acids in its sequence.

```
In[29]:= {#, ProteinData[#, "SequenceLength"]} & /@
           Take[ProteinData[], 10] // TableForm
Out[29]//TableForm=
         A1BG      495
         A2M       1474
         NAT1      290
         NAT2      290
         SERPINA3  423
         AADAC     399
         AAMP      434
         AANAT     207
         AARS      968
         ABAT      500
```

Find five other chromosomes that have sequences that match the first 50 bases of chromosome-1 in the human genome. Strands of the chromosome are indicated as 1 or -1.

```
In[30]:= GenomeLookup[GenomeData[{"Chromosome1", {1, 50}}], 5]
Out[30]= {{{Chromosome1, 1}, {1, 50}}, {{Chromosome1, 1}, {7, 56}},
         {{Chromosome1, 1}, {13, 62}}, {{Chromosome3, -1}, {116621, 116670}},
         {{Chromosome3, -1}, {116615, 116664}}}
```

Discussion

At the time of writing, Mathematica has data on 27,479 proteins and 39,920 genes.

```
In[31]:= {Length[ProteinData[]], Length[GenomeData[]]}
Out[31]= {27479, 39920}
```

The following is a list of properties of the proteins. This data is somewhat incomplete: some of the values are not known or have not been updated in Wolfram's database. The good news is that it improves over time, so there is likely more data when you're reading this than when I wrote it. Notice how this sample is ordered in columns, whereas prior recipes showed similar lists in rows. All you need is Transpose and a bit of math to get the desired number of columns.

```
In[32]:= Module[{props = ProteinData["Properties"]},
           With[{nCols = Ceiling[Length[props]/3]},
             Transpose[Partition[props, nCols, nCols, 1, ""]]]] // TableForm
```

```
Out[32]//TableForm=
            AdditionalAtomPositions  DNACodingSequence        MolecularWeight
            AdditionalAtomTypes      DNACodingSequenceLength   MoleculePlot
            AtomPositions            DomainIDs                 Name
            AtomRoles                DomainPositions           NCBIAccessions
            AtomTypes                Domains                   PDBIDList
            BiologicalProcesses      Gene                      PrimaryPDBID
            CellularComponents       GeneID                    SecondaryStructureRules
            ChainLabels              GyrationRadius            Sequence
            ChainSequences           Memberships              SequenceLength
            DihedralAngles           MolecularFunctions       StandardName
```

One property that is sparsely populated is MoleculePlot. At the time of writing, the
only protein beginning with "ATP" that has a MolecularPlot is ATP7BIsoformA.

```
In[33]:= ProteinData["ATP7BIsoformA", "MoleculePlot"]
```

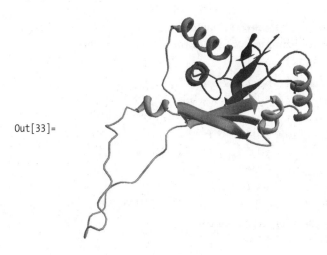

Out[33]=

GenomeData likewise contains a wealth of information. Here I show the properties
available.

```
In[34]:= Module[{props = GenomeData["Properties"]},
          With[{nCols = Ceiling[Length[props]/3]},
            Transpose[Partition[props, nCols, nCols, 1, ""]]]] // TableForm
```

```
Out[34]//TableForm=
            AlternateNames          GBandStainingLevels  Orientation
            AlternateStandardNames  GenBankIndices       ProteinGenBankIndices
            BiologicalProcesses     GeneID               ProteinNames
            CellularComponents      GeneOntologyIDs      ProteinNCBIAccessions
            Chromosome              GeneType             ProteinStandardNames
            CodingSequenceLists     InteractingGenes     PubMedIDs
            CodingSequencePositions IntronSequences      SequenceLength
            CodingSequences         LocusList            StandardName
            ExonSequences           LocusString          TranscriptGenBankIndices
            FullSequence            Memberships          TranscriptNCBIAccessions
            FullSequencePosition    MIMNumbers           UniProtAccessions
            GBandLocusStrings       MolecularFunctions   UnsequencedPositions
            GBandScaledPositions    Name                 UTRSequences
            GBandStainingCodes      NCBIAccessions
```

```
In[35]:=  GenomeData["ACOT9", "ProteinNames"]

Out[35]=  {acyl-Coenzyme A thioesterase 2, mitochondrial isoform a,
           acyl-Coenzyme A thioesterase 2, mitochondrial isoform b}

In[36]:=  GenomeData["ACOT9", "Memberships"]

Out[36]=  {ChromosomeXGenes, Genes, Hydrolase,
           Mitochondrion, ProteinBinding, ProteinCoding}

In[37]:=  GenomeData["ACOT9", "CellularComponents"]

Out[37]=  {Mitochondrion}

In[38]:=  GenomeData["ACOT9", "MolecularFunctions"]

Out[38]=  {AcetylCoAHydrolaseActivity,
           CarboxylesteraseActivity, HydrolaseActivity, ProteinBinding}
```

13.5 Modeling Predator-Prey Dynamics

Problem

You want to model a dynamic system consisting of populations of predators and prey to see how population levels evolve over time.

Solution

Consider a population of rabbits (prey) and foxes (predators) with a specific growth rate for rabbits G and carrying capacity of their environment K. The population dynamics can be modeled by a pair of difference equations. See the "Discussion" section on page 520 for more insight into the form of these equations and the meaning of the constants.

$$R_{t+1} = R_t + G\,R_t\left(1 - \frac{R_t}{K}\right) - 0.0001\,F_t\,R_t$$

$$F_{t+1} = F_t + 0.0001\,F_t\,R_t - 0.02\,F_t$$

`NestList` presents one possible solution for deriving the dynamics of the population over time from an initial starting point.

```
In[39]:= RabFox[{r_, f_}, G_: 0.02, K_: 500] :=
           {r + (G (1 - (r/K)) r) - 0.0001 r f, f + (0.0001 r f) - (0.02 f)}
         initPop = {50, 10};
         ListLinePlot[ NestList[RabFox, initPop, 1500],
           PlotRange → {{0, 500}, {0, 200}}, AxesLabel → {"Rabbits", "Foxes"}]
```

Out[41]=

This shows the rabbit population doing what rabbits do for many generations as the fox population slowly increases due to the increasing food supply. An inflection point is reached, and the fox population begins to take off with a resulting collapse in the rabbit population. Eventually the system reaches equilibrium.

Discussion

The equation for rabbits assumes that rabbits follow the logistic model of exponential growth limited by the carrying capacity of the environment and then subtracts a term proportional to the number of rabbits and foxes where the constant 0.0001 reflects the efficiency of the predators. The equation for foxes assumes that the fox population is proportional to the ability to catch rabbits (same term from first equation) minus some natural death rate (here 2 percent of the population).

`NestList` provides a very simple solution to this model, but it is not the best choice if, due to efficiency, you want to create an interactive model using `Manipulate`. Luckily, Mathematica 7 has new capabilities for discrete math that provide an alternate solution path. `RecurrenceTable` is a new function that will generate the list of solutions of specified length given a recurrence relation.

```
In[42]:=  DynamicModule[{pop},
            Manipulate[
              pop = RecurrenceTable[{
                R[t + 1] == R[t] + G * (1 - (R[t] / k)) * R[t] - 0.0001 R[t] F[t],
                F[t + 1] == F[t] + 0.0001 R[t] F[t] - 0.02 F[t],
                R[0] == P[[1]],
                F[0] == P[[2]]}, {R, F}, {t, 0, T}, Method → {Compiled → False}];
              ListLinePlot[pop, PlotRange → {{0, 500}, {0, 200}},
              AxesLabel → {"Rabbits", "Foxes"}, PlotLabel :→ Floor[Last[pop]]],
              {{G, 0.02}, 0.00, 0.03}, {{k, 500}, 300, 800}, {{P, {50, 10}}, Locator},
              {{T, 1000}, 1, 5000, 1}, SaveDefinitions → True]]
```

Out[42]=

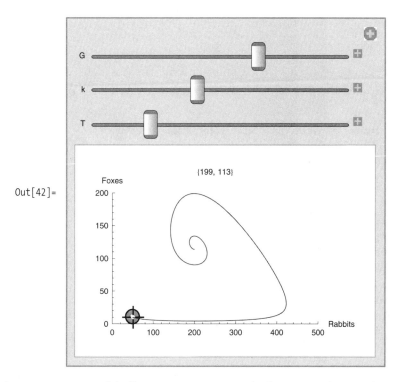

This interactive model allows you to position the locator at the initial population levels for rabbits and foxes and allows you to adjust the growth rate, carrying capacity, and number of iterations. The plot title displays the end value of rabbits and foxes.

See Also

More elaborate predator-prey models can be found at the Wolfram Demonstration Project: *http://bit.ly/mUVGS* and *http://bit.ly/21GfLm*.

13.6 Solving Basic Rigid Bodies Problems

Problem

You want to compute mass, center of mass, and moment of inertia as a prerequisite to solving dynamical problems involving rigid bodies.

Solution

The basic equation for computing the center of mass given a collection of discrete point masses is

$$\frac{\sum_{i=1}^{n} cm_i \, m_i}{\sum_{i=1}^{n} m_i}$$

where cm_i is the center of mass of each point and m_i is its mass. The numerator of this equation is called the *first moment*. Another name for the center of mass is the *centroid*.

```
In[43]:=  centerMass[particles_] := Module[{totalMass, firstMoment},
            {firstMoment, totalMass } =
            Sum[{mass@particles[[i]] centroid@particles[[i]],
              mass@particles[[i]]}, {i, Length[particles]}];
            firstMoment / totalMass]

In[44]:=  mass@car = 1000.;
          centroid@car = {100, 100};
          mass@driver = 86.;
          centroid@driver = {103, 101} ;
          mass@fuel = 14.2;
          centroid@fuel = {93, 100};
          centerMass[{car, driver, fuel}]
Out[50]=  {100.144, 100.078}
```

Discussion

The solution is fairly elementary from a physical point of view, but it may look a bit mysterious from a Mathematica coding point of view. The solution is coded using Mathematica's prefix notion. Recall that f@x is prefix notation for f[x]. This notation is appealing for modeling problems because it is concise and readable (simply replace the @ with "of" as you read the code). Notice how I use the same notation with the problem objects car, driver, and fuel.

Now suppose this notation does not appeal to you; perhaps you like to model the physical objects as lists or some other notation like object[{mass,centroid}]. Does this mean you need to reimplement the centerMass function? Not at all. Simply define the function's mass and centroid for your preferred representation, and you are all set.

```
In[51]:= mass[object[{m_, ___}]] := m

In[52]:= centroid[object[{_, c_, ___}]] := c

In[53]:= centerMass[{object[{1000, {100, 100}}],
            object[{86, {103, 101}}], object[{14.2, {93, 100}}]}]

Out[53]= {100.144, 100.078}
```

Another important property of rigid bodies is the mass moment of inertia about an axis. These values are important when solving problems involving rotation of the body. The general equation for the mass moment of inertia involves integration over infinitesimal point masses that make up the body, but in practice problems, equations for known geometries are typically used. One way to approach this in Mathematica is to use a property called shape and rely on pattern matching to select the appropriate formula. Each of these functions returns a list in the form {Ixx, Iyy, Izz}, giving the moment of inertia about the x-, y-, and z-axis, respectively.

```
In[1]:= massMomentOfInertia[o_] /; shape@o == "circularCylinder" :=
        Module[{i1, i2},
          i1 = ((mass@o radius@o^2) /4) + ((mass@o length@o ^2) /12);
          i2 = ((mass@o radius@o^2) /2) ;
          {i1, i1, i2} ]
        massMomentOfInertia[o_] /; shape@o == "circularCylindricalShell" :=
        Module[{i1, i2},
          i1 = ((mass@o radius@o^2) /2) + ((mass@o length@o ^2) /12);
          i2 = ((mass@o radius@o^2)) ;
          {i1, i1, i2} ]
        massMomentOfInertia[o_] /; shape@o == "rectangularCylinder" :=
        Module[{ixx, iyy, izz},
          ixx = ((mass@o (height@o + length@o) ^2) /12) ;
          iyy = ((mass@o (width@o + length@o) ^2) /12) ;
          izz = ((mass@o (width@o + height@o) ^2) /12) ;
          {ixx, iyy, izz} ]
        massMomentOfInertia[o_] /; shape@o == "sphere" := Module[{i},
          i = (mass@o (2 radius@o ^2) /5) ;
          {i, i, i} ]
        massMomentOfInertia[o_] /; shape@o == "sphericalShell" := Module[{i},
          i = (mass@o (2 radius@o ^2) /3) ;
          {i, i, i} ]
```

```
In[59]:=  shape@car = "rectangularCylinder";
          length@car = 4.73;
          width@car = 1.83;
          height@car = 1.25;

In[63]:=  massMomentOfInertia[car]
Out[63]=  {2980.03, 3586.13, 790.533}

In[64]:=  shape@car = "circularCylindricalShell";
          radius@car = 1.83;

In[66]:=  massMomentOfInertia[car]
Out[66]=  {3538.86, 3538.86, 3348.9}
```

13.7 Solving Problems in Kinematics

Problem

You want to demonstrate standard problems in kinematics, like those you typically find in first-year physics studies.

Solution

The basic equations of kinematics are as follows.

```
In[67]:=  acceleration1[deltaT_, v1_, v2_] := (v2 - v1) / deltaT
          acceleration2[deltaT_, v1_, deltaS_] :=
            2 (deltaS - v1 deltaT) / (deltaT^2)
          acceleration3[v1_, v2_, deltaS_] := (v2^2 - v1^2) / (2 deltaS)
          distance[a_, v1_, deltaT_] := (a deltaT^2 /2) + v1 deltaT
          distance1[a_, v1_, v2_] := (v2^2 - v1^2) / (2 a)
          distance2[deltaT_, v1_, v2_] := (deltaT / 2) (v1 + v2)
          time1[a_, v1_, v2_] := (v2 - v1) / a
          time2[a_, v1_, deltaS_] := (Sqrt[v1^2 + 2 + 2 a deltaS] - v1) / a
          time3[v1_, v2_, deltaS_] := ( 2 deltaS) / (v1 + v2)
          velocity1[a_, v2_, deltaT_] := v2 - a deltaT
          velocity2[a_, deltaS_, deltaT_] := (deltaS / deltaT) - ( a deltaT / 2)
          velocity3[a_, v2_, deltaS_] := Sqrt[v2^2 - 2 a deltaS]
```

Given these equations, you can solve a variety of problems. For example, how far will a bullet drop if shot horizontally from a rifle at a target 500 m away if the initial velocity is 800 m/s? Ignore drag, wind, and other factors.

First, compute how long the bullet remains in flight before hitting the target by taking the initial and final velocity to be the same.

```
In[79]:= timeTraveled = time3[800, 800, 500] // N
Out[79]= 0.625
```

Given the acceleration due to gravity is 9.8 m/s², compute the distance dropped by setting the initial vertical velocity component to zero.

```
In[80]:= distanceDropped = distance[9.8, 0, timeTraveled]
Out[80]= 1.91406
```

The bullet drops almost 2 meters.

Discussion

The solution works out a simple problem by working first in the x direction and then plugging the results into an equation in the y direction. In more complex problems, it is often necessary to use vectors to capture the velocity components in the x, y, and z directions. Consider a game or simulation involving a movable cannon and a movable target of varying size.

Imagine the cannon is fixed to the side of a fortress such that the vertical height (z direction in this example) is variable but the x and y position is fixed. The length, angle of elevation (alpha), left-right angle (gamma), and muzzle velocities are also variable. You require a function that gives the locus of points traversed by the shell given the cannon settings and the time of flight. Here we use Select to filter the points above ground level (positive in the z direction). The function returns a list of values of the form {{x1,y1,z1,t1}, ..., {xn,yn,zn,tn}}, where each entry is the position of the shell at the specified time. Chop is used only to replace numbers close to zero by zero. Note that in each dimension, the basic kinematic equations are in play, but since the inputs are in terms of angles, some basic trigonometry is needed to get the separate x, y, and z components. Velocity is constant in the x-y plane (we are still ignoring drag), and the z-axis uses the initial velocity component and the fall of the shell due to gravity.

```
In[81]:= displacement[origin_List, velocity_, alpha_, gamma_, tEnd_] :=
           With[{g = 9.8},
             Select[If[tEnd ≤ 0, {},
               Chop[Table[{
                 origin[[1]] + velocity * t * Cos[alpha * Pi / 2],
                 origin[[2]] + velocity * t * Cos[gamma * Pi],
                 origin[[3]] + velocity * t * Sin[alpha * Pi / 2] - 0.5 g t^2,
                 t},
                 {t, 0, tEnd, 0.25}]]], #[[3]] ≥ 0 &]
           ]
```

You can also create a function that computes the instantaneous velocity components at a specified time.

```
In[82]:= velocity[velocity_, alpha_, gamma_, t_] :=
          With[{g = 9.8},
            Chop[
             If[t > 0,
               {velocity * Cos[alpha * Pi / 2],
                velocity * Cos[gamma * Pi],
                velocity Sin[alpha * Pi / 2] - g t}, {0., 0., 0.}]
            ]
          ]
```

Since the plan is to create a simulation, you need a function that figures out when the shell intersects with the target. For simplicity, assume the shape of the target is a box.

```
In[83]:= intersect[point_List, corner1_List, corner2_List] :=
          point[[1]] ≥ corner1[[1]] && point[[1]] ≤ corner2[[1]] &&
           point[[2]] ≥ corner1[[2]] && point[[2]] ≤ corner2[[2]] &&
           point[[3]] ≥ corner1[[3]] && point[[3]] ≤ corner2[[3]]
         (*The shell hit the target if any point in the locus
         of points intersects. Apply Or to list of Booleans.*)
         intersection[points_List, corner1_List, corner2_List] :=
          Or @@ (intersect[#, corner1, corner2] & /@ points)
```

You can set the simulation up inside of a Manipulate so that you can play around with all the variables.

```
In[85]:=  With[{width = 200, height = 200, length = 200, limit = 10},
          Manipulate[
            DynamicModule[{b, Lx, Ly, Lz, cannonAlpha,
               cannonGamma, targetX, targetY, path, text, color, Vx, Vy, Vz},
              {cannonGamma, cannonAlpha} = cannonOrient;
              {targetX, targetY} = targetPos;
              b = cannonL * Cos[(1 - cannonAlpha) * Pi / 2];
              Lx = cannonL Cos[cannonAlpha * Pi / 2];
              Ly = length / 2 + cannonL * Cos[cannonGamma * Pi];
              Lz = cannonL Sin[cannonAlpha * Pi / 2];
              path = displacement[{Lx, Ly, cannonZb + Lz},
                cannonVM, cannonAlpha, cannonGamma, time];
              tLast = If[Length[path] > 1, Last[path][[4]], 0];
              {Vx, Vy, Vz} = velocity[cannonVM, cannonAlpha, cannonGamma, tLast];
              color =
               If[intersection[path, {targetX, targetY, targetZ}, {targetX + targetL,
                   targetY + targetW, targetZ + targetH}], Red, Green];
              Column[{
                Grid[{{"Vx", "Vy", "Vz"}, {Vx, Vy, Vz}}],
                Graphics3D[{{Thickness[0.02],
                    Line[{{0, length / 2, cannonZb}, {Lx, Ly, Lz + cannonZb}}]}, {color,
                    Cuboid[{targetX, targetY, targetZ}, {targetX + targetL, targetY +
                        targetW, targetZ + targetH}]}, Point[Most[#]] & /@ path},
                  PlotRange -> {{0, width}, {0, length}, {0, height}},
                  ImageSize -> 300]}]
             ],
             {{cannonVM, 50}, 10, 100}, {{cannonOrient, {0.5, 0.5}}, {0, 0}, {1, 1}},
             {cannonL, 20, length / 2}, {cannonZb, 0, height / 2},
             {{targetPos, {100, 100}}, {5 * limit, 0},
              {width - limit, length - limit}},
             {targetZ, 0, height - limit}, {targetL, limit, length / 2},
             {targetW, limit, width / 2}, {targetH, limit, height / 2},
             {time, 0, 25},
             {time, 0, 25, ControlType -> Trigger}, SaveDefinitions -> True]]
```

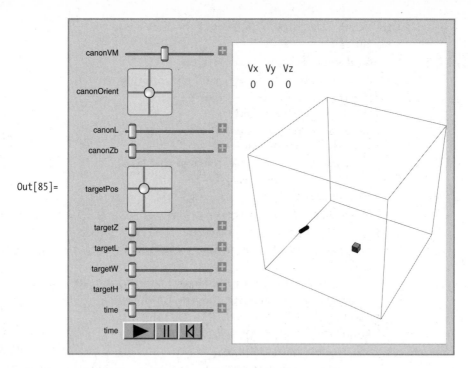

Out[85]=

The initial output of the Manipulate is shown in Out[85] above. The path of the bullet is displayed up until the point in time specified by the time control, so the box turns red after it is hit by a shell. The instantaneous velocity of the shell is displayed for the current value of time. The Vz will be negative when the shell is falling. Figure 13-1 shows two frames from the Manipulate, at a time before impact and a time after.

See Also

David M. Bourg's *Physics for Game Developers* (O'Reilly) has an example of the cannon problem where wind drag is introduced. Keep in mind that the author uses the y-axis as the vertical whereas the code in this recipe uses the z-axis.

Mathematical Methods Using Mathematica by Sadri Hassani (Springer) has solutions to similar problems using differential equations which consider drag, curvature of the earth, and nonconstant acceleration at large distances from the earth's surface (see Chapter 6).

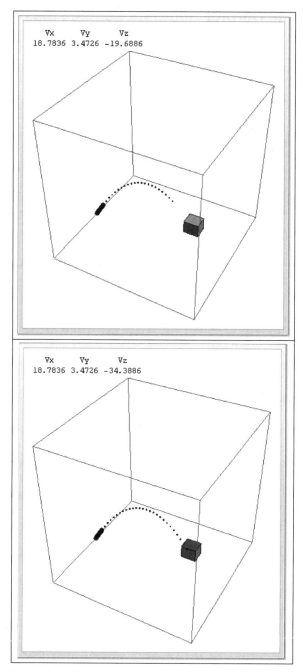

Figure 13-1. Two frames from the cannon simulation

13.8 Computing Normal Modes for Coupled Mass Problems

Problem

You want to compute the normal modes for a system of identical masses connected by identical springs. Normal modes are natural or resonant frequencies of the entire system. The system this recipe considers consists of n>1 masses connected by n-1 springs on a frictionless surface. Figure 13-2 shows an example for n=3.

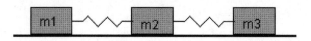

Figure 13-2 Coupled masses

Solution

Here I state, without proof (refer to "See Also" section on page 532), that these systems take the form of *n* simultaneous linear equations whose matrix representation is tridiagonal. That is a matrix with nonzero entries along the main diagonal and adjacent minor diagonals and zero entries in all other elements. The corner entries of the main diagonal are special since they represent masses that are free on one side and take the form k - m*ω^2, where k is the spring constant, m is the mass, and ω is the angular frequency. The off corner entries represent the masses with springs on both sides and take the form 2*k - m*ω^2. The minor diagonals are all -k. Here I solve the three mass problems, and in the discussion, I show how to create a general solver for the n mass case.

$$\text{In[86]:= } \mathbf{matrix} = \begin{pmatrix} k - 2\,\omega\texttt{^}2 & -k & 0 \\ -k & 2\,k - 2\,\omega\texttt{^}2 & -k \\ 0 & -k & k - 2\,\omega\texttt{^}2 \end{pmatrix}$$

$$\text{Out[86]= } \{\{k - 2\,\omega^2, -k, 0\}, \{-k, 2\,k - 2\,\omega^2, -k\}, \{0, -k, k - 2\,\omega^2\}\}$$

Nontrivial solutions to this system leave the matrix as noninvertible; hence, the determinant is zero. Use Solve to find the frequencies in terms of k.

```
In[87]:= sol = Solve[Det[matrix] == 0, ω]
```

$$Out[87]= \left\{ \{\omega \to 0\}, \{\omega \to 0\}, \left\{\omega \to -\sqrt{\frac{3}{2}} \sqrt{k}\right\}, \right.$$

$$\left. \left\{\omega \to \sqrt{\frac{3}{2}} \sqrt{k}\right\}, \left\{\omega \to -\frac{\sqrt{k}}{\sqrt{2}}\right\}, \left\{\omega \to \frac{\sqrt{k}}{\sqrt{2}}\right\}\right\}$$

You don't care about the solutions with negative or zero frequencies, so you can filter these out to obtain two physically interesting resonant frequencies.

```
In[88]:= sol = Cases[sol, Except[{_ → 0} | {_ → -_}]]
```

$$Out[88]= \left\{\left\{\omega \to \sqrt{\frac{3}{2}} \sqrt{k}\right\}, \left\{\omega \to \frac{\sqrt{k}}{\sqrt{2}}\right\}\right\}$$

Given the frequencies, you can solve the system to get the amplitudes. The first solution gives a1 == a3 and a2 == -2a1, with the alternative of k == 0 being physically uninteresting. This solution has the outer masses moving in unison in the same direction while the inner mass compensates by moving in the opposite direction with twice the amplitude.

```
In[89]:= Reduce[Dot[(matrix /. sol[[1]]) , {a1, a2, a3}] == 0, {a1, a2, a3}]
Out[89]= (a2 == -2 a1 && a3 == a1) || k == 0
```

The second solution gives a2 == 0 and a3 == -a1 with the alternative of k == 0 being physically uninteresting. This is a solution with the center mass at rest and the outer masses moving toward and then away from the center.

```
In[90]:= Reduce[Dot[(matrix /. sol[[2]]) , {a1, a2, a3}] == 0, {a1, a2, a3}]
Out[90]= (a2 == 0 && a3 == -a1) || k == 0
```

Discussion

To solve the general *n*-mass system, we need a way to synthesize a tridiagonal matrix of the proper form. For this, SparseArray and Band are just what the doctor ordered. When using sparse matrix, rules that come earlier override rules that come later. This works to your favor because it allows the case where n == 2 to be handled without any conditional logic stemming from the fact that there are no 2*k - m*ω^2 terms when n == 2.

```
In[91]:=  Clear[massMatrix];
          massMatrix[n_ /; n > 1] := SparseArray[{
              {1, 1} -> k - m ω^2,
              {n, n} -> k - m ω^2,
              Band[{2, 1}] → -k,
              Band[{1, 2}] → -k,
              Band[{1, 1}] → 2 k - m ω^2}, n]
In[93]:=  massMatrix[2] // MatrixForm
Out[93]//MatrixForm=
```

$$\begin{pmatrix} k - m\,\omega^2 & -k \\ -k & k - m\,\omega^2 \end{pmatrix}$$

```
In[94]:=  massMatrix[5] // MatrixForm
Out[94]//MatrixForm=
```

$$\begin{pmatrix} k - m\,\omega^2 & -k & 0 & 0 & 0 \\ -k & 2\,k - m\,\omega^2 & -k & 0 & 0 \\ 0 & -k & 2\,k - m\,\omega^2 & -k & 0 \\ 0 & 0 & -k & 2\,k - m\,\omega^2 & -k \\ 0 & 0 & 0 & -k & k - m\,\omega^2 \end{pmatrix}$$

For the general solution, you want to use NSolve with specific values of m and k because roots of polynomials with degree greater than five are likely to give Solve trouble. Here I solve a 10-mass system with k == 1 and m == 1. Chop is used to remove residual imaginary values and Cases filters out zero and negative solutions because they are physically uninteresting.

```
In[95]:=  Cases[Chop[NSolve[Det[massMatrix[10]] == 0 /. {k → 1, m → 1}, ω]],
              {_ → a_ /; a > 0}]
Out[95]=  {{ω → 0.312869}, {ω → 0.618034}, {ω → 0.907981}, {ω → 1.17557},
              {ω → 1.41421}, {ω → 1.61803}, {ω → 1.78201}, {ω → 1.90211}, {ω → 1.97538}}
```

See Also

You can find derivations of the systems solved in this recipe in many advanced physics and linear algebra books. In particular, *Mathematical Methods Using Mathematica* by Sadri Hassani provides a nice mix of practical physics and Mathematica techniques, although the most recent edition is written for versions of Mathematica prior to 6 and therefore does not always indicate the best technique to use for current versions.

13.9 Modeling a Vibrating String

Problem

You want to model the dynamics of a vibrating string after it is released from a particular deformation.

Solution

This solution is a particular solution to the one-dimensional wave equation D[u[x,t], {x,2}] == c^2 D[u[x,t],{t,2}] where u[x,t] gives the position of the string at point x and time t. The general solution to the wave equation can be obtained using DSolve.

```
In[96]:= DSolve[D[u[x, t], {x, 2}] == c^2 D[u[x, t], {t, 2}], u[t, x], {t, x}]
```

$$Out[96]= \left\{\left\{u[x, t] \to C[1]\left[t - \sqrt{c^2}\ x\right] + C[2]\left[t + \sqrt{c^2}\ x\right]\right\}\right\}$$

The general solution is not very helpful because it is specified in terms of two unknown functions, C[1] and C[2]. In theory, you could specify boundary conditions and initial conditions, but DSolve is very limited in its ability to find solutions to partial differential equations. This problem is better handled numerically with NDSolve.

First we need a specification for the shape of the string at $t = 0$. For simplicity, I'll use the Sin function that will give a width of L units. Here I use Plot to show the initial defection of the string.

```
In[97]:= string[x_, L_] := 0.35 Sin[ (π x)/L ];
```

```
In[98]:= With[{L = 5}, Plot[string[ x, L], {x, 0, L}, AspectRatio → 1/L]]
```

To use NDSolve to model the vibrating string, you must provide initial and boundary conditions. The initial condition states that u[0,x] = string[x]. In other words, at the start, the string has the position depicted previously. You must also specify the initial velocity of the string, which is the first derivative with respect to time. The obvious choice for initial velocity is zero. Using input form, this would be entered as Derivative[1, 0][u][0, x] == 0. This operator notation was explained in Recipe 11.4. The two boundary conditions specify that the ends of the string are anchored at position 0 and L, u[t, 0] == 0, and u[t, L] == 0.

```
In[99]:=  With[{L = 5, T = 10, waveEq = D[u[t, x], t, t] == D[u[t, x], x, x]},
          sol = NDSolve[
            {waveEq, u[0, x] == string[x, L], Derivative[1, 0][u][0, x] == 0,
            u[t, 0] == 0, u[t, L] == 0}, u, {t, 0, 10}, {x, 0, L}];
          Animate[Plot[Evaluate[u[t, x] /. sol[[1]]], {x, 0, L},
            AspectRatio -> 1 / L, PlotRange → {{0, L}, {-0.4, 0.4}}],
            {t, 0, T, 0.5}, SaveDefinitions → True]]
```

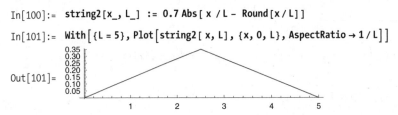

Out[99]=

Discussion

Although DSolve can deal with some partial differential equations (PDEs), it is limited in its ability to derive specific solutions given initial and boundary conditions.
Therefore, it is better to use NDSolve on PDEs, as I've done in the solution. However,
it is not difficult to pose problems that NDSolve will have a hard time with and ultimately fail to solve. Consider trying to solve the wave equation with an initial position that contains a discontinuity.

```
In[100]:=  string2[x_, L_] := 0.7 Abs[x / L - Round[x / L]]
```

```
In[101]:=  With[{L = 5}, Plot[string2[x, L], {x, 0, L}, AspectRatio → 1 / L]]
```

Out[101]=

If you try to use string2 in the solution shown in In[99] above, it will likely run for a
very long time, consuming memory and finally failing. However, this situation is not
entirely hopeless. One technique is to produce an approximation to string2 using Fourier
series. Using Fourier series, I obtained the following Sin expansion, called sinString2:

```
In[102]:= sinString2[x_] = 0.285325252629769` Sin[(Pi*x)/5] -
              0.033193742967516204` Sin[(3*Pi*x)/5] +
              0.013117204588138661` Sin[π x] - 0.007723288156504195`
              Sin[(7*Pi*x)/5] + 0.005695145921372713` Sin[(9*Pi*x)/5] -
              0.004945365736699312` Sin[(11*Pi*x)/5];
```

Below I plot both functions to demonstrate how closely sinString2 approximates string2 while smoothing out the discontinuity at the apex.

```
In[103]:= With[{L = 5}, Plot[{string2[x, L], sinString2[x]},
             {x, 0, L}, AspectRatio → 1/L, PlotStyle → {Dashed, Thin}]]
```

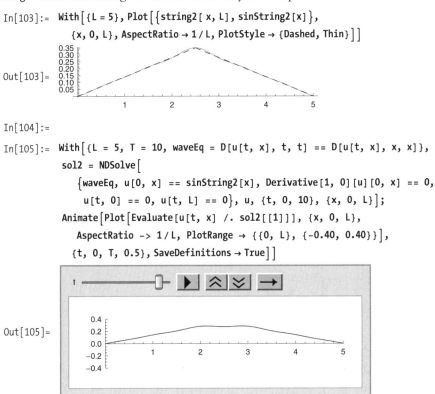

Out[103]=

```
In[104]:=
```

```
In[105]:= With[{L = 5, T = 10, waveEq = D[u[t, x], t, t] == D[u[t, x], x, x]},
             sol2 = NDSolve[
               {waveEq, u[0, x] == sinString2[x], Derivative[1, 0][u][0, x] == 0,
                u[t, 0] == 0, u[t, L] == 0}, u, {t, 0, 10}, {x, 0, L}];
             Animate[Plot[Evaluate[u[t, x] /. sol2[[1]]], {x, 0, L},
               AspectRatio -> 1/L, PlotRange → {{0, L}, {-0.40, 0.40}}],
               {t, 0, T, 0.5}, SaveDefinitions → True]]
```

Out[105]=

There is an exact solution to the triangular wave, although it isn't derived here (refer to the "See Also" section on page 536). It is given by this infinite sum, which Mathematica can solve using a special function LerchPhi. This solution is too complex to use in an animation, but you can use it to verify that the approximate solution is quite good.

```
In[106]:= triangular[t_, x_] = With[{L = 5}, FullSimplify[
            ((0.35 * 8) / Pi^2) * Sum[(-1) ^ (i + 1) * Sin[(2 * i - 1) * Pi * (x / L)] *
            (Cos[(2 * i - 1) * Pi * (t / L)]) / (2 * i - 1) ^2), {i, 1, Infinity}]]]
```

$$
\text{Out[106]= } e^{-\frac{1}{5} i \pi (5t+x)} \left((0. - 0.0177312\, i)\, e^{\frac{2}{5} i \pi (2t+x)} \text{ LerchPhi}\left[-e^{-\frac{2}{5} i \pi (t-x)}, 2, \frac{1}{2}\right] + \right.
$$

$$
(0. + 0.0177312\, i)\, e^{\frac{6 i \pi t}{5}} \text{ LerchPhi}\left[-e^{\frac{2}{5} i \pi (t-x)}, 2, \frac{1}{2}\right] +
$$

$$
(0. + 0.0177312\, i)\, e^{\frac{4 i \pi t}{5}} \text{ LerchPhi}\left[-e^{-\frac{2}{5} i \pi (t+x)}, 2, \frac{1}{2}\right] -
$$

$$
\left. (0. + 0.0177312\, i)\, e^{\frac{2}{5} i \pi (3t+x)} \text{ LerchPhi}\left[-e^{\frac{2}{5} i \pi (t+x)}, 2, \frac{1}{2}\right] \right)
$$

Plotting a few snapshots of the exact solution over time tells us that the approximate solution is more than adequate and, in some sense, superior because it is far less computationally intense.

```
In[107]:= Grid[With[{L = 5, T = 5},
            Partition[Table[Plot[triangular[t, x] , {x, 0, L},
              AspectRatio -> 1 / L, Ticks → None,
              PlotRange → {{0, L}, {-0.40, 0.40}}], {t, 0, T}], 3]]]
```

Out[107]=

See Also

There are many ways to approach the solution to the wave equation. When this problem is solved by hand, separation of variables is often employed. See *Advanced Engineering Mathematics* by Erwin Kreyszig (John Wiley) for a step-by-step example. Warning: this book is not a Mathematica reference, but the problems are worked out in enough detail that you can easily see your way to creating your own Mathematica-based solutions.

13.10 Modeling Electrical Circuits

Problem

You want to understand how electrical circuits consisting of resistors, capacitors, and inductors behave.

Solution

The differential equation governing an RLC circuit is L I'' + R I' + I/C = E(t), where I is current, L is inductance, R is resistance, C is capacitance, and E(t) is the electromotive force (commonly known as voltage). Modeling the system means understanding how the current varies as you drive the system with a particular timing varying voltage. Let's consider a common sinusoidal voltage and solve the system assuming that the charge and current are zero at t=0. Setting the problem up with the context of a With allows you to solve the problem for different values of inductance, capacitance, resistance, frequency, and voltage.

```
In[108]:= sol = With[{L = 0.01, R = 100, C = 0.001, f = 60, V = 1},

            DSolve[{L Iout''[t] + R Iout'[t] + 1/C Iout[t] == V 2 Pi f Cos[2 Pi f t],

                Iout[0] == 0, Iout'[0] == 0}, Iout[t], t]]
```

Out[108]= {{Iout[t] →
    $e^{-10000. t}$ (0.000377588 $e^{10.01 t}$ − 0.000265869 $e^{9989.99 t}$ − (0.000111719 + 0. i)
    $e^{10000. t}$ Cos[376.991 t] + (0.00999875 + 0. i) $e^{10000. t}$ Sin[376.991 t])}}

```
In[109]:= fIout[t_] = Chop[FullSimplify[Iout[t] /. sol[[1]]]]
```

Out[109]= 0.000377588 $e^{-9989.99 t}$ − 0.000265869 $e^{-10.01 t}$ −
    0.000111719 Cos[376.991 t] + 0.00999875 Sin[376.991 t]

By plotting the input voltage and output current, you can see they have the same basic shape and frequency except for a phase shift.

```
In[110]:= With[{f = 60, V = 1},
            GraphicsRow[{Plot[{V 2 Pi f Cos[2 Pi f t]}, {t, 0, 0.1}, PlotLabel → Vin],
                Plot[{fIout[t]}, {t, 0, 0.1}, PlotLabel → Iout]}]
            ]
```

Out[110]=

Discussion

A more interesting example uses a nonsinusoidal wave, such as a triangular wave. Conveniently, Mathematica 7 has a function TriangleWave[t] that suits our purpose.

```
In[111]:= Et[V_, t_] = V TriangleWave[t];
```

```
In[112]:= Plot[Et[1, t], {t, 1, 3}, ImageSize → Small]
```

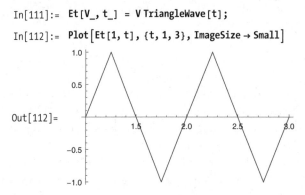

Out[112]=

However, the discontinuities in this waveform throw DSolve for a loop. To work around this, represent the triangular wave by its Fourier series. This will give a very close approximation without the discontinuities at the extremes. This will allow you to use DSolve.

```
In[113]:= Et2[V_, t_] =
            FourierSinSeries[Et[V, t], t, 10, FourierParameters → {1, 2 Pi}]
```

$$
Out[113]= \frac{8\,V\,\text{Sin}[2\,\pi\,t]}{\pi^2} - \frac{8\,V\,\text{Sin}[6\,\pi\,t]}{9\,\pi^2} +
$$
$$
\frac{8\,V\,\text{Sin}[10\,\pi\,t]}{25\,\pi^2} - \frac{8\,V\,\text{Sin}[14\,\pi\,t]}{49\,\pi^2} + \frac{8\,V\,\text{Sin}[18\,\pi\,t]}{81\,\pi^2}
$$

```
In[114]:= Plot[Et2[1, t], {t, 1, 3}, ImageSize → Small]
```

Out[114]=

```
In[115]:= sol2 = With[{L = 0.01, R = 100, C = 0.001, V = 1},
            DSolve[{L * Derivative[2][Ii][t] +
                R * Derivative[1][Ii][t] + (1/C) * Ii[t] ==
            Et2[V, t], Ii[0] == 0, Derivative[1][Ii][0] == 0}, Ii[t], t]];
```

```
In[116]:= fIout2[t_] = Ii[t] /. sol2[[1]];
```

Notice how the RLC circuit responds to the triangular wave input by smoothing the current flow to an approximately sinusoidal form. As an exercise, you can try this same example using SquareWave, SawtoothWave, or other functions of your own design.

```
In[117]:=  With[{f = 60, V = 1},
              GraphicsRow[{Plot[{Et2[1, t]}, {t, 0, 3}, PlotLabel → Vin],
                Plot[{fIout2[t]}, {t, 0, 3}, PlotLabel → Iout]}]
           ]
```

Out[117]=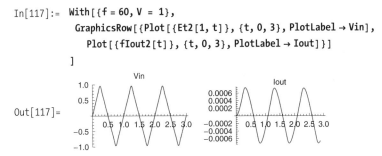

13.11 Modeling Truss Structures Using the Finite Element Method

Problem

You want to build a model based on the finite element method (FEM). You want to organize the model in a manner that allows you to obtain the solution as well as other intermediate results and structural diagrams.

Solution

The FEM has a wide range of engineering applications. In this recipe, I will limit the discussion to structures composed of linear elements known as trusses. See the figure shown in the "Discussion" section on page 545. Here my focus will be on the organization of the solution within Mathematica rather than on the underlying theory. Therefore, all results will be present without derivation of the underlying mathematics. Please refer to the references in the "See Also" section on page 547.

To begin, you will need a means to represent the elements. I use a structure called linearElement that specifies two endpoints called nodes ({{x1, y1}, {x2, y2}}), an area, and a measure of stiffness called *Young's Modulus* (YM).

> linearElement[{{x1, y1}, {x2, y2}}, area, YM]

In addition, you need a means for specifying the *x* and *y* components of the force at each node.

> force[{x, y}, fx, fy]

Furthermore, at each node there is a computed displacement in the x and y direction. The FEM literature uses the variable u for x displacements and v for y displacements Typically, each node is sequentially numbered, so you would have $u1$, $v1$, $u2$, $v2$, and so on. I will not use a sequential numbering here, because each node is uniquely identified by its coordinates, and given Mathematica's liberal representation of variables, it is much more convenient to specify nodal displacements using coordinates.

```
u[x1, y1]
(*The displacement in the x direction at node {x1,y1}*)
v[x1, y1] (*The displacement in the y direction at node {x1,y1}*)
```

With these conventions established, I proceed by defining a series of helper functions that will be needed later. I provide a brief description of each function but, for brevity, defer more detail to the "Discussion" section on page 543.

Each element in the model is governed by a system of linear equations. The system is naturally represented by a symmetric matrix. The symmetry takes the form `{{A,-A},{-A,A}}` where A is a block matrix.

```
In[118]:= linearElementMatrix[
            linearElement[{{x1_, y1_}, {x2_, y2_}}, area_, YM_]] :=
            Module[{L, BlockMatrix, LocalMatrix, A, l, m},
             L = EuclideanDistance[{x1, y1}, {x2, y2}];
             BlockMatrix = {{A, -A}, {-A, A}};
             LocalMatrix =
             ArrayFlatten[ BlockMatrix /. {A → {{l l, l m}, {l m, m m}}}];
             ( LocalMatrix /. {l → (x2 - x1) / L , m → (y2 - y1) / L})
              (( YM area) / L)
            ]
```

A location vector provides a means for locating the position of the local element matrices computed by `linearElementMatrix` within a larger global matrix that represents the system over all elements.

```
In[119]:= assemblyLocationVector[linearElement[{n1_, n2_}, __], allnodes_] :=
            Flatten[Position[allnodes, #] & /@ {u @@ n1, v @@ n1, u @@ n2, v @@ n2}]
```

This helper maps a node of the form `{{x1,y1},{x2,y2}}` to the corresponding force components `{{fx1,fy1},{{fx2,fy2}}}`. It does this by searching for the first match of the node within the list of forces and transforming it to the desired form.

```
In[120]:= getExternalForces[{forces__force}, node_] :=
            Cases[{forces}, force[node, fu_, fv_] :> {fu, fv}, 1, 1]
```

This helper extracts the unique set of nodes from the elements and places them in a canonical order, as defined by Union. This ordering is essential to the construction of a consistent system of equations. See the "Discussion" section on page 543 for details.

```
In[121]:= getNodes[{elements__linearElement}] :=
            Union[{elements} /. linearElement[{n1_, n2_}, __] :> Sequence[n1, n2]]
```

This helper is used to construct a replacement rule for forces.

```
In[122]:= makeForceRule[force[p_, fx_, fy_]] := force[p, _, _] -> force[p, fx, fy]
```

Construct a global vector of all forces using a set of nodes in canonical order.

```
In[123]:= getForceVector[{forces__force}, nodes_] :=
            Flatten[getExternalForces[{forces}, #] & /@ nodes]
```

Assemble the global matrix that defines the system of equations over all elements using the local matrices for individual elements and the location vectors that define the position of the local matrices with the global matrix. Note that the global matrix is obtained by summing the local matrices into the appropriate positions within the global matrix. In other words, think of each member of locationVectors as specifying a submatrix within the global matrix for which the corresponding member of localMatrices is added.

```
In[124]:= assembleGlobalMatrix[localMatricies_,
              locationVectors_, numElements_, dimension_] :=
            Module[{g},
              g = Table[0, {dimension}, {dimension}];
              Do[g[[ locationVectors[[i]], locationVectors[[i]] ]] +=
                localMatricies[[i]], {i, 1, numElements}];
              g
            ]
```

A model consists of a collection of connected elements, the external forces applied to the structure at one or more nodes, and the boundary conditions that typically manifest as points where a node is anchored, rendered immobile in the *x*, *y*, or both directions. Here I organize a solution in the spirit of LinearModelFit covered in Chapter 12. That is, I construct an object called a TrussModel, the function of which is to organize the underlying data and then use that object as the target for requests for certain properties relevant to the FEM. As of Mathematica 6 and particularly in Mathematica 7, this object-based methodology has emerged as a design pattern for organizing solutions that involve large quantities of data or collections of related functionality.

To proceed in this manner, you need a function for creating the TrussModel and a Format for displaying it. The Format is syntactic sugar that hides the details of the TrussModel, which could be quite large.

```
In[125]:= createTrussModel[{elements__linearElement},
             {forces__force}, boundaryNodes_] :=
         Module[{localMatrices, nodes, nodalVar, forceVec, locationVectors,
             degreesOfFreedom, globalMatrix, allForces, forceRules},
           nodes = getNodes[{elements}];
           nodalVar = Flatten[{u @@ #, v @@ #} & /@ nodes];
           localMatrices = linearElementMatrix /@ {elements};
           locationVectors = assemblyLocationVector[#, nodalVar] & /@ {elements};
           globalMatrix = assembleGlobalMatrix[localMatrices,
             locationVectors, Length[{elements}], Length[nodalVar]];
           degreesOfFreedom = Complement[Range[Length[nodalVar]],
             Flatten[Position[nodalVar, #] & /@ boundaryNodes]];
           allForces = force[#, 0, 0] & /@ nodes;
           forceRules = makeForceRule /@ {forces} ;
           allForces = allForces /. forceRules;
           forceVec = getForceVector[allForces, nodes];
           TrussModel[{elements}, boundaryNodes, localMatrices,
             globalMatrix, nodalVar, forceVec, degreesOfFreedom, forces]]

         Format[TrussModel[elements_, boundaryNodes_, __]] :=
           ToString[TrussModel[{Length[elements]}, {Length[boundaryNodes]}]]
```

The goal of a FEM analysis is to determine the behavior of the structure from the behavior of the elements. For a system of trusses, solve for the displacements at the joints, the axial forces, and axial stresses. Following the proposed methodology, these will be accessed as properties of the TrussModel.

The displacements property is implemented as a functional pattern associated with the TrussModel. This notation may look somewhat unusual but is quite natural from the standpoint of Mathematica's design. It simply states that when you see a pattern consisting of a TrussModel and a literal argument, "displacements", replace it with the results of computing the displacements using data from the TrussModel.

```
In[127]:= TrussModel[_, _, _, globalMatrix_, nodalVars_,
             forceVec_, degreesOfFreedom_, ___]["displacements"] :=
         Flatten[Solve[Dot[globalMatrix[[degreesOfFreedom, degreesOfFreedom]],
             nodalVars[[degreesOfFreedom]]] ==
             forceVec[[degreesOfFreedom]], nodalVars[[degreesOfFreedom]]]]
```

As a matter of convenience, you can make a property the default property of the model by associating it with the invocation of the model with no arguments. Of course, thus far I have defined only one property, displacements, but it was my intent to make this the default. In the discussion I derive other properties of this model.

```
In[128]:= TrussModel[model__][] := TrussModel[model]["displacements"]
```

All this tedious preparation leads us to a solution that is very easy to use. Here is the TrussModel, depicted in Out[136] on page 545. The example data is borrowed from a problem presented in Bhatti's book (refer to the "See Also" section on page 547).

```
In[129]:= tm = createTrussModel[
             {linearElement[{{0, 0}, {1500, 3500}}, 4000., 200 * 10^3],
              linearElement[{{1500, 3500}, {5000, 5000}}, 4000., 200 * 10^3],
              linearElement[{{0, 0}, {0, 5000}}, 3000., 200 * 10^3],
              linearElement[{{0, 5000}, {5000, 5000}}, 3000., 200 * 10^3],
              linearElement[{{0, 5000}, {1500, 3500}}, 2000., 70 * 10^3]},
             {force[{1500, 3500}, 0, -150000]},
             {u[0, 0], v[0, 0], u[5000, 5000], v[5000, 5000]}]
Out[129]= TrussModel[{5}, {4}]
```

Now you can compute the nodal displacements at the nodes that are unsupported.

```
In[130]:= tm["displacements"]
Out[130]= {u[0, 5000] → 0.264704, v[0, 5000] → -0.264704,
           u[1500, 3500] → 0.538954, v[1500, 3500] → -0.953061}
```

Discussion

To complete the TrussModel, we need to define more properties. It is nice to have a visual aid to help diagnose problems in the setup of the model. A "diagram" property generates graphics. As before, I need to develop some helper functions to take care of certain tails. Each helper function has a placeholder for options (opts__), but to keep the implementation from getting any more complicated, I do not implement any options. You could add options to control the level of detail, for example, to include or suppress displacement arrows and labels. Other options might be pass-through options to Graphics.

The diagram uses a convention where supported nodes are filled-in points, whereas unsupported nodes are hollow circles with associated displacement arrows. It is possible that a node can be stationary in one direction but not the other. For example, a roller would be free to move in the x direction but not the y. Professional FEM software handles a much wider variety of boundary conditions, and standard icons are used in the industry to depict these. The goal here is simplicity over sophistication.

The function trussGraphicsNodes does most of the work of mapping the various types of nodes onto the specific graphics element. The complexity of the code is managed by judicious use of patterns and replacement rules. Some of the scaling and text placement was largely determined by trial and error, so you may need to tweak these settings for your own application or add additional code to help generalize the solution.

```
In[131]:= trussGraphicsElement[
            linearElement[{{x1_, y1_}, {x2_, y2_}}, ___], opts___] :=
          {Opacity[0.6], Line[{{x1, y1}, {x2, y2}}]}

          trussGraphicsNodes[nodalVars_, boundaryNodes_, arrowLen_, opts___] :=
          Module[{freeNodes, arrows, circles, disks},
            freeNodes = Complement[nodalVars, boundaryNodes] ;
            arrows = { Arrowheads[.02],
              freeNodes /. {u[x_, y_] :> {Arrow[{{x, y}, {x + arrowLen, y}}],
                Text[u[x, y], Offset[{12, 12}, {x + arrowLen, y}]]]},
              v[x_, y_] :> {Arrow[{{x, y}, {x, y + arrowLen}}],
                Text[v[x, y], Offset[{12, 12}, {x, y + arrowLen}]]]}}
            };
            circles =
            Union[freeNodes /. (u | v)[x_, y_] :> Circle[{x, y}, arrowLen / 6]];
            disks = Union[boundaryNodes /.
              (u | v)[x_, y_] :> Disk[{x, y}, arrowLen / 6]];
            Flatten[{circles, disks, arrows}]
          ]

          trussForceGraphics[force[{x_, y_}, fx_, fy_], scale_, opts___] :=
          Module[{a1, a2},
            a1 = {Arrow[{{x, y}, {x + fx * scale, y}}],
              Text[fx, Offset[{Sign[fx] 12, 0}, {x + fx * scale, y}]]};
            a2 = {Arrow[{{x, y}, {x, y + fy * scale}}],
              Text[fy, Offset[{0, Sign[fy] 12}, {x, y + fy * scale}]]};
            {a1, a2}
          ]

          trussBoundary[force[{x_, y_}, fx_, fy_], scale_, opts___] :=
          Module[{a1, a2},
            a1 = Arrow[{{x, y}, {x + fx * scale, y}}];
            a2 = Arrow[{{x, y}, {x, y + fy * scale}}];
            {a1, a2}
```

```
    ]

TrussModel[{elements__linearElement}, boundaryNodes_, _, _, nodalVars_,
    forceVec_, degreesOfFreedom_, forces_]["diagram", opts___] :=
  Module[{dispLen, forceScale, min, max},
    {max, min} = {Max[##], Min[##]} & @@ Flatten[List @@@ nodalVars];
    dispLen = (max - min) / 15;
    forceScale = (max - min) / (3 Max[Abs[forceVec]]);
    Graphics[{
      trussGraphicsElement[#, opts] & /@ {elements},
      trussGraphicsNodes[nodalVars, boundaryNodes, dispLen, opts],
      Flatten[trussForceGraphics[#, forceScale, opts] & /@ {forces}]
      }, Axes → True, ImagePadding → All, AxesOrigin → {-max / 10, -max / 10}]]
```

As before, once the infrastructure is in place, the diagram is easy to create by simply asking the model for the "diagram" property.

In[136]:= tm["diagram"]

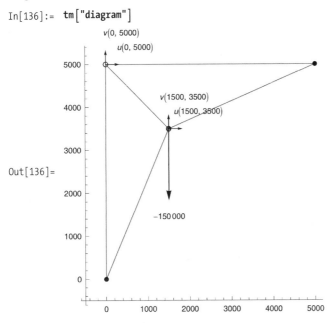

Out[136]=

Other important properties are axialStrain, axialStress, and axialForce. These will be implemented to return all or specific values for a specified element.

```
In[137]:= Clear[axialStrain]
          axialStrain[
            linearElement[{{x1_, y1_}, {x2_, y2_}}, _], displacements_] :=
            Module[{l, m, L, dv},
              dv = {u[x1, y1], v[x1, y1], u[x2, y2], v[x2, y2]} /. displacements /.
                (u | v)[__] → 0;
              L = EuclideanDistance[{x1, y1}, {x2, y2}];
              l = (x2 - x1) / L;
              m = (y2 - y1) / L;
              Plus[-#1, #2] & @@ Dot[{{l, m, 0, 0}, {0, 0, l, m}}, dv] / L]

          axialStress[linearElement[_, _, YM_], strain_] := strain * YM;

          axialForce[linearElement[_, A_, _], stress_] := stress * A ;

In[141]:= TrussModel[{elements__linearElement}, _]["elements"] := {elements}

In[142]:= TrussModel[model_]["axial strain", element_ : All] :=
          Module[{thisModel, disp, elements},
            thisModel = TrussModel[model];
            disp = thisModel["displacements"];
            elements = Cases[thisModel["elements"], element /. {All → _}];
            axialStrain[#, disp] & /@ elements]

          TrussModel[model_]["axial stress", element_ : All] :=
          Module[{thisModel, strain, elements},
            thisModel = TrussModel[model];
            elements = Cases[thisModel["elements"], element /. {All → _}];
            strain = thisModel["axial strain", element];
            MapThread[axialStress , {elements, strain}]]

In[144]:= TrussModel[model_]["axial force", element_ : All] :=
          Module[{thisModel, stress, elements},
            thisModel = TrussModel[model];
            elements = Cases[thisModel["elements"], element /. {All → _}];
            stress = thisModel["axial stress", element];
            MapThread[axialForce , {elements, stress}]]

In[145]:= tm["axial strain"]
Out[145]= {-0.000174295, -0.0000314997, -0.0000529407, -0.0000529407, 0.000320869}

In[146]:= tm["axial strain", linearElement[{{0, 0}, {1500, 3500}}, _]]
Out[146]= {-0.000174295}

In[147]:= tm["axial stress"]
Out[147]= {-34.8591, -6.29994, -10.5881, -10.5881, 22.4608}
```

```
In[148]:=  tm["axial force"]
Out[148]=  {-139436., -25199.8, -31764.4, -31764.4, 44921.7}
```

See Also

There are many books and online resources that cover FEM. For example, the theory relevant to truss structures can be found at Jason Midkiff's Virginia Tech science and engineering website: *http://bit.ly/32BUq1*.

If you are looking for books with a Mathematica focus, look no further than *Fundamental Finite Element Analysis and Applications: With Mathematica and Matlab Computations* (John Wiley) and—if you are really into FEM—*Advanced Topics in Finite Element Analysis of Structures: With Mathematica and MATLAB Computations* (John Wiley), both by M. Asghar Bhatti. The code in these books is pre-version 6, but I found few incompatibilities.

Financial Engineering

14.0 Introduction

Financial engineering (also known as computational finance) is the use of computers to create mathematical models and simulations that attempt to price financial instruments, model their sensitivity to changes in the market, hedge against these changes, and measure and manage risk. This is a high-stakes game, where there can be great reward for getting things right but even greater loss if you get things wrong. This became acutely evident during the financial crisis that started around July 2007. It might be tempting to conclude that attempts to bring mathematical rigor to the chaos of the market is foolhardy, but this would be like concluding that traditional engineering is foolhardy because a plane crashed or a bridge fell. Such failings are human failings, not mathematical ones. They only point to the need to use computational tools more diligently and more responsibly.

One goal for this chapter was to create a variety of recipes with a range of difficulties. This means that there are some recipes that may seem trivial and others that a novice might find difficult. Almost every recipe tries to demonstrate techniques that are unique to Mathematica; I hope readers of every skill level will take away techniques that they can apply to financial problems that interest them.

Mathematica has unique characteristics lacking in many other tools commonly used in the financial industry. As of version 6, Mathematica has integrated financial data that is essential to testing your models. This is a big plus; having worked in the industry, I have seen how hard it can be for *quants* (quantitative analysts) to get data easily that is immediately usable. This may seem counterintuitive; it seems that investment banks and hedge funds would be swimming in data. They are, but you often must exert great effort to access it because of technical, logistical, and political barriers. Recipe 14.1 explains how to use `FinancialData` to get access to historical and delayed market data. Unfortunately, `FinancialData` is still incomplete. As of version 7, it concentrates mainly on equities, commodities, and currency data. There is nothing related to government, municipal, or corporate bonds; options; or interest rates. Luckily, Mathematica will import data from other sources; Recipe 14.2 shows an example of that.

Another important feature of Mathematica is its ability to find exact solutions using its unparalleled symbolic capabilities. Exact solutions, when you can get them, overcome the errors and inaccuracies introduced by numerical methods, especially around the boundaries of a solution. For example, when computing Greeks it is advantageous if you can compute a symbolic derivative (D) rather than a numerical one (ND). Recipe 14.6 shows how the symbolic capabilities of Mathematica can be used to compute and visualize the Greeks for European style options. See the introductory sidebar on page 551 if this is all Greek to you!

Performance is important in financial engineering, and getting Mathematica to perform well can be tricky for the novice. Recipes 14.8, 14.9, and 14.10 show how to use some of the optimized special functions that execute at machine speed and how to use `Compile` to eliminate the overhead of handwritten interpreted code. When writing numerically intense financial functions, you should try to compile as much as possible, but there are cases where functions cannot be compiled fully and where doing so may influence results.

Finally, Mathematica has some of the best visualization tools for checking your models and developing an intuition for their behaviors across different regions of the solution. Almost every recipe includes 2D or 3D plots, but Recipe 14.12 shows how you can use lower-level graphics primitives to create useful diagrams.

A Brief Introduction to Computational Finance for the Nonquant

It is impossible to do justice to this topic in a few paragraphs, but since this is a general purpose book and computational finance is littered with specific terminology, I attempt to define some basic ideas that are assumed in the recipes in the book. The references below can help you dig deeper.

Bonds are debt instruments that allow the lending of money under set terms. Typically, the issuer (borrower) of a bond is obligated to pay the holder (lender) interest in the form of fixed payments at specified dates (the *coupon*). A wide variety of terms are associated with various bonds that influence the computation of price, yield, risk characteristics, and so forth. Some bonds may be convertible to a different security (e.g., common stock) and some may be callable (the issuer can cancel their obligation by paying back the holder before the bonds expire). A fixed-rate bond is initially issued at a set price for a standardized amount (e.g., 1000 × $100.00) at a set interest rate (e.g., 6%). After the bond is issued, its price fluctuates (based on factors such as interest rates, credit ratings, and so forth). The change in price alters the bond's yield or effective interest rate, since the interest remains fixed. So, for example, if the bond was issued at $100 but falls to $95, its yield would increase because a buyer would be getting the same interest payments for less up-front cost. Thus, price and yield have an inverse relation.

An *option* on a security is a contract that gives the holder the right (but not the obligation) to buy or sell that stock at a specific price (the strike price) on a specific date. The owner of a *call* has the right to buy; the owner of a *put* has the right to sell to the buyer. In contrast, the seller of a call is obligated to sell the security at the strike if it is *exercised* by the owner, and the seller of the put is obligated to buy. It would only make sense for an owner of an option to exercise it if it were *in the money*, if the option's strike were favorable relative to the market price of the underlying security. For example, a call for IBM at strike $100 would be favorable to the call owner if IBM were trading at $120 when the call was exercised: there would be an immediate profit of $20 less transaction fees.

Options come in different flavors. European options can only be exercised at the expiration date. These are the simplest to model. American options can be exercised at any time up to expiration. If the underlying security pays dividends, it creates further complications that must be accounted for in the model. There are also more exotic flavors of options, such as Asian and Bermudian, that you can read about in the references.

The *Greeks* are important measures for an options trader. The Greeks are computed as derivatives of the option's pricing function with respect to various parameters. For example, *delta* is the derivative with respect to the price of the underlying security. Thus, delta measures the sensitivity of the option's price with respect to changes in the underlying. *Gamma* is a second derivative with respect to price and measures the sensitivity of delta. Other important Greeks are *theta* (time), *rho* (interest rates), and *vega* (volatility). These are discussed in Recipe 14.6.

See Also

The classic text in this area is *Options, Futures, and Other Derivatives* by John C. Hull (Prentice Hall).

The *Wilmott Journal* and magazine discuss modern ideas in quantitative finance: *http://bit.ly/rm9hO*.

If you have more of a passing interest, Wikipedia has good definitions and basic explanations of most of the ideas discussed here.

An excellent book that teaches Mathematica programming in parallel with financial engineering is *Computational Financial Mathematics Using Mathematica* by Srdjan Stojanović (Springer).

14.1 Leveraging Mathematica's Bundled Financial Data

Problem

You need financial data to test your mathematical models.

Solution

Use Mathematica's curated financial data, FinancialData. This is a data source that you can query to extract quite a variety of up-to-date data (15-minute delayed and historical) on a variety of security types, what Mathematica calls "Groups". To see the available groups, execute the following. If this is the first time you are doing this, you will see the status message "Initializing Financial Indices", and the groups will display.

```
In[1]:=  FinancialData["Groups"]
Out[1]=  {Currencies, Exchanges, ExchangeTradedFunds,
          Futures, Indices, MutualFunds, Sectors, Stocks}
```

The next thing you will want to find is the available properties of the data.

```
In[2]:= FinancialData["Properties"]
```

```
Out[2]= {Ask, AskSize, Average200Day, Average50Day, AverageVolume3Month,
    Bid, BidSize, BookValuePerShare, Change, Change200Day, Change50Day,
    ChangeHigh52Week, ChangeLow52Week, CIK, Close, Company,
    CumulativeFractionalChange, CumulativeReturn, CUSIP, Dividend,
    DividendPerShare, DividendYield, EarningsPerShare, EBITDA, Exchange,
    FloatShares, ForwardEarnings, ForwardPERatio, FractionalChange,
    FractionalChange200Day, FractionalChange50Day, FractionalChangeHigh52Week,
    FractionalChangeLow52Week, High, High52Week, ISIN, LastTradeSize,
    LatestTrade, Lookup, Low, Low52Week, MarketCap, Name, Open, PEGRatio,
    PERatio, Price, PriceTarget, PriceToBookRatio, PriceToSalesRatio,
    QuarterForwardEarnings, Range, Range52Week, RawClose, RawHigh,
    RawLow, RawOpen, RawRange, Return, Sector, SEDOL, ShortRatio,
    SICCode, StandardName, Symbol, Volatility20Day, Volatility50Day,
    Volume, Website, YearEarningsEstimate, YearPERatioEstimate}
```

Now you can retrieve data for a specific symbol. By default, you will get the current price, but you can also ask for data from a specific date or within a date range.

```
In[3]:= FinancialData["IBM", "Price"]
```

```
Out[3]= 127.17
```

```
In[4]:= DateListPlot[{FinancialData["IBM", "Price", "Jan 1,2005"],
    FinancialData["AAPL", "Price", "Jan 1,2005"]}]
```

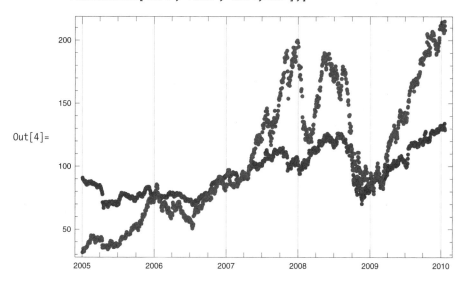

Discussion

FinancialData has a rich interface that allows you to perform many types of queries. First, let's see how you can use the interface to find what is available. Suppose you are curious to see what coverage there is for a specific symbol.

```
In[5]:=  FinancialData["IBM", "Properties"]
Out[5]=  {Ask, AskSize, Average200Day, Average50Day, AverageVolume3Month,
          Bid, BidSize, BookValuePerShare, Change, Change200Day, Change50Day,
          ChangeHigh52Week, ChangeLow52Week, CIK, Close, Company,
          CumulativeFractionalChange, CumulativeReturn, CUSIP, Dividend,
          DividendPerShare, DividendYield, EarningsPerShare, EBITDA, Exchange,
          FloatShares, ForwardEarnings, ForwardPERatio, FractionalChange,
          FractionalChange200Day, FractionalChange50Day, FractionalChangeHigh52Week,
          FractionalChangeLow52Week, High, High52Week, ISIN, LastTradeSize,
          LatestTrade, Lookup, Low, Low52Week, MarketCap, Name, Open, PEGRatio,
          PERatio, Price, PriceTarget, PriceToBookRatio, PriceToSalesRatio,
          QuarterForwardEarnings, Range, Range52Week, RawClose, RawHigh,
          RawLow, RawOpen, RawRange, Return, Sector, SEDOL, ShortRatio,
          SICCode, StandardName, Symbol, Volatility20Day, Volatility50Day,
          Volume, Website, YearEarningsEstimate, YearPERatioEstimate}
```

One difficulty is that every security is not guaranteed to have every property populated. There seem to be two possibilities when a property is not present. You may get Missing["NotAvailable"] or you may get an unevaluated expression like Financial-Data["IBM", "CumulativeFractionalChange"]. One way to see what properties are populated and also get a sample of the associated data is to execute the following (I elide the results with Short).

```
In[6]:=  With[{sec = "IBM"},
            Select[
              Table[{prop, FinancialData[sec, prop]},
                {prop, FinancialData[sec, "Properties"]}],
              FreeQ[#, {_, Missing["NotAvailable"] |
                  HoldPattern[FinancialData[__]]}] &]] // Short
Out[6]//Short=
            {{Average200Day, 122.097}, {Average50Day, 129.82}, <<54>>,
             {YearEarningsEstimate, 11.08}, {YearPERatioEstimate, 11.64}}
```

Let's look at other types of financial data and see some of the additional capabilities that are provided. Industry sectors are especially useful for studying and comparing different industries' performance.

```
In[7]:= Length[FinancialData["Sectors"]]
Out[7]= 169
```

There are 169 sectors. Here I use a pattern to find those with the string "Service" in the name.

```
In[8]:= Select[FinancialData["Sectors"], StringMatchQ[#, __ ~~ "Service" ~~ __] &]
Out[8]= {CommunicationsServicesNotElsewhere,
         LegalServices, MiscellaneousBusinessServices,
         MiscellaneousHealthAndAlliedServicesNot, OilNaturalGasFieldServices,
         RefrigerationServiceMachinery, ResearchDevelopmentAndTestingServices,
         TruckingAndCourierServicesExceptAir}
```

Given a sector, you can ask for its members. You can also use "Members" with an index, such as the S&P 500, or an exchange like the New York Stock Exchange (NYSE). Here I pick 10 OilNaturalGasFieldServices members at random.

```
In[9]:= RandomChoice[FinancialData["OilNaturalGasFieldServices", "Members"], 10]
Out[9]= {DE:HRL, PK:ONXC, PK:ASRPF, F:SJR,
         PK:VTHC, F:DG1, NYSE:WG, TO:POU, TO:POU, DE:DO1}
```

```
In[10]:= Mean[Select[Quiet[FinancialData[#, "Price"] & /@
               FinancialData["OilNaturalGasFieldServices", "Members"]], NumberQ]]
Out[10]= 13.025
```

FinancialData provides information on 153 currencies. You can get the exchange rate by using a string or list notation.

```
In[11]:= Length[FinancialData["Currencies"]]
Out[11]= 153
```

```
In[12]:= FinancialData["USD/EUR"]
Out[12]= 0.7065
```

```
In[13]:= FinancialData[{"USD", "EUR"}]
Out[13]= 0.7065
```

FinancialData does not provide a notation to get more than a single property at a time, which is unfortunate. You can use Outer to get this behavior, but it seems it could be done more efficiently if this were native to FinancialData. First I extract U.S. oil and gas service companies using FinancialData's ability to list the members of a sector.

```
In[14]:= americanOilGasCos =
            Select[FinancialData["OilNaturalGasFieldServices", "Members"],
              StringMatchQ[#, ("AMEX:" | "NYSE:" | "NASDAQ:") ~~ __] &];
```

Then, using Outer, I extract the market cap and a price. Recalling that market cap equals *share price * shares outstanding*, it is easy to compute a share-weighted average price for the sector by summing the market cap and dividing by the sum of the shares outstanding. I put this in a function sharedWeightedAvg so we can reuse it later.

```
In[15]:= sharedWeightedAvg[symbols_List, price_] := Module[{data},
            data = Select[
              Quiet[Outer[FinancialData[#1, #2] &, symbols, {"MarketCap", price}]],
              And @@ (NumberQ /@ #) &];
            Total[data][[1]] / Total[Divide @@ # & /@ data]]
          sharedWeightedAvg[americanOilGasCos, "Close"]
Out[16]= 33.619
```

You can add as many properties as you need to the second argument of Outer. As usual, it is a good idea to filter out invalid data, as I do here by using Select and testing for numeric values in both entries using And @@ (NumberQ /@ #) & as the filter function.

You can use "Members" with indices and exchanges. Here I get the share-weighted average for the Dow Jones Industrial Average (DJIA) stocks.

```
In[17]:= sharedWeightedAvg[FinancialData["^DJI", "Members"], "Close"]
Out[17]= 35.3389
```

```
In[18]:= FinancialData["Exchanges"]
Out[18]= {AMEX, Amsterdam, AustraliaASX, Barcelona, Berlin, Bilbao, Bombay, Brussels,
          BuenosAires, Cairo, CBOE, CBOT, CME, Colombo, COMEX, Copenhagen,
          Dusseldorf, Eurex, Euronext, Frankfurt, Hamburg, Hanover, HongKong,
          IndiaNSE, Ireland, Jakarta, KCBT, KoreaKOSDAQ, KoreaKSE, Lisbon,
          LondonIOB, LSE, Madrid, MadridCATS, MexicoBMV, Milan, Munich, NASDAQ,
          NewZealandNZX, NYBOT, NYMEX, NYSE, Oslo, OTCBB, Paris, PhilippinesPSE,
          Pinksheets, Prague, RussiaRTS, Santiago, SaoPaulo, Shanghai,
          Shenzhen, Singapore, Stockholm, Stuttgart, SwitzerlandSWX, TaiwanOTC,
          TaiwanTSEC, TelAviv, Toronto, TSXVenture, Valencia, Vienna, Xetra}
```

A special property called "Lookup" allows you to search using patterns. Here I search for New York Mercantile Exchange (NYMEX) symbols that begin with "A" and retrieve the full name.

```
In[19]:= FinancialData[#, "Name"] & /@ FinancialData["NYM:A*", "Lookup"]
Out[19]= {Ardour Global XL Mar 2009, Ardour Global XL Jun 2009,
          Ardour Global XL Sep 2009, Ardour Global XL Dec 2008}
```

You can use dynamic features to create a mini interface for exploring the data. Here I use PopMenu to create an interface over all the symbols in the Dow Jones Industrials and all available properties.

```
In[20]:= DynamicModule[{symbol = "MSFT", prop},
           Row[{PopupMenu[Dynamic[symbol], FinancialData["^DJI", "Members"]],
             PopupMenu[Dynamic[prop], FinancialData["Properties"]],
             Dynamic[FinancialData[symbol, prop]]}, " "]]
```

Out[20]= | MSFT ∨ | Ask ∨ | 28.56

In the solution, we saw that data can be retrieved over intervals of time. The intervals can specify a start date, a start and an end date, and also a period, such as "Day", "Week", "Month", or "Year".

```
In[21]:= FinancialData["^DJI", {"Jan 1,2008", "Jan 1,2009", "Month"}]
Out[21]= {{{2008, 1, 2}, 12650.4}, {{2008, 2, 1}, 12266.4}, {{2008, 3, 3}, 12262.9},
          {{2008, 4, 1}, 12820.1}, {{2008, 5, 1}, 12638.3}, {{2008, 6, 2}, 11350.},
          {{2008, 7, 1}, 11378.}, {{2008, 8, 1}, 11543.6}, {{2008, 9, 2}, 10850.7},
          {{2008, 10, 1}, 9325.01}, {{2008, 11, 3}, 8829.04}, {{2008, 12, 1}, 8776.39}}
```

14.2 Importing Financial Data from Websites

Problem

The data you want is not yet available from FinancialData but it is available from another website.

Solution

The Import function can retrieve data directly from websites like Yahoo! Finance that support an interface that uses HTTP GET-style queries. Here I extract options data for IBM.

```
In[22]:= With[{optSymbol = "IBMGM.X"},
           Import["http://download.finance.yahoo.com/d/quotes.csv?s=" <>
             optSymbol <> "&f=sl1d1t1c1ohgv&e=.csv"]]
Out[22]= {{IBMGM.X, 0., N/A, N/A, 0., 0., 0., 0., 0}}
```

Discussion

The Yahoo! URL structure is self-explanatory except for the f=sl1d1t1c1ohgv portion. The *f* stands for "format," and the characters define the types of data you want to download. For example, *s* stands for symbol, *l1* last trade price, and *d1* is the trade date. The entire set is available on a website (see the "See Also" section on page 559).

To get more data on options chains it is useful to be able to encode an option symbol. Each option symbol is made up of a base symbol, an expiration month letter in the range A-L for calls and M-X for puts, and a strike price letter. Standard strike prices are in increments of 5 and use the letters A-T, but there are also fractional strike prices using letters U-Z (see the "See Also" section on page 559).

```
In[23]:= strikePriceCode[strike_Integer] /; Mod[strike, 5] == 0 :=
           FromCharacterCode[ToCharacterCode["A"] + Mod[strike / 5 - 1, 20]]
         strikePriceCode[strike_Real] :=
           FromCharacterCode[ToCharacterCode["U"] + Floor[Mod[(strike - 2.5) / 5 - 1, 6]]]
         expirationCall[month_] :=
           FromCharacterCode[ToCharacterCode["A"] + month - 1]
         expirationPut[month_] :=
           FromCharacterCode[ToCharacterCode["M"] + month - 1]
```

Now it is easy to download a range of options data, such as these July (month 7) calls for IBM at various strike prices.

```
In[27]:= With[{symbols = Flatten[Table["IBM" <> expirationCall[7] <>
               strikePriceCode[strike] <> ".X", {strike, 60, 135, 5}]]},
           Table[Import["http://download.finance.yahoo.com/d/quotes.csv?s=" <>
               optSymbol <> "&f=s11d1t1c1ohgv&e=.csv"], {optSymbol, symbols}]]
Out[27]= {{{IBMGL.X, 0., N/A, 2:56pm, N/A, N/A, N/A, N/A, N/A}},
          {{IBMGM.X, 0., N/A, N/A, 0., 0., 0., 0., 0}},
          {{IBMGN.X, 0., N/A, N/A, 0., 0., 0., 0., 0}},
          {{IBMGO.X, 0., N/A, N/A, 0., 0., 0., 0., 0}},
          {{IBMGP.X, 51.4, 1/22/2010, 10:54am, 0., 51.4, 51.4, 51.4, 10}},
          {{IBMGQ.X, 46.45, 1/22/2010, 10:55am, 0., 46.45, 46.45, 46.45, 10}},
          {{IBMGR.X, 39.15, 1/22/2010, 10:54am, 0., 39., 39.15, 39.15, 34}},
          {{IBMGS.X, 35., 1/22/2010, 10:54am, 0., 34.85, 35., 35., 52}},
          {{IBMGT.X, 29.45, 1/22/2010, 10:54am, 0., 29.45, 29.45, 29.45, 2}},
          {{IBMGA.X, 24.78, 1/22/2010, 10:54am, 0., 25.73, 24.78, 24.78, 106}},
          {{IBMGB.X, 18.7, 1/22/2010, 10:55am, -2., 21.52, 19.8, 18.7, 16}},
          {{IBMGC.X, 15.65, 1/22/2010, 10:54am, -0.45, 16.6, 15.65, 15.65, 55}},
          {{IBMGD.X, 11.45, 1/22/2010, 10:55am, -0.9, 11.15, 11.95, 11.15, 49}},
          {{IBMGE.X, 8.05, 1/22/2010, 10:54am, -0.95, 8.55, 8.75, 8.05, 111}},
          {{IBMGF.X, 5.59, 1/22/2010, 10:55am, -0.76, 6.4, 6.2, 5.5, 62}},
          {{IBMGG.X, 3.6, 1/22/2010, 10:54am, -0.6, 4.5, 4.05, 3.6, 63}}}
```

You can also import data from files in a variety of formats and from databases (provided you have access to such databases). See Recipe 17.9 for Mathematica's database connectivity capabilities.

See Also

An explanation of the Yahoo! interface can be found at: *http://bit.ly/dyiIPO*.

The encoding of options ticker symbols is explained here *http://bit.ly/24yb0p*.

14.3 Present Value of Future Cash Flows

Problem

You want to compute the present value of a set of cash payments or receipts over time.

Solution

Use the standard formula for compound interest calculations to discount future cash flows to the present.

```
In[28]:= pv[cashFlows_List, times_List, rate_Real] :=
```

$$Module\left[\{T = Length[cashFlows]\}, \sum_{t=1}^{T} \frac{cashFlows[[t]]}{(1 + rate)^{times[[t]]}}\right]$$

For example, if you pay $1000 today to receive income of $100, $300, $600, and $600 in the next four years with a rate of 5%, the present value is

```
In[29]:= pv[{-1000.0, 100.0, 300.0, 600.0, 600.0}, {0, 1, 2, 3, 4}, 0.05]
Out[29]= 379.271
```

Discussion

Cash in hand today is worth more then the same amount in the future. Present value is determined by discounting future cash flows by a *discount factor*. The solution follows from the formula for a discount factor in terms of an interest rate r and a time t, which is $(r + 1)^{-t}$. There are some standard types of cash flow arrangements, and you can use Simplify to derive them from the standard present value formula in the solution. For example, a *perpetuity* is a set of fixed cash flows X that repeat forever.

```
In[30]:= Simplify[Sum[X / (1 + r)^t, {t, 1, Infinity}]]
```

$$Out[30]= \frac{X}{r}$$

```
In[31]:= 1 / ((1 + r)^t) // TraditionalForm
```

```
Out[31]//TraditionalForm=
```

$$(r + 1)^{-t}$$

Hence...

```
In[32]:= pvPerpetuity[cash_Real, rate_Real] := cash / rate
```

An *annuity* is a set of fixed cash flows X that repeat for a specified number of periods T.

```
In[33]:= Simplify[Sum[X / (1 + r)^t, {t, 1, T}]]
```

$$Out[33]= \frac{X - (1 + r)^{-T} X}{r}$$

```
In[34]:= pvPerpetuity[100.00, 0.03]
Out[34]= 3333.33
```

Hence...

```
In[35]:= pvAnuity[cash_Real, rate_Real, periods_Integer] :=
```

$$\frac{cash - (1 + rate)^{-periods} cash}{rate}$$

```
In[36]:= pvAnuity[100.00, 0.03, 10]
Out[36]= 853.02
```

Closely related to present value is the *internal rate of return*, the rate that would make the present value equal to zero. You can use FindRoot to calculate the internal rate of return for a set of cash flows. Here we tell FindRoot to begin searching for a solution at irr of 0.0.

```
In[37]:= internalRateOfReturn[cashFlows_List, times_List] :=
            FindRoot[pv[cashFlows, times, irr], {irr, 0.0}]

In[38]:= internalRateOfReturn[{-1000.0, 100.0, 300.0, 600.0, 600.0}, {0, 1, 2, 3, 4}]
Out[38]= {irr → 0.169775}
```

In finance, it is more common to deal with continuously compounding interest than the discrete compounding formulas discussed. The present value in terms of continuously compounding interest is

```
In[39]:= pvCC[cashFlows_List, times_List, rate_Real] :=
            Module[{N = Length[cashFlows]},
              Sum[cashFlows[[i]] / E^(rate * times[[i]]),
              {i, 1, N}]]

In[40]:= pvCC[{-1000.0, 100.0, 300.0, 600.0, 600.0}, {0, 1, 2, 3, 4}, 0.05]
Out[40]= 374.237
```

See Also

You may want to play with (and download the source code for) some of the Wolfram demonstrations that cover present value and related basic financial concepts. See, for example, *http://bit.ly/1D7JVU*.

14.4 Interest Rate Sensitivity of Bonds

Problem

You want to determine the fair value of a bond and analyze its performance under varying market conditions.

Solution

Before you can analyze a bond, you need to know how to compute its price and yield to maturity. The price of a fixed-rate bond is equivalent to the present value of the bond's coupon payments. For example, if a three-year bond has a face value of $100 and makes yearly payments of 10% and the present interest rate is 8%, then the fair bond price should be

```
In[41]:= pv[{10, 10, 110}, {1, 2, 3}, 0.08]
Out[41]= 105.154
```

The price only captures one aspect of a bond. You may also want to know the effective interest rate of the bond if it is held to maturity (*yield to maturity*). This is the same as the internal rate of return calculation of Recipe 12.1. The first cash flow is the bond's price, then the two coupon payments, and the final is coupon plus face value.

```
In[42]:= (*Yield to maturity for a bond is the same
            calculation as IRR with bond price as first cash flow.*)
          internalRateOfReturn[{-105.154, 10, 10, 110}, {0, 1, 2, 3}]
Out[42]= {irr → 0.0800007}
```

It is no accident that the yield to maturity is equal (modulo rounding errors) to the current interest rate. This is a sign that the bond is priced correctly.

Investors in bonds want to understand a bond's sensitivity to changes in current interest rates. The price of an asset with long-term cash flows has more interest-rate sensitivity than an asset with cash flows in the near future. The *duration* is a weighted average maturity of a bond.

```
In[43]:= duration[cashFlows_List, times_List, rate_Real] :=
           Module[{T = Length[cashFlows], D, B},
             {D, B} = Sum[{(times[[t]] * cashFlows[[t]]) / (1 + rate)^times[[t]],
                 cashFlows[[t]] / (1 + rate)^times[[t]]}, {t, 1, T}]; D/B]

In[44]:= duration[{10, 10, 110}, {1, 2, 3}, 0.08]
Out[44]= 2.74236

In[45]:= convexity[cashFlows_List, times_List, rate_Real] :=
           Module[{T = Length[cashFlows], B},
             B = pv[cashFlows, times, rate]; (1/B) * (1/(1 + rate)^2) *
               Sum[(times[[t]] + times[[t]]^2) *
                 (cashFlows[[t]] / (1 + rate)^times[[t]]), {t, 1, T}]]

In[46]:= convexity[{10, 10, 110}, {1, 2, 3}, 0.08]
Out[46]= 9.11374
```

Discussion

```
In[47]:= Plot[pv[{10, 10, 10, 10, 10, 110}, {1, 2, 3, 4, 5, 6}, r], {r, 0.0, 0.20}]
```

Out[47]=

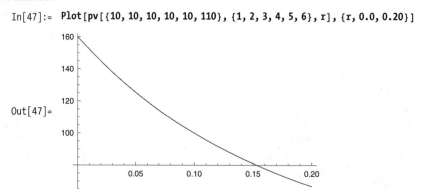

```
In[48]:= Plot[pv[Append[Table[10, {119}], 110], Range[1, 120], r], {r, 0.0, 0.20}]
```

Out[48]=

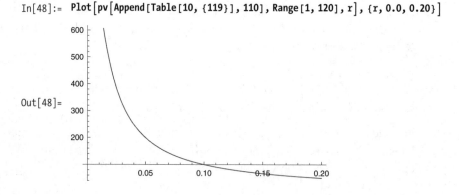

14.5 Constructing and Manipulating Yield Curves

Problem

You want to build a yield curve from underlying spot rates and then model changes in the curve so you can model the return of a portfolio of rate-sensitive securities.

Solution

If you are only interested in changes in the yield curve at a particular maturity, you can use published yields for various maturities and use interpolation. For example, here is some interest rate data taken from Bloomberg in late June 2009. The pairs are {days, rate}.

```
In[49]:= rates = {{7, 0.01}, {14, 0.04}, {30, 0.05}, {60, 0.17}, {180, 0.29},
            {360, 0.4}, {730, 1.11}, {1095, 1.63}, {1825, 2.56}, {2555, 3.20},
            {3650, 3.54}, {5475, 4.12}, {7300, 4.49}, {10950, 4.86}};
```

```
In[50]:= iRates = Interpolation[rates, Method → "Spline"];
```

```
In[51]:= Show[ListPlot[rates, PlotStyle → {PointSize[0.01]},
            PlotRange → {{0, 11000}, {0, 6}}],
          Plot[iRates[t], {t, 7, 11000}]
        ]
```

Out[51]=

Interpolation is all well and good, but if you want to understand the dynamics of the curve, you need a model. The Nelson-Siegel function is a popular parametric model of the yield curve.

In[52]:= nsYieldCurve[m_, β0_, β1_, β2_, τ_] :=
$$\beta0 + \frac{\beta1 \, (1 - \text{Exp}[-m / \tau])}{(m / \tau)} +$$
$$\beta2 \left(\frac{(1 - \text{Exp}[-m / \tau])}{(m / \tau)} - \text{Exp}[-m / \tau] \right)$$

In[53]:= fit = FindFit[rates, nsYieldCurve[m, b0, b1, b2, t],
        {b0, b1, b2, t}, m, Method → NMinimize]

Out[53]= {b0 → 5.28846, b1 → −5.26294, b2 → −3.75868, t → 651.468}

Here I use the fitted curve to initialize a Manipulate. You can then play with the parameters to get a feel for their effect.

In[54]:= Manipulate[Show[ListPlot[rates,
          PlotStyle → {PointSize[0.01]}, PlotRange → {{0, 11000}, {0, 6}}],
        Plot[nsYieldCurve[m, beta0, beta1, beta2, tau],
          {m, 1, 11000}, PlotRange → {{0, 11000}, {0, 6}}]],
      {{beta0, b0}, 3, 6, 0.1},
      {{beta1, b1}, 2, −6, 0.1},
      {{beta2, b2}, −5, −1, 0.1},
      {{tau, t}, 100, 1000, 10}, SaveDefinitions → True] /. fit

Out[54]=

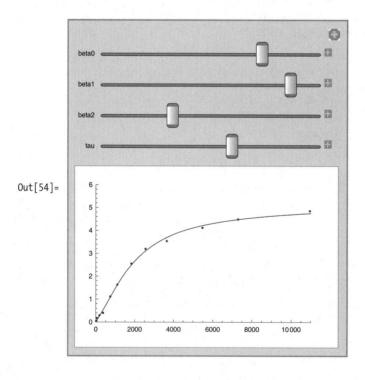

Discussion

An extension of the Nelson-Siegel model is the Svensson model, which addresses problems with convexity, inaccuracies introduced for large changes in yield due to the nonlinear relationship between prices and yields. The capital gain induced by a decline in the yield is larger than the capital loss induced by an equal-sized increase in the yield.

Given the Svensson model for the forward curve, you can use Mathematica's symbolic integration capabilities to find the zero coupon (or spot) model.

```
In[55]:=  Clear[svForwardCurve, svSpotCurve];
          svForwardCurve[m_, β0_, β1_, β2_, β3_, τ1_, τ2_] :=
           β0 + β1 Exp[-m/τ1] + β2 (m/τ1) Exp[-m/τ1] + β3 (m/τ2) Exp[-m/τ2]
In[57]:=  svSpotCurve[m_, β0_, β1_, β2_, β3_, τ1_, τ2_] =
          FullSimplify[ (1/m) *
             Integrate[svForwardCurve[m, β0, β1, β2, β3, τ1, τ2], {m, 0, m}]]
```

$$Out[57]= \frac{m\,\beta0 + \beta1\left(\tau1 - e^{-\frac{m}{\tau1}}\,\tau1\right) + \beta2\left(\tau1 - e^{-\frac{m}{\tau1}}\,(m + \tau1)\right) + \beta3\left(\tau2 - e^{-\frac{m}{\tau2}}\,(m + \tau2)\right)}{m}$$

The solution demonstrates a so-called parametric method (i.e., a method based on parameters that have real-world meaning). There are also nonparametric methods that are in use where curves are fit using polynomials and tension splines. See the following references.

See Also

This recipe is based on *Parsimonious Modeling of Yield Curves* by Charles R. Nelson and Andrew F. Siegel (*Journal of Business*, Vol. 60, No. 4 [Oct. 1987]: 473-489), which can be found online at *http://bit.ly/1mQ3mq*.

A library of Mathematica code for working with the term structure of interest rates can be found on Mark Fisher's website at *http://bit.ly/3hW4KC*, with documentation at *http://bit.ly/1ormSc*.

A more thorough investigation of yield curve models can be found in this notebook at the Wolfram Library Archives, *http://bit.ly/17OU4U*, which was developed by Jan Hurt of the Charles University of Prague.

14.6 Black-Scholes for European Option Pricing

Problem

You want to price European puts and calls using the Black-Scholes formula.

Solution

We give the solution to the Black-Scholes formula here without derivation. There are many excellent resources listed in the "See Also" section on page 572 for readers interested in the theory underlying this solution. The helper functions d1 and d2 have become fairly standard within the literature, so I use them here despite my personal aversion to short, cryptic names. The expression involving the d1 term in the pricing functions is related to the value of acquiring the stock; the expression involving the d2 term relates to the value of exercising the option on expiration.

```
In[58]:= Clear[d1, d2, priceEuroCall, priceEuroPut]
```

These helper functions are used by both priceEuroCall and priceEuroPut.

```
In[59]:= d1[price_Real, strike_Real, volatility_Real, maturityT_Real, rate_Real] :=
           (Log[price / strike] + (rate + volatility^2. / 2.) * maturityT) /
           (volatility * Sqrt[maturityT]);
         d2[price_Real, strike_Real, volatility_Real, maturityT_Real, rate_Real] :=
           d1[price, strike, volatility, maturityT, rate] -
           volatility * Sqrt[maturityT];
         cumNormDist[x_ ?NumberQ] := CDF[NormalDistribution[], x];
```

Given the price of a stock, the strike price of the option, the volatility, time to option maturity in fractions of a year, and the risk-free interest rate, compute the value of a call or put option.

```
In[62]:= priceEuroCall[price_Real, strike_Real,
             volatility_Real, maturityT_Real, rate_Real] :=
           price * cumNormDist[d1[price, strike, volatility, maturityT, rate]] -
           strike * Exp[-rate * maturityT] *
           cumNormDist[d2[price, strike, volatility, maturityT, rate]]
```

The fact that a put can be priced in terms of a call is called put-call parity.

```
In[63]:= priceEuroPut[price_Real, strike_Real, volatility_Real, maturityT_Real,
             rate_Real] := priceEuroCall[price, strike, volatility, maturityT, rate] +
           strike * Exp[-rate * maturityT] - price
```

Here we compute the value of a call option with strike $60 and 1/2 year to maturity, with the underlying stock trading at $70, with a volatility of 0.29, and a risk-free rate of 4%. The volatility is usually measured as the standard deviation of the stock price.

```
In[64]:= priceEuroCall[70., 60., 0.29, 0.5, 0.04]
Out[64]= 12.6323
```

Here we show the opposing relationship between a call and a put with equal attributes by plotting their values against the price of the underlying stock. A call increases in value with the stock price, whereas a put decreases in value.

```
In[65]:= Plot[{priceEuroCall[s, 60., 0.29, 0.5, 0.04],
        priceEuroPut[s, 60., 0.29, 0.5, 0.04]}, {s, 40, 80},
      PlotRange -> All, AxesLabel -> {"stock price", "option price"},
      PlotRange → {{0, 15}, {2, 15}}, ImageSize → Small]
```

Out[65]=

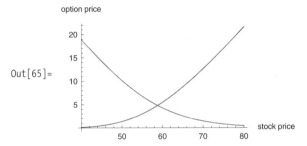

Discussion

Although the ability to price an option is vital to successful trading, it is equally vital to measure the sensitivity of an option (or any other derivative security) to changes in the economic environment. These measures are based on mathematical derivatives of the pricing function. These measures are collectively known as *the Greeks* because each is associated with a Greek letter.

```
In[66]:= Clear[deltaEuroCall, deltaEuroPut,
      gammaEuroCall, gammaEuroPut, thetaEuroCall, thetaEuroPut,
      rhoEuroCall, rhoEuroPut, vegaEuroCall, vegaEuroPut]
```

Delta is a measure of the sensitivity of an option to changes in the stock price. It is computed as the first derivative of the pricing function with respect to the underlying stock price.

```
In[67]:= deltaEuroCall[price_Real, strike_,
        volatility_Real, maturityT_Real, rate_Real] :=
      Module[{s}, D[priceEuroCall[s, strike, volatility, maturityT, rate], s] /.
        s :→ price]
      deltaEuroPut[price_Real, strike_, volatility_Real,
        maturityT_Real, rate_Real] :=
      D[priceEuroPut[s, strike, volatility, maturityT, rate], s] /. s :→ price
```

Gamma is a measure of the sensitivity of the delta to changes in the stock price. It is computed as the second derivative of the pricing function with respect to the underlying stock price.

```
In[69]:= gammaEuroCall[price_Real, strike_, volatility_, maturityT_, rate_] :=
         Module[{s},
          D[priceEuroCall[s, strike, volatility, maturityT, rate], {s, 2}] /.
           s :> price]
         gammaEuroPut[price_Real, strike_, volatility_, maturityT_, rate_] :=
          Module[{s},
           D[priceEuroPut[s, strike, volatility, maturityT, rate], {s, 2}] /.
            s :> price]
```

Theta is a measure of the sensitivity of the option price to time. It is computed as the
first derivative of the pricing function with respect to the time to expiration (maturity).

```
In[71]:= thetaEuroCall[price_Real, strike_,
          volatility_Real, maturityT_Real, rate_Real] :=
         Module[{t}, -D[priceEuroCall[price, strike, volatility, t, rate], t] /.
          t :> maturityT]
         thetaEuroPut[price_Real, strike_, volatility_Real,
          maturityT_Real, rate_Real] :=
          Module[{t}, -D[priceEuroPut[price, strike, volatility, t, rate], t] /.
           t :> maturityT]
```

Rho is a measure of the sensitivity of the option price to changes in the risk-free rate.
It is computed as the first derivative of the pricing function with respect to the interest rate.

```
In[73]:= rhoEuroCall[price_Real, strike_Real,
          volatility_Real, maturityT_Real, rate_Real] :=
         Module[{r}, D[priceEuroCall[price, strike, volatility, maturityT, r],
          r] /. r :> rate]
         rhoEuroPut[price_Real, strike_Real, volatility_Real,
          maturityT_Real, rate_Real] :=
         Module[{r}, D[priceEuroPut[price, strike, volatility, maturityT, r], r] /.
          r :> rate]
```

Vega (also known as kappa) is a measure of the sensitivity of the option price to
changes in the volatility. It is computed as the first derivative of the pricing function
with respect to the volatility.

```
In[75]:= vegaEuroCall[price_Real, strike_Real,
            volatility_Real, maturityT_Real, rate_Real] :=
          Module[{v}, D[priceEuroCall[price, strike, v, maturityT, rate], v] /.
            v :→ volatility]
        vegaEuroPut[price_Real, strike_Real, volatility_Real,
            maturityT_Real, rate_Real] :=
          Module[{v}, D[priceEuroPut[price, strike, v, maturityT, rate], v] /.
            v :→ volatility]
```

Here we compute delta of a call with strike $60 with 6 months left to maturity when the stock is trading at $40. This shows that the option will change value by roughly 3.7 cents for a dollar move. We can confirm this using the pricing function.

```
In[77]:= deltaEuroCall[40.00, 60., 0.29, 0.5, 0.04]
Out[77]= 0.0377654
```

This is in basic agreement with the difference between the value of the option at a stock price of $40.50 and $39.50 (we choose a dollar spread that places the delta stock price at the center).

```
In[78]:= priceEuroCall[40.50, 60., 0.29, 0.5, 0.04] -
            priceEuroCall[39.50, 60., 0.29, 0.5, 0.04]
Out[78]= 0.0378454
```

You can get an intuitive feel for the behavior of options by creating a 3D plot of each Greek with respect to stock price and time.

Note how delta increases sharply as the stock price approaches the strike and how this sensitivity is stronger near expiration ($t = 0$).

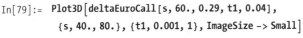

```
In[79]:= Plot3D[deltaEuroCall[s, 60., 0.29, t1, 0.04],
            {s, 40., 80.}, {t1, 0.001, 1}, ImageSize -> Small]
```

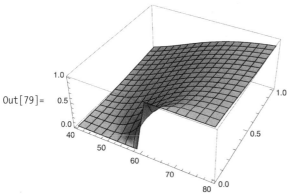

Out[79]=

The sensitivity of the delta to shrinking time to maturity and strike price is rein-
forced by the plot of the gamma, which is the second derivative of the price, or the
first derivative of the delta.

In[80]:= Plot3D[gammaEuroCall[s1, 60., 0.29, t1, 0.04],
{s1, 40., 80.}, {t1, 0.001, 1.}, ImageSize -> Small]

Out[80]=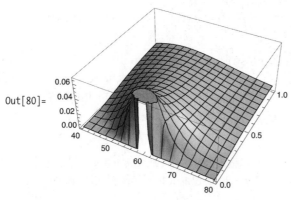

The plot of theta shows that the value of an option will decay more rapidly with ad-
verse moves of the underlying stock when there is a short time to expiration compared to when there are longer times.

In[81]:= Plot3D[thetaEuroCall[s1, 60, 0.29, t1, 0.04],
{s1, 40, 80}, {t1, 0.001, 1.}, ImageSize → Small]

Out[81]=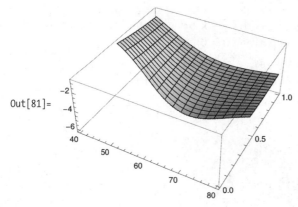

```
In[82]:= Plot3D[rhoEuroCall[s1, 60., 0.29, t1, 0.04],
            {s1, 40, 80}, {t1, 0.001, 1}, ImageSize → Small]
```

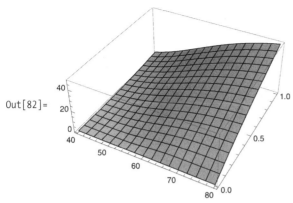

Note how sensitivity to volatility increases near the strike price and with increasing time. This follows from the fact that high volatility has more impact over longer time periods and for options that are in the money (because of the larger delta and gamma of in-the-money options).

```
In[83]:= Plot3D[vegaEuroCall[s1, 60, 0.29, t1, 0.04],
            {s1, 20, 100}, {t1, 0.01, 0.5}, ImageSize → Small]
```

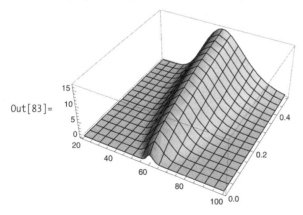

The interactive capabilities of Mathematica 6 provide an excellent platform for getting the feel of the behavior of the Greeks. However, for sake of responsiveness, it is a good idea to evaluate the derivative outside the Manipulate. You can use With to evaluate the derivative before the call to Manipulate and FullSimplify to make sure it is in simplest form.

```
In[84]:=  manipulateDeltaEuroCall[] := Block[{k, v, t1, r},
            With[{deltaCall = FullSimplify[D[priceEuroCall[s, k, v, t1, r], s]]},
              Manipulate[Plot3D[Evaluate[deltaCall], {s, 40., 80.}, {t1, 0.001, 1.},
                PerformanceGoal → "Speed"], {{k, 60., "Strike"}, 10., 100.},
                  {{r, 0.04, "Rate"}, 0.01, 0.12}, {{v, 0.29, "Volatility"}, 0.01, 0.40},
                    ContinuousAction → False, AppearanceElements → All]]]

In[85]:=  manipulateDeltaEuroCall[]
```

Out[85]=

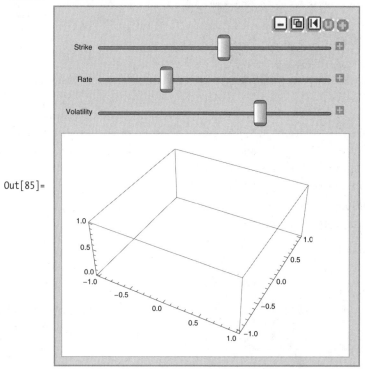

See Also

Modeling Financial Derivatives with Mathematica (Cambridge University Press) by William Shaw is an excellent resource for the quant interested in modeling vanilla and more exotic flavors (such as Asian options) in Mathematica. It concentrates on analytical solutions rather than solutions based on numerical methods.

Black-Scholes and Beyond: Option Pricing Models by Neil A. Chris (McGraw-Hill) covers the basics of modern option pricing. Wikipedia also provides basic information on the Black-Scholes model: *http://bit.ly/c8IrYX*.

14.7 Computing the Implied Volatility of Financial Derivatives

Problem

You want to compute the volatility of an option that is implied by its current market price.

Solution

Use FindRoot to solve for the volatility.

```
In[86]:= impliedVolEuroCall[price_, strike_, maturityT_, rate_, optionsPrice_] :=
           volatility /.
             FindRoot[priceEuroCall[price, strike, volatility, maturityT, rate] ==
               optionsPrice, {volatility, 0.2}]

In[87]:= impliedVolEuroPut[price_, strike_, maturityT_, rate_, optionsPrice_] :=
           volatility /.
             FindRoot[priceEuroPut[price, strike, volatility, maturityT, rate] ==
               optionsPrice, {volatility, 0.2}]

In[88]:= impliedVolEuroCall[58.00, 60., 0.5, 0.04, 3.8]
Out[88]= 0.254867
```

Discussion

Implied volatility is the volatility that is implied by the market price of the option given the pricing model. The idea is that the market will find the fair price for the option, and from that, you can back out the volatility of the underlying security that the market is pricing in. This is in contrast to historical volatility, which is a direct measure of the movement of the underlying's price over recent history.

In the solution, FindRoot searches for a numerical root of the pricing function that will yield the observed price, given the other option parameters.

14.8 Speeding Up NDSolve When Solving Black-Scholes and Other PDEs

Problem

You want to compute numerical solutions to partial differential equations (PDEs), such as the Black-Scholes PDE. NDSolve can sometimes take too much time or lose accuracy near critical values. You would like to speed up NDSolve without loss of accuracy where it matters.

$$-\partial_t u[x,t] == \frac{1}{2}\, \sigma^2 x^2 \partial_{x,x} u[x,t] + r\, x\, \partial_x u[x,t] - r\, u[x,t];$$

Solution

This recipe was motivated by work done by Andreas Lauschke and used with permission. Refer to the "See Also" section on page 578 for more information.

To illustrate the problem, I use the PDE for a European put on a dividend-paying security. For the interest and dividend, I use fixed rate plus time-varying rate that is strictly increasing. For volatility, I use a volatility smile, which reflects the observation that volatility is higher for in- and out-of-the-money options and lower for at-the-money options. In the PDE, x represents the price of the underlying and t is time.

```
In[89]:= Clear[iRate, dividend, sigma, makePutEuropean];
         iRate[t_] := 0.035 + t 0.01 / 3
         dividend[t_] := 0.01 + t 0.01 / 3;
         sigma[price_, strike_, time_] := 1. / 10000 (price - strike) ^2 + 0.25
         Options[makePutEuropean] = {Method → Automatic};
         makePutEuropean[strike_, lower_,
           upper_, timeToExp_, opts : OptionsPattern[]] :=
         Module[{},
           NDSolve[{D[u[x, t], t] + 1 / 2 D[u[x, t], x, x] x^2 sigma[x, strike, t] ^2 +
               (iRate[t] - dividend[t]) x D[u[x, t], x] - iRate[t] u[x, t] == 0,
             u[x, timeToExp] == Max[0, strike - x],
             u[lower, t] == strike,
             u[upper, t] == 0}, u, {x, lower, upper}, {t, 0, timeToExp}, opts]]
```

You can adjust different aspects of this model to suit your needs. The main point here is to consider the performance of NDSolve using different options.

```
In[95]:= Off[NDSolve::"mxsst"]
         {timePut1, put1} = makePutEuropean[50, 0, 250, 1] // Timing
Out[96]= {3.01551, {{u → InterpolatingFunction[{{0., 250.}, {0., 1.}}, <>]}}}
```

It took just over eight seconds to solve this PDE numerically. However, you can do better using an adaptive grid method where you instruct NDSolve to sample more points around the strike price while being looser away from the strike. Here I define a function for the adaptive grid but defer explanation until the discussion.

```
In[97]:= Clear[makeAdaptiveGrid, makePutEuropeanAdaptive]
         makeAdaptiveGrid[strike_, size_ : 200, deg_ : 1] :=
           Module[{a = 2 deg + 1, incr = 2 strike / size},
             Table[((x - strike)^a / strike^(a - 1)) + strike, {x, 0, strike * 2, incr}]]

In[99]:= makePutEuropeanAdaptive[strike_, lower_, upper_, timeToExp_] :=
           Module[{},
             NDSolve[{D[u[x, t], t] + 1/2 D[u[x, t], x, x] x^2 sigma[x, strike, t]^2 +
                 (iRate[t] - dividend[t]) x D[u[x, t], x] == iRate[t] u[x, t],
               u[x, timeToExp] == Max[0, strike - x],
               u[lower, t] == strike,
               u[upper, t] == 0}, u, {x, lower, upper},
               {t, 0, timeToExp}, Method :> {"MethodOfLines",
                 "SpatialDiscretization" -> {"TensorProductGrid", "Coordinates" -> N@
                   Union[makeAdaptiveGrid[strike], Range[2 strike, 5 strike, 2]]}}]]

In[100]:= Off[NDSolve : : "eerri", NDSolve::"eerr"]
          {timePut2, put2} = makePutEuropeanAdaptive[50, 0, 250, 1] // Timing
Out[101]= {0.129383, {{u -> InterpolatingFunction[{{0., 250.}, {0., 1.}}, <>]}}}
```

You can see the speedup is quite substantial.

```
In[102]:= timePut1 / timePut2
Out[102]= 23.3068
```

Discussion

You can see that the result of pricing the option appears the same for both versions.

```
In[103]:= GraphicsColumn[{Plot3D[Evaluate[u[x, 1 - t] /. First@put1], {x, 40, 60},
            {t, 0, 1}, PlotRange -> All, ImageSize -> {300, 300}, AxesLabel ->
              {"Underlying Price", "Time to\nExpiration", "Option\nPrice"}],
            Plot3D[Evaluate[u[x, 1 - t] /. First@put2], {x, 40, 60}, {t, 0, 1},
            PlotRange -> All, ImageSize -> {300, 300}, AxesLabel -> {"Underlying Price",
              "Time to\nExpiration", "Option\nPrice"}]}, Spacings -> 0]
```

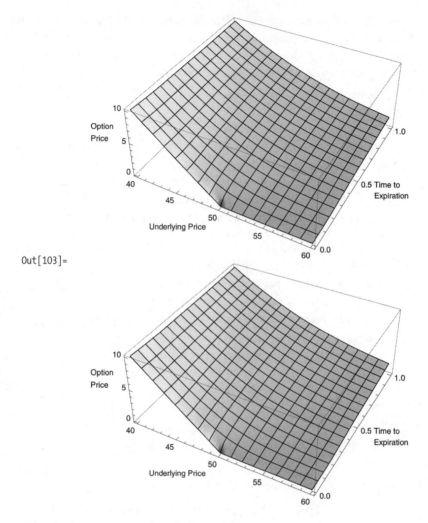

Out[103]=

And, indeed, you can see that the max difference in both approaches is negligible.

```
In[104]:= Max@
            Flatten@Abs[Table[(u[x, t] /. First@put1), {x, 40, 60}, {t, 0, 1, 0.01}] -
                Table[(u[x, t] /. First@put2), {x, 40, 60}, {t, 0, 1, 0.01}]]
Out[104]= 0.0000251351
```

A few words about the function makeAdaptiveGrid are in order. The motivation for this function can be seen considering the plot of x^3.

In[105]:= **Plot[x^3, {x, -3, 3}, ImageSize → Small]**

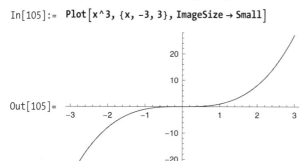

Out[105]=

The slope about the origin is small compared to the slope at the extremes. This is perfect for our application because it means that simply shifting the origin to the strike will give a function that generates a dense grid around the strike and a looser one at the wings of the option (away from the strike). The two optional parameters of makeAdaptiveGrid control the number of grid points (size) generated and the extent of the density around the slope (deg).

In[106]:= **Needs["PlotLegends`"]**
With[{strike = 50},
  ListLinePlot[{makeAdaptiveGrid[strike, 200, 1],
    makeAdaptiveGrid[strike, 200, 2]}, DataRange → {0, 2 strike},
    PlotStyle → {Thin, Dashed}, PlotLegend → {"deg = 1", "deg = 2"},
    LegendPosition → {-0.75, 0.25}, LegendSize → 0.5]]

Out[107]=

In the NDSolve options, I use MethodOfLines, which is a very efficient way to numerically solve a PDE provided it is an initial value problem. In particular, the solution uses the suboption "SpatialDiscretization", which itself allows the coordinates to be passed in. Here the expression N@Union[makeAdaptiveGrid[strike], Range[2 strike, 5 strike, 2]] simply tacks on some coarsely spaced points far from the strike so we can ensure the solution is valid for a reasonably liberal range of prices on the high end. Refer to the references in the following "See Also" section for more details about MethodOfLines, which is quite feature rich and worth learning if you plan to use NDSolve.

See Also

This recipe was motivated by the notebook penalty.nb developed by Andreas Lauschke. The original notebook is available in the downloads section of this book's website: *http://bit.ly/xIgx7*. Also see Lauschke's site at *http://bit.ly/1Zhdfv* for useful Mathematica and web Mathematica samples, products, and services.

NDSolve was introduced in Recipe 13.9.

The MethodOfLines can be found in *tutorial/NDSolvePDE* in the Mathematica documentation.

14.9 Developing an Explicit Finite Difference Method for the Black-Scholes Formula

Problem

You want to use the finite difference method (FDM) to compute solutions to the Black-Scholes formula in an efficient manner.

Solution

This solution was developed by Thomas Weber and rearranged to conform to the format of this book. Refer to the "See Also" section on page 582 for references to the original notebook.

In this solution we will price a European call option with the following attributes:

```
In[108]:=  strike = 100.; (*strike price at maturity of the option*)
           sigma = 0.2;   (*volatility of the prices of the underlying*)
           tau = 1.0;     (*time to maturity of the option*)
           rate  = 0.05 ; (*riskless interest rate*)
```

The presented calculation scheme is a version of the explicit *finite difference method* (FDM). While applying this calculation scheme, the new values for the derivative $V_{j,i-1}$ are stepwise calculated from $V_{j+1,i}$, $V_{j,i}$, and $V_{j-1,i}$. The concepts are elaborated in the "Discussion" section on page 580.

In this solution, the number of grid points for the discrete prices of the stock n can freely be chosen within a specific range. Increasing the number of time steps improves the accuracy but also increases the overall calculation time. For a first demonstration, the number of discrete stock prices is set to 20.

```
In[112]:= n = 20;
```

The grid points for the stock price should be placed in a range not too tight around the current stock price. In this example, the range is chosen from zero up to twice the strike price. From the chosen region results the step size $\triangle S$ for the discretization of the stock prices range. One way to generate the list of grid points is to use NestList. #+$\triangle S$& within NestList is a generic function defined for local use.

On the list of discrete stock prices, the exercise function of the option can be applied. The resulting list provides the starting or initial values for the numerical method.

```
In[113]:= δS = (2 * strike) / n;
          S = NestList[#1 + δS & , 0, n];
          V = (Max[#1 - strike, 0] & ) /@ S;
```

The necessary number of time steps for the explicit FDM to converge depends on the step size for the discretization of the stock price, the volatility, and the strike price. The number of time steps can be calculated as follows (for more information, see the Wilmott reference in the "See Also" section on page 582):

```
In[116]:= nt = Floor[τ / (δS / (2 * X * σ)) ^2] + 1;
```

Then the size of the time steps are

```
In[117]:= δt = τ/nt;
```

In pricingFunc, two terms Γ and $\triangle$ (see the "Discussion" section on page 580) are the speed-critical computations since they are inside the Do loop. The Mathematica function ListConvolve is used because it is a very fast way to compute finite differences. After the Do loop is finished, V contains a list of option values. Each option value corresponds to a discrete stock price on the grid. Interpolation on these numbers produces an interpolating function for the option price given current price of the underlying S_0.

```
In[118]:= pricingFunc[X_, r_, t_, σ_, n_] :=
            Module[{Δ, Γ, s, v, V, S, δS}, δS = (2*X)/n;
              S = NestList[#1 + δS &, 0, n];
              V = (Max[#1 - X, 0] &) /@ S;
              Do[Δ = ListConvolve[{1, 0, -1}, V]/(2*δS);
                Γ = ListConvolve[{1, -2, 1}, V]/δS^2;
                s = Take[S, {2, -2}];
                v = Take[V, {2, -2}];
                V = Join[{0}, v + δt*((1/2)*σ^2*s^2*Γ + r*s*Δ - r*v),
                {Last[S] - X/E^(r*i*δt)}], {i, nt}
              ];
              Interpolation[Transpose[{S, V}]]]
```

```
In[119]:= pf = pricingFunc[V, S, X, r, δS, δt, σ, nt];
          S0 = 100.;   (*price of the stock at valuation time*)
          pf[S0]
```

$$\text{Out[121]= } \text{pricingFunc}\left[\{0, 0, 0, 0, 0, 0, 0, 0, 0, 0, 0, 0., 10., 20., 30., 40., 50., 60.,\right.$$
$$70., 80., 90., 100.\}, \{0, 10., 20., 30., 40., 50., 60., 70., 80., 90.,$$
$$100., 110., 120., 130., 140., 150., 160., 170., 180., 190., 200.\}, X,$$
$$\left. r, 10., \frac{\tau}{1 + \text{Floor}\left[0.04\, X^2\, \sigma^2\, \tau\right]}, \sigma, 1 + \text{Floor}\left[0.04\, X^2\, \sigma^2\, \tau\right]\right][100.]$$

Discussion

The PDE from the Black-Scholes formula for a derivative V on the security S is given as:

```
In[122]:= Clear[S, δS, t, δt, σ, r, V];
          pde = -D[V[S, t], t] ==
            (1/2)*σ^2*S^2*D[V[S, t], S, S] + r*S*D[V[S, t], S] - r*V[S, t];
```

Numerical approximation for the partial derivative follows, for example from the Taylor series. The partial derivatives in the equation are replaced through the appropriate Taylor series.

```
In[124]:= rls = {D[V[S, t], t] -> (V[S, t - δt] - V[S, t])/δt,
            D[V[S, t], S] -> (V[S + δS, t] - V[S - δS, t])/(2*δS),
            D[V[S, t], S, S] ->
              (V[S + δS, t] - 2*V[S, t] + V[S - δS, t])/δS^2};
          prox = pde /. rls
```

$$\text{Out[125]= } -\frac{-V[S, t] + V[S, t - δt]}{δt} == -r\, V[S, t] + \frac{r\, S\, (-V[S - δS, t] + V[S + δS, t])}{2\, δS} +$$
$$\frac{S^2\, σ^2\, (-2\, V[S, t] + V[S - δS, t] + V[S + δS, t])}{2\, δS^2}$$

In the next step, the notation is changed to make it more consistent with a grid scheme.

In[126]:= **prox = prox /. {V[S, t] → V$_{j,i}$,**
        V[S, t - δt] → V$_{j,i-1}$, V[S + δS, t] → V$_{j+1,i}$, V[S - δS, t] → V$_{j-1,i}$}

Out[126]= $-\dfrac{V_{j,-1+i} - V_{j,i}}{\delta t} == -r\,V_{j,i} + \dfrac{r\,S\,(-V_{-1+j,i} + V_{1+j,i})}{2\,\delta S} + \dfrac{S^2\,\sigma^2\,(V_{-1+j,i} - 2\,V_{j,i} + V_{1+j,i})}{2\,\delta S^2}$

To better illustrate the structure of the equation, more notational adjustments are made. The new structure will later help to simplify the calculations.

In[127]:= **prox = prox /. $\left\{\dfrac{V_{j+1,i} - 2\,V_{j,i} + V_{j-1,i}}{\delta S^2} → Γ_{i,j}, \dfrac{V_{j+1,i} - V_{j-1,i}}{2\,\delta S} → Δ_{i,j}\right\}$**

Out[127]= $-\dfrac{V_{j,-1+i} - V_{j,i}}{\delta t} == -r\,V_{j,i} + \dfrac{1}{2}\,S^2\,\sigma^2\,Γ_{i,j} + r\,S\,Δ_{i,j}$

Solving the last expression for $V_{j,i}$ and simplifying leads to

In[128]:= **diff = Solve[prox, V$_{j,i-1}$] // Simplify // First;**
        diff // TraditionalForm
Out[129]//TraditionalForm=

$$\left\{V_{j,i-1} → (r\,\delta t + 1)\,V_{j,i} - \frac{1}{2}\,S\,\delta t\,(2\,r\,Δ_{i,j} + S\,\sigma^2\,Γ_{i,j})\right\}$$

The presented calculation scheme is a version of the explicit FDM. While applying this calculation scheme, the new values for the derivative $V_{j,i-1}$ are stepwise calculated from $V_{j+1,i}$, $V_{j,i}$, and $V_{j-1,i}$. Figure 14-1 illustrates this approach.

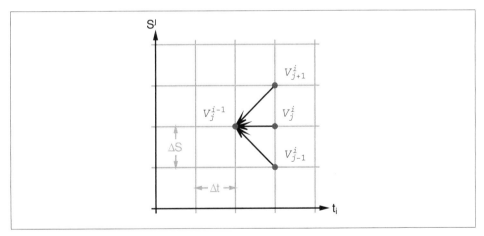

Figure 14-1. Explicit FDM

An efficient Mathematica function for the calculation of the differences needed in Δ and Γ is available through ListConvolve. To demonstrate this, ListConvolve is applied to a list of symbols.

```
In[130]:= Clear[V, δS];
          v = Table[V_j, {j, 6}]
Out[131]= {V₁, V₂, V₃, V₄, V₅, V₆}
```

ListConvolve used for Δ results in the following expression.

```
In[132]:= Δ = ListConvolve[{1, 0, -1}, v] / (2 δS) // TraditionalForm
Out[132]//TraditionalForm=
```

$$\left\{ \frac{V_3 - V_1}{2\,\delta S},\ \frac{V_4 - V_2}{2\,\delta S},\ \frac{V_5 - V_3}{2\,\delta S},\ \frac{V_6 - V_4}{2\,\delta S} \right\}$$

The first list in ListConvolve, the kernel {1,0,1}, is applied piecewise to the second list, multiplies the elements of the second list, and adds them up according to the values given in the kernel. This operation runs internally in Mathematica and is much faster than any loop written in Mathematica code.

The approach used for Δ can also be applied for the calculation of Γ. ListConvolve can replace loops that are common to the explicit approximation of PDEs.

```
In[133]:= Γ = ListConvolve[{1, -2, 1}, v] / (δS ^ 2) // TraditionalForm
Out[133]//TraditionalForm=
```

$$\left\{ \frac{V_1 - 2\,V_2 + V_3}{\delta S^2},\ \frac{V_2 - 2\,V_3 + V_4}{\delta S^2},\ \frac{V_3 - 2\,V_4 + V_5}{\delta S^2},\ \frac{V_4 - 2\,V_5 + V_6}{\delta S^2} \right\}$$

See Also

Derivatives: The Theory and Practice of Financial Engineering (Wiley) by P. Wilmott contains the technical background underlying this recipe.

This recipes was derived from work done by Thomas Weber of Weber & Partner. The original notebook and other interesting financial applications in Mathematica can be found at *http://bit.ly/bR0bF*.

The method used in this recipe is based on the explicit FDM. There are also implicit methods. See Wikipedia for a general explanation of the difference and the trade-offs (*http://bit.ly/tr3IN*).

14.10 Compiling an Implementation of Explicit Trinomial for Fast Pricing of American Options

Problem

You need a very fast pricer for American options. You want to make sure the implementation can be compiled for fastest possible execution without any calls to non-compiled code.

Solution

This solution was contributed by Andreas Lauschke. See Recipe 14.8 for more information.

Mathematica has a built-in compiler that creates optimized code for a Mathematica-specific virtual machine. Compile is discussed fully in Recipe 18.5. Here we simply show an application that creates a pricer for American options using *trinomial scheme* (see discussion).

```
In[134]:= americanPutCompiled = Compile[{kk, r, sigma, tt},
            With[{a = 5, nn = 100, mm = 20, tt0 = sigma^2 tt / 2, k = 2 r / sigma^2},
              Module[{alpha, h = 2 a / nn, s = tt0 / mm, x, ss, tmax, f, pp0, u, z},
                alpha = s / h^2;
                x = Range[-a, a, h];
                ss = kk Exp@x;
                tmax = MapThread[Max, {Table[0, {nn + 1}], 1 - Exp@x}];
                f =
                  Exp[1 / 2 (k - 1) x + 1 / 4 (k + 1)^2 (# - 1) s] tmax & /@ Range[mm + 1];
                pp0 = Max[0, kk - #] & /@ ss;
                u = Exp[1 / 2 (k - 1) x] pp0 / kk;
                Do[z = alpha (Take[u, {3, nn + 1}] + Take[u, {1, nn - 1}]) -
                    (2 alpha - 1) Take[u, {2, nn}];
                  z = Append[Prepend[z, alpha u[[2]] - (2 alpha - 1) u[[1]] +
                        alpha / kk Exp[1 / 2 (k - 1) a + 1 / 4 (k + 1)^2 (j - 1) s]], 0];
                  u = MapThread[Max, {z, f[[j]]}];, {j, mm}];
                {ss, kk Exp[-1 / 4 (k + 1)^2 tt0] Exp[-1 / 2 (k - 1) x] u}]]];
```

You can see that 10 runs of the pricer over various strike prices execute in 32 milliseconds.

```
In[135]:= {time, pricing} = Timing[
              Table[Take[Transpose@americanPutCompiled[strike, 0.05, 0.4, 1], 60],
                {strike, 50, 100, 5}]];
            ListLinePlot[pricing, PlotLabel → ToString[time * 10^3] <> " millisecs"]
```

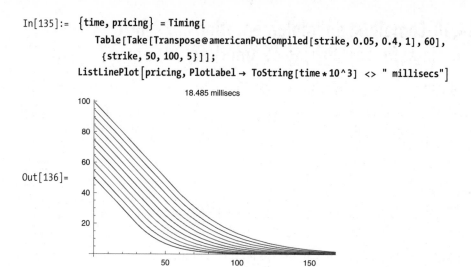

Out[136]=

Discussion

The function americanPutCompiled returns a packed array of two lists: the first is a list of nodes in the spatial (stock price) direction, and the second is a list of American option prices at these nodes. The two lists can now be interpolated with Mathematica's Interpolation function to obtain intermediate values.

The function americanPutCompiled is fully compiled, as can be seen by inspecting americanPutCompiled[[4]] and noting that all list elements are numeric.

```
In[137]:= DeleteCases[Flatten[americanPutCompiled[[4]]], _?NumericQ]
Out[137]= {}
```

The algorithm implements a method to price American options based on the linear complementarity formulation of the free boundary value problem. The numbers a, nn, T0, and mm (and, correspondingly, s and h) are parameters that define the grid to be used. a and nn determine the grid along the space (stock price) axis, and T0 and mm determine the grid along the time axis. For explicit methods, it is crucial to keep the spatial and temporal spacing in certain limits, otherwise local blow-up will occur. For a 100% explicit method, it is necessary that alpha=s/h^2<=1/2. That means that if the spatial step size h is reduced by a factor of 10, the time step size s has to be reduced by a factor of 100. This is not due to reasons of precision, but due to reasons of stability. If, for example, mm is lowered to 15, alpha is no longer <=1/2, and the instability becomes quite visible. For numbers like 5 or 10 for mm, the method wreaks havoc. Traditional American option pricing methods use binomial trees and exhibit this problem with what is called *oscillations*. (All tree methods are necessarily 100% explicit.) It's the same stability problem that is inherent to all explicit methods.

What makes this rectangular grid method so powerful is the fact that although it is faster than most tree-based implementations, it computes the option prices for the whole interval, not just for *one* particular price of the underlying, which is a limitation all tree-based methods possess.

See Also

Recipe 18.5 explains the mechanics of compiled functions and the performance implications of functions that don't fully compile.

See Ansgar Jüngel, "Modellierung und Numerik von Finanzderivaten," Vorlesungsmanuskript 2002, Johannes-Gutenberg Universität Mainz.

14.11 Modeling the Value-at-Risk of a Portfolio Using Monte Carlo and Other Methods

Problem

You want to understand the worst expected loss of a portfolio of securities. This is referred to as *Value-at-Risk* or *VaR*. Specifically, you want to use Monte Carlo methods because these allow you to trade accuracy for speed by varying the number of samples.

 Since the financial disaster that began in 2007, the notion of Value-at-Risk has become quite controversial. Some, like Nassim Taleb, have called it an intellectual fraud, while others have called it an invaluable tool, if used properly. I include this recipe as an illustration of the math behind *one particular implementation* of VaR and without judgment as to its effectiveness. Please refer to the link in the "See Also" section on page 587 for a thorough discussion of the efficacy of VaR in practice.

Solution

In its simplest form, VaR is a measure of the worst expected loss under *normal market conditions* over some time interval, usually days or weeks. The simplest (and highly artificial) illustration of VaR concerns a portfolio consisting of a single security. Let's assume it is worth $10 million, the average return is 0.085, and the standard deviation is 0.26. The distribution of the portfolio's value is

```
In[138]:=  With[{portfolio = 10^7, return = 0.085, stddev = 0.26},
            Plot[PDF[NormalDistribution[portfolio * (1.0 + return),
              portfolio * stddev ], x], {x, 0, 2 portfolio}]]
```

Out[138]=

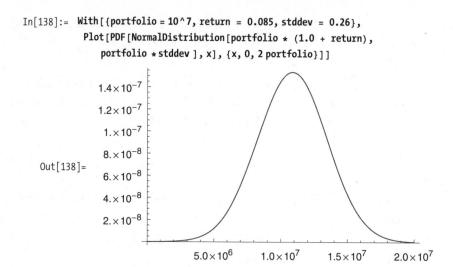

From this we can compute the probability of a loss of 25% using the CDF.

```
In[139]:=  With[{portfolio = 10000000, return = 0.085, stddev = 0.26, loss = 0.25},
            CDF[NormalDistribution[portfolio * (1.0 + return), portfolio * stddev ],
              portfolio (1 - loss) ]]
Out[139]=  0.0987927
```

VaR is computed in terms of worst expected loss in dollars at a certain probability level, say 1%.

```
In[140]:=  valueAtRisk[startingValue_, meanReturn_, var_, level_] :=
            Module[{expected = startingValue * (1 + meanReturn)},
              startingValue -
              Quantile[NormalDistribution[expected, startingValue * var], level]]
In[141]:=  With[{portfolio = 10000000,
              meadReturn = 0.085, stddev = 0.26, loss = 0.25},
            valueAtRisk[portfolio, meadReturn, stddev, 0.01]]
Out[141]=  5.1985 × 10^6
```

Thus the VaR at 1% is about 5.2 million.

Discussion

The solution merely shows the statistical ideas behind VaR. In real-life scenarios, portfolios are more complexly structured, and you need to measure and account for correlations in the movements of these assets' values. The rest of this discussion deals with these issues.

The first issue to address is that prices don't typically follow a NormalDistribution but rather a LogNormal one. Second, portfolio managers and traders are typically interested in VaR over much shorter time periods than one year. So a more useful function is

```
In[142]:=  Clear[valueAtRisk]
           valueAtRisk[startingValue_, mean_,
             var_, level_, days_, tradingDays_: 365] :=
               Module[{T = days / tradingDays},
                 startingValue - Exp[Quantile[NormalDistribution[
                   Log@startingValue + (mean - var^2 / 2) * T, var * T], level]]
               ]
```

Here we compute the VaR assuming 250 trading days.

```
In[144]:=  With[{portfolio = 10 000 000,
             return = 0.085, stddev = 0.26, loss = 0.25, days = 1},
             valueAtRisk[portfolio, return, stddev, 0.01, days, 250]]
Out[144]=  22 121.5
```

See Also

An extensive discussion of VaR in light of the financial crisis of 2007-2009 (and counting) can be found in this excellent *New York Times* article by Joe Nocera: *http://bit.ly/2SgV68*.

14.12 Visualizing Trees for Interest-Rate Sensitive Instruments

Problem

You are using a tree-based approach to pricing (such as the Hull-White trees) and you want to visualize these trees using Mathematica's graphics abilities. Such visualizations are often useful for pedagogical or diagnostic purposes.

Solution

In this recipe, I am only concerned with using Mathematica for visualizing Hull-White trees. See the "See Also" section on page 591 for the theory and Mathematica implementation of the same for pricing purposes.

The usual way to implement tree valuation methods is to state results in two or more new states, thereby modeling the diffusion of the stochastic process. The idea of Hull-White to model mean reverting processes is to add boundary conditions to this tree structure. The boundary conditions are valid for a given maximum state.

The graphical building blocks of the tree can then be defined as follows. The variable nmax is global. There are three primitive elements: a nonboundary element, an upper-boundary element, and a lower-boundary element. The function path returns a triple that defines the terminal points of the path.

```
In[145]:= path[j_] := j + {1, 0, -1}
          path[j_ /; j == nmax] := j - {0, 1, 2}
          path[j_ /; j == -nmax] := j + {0, 1, 2}
```

The function grpath then constructs the graphical representation in terms of Line elements emanating from a starting point.

```
In[148]:= grpath[pt : {i_, j_}] := Line[{pt, {i + 1, #}}] & /@ path[j]
```

Here then are the three primitive components used to build the tree.

```
In[149]:= Block[{nmax = 2},
            GraphicsGrid[{{Graphics[grpath[{0, 1}], PlotLabel → "Unbounded"],
              Graphics[grpath[{0, nmax}], PlotLabel → "Upper Boundary"],
              Graphics[grpath[{0, -nmax}], PlotLabel → "Lower Boundary"]}},
            AspectRatio → 0.3] /. Line → Arrow]
```

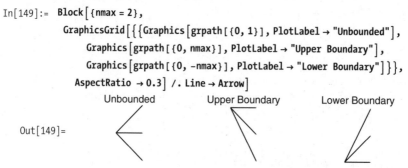

Out[149]=

Given these primitives, it's a straightforward process to generate a tree with a particular boundary and depth.

```
In[150]:=  Block[{nmax = 4, depth = 10},
             Module[{n},
               n[m_] := Min[nmax, m];
               Graphics[Table[grpath[{m, j}],
                 {m, 0, depth - 1}, {j, -n[m], n[m]}], Axes -> True]]]
```

Out[150]=

Discussion

The solution is really just a skeleton to illustrate the general technique. For purposes
of visualization, we need trees with labels that suggest the underlying semantics of
Hull-White. A particularly nice way to proceed is to augment the tree with node
labels that are purely coordinates. This is just a matter of adding text elements to the
solution version. The resulting gr becomes a template, and you can leverage Mathematica's pattern-directed replacement to assign meaningful labels to the nodes.

```
In[151]:=  gr = Block[{nmax = 2, depth = 3},
             Module[{n},
               n[m_] := Min[nmax, m];
               Flatten[Table[{If[m < depth, grpath[{m, j}], {}],
                 Text[{m, j}, {m, j}, Background -> White]},
                 {m, 0, depth}, {j, -n[m], n[m]}]]
             ]];
```

In[152]:= `Graphics[gr, AspectRatio → 1 / GoldenRatio]`

Out[152]=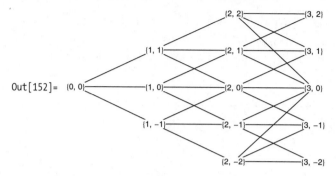

The process you want to visualize is a single-factor interest rate model described by the following formula:

$$dr = (\theta(t) - a\, r_t)\, dt + \sigma\, dz.$$

Here r is the short-term rate, and a and σ are constants.

In[153]:= `a = 0.1;`
`σ = 0.01;`
`Δt = 1;`
`Δr = σ * Sqrt[3 * Δt];`

Using the template gr, replace the nodes with the rate deltas using the node coordinates in the computation of the labels. Here you use depth `Infinity` with `Replace` so you need not worry about the actual depth of the graphics elements.

In[157]:= `Graphics[Replace[gr, {{x_Integer, y_Integer} :> {x, y Δr},`
`    Text[{m_, j_}, y__] :> Text[j 100, y]}, Infinity],`
`    AspectRatio → 1 / GoldenRatio]`

Out[157]=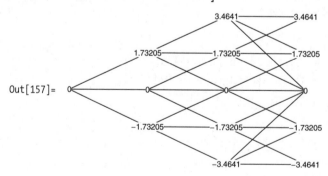

See Also

This recipe contains content originally developed by Thomas Weber of Weber & Partner (*http://bit.ly/3Dz1wg*) and is used with permission. A complete notebook showing both the theory and visualization is available at this cookbook's website: *http://bit.ly/xIgx7*.

CHAPTER 15

Interactivity

I'm alive
Oh oh, so alive
I'm alive
Oh oh, so alive
...
My head is full of magic, baby
And I can share this with you
The feel I'm on top again, baby
That's got everything to do with you

Love and Rockets, "So Alive"

15.0 Introduction

The pièce de résistance of Mathematica 6 is its dynamic interactivity features. These features forced Wolfram to completely rethink and redesign its frontend. This had the unfortunate consequence of breaking many notebooks from version 5 and earlier, especially those that used graphics. However, it is my opinion that the gain was well worth the pain!

The interactive features of Mathematica 6 are even more impressive when one considers that they sit on relatively few new functions. The centerpiece of interactivity is the function Manipulate. Think of Manipulate as a very intelligent user-interface generator. Manipulate's power comes by virtue of its ability to take any Mathematica expression plus a declarative description of the expression's variables and generate a mini embedded GUI within the notebook for interacting with that expression. Of course, there are always caveats, and an important feature of this chapter is to help you get the best possible results with nontrivial Manipulate use cases.

The first five recipes of this chapter are intended to gradually introduce the reader to Manipulate by demonstrating increasingly sophisticated examples. These recipes are not necessarily intended for direct use but rather to illustrate the basic features and generality of Manipulate. Each recipe highlights a feature of Manipulate or a subtlety of its use in a particular context. Animate is a relative of Manipulate that puts its interactive features in autonomous mode. Recipe 15.15 focuses on Animate and shows how animations can be exported to Flash and other Web-friendly formats.

Many users will never need anything beyond Manipulate, but more advanced applications require you to dig deeper and understand lower-level dynamic primitive functions called Dynamic, DynamicModule, and DynamicWrapper. Recipe 15.4 shows how Dynamic is used in conjunction with Manipulate to achieve better performance or smoother operation. DynamicModule is a preferred alternative to Module when working with dynamic content, and I use it liberally before introducing it formally. The initial usage does not require you to know more than its function as a scoping construct. Recipe 15.11 illustrates the intimate relationship between Manipulate and Dynamic-Module and shows why you often want to use DynamicModule directly. Many useful dynamic techniques require the use of DynamicWrapper but, unfortunately (as of version 7), this important function is undocumented in the help system. Recipes 15.8, 15.11, and 15.16 show some interesting use cases for this hidden gem.

 You will get the most out of this chapter by downloading its associated notebook from the book's website and playing along; see *http://oreilly.com/catalog/9780596520991*.

15.1 Manipulating a Variable

Problem

You want to control the value of one or more variables via an interactive interface and see their values update as you interact with the interface.

Solution

Use Manipulate with the desired variables and (optionally) their ranges.

In[1]:= `Manipulate[a, {a, 1, 10}]`

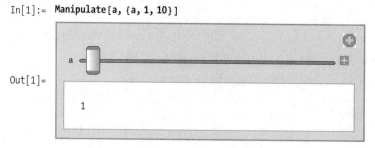

```
In[2]:= Manipulate[{a, b, c, d, pt},
        {a, 1, 10},     (*a varies from 1 - 10.*)
        {b, 1, 10, 1},  (*b varies from 1 - 10 in steps of 1.*)
        {{c, 5}, 1, 10}, (*c varies 1 - 10. Initial value 5*)
        {d},  (*d can have any value.*)
        {pt, {1, 1}, {10, 10}},  (*Creates a 2D slider*)
        {{d, 7, "d again"}, {1, 3, 5, 7, 9}} (*Creates buttons*)
        ]
```

Out[2]=

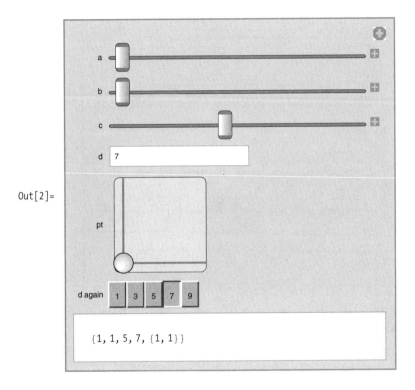

Discussion

This solution is strictly intended as a simple introduction to Manipulate. As it stands, it is not very practical because the variables are displayed rather than used to compute. Still, there are some important concepts.

The first concept is that Manipulate will automatically choose a control type based on the structure of the constraints you place on a variable's value. The most common control is a slider. It is chosen when a variable is specified with a minimum and maximum value. Out[3] below shows three variations of this idea. The second example uses a specified increment, and the third adds an initial value.

```
In[3]:= Column[{Manipulate[a, {a, -10, 10}], Manipulate[b, {b, -10, 10, 0.1}],
           Manipulate[c, {{c, 0}, -10, 10, 0.1}]}, Spacer[2]]
```

Out[3]=

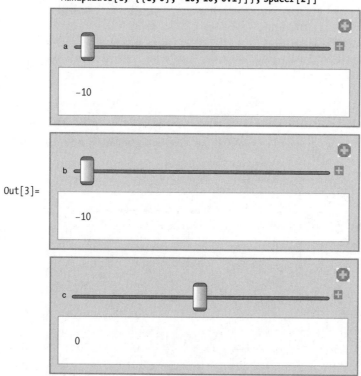

When a multiple-choice list is specified, you will get either a series of buttons or a drop-down list, depending on the number of choices.

```
In[4]:= Row[{Manipulate[a, {a, {0, 1, 2, 3}}],
           Manipulate[b, {b, Table[i, {i, 10}]}]}, Spacer[5]]
```

Out[4]=

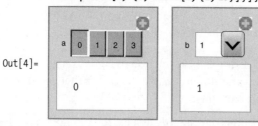

When a variable is unconstrained or just specified with an initial value, Manipulate infers an edit control. In the first case, the variable begins with a null value, so it is probably a good idea to provide an initial value.

In[5]:= `Row[{Manipulate[a, {a}], Manipulate[b, {b, 3.3}]}, Spacer[2]]`

Out[5]=

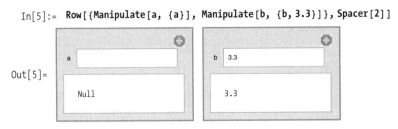

A second concept, illustrated in Out[6], is that a single variable can be bound to multiple controls. This has the effect of tying the controls together so a change in one control changes the variable and is automatically reflected in the other controls bound to that variable. It's possible in this circumstance to violate the constraints of one of the controls. In this case, `Manipulate` will display a red area in the control that has the violated constraint.

In[6]:= `Manipulate[a, {a, -10, 10}, {a, -20, 20}]`

Out[6]=

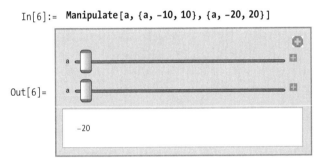

A third concept is the ability to provide an arbitrary label by specifying the label after the initial value. The label can be any Mathematica expression.

In[7]:= `Column[{Manipulate[Sin[N[a]], {{a, -10, Sin[a]}, -10, 10}], Manipulate[a,`
`{{a, -10, Rasterize[Text[Style["a", Blue, Italic, Bold, 20]]]},`
`-10, 10}]}, Spacer[2]]`

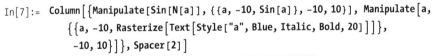

Out[7]=

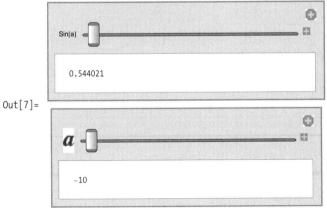

15.2 Manipulating a Symbolic Expression

Problem

You want to vary the structure of a symbolic expression interactively.

Solution

This recipe is intended to illustrate that any Mathematica expression that can be parametrized can be used with Manipulate.

```
In[8]:= Clear[x];
        Grid[Partition[Table[Manipulate[Expand[(x + 1)^r], {{r, init}, 0, 30, 1},
          FrameMargins → 0, ImageMargins → 0, ContentSize → {250, 75}],
          {init, {1, 2, 10, 15}}], 2], Spacings → 0.5, Alignment → Left]
```

Out[8]=

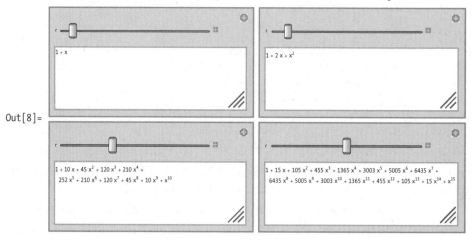

Discussion

Here are a few examples to reinforce the idea that any aspect of an expression can be manipulated. In Out[9] on page 599, both of the function's integration limits are variable. In Out[10] on page 599, every aspect of the expression, including its display form, is subject to user manipulation. Finally, in Out[11] on page 600, you see that tables of values can be dynamically generated and that Manipulate will adjust the display area to accommodate the additional rows. The ability of Manipulate to mostly do the right thing is immensely liberating: it allows you to focus on the concept you are illustrating rather than the GUI programming.

In[9]:= Module$\left[\{x\}, \text{Manipulate}\left[\int_a^b \left(g[f][x]\right) dx, \{\{a, 0\}, 0., 10\}, \{\{b, 10\}, 0., 10\},\right.\right.$

$\left.\left.\{f, \{\text{Identity, Sin, Cos, Exp, Sqrt}\}\}, \{g, \{\text{Identity, InverseFunction}\}\}\right]\right]$

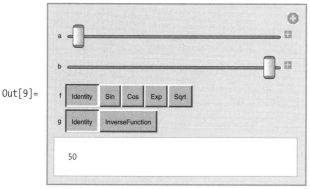

Out[9]=

In[10]:= Manipulate$\left[f\left[\begin{pmatrix} a & b \\ c & d \end{pmatrix}\right]\right]$ // form, {{f, Inverse}, {Det, Transpose, Inverse}},

{{a, x^2}, {0, 1, x, x^2}}, {{b, x}, {0, 1, x, x^2}},

{{c, I}, {0, 1, -1, I, x, Sqrt[x]}}, {{d, x}, {-1, 0, 1, x}},

{form, {MatrixForm, StandardForm, TraditionalForm, InputForm}},

BaseStyle → {Large}$\Big]$

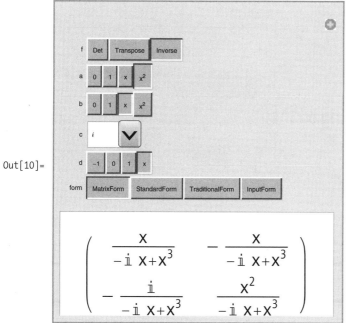

Out[10]=

```
In[11]:= Grid[{{
        Manipulate[
         Framed[TableForm[{#, N[f[#]]} & /@ Table[i, {i, 0, 2 Pi, incr}],
           TableSpacing → {1, 2}, TableHeadings → {None, {"x", f}}]],
         {incr, 1, 0.1, -0.1}, {{f, Sin}, {Sin, Cos, Tan, Sec, Csc, Cot}},
         {incr}], Manipulate[
         Framed[TableForm[{#, N[f[#]]} & /@ Table[i, {i, 0, 2 Pi, incr}],
           TableSpacing → {1, 2}, TableHeadings → {None, {"x", f}}]],
         {{incr, 0.5}, 1, 0.1, -0.1}, {{f, Cos}, {Sin, Cos, Tan, Sec, Csc, Cot}},
         {incr}]}}, Alignment → Top, Spacings → 3]
```

Out[11]=

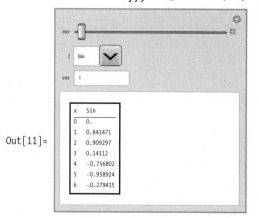
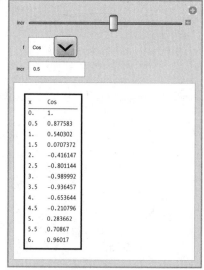

15.3 Manipulating a Plot

Problem

You want to create an interactive graph.

Solution

Possibly one of the most popular use cases for Manipulate is to create an interactive plot. However, a common stumbling block is forgetting to specify the PlotRange, causing a plot for which the axes vary instead of the plot itself varying.

```
In[12]:= Manipulate[Plot[m x + b, {x, -10, 10}, PlotRange → {Automatic, {-30, 30}}],
         {{m, 1}, -3, 3}, {{b, 0}, -10, 10}]
```

Out[12]=

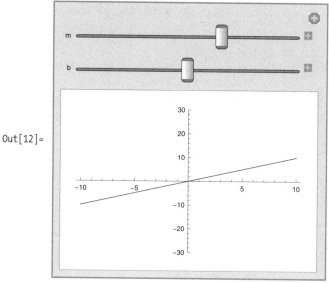

Discussion

Use Mathematica to compare the solution to the following variation and you will
immediately see why PlotRange is essential.

```
In[13]:= Manipulate[Plot[m x + b, {x, -10, 10}], {{m, 1}, -3, 3}, {{b, 0}, -10, 10}]
```

Out[13]=

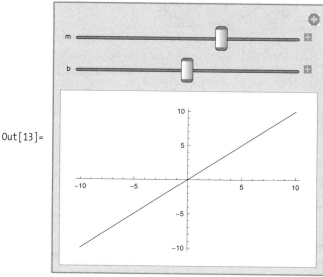

Another common problem when manipulating graphics is sluggishness when controls are varied. A crude way of dealing with this problem is to tell Manipulate to not update the display until the control is released. You do this with the option ContinuousAction→False .

```
In[14]:= Manipulate[
           SphericalPlot3D[{1, If[ϕ < 3 Pi / 2, 2, None], If[ϕ < 3 Pi / 2, 3, None]},
             {θ, 0, l1}, {ϕ, 0, l2}], {{l1, Pi}, Pi / 4, 2 Pi},
             {{l2, 2 Pi}, Pi / 4, 2 Pi}, ContinuousAction → False]
```

Out[14]=

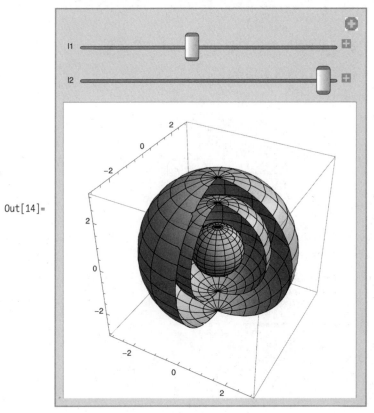

A more refined alternative is to perform a low-resolution plot while controls are changing and then switch automatically to a full-resolution plot when the control is released. The ControlActive function along with PlotPoints is exactly what the doctor ordered. Many graphics functions are self-adaptive when used inside a Manipulate, but ControlActive allows you to fine-tune this behavior to match the complexity of the graph and the speed of your computer.

```
In[15]:= Manipulate[
          SphericalPlot3D[{1, If[φ < 3 Pi / 2, 2, None], If[φ < 3 Pi / 2, 3, None]},
           {θ, 0, l1}, {φ, 0, l2}, PlotPoints → ControlActive[12, 25]],
          {{l1, Pi}, Pi / 4, 2 Pi}, {{l2, 2 Pi}, Pi / 4, 2 Pi}]
```

Out[15]=

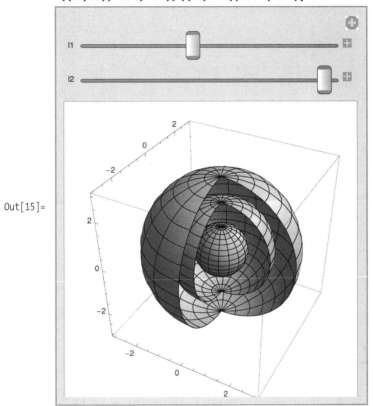

Another way to fine-tune interactive plots is to separate those options that can be rendered quickly from those that require a lot of computation. A classic example is a plot with variable parameters that change the shape of the plot (expensive) and parameters that change the orientation of the plot (inexpensive). Ideally, parameters that are inexpensive to compute should not trigger computation of the expensive parts. You achieve this by wrapping the inexpensive parts in Dynamic[]. I discuss this use of Dynamic in detail in Recipe 15.11.

```
In[16]:= Manipulate[Plot3D[a Sin[2 Pi a x] + b Sin[2 Pi b y], {x, 0, 2 Pi}, {y, 0, 2 Pi},
           ViewPoint → Dynamic[{2, v, 2}]], {a, 0.1, 1}, {b, 0.1, 1}, {v, -3, 3}]
```

Out[16]=

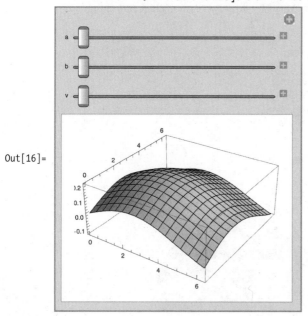

15.4 Creating Expressions for Which Value Dynamically Updates

Problem

You want to create output cells that have values that change in real time as variables used in computing the cell values change.

Solution

Normally an expression is evaluated and produces an output that remains static. You can wrap an expression in Dynamic[] to indicate you want Mathematica to update the value whenever a variable in the expression acquires a new value. Here I initialize three variables and create a list in which the first element is their sum and the second is the sum wrapped in Dynamic. Initially the result is {6,6} as you would expect. However, you are looking at the output after the variable x1 was given a new value of 100. Notice how the second element reflects the new sum of 105.

```
In[17]:= x1 = 1; x2 = 2; x3 = 3; {x1 + x2 + x3, Dynamic[x1 + x2 + x3]}
Out[17]= {6, 105}

In[18]:= x1 = 100
Out[18]= 100
```

Discussion

Dynamic is one of the low-level primitives that make the functionality of Manipulate possible. A typical use case of Dynamic is creating free controls that update a variable.

```
In[19]:= a1 = 3;
         Row[{Slider[Dynamic[a1], {1, 5}], Dynamic[a1]}, "\t"]
Out[20]=
```

Dynamic expressions can appear in a variety of contexts and work across multiple cells. Each output cell here will update as the slider changes the value of a1.

```
In[21]:= Module[{x}, Dynamic[Integrate[Exp[x], {x, a1, 10}]]]
Out[21]= 22 023.7
```

```
In[22]:= Dynamic[Plot[Sin[a1 x], {x, 0, 2 Pi}, PlotRange → {Automatic, {-1, 1}}]]
```

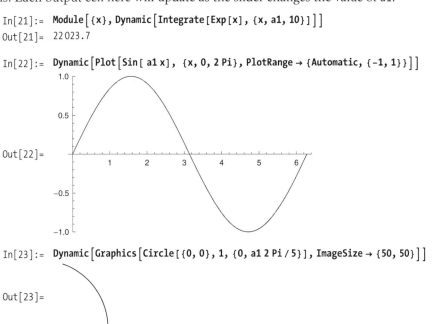

```
In[23]:= Dynamic[Graphics[Circle[{0, 0}, 1, {0, a1 2 Pi / 5}], ImageSize → {50, 50}]]
```

There are two key principles that underlie Dynamic, and you must keep these in mind to avoid common pitfalls. The first principle is that Dynamic has the attribute Hold-First. This means that it does not immediately update its expression until it needs to and does so only to produce output.

```
In[24]:= Attributes[Dynamic]
Out[24]= {HoldFirst, Protected, ReadProtected}
```

This leads to the second key concept. Dynamic is strictly a frontend function and can't be used to produce values that will be passed to other functions. The following example underscores this important point.

```
In[25]:= DynamicModule[{x}, Row[{Slider[Dynamic[x], {1, 5}],
           Plot[Sin[Dynamic[x] i], {i, 0, 2 Pi}]}, Spacer[2]]]
```

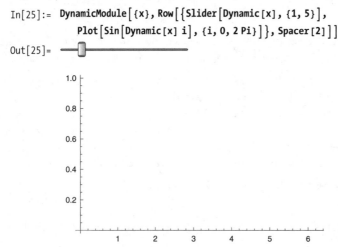

Moving the slider does nothing because passing the output of Dynamic to a kernel function like Sin can never work.

 As a general rule, if Dynamic is not in a context where its output will be displayed directly or embedded in an expression that will be displayed (like a control or a graphics primitive), then you are almost certainly using Dynamic incorrectly.

See Also

See the tutorial "Introduction to Dynamic" under *tutorial/IntroductionToDynamic* in the Wolfram help system.

15.5 Intercepting the Values of a Control Attached to a Dynamic Expression

Problem

You want to apply a function to the output of a control before it affects the value of a Dynamic expression.

Solution

Normally when you adjust a control, the value produced is assigned to the expression in the first argument of Dynamic. However, if the expression is not a variable that can be assigned, this will lead to errors. The solution is provided by the second argument of Dynamic, which allows you to provide a function that can override the default behavior. A classic example is the creation of a control that inverts the value of the slider. Here are a normal slider and an inverted slider that uses an inversion function as its second argument.

```
In[26]:= DynamicModule[{x1},
            {Slider[Dynamic[x1, Automatic]], Slider[Dynamic[1 - x1, (x1 = 1 - #) &]]}]
Out[26]= {⟨slider⟩, ⟨slider⟩}
```

Discussion

The solution shows a case where the second argument of Dynamic is a function. Dynamic also supports a more advanced variation where a list of functions is passed in the second argument. A list with two functions tells Dynamic to evaluate the first function as the control is varied and the second function when interaction with the control is complete. A list with three functions defines a start function, a during function, and an end function.

```
In[27]:= DynamicModule[{x1}, Slider[Dynamic[x1, { (x1 = #) &, Print["End ", #] &}]]]
Out[27]= ⟨slider⟩
```

End 0.

```
In[28]:= DynamicModule[{x1}, Slider[
            Dynamic[x1, {Print["Start ", #] &, (x1 = #) &, Print["End ", #] &}]]]
Out[28]= ⟨slider⟩
```

Start 0.

End 0.

Here is an example illustrating Ohm's law (voltage = current * resistance) as a set of three coupled sliders. The goal is for voltage to be computed when the current or resistance sliders change. However, if voltage is changed, then current must be recomputed. The problem with such an example is that if you allow voltage to change when resistance is high, it can easily lead to very large currents that would violate the limits of the current slider. The solution is to make the sliders' limits dynamic as well, but that requires the whole slider to be dynamic! Of course, you don't want the interface to be constantly generated as a slider is moved. This is where the finish function comes in handy. When a slider interaction ends, the limits of the other sliders are recomputed, triggering the creation of a new slider.

```
In[29]:= DynamicModule[{current = 0., resistance = 1., voltage,
         maxCurrent = 1, maxResistance = 100, maxVoltage = 100},
       DynamicWrapper[
        Grid[{{"current",
          Dynamic[Slider[Dynamic[current, {
             (*The interactive function updates current and computes voltage.*)
             ({current, voltage} = {#, resistance * #}) &,
             (*The finish function updates voltage and resistance limits.*)
             ({maxVoltage, maxResistance} = {Max[maxVoltage, # * resistance],
                Max[maxResistance, voltage / Max[#, 1]]}) &}],
            {0., maxCurrent}]], Dynamic[current]},

         {"resistance",
          Dynamic[Slider[Dynamic[resistance, {
             (*The interactive function
              updates resistance and computes voltage.*)
             ({resistance, voltage} = {#, # * current}) &,
             (*The finish function updates current and voltage limits.*)
             ({maxCurrent, maxVoltage} = {Max[maxCurrent, voltage/#],
                Max[maxVoltage, current * #]}) &}],
            {1., maxResistance}]], Dynamic[resistance]},
```

```
{"voltage",
    Dynamic[Slider[Dynamic[voltage, {
        (*The interactive function updates voltage and computes current.*)
        ({voltage, current} = {#, # / resistance }) &,
        (*The finish function updates current and resistance limits.*)
        ({maxCurrent, maxResistance} = {Max[maxCurrent, # / resistance],
            Max[maxResistance, # / Max[current, 1]]}) &}],
      {0., Max[100., maxVoltage]}]],
    Dynamic[voltage]},

    (*Reset to starting conditions.*)
    {Button["Reset", current = 0.;
      resistance = 1.; voltage = current * resistance;
      maxCurrent = 1; maxResistance = 100; maxVoltage = 100;]}
    }
  ], voltage = current * resistance]]
```

current ⊲▭━━━━━━━━━ 0.

resistance ⊲▭━━━━━━━━━ 1.

Out[29]= voltage ⊲▭━━━━━━━━━ 0.

Reset

See Also

See Recipe 15.7 for an explanation of why DynamicModule is used in the Ohm's law example.

15.6 Controlling Updates of Dynamic Values

Problem

You want to control the timing or variable dependencies that trigger and update to a dynamic value.

Solution

Use Refresh to explicitly control dynamic updates. The following dynamic expression will generate a random number once every second.

```
In[30]:= Dynamic[Refresh[RandomInteger[{1, 100}], UpdateInterval → 1]]
Out[30]= 42

In[31]:= 9
Out[31]= 9
```

Also use Refresh to control dependencies between dynamic variables. Here you create two sliders that update the variables x and y and two dynamic sums of x and y, but you use Refresh to make the first sum respond to changes in x alone, whereas the second responds only to changes in y.

```
In[32]:= DynamicModule[{x, y},
           Grid[
             {{Slider[Dynamic[x]], Dynamic[x + y, TrackedSymbols → {x}]},
              {Slider[Dynamic[y]], Dynamic[x + y, TrackedSymbols → {y}]}}]]
```

Out[32]=   ⊏────────────   0.
           ⊏────────────   0.

Discussion

Refresh should be used with caution because it subverts the expected behavior of Dynamic. One legitimate use of Refresh is with functions that will not be triggered by Dynamic. Theodore Gray of Wolfram Research refers to these functions as nonticklish. The function Set normally written as = is ticklish, as you can see by evaluating the following expression.

```
In[33]:= DynamicModule[{x = 1}, Dynamic[x = x + 1]]
Out[33]= 32 863
```

This will create an output cell that increments about 20 times per second, which is the standard refresh rate for Dynamic. Contrast this with the evaluation of a nonticklish function, RandomReal.

```
In[34]:= Dynamic[RandomReal[]]
Out[34]= 0.385954
```

This creates a single random number that will not update. However, wrapping it with a Refresh, like we did in the "Solution" section above, will force it to update.

See Also

See the tutorial "Advanced Dynamic Functionality" at *tutorial/AdvancedDynamicFunctionality* in the Wolfram help.

15.7 Using DynamicModule As a Scoping Construct in Interactive Notebooks

Problem

You want to create dynamic content with local, statically scoped variables (similar to Module) that maintain values across sessions.

Solution

DynamicModule is similar to Module in that it restricts the scope of variables, but DynamicModule has the additional behavior of preserving the values of the local variables in the output so that they are retained between Mathematica sessions. Further, if you copy and paste the output of a DynamicModule, the values of the pasted copy are also localized in the copy, leaving the original unchanged as the copy varies.

```
In[35]:= DynamicModule[{pts = {{0, 0}, {1, 1}, {2, 0}, {3, 2}}},
            LocatorPane[Dynamic[pts],
              Dynamic[Plot[InterpolatingPolynomial[pts, x], {x, 0, 3}, PlotRange → 3]]]]
```

Out[35]=

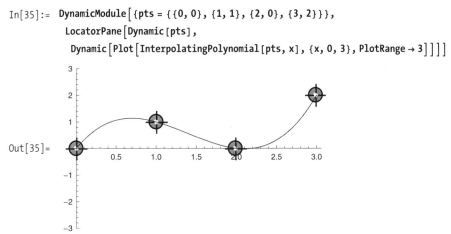

The dynamic plot on page 612 was copied from Out[35] above, pasted here, and then the locators manipulated. Each variable has its own independent state that will be retained after Mathematica is shut down and restarted with this notebook. This works because the values are bundled with the expression that underlies the output cells of a dynamic module.

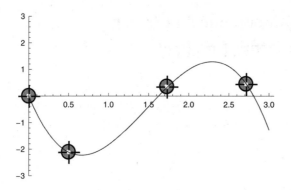

Discussion

Normal variables (including global variables and scoped variables inside a `Block` or `Module`) are stored inside the Mathematica kernel's memory. When the kernel exits, the values are lost. `DynamicModule` variables are stored in the notebook output cells. Below are a trivial `DynamicModule` and a trivial `Module`. Each simply sets a local variable to 1 and outputs the value. In Figures 15-1 and 15-2 you can see the difference in the underlying notebook representation (via `ShowExpression`).

```
In[36]:=  DynamicModule[{x = 1}, x]
Out[36]=  1

          Cell[BoxData[
            DynamicModuleBox[{$CellContext`x$$ = 1}, "1",
             DynamicModuleValues:>{}]], "Output",
            CellChangeTimes->{3.4346288561668787`*^9}]
```

Figure 15-1. Cells resulting from `DynamicModule`

```
In[37]:=  Module[{x = 1}, x]
Out[37]=  1

          Cell[BoxData["1"], "Output",
            CellChangeTimes->{3.4346290869012537`*^9}]
```

Figure 15-2. Cells resulting from `Module`

15.8 Using Scratch Variables with DynamicModule to Balance Speed Versus Space

Problem

You want to avoid doing duplicate computations in a dynamic module by caching data, but you don't want to create a bloated notebook when saved.

Solution

Use the UnsavedVariables option of DynamicModule to prevent saving in the notebook while keeping the variable localized in the frontend. Also use DynamicWrapper to guarantee cached data is calculated before any of the dynamic expressions. In this example, you wish to compute plotPoints once since we plot the points and their squares. You neither need nor want plotPoints to be saved in the notebook; saving the locator point is sufficient.

```
In[38]:= DynamicModule[{pt = {1, 1}, plotPoints},
           DynamicWrapper[
             Row[{LocatorPane[Dynamic[pt], Graphics[{Gray, Opacity[0.5], Disk[]},
                 Axes → True, ImageSize → 150]],
               Dynamic[ListPlot[plotPoints, AspectRatio → 1, ImageSize → 150]],
               Dynamic[ListPlot[plotPoints^2, AspectRatio → 1, ImageSize → 150]]},
               " "],
             plotPoints = {Re[#], Im[#]} & /@ Table[(Complex[#1, #2] & @@ pt)^n,
               {n, 0, 16, 0.1}]], UnsavedVariables → {plotPoints}]
```

Out[38]=
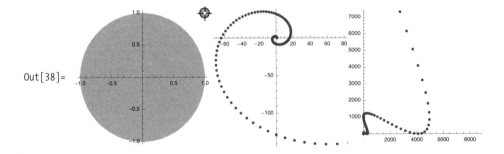

Discussion

My first attempt at the solution did not use DynamicWrapper and seemed to work fine. However, as explained by Theodore Gray of Wolfram, there is a subtle bug that will likely cause this to break in future versions of Mathematica. The assumption is that the first Dynamic will be computed before the second, and Mathematica provides no such evaluation order guarantee. In contrast, the solution using Dynamic-Wrapper will always guarantee that the second argument of DynamicWrapper will be computed before any dynamic expressions contained in the first argument.

```
In[39]:= DynamicModule[{pt = {1, 1}, plotPoints},
           Row[{LocatorPane[Dynamic[pt],
             Graphics[{Gray, Opacity[0.5], Disk[]}, Axes → True, ImageSize → 150]],
             Dynamic[ListPlot[plotPoints = {Re[#], Im[#]} & /@
               Table[(Complex[#1, #2] & @@ pt)^n, {n, 0, 16, 0.1}],
               AspectRatio → 1, ImageSize → 150]],
             Dynamic[ListPlot[plotPoints^2, AspectRatio → 1, ImageSize → 150]]}, " "],
           UnsavedVariables → {plotPoints}]
```

Out[39]=

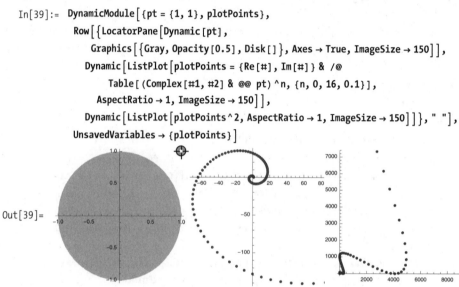

See Also

DynamicWrapper is further discussed in the "DynamicWrapper" sidebar on page 615 and the "Discussion" section of Recipe 15.11.

DynamicWrapper: A Useful Undocumented Function

If you search the Mathematica documentation as of version 7, you will not find reference to DynamicWrapper, and as I write this, Google will fail to turn up anything as well. I was alerted to the existence of DynamicWrapper by Theodore Gray of Wolfram, who stated that it is definitely an approved function that just slipped through the documentation cracks. In fact, you can find an instance of its use in a Wolfram demonstration at *http://bit.ly/jds9Z*. This sidebar will provide you with the information you need until Wolfram fills this hole.

DynamicWrapper[appearance, expr] - appearance is typeset and displayed normally as a static (nondynamic) box structure. Associated with that box structure (wrapped around it) is an invisible Dynamic[expr] that is tracked and evaluated just like any other Dynamic, but the result of evaluating expr is not displayed anywhere. An important feature is that it is guaranteed, now and in the future, that expr will be evaluated before any Dynamics there may be inside appearance. This allows you to use DynamicWrapper to set up, initialize, and update variables used by Dynamics inside it.

15.9 Making a Manipulate Self-Contained

Problem

You want to make sure a Manipulate encapsulates all definitions necessary for its operation so it always starts up in a working state.

Solution

Manipulate can reference functions and variables from the current kernel's environment. There is no guarantee that these will be defined or defined equivalently when a notebook is saved and reopened. Compare the following two cases. Although each Manipulate below will behave the same after initial evaluation, you are seeing the results after restarting Mathematica and reloading this notebook without reevaluating the definitions of f1 and f2. Note how the first does not know what f1 is, whereas the second remembers the definition of f2 as before.

```
f1[x_] := Sin[x^2] + Cos[x]
f2[x_] := Sin[x^2] + Cos[x]
Manipulate[f1[x], {{x, N[Pi]}, 0, 2 Pi},
 FrameLabel → "Definitions UnSaved"]
Manipulate[f2[x], {{x, N[Pi]}, 0, 2 Pi},
 SaveDefinitions → True, FrameLabel → "Definitions Saved"]
```

In[40]:=

f1[3.14159]

Definitions UnSaved

Out[40]=

f1[3.14159]

Definitions UnSaved

In[41]:=

−1.4303

Definitions Saved

Out[41]=

−1.4303

Definitions Saved

Discussion

For simple cases of self-contained formulas, the solution using SaveDefinitions is appropriate, but it has limitations. Although the definition of the function is saved within the context of the manipulate output, it is still in the Global` scope. This means a Clear[f2] will break the manipulation. To localize functions and variable definitions, you can wrap the Manipulate in a DynamicModule. Now the variables defined in the DynamicModule will be localized and values will be preserved across Mathematica sessions.

```
In[42]:= DynamicModule[{f},
            f[x_] := Sin[x^2] + Cos[x];
            Manipulate[f[x], {{x, N[Pi]}, 0, 2 Pi},
              FrameLabel -> "Definitions Localized"]]
          Clear[
            f]
```

```
Out[42]=
```

Another potential problem with SaveDefinitions is that a great deal of code can get pulled into the Manipulate output. Imagine your Manipulate uses a function that depends on code from an external package pulled in by Needs. All the code in the package could potentially be pulled into the Manipulate cell by SaveDefinitions. This will bloat the notebook and affect the time it takes the control to initialize each time. In situations like this, it is better to use the option Initialization. Further, if the Initialization code must complete before the results are displayed, you should also specify option SynchronousInitialization → True.

```
In[44]:= Manipulate[Histogram[RandomReal[dist, {1000}], PlotRange → All],
            {dist, {{0, 1}, NormalDistribution[0, 1], HalfNormalDistribution[1],
              StudentTDistribution[2], StudentTDistribution[3]}},
            Initialization :> (If[TrueQ[$VersionNumber < 7], Needs["Histograms`"]]),
            SynchronousInitialization → True]
```

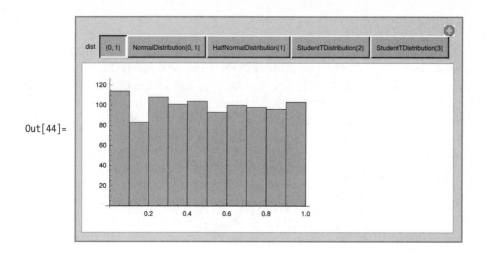

Out[44]=

Mathematica 7 was released midway through the production of this book, hence I conditionalized the Initialization since Histogram is a built-in function in version 7.

15.10 Remembering the Values Found Using Manipulate

Problem

You found some interesting results using Manipulate and want to preserve them for future use.

Solution

Use the + icon in the Manipulate to select either "Paste Snapshot " or "Add To Bookmarks."

```
In[45]:= Manipulate[-0.07 x^5 - 0.42 x^4 + 0.94 x^3 - 4.25 x^2 + 86.5 x - 0.13,
          {x, 4.873, 4.874}]
```

Out[45]=

0.0617716

```
In[46]:= DynamicModule[{x = 4.8732500000000005`},
        -0.07` x^5 - 0.42` x^4 + 0.94` x^3 - 4.25` x^2 + 86.5` x - 0.13`]

Out[46]= -0.00816536

In[47]:= DynamicModule[{x = 4.873219000000001`},
        -0.07` x^5 - 0.42` x^4 + 0.94` x^3 - 4.25` x^2 + 86.5` x - 0.13`]

Out[47]= 0.000507714
```

Discussion

You can bookmark specific settings by adjusting the dynamic module output to the desired values and then choosing "Add To Bookmarks." You will be prompted for a bookmark name. From that point on you can return to those settings by selecting the bookmark. In the figure below I have added two bookmarks: "Initial Settings" and "Interesting."

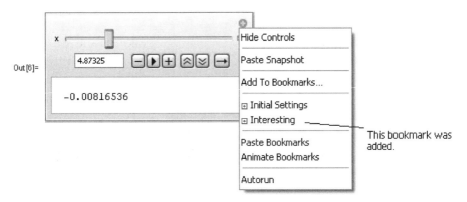

15.11 Improving Performance of Manipulate by Segregating Fast and Slow Operations

Problem

You have a sluggish Manipulate with several controls and you would like to improve some aspects of its performance.

Solution

Isolate fast dynamic computations from computationally intensive ones by performing the fast computations local to an internal Dynamic. In the example below, the generation of the 50,000 data points using NestList is significantly more expensive than raising the values in the list to a power. You need not pay the price of the generation when manipulating the variable z, but to isolate that computation you need to wrap it in a Dynamic, as shown.

```
In[48]:=  Manipulate[
            DynamicModule[{data}, data = NestList[r # (1.0 - #) &, x, 50000];
              Dynamic[ListPlot[data^z, PlotRange -> {{0, 10000}, {0, 1}}]]],
            {{r, 3.58}, 2, 4}, {{x, 0.4}, 0, 1}, {{z, 1}, 0.1, 5}]
```

Out[48]=

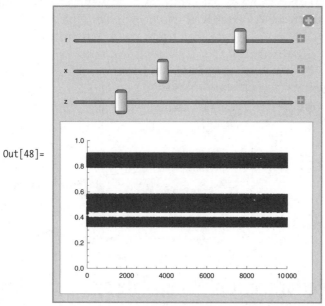

Discussion

This technique works because internally Manipulate wraps its expression with a Dynamic and the net result is a Dynamic nested inside another Dynamic. In the solution, the inner Dynamic is monitoring changes in data and z but not r or x, and since data does not recompute when z changes, data need not be recomputed. The general rule is that changes that trigger only updates to an inner Dynamic will not trigger updates to any outer Dynamic.

You can also exploit this property when combining plots where one is slow and the other is fast. To make this work, you need to solicit the services of DynamicWrapper because Show cannot combine Dynamic output. The trick here is to use DynamicWrapper to capture the output of each plot, nesting the DynamicWrapper that computes the ReliefPlot (less expensive) inside the DynamicWrapper that computes the ListContour-Plot (more expensive). The result is that you can change the color function cf or the plot points p of the ReliefPlot and get fast updates while paying for the updates to n or the number of contours c only when these are changed.

```
In[49]:=  Manipulate[DynamicModule[{p1 = 0, p2 = 0, data},
           data = Table[i + Sin[i^n + j^n], {i, -4, 4, .03}, {j, -4, 4, .03}];
           DynamicWrapper[DynamicWrapper[Dynamic[Show[{p2, p1}]]],
             p1 = ListContourPlot[data, ContourShading -> None, Contours -> c,
               ContourStyle -> {Opacity[.5], Opacity[.8]}, ImageSize -> 300]],
             p2 = ReliefPlot[data, MaxPlotPoints -> p, ColorFunction -> cf,
               ImageSize -> 300]]], {{n, 2}, 1, 10, 1},
           {{c, 3}, 3, 10, 1}, {{p, 50}, 20, 200, 1},
           {cf, {Automatic, "SunsetColors", "BlueGreenYellow"}}]
```

Out[49]=

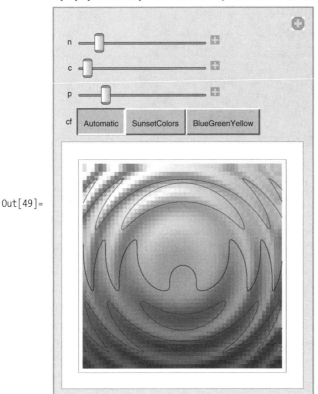

```
In[50]:=  DynamicModule[{cf = "SunsetColors", c = 5, n = 6, p = 110},
          DynamicModule[{p1, p2, data},
           data = Table[i + Sin[i^n + j^n], {i, -4, 4, 0.03`}, {j, -4, 4, 0.03`}];
           DynamicWrapper[DynamicWrapper[Dynamic[Show[{p2, p1}]],
             p1 = ListContourPlot[data, ContourShading → None, Contours → c,
               ContourStyle → {Opacity[0.5`], Opacity[0.8`]}, ImageSize → 500]],
             p2 = ReliefPlot[data, MaxPlotPoints → p, ColorFunction → cf,
               ImageSize → 300]]]]
```

Out[50]=

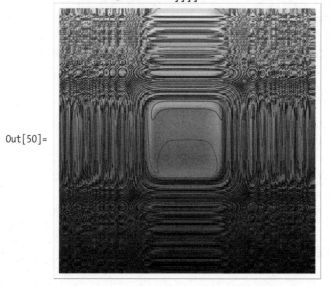

15.12 Localizing a Function in a Manipulate

Problem

You want to manipulate a function while keeping the function's definition localized.

Solution

Wrap the Manipulate in a DynamicModule and use the Initialization option to establish the function's definition. Below we define a global function f[x] and two Manipulates using localized definitions of f[x] that remain independent.

```
In[51]:=  f[x_] := 1
```

```
In[52]:= DynamicModule[{f}, Manipulate[f[x], {x, -2 Pi, 2 Pi}],
            Initialization :> (f[x_] := Sin[x])]
```

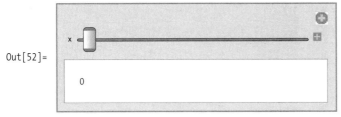

Out[52]=

```
In[53]:= DynamicModule[{f}, Manipulate[f[x], {x, -2 Pi, 2 Pi}],
            Initialization :> (f[x_] := Cos[x])]
```

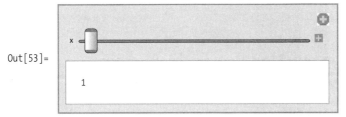

Out[53]=

Discussion

Manipulate only localizes variables associated with control variables. This can cause problems when you have multiple Manipulates that use the same function name in different ways. In Out[54] below, it is clear that the second definition of g[x] modified the first since Sin[x] takes on values between -1 and 1.

```
In[54]:= Manipulate[g[x], {x, -2. Pi, 2. Pi}, Initialization :> (g[x_] := Sin[x])]
```

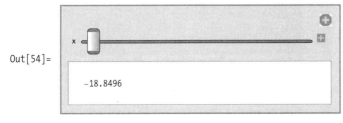

Out[54]=

```
In[55]:= Manipulate[g[x], {x, 1., 2.}, Initialization :> (g[x_] := 3 x)]
```

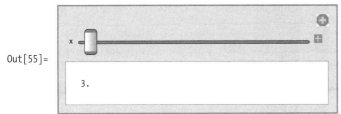

Out[55]=

Note that SaveDefinitions→True as discussed in Recipe 15.9 does not localize the symbol, so it is not a solution to this problem.

```
In[56]:=  f[x_] := Exp[x]
          Manipulate[f[x],  {x, -2 Pi, 2 Pi}, SaveDefinitions → True]
```

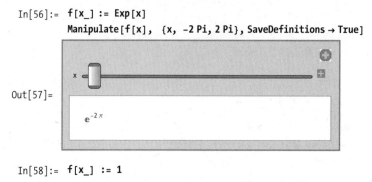

Out[57]=

```
In[58]:=  f[x_] := 1
```

15.13 Sharing DynamicModule Variables across Cell or Window Boundaries

Problem

You want to create an interface that is divided across multiple cells or notebooks but interacts with shared variables. However, you don't want these variables to be global.

Solution

Create a *DynamicModule Wormhole* using InheritScope→True from within a Manipulate or DynamicModule you want to inherit from.

Discussion

Variables defined in the first argument of a DynamicModule or as control variables in a Manipulate have their scope restricted to the resulting output cell. This concept is explained in Recipe 15.7. Generally, this is exactly the behavior you want when using Manipulate. An obvious exception is when you want to create a more complex application composed of multiple notebooks (a palette is implemented as a notebook). The whimsical term *wormhole* is used to suggest the sharing of scope between different physical locations (e.g., output cells).

Here is an example that uses the same technique as the solution but with DynamicModule instead of Manipulate and multiple output cells instead of a palette. Each time the button is pressed, a new cell is printed that inherits the scope from the original DynamicModule.

```
In[59]:= DynamicModule[{x = 0, d},
          {Dynamic[x], Slider[Dynamic[x], {-10, 10}], Button["MakeCell",
           Print[DynamicModule[{}, Dynamic[x], InheritScope → True]]]}]

Out[59]= {0, ————————[]————————, [ MakeCell ]}
```

See Also

The "Advanced Dynamic Functionality" tutorial (*http://bit.ly/3u8fXo*) explains some of the technical details underlying DynamicModule wormholes. It hints at the ability to link up arbitrary existing DynamicModules but, unfortunately, provides no additional information.

15.14 Creating Your Own Custom Controls

Problem

You want to create a control of your own design that can be used inside a Manipulate or notebook cell.

Solution

Manipulate allows you to associate a control variable with a function and thus provides a means to specify controls with nonstandard behavior and appearance. The function incUntilButton creates a button that increments the dynamic variable until it hits a specified value, at which point it sets it back to the minimum specified in the Manipulate definition. Notice how the slider can change the x through its full range while the button immediately resets x to -10 if it exceeds 5.

```
In[60]:= incUntilButton[name_String, limit_Integer, Dynamic[val_],
          {min_, max_}] := Button[name, If[val < limit, ++val, val = min]]
        Manipulate[x, {x, -10, 10}, {{x, 0}, -10, 10,
          incUntilButton["Inc Until 5", 5, ##] &}]
```

Out[61]=

```
  x ⊂[]——————————————————————————————————————⊞

  x  incUntilButton[Inc Until 5, 5, -10, {-10, 10}]

   ┌──────────────────────────────────────────┐
   │  -10                                       │
   │                                            │
   └──────────────────────────────────────────┘
```

Discussion

The function you use to create a custom control can take two forms. In the simple form, it is passed only the control variable wrapped in Dynamic (e.g., Dynamic[x]).

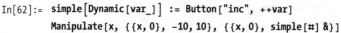

```
In[62]:= simple[Dynamic[var_]] := Button["inc", ++var]
        Manipulate[x, {{x, 0}, -10, 10}, {{x, 0}, simple[#] &}]
```

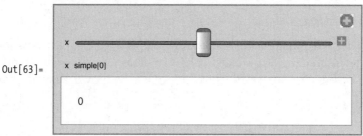

Out[63]=

The solution shows the advanced form that gives the function access to the minimum and maximum values specified in the definition. In this case, the function Manipulate sees must have the form f[Dynamic[var_], {min_,max_}]. As the solution shows, this does not mean you can't use a function that takes additional arguments. However, those arguments must be bound when the anonymous function is created inside the Manipulate, as I did by providing "Inc Until 5" and 5 in the solution.

You may argue that a button hardly qualifies as a "custom control" even though the solution gives it custom behavior. Have no fear, because you have all the user interface primitives Mathematica has to offer at your disposal for creating interesting controls. Here is an example that shows how the angular slider (adapted from the "Applications" section DynamicModule in the Mathematica documentation) can be incorporated as a control in a Manipulate.

This example uses the function Control and the option ContentSize, which are only available in Mathematica 7.

```
In[64]:= angularSlider[Dynamic[angle_]] :=
            Control[{angle, (DynamicModule[{p = {1, 0}, angleCalc},
                LocatorPane[Dynamic[p, (angleCalc @@ Normalize /@ {#, p}) &],
                  Graphics[{Circle[], Arrowheads[0.15], Arrow[
                    Dynamic[{{0, 0}, p}]]}], ImageSize → Tiny], Appearance → None],
                Initialization :→ (angle = 0; angleCalc[newp_, oldp_] := (angle =
                    angle + ArcCos[newp.oldp] Sign[Cross[newp].(newp - oldp)];
                    p = {Cos[angle], Sin[angle]}))]) &}]
          Manipulate[{angle, Sin[angle], Cos[angle]}, {angle, angularSlider[#] &},
            ContentSize → 275]
```

Out[65]=

angle angularSlider[0]

{0, 0, 1}

15.15 Animating an Expression

Problem

You want to see how an expression evolves without having to manually adjust controls.

Solution

Use Animate to create instructive self-running demonstrations. Here Animate drives an illustration of the cycloid, which is the locus of points traced by a point on a wheel as it rolls across a flat surface.

```
In[66]= Animate[
          Show[ParametricPlot[{t - Sin[t], 1 - Cos[t]}, {t, 0, x + $MachineEpsilon},
            PlotRange → {{0, 4 Pi}, {0, 2}}, Axes → None], Graphics[Translate[
            Rotate[{Circle[{0, 1}], Point[{0, 0}]}, -x], {x, 0}]]], {x, 0, 4 Pi}]
```

x

Out[66]=

Discussion

Animate can drive a variety of demonstrations. Here we can get some insight into the implementation of the Sort function by providing a parameter limit within a custom comparison function that short-circuits the sort after that many steps. You use Animate with BarChart to visualize the partialSort at each step. Here the option DisplayAllSteps keeps Animate from skipping over steps. DisplayAllSteps will slow things down, so only use it if the animation suffers without it.

```
In[67]= DynamicModule[{list, len},
        list = RandomReal[{1, 100}, 50];
        len = Length[list];
        max = Floor[len * Log[2, len]];
        Animate[BarChart[partialSort[list, t], Axes → None,
          ColorFunction → Function[{height}, ColorData["Rainbow"][1 - height]]],
         {t, 0, max, 1}, DisplayAllSteps → True],
        Initialization :→ (

          partialSort[list_, limit_] :=
           Module[{step = 0}, Sort[list, (step++ < limit && #1 < #2) &]]

        )]
```

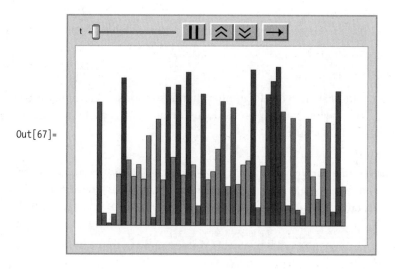

Out[67]=

Other useful options are AnimationRunning→True, which starts the animation running immediately; AnimationRate, which sets the initial speed of the animation; and AnimationRepetitions, which controls how many times the animation repeats before stopping.

As you might expect, there is a close relationship between Animate and Manipulate. Animate is implemented in terms of Manipulate with the help of a low-level control called an Animator. You can use an Animator directly to get more control over the details of the animation layout. Stare at the next animation for 10 seconds, and when you awaken, you will have the strong urge to tell all your friends to buy the *Mathematica Cookbook*!

```
In[68]:= DynamicModule[{x},
            Grid[{{Animator[Dynamic[x]], Dynamic[Graphics[{Opacity[0.5],
                Disk[{0, 0}, 0.5], Disk[{0, 0}, x]}]]}, {"You are getting...",
                Dynamic[Text[Style["Sleepy", Bold, 12 + 5 x]]]}}]]
```

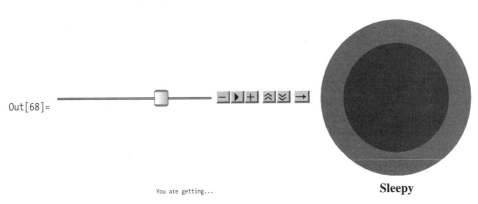

Out[68]=

You are getting...   **Sleepy**

You can share your animations over the Web by exporting them to several common video formats, such as Microsoft AVI or Adobe Flash. You may need to experiment with the options AnimationRate, RefreshRate, and DefaultDuration to get a smooth animation.

```
In[69]:= Export["cycloid.avi",
            Animate[Show[ParametricPlot[{t - Sin[t], 1 - Cos[t]},
                {t, 0, x + $MachineEpsilon}, PlotRange → {{0, 4 Pi}, {0, 2}},
                Axes → None], Graphics[Translate[
                Rotate[{Circle[{0, 1}], Point[{0, 0}]}, -x], {x, 0}]]],
            {x, 0, 4 Pi}, AnimationRate → 0.1, RefreshRate → 1,
            AnimationRunning → True, DefaultDuration → 20.`,
            AnimationDirection → ForwardBackward]];
```

See Also

The function ListAnimate provides an alternative to Animate in which the animation is derived by cycling through the elements of a list. This is useful in a case where each step in the animation takes a lot of computation; you can precompute all the frames of the animation and play them back using ListAnimate. See the Mathematica documentation for examples.

15.16 Creating Custom Interfaces

Problem

You want to create a custom interface that requires handling of low-level events such as mouse clicks.

Solution

Mathematica's higher level interactive functionality is adequate for most casual users, but sometimes you want to achieve something cool. Luckily, Mathematica lets you intercept low-level GUI events generated by your operating system using EventHandler. When you execute the following code, you can increase the size of the text by dragging (moving the mouse with the left button depressed) over the word Start. When you release the mouse, the text changes to Done.

```
In[70]:= DynamicModule[{text = "Start", points = 12},
          EventHandler[Dynamic[Text[Style[text, points]]],
           "MouseDown" :> (text = "Start"; points = 12),
           "MouseUp" :> (text = "Done"), "MouseDragged" :> (points += 0.5)]]

Out[70]= Start
```

Discussion

You can use event handlers to add interactive features to existing plotting and graphics functions. In these applications, you will often use MousePosition["Graphics"] to query the position of the mouse relative to the enclosing graphic. Here interactive-Plot creates a plot of a function and annotates it with a point based on the position of the mouse when you click. The coordinates of the point are displayed in the upper left.

```
In[71]:= SetAttributes[interactivePlot, HoldAll];
         interactivePlot[f_, range_] := DynamicModule[{m, p = {0, 0}, plot, dot},
           Column[{Dynamic[Row[p, Spacer[4]]], EventHandler[
             plot = Plot[f, range];
             DynamicWrapper[Dynamic[Show[plot, dot]],
               dot = Graphics[Point[{p[[1]], p[[2]]}], AspectRatio → 0.1]],
             "MouseDown" :→ (m = MousePosition["Graphics"];
               p = {m[[1]], Head[f][m[[1]]]})]}]]

In[73]:= interactivePlot[Cos[x], {x, 0, 4 Pi}]
```

Out[73]=

Event handlers can nest with the options PassEventsDown and PassEventsUp, control-ling event propagation. By default, inner event handlers get to act on events first, but outer event handlers see the event first and thus can control propagation of the event downward. The program below creates a simple game using the keyboard. The idea is to try to catch the dot with the arrow. Notice that there is an outer event handler that is used to control the difficulty of the game using the d and e keys. The outer event handler uses PassEventsDown → False, which means that if it handles the event, then the inner handler will not see it. This prevents the dot from moving when the d or e key is handled.

EventHandler using arrow keys does not work well in Mac OS X because selection is lost when the arrow is pressed. I do not know a workaround except to use other keys or mouse events.

```
In[74]:= DynamicModule[{line = {{0, 0}}, dot, inc = 0.1, difficulty = 0.5},
            dot = Disk[Round[RandomReal[{0, 1}, 2], 0.1], 0.025];
            (*This event handler controls difficulty.*)
            EventHandler[Dynamic[
               (*This event handler controls the game play.*)
               EventHandler[
               Dynamic[
                 Column[{Row[{"Difficulty", difficulty}, Spacer[2]], Graphics[{White,
                     EdgeForm[Thick], Rectangle[], Black, Arrow[line], dot}]}]],
               (*Arrow keys extend the line.*)
               "RightArrowKeyDown" :> AppendTo[line, Last[line] + {inc, 0}],
               "LeftArrowKeyDown" :> AppendTo[line, Last[line] + {-inc, 0}],
               "UpArrowKeyDown" :> AppendTo[line, Last[line] + {0, inc}],
               "DownArrowKeyDown" :> AppendTo[line, Last[line] + {0, -inc}],
               (*Any key, including arrows, may move the dot or declare a winner.*)
               "KeyDown" :> (dot = If[inc > 0 && dot[[1]] == Last[line],
                   inc = 0; Text[Style["Winner", Bold, 16], dot[[1]]],
                   If[inc == 0 || RandomReal[] > difficulty, dot,
                   Disk[Round[RandomReal[{0, 1}, 2], 0.1], 0.025]]])],
               {"KeyDown", "d"} :> (difficulty = Min[0.8, difficulty + 0.05]),
               {"KeyDown", "e"} :> (difficulty = Max[0.1, difficulty - 0.05]),
               (*Escape key resets the game.*)
               "EscapeKeyDown" :> (line = {{0, 0}}; inc = 0.1;
                 dot = Disk[Round[RandomReal[{0, 1}, 2], 0.1], 0.025]),
               (*Don't pass events handled on this layer down.*)
               PassEventsDown -> False]]
```

Difficulty 0.5

Out[74]=

See Also

FrontEndEventActions, NotebookEventActions, and CellEventActions are other event handlers with differing levels of granularity. See the Mathematica documentation for details.

15.17 Managing a Large Number of Controls in Limited Screen Real Estate

Problem

You want to go beyond what Manipulate has to offer and create your own custom interfaces. You may need to manage a large number of controls in a sensible manner or need a custom layout that Manipulate does not support.

Solution

The building blocks of sophisticated user interfaces are PaneSelector and Opener-View, for managing many controls; Control, for selection of appropriate controls; and Item, Row, Column, and Grid, for layout. The following Manipulate initially presents a simple interface for modifying the parameters to a 3D plot. You use Opener-View to provide an advanced set of controls that remain hidden until selected. Within this OpenerView, you use PaneSelector to alternate between sets of controls, depending on a checkbox that allows modification of PlotStyle or ColorFunction.

 Control is a Mathematica 7 feature, so the following code will not work in version 6.

```
In[75]:=  DynamicModule[{color, specularity, colorFunc, colorScale, vxy, vz},
            Manipulate[Plot3D[Sin[a Pi x + y^2] b Cos[c Pi y], {x, -1, 1},
              {y, -1, 1}, PlotRange → {{-1, 1}, {-1, 1}, {-5, 5}},
              PlotStyle → {Specularity[White, specularity], color},
              ColorFunction →
                If[colorFunc, Function[{x, y, z}, Hue[colorScale (1 - z)]], None],
              (*Here I use Dynamic as per Recipes 15.6 and 15.5 so that updates
              are fast and viewpoint drags of plot sync with controls.*)
              ViewPoint → Dynamic[Flatten[{vxy, vz}],
                ({vxy[[1]], vxy[[2]], vz} = #) &]],
              {a, -5, 5}, {b, -5, 5}, {c, -5, 5},
              (*Advanced set of controls*)
              OpenerView[{"Advanced", Column[{
                Item["Plot Style", Alignment → Center],
                Control[{{colorFunc, False}, {True, False}}],
                (*PlotStyle and ColorFunction are mutually exclusive.*)
                PaneSelector[{True ->
                  Control[{{colorScale, 0.65}, 0, 1}],
                  False → Column[{Control[{color, Orange}],
                    Control[{{specularity, 3}, 5, 1}]}]}, Dynamic[colorFunc]],
                Item["View", Alignment → Center],
                Row[{Control[{{vxy, {2, 2}, "x-y"}, {-2 Pi, -2 Pi}, {2 Pi, 2 Pi}}],
                  Control[{{vz, 2, "z"}, -2 Pi, 2 Pi,
                    ControlType → VerticalSlider, ImageSize → Tiny}]}]
              }]}]]]]
```

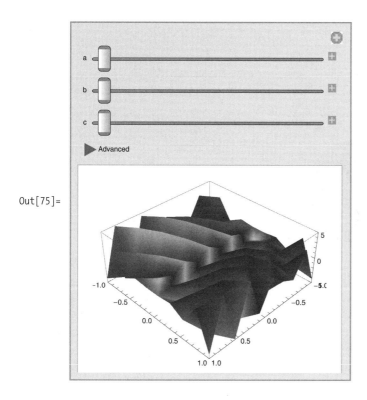

Out[75]=

Discussion

In addition to OpenerView and PaneSelector, there is a whole family of controls for managing limited screen real estate. These include FlipView, MenuView, SlideView, and TabView. I provide a sample of each without going into much detail because they are fairly self-explanatory and follow the same basic syntax.

A FlipView cycles through a list of expressions as you click on the output. Here I use FlipView over a list of graphics. Click on the graphic to see the next in the series.

```
In[76]:= FlipView[
           Graphics[#, ImageSize → Tiny] & /@ {Disk[], Circle[], Rectangle[]}]
```

Out[76]=

`SlideView` is similar to `FlipView` but uses VCR-style controls to give more control of the progression.

In[77]:= `SlideView[`
      `Graphics[#, ImageSize → Tiny] & /@ {Disk[], Circle[], Rectangle[]}]`

Out[77]=

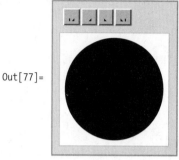

A `MenuView` allows you random access to the items via a menu that you specify as a list of rules: `MenuView[{lbl1→expr1, label2→expr2, ...}]`. This is similar syntax to that used by `PaneSelector` in the solution. Don't be afraid to build up these expressions using a bit of functional programming as I do here, especially if it cuts down on repetition. In Out[78] below, I use the `Head` of each graphic primitive as the label for convenience, but you can also provide the label explicitly, as in Out[79] on page 637, which builds the list of rules using `Inner`.

In[78]:= `MenuView[ (Head[#] :→ Graphics[#, ImageSize → Tiny]) & /@`
      `{Disk[], Circle[], Rectangle[]}]`

Out[78]=

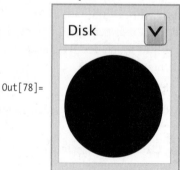

In[79]= MenuView[Inner[(#1 → Graphics[#2, ImageSize → Tiny]) &,
         {"aDisk", "aCircle", "aRectangle"},
         {Disk[], Circle[], Rectangle[]}, List]]

Out[79]=

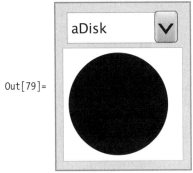

TabView is similar to MenuView but uses the familiar tabbed folder theme that has become popular in a variety of modern interfaces, including most web browsers.

In[80]:= TabView[Inner[(#1 → Graphics[#2, ImageSize → Tiny]) &,
         {"aDisk", "aCircle", "aRectangle"},
         {Disk[], Circle[], Rectangle[]}, List]]

Out[80]=

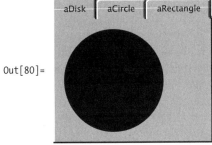

Clearly these controls can be mixed, combined with Manipulate, or used alone to create an unlimited variety of sophisticated interfaces. For example, here is a tabbed set of Manipulates.

```
In[81]:= TabView[Inner[
            (#1 → Manipulate[ Plot[a #2[b x], {x, 0, Pi}], {a, 1, 5}, {b, 1, 5}]) &,
            {"Sin", "Cos", "Tan"}, {Sin, Cos, Tan}, List]]
```

Out[81]=

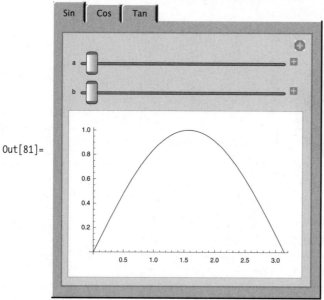

Contrast this to a single Manipulate that can switch between a TabView or a MenuView, or even one that lets you switch back and forth. This is actually a useful technique when building an interface for someone's approval. You can switch among various design choices without touching the code.

```
In[82]:= Manipulate[control[Inner[(#1 → Plot[a #2[b x], {x, 0, Pi}]) &,
            {"Sin", "Cos", "Tan"}, {Sin, Cos, Tan}, List]],
          {a, 1, 5}, {b, 1, 5}, {{control, TabView}, {TabView, MenuView}}]
```

Out[82]=

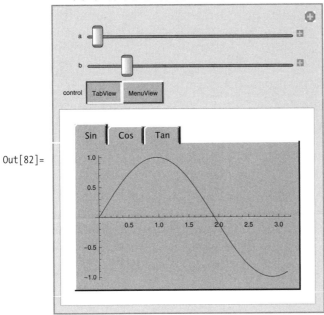

See Also

Inspiration for this recipe came from a presentation by Lou D'Andria of Wolfram during the 2008 International Mathematica User Conference. Presentations from this conference can be found at *http://bit.ly/41BMSZ*.

CHAPTER 16

Parallel Mathematica

splintered dreams of unity (our lives are parallel)
so far from reality (our lives are parallel)
independent trajectories (our lives are parallel)
separate terms of equality (our lives are parallel)

our lives are parallel

is there no redemption? no common good?
is there nothing we can do for ourselves?
or only what we should?
comes the hard admission of what we don't provide
goes the insistence on the ways
and means that so divide

Bad Religion, "Parallel"

16.0 Introduction

Mathematica has impressive performance on many types of problems. The majority of Mathematica users are not drawn to Mathematica for its brute speed, but rather for its unparalleled depth of features in the realm of symbolic processing. Yet, there are certainly problems that you will solve in Mathematica that you will want to scale to larger data sets or more complex models. In the past, the only viable solution might be to port your Mathematica solution to C or Fortran. Today relatively cheap multiprocessor and multicore computers have become commonplace. My primary development machine has eight cores available. Wolfram provides two solutions for exploiting multiple CPUs. The first solution, called Grid Mathematica, has been available as a separate (and somewhat costly) product distinct from your vanilla Mathematica product. The second solution is available to everyone who has updated to Mathematica 7. One of the big feature enhancements in version 7 is integrated parallelism that can exploit up to four CPU cores. At the present time, going beyond four cores requires the Grid Mathematica solution, even with version 7.

Whether you use Mathematica 7, Grid Mathematica 7, or Grid Mathematica prerelease 7, the road to parallelizing your Mathematica code is essentially the same, although it has become significantly more user friendly in version 7. Mathematica's concurrency model revolves around running multiple communicating kernels. These kernels can be on the same machine (which only makes sense if that machine has multiple cores) or on several networked machines. In the networked case, the machines can be of any architecture and operating system for which a Mathematica version exists.

Mathematica's concurrency model uses one master kernel and multiple slave kernels. The designations *master* and *slave* do not denote different versions of the kernel: any kernel can play the role of the master. The master coordinates the activity of the slaves, ships work to the slave kernels, and integrates results to present back to the end users. There are several possible configurations of master and slaves that will vary based on your particular arrangement of computer resources and possibly third-party tools. The simplest configuration uses all local kernels and is appropriate when working on a multicore machine. The next level of complexity is based on Wolfram's Lightweight Grid Service technology and represents the simplest option for users who need to distribute computations over a network of computers. The third option is ideal for enterprise users who already deploy some third-party vendor's clustering solution (e.g., Microsoft Cluster Server, Apple Workgroup Cluster, Altair PBS GridWorks, etc.). A final option is based on the ability of the master kernel to launch remote kernels using the remote shell (rsh), but this is largely a legacy option and is typically harder to set up and maintain. Recipes 16.1 and 16.2 explain how to set up the two most common configurations.

 The recipes in this chapter assume you have Mathematica 7, which no longer relies on the Parallel Computing Toolkit that was the foundation of parallel operations for Mathematica 6 and earlier versions. However, many of the recipes will port easily to the Parallel Computing Toolkit since many of commands have the same names.

There are some common pitfalls you need to avoid so your experience with parallelization does not end in utter frustration.

Never attempt to test your code for the first time in parallel evaluation. If you are writing a function that you plan to evaluate in parallel, first test it in the normal way on a single kernel. Make sure it is as bug free as possible so you can separate any problems you encounter under parallel operation from problems that have nothing to do with parallel evaluation.

Don't forget that slave kernels do not have access to variables and definitions created in the master unless you specifically grant them access. A very common pitfall is to forget to use `DistributeDefinitions`.

Try structuring your code so that it is side-effect free. Code with side effects, including code that may create new definitions within the kernel, perform writes to files, or create visual content in the frontend, may still be parallelizable, but you need to know what you are doing. A function that saves some state in one slave kernel will not see that change when it runs again in a different slave kernel.

Race conditions may be another problem. Consider a function that checks if a file exists, opens it, and writes some data to the end. If the file was not found, it creates it. Parallelizing the function is going to be fraught with difficulties unless special precautions are taken. If the function is running on two kernels, both may see that the file does not exist, and both may then attempt to create it. This will most likely result in the initial output of one kernel getting lost. Race conditions are extremely frustrating because a program may work 99 times in a row but then suddenly fail on the hundredth try. Recipe 16.11 provides techniques for avoiding these kinds of problems.

16.1 Configuring Local Kernels

Problem

You want to exploit your multicore computer by running two or more local kernels in parallel.

Solution

Use Edit, Preferences and navigate to the Parallel tab (see Figure 16-1). Within this top-level tab there is a subtab group where the first subtab is called Local Kernels. If you are configuring parallel preferences for the first time, this tab is probably already selected. Notice the button called Enable Local Kernels. Pressing that button will cause the display to change to that in Figure 16-2.

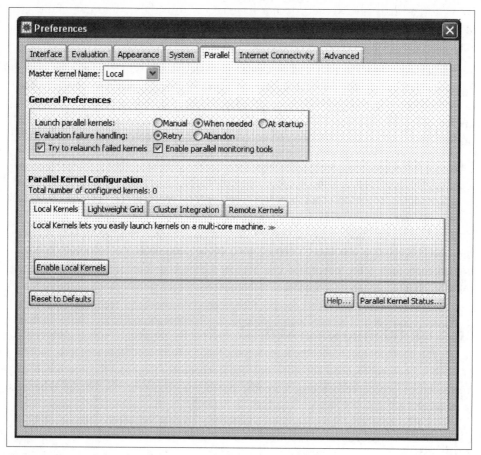

Figure 16-1. Parallel preferences for local kernel configuration

There are a few radio buttons for specifying how many slave kernels to run. The default setting is Automatic, meaning it will run as many kernels as there are cores, up to the standard license limit of four. For most users, this is exactly the setting you want, and you can now close the Preferences dialog and begin using the parallel programming primitives described in the remaining recipes of this chapter.

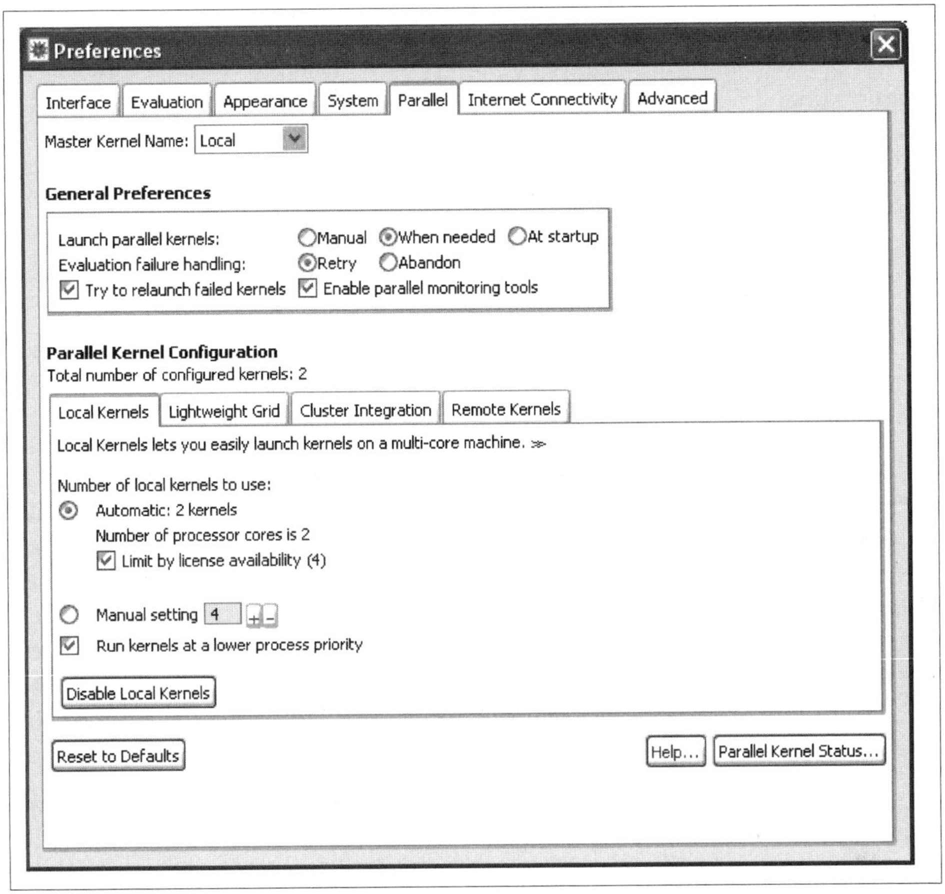

Figure 16-2. Preferences after enabling local kernels

Discussion

The simplest way to get started with parallel computing in Mathematica is to run on a computer with more than one core. A four-core machine is ideal because that is the number of slave kernels Mathematica allows in a standard configuration. If you are using the computer to do other work, you may want to leave "Run kernels at lower process priority" checked, but on my Mac Pro eight-core processor, I uncheck this since there is plenty of CPU available to the system even with the four slaves, one master, and the frontend.

Once you have enabled local kernels, you can use Parallel Kernel Status to check the status of the slaves and launch or close them.

See Also

See Recipe 16.2 for configuring access to kernels running on other computers on your network.

16.2 Configuring Remote Services Kernels

Problem

You want to exploit the computing resources of your network by running two or more kernels across multiple networked computers.

Solution

If you have not already done so, you must obtain the Lightweight Grid Service from Wolfram and install it on all computers that you wish to share kernels. The Lightweight Grid Service is available free to users who have Premier Service. Contact Wolfram for licensing details. By default, the Lightweight Grid Service is associated with port 3737, and assuming this default, you can administer the service remotely via a URL of the form *http://<server name>:3737/WolframLightweightGrid/*, where *<server name>* is replaced by the server or IP address. For example, I use *http://maxwell.local:3737/WolframLightweightGrid/* for my Mac Pro. I could also access this machine via its IP address on my network *http://10.0.1.4:3737/WolframLightweightGrid/*.

Use the Lightweight Grid tab under Parallel Preferences tab to configure the Lightweight Grid. This tab should automatically detect machines on your local subnet. You can also find machines on other subnets (provided they are running Lightweight Grid) by using the "Discover More Kernels" option, and entering the name of the machine manually.

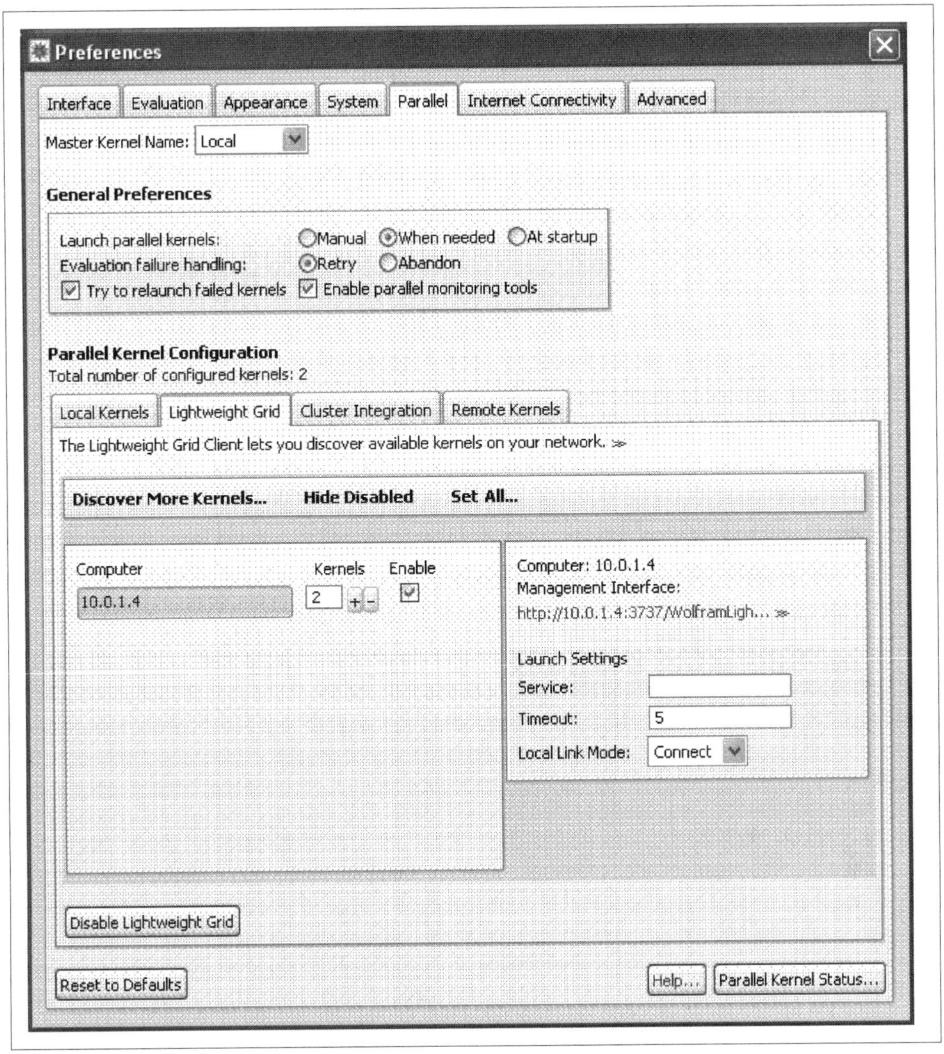

Figure 16-3. Parallel preferences for Lightweight Grid

Discussion

Once you have the Lightweight Grid configured, remote kernels are as easy to use as local ones. Mathematica will launch the specified number of remote kernels on the computers you selected provided the kernels are available. The kernels may not be available if they are being used by another user on the network since each computer will typically have a maximum number of kernels that can be launched, and launching more kernels than there are cores on a specific computer does not usually make sense.

You can use the LaunchKernels command to launch kernels associated with a specific computer running the Lightweight Grid Service.

```
In[1]:= LaunchKernels["http://10.0.1.4:3737/WolframLightweightGrid/"];
```

See Also

Documentation and download links for the Lightweight Grid can be found at *http://www.wolfram.com/products/lightweightgrid/*.

16.3 Sending a Command to Multiple Kernels for Parallel Evaluation

Problem

You want to run a command on several kernels simultaneously.

Solution

Use ParallelEvaluate to send commands to multiple kernels and wait for results to complete. Use With to bind locally defined variables before distribution.

Imagine you need to generate many random numbers and you want to distribute the calculation across all available kernels. Here I use $KernelCount to make the computation independent of the number of kernels and Take to compensate for the extra numbers returned if $KernelCount does not divide 100 evenly.

```
In[2]:= Take[Flatten[ParallelEvaluate[
          RandomInteger[{-100, 100}, Ceiling[100/$KernelCount]]]], 100]
Out[2]= {83, -11, 5, -15, -11, -24, 6, -75, 74, 27, -42, 95, 100, -83, -91, -81, 25,
         -91, -96, -98, 9, 47, 44, 44, -81, 17, 10, -66, -40, -31, -30, 96, -55,
         92, -76, 5, -44, -79, -83, 51, -36, -93, -1, 12, 34, -68, -8, 29, 9, 1,
         44, 39, -1, 10, -80, -25, 62, 58, 88, -49, 77, 44, -48, 13, -69, -80, -39,
         -44, -37, 95, 34, -81, -8, 33, -79, 86, -97, 29, -29, -19, 22, 50, 4, 95,
         -55, -99, -98, 9, -61, -7, 0, -66, -14, -26, 95, 47, -35, -24, -29, -23}

In[3]:= Length[%]
Out[3]= 100
```

If you want to make the number of random numbers into a variable, you need to use With since variable values are not known across multiple kernels by default.

```
In[4]:= vars = With[{num = 1000}, Take[Flatten[ParallelEvaluate[
          RandomInteger[{-100, 100}, Ceiling[num/$KernelCount]]]], num]];
        Length[
          vars]
Out[5]= 1000
```

Discussion

Since ParallelEvaluate simply ships the command as stated to multiple kernels, there needs to be something that inherently makes the command different for each kernel; otherwise you just get the same result back multiple times.

```
In[6]:= ParallelEvaluate[Sin[Pi/3]]
```
$$Out[6]= \left\{ \frac{\sqrt{3}}{2}, \frac{\sqrt{3}}{2}, \frac{\sqrt{3}}{2}, \frac{\sqrt{3}}{2} \right\}$$

You can control which kernels ParallelEvaluate uses by passing as a second argument the list of kernel objects you want to use. The available kernel objects are returned by the function Kernels[].

```
In[7]:= Kernels[]
Out[7]= {KernelObject[1, local], KernelObject[2, local],
         KernelObject[3, local], KernelObject[4, local]}
```

Here you evaluate the kernel ID and process ID of the first kernel returned by Kernels[] and then for all but the last kernel.

```
In[8]:= link = Kernels[][[1]];
        ParallelEvaluate[{$KernelID, $ProcessID}, link]
Out[9]= {1, 2478}
```

```
In[10]:= ParallelEvaluate[{$KernelID, $ProcessID}, Drop[Kernels[], 1]]
Out[10]= {{2, 2479}, {3, 2480}, {4, 2481}}
```

If you use Do or Table with ParallelEvaluate, you may not get the result you expect since the iterator variable will not be known on remote kernels. You must use With to bind the iteration variable before invoking ParallelEvaluate.

```
In[11]:= Table[With[{i = i}, ParallelEvaluate[Sin[Pi/i],
           Kernels[][[Mod[i, $KernelCount] + 1]]]], {i, 1, 10}]
```

$$Out[11]= \left\{0, 1, \frac{\sqrt{3}}{2}, \frac{1}{\sqrt{2}}, \sqrt{\frac{5}{8} - \frac{\sqrt{5}}{8}}, \frac{1}{2}, \sin\left[\frac{\pi}{7}\right], \sin\left[\frac{\pi}{8}\right], \sin\left[\frac{\pi}{9}\right], \frac{1}{4}\left(-1 + \sqrt{5}\right)\right\}$$

In any case, you don't want to use ParallelEvaluate with Table because this will effectively serialize the computation across multiple kernels rather than execute them in parallel. You can see this by using AbsoluteTiming.

```
In[12]:= AbsoluteTiming[Table[ParallelEvaluate[Pause[1];
           0, Kernels[][[Mod[j, $KernelCount] + 1]]], {j, 1, 4}]]
Out[12]= {4.010592, {0, 0, 0, 0}}
```

ParallelEvaluate is useful for interrogating the remote kernels to check their state. For example, a common problem with parallel processing occurs when the remote kernels are not in sync with the master with respect to definitions of functions.

```
In[13]:= Clear[myFunc];
         Options[myFunc] = {option1 -> 2};
         myFunc[x_, opts : OptionsPattern[]] := OptionValue[option1] * x;
         DistributeDefinitions[myFunc];
         Options[myFunc] = {option1 -> 3};
         ParallelEvaluate[Options[myFunc]]
Out[14]= {{option1 -> 2}, {option1 -> 2}, {option1 -> 2}, {option1 -> 2}}

In[15]:= Options[myFunc]
Out[15]= {option1 -> 3}
```

See Also

See the Mathematica documentation for ParallelTable and ParallelArray for better ways to parallelize Table-like operations.

16.4 Automatically Parallelizing Existing Serial Expressions

Problem

You have code that you wrote previously in a serial fashion and you want to experiment with parallelization without rewriting.

Solution

Use `Parallelize` to have Mathematica decide how to distribute work across multiple kernels. To demonstrate, I first generate 1,000 large random semiprimes (composite numbers with only two factors).

```
In[16]:= semiprimes =
             Times @@@ Map[Prime, RandomInteger[{10 000, 1 000 000}, {1000, 2}], {2}];

In[17]:= Prime[10 000]
Out[17]= 104 729
```

Using `Parallelize`, these semiprimes are factored in ~0.20 seconds.

```
In[18]:= {timing1, result} =
             AbsoluteTiming[Parallelize[Map[FactorInteger, semiprimes]]]; timing1

Out[18]= 0.206849
```

Running on a single kernel takes ~0.73 seconds, giving a 3.6 times speedup on my eight-core machine.

```
In[19]:= {timing2, result} = AbsoluteTiming[Map[FactorInteger, semiprimes]]; timing2
Out[19]= 0.737002

In[20]:= timing2 / timing1
Out[20]= 3.563
```

If you replace `AbsoluteTiming` with `Timing`, you measure an 8 times speedup on this problem, so the cost of communicating results back to the frontend is significant.

Discussion

In the solution, I did not use any user-defined functions, so `Parallelize` was all that was necessary. In a more realistic situation, you will first need to `DistributeDefinitions` of user-defined functions and constants to all kernels before using `Parallelize`.

```
In[21]:= fmaxFactor[x_Integer] := Max[Power @@@ FactorInteger[x]]
         fmaxFactor[1000]
Out[22]= 125

In[23]:= DistributeDefinitions[fmaxFactor];
         Parallelize[Map[fmaxFactor, semiprimes]] // Short
Out[24]= {11 124 193, 11 988 217, 12 572 531, 3 331 357, 15 447 821, 11 540 261,
          715 643, 5 844 217, 9 529 441, 8 574 353, 3 133 597, 9 773 531, ≪976≫,
          10 027 051, 7 012 807, 13 236 779, 13 258 519, 11 375 971, 7 156 727,
          13 759 661, 15 155 867, 13 243 157, 8 888 531, 11 137 717, 1 340 891}
```

Parallelize will consider listable functions, higher-order functions (e.g., Apply, Map, MapThread), reductions (e.g., Count, MemberQ), and iterations (Table).

There is a natural trade-off in parallelization between controlling the overhead of splitting a problem or keeping all cores busy. A coarse-grained approach splits the work into large chunks based on the number of kernels. If a kernel finishes its chunk first, it will remain idle as the other kernels complete their work. In contrast, a fine-grained approach uses smaller chunks and therefore has a better chance of keeping cores occupied, but the trade-off is increased communications overhead.

```
In[26]:= {timing1, result} = AbsoluteTiming[Parallelize[
             Map[FactorInteger, semiprimes], Method → "CoarsestGrained"]]; timing1
Out[26]= 0.240895

In[27]:= {timing2, result} = AbsoluteTiming[Parallelize[
             Map[FactorInteger, semiprimes], Method → "FinestGrained"]]; timing2
Out[27]= 0.862007

In[28]:= timing2 / timing1
Out[28]= 3.57835
```

You can use Parallelize to implement a parallel version of MapIndexed since Mathematica 7 does not have this as a native operation (it does have ParallelMap, which I will discuss in Recipe 16.6).

```
In[29]:= parallelMapIndexed[func_, expr_, opts : OptionsPattern[]] := Parallelize[
             MapIndexed[func, expr], FilterRules[opts, Options[Parallelize]]]
         parallelMapIndexed[func_, expr_, levelspec_, opts : OptionsPattern[]] :=
             Parallelize[MapIndexed[func, expr, levelspec],
             FilterRules[opts, Options[Parallelize]]]
```

```
In[31]:= parallelMapIndexed[#1^First[#2] &, Range[10]]
```

$$\text{Out[31]= } \text{Parallelize}\left[\text{MapIndexed}\left[\#1^{First[\#2]} \&, \{1, 2, 3, 4, 5, 6, 7, 8, 9, 10\}\right],\right.$$
$$\left.\text{FilterRules}[\{Method \rightarrow Automatic\}]\right]$$

16.5 Distributing Data Segments in Parallel and Combining the Results

Problem

You want to parallelize a function that can be fed chunks of a list in parallel and the intermediate results combined to yield the final answer.

Solution

Use `ParallelCombine` to automatically divvy up the processing among available kernels. Here we generate a list of integers and ask Mathematica to feed segments of the list to `Total` with each segment running on a different kernel. The individual totals are then combined with the function `Plus` to arrive at the grand total.

```
In[32]:= integersList = RandomInteger[{0, 10^8}, 10 000 000];
         ParallelCombine[Total, integersList, Plus]
Out[33]= 500 152 672 039 330

In[34]:= Flatten[{Outer[Min, {9, 9, 9, 10}, {3, 4}], Outer[Max, {9, 9, 9, 10}, {3, 4}]}]
Out[34]= {3, 4, 3, 4, 3, 4, 3, 4, 9, 9, 9, 9, 9, 9, 10, 10}
```

Discussion

`ParallelCombine` can be applied to optimization problems where the goal is to find the best of a list of inputs. Here I use `Max` as the objective function, but in practice this would only be useful if the objective function was computationally intense enough to justify the parallel processing overhead. If the objective function is equally expensive for all inputs, you will want to specify `Method→"CoarsestGrained"`.

```
In[35]:= data = Union[RandomReal[{0, 10.0}, 100 000]];
         ParallelCombine[Max, data, Max, Method → "CoarsestGrained"]
Out[36]= 9.99998
```

To get actual speedup with `ParallelCombine`, you must pick problems for which the data returned from each kernel is much smaller than the data sent. Here is an example that has no hope for speedup even though on the surface it may seem compelling. Here, the idea is to speed up a Sort by using ParallelCombine to Sort smaller segments, and then perform a final merge on the sorted sections.

```
In[37]:= data = RandomInteger[{1, 100}, 100 000];
         AbsoluteTiming[ParallelCombine[Sort, data,
            Sort[Flatten[#]] &, Method → "CoarsestGrained"]] // Short
Out[38]= {0.047581, {1, 1, 1, 1, 1, 1, 1, 1, 1, 1, 1, 1, 1, 1, 1, 1, 1,
          1, 1, 1, 1, 1, 1, 1, 1, 1, 1, 1, 1, 1, ≪24 942≫, 100, 100, 100,
          100, 100, 100, 100, 100, 100, 100, 100, 100, 100, 100, 100, 100,
          100, 100, 100, 100, 100, 100, 100, 100, 100, 100, 100, 100, 100}}
```

Here you can see that a plain Sort in a single kernel is an order of magnitude faster. If you think this has to do with using Sort[Flatten[#]] as the merge function, think again.

```
In[39]:= AbsoluteTiming[Sort[data]] // Short
Out[39]= {0.018599, {1, 1, 1, 1, 1, 1, 1, 1, 1, 1, 1, 1, 1, 1, 1, 1, 1,
          1, 1, 1, 1, 1, 1, 1, 1, 1, 1, 1, 1, 1, ≪99 942≫, 100, 100, 100,
          100, 100, 100, 100, 100, 100, 100, 100, 100, 100, 100, 100, 100,
          100, 100, 100, 100, 100, 100, 100, 100, 100, 100, 100, 100, 100}}
```

Even if you use Identity to make the merge a no-op, the distributed "Sort" will be significantly slower. Adding more data or more process will not help because it only exacerbates the communications overhead.

```
In[40]:= AbsoluteTiming[ParallelCombine[Sort, data,
            Identity[Flatten[#]] &, Method → "CoarsestGrained"]] // Short
Out[40]= {0.091931, {1, 1, 1, 1, 1, 1, 1, 1, 1, 1, 1, 1, 1, 1, 1, 1, 1,
          1, 1, 1, 1, 1, 1, 1, 1, 1, 1, 1, 1, 1, ≪24 942≫, 100, 100, 100,
          100, 100, 100, 100, 100, 100, 100, 100, 100, 100, 100, 100, 100,
          100, 100, 100, 100, 100, 100, 100, 100, 100, 100, 100, 100, 100}}
```

16.6 Implementing Data-Parallel Algorithms by Using ParallelMap

Problem

You want to map a function across a list of data by executing the function in parallel for different items in a list.

Solution

Functional styles of programming often lead naturally to parallel implementation, especially when functions are side-effect free. `ParallelMap` is the parallel counterpart to `Map` (`/@`). It will spread the execution of the `Map` operation across available kernels.

```
In[41]:= ParallelMap[PrimeOmega, RandomInteger[{10^40, 10^50}, 32]]
Out[41]= {5, 5, 5, 5, 4, 2, 1, 6, 1, 7, 10, 7, 5, 7,
          6, 7, 7, 5, 4, 9, 10, 5, 7, 6, 4, 6, 8, 3, 12, 7, 7, 4}
```

Discussion

Here I compare the performance of `ParallelMap` with regular `Map` on a machine running four slave kernels. You can see that the speedup is less than the theoretical limit due to overhead caused by communication with the kernels and other inefficiencies inherent in `ParallelMap`'s implementation.

```
In[42]:= Module[{data = RandomInteger[{10^40, 10^50}, 32]},
           SeedRandom[8];
           Column[{
             AbsoluteTiming[ParallelMap[PrimeOmega, data]],
             AbsoluteTiming[Map[PrimeOmega, data]]}]]

         {11.794302, {5, 6, 8, 7, 5, 5, 2, 7, 6, 5, 9, 6,
           6, 8, 7, 4, 6, 5, 14, 8, 2, 5, 3, 5, 6, 5, 7, 4, 5, 3, 3, 5}}
Out[43]=
         {18.872163, {5, 6, 8, 7, 5, 5, 2, 7, 6, 5, 9, 6,
           6, 8, 7, 4, 6, 5, 14, 8, 2, 5, 3, 5, 6, 5, 7, 4, 5, 3, 3, 5}}
```

`ParallelMap` is a natural way to introduce parallelism using a functional style. When you have a computationally intensive function you need to execute over a large data set, it often makes sense to execute the operations in parallel by allowing Mathematica to split the mapping among multiple kernels.

Like `Map`, `ParallelMap` can accept a levelspec as a third argument to control the parts of the expression that are mapped. For example, here I count the satisfiability count for all Boolean functions of one to four variables, where each function of a particular variable count is grouped together at level two in the list. The entire output is large, so I abbreviate using `Short`.

```
In[44]:=  ParallelMap[SatisfiabilityCount[BooleanFunction @@ #] &,
             Table[{n, v}, {v, 1, 4}, {n, 1, 2^2^v}], {2}] // Short
Out[44]=  {{1, 1, 2, 0}, <<2>>, {1, 1, 2, 1, 2, 2, 3, 1, 2, 2, 3, 2, 3, 3, 4, 1, 2, 2, 3, 2,
            3, 3, 4, 2, 3, 3, 4, 3, 4, 4, 5, 1, 2, 2, 3, 2, 3, 3, <<65460>>, 14, 13,
            14, 14, 15, 11, 12, 12, 13, 12, 13, 13, 14, 12, 13, 13, 14, 13, 14, 14,
            15, 12, 13, 13, 14, 13, 14, 14, 15, 13, 14, 14, 15, 14, 15, 15, 16, 0}}
```

16.7 Decomposing a Problem into Parallel Data Sets

Problem

You have a problem that involves computation across a large data set, and you partition the data set into chunks that can be processed in parallel.

Solution

A simple example of this problem is where the computation occurs across a data set that can be generated by Table. Here you can simply substitute ParallelTable. For example, visualizing the Mandelbrot set requires performing an iterative computation on each point across a region of the complex plane and assigning a color based on how quickly the iteration explodes toward infinity. Here I use a simple grayscale mapping for simplicity.

```
In[45]:=  Clear[mbrotColor]
          mbrotColor[c_Complex] := Module[{max = 100, r},
             r = NestWhile[{#[[1]] + 1, #[[2]]^2 + c} &,
                {0, c}, Norm[#[[2]]] < 2 &, 1, max][[1]];
             (*Map r onto a grayscale value. Squaring is for finer detail.*)
             1.0 - ((max - r) / max)^2]
          DistributeDefinitions[mbrotColor]
          With[{granularity = 0.004},
           ArrayPlot[Transpose[ParallelTable[mbrotColor[i + j I],
              {i, -2, 0.75, granularity},
              {j, -1, 1, granularity}]], ImageSize → 450]]
```

Out[46]=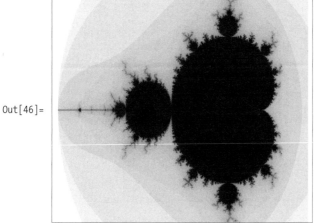

Discussion

ParallelTable has many useful applications. Plotting a large number of graphics is a
perfect way to utilize a multicore computer. Parallel processing makes you a lot
more productive when creating animations, for example.

```
In[47]:= images = ParallelTable[
         SphericalPlot3D[If[θ < Pi / 4, None, 1 / (φ + 5)], {θ, 0, Pi}, {φ, 0, i Pi},
          PlotStyle → Directive[Orange, Specularity[White, 10]], Mesh → None,
          PlotPoints → 30, Axes → None, Boxed → False], {i, 1, 8, 0.25}];
       ListAnimate[images, ImageSize → Small]
```

Out[48]=

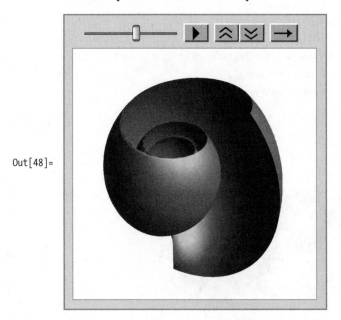

You can also generate multiple data sets in parallel, which you can then plot or process further.

```
In[49]:= ListLinePlot[ParallelTable[ Sin[n Pi x] / n, {n, 1, 4}, {x, 0, 2 Pi, 0.01}]]
```

Out[49]=

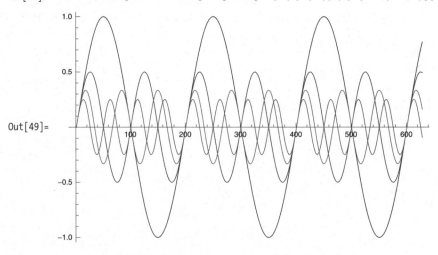

16.8 Choosing an Appropriate Distribution Method

Problem

You want to parallelize an operation whose runtime varies greatly over different inputs.

Solution

The parallel primitives Parallelize, ParallelMap, ParallelTable, ParallelDo, ParallelSum, and ParallelCombine support an option called Method, which allows you to specify the granularity of subdivisions used to distribute the computation across kernels.

Use Method → "FinestGrained" when the completion time of each atomic unit of computation is expected to vary widely. "FinestGrained" prevents Mathematica from committing work units to a kernel until a scheduled work unit is complete. To illustrate this, create a function for which the completion time can be controlled via Pause. Then generate a list of small random delays and prepend to that a much larger delay to simulate a long-running computation.

```
In[50]:= SeedRandom[11];
         delays = RandomReal[{0.1, 0.15}, 200];
         (*Add a long
           20-second delay to simulate a bottleneck in the computation.*)
         PrependTo[delays, 20.0];
         funcWithDelay[delay_] := Module[{}, Pause[delay]; delay]
         DistributeDefinitions[funcWithDelay];
```

Since the pauses are distributed over several cores, we expect the actual delay to be less than the total delay, and that is what we get. However, by specifying "CoarsestGrained", we tell Mathematica to distribute large chunks of work to the kernels. This effectively results in jobs backing up behind the ~20-second delay.

```
In[52]:= AbsoluteTiming[
           Total[ParallelMap[funcWithDelay, delays, Method → "CoarsestGrained"]]]
Out[52]= {26.403951, 44.8136}
```

When we run the same computation with Method → "FinestGrained", our actual completion time drops by 6 seconds since the remaining cores are free to receive more work units as soon as they complete a given work unit.

```
In[53]:=   AbsoluteTiming[
             Total[ParallelMap[funcWithDelay, delays, Method → "FinestGrained"]]]
Out[53]=   {20.040469, 44.8136}
```

Contrast this to the case where the expected computation time is very uniform. Here Method → "CoarsestGrained" has a distinct advantage since there is less overhead in distributing work in one shot than incrementally.

```
In[54]:=   delays = Table[0.1, {800}];

In[55]:=   AbsoluteTiming[
             Total[ParallelMap[funcWithDelay, delays, Method → "CoarsestGrained"]]]
Out[55]=   {20.112191, 80.}
```

Here we see that Method → "FinestGrained" only has a slight disadvantage, but that disadvantage would increase with larger payloads and remotely running kernels.

```
In[56]:=   AbsoluteTiming[
             Total[ParallelMap[funcWithDelay, delays, Method → "FinestGrained"]]]
Out[56]=   {20.973056, 80.}
```

Discussion

If you have ever been to the bank, chances are you stood in a single line that served several tellers. When a teller became free, the person at the head of the line went to that window. It turns out that this queuing organization produces higher overall throughput because different customers' bank transactions take varying amounts of time, while presumably each teller is equally skilled at handling a variety of transactions. This setup is analogous to the effect you get when using "FinestGrained".

If there were no overhead involved in communication, "FinestGrained" would be ideal. But, returning to the analogy with the bank, it is often the case that the person who is next in line fails to notice a teller has become free and a delay is introduced. This is analogous to the master-slave overhead: the master must receive a result from the slave and move the next work unit into the freed-up slave. Each such action has overhead, and this overhead can swamp any gains obtained from making immediate use of an available slave.

In many problems, it is best to let Mathematica balance these trade-offs by using Method→Automatic, which is what you get by default when no Method is explicitly specified. Under this scenario, Mathematica performs a moderate amount of chunking of work units to minimize communication overhead while not committing too many units to a single slave and thus risking wasted computation when one slave finishes before the others.

See Also

There are a few less important `Method` options (`"EvaluationsPerKernel"` and `"ItemsPerEvaluation"`) that are covered under the `Parallelize` function in Mathematica's documentation. These give you more precise control over the distribution of work.

16.9 Running Different Algorithms in Parallel and Accepting the First to Complete

Problem

You have several different ways to solve a problem and are uncertain which will complete fastest. Typically, one algorithm may be faster on some inputs, while another will be faster on other inputs. There is no simple computation that makes this determination at lower cost than running the algorithms themselves.

Solution

Use `ParallelTry` to run as many versions of your algorithm as you have available slave kernels. There are several ways to use `ParallelTry`, but the differences are largely syntactical. If your algorithms are implemented in separate functions (e.g., `algo1[data_]`, `algo2[data_]`, and `algo3[data_]`), you can use `ParallelTry`, as in the following example. Here I merely simulate the uncertainty of first completion using a random pause.

```
In[57]:= RandomSeed[13];
         algo1[data_] := Module[{}, Pause[RandomInteger[{1, 10}]]; data^2]
         algo2[data_] := Module[{}, Pause[RandomInteger[{1, 10}]]; data^3]
         algo3[data_] := Module[{}, Pause[RandomInteger[{1, 10}]]; data^4]
         DistributeDefinitions[algo1, algo2, algo3]
         algo[data_] := ParallelTry[Composition[#][data] &, {algo1, algo2, algo3}]

In[59]:= algo[2]
Out[59]= 4
```

Discussion

Sometimes you can choose variations to try by passing different function arguments. Here I minimize a `BooleanFunction` of 30 variables using `ParallelTry` with four of the forms supported by `BooleanMinimize`.

```
In[60]:= ParallelTry[{#, BooleanMinimize[BooleanFunction[10000, 30], #]} &,
            {"DNF", "CNF", "NAND", "NOR"}]
Out[60]= {CNF, ! #1 && ! #2 && ! #3 && ! #4 && ! #5 && ! #6 && ! #7 && ! #8 &&
            ! #9 && ! #10 && ! #11 && ! #12 && ! #13 && ! #14 && ! #15 && ! #16 &&
            ! #17 && ! #18 && ! #19 && ! #20 && ! #21 && ! #22 && ! #23 && ! #24 &&
            ! #25 && ! #26 && (! #27 || ! #28 || #30) && (#27 || #28) &&
            (#27 || ! #30) && (! #28 || ! #29) && (! #29 || ! #30) &}
```

Another possibility is that you have a single function that takes different options,
indicating different computational methods. Many advanced numerical algorithms
in Mathematica are packaged in this manner.

```
In[61]:= WeierstrassFunction[a_, x_] := Sum[Sin[Pi k^a x] / (Pi k^a), {k, 100}]
          DistributeDefinitions[WeierstrassFunction]

In[63]:= ParallelTry[
            {#, FindMinimum[Sin[WeierstrassFunction[Sin[x], Sin[2 y]]],
                {{x, 0.6}, {y, 0.6}}, WorkingPrecision → 48, Method → #]} &,
            {"Gradient", "ConjugateGradient", "InteriorPoint", "QuasiNewton", "Newton"}]
Out[63]= {QuasiNewton, {-1.000000000000000000000000000000000000000000000000,
            {x → 0.104539716554326205174773982146950548720470352834,
             y → 0.510629205999258520978426706655563835929211167845}}}
```

16.10 Sharing Data Between Parallel Kernels

Problem

Your parallel implementations need to communicate via one or more variables
shared across kernels.

Solution

Mathematica provides SetSharedVariable as a means of declaring one or more variables as synchronized across all parallel kernels. Similarly, SetSharedFunction is used
to synchronize the down values of a symbol. In the following example, the variable
list is shared and each slave kernel is thus able to prepend its $KernelID.

```
In[64]:= SetSharedVariable[list]; list = {};
          ParallelEvaluate[PrependTo[list, $KernelID]];
          list
Out[65]= {4, 3, 2, 1}
```

Discussion

Consider a combinatorial optimization problem like the traveling salesperson problem (TSP). You might want all kernels to be aware of the best solution found by any given kernel thus far so that each kernel can use this information to avoid pursuing suboptimal solutions. Here I use a solution to the TSP based on simulated annealing.

```
In[66]:= dist = Table[If[i <= j, 0, RandomReal[{1, 10}]], {i, 1, 10}, {j, 1, i}];
```

16.11 Preventing Race Conditions When Multiple Kernels Access a Shared Resource

Problem

Prior to Mathematica 7, users never had to think about problems like race conditions because all processing occurred in a single thread of execution. Parallel processing creates the possibility of subtle bugs caused by two or more kernels accessing a shared resource such as the file system or variables that are shared. These resources are not subject to atomic update or synchronization unless special care is taken.

Solution

Consider a situation where each parallel task needs to update a shared data structure like a list. Here I create a simplified example with a shared list. Each kernel is instructed to prepend its $KernelID to the list 10 times. If all goes well, we should see 10 IDs for each kernel. I use Tally to see if that is the case. The random pause is there to inject a bit of unpredictability into each computation to simulate a more realistic computation.

```
In[67]:= SetSharedVariable[aList]; aList = {};
         ParallelEvaluate[Do[aList = Prepend[aList, $KernelID];
            Pause[RandomReal[{0.01, 0.1}]], {10}]];
         Tally[
          aList]
Out[68]= {{2, 7}, {1, 8}, {3, 4}, {4, 7}}
```

Clearly this is not the result expected, since not one of the $KernelID's showed up 10 times. The problem is that each kernel may interfere with the others as it attempts to modify the shared list. This problem is solved by the use of CriticalSection.

```
In[69]:= SetSharedVariable[aList]; aList = {};
         ParallelEvaluate[
            Do[CriticalSection[{aListLock}, aList = Prepend[aList, $KernelID]];
              Pause[RandomReal[{0.01, 0.1}]], {10}]];
         Tally[
          aList]
Out[70]= {{4, 10}, {3, 10}, {1, 10}, {2, 10}}
```

Much better. Now each kernel ID appears exactly 10 times.

Discussion

A critical section is a mutual exclusion primitive implemented in terms of one or more locks. The variables passed, as in the list (first argument to CriticalSection), play the role of the locks. A kernel must get control of all locks before it is allowed to enter the critical section. You may wonder why you would ever need more than one lock variable. Consider the case where there are two shared resources and three functions that may be executing in parallel. Function f1 accesses resource r1, which is protected by lock l1. Function f2 accesses resource r2, which is protected by lock l2. However, function f3 accesses both r1 and r2, so it must establish both locks. The following example illustrates.

```
In[71]:= SetSharedVariable[r1, r2, r3];
         r1 = {}; r2 = {}; r3 = {};
         f1[x_] :=
          Module[{}, CriticalSection[{l1}, PrependTo[r1, x]]]
         f2[x_] :=
          Module[{}, CriticalSection[{l2}, PrependTo[r2, x]]]
         f3[] :=
          Module[{}, CriticalSection[{l1, l2}, r3 = Join[r1, r2]]]
```

If f1, f2, and f3 happen to be running in three different kernels, f1 and f2 will be able to enter their critical sections simultaneously because they depend on different locks, but f3 will be excluded. Likewise, if f3 has managed to enter its critical section, both f1 and f2 will be locked out until f3 exits its critical section.

Keep in mind that shared resources are not only variables used with SetShared-Variable. They might be any resource that a kernel could gain simultaneous access to, including the computer's file system, a database, and so on.

It should not come as a surprise that critical sections can reduce parallel processing performance since they effectively define sections of code that can only execute in one kernel at a time. Further, there is a loss of *liveliness* since a kernel that is waiting on a lock cannot detect instantaneously that the lock has been freed. In fact, if you dig into the implementation (the entire source code for Mathematica 7's parallel processing primitives is available in *Parallel.m* and *Concurrency.m*) you will see that a kernel enters into a 0.1-second pause while waiting on a lock. This implies that `CriticalSection` should be used sparingly, and if possible, you should find ways to structure a program to avoid it altogether. One obvious way to do this is to rely largely on the data parallelism primitives like `ParallelMap` and `ParallelTable` and only integrate results of these operations in the master kernel. However, advanced users may want to experiment with more subtle parallel program designs, and it is handy that synchronization is available right out of the box.

See Also

In Recipe 16.13, I implement the `map-reduce` algorithm where `CriticalSection` is necessary to synchronize access to the file system.

16.12 Organizing Parallel Processing Operations Using a Pipeline Approach

Problem

You have a computation that involves processing many data sets where the computation can be viewed as data flowing through several processing steps. This type of computation is analogous to an assembly line.

Solution

An easy way to organize a pipeline is to create a kind of to-do list and associate it with each data set. The master kernel loads the data, tacks on the to-do list and a job identifier, and then submits the computations to an available slave kernel using `ParallelSubmit`. The slave takes the first operation off the to-do list, performs the operation, and returns the result to the master along with the to-do list and job identifier it was given. The master then records the operation as complete by removing the first item in the to-do list and submits the data again for the next step. Processing is complete when the to-do list is empty. Here I use `Reap` and `Sow` to collect the final results.

```
In[73]:=  slaveHandler[input_, todo_, jobId_] := Module[{result},
            result = First[todo][input];
            {todo, result, jobId}
          ]

          DistributeDefinitions[slaveHandler];

          pipelineProcessor[inputs_, todo_] :=
           Module[{pids, result, id},
             Reap[
               pids = With[{todo1 = todo},
                 MapIndexed[ParallelSubmit[slaveHandler[#, todo1,
                   First[#2]]] &, inputs]];
               While[pids =!= {},
                 {result, id, pids} = WaitNext[pids];
                 If[Length[result[[1]]] > 1,
                   AppendTo[pids,
                     With[{todo1 = Rest[result[[1]]], in = result[[2]], jobId =
                       result[[3]]}, ParallelSubmit[slaveHandler[in, todo1, jobId]]]],
                   Sow[{Last[FileNameSplit[inputs[[result[[3]]]]]], result[[2]]}
                   ];
                 ]
               ];
             True
             ]
           ]
```

To illustrate this technique, I use an image-processing problem. In this problem, a number of images need to be loaded, resized, sharpened, and then rotated. For simplicity, I assume all images will use the same parameters. You can see that the to-do list is manifested as a list of functions.

```
In[75]:=  files = FileNameJoin[{NotebookDirectory[], "..", "images", #}] & /@
            {"image1.jpg", "image2.jpg", "image3.jpg"};
          todoList = {Import[#] &, ImageResize[#, 100] &,
            Sharpen[#] &, ImageRotate[#, Right] &};

          Grid @@ pipelineProcessor[files, todoList][[2]]
```

image2.jpg

Out[76]= image1.jpg

image3.jpg

Discussion

The solution illustrates a few points about using `ParallelSubmit` that are worth noting even if you have no immediate need to use a pipeline approach to parallelism.

First, note the use of `MapIndexed` as the initial launching pad for the jobs. `MapIndexed` is ideal for this purpose because the generated index is perfect as a job identifier. The `jobId` plays no role in `slaveHandler` but is simply returned back to the master. This `jobId` allows the master to know what initial inputs were sent to the responding slave. Similarly, you may wonder why the whole to-do list is sent to the slave if it is only going to process the first entry. The motivation is simple. This approach frees `pipelineProcessor` from state management. Every time it receives a response from a slave, it knows immediately what functions are left for that particular job. This approach is sometimes called *stateless* because neither the master nor the slaves need to maintain state past the point where one transfers control to the other.

Also note the use of With as a means of evaluating expressions before they appear inside the arguments of ParallelSubmit. This is important because ParallelSubmit keeps expressions in held form and evaluating those expressions on slave cores is likely to fail because the data symbols (like todo and result) don't exist there.

A reasonable question to ask is, why use this approach at all? For instance, if you know you want to perform five operations on an image in sequence, why not just wrap them up in a function and use ParallelMap to distribute images for processing? For some cases, this approach is indeed appropriate. There are a few reasons why a pipeline technique might still make sense.

Intermediate results

For some problems, you want to keep the intermediate results of each step. By returning the intermediate results back to the master, you can keep the code that knows what needs to be done with the result out of the logic that is distributed to the slaves. This is a nice way to reduce overall complexity, and it works when the slaves don't have the appropriate access to a database or other storage area where the intermediate results are to be archived.

Checkpointing

Even if you don't care about intermediate steps, you may want to checkpoint each immediate calculation, especially if that calculation was quite expensive to compute. Then, if some later step fails, you do not lose everything computed up to that point.

Managing complexity

The solution showed a very simplistic use case where there is a fixed to-do list for each input. This is not the only possibility. It might be the case that each input needs a specialized to-do list or, more ambitiously, the to-do list for any input will change based on the results that return from intermediate steps. This can, of course, be done with complex conditional logic distributed to the slaves, but overall complexity might be reduced by keeping these decisions in the master pipeline logic.

Branching pipelines

Slave kernels can't initiate further parallel computations, so if an intermediate result suggests a further parallel computation, control needs to be returned to the master in any case. Of course, branching introduces a degree of complexity, since the master kernel must now do state management to keep track of progress along each branch.

16.13 Processing a Massive Number of Files Using the Map-Reduce Technique

Problem

You have a large number of data files that you need to process. Typically you need to integrate information from these files into some global statistics or create an index, sort, or cross-reference. The data from these files is too large to load into a single Mathematica kernel.

Solution

Here I show a toy use case traditionally used to introduce mapReduce. The problem is to process a large number of text files and calculate word frequencies. The principle that makes mapReduce so attractive is that the user need only specify two, often simple, functions called the map function and the reduce function. The framework does the rest. The map function takes a key and a value and outputs a different key and a different value. The reduce function takes the key that was output by map and the list of all values that map assigned to the specific key. The framework's job is to distribute the work of the map and reduce functions across a large number of processors on a network and to group by key the data output by map before passing it to reduce.

To make this concrete, I show how to implement the word-counting problem and the top-level mapReduce infrastructure. In the discussion, I dive deeper into the nuts and bolts.

First we need a map function. Recall that it takes a key and a value. Let's say the key is the name of a file and the value is a word that has been extracted from that file. The output of the map function is another key and value. What should these outputs be to implement word counting? The simplest possible answer is that the output key should be the word and the output value is simply 1, indicating the word has been counted. Note that the input key (the filename) is discarded, which is perfectly legitimate if you have no need for it. In this case, I do not wish to track the word's source.

```
In[77]:= countWords[key_, value_] := {value, 1}
```

Okay, that was easy. Now we need a reduce function. Recall that the reduce function will receive a key and a list of all values associated to the key by the map function. For the case at hand, it means reduce will receive a word and a list of 1's representing each time that word was seen. Since the goal is to count words, the reduce function simply performs a total on the list. What could be easier?

```
In[78]:= totalWords[key_, value_List] := Total[value]
```

Here again I discard the key because the framework will automatically associate the key to the output of reduce. In other applications, the key might be required for the computation.

Surprisingly enough, these two functions largely complete the solution to the problem! Of course, something is missing, namely the map-reduce implementation that glues everything together. Here is the top-level function that does the work.

```
In[79]:=  Clear[mapReduce];
          Options[mapReduce] = {
              fileDisposition → DeleteFile,
              intermediateFile → True,
              saveDirectory :→ $UserDocumentsDirectory,
              keyToFilenamePrefix → Identity};
          mapReduce[inputs_List, map_,
            reduce_, parser_, opts : OptionsPattern[]] :=
          Module[{},
           ParallelMap[
              reducer[#, reduce, FilterRules[{opts}, Options[reducer]]] &,
              mergeAll[ParallelMap[mapper[#, parser, map,
                  FilterRules[{opts}, Options[mapper]]] &, inputs],
                FilterRules[{opts}, Options[mergeAll]]]]]
          ]
```

You can see from this function that it requires a list of inputs. That will be the list of files to process. It needs a function map, which in this example will be count-Words, and a function reduce, which will be totalWords. It also needs something called a *parser*. The parser is a function that breaks up the input file into the units that map will process. Here I use a simple parser that breaks up a file into words. This function leverages Mathematica's I/O primitive ReadList, which does most of the work. The only bit of postprocessing is to strip some common punctuation that Read-List does not strip and to convert words to lowercase so counting is case insensitive.

```
In[81]:=  parseFileToWords[file_] := Module[{stream, words},
            stream = OpenRead[file];
            words = ToLowerCase[Select[ReadList[stream, Word], StringMatchQ[#,
                RegularExpression["^[A-Za-z0-9][A-Za-z0-9-]*$"]] &]];
            Close[stream];
            words
            ]
```

Here is how you use the framework in practice. For test data, I downloaded a bunch of files from *http://www.textfiles.com/conspiracy/*. I placed the names of these files in another file called wordcountfiles and use Get to input this list. This is to avoid cluttering the solution with all these files.

```
In[82]:= files = Get[FileNameJoin[{$UserDocumentsDirectory, "oreilly",
          "Mathematica Cookbook", "data", "textfiles", "filelist.m"}]];
```

```
In[83]:= mapReduce[files, countWords, totalWords, parseFileToWords]
```

```
Out[83]= mergeAll[reducer[{mapper[/Users/smangano/Documents/oreilly/Mathematica
          Cookbook/data/textfiles//a-z-cons.txt, parseFileToWords,
          countWords, {}], mapper[/Users/smangano/Documents/oreilly/Mathematica
          Cookbook/data/textfiles//africa.txt,
          parseFileToWords, countWords, {}], mapper[
          /Users/smangano/Documents/oreilly/Mathematica
          Cookbook/data/textfiles//aids-2.txt,
          parseFileToWords, countWords, {}], mapper[
          /Users/smangano/Documents/oreilly/Mathematica
          Cookbook/data/textfiles//aids-war.txt,
          parseFileToWords, countWords, {}], mapper[
          /Users/smangano/Documents/oreilly/Mathematica
          Cookbook/data/textfiles//aids.txt,
          parseFileToWords, countWords, {}], mapper[
          /Users/smangano/Documents/oreilly/Mathematica
          Cookbook/data/textfiles//aids02.txt,
          parseFileToWords, countWords, {}], mapper[
          /Users/smangano/Documents/oreilly/Mathematica
          Cookbook/data/textfiles//aidsconsp.txt,
          parseFileToWords, countWords, {}], mapper[
          /Users/smangano/Documents/oreilly/Mathematica
          Cookbook/data/textfiles//air-rail.txt,
          parseFileToWords, countWords, {}], mapper[
          /Users/smangano/Documents/oreilly/Mathematica
          Cookbook/data/textfiles//alt3.txt,
          parseFileToWords, countWords, {}], mapper[
          /Users/smangano/Documents/oreilly/Mathematica
          Cookbook/data/textfiles//anti-jew.txt,
          parseFileToWords, countWords, {}], ≪···≫ mapper[
          /Users/smangano/Documents/oreilly/Mathematica
          Cookbook/data/textfiles//pvt-prop.txt,
          parseFileToWords, countWords, {}], mapper[
          /Users/smangano/Documents/oreilly/Mathematica
          Cookbook/data/textfiles//pvtprop2.txt,
          parseFileToWords, countWords, {}], mapper[
          /Users/smangano/Documents/oreilly/Mathematica
          Cookbook/data/textfiles//rat11.txt,
```

```
      parseFileToWords, countWords, {}], mapper[
      /Users/smangano/Documents/oreilly/Mathematica
        Cookbook/data/textfiles//realene.txt,
      parseFileToWords, countWords, {}], mapper[
      /Users/smangano/Documents/oreilly/Mathematica
        Cookbook/data/textfiles//rfk1.txt,
      parseFileToWords, countWords, {}], mapper[
      /Users/smangano/Documents/oreilly/Mathematica
        Cookbook/data/textfiles//right-lf.txt,
      parseFileToWords, countWords, {}], mapper[
      /Users/smangano/Documents/oreilly/Mathematica
        Cookbook/data/textfiles//rightday.txt,
      parseFileToWords, countWords, {}], mapper[
      /Users/smangano/Documents/oreilly/Mathematica
        Cookbook/data/textfiles//scrtgovt.txt,
      parseFileToWords, countWords, {}], mapper[
      /Users/smangano/Documents/oreilly/Mathematica
        Cookbook/data/textfiles//secret.txt,
      parseFileToWords, countWords, {}]]}, totalWords,
    {}], reducer[{}, totalWords,
    {}]]
```

In[84]:= **% >> "mapReduce.out"**

In[85]:= **? countWords**

```
Global`countWords
```

```
countWords[key_, value_] := {value, 1}
```

Discussion

If you want to try map-reduce, use the package files *Dictionary.m* and *MapReduce.m*. The code here is laid out primarily for explanation purposes. You will need to add the following code to your notebook, and don't forget to use DistributeDefinitions with the functions you create for map, reduce, and parse.

```
Needs["Cookbook`Dictionary`"]
Needs["Cookbook`MapReduce`"]
ParallelNeeds["Cookbook`Dictionary`"]
ParallelNeeds["Cookbook`MapReduce`"]
```

You can find examples of usage in *mapReduce.nb*.

If you are new to map-reduce you should refer to references listed in the "See Also" section on page 678 before trying to wrap your mind around the low-level implementation. The original paper by the Google researchers provides the fastest high-level overview and lists additional applications beyond the word-counting problem. The most important point about map-reduce is that it is not an efficient way to use parallel processing *unless* you have a very large number of files to process and a very large number of networked CPUs to work on the processing. The ideal use case is a problem for which the data is far too large to fit in the memory of a single computer, mandating that the processing be spread across many machines. To illustrate, consider how you might implement word counting across a small number of files.

```
In[86]:= baseDir = FileNameJoin[
              {$UserDocumentsDirectory, "oreilly", "Mathematica Cookbook", "data"}];
         files = FileNameJoin[{baseDir, #}] & /@ {"adventur.txt", "solitary.txt"};
         AbsoluteTiming[Tally[Flatten[parseFileToWords[#] & /@ files]]] // Short
         AbsoluteTiming[mapReduce[files, countWords, totalWords,
              parseFileToWords, intermediateFile → False]] // Short
Out[86]= {0.089739, {{adventure, 3}, {solving, 1}, {it, 77}, {in, 123},
           {easy, 3}, {steps, 1}, ≪1562≫, {viewed, 1}, {gravely, 1},
           {reputation, 1}, {sufficient, 1}, {satisfy, 1}, {demands, 1}}}
Out[87]= {0.014468,
           mergeAll[reducer[{mapper[/Users/smangano/Documents/oreilly/Mathematica
                Cookbook/data/adventur.txt, parseFileToWords, countWords, {}],
              mapper[≪1≫]}, totalWords, {}], reducer[{}, ≪10≫, {}]]]}
```

The guts of our map-reduce implementation are a bit more complex than the other parallel recipes. The low-level implementation details have less to do with parallel processing than with managing the data as it flows though the distributed algorithm. A key data structure used is a dictionary which stores the intermediate results of a single file in memory. This makes use of a packaged version of code I introduced in Recipe 3.13 and won't repeat here.

The function mapAndStore is responsible for applying the map function to a key value pair and storing the result in a dictionary. The dictionary solves the problem of grouping all identical keys for a given input file.

```
In[88]:= mapAndStore[{key1_, value1_}, map_, dict_Dictionary] :=
         Module[{key2, value2},
           {key2, value2} = map[key1, value1];
           If[key2 =!= Null,
             dictStore[dict, key2, value2]]
         ]
```

The default behavior of mapReduce is to store intermediate results in a file. The functions uniqueFileName, nextUniqueFile, and saver have the responsibility of synthesizing the names of these files and storing the results. The filename is derived from the key, and options saveDirectory and keyToFilenamePrefix help to customize the behavior. These options are provided in the top-level mapReduce call. Here saveDirectory provides a directory where the intermediate files will be stored. This directory must be writable by all slave kernels. Use keyToFilenamePrefix to specify a function that maps the key to a filename prefix. This function is necessary for cases where the key might not represent a valid filename.

```
In[89]:= nextUniqueFile[existingFile_] := StringReplace[existingFile,
          num : RegularExpression["\d+"] :> With[{n = ToExpression[num]},
            ToString[
              If[n < 999, PaddedForm[n + 1, 3, NumberPadding -> {"0", ""}],
                n + 1]]]
        ]

        uniqueFilename[base_, dir_] := Module[{baseFile, existingFiles},
          baseFile = FileNameJoin[{dir, ToString[base]}];
          (*Ensure only one kernel goes for the next file.*)
          CriticalSection[{uniqueFilenameLock},
            existingFiles = Sort[FileNames[baseFile <> ".*." <> "mr"]];
            If[existingFiles === {}, baseFile <> ".0001.mr",
              nextUniqueFile[Last[existingFiles]]]
          ]
        ]

        Clear[saver];
        Options[saver] = {
            saveDirectory :> $UserDocumentsDirectory,
            keyToFilenamePrefix -> Identity
          };
        saver[{key_, values_List}, OptionsPattern[]] :=
         Module[{filename, stream, prefix},
          prefix = OptionValue[keyToFilenamePrefix][key];
          filename =
           uniqueFilename[ReleaseHold[prefix], OptionValue[saveDirectory]];
          stream = OpenWrite[filename];
          Write[stream, values];
          Close[stream];
          {key, filename}]

        Clear[saveKeyValues];
        Options[saveKeyValues] = {
            saveDirectory :> $UserDocumentsDirectory,
            keyToFilenamePrefix -> Identity
          };
        saveKeyValues[dict_Dictionary, opts : OptionsPattern[]] :=
         Module[{keyValues},
          keyValues = dictKeyValuePairs[dict] ;
          saver[#, FilterRules[{opts}, Options[saver]]] & /@ keyValues]
```

The function mapper provides the glue between the parser, the map function, and the intermediate storage of the output of map. As mentioned above, the default behavior is to store the output in a file whose name is derived from the key. However, for small toy problems you might wish to dispense with the intermediate storage and return the actual output to the next stage of processing in the master kernel. This feature is available by specifying intermediateFile → False (the default is True).

```
In[91]:=  (*mapper*)
          Clear[mapper];
          Options[mapper] =
            {intermediateFile → True, keyToFilenamePrefix → Identity};
          mapper[input_, parser_, map_, opts : OptionsPattern[]] :=
           Module[{parseList, dict, result, useFile},
            parseList = parser[input];
            dict = makeDictionary[];
            Scan[mapAndStore[{input, #}, map, dict] &, parseList];
            useFile = OptionValue[intermediateFile];
            result = If[useFile,
               saveKeyValues[dict, FilterRules[{opts}, Options[saveKeyValues]]],
               dictKeyValuePairs[dict]];
            destroyDictionary[dict];
            result
           ]
```

Before the results of mapper can be passed to the reduce stage of processing, it is necessary to group all intermediate results together. For example, in the solution, we presented the problem of counting words in files. Consider a common word like *the*. Clearly, this word will have been found in almost all of the files. Thus, counts of this word are distributed across a bunch of intermediate files (or lists if intermediate-File→False was specified). Before the final reduction, the intermediate files (or lists) must be grouped by key and merged. This is the job of the functions mergeAll and merge. The grouping task is solved by the Mathematica 7 function GatherBy, and the actual merging is implemented as a parallel operation since each key can be processed independently.

```
In[92]:=  Clear[merge, put];
          (*Put is a helper function around the Mathematica
           Put that saves the merged results and deletes
           the now redundant files.*)
          Options[put] = {fileDisposition → DeleteFile};
          put[list_, files_, opts : OptionsPattern[]] :=
           (Put[list, First[files]];
            OptionValue[fileDisposition][Rest[files]]; First[files])

          (*Merge either merges files into a
           single file or lists into a single list.*)
          Options[merge] = {intermediateFile → True};
          merge[list_, opts : OptionsPattern[]] :=
           Module[{useFile, getFunc, putFunc},
            useFile = OptionValue[intermediateFile] ;
            {getFunc, putFunc} = If[useFile, {Get, put[#, list] &},
              {Identity, Identity}, {Identity, Identity}];
            putFunc[Join @@ getFunc /@ list]]

          Clear[mergeAll]
          Options[mergeAll] = {intermediateFile → True};
          mergeAll[result_, opts : OptionsPattern[]] := Module[{groupResult},
            (*Gather by key,
            which is the First element of each list in the flattened result.*)
            groupResult = GatherBy[Flatten[result, 1], First];
            (*Transform grouped results into single key and merged values.
              Here Transpose is used to take results of the form:
                {{key, value1}, {key, value2}, ..., {key, valueN}} to
                 {{key, ...}, {value1, value2, ...}} so the duplicate keys are easily
                discarded and the values passed to merge.*)
            ParallelMap[
             ({First[#1], merge[#2, opts]} & @@ Transpose[#]) & , groupResult]
           ]
```

The final stage is the reducer, which accepts the merged results (in file or list form) for each key and passes the key and resulting list to the reduce function. An option, fileDisposition, is used to determine what should happen to the intermediate file. The default disposition is DeleteFile, but you could imagine adding some more complex processing at this stage, such as logging or checkpointing a transaction that began during the parsing stage.

```
In[94]:=  (*reducer*)
          Clear[reducer];
          Options[reducer] =
            {fileDisposition → DeleteFile, intermediateFile → True};
          reducer[{key_, value_}, reduce_, opts : OptionsPattern[]] :=
           Module[{stream, list, temp, useFile},
             useFile = OptionValue[intermediateFile];
             list = If[useFile,
               temp = Get[value];
               OptionValue[fileDisposition][value];
               temp,
               value];
             {key, reduce[key, list]}
            ]
In[95]:=  DistributeDefinitions[countWords, destroyDictionary, dictName,
            dictKeyValuePairs, dictLookup, makeDictionary, mapAndStore, mapper,
            mapReduce, merge, mergeAll, nextUniqueFile, parseFileToWords, put,
            reducer, saveKeyValues, saver, dictStore, totalWords, uniqueFilename]
```

See Also

The original paper on map-reduce can be found at *http://bit.ly/cqBSTH*.

More details that were left out of the original paper can be found in the analysis at *http://bit.ly/bXsWsD*.

16.14 Diagnosing Parallel Processing Performance

Problem

You are trying to understand why your parallel program is not achieving the expected speedup.

Solution

You can enable parallel tracing by setting options associated with the symbol $Parallel. Use Tracers to specify the types of trace information you want to output and TraceHandler to specify how the trace information should be processed.

```
In[96]:= SetOptions[$Parallel, Tracers → {SendReceive}, TraceHandler → Print]
Out[96]= {Tracers → {SendReceive}, TraceHandler → Print}

In[97]:= ParallelTable[Prime[i], {i, 99 990, 100 010}]
```

```
SendReceive:
  Sending to kernel 4: iid_8600[Table[Prime[i], {i, 99990, 99992, 1}]]  (q=0)
```

```
SendReceive:
  Sending to kernel 3: iid_8601[Table[Prime[i], {i, 99993, 99995, 1}]]  (q=0)
```

```
SendReceive:
  Sending to kernel 2: iid_8602[Table[Prime[i], {i, 99996, 99998, 1}]]  (q=0)
```

```
SendReceive:
  Sending to kernel 1: iid_8603[Table[Prime[i], {i, 99999, 100001, 1}]]  (q=0)
```

```
SendReceive:
  Receiving from kernel 2: iid_8602[{1299647, 1299653, 1299673}]  (q=0)
```

```
SendReceive:
  Sending to kernel 2: iid_8604[Table[Prime[i], {i, 100002, 100004, 1}]]  (q=0)
```

```
SendReceive:
  Receiving from kernel 3: iid_8601[{1299601, 1299631, 1299637}]  (q=0)
```

```
SendReceive:
  Sending to kernel 3: iid_8605[Table[Prime[i], {i, 100005, 100006, 1}]]  (q=0)
```

```
SendReceive:
  Receiving from kernel 2: iid_8604[{1299743, 1299763, 1299791}]  (q=0)
```

```
SendReceive:
  Sending to kernel 2: iid_8606[Table[Prime[i], {i, 100007, 100008, 1}]]  (q=0)
```

```
SendReceive: Receiving from kernel 3: iid_{8605}[{1299811, 1299817}]  (q=0)
```

```
SendReceive:
  Sending to kernel 3: iid_{8607}[Table[Prime[i], {i, 100009, 100010, 1}]]  (q=0)
```

```
SendReceive: Receiving from kernel 2: iid_{8606}[{1299821, 1299827}]  (q=0)
```

```
SendReceive: Receiving from kernel 3: iid_{8607}[{1299833, 1299841}]  (q=0)
```

```
SendReceive:
  Receiving from kernel 4: iid_{8600}[{1299541, 1299553, 1299583}]  (q=0)
```

```
SendReceive:
  Receiving from kernel 1: iid_{8603}[{1299689, 1299709, 1299721}]  (q=0)
```

```
Out[97]=  {1 299 541, 1 299 553, 1 299 583, 1 299 601, 1 299 631, 1 299 637, 1 299 647,
           1 299 653, 1 299 673, 1 299 689, 1 299 709, 1 299 721, 1 299 743, 1 299 763,
           1 299 791, 1 299 811, 1 299 817, 1 299 821, 1 299 827, 1 299 833, 1 299 841}
```

Be sure to disable tracing when you are done.

```
In[98]:=  SetOptions[$Parallel, Tracers → {}]
Out[98]=  {Tracers → {}}
```

Discussion

There are four kinds of Tracers, and you can enable any combination of these. Each
focuses on a different aspect of Mathematica's parallel architecture.

```
In[99]:=  OptionValues[Tracers]
Out[99]=  {MathLink, Queueing, SendReceive, SharedMemory}
```

In addition, there are three ways to present the data via the TraceHandler option.
Print and Display are similar, but Save is interesting because it defers output until
the TraceList[] command is invoked.

```
In[100]:=  OptionValues[TraceHandler]
Out[100]=  {Print, Save, Display}
```

```
In[101]:=  SetOptions[$Parallel, Tracers → {SendReceive, Queueing}];
           SetOptions[$Parallel, TraceHandler → "Save"];
           newTraceList[];
           ParallelTable[Prime[i], {i, 99 990, 100 010}];
```

Now when you execute TraceList, it will return the trace information in a list instead of printing it. This is useful if you want to further process this data in some way.

```
In[103]:= TraceList[]
Out[103]= {{SendReceive,
              Sending to kernel 4: iid_{8608}[Table[Prime[i], {i, 99990, 99992, 1}]]
                 (q=0)}, {SendReceive, Sending to kernel 3:
              iid_{8609}[Table[Prime[i], {i, 99993, 99995, 1}]]  (q=0)}, {SendReceive,
              Sending to kernel 2: iid_{8610}[Table[Prime[i], {i, 99996, 99998, 1}]]
                 (q=0)}, {SendReceive,
              Sending to kernel 1: iid_{8611}[Table[Prime[i], {i, 99999, 100001, 1}]]
                 (q=0)}, {SendReceive,
              Receiving from kernel 4: iid_{8608}[{1299541, 1299553, 1299583}]  (q=0)},
              {Queueing, eid_{8608}[Table[Prime[i], {i, 99990, 99992, 1}]] done},
              {SendReceive,
              Sending to kernel 4: iid_{8612}[Table[Prime[i], {i, 100002, 100004, 1}]]
                 (q=0)}, {SendReceive,
              Receiving from kernel 3: iid_{8609}[{1299601, 1299631, 1299637}]  (q=0)},
              {Queueing, eid_{8609}[Table[Prime[i], {i, 99993, 99995, 1}]] done},
              {SendReceive,
              Sending to kernel 3: iid_{8613}[Table[Prime[i], {i, 100005, 100006, 1}]]
                 (q=0)}, {SendReceive,
              Receiving from kernel 2: iid_{8610}[{1299647, 1299653, 1299673}]  (q=0)},
              {Queueing, eid_{8610}[Table[Prime[i], {i, 99996, 99998, 1}]] done},
              {SendReceive,
              Sending to kernel 2: iid_{8614}[Table[Prime[i], {i, 100007, 100008, 1}]]
                 (q=0)}, {SendReceive,
              Receiving from kernel 1: iid_{8611}[{1299689, 1299709, 1299721}]  (q=0)},
              {Queueing, eid_{8611}[Table[Prime[i], {i, 99999, 100001, 1}]] done},
              {SendReceive,
              Sending to kernel 1: iid_{8615}[Table[Prime[i], {i, 100009, 100010, 1}]]
                 (q=0)}, {SendReceive,
              Receiving from kernel 4: iid_{8612}[{1299743, 1299763, 1299791}]  (q=0)},
              {Queueing, eid_{8612}[Table[Prime[i], {i, 100002, 100004, 1}]] done},
              {SendReceive, Receiving from kernel 3: iid_{8613}[{1299811, 1299817}]  (q=0)},
              {Queueing, eid_{8613}[Table[Prime[i], {i, 100005, 100006, 1}]] done},
              {SendReceive, Receiving from kernel 2: iid_{8614}[{1299821, 1299827}]  (q=0)},
              {Queueing, eid_{8614}[Table[Prime[i], {i, 100007, 100008, 1}]] done},
              {SendReceive, Receiving from kernel 1: iid_{8615}[{1299833, 1299841}]  (q=0)},
              {Queueing, eid_{8615}[Table[Prime[i], {i, 100009, 100010, 1}]] done}}
```

You can get a better understanding of the use of shared memory and critical sections by using the SharedMemory tracer.

```
In[104]:= SetSharedVariable[list]; list = {}
          SetOptions[$Parallel, Tracers → {SendReceive, SharedMemory}];
          SetOptions[$Parallel, TraceHandler → "Save"];
          newTraceList[];
          ParallelEvaluate[
           CriticalSection[{listLock}, list = Prepend[list, $KernelID]]]
In[104]:= {}

Out[105]= {{1}, {2, 1}, {3, 2, 1}, {4, 3, 2, 1}}
```

Now executing TraceList shows how a shared variable was accessed and modified over the parallel evaluation as well as how locks were set and released.

```
In[106]:= TraceList[]
Out[106]= {{SendReceive, Sending to kernel 1:
               CriticalSection[{listLock}, list = Prepend[list, $KernelID]]  (q=0)},
            {SendReceive, Sending to kernel 2:
               CriticalSection[{listLock}, list = Prepend[list, $KernelID]]  (q=0)},
            {SendReceive, Sending to kernel 3:
               CriticalSection[{listLock}, list = Prepend[list, $KernelID]]  (q=0)},
            {SendReceive, Sending to kernel 4:
               CriticalSection[{listLock}, list = Prepend[list, $KernelID]]
               (q=0)}, {SharedMemory,
             kernel 1: Parallel`Concurrency`Private`acquire[{listLock}, 1] ⟶ True},
            {SharedMemory,
             kernel 2: Parallel`Concurrency`Private`acquire[{listLock}, 2] ⟶ False},
            {SharedMemory,
             kernel 3: Parallel`Concurrency`Private`acquire[{listLock}, 3] ⟶ False},
            {SharedMemory,
             kernel 4: Parallel`Concurrency`Private`acquire[{listLock}, 4] ⟶ False},
            {SharedMemory, kernel 1: list ⟶ {}},
            {SharedMemory,
             kernel 1: list = {1} ⟶ {1}}, {SharedMemory,
             kernel 1: Parallel`Concurrency`Private`release[{listLock}] ⟶ True},
            {SendReceive, Receiving from kernel 1: {1} (q=0)},
            {SharedMemory,
             kernel 2: Parallel`Concurrency`Private`acquire[{listLock}, 2] ⟶ True},
            {SharedMemory,
             kernel 3: Parallel`Concurrency`Private`acquire[{listLock}, 3] ⟶ False},
            {SharedMemory,
```

```
   kernel 4: Parallel`Concurrency`Private`acquire[{listLock}, 4] → False},
 {SharedMemory, kernel 2: list → {1}},
 {SharedMemory, kernel 2: list = {2, 1} → {2, 1}},
 {SharedMemory,
  kernel 2: Parallel`Concurrency`Private`release[{listLock}] → True},
 {SendReceive, Receiving from kernel 2: {2, 1} (q=0)},
 {SharedMemory,
  kernel 3: Parallel`Concurrency`Private`acquire[{listLock}, 3] → True},
 {SharedMemory,
  kernel 4: Parallel`Concurrency`Private`acquire[{listLock}, 4] → False},
 {SharedMemory, kernel 3: list → {2, 1}},
 {SharedMemory, kernel 3: list = {3, 2, 1} → {3, 2, 1}},
 {SharedMemory,
  kernel 3: Parallel`Concurrency`Private`release[{listLock}] → True},
 {SendReceive, Receiving from kernel 3: {3, 2, 1} (q=0)},
 {SharedMemory,
  kernel 4: Parallel`Concurrency`Private`acquire[{listLock}, 4] → True},
 {SharedMemory, kernel 4: list → {3, 2, 1}},
 {SharedMemory, kernel 4: list = {4, 3, 2, 1} → {4, 3, 2, 1}},
 {SharedMemory,
  kernel 4: Parallel`Concurrency`Private`release[{listLock}] → True},
 {SendReceive, Receiving from kernel 4: {4, 3, 2, 1} (q=0)}}

TraceList[]

{{SendReceive,
  StringForm[Sending to `1`: `2` (q=`3`), StringForm[kernel `1`, 1],
HoldForm[CriticalSection[{listLock}, list = Prepend[list, $KernelID]]], 0]},
 {SendReceive,
  StringForm[Sending to `1`: `2` (q=`3`), StringForm[kernel `1`, 2],
HoldForm[CriticalSection[{listLock}, list = Prepend[list, $KernelID]]], 0]},
 {SendReceive,
  StringForm[Sending to `1`: `2` (q=`3`), StringForm[kernel `1`, 3],
HoldForm[CriticalSection[{listLock}, list = Prepend[list, $KernelID]]], 0]},
 {SendReceive,
  StringForm[Sending to `1`: `2` (q=`3`), StringForm[kernel `1`, 4],
HoldForm[CriticalSection[{listLock}, list = Prepend[list, $KernelID]]], 0]},
 {SharedMemory, StringForm[`1`: `2` → `3`, StringForm[kernel `1`, 1],
HoldForm[Parallel`Concurrency`Private`acquire[{listLock}, 1]],
    HoldForm[True]]},
 {SharedMemory, StringForm[`1`: `2` → `3`, StringForm[kernel `1`, 2],
HoldForm[Parallel`Concurrency`Private`acquire[{listLock}, 2]],
```

```
      HoldForm[False]]},
  {SharedMemory, StringForm[`1`: `2` ⟶ `3`, StringForm[kernel `1`, 3],
HoldForm[Parallel`Concurrency`Private`acquire[{listLock}, 3]],
      HoldForm[False]]},
  {SharedMemory, StringForm[`1`: `2` ⟶ `3`, StringForm[kernel `1`, 4],
HoldForm[Parallel`Concurrency`Private`acquire[{listLock}, 4]],
      HoldForm[False]]},
  {SharedMemory, StringForm[`1`: `2` ⟶ `3`, StringForm[kernel `1`, 1],
HoldForm[list], HoldForm[{}]]},
  {SharedMemory, StringForm[`1`: `2` ⟶ `3`, StringForm[kernel `1`, 1],
HoldForm[list = {1}], HoldForm[{1}]]},
  {SharedMemory, StringForm[`1`: `2` ⟶ `3`, StringForm[kernel `1`, 1],
HoldForm[Parallel`Concurrency`Private`release[{listLock}]],
      HoldForm[True]]}, {SendReceive,
   StringForm[Receiving from `1`: `2` (q=`3`), StringForm[kernel `1`, 1],
HoldForm[{1}], 0]}, {SharedMemory,
   StringForm[`1`: `2` ⟶ `3`, StringForm[kernel `1`, 2],
HoldForm[Parallel`Concurrency`Private`acquire[{listLock}, 2]],
      HoldForm[True]]},
  {SharedMemory, StringForm[`1`: `2` ⟶ `3`, StringForm[kernel `1`, 3],
HoldForm[Parallel`Concurrency`Private`acquire[{listLock}, 3]],
      HoldForm[False]]},
  {SharedMemory, StringForm[`1`: `2` ⟶ `3`, StringForm[kernel `1`, 4],
HoldForm[Parallel`Concurrency`Private`acquire[{listLock}, 4]],
      HoldForm[False]]},
  {SharedMemory, StringForm[`1`: `2` ⟶ `3`, StringForm[kernel `1`, 2],
HoldForm[list], HoldForm[{1}]]},
  {SharedMemory, StringForm[`1`: `2` ⟶ `3`, StringForm[kernel `1`, 2],
HoldForm[list = {2, 1}], HoldForm[{2, 1}]]}, {SharedMemory,
   StringForm[`1`: `2` ⟶ `3`, StringForm[kernel `1`, 2], HoldForm[
      Parallel`Concurrency`Private`release[{listLock}]], HoldForm[True]]},
  {SendReceive, StringForm[Receiving from `1`: `2` (q=`3`),
    StringForm[kernel `1`, 2], HoldForm[{2, 1}], 0]},
  {SharedMemory, StringForm[`1`: `2` ⟶ `3`, StringForm[kernel `1`, 3],
    HoldForm[Parallel`Concurrency`Private`acquire[{listLock}, 3]],
    HoldForm[True]]},
  {SharedMemory, StringForm[`1`: `2` ⟶ `3`, StringForm[kernel `1`, 4],
    HoldForm[Parallel`Concurrency`Private`acquire[{listLock}, 4]],
    HoldForm[False]]}, {SharedMemory, StringForm[`1`: `2` ⟶ `3`,
    StringForm[kernel `1`, 3], HoldForm[list], HoldForm[{2, 1}]]]},
```

```
{SharedMemory, StringForm[`1`: `2` ⟶ `3`, StringForm[kernel `1`, 3],
  HoldForm[list = {3, 2, 1}], HoldForm[{3, 2, 1}]]},
{SharedMemory, StringForm[`1`: `2` ⟶ `3`, StringForm[kernel `1`, 3],
  HoldForm[Parallel`Concurrency`Private`release[{listLock}]],
  HoldForm[True]]},
{SendReceive, StringForm[Receiving from `1`: `2` (q=`3`),
  StringForm[kernel `1`, 3], HoldForm[{3, 2, 1}], 0]},
{SharedMemory, StringForm[`1`: `2` ⟶ `3`, StringForm[kernel `1`, 4],
  HoldForm[Parallel`Concurrency`Private`acquire[{listLock}, 4]],
  HoldForm[True]]}, {SharedMemory, StringForm[`1`: `2` ⟶ `3`,
  StringForm[kernel `1`, 4], HoldForm[list], HoldForm[{3, 2, 1}]]},
{SharedMemory, StringForm[`1`: `2` ⟶ `3`, StringForm[kernel `1`, 4],
  HoldForm[list = {4, 3, 2, 1}], HoldForm[{4, 3, 2, 1}]]},
{SharedMemory, StringForm[`1`: `2` ⟶ `3`, StringForm[kernel `1`, 4],
  HoldForm[Parallel`Concurrency`Private`release[{listLock}]],
  HoldForm[True]]},
{SendReceive, StringForm[Receiving from `1`: `2` (q=`3`),
  StringForm[kernel `1`, 4], HoldForm[{4, 3, 2, 1}], 0]}}
```

It is enlightening to do the same trace without the use of CriticalSection. Here you can see the problems caused by unsynchronized modification of shared memory.

```
In[107]:= SetSharedVariable[list]; list = {}
          SetOptions[$Parallel, Tracers → {SendReceive, SharedMemory}];
          SetOptions[$Parallel, TraceHandler → "Save"];
          newTraceList[];
          ParallelEvaluate[list = Prepend[list, $KernelID]]
In[107]:= {}
Out[108]= {{1}, {2}, {3}, {4}}
```

```
In[109]:=  TraceList[]
Out[109]=  {{SendReceive, Sending to kernel 1: list = Prepend[list, $KernelID]  (q=0)},
            {SendReceive, Sending to kernel 2: list = Prepend[list, $KernelID]  (q=0)},
            {SendReceive, Sending to kernel 3: list = Prepend[list, $KernelID]  (q=0)},
            {SendReceive, Sending to kernel 4: list = Prepend[list, $KernelID]  (q=0)},
            {SharedMemory, kernel 1: list ⟶ {}},
            {SharedMemory, kernel 2: list ⟶ {}},
            {SharedMemory, kernel 3: list ⟶ {}},
            {SharedMemory, kernel 4: list ⟶ {}},
            {SharedMemory, kernel 1: list = {1} ⟶ {1}},
            {SharedMemory, kernel 2: list = {2} ⟶ {2}},
            {SharedMemory, kernel 3: list = {3} ⟶ {3}},
            {SharedMemory, kernel 4: list = {4} ⟶ {4}},
            {SendReceive, Receiving from kernel 1: {1}  (q=0)},
            {SendReceive, Receiving from kernel 2: {2}  (q=0)},
            {SendReceive, Receiving from kernel 3: {3}  (q=0)},
            {SendReceive, Receiving from kernel 4: {4}  (q=0)}}
```

16.15 Measuring the Overhead of Parallelization in Your Environment

Problem

You want to get a handle on the inherent data communications overhead of parallel Mathematica in your environment.

Solution

Given that Mathematica is available on many operating systems and classes of computer, and also given that computational cores may be local or networked, and given network topologies and throughput, it is important to benchmark your environment to get a sense of its parallel performance characteristics.

One solution is to plot the time it takes to send various amounts of data to kernels with and without computation taking place on the data. The code below generates random data of various sizes and measures the time it takes to execute a function on that data on all kernels using ParallelEvaluate. Here I plot the Identity versus Sqrt versus Total to show the effect of no computation versus computation on every element of data versus computation on every element with a single return value. The key here is that the amount of data sent to slaves and returned to master is the same in the first two cases, whereas for the third case (dotted), less data is returned than sent. Also, the first case (solid) does no computation, and the second (dashed) and third (dotted) do.

```
In[110]:= sendReceiveTime[complexity_, op_] :=
            Module[{data = RandomReal[{0, 100}, 2^complexity]},
             With[{d = data, now = AbsoluteTime[]},
              ParallelEvaluate[op[d]]; {2^complexity, AbsoluteTime[] - now}]]
          ListLinePlot[Transpose[Table[{sendReceiveTime[c, Identity],
              sendReceiveTime[c, Sqrt], sendReceiveTime[c, Total]}, {c, 0, 24}]],
            PlotStyle → {Black, Directive[Black, Dashed], Directive[Black, Dotted]}]
```

Out[2]=

The plot shows that communication overhead of sending data to kernels dominates since the effect of computing Sqrt is negligible. Also, Total (dotted) performs better because less data is returned to the master. Notice how the overhead is roughly linear within my configuration, which consists of four local cores on a Mac Pro with 4 GB of memory.

Discussion

Many users who experiment casually with parallelization in Mathematica 7 come away disappointed. This is unfortunate because there are quite a few useful problems where parallel primitives can yield real gains. The trick is to understand the inherent overhead of your computational setup. Running simple experiments like the one in the solution can give you a sense of the limitations. There are many calculations Mathematica can do that take well under 0.05 seconds, but that is how long it might take to get your data shipped to another kernel. This can make parallelization impractical for your problem.

Consider the Mandelbrot plot from Recipe 16.7. Why did I achieve speedup there? The key characteristics of that problem are that very little data is shipped to the kernels, much computation is done with the data sent, and no coordination is needed with kernels solving other parts of the problem. Such problems are called embarrassingly parallel because it is virtually guaranteed that you will get almost linear speedup with the number of cores at your disposal.

Unfortunately, many problems you come across are not embarrassingly parallel, and you will have to work hard to exploit any parallelism that exists. In many cases, if you can achieve any speedup at all, you will need to expend much effort in reorganizing the problem to fit the computational resources you have at your disposal. The keys to success are:

1. Try to ship data to kernel only once.

2. Try to ship data in large chunks, provided computation does not become skewed.

3. Try to compute as much as possible and return as little data as possible.

4. Try to avoid the need to communicate between kernels via shared data.

5. Try to return data in a form that can be efficiently combined by the master into a final result.

6. Try to avoid repeating identical computations on separate kernels.

CHAPTER 17

Interfacing Mathematica

I want somebody to share
Share the rest of my life
Share my innermost thoughts
Know my intimate details
Someone who'll stand by my side
And give me support
And in return
She'll get my support
She will listen to me
When I want to speak

Depeche Mode, "Somebody"

17.0 Introduction

As wonderful as Mathematica is, there are many practical reasons for needing to interact with other languages and data sources. Luckily, Mathematica is designed to interoperate well with third-party tools. The foundation of much of this interoperability is MathLink. The MathLink protocol is central to Mathematica because it is how the frontend communicates with the kernel. A link (LinkObject) is a communications channel that allows Mathematica expressions and data values to be transmitted between the kernel and programs written in C, Java, .NET, and even scripting languages like Python. Recipes 17.5, 17.6, 17.7, and 17.8 solve some of the most common language interoperability problems.

Equally important to programming language interoperability is database interoperability. A powerful language like Mathematica would be far less useful if it did not allow full access to enterprise data. In the past, the ability to read in data from flat files would suffice, but today most enterprises keep data in some form of relational database. Mathematica supports a variety of database linkages, such as generic Open Database Connectivity (ODBC), Java Database Connectivity (JDBC), as well as specific database products like MySQL (*http://www.mysql.com/*) and HSQL (*http://hsqldb.org/*). Recipes 17.9 and 17.10 show typical database connectivity use cases. Recipe 17.11 shows how to extract metadata from a database.

More mundane, but nonetheless useful, interfacing problems involve launching external programs and using remote kernels. See Recipes 17.1, 17.2, and 17.3.

17.1 Calling External Command Line Programs from Mathematica

Problem

You have an executable program that you would like to launch from Mathematica.

Solution

Use Run to execute command line programs. Run returns the exit code of the program. Results can be read in from a file written by the program. Here is an example that will work on the Windows operating system. This is only to illustrate the technique. Mathematica is perfectly capable of telling you the date itself.

```
Run["\"date /T > date.txt\""]; FilePrint["date.txt"]
```

```
Sat 11/15/2008
```

Discussion

You can also read the output of external programs by using the escape character ! and the function ReadList. This example uses the GNU program wget to retrieve a web page and extract the unique URLs. Note that this example assumes you have wget installed on your system and that it is in the path the Operating System (OS) uses to find programs.

```
webpage = ReadList["!wget -O - http://www.wolfram.com", String];
Union[Flatten[StringCases[webpage, RegularExpression[
    "https?://([-\w\.]+)+(:\d+)?(/([\w/_\.]*(\?\S+)?)?)?"]]]]
{http://blog.wolfram.com/,
 http://demonstrations.wolfram.com/, http://functions.wolfram.com/,
 http://integrals.wolfram.com/index.jsp, http://library.wolfram.com/,
 http://mathworld.wolfram.com/, http://partnerships.wolfram.com/,
 http://reference.wolfram.com/alphaindex/,
 http://reference.wolfram.com/mathematica/guide/Mathematica.html,
 http://register.wolfram.com/, http://search.wolfram.com/,
 http://store.wolfram.com/, http://store.wolfram.com/catalog/,
 http://store.wolfram.com/view/app/mathematica/upgrade.upg,
 http://support.wolfram.com/, http://tones.wolfram.com/,
 http://www.mathematica-journal.com/issue/v10i3/,
 http://www.stephenwolfram.com/, http://www.w3.org/1999/xhtml,
 http://www.w3.org/TR/xhtml1/DTD/xhtml1,
 http://www.wolfram.com/services/education/seminars/,
 http://www.wolframscience.com/}
```

See Also

Additional details about running external programs can be found in the Mathematica tutorial /*ExternalPrograms*.

17.2 Launching Windows Programs from Mathematica

Problem

You want to launch a Windows-based program from the frontend and Run["Program"] does not work.

Solution

Use the Windows Start command in the Run so the program is launched indirectly.

```
Run["Start WinWord"]; (*starts MS Word*)
```

Discussion

I ran across this problem while preparing a presentation in Mathematica for which I wanted to have a button that launched XMLSpy to show some XML. Without the use of Start, you need to specify the full path to the executable; Mathematica complains because it expects the command to be short-lived. Note that Start is a Windows command and not a Mathematica one.

```
Button["Show some XML",
   Run["\"c:/Program Files/Altova/XMLSpy2006/XmlSpy.exe\""]]
```

```
Show some XML
```

The above problem could be solved using Method → "Queued" as an option to Button, but using Start is much simpler.

```
Button["Show some XML", Run["Start XMLSpy"]]
```

```
Show some XML
```

17.3 Connecting the Frontend to a Remote Kernel

Problem

You want to use the Mathematica kernel from a different computer than the one you are using to run the frontend.

Solution

Use the menu Evaluation, Kernel Configuration to create a configuration for a remote kernel. Select Add from the dialog. You will then be presented with the Kernel Properties dialog shown in Figure 17-1. It makes sense to give the kernel a meaningful name that will remind you what server it is connected to, but you can name it after your spouse or your dog if you like. Select the radio button Remote Machine and then enter the machine's name, a login name, and the kernel program (which is often "math," but see the "Discussion" section on page 693). I like to check the option "Append name to In/Out prompts" to remind me I am working with a remote kernel, but this is a matter of taste. If you will mostly be working with this specific remote kernel, you can also check the automatic launch option.

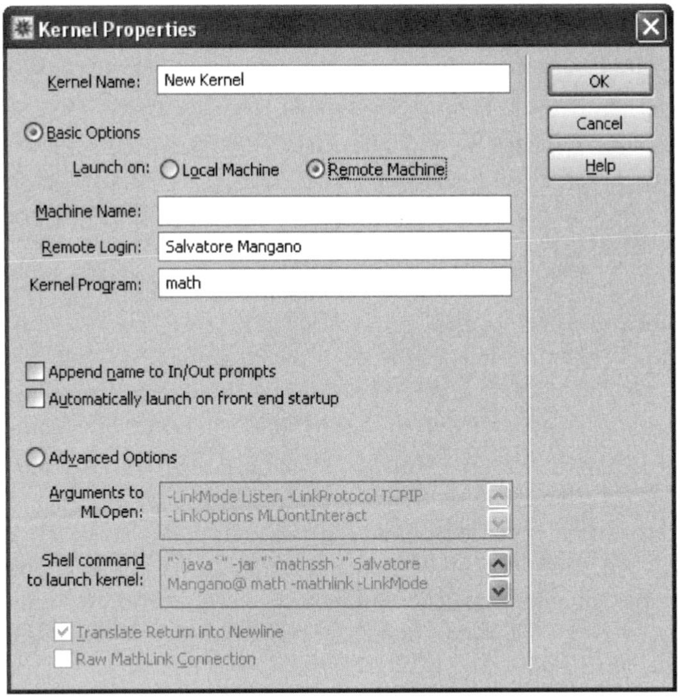

Figure 17-1. Kernel Properties dialog

When you have the kernel configured, you can use Evaluation, Start Kernel to start it and Evaluation, Notebook Kernel to associate it with the current notebook.

Discussion

If you have network access to a more powerful computer than the one you use daily and that computer has Mathematica installed, then you can reap a lot of benefit from using a remote kernel. For example, I like to work on my laptop because it gives me the flexibility to work anywhere in my house. However, my basement has my powerful Mac Pro, so I usually run my kernel there. This not only gives me access to a faster machine, but frees resources on the laptop that would otherwise be used by the local kernel.

There is a caveat to the solution. If the machine you are connected to is a Mac, there is no program called "math." You must instead give the full path to the program called MathKernel in the edit box for Kernel Program. The location will depend on where Mathematica was installed. For example, I installed Mathematica under *Applications/Wolfram,* so I entered */Applications/Wolfram/Mathematica.app/ Contents/MacOS/MathKernel.*

If you have trouble connecting to the remote kernel you should take the following steps.

1. Make sure you can ping the computer you entered on the command line. You can run ping from the Windows cmd.exe shell or Unix or Mac OS X shell. If you can't ping the machine, it is either off or there is some network issue you need to resolve.

2. If you can ping the computer but the kernel fails to start, make sure Mathematica is properly installed on the remote computer. Do this by running Mathematica directly from the remote computer or ask your systems administrator to verify. A common problem is for Mathematica to be installed but to rely on a license manager (MathLM) that is not running.

3. If you get an error like "SSH could not launch kernel '*<kernel name>*' because the remote machine refused the connection. Error code = 113", then there is most likely a permissions problem with the login name and the password you provided when prompted by the frontend. Make sure you can remotely log in to the machine using Secure Shell (SSH) or PuTTY from the command line (PuTTY is a free SSH program for Windows that you can download from *http://www.putty.org/*).

17.4 Using Mathematica with C and C++

Problem

You want to call C functions from Mathematica.

Solution

Here I demonstrate the process of creating a C program with functions that can be invoked from Mathematica. This example uses Microsoft Visual C++ 2005. Refer to the "See Also" section on page 699 for information on using other programming environments. The simplest way to interface Mathematica to C is to utilize the pre-processor mprep, which takes a template file describing one or more C functions, and generate the glue code needed to interface those functions to Mathematica. Here is an example of an mprep file describing three different functions.

```
:Begin:

:Function:      fExample1
:Pattern:       fExample1[x_Integer, y_Integer]
:Arguments:     {x, y}
:ArgumentTypes: {Integer, Integer}
:ReturnType:    Integer

:Function:      fExample2
:Pattern:       fExample2[x_List, y_List]
:Arguments:     {x, y}
:ArgumentTypes: {IntegerList, RealList}
:ReturnType:    Integer

:Function:      fExample3
:Pattern:       fExample3[aStr_String]
:Arguments:     {aStr}
:ArgumentTypes: {String}
:ReturnType:    String

:End:
```

The C source code corresponding to these definitions follows. Note that lists are passed as pointers to arrays and that an extra integer parameter is needed for each such list to receive the length of the array. In this listing, you will also find the definition of WinMain that is required for Windows executables built with Microsoft Visual Studio. The body of WinMain is standard boilerplate that you can copy into your own project. The implementation of the functions themselves is really not important in this code as its main purpose is to demonstrate the C interface mechanics.

```
//functions.h

extern "C"
{
int fExample1(int x, int y);
double fExample2(int * x, long xLen, double* y, long yLen);
char * fExample3(char * aStr);
}
//functions.cpp

#include "functions.h"
#include <mathlink.h>
```

```c
#include <stdio.h>
#include <ctype.h>


int fExample1(int x, int y)
{
    return (x >> y) + 1;
}

double fExample2(int * x, int xLen, double* y, int yLen)
{
    double result = 0.0;
    int i = 0;
    for (; i<xLen && i<yLen; ++i)
    {
        result += x[i] * y[i] ;
    }
    for (;i < yLen; ++i)
    {
        result += y[i];
    }
    return result ;
}

char * fExample3(char * aStr)
{
    for(char *p=aStr;*p;++p)
    {
        *p = toupper(*p) ;
    }
    return aStr ;
}


int PASCAL WinMain( HINSTANCE hinstCurrent, HINSTANCE hinstPrevious,
LPSTR lpszCmdLine, int nCmdShow)
{
    char  buff[512];
    char FAR * buff_start = buff;
    char FAR * argv[32];
    char FAR * FAR * argv_end = argv + 32;
```

```
        hinstPrevious = hinstPrevious; /*suppress warning*/

        if( !MLInitializeIcon( hinstCurrent, nCmdShow)) return 1;
        MLScanString( argv, &argv_end, &lpszCmdLine, &buff_start);
        return MLMain( (int)(argv_end - argv), argv);
    }
```

Once you have a MathLink program compiled to an executable, you can install it using Install. By default, Install will look in the current directory for the executable; either change the current directory or give Install the full path. Install returns a LinkObject, which can be used to get information about available functions and also to terminate the connection using Uninstall.

```
saveCurDir = Directory[];
SetDirectory[
    "oreilly\\Mathematica Cookbook\\code\mathLinkExample\\Debug"];
link = Install["mathLinkExample"];
SetDirectory[saveCurDir];
```

You can interrogate a link for the available functions.

```
LinkPatterns[link]
{fExample1[x_Integer, y_Integer],
 fExample2[x_List, y_List], fExample3[aStr_String]}
```

You call installed MathLink functions just like normal Mathematica functions.

```
fExample1[2000, 4]
126

fExample2[{1, 2, 3}, {2.0, 4.0, 6.0, 8.0}]
36.

fExample3["Testing"]
TESTING

Uninstall[link]
mathLinkExample
```

Discussion

Although the solution is fairly straightforward, there are numerous details that are specific to the OS and compilation environment (compiler and IDE or make system). The Mathematica documentation for MathLink contains detailed instructions for many common environments, and you should follow those directions carefully. It is highly recommended that you use either the example in the solution given or some of the simple examples that are installed with Mathematica to become familiar with the process before trying to interface your own C functions.

Often you will need to return objects more complex than integers and doubles from your C functions. If this is the case, you should specify a return type of Manual in the template file. Manual means that you will manually code the function to call the appropriate low-level MathLink C API functions needed to return the correct data to Mathematica.

```
//randomList.tm

#include <stdlib.h>
#include <mathlink.h>

:Begin:
:Function:       randomIntList
:Pattern:        randomIntList[n_Integer]
:Arguments:      {n}
:ArgumentTypes:  {Integer}
:ReturnType:     Manual
:End:

extern "C" void randomIntList(int n)
{
    int* randData = new int [n] ;
    if (randData)
    {
        for(int i=0; i<n; ++i)
        {
            randData[i] = rand() ;
        }
        MLPutInteger32List(stdlink, randData , n);
        delete [] randData;
    }
}
```

```
        else
        {
            MLPutInteger32List(stdlink,0,0) ;
        }
    }
    saveCurDir = Directory[];
    SetDirectory[
       "oreilly\\Mathematica Cookbook\\code\mathLinkExample2\\Debug"];
    link2 = Install["mathLinkExample2"];
    SetDirectory[saveCurDir];

    LinkPatterns[link2]
    {randomIntList[n_Integer]}

    randomIntList[12]
    {2287, 5306, 19 753, 3868, 19 313,
     1043, 29 879, 26 846, 14 625, 1380, 24 555, 28 439}

    Uninstall[link2];
```

The example given illustrates the use of MLPutInteger32List to return an array of data as a list. The MathLink API contains many related functions for returning a variety of types, including integers, strings, lists, multidimensional arrays, and the like. This example also demonstrates that template files processed by mprep can mix source code with template directives.

Another common requirement is the need to execute initialization code once when you install the MathLink program. C-based initialization code can easily be added to the applications main() or WinMain(), but what about Mathematica code? A typical example is code that installs documentation for the installed functions. For this you use mprep's :Evaluate: specifications. For an example of this see *http://bit.ly/duSEnb*.

See Also

Information on how to set up your C-built environment can be found at *tutorial/ MathLinkDeveloperGuide* (Mac OSX), *tutorial/MathLinkDeveloperGuide* (Windows), and *tutorial/MathLinkDeveloperGuide* (Unix and Linux).

See *ref/program/mprep* in the Mathematica documentation.

17.5 Using Mathematica with Java

Problem

You want to use Mathematica as a Java scripting language to prototype a Java application or leverage the functionality of Java classes.

Solution

Use the JLink` package and call InstallJava to make the Java runtime environment available to Mathematica. You can then create objects and call methods or load classes to access static methods just as if they were Mathematica functions.

```
Needs["JLink`"]
InstallJava[];
(*Create an instance of decimal format and
  call a method using prefix notation obj@method.*)
fmt = JavaNew["java.text.DecimalFormat", "#.0000"];
fmt@format[#] & /@ {1.0, 7.333, N[Pi], 1/3.}
{1.0000, 7.3330, 3.1416, .3333}

(*Load a class and call a static method using
  the full class name as if it were a package.*)
LoadJavaClass["java.lang.System"];
java`lang`System`currentTimeMillis[]
1 226 852 744 984
```

Discussion

```
Options[InstallJava]
{ClassPath → Automatic, CommandLine → Automatic, JVMArguments → None,
 ForceLaunch → False, Default → Automatic, CreateExtraLinks → Automatic}
```

InstallJava takes options that control how the Java is loaded. CommandLine → **java-path** allows you to specify the particular version of Java you want to load if you have several versions available. For example, CommandLine → "c:\\Program Files\\Java\\jre1.6.0_07\\bin\\java". ClassPath → **classpath** is used to provide a classpath that is different from the default obtained from the CLASSPATH environment variable. If you require special Java Virtual Machine (JVM) options, use JVMArguments → **arguments**.

When InstallJava is invoked several times during a Mathematica session, the subsequent invocations are ignored. However, sometimes you want to clear out the old JVM and start fresh. In that case, use ReinstallJava to exit and reload Java. This is especially useful if you are making changes to a Java Archive (JAR) that you are developing alongside the Mathematica notebook that uses it. ReinstallJava takes the same options as InstallJava.

```
ReinstallJava[
    CommandLine → "c:\\Program Files\\Java\\jre1.6.0_07\\bin\\java"];
```

The following example uses a *genetic algorithm* (GA) Java library called JGAP (see *http://jgap.sourceforge.net/*). GAs are in the class of evolutionary inspired algorithms typically used to tackle complex optimization problems. This example demonstrates an ideal blend of Mathematica and Java because it shows how easy it is to script a Java application and exploit the visualization features of Mathematica to investigate its behavior.

The example also illustrates the use of JavaBlock as a means of automatically cleaning up Java objects when they are no longer needed. It also shows how Java arrays of objects are replaced by Mathematica lists and how the translation is automated by JLink.

```
Needs["JLink`"]
ReinstallJava[ClassPath →
    "C:\\code\\jgap;C:\\code\\jgap\jgap-examples.jar;C:\\code\\jgap\jgap.jar
        ;C:\\code\\jgap\jgapMathematica.jar"];
(*The volumes of items we wish to be packed*)
itemVolumes = {1.2, 2.8, 3.5, 4.0, 25.0, 6.75, 14.36, 36.7, 78.9, 325.1};
(*The names of the items*)
itemNames = {"item1", "item2", "item3", "item4", "widget",
    "thingie", "thingie2", "fooBar", "WingWam", "ThingAMaBob"};
targetVolume = 1000.0;
popSize = 1500;
generations = 150;
```

I implement the problem using a function called knapsack, which takes an optional fitness function. The reason for this will become apparent later. Most of the code within knapsack is straightforward use of JLink facilities interspersed with standard Mathematica code. The comments in the code point out what's going on, and much of the detail is specific to the JGAP library and the knapsack problem. One thing that might trip you up in your own Java-interfacing projects is dealing with Java arrays of objects. There is no JLink function specifically designed to construct arrays. Instead, wherever you need to call a Java function that expects an array, simply pass it a Mathematica list of objects created with JavaNew and Jlink will translate. Mathematica's Table is convenient for that purpose and it is how the following code creates an array of Gene objects. Likewise, when calling a Java function that returns an array, expect Mathematica to convert it to a list.

```
knapsack[fitnessFunc_ : None] :=
 (*Use a JavaBlock to release all Java objects when block completes.*)
 JavaBlock[
  Module[{conf, fitnessFunc2, sampleGenes, sampleChromosome, population,
    individuals, bestSolutionSoFar, packing, volumeFound, dummy},
   (*JGAP uses a configuration object to organize the
    genetic algorithm's parameters and objects.*)
   LoadJavaClass["org.jgap.Configuration"];
   Configuration`reset[];
   conf = JavaNew["org.jgap.impl.DefaultConfiguration"];
(*We want to preserve the fittest individual.*)
conf@setPreservFittestIndividual[True];
   (*The fitness function is
    implemented as a class in the example code.*)
   fitnessFunc2 = If[fitnessFunc === None,
    JavaNew["examples.knapsack.KnapsackFitnessFunction", targetVolume],
    JavaNew["jgapMathematica.FitnessFunction", fitnessFunc]];
   conf@setFitnessFunction[fitnessFunc2];
   (*In the original Java code sampleGenes is a Java array of class
    Gene. However, in Mathematica you create lists of objects, and the
    JLink code will take care of translating to arrays when necessary.*)
   sampleGenes = Table[JavaNew["org.jgap.impl.IntegerGene",
     conf, 0, Ceiling[0.75 targetVolume / itemVolumes[[i]]]],
    {i, 1, Length[itemVolumes]}];

   sampleChromosome = JavaNew["org.jgap.Chromosome", conf, sampleGenes];
conf@setSampleChromosome[sampleChromosome];
   conf@setPopulationSize[popSize];
   LoadJavaClass["org.jgap.Genotype"];
   population = org`jgap`Genotype`randomInitialGenotype[conf];
   (*Let's run the evolution for 200 generations and
    capture the fittest at each generation.*)
   {dummy, {saveFitnessValues }} = Reap[Do[population@evolve[];
     Sow[population@getFittestChromosome[]@getFitnessValue[]],
     {generations}]];
   bestSolutionSoFar = population@getFittestChromosome[];
Print["Fitness of Best:", bestSolutionSoFar@getFitnessValue[]];
 (*Here we decode the best solution to get the qty of each item.*)
```

```
packing =
    Table[{bestSolutionSoFar@getGene[i]@getAllele[],
        itemNames[[i + 1]]}, {i, 0, bestSolutionSoFar@size[] - 1}];
Print["Packing found: ", packing];
  volumeFound = Total[packing[[All, 1]] * itemVolumes];
Print["Volume used ", volumeFound];
  Print["Difference from desired volume: ", targetVolume - volumeFound];
  ]
]
```

Using a fairly healthy population size and a large number of generations, we unfortunately get a fairly poor solution! This indicates a problem with the design of our GA. Let's see how we can draw on Mathematica to help resolve this.

```
popSize = 1500;
generations = 200;
knapsack[]
```

```
Fitness of Best: 4.58099×10^8
```

```
Packing found:
  {{78, item1}, {27, item2}, {38, item3}, {0, item4}, {26, widget},
   {86, thingie}, {11, thingie2}, {0, fooBar}, {0, WingWam}, {0, ThingAMaBob}}
```

```
Volume used 1690.66
```

```
Difference from desired volume: -690.66
```

By plotting the logarithm of the fitness at each generation, we can see that the fitness landscape of this problem is extremely steep since we make a rapid transition from very low fitness to very high fitness. This suggests the fitness function provided with this JGAP sample might not be ideal. The poor quality of the solution is further indication of a poorly designed fitness function. The real lesson is that Mathematica is an ideal experimental playground for Java libraries because the full wealth of analytic and visual tools is at your disposal. In fact, I use Mathematica to help find a better fitness function, so read on.

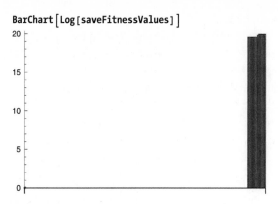

BarChart[Log[saveFitnessValues]]

If you want to experiment with Java libraries, it is ideal to be able to implement interfaces defined by those libraries directly in Mathematica. In fact, this can be done rather easily using ImplementJavaInterface. The following example uses Implement-JavaInterface to try an alternate fitness function for the knapsack problem. There is a caveat, however. ImplementJavaInterface will only work with true interfaces, not abstract classes. In JGAP, FitnessFunction is an abstract class, hence we can't implement it using ImplementJavaInterface. The solution in cases like this is to create an adapter like the one in the following listing.

```
package jgapMathematica;

import org.jgap.IChromosome;

public class FitnessFunction extends org.jgap.FitnessFunction {

    private IMathematicFitness m_fitness;

    public FitnessFunction(IMathematicFitness fitness) {
        m_fitness = fitness ;
    }

    @Override
    protected double evaluate(final IChromosome chromosome) {
        return m_fitness.evaluate(chromosome);
        }

}
```

The above fitness function allows us to use the following interface within Mathematica code.

```
package jgapMathematica;

import org.jgap.IChromosome;

public interface IMathematicFitness {
    public double evaluate(final IChromosome chromosome) ;
}
```

Once this is done, we can write any fitness function we like in pure Mathematica code. This solution is general in that any abstract class you find in any Java library can be adapted in a similar manner. Below, we exploit the adapter to write a new fitness function for the knapsack problem. The function penalizes solutions that use more volume than specified, while giving increasing reward to solutions that use close to the available volume.

```
knapsackEvaluate[subject_] := Module[{subjPacking, subjVol},
   (*Figure out the volume used by the solution being evaluated.*)
   subjPacking =
    Table[subject@getGene[i]@getAllele[], {i, 0, subject@size[] - 1}];
   subjVol = Total[subjPacking * itemVolumes];
   (*This function gives small fitness to
    volumes that are far from the target volume; however,
    it rewards underfitting twice as much as overfitting.*)
   If[subjVol > targetVolume, targetVolume/subjVol,
     (subjVol/targetVolume) * 2.0]
  ]
(*Implementing an interface is nothing more than mapping the interface
 methods to the Mathematica function. Here our interface has only a single
 function called evaluate and it gets mapped to knapsackEvaluate.*)
ff = ImplementJavaInterface["jgapMathematica.IMathematicFitness",
    {"evaluate" → "knapsackEvaluate"}];

popSize = 50;
generations = 20;
knapsack[ff]
```

```
Fitness of Best: 1.99776
```

```
Packing found:
 {{20, item1}, {95, item2}, {67, item3}, {20, item4}, {2, widget},
  {34, thingie}, {8, thingie2}, {0, fooBar}, {0, WingWam}, {0, ThingAMaBob}}
```

```
Volume used 998.88
```

```
Difference from desired volume: 1.12
```

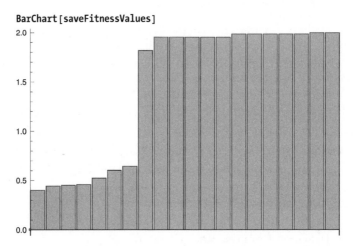

Keep in mind that implementing interface in Mathematica code is convenient but comes at a very high cost. In our case, it makes the GA run much slower and forces the use of a much smaller population size. This is especially true because the fitness function is called many times, and it must call back into Java, making it extremely costly. This is not a real issue because the goal here is experimentation. When a reasonable fitness function is found, it can be ported back to Java. You can use the same methodology when working with other Java libraries. Of course, if the interface you implement in Mathematica is called infrequently, the hassle of porting back to Java may seem unnecessary.

See Also

The J/Link tutorial is an excellent way to round out your knowledge of the Mathematica-to-Java interface. See *JLink/tutorial/Overview*.

Mathematica is bundled with notebooks illustrating different aspects of Mathematica-Java interaction (such as using the GUI features of Java Swing). These can be found in the Mathematica installation directory (evaluate $InstallationDirectory) under subdirectory *SystemFiles/Links/JLink/Examples*.

17.6 Using Mathematica to Interact with Microsoft's .NET Framework

Problem

You want to use Mathematica as a .NET scripting language to prototype a .NET application or leverage Windows-specific functionality not directly available in Mathematica.

Solution

Use the NETLink` package and InstallNET to initialize Mathematica's .NET interface. You then can use functions like LoadNETAssembly to load custom .NET assemblies and NETNew to create instances of objects. Methods and properties of objects are accessed using Mathematica prefix notation **object@property** and **object@method** **[args]**.

As an example, you can use Mathematica 6's dynamic functionality with a .NET timer to display a ticking clock.

```
Needs["NETLink`"]
InstallNET[];
timeOut = "Not Set";
timer = NETNew["System.Timers.Timer", 1000];
(*1 sec timer = 1000 msec*)
onTimedEvent[source_, eventArgs_] :=
  Module[{}, timeOut = eventArgs@SignalTime@ToString["G"]];
(*Use AddEventHandler to bind a Mathematica function to an event.*)
AddEventHandler[timer@Elapsed, onTimedEvent];
timer@Enabled = True;
Dynamic[timeOut]
timeOut

timer@Enabled = False; (*Stop the timer*)
```

Discussion

When you use NETNew, Mathematica implicitly loads the .NET type of the class you are creating. For some cases, you need to load the type explicitly. For example, many .NET components use Enums in their interface. To reference these in Mathematica code, you need to load them. In Mathematica, you use LoadNETType for this purpose. In the following example, you use LoadNETType to get the enumerations associated with dialog box results. This allows you to use the OpenFileDialog component to select a file. If you run this code, you may need to press Alt-Tab to switch to the dialog.

```
Needs["NETLink`"]
InstallNET[];
LoadNETType["System.Windows.Forms.DialogResult"];
openFileDialog1 = NETNew["System.Windows.Forms.OpenFileDialog"];
openFileDialog1@InitialDirectory =
  "c:\\Documents And Setting\\Salvtore Mangano"; openFileDialog1@Filter =
  "image files (*.jpg;*.gif;*.bmp)|*.jpg;*.gif;*.bmp|All
    files (*.*)|*.*"; openFileDialog1@FilterIndex = 1;
openFileDialog1@RestoreDirectory = True;
If[openFileDialog1@ShowDialog[] === DialogResult`OK,
  Import[openFileDialog1@FileName], "No Image Selected"]
```

You also use LoadNETType to load a class that has a static method you want to call. Static methods are then accessible as normal Mathematica functions.

```
Needs["NETLink`"]
InstallNET[];
LoadNETType["System.Diagnostics.Stopwatch"];
System`Diagnostics`Stopwatch`GetTimestamp[]
5 674 487 004
```

The default value for the LoadNETType option StaticsVisible is False, but you can set it to True to avoid having to specify the full namespace path to invoke the function. You should use this feature with caution since it can lead to name conflicts.

See Also

An extensive tutorial on NETLink can be found in the Mathematica documentation at *NETLink/tutorial/Overview*.

17.7 Using the Mathematica Kernel from a .NET Application

Problem

You want to leverage the advanced Mathematica algorithms from within a .NET application.

Solution

Use the classes in the Wolfram.NETLink.dll from your .NET application. This recipe will use C#, but the Mathematica kernel is accessible from any .NET language. The simplest way to interact with Mathematica is through passing strings of Mathematica code using an instance of IKernelLink. You acquire an instance via MathLinkFactory.CreateKernelLink. IKernelLink has several methods for evaluating Mathematica code, but the function EvaluateToOutputForm is one of the most convenient.

```
using System;
using Wolfram.NETLink;

namespace TestNetLink1
{
    public class TestNetLink
    {
        public static void Main (String[] args)
        {
            //Launch the Mathematica Kernel
            IKernelLink ml = MathLinkFactory.CreateKernelLink ();
            //Discard the initial response kernel will send when launched.
            ml.WaitAndDiscardAnswer ();
            //Solve a differential equation and evaluate at the value 2
             string expr = "s = NDSolve[{y''[x]+Sin[y[x]] y[x] == 0,
                y[0] == 1," +
                   "y'[0] == 0},y,{x, 0,30}]; y[2] /. s";
            string result = ml.EvaluateToOutputForm(expr, 0);
                Console.WriteLine ("Result = " + result);
        }
    }
}
```

Discussion

Receiving numerical data back in string form is fine when you just want to display the result of a computation, but if you want to feed the results Mathematica returns into further computations, it is less than ideal. There are other ways to read the data returned by evaluation expressions, but these involve being cognizant of the types you expect back.

```
using System;
using Wolfram.NETLink;

namespace TestNetLink2
{
    public class TestNetLink2
    {
        public static void Main(String[] args)
        {
            //Launch the Mathematica Kernel
            IKernelLink ml = MathLinkFactory.CreateKernelLink();
            //Discard the initial response kernel will send when launched.
            ml.WaitAndDiscardAnswer();
            //Solve a differential equation and evaluate at the value 2.
            string expr = "s = NDSolve[{y''[x]+Sin[y[x]] y[x] == 0, y[0] ==
                1," +
                "y'[0] == 0},y,{x, 0,30}]; y[2] /. s";
            //Evaluate expression. Notice this does not return anything.
            ml.Evaluate(expr);
            //Wait for results to be ready.
            ml.WaitForAnswer();
            //Read the result being sure to use the method that retrieves a
n
                appropriate
            //type. In this case, we expect a list of doubles but MathLink
                converts
            //these into arrays. Here you get the first element of the arra
y
                and can then
            //perform additional computations such as adding 10.
            double result = ml.GetDoubleArray()[0] + 10.0;
            Console.WriteLine("Result = " + result);
        }
    }
}
```

The IKernelLink interface has a variety of methods for retrieving typed results. These include GetBoolean, GetDouble, GetInteger, GetString, GetDecimal, GetDouble-Array, and quite a few others. Refer to the NETLink documentation for the full set of methods.

In addition to IKernelLink, there is a very high-level interface to Mathematica implemented as a class called MathKernel that is ideal for creating a custom frontend to Mathematica. MathKernel derives from System.ComponentModel.Component and follows the conventions of .NET components. A nice example of using MathKernel can be found in the Mathematica installation directory ($InstallationDirectory) under *SystemFiles/Links/NETLink/Examples/Part2/MathKernelApp*.

See Also

You can find more information on interacting with the kernel from .NET languages at *NETLink/tutorial/CallingMathematicaFromNET*. There are examples there using both C# and Visual Basic.

17.8 Querying a Database

Problem

You want to compute with data retrieved from an external database.

 The examples in Recipes 17.9 and 17.10 assume the existence of certain databases. If you don't have access to a database system where you can set up these databases, the examples will obviously not work. If you have a database system or know how to install one, you can get files to initialize the database for these examples from the book's website. Naturally, these examples are only for illustrating techniques that you can employ on real databases you wish to interface to Mathematica.

Mathematica supports several flavors of database connectivity, including ODBC, JDBC, MySQL, and HSQLDB (Hyper Structured Query Language Database).

Solution

Here I open a connection to a SupplierParts database previously set up on my system and then query all rows of the part table. SQLSelect is the best way to retrieve all data from a single table. See the discussion for variations and alternatives.

```
Needs["DatabaseLink`"];
conn = OpenSQLConnection["SupplierParts"];
SQLSelect[conn, "part"]
```

{{p1, Nut, Red, 12., London}, {p2, Bolt, Green, 17., Paris},
 {p3, Screw, Blue, 17., Rome}, {p4, Screw, Red, 14., London},
 {p5, Cam, Blue, 12., Paris}, {p6, Cog, Red, 19., London}}

Discussion

SQLSelect provides a stylized means to perform simple database queries without knowing SQL. Below are three increasingly complex queries you can do with
SQLSelect.

```
(*Restrict to specific columns.*)
SQLSelect[conn, "supplier", {"name", "city"}]
```
{{Smith, London}, {Jones, Paris},
 {Blake, Paris}, {Clark, London}, {Adams, Athens}}

```
(*Specify selection criteria.*)
SQLSelect[conn, "supplier", {"name", "city"}, SQLColumn["id"] == "s1"]
```
{{Smith, London}}

```
(*Join data from multiple tables. Here I show
 collocated suppliers and parts, and specify a sort.*)
SQLSelect[conn, {"supplier", "part"},
   {{"supplier", "id"}, {"part", "id"}, {"supplier", "city"}},
   SQLColumn[{"supplier", "city"}] == SQLColumn[{"part", "city"}],
   "SortingColumns" -> {SQLColumn[{"supplier", "id"}],
                        SQLColumn[{"part", "id"}]}] // TableForm
```
s1 p1 London
s1 p4 London
s1 p6 London
s2 p2 Paris
s2 p5 Paris
s3 p2 Paris
s3 p5 Paris
s4 p1 London
s4 p4 London
s4 p6 London

Of course, the conventions used by SQLSelect create a very thin veneer over SQL, so if you plan to do quite a bit of database work, you will benefit from learning and using SQL directly via SQLExecute.

```
SQLExecute[conn,
  "SELECT supplier.id sid, part.id pid, supplier.city city
  FROM supplier, part
  WHERE supplier.city = part.city
  ORDER BY sid,pid", "ShowColumnHeadings" → True] // TableForm
sid pid city
s1  p1  London
s1  p4  London
s1  p6  London
s2  p2  Paris
s2  p5  Paris
s3  p2  Paris
s3  p5  Paris
s4  p1  London
s4  p4  London
s4  p6  London
```

Nevertheless, using straight SQL can sometimes be a pain when you need to build the query from data stored in variables. SQLArgument, along with argument placeholders (e.g., `1`, `2`), is the recommended solution. You can use SQLArgument directly with values, but if you are parameterizing a query on column or table names, you must also use SQLColumn and SQLTable, respectively.

```
table = "supplier"; id = "s2"; col = "city";
SQLExecute[conn,
  "SELECT `1` FROM `2` WHERE id = `3`", {SQLArgument[SQLColumn[col]],
    SQLArgument[SQLTable[table]], SQLArgument[id]}]
{{Paris}}

CloseSQLConnection[conn];
```

See Also

Detailed discussion of query commands can be found in *DatabaseLink/tutorial/SelectingData* in the Mathematica documentation.

17.9 Updating a Database

Problem

You want to store results of computations to a database.

Solution

Use SQLInsert to add new records and SQLUpdate to modify existing records.

```
Needs["DatabaseLink`"];
conn = OpenSQLConnection["MySQLTest"];
SQLInsert[conn, "data1", {"x1", "x2", "x3"},
  Table[{i, Prime[i], RandomReal[]}, {i, 1, 100}]];
SQLUpdate[conn, "data1", {"x1", "x2", "x3"},
  {0.0, 1.0, 2.0}, SQLColumn["data1.key"] == 4]
1
```

Use SQLDelete to remove records.

```
SQLDelete[conn, "data1", SQLColumn["data1.key"] == 10]
0
```

Discussion

If you need to update multiple tables in an all-or-nothing manner and your database management system supports transactions, you should use SQLBeginTransaction and SQLCommitTransaction to bracket the updates. If an error occurs you can use SQLRollbackTransaction, which rolls back to the beginning of the transaction or to a named save point (which is set using SQLSetSavepoint).

Inserting, updating, and deleting are the most common operations for changing a database, but Mathematica also gives you the ability to create and drop tables.

```
SQLExecute[conn, "UPDATE data1 SET x1=0,x2=1,x3=2 WHERE data1.key=104"]
1
```

See Also

Detailed discussion of transactions can be found in *DatabaseLink/tutorial/Transactions* in the Mathematica documentation.

17.10 Introspection of Databases

Problem

You want to query a database to find out what entities (tables, columns, etc.) are available.

Solution

Mathematica contains a variety of methods that return information about the data sources available, their tables, and the schema of those tables.

```
Needs["DatabaseLink`"]
```

The command `DataSourceNames[]` lists all data sources known to the Mathematica instance.

```
DataSourceNames[]
{demo, graphs, publisher, MySQLMeta, MySQLTest, SupplierParts}
```

Given a connection to one of these sources, list all the tables.

```
conn = OpenSQLConnection["SupplierParts"];
SQLTables[conn]
{SQLTable[inventory, TableType → TABLE],
 SQLTable[part, TableType → TABLE], SQLTable[supplier, TableType → TABLE]}
```

Given a connection, list all columns with their associated tables.

```
SQLColumnNames[conn] // TableForm
inventory  sid
inventory  pid
inventory  qty
part       id
part       name
part       color
part       weight
part       city
supplier   id
supplier   name
supplier   status
supplier   city
```

You can also find out all the data types supported by your particular database.

```
SQLDataTypeNames[conn]
{BIT, BOOL, TINYINT, TINYINT UNSIGNED, BIGINT, BIGINT UNSIGNED,
 LONG VARBINARY, MEDIUMBLOB, LONGBLOB, BLOB, TINYBLOB, VARBINARY, BINARY,
 LONG VARCHAR, MEDIUMTEXT, LONGTEXT, TEXT, TINYTEXT, CHAR, NUMERIC,
 DECIMAL, INTEGER, INTEGER UNSIGNED, INT, INT UNSIGNED, MEDIUMINT,
 MEDIUMINT UNSIGNED, SMALLINT, SMALLINT UNSIGNED, FLOAT, DOUBLE,
 DOUBLE PRECISION, REAL, VARCHAR, ENUM, SET, DATE, TIME, DATETIME, TIMESTAMP}

CloseSQLConnection[conn];
```

Discussion

The introspection commands demonstrated in the solution can take different arguments and options that restrict results or return additional information.

```
Needs["DatabaseLink`"]
conn = OpenSQLConnection["MySQLTest"];
```

For example, the SQLTables command can retrieve specific tables by name or using wildcards % (zero or more characters) and _ (any single character). By default, only tables are returned, but you can use the option TableType to list other tablelike entities, such as views.

```
SQLTables[conn]
{SQLTable[data1, TableType → TABLE], SQLTable[data2, TableType → TABLE]}

SQLTables[conn, "data1%", "TableType" → {"TABLE", "VIEW"}]
{SQLTable[data1, TableType → TABLE],
 SQLTable[data1view100, TableType → VIEW]}

SQLTables[conn, "data_", "TableType" → {"TABLE", "VIEW"}]
{SQLTable[data1, TableType → TABLE], SQLTable[data2, TableType → TABLE]}
```

If you are unsure what kinds of table types your database supports, you can list them with SQLTableTypeNames.

```
SQLTableTypeNames[conn]
{TABLE, VIEW, LOCAL TEMPORARY}
```

SQLColumnNames provides similar functionality. Here you can restrict columns to a particular table or columns in a table that match a pattern.

```
SQLColumnNames[conn]
{{data1, key}, {data1, x1}, {data1, x2}, {data1, x3},
 {data2, akey}, {data2, avalue}, {data1view100, key},
 {data1view100, x1}, {data1view100, x2}, {data1view100, x3}}
```

```
SQLColumnNames[conn, "data_"]
{{data1, key}, {data1, x1}, {data1, x2},
 {data1, x3}, {data2, akey}, {data2, avalue}}
```

```
SQLColumnNames[conn, {"data_", "x_"}]
{{data1, x1}, {data1, x2}, {data1, x3}}
```

See Also

Detailed discussion of descriptive commands can be found in *DatabaseLink/tutorial/TableStructure* and *DatabaseLink/tutorial/ColumnStructure* in the Mathematica documentation.

CHAPTER 18

Tricks of the Trade

Meine tricks
Don't know what I would do without
Tricks yeah yeah
Gimme tricks
Ihr wisst ich bin alleine ohne meine meine
Tricks yeah
That's the only reason my heart still ticks
Vishnu, Batu, Fu Manchu too
Hu-Hu, Jonny Manushutu
Dr. Wu, Peggy Sue
Randy Andy too
One thing in common when they get up to their tricks
They do it for kicks
So if you ever see me acting
Like a kid from outer space
And you think of lending a hand
But if you look real close
You'll see a smile on my face
Then I'm sure you'll understand

Falco, "Tricks"

18.0 Introduction

This chapter's recipes consist of Mathematica techniques and capabilities that every serious user should have in their tool box. Unlike other chapters, the recipes here are not tied together by any one theme. I include them because each recipe will give you some deeper insight into details that are unique to the Mathematica architecture. Each recipe has been a lifesaver to me at various times, and I hope that one or more of them will be helpful to you.

18.1 Cleaning Up During Incremental Development

Problem

You are solving a problem by incremental refinement of a set of functions. As you proceed to refactor and introduce alternative definitions for symbols, you find that code that was working before mysteriously breaks.

Solution

Make judicious use of Clear before every group of functions that are still undergoing development. First, I illustrate what can go wrong if you are sloppy. Suppose you define this function f.

```
f[x_Integer] := x^2;
```

Later, you decide that you should be more general about the valid types for argument x and also realize you really meant to compute x^2 +1, so you change the line to this (deleting the previous line from the notebook):

```
f[x_?NumericQ] := x^2 + 1
```

Later (possibly after you have forgotten the old version even existed), you try out your code and are surprised by the result.

```
f[2]
4
```

To avoid problems like this, you should clear old definitions before defining a function. Then you can redefine f to your heart's content without worrying that old definitions will interfere.

```
Clear[f]
f[x_?NumericQ] := x^2 + 1
```

Discussion

Developers coming from other programming environments easily fall into the trap caused by the fact that the kernel holds all definitions created during a session unless they are specifically cleared or exactly redefined. This is not the expected behavior of languages that are compiled or interpreted, since in those environments old definitions do not persist. The solution shows one way problems can arise, but there are others. It is just as likely that conflicts can come from other notebooks that are sharing the same kernel instance. Many Mathematica veterans begin their notebooks with an expression to clear every symbol in the global context (a context is similar to what other languages call *namespaces*).

```
Clear["Global`*"]
```

The Global` context is the default context in which new symbols are defined.

You can also clear the command history. This is useful for freeing memory. Consider the following example.

```
In[192]:= MemoryInUse[]
Out[192]= 132430904
```

Let's use a lot of memory.

```
In[193]:= x = Array[f, {1000, 1000}];
          MemoryInUse[]
Out[194]= 188470896
```

Simply clearing x does not get the memory back because it is cached in the history.

```
In[196]:= Clear[x];
          MemoryInUse[]
Out[197]= 188473032
```

However, you can clear the In and Out history by unprotecting, clearing, and reprotecting In and Out.

```
In[198]:= Unprotect[In, Out];
          Clear[In, Out];
          Protect[In, Out];
          MemoryInUse[]
Out[201]= 132287208
```

See Also

Problems with name conflicts can also be mitigated by use of packages. See Recipe 18.4.

18.2 Modifying Built-in Functions and Constants

Problem

You want to extend or alter the meaning of intrinsic functions that are built in to Mathematica. Perhaps you want to introduce a mathematical object that has its own natural definitions for the standard operations Plus, Times, etc.

Solution

The most straightforward way to modify Mathematica operations is to unprotect them, augment their meaning, and protect them again. However, the easiest way is frequently not the best or safest way, so be sure not to skip the "Discussion" section.

It is common in certain applications to consider 0^0 to be defined as 1; however, Mathematica considers this expression to be indeterminate and will issue a warning when it evaluates it (hence, the use of Quiet here).

```
0^0 // Quiet
Indeterminate
```

You can change this behavior quite easily.

```
Unprotect[Power];
Power[0, 0] = 1;
Protect[Power];
0^0
1
```

This new behavior will persist only within the Mathematica kernel session and will be known to all notebooks associated with the notebook's kernel. See Recipe 18.9 for a way to make such changes automatically active each time you use Mathematica.

Discussion

The solution shows a reasonable change to the meaning of an intrinsic function. It is reasonable because it is unlikely to change the behavior of Mathematica in a detrimental way since you are simply supplying meaning to an expression that had no meaning. Technically speaking, it is possible that third-party code you are also using depended on Power[0,0] evaluating to indeterminate; however, this possibility is far-fetched. This is not the case for other seemingly reasonable changes. For example, you might be irked by the following result:

```
(-1) ^ (1 / 3) // N
0.5 + 0.866025 i
```

Clearly, an equally valid answer is -1. In fact, there are three valid answers. This is a question of which branch Mathematica takes by default.

```
Solve[x ^ 3 == -1, x] // N
{{x → -1.}, {x → 0.5 + 0.866025 i}, {x → 0.5 - 0.866025 i}}
```

To remedy this choice, you might decide to take matters into your own hands and force Mathematica to take a different branch whenever it needs to evaluate a rational power of a negative number.

```
Unprotect[Power];
Power[a_?Negative, n_Rational] = Exp[n Log[a] + n 2 Pi I];
Protect[Power];
(-1)^(1/3) // N
-1.
```

This has an unfortunate consequence if you want Solve to work as before!

```
Solve[x^3 == -1, x] // N
{{x → -1.}, {x → -1.}, {x → -1.}}
```

Quitting the kernel will revert to the old behavior.

```
Quit[]
Solve[x^3 == -1, x] // N
{{x → -1.}, {x → 0.5 + 0.866025 i}, {x → 0.5 - 0.866025 i}}
```

Sometimes you want to temporarily change the meaning of a symbol. In that case, use of Unprotect is overkill, and it is better to introduce the new value within a Block. For example, E is the built-in symbol for the base of the natural logarithm, but in this block we use E as hex digit 14.

```
Block[{A = 10, B = 11, C = 12, D = 13, E = 14, F = 15}, A * 16 + E]
174
```

This technique is often used to temporarily change special global variables like $RecursionLimit. The following is a recursive implementation of the Ackermann function that would easily overflow the default stack limit of 256. This is for illustration purposes and not a good way to implement Ackermann.

```
(*Ackermann function*)
Block[{$RecursionLimit = 100 000, A},
 A[0, n_] := n + 1; A[m_, 0] := A[m, 0] = A[m - 1, 1];
 A[m_, n_] := A[m, n] = A[m - 1, A[m, n - 1]]; A[4, 1]]
65 533
```

18.3 Locating Undocumented Functions

Problem

You are wondering what undocumented functions might be hiding in your current version of Mathematica.

Solution

Inspect the Developer` and Experimental` contexts for hidden treasures. Here, //Short is used only to reduce clutter, so remove that before evaluating.

```
In[891]:=  Names ["Developer`*"] // Short
Out[891]//Short=
```

$$\{\text{Developer`BesselSimplify}, \ll 69\gg, \text{Developer`\$SymbolSystemShadowing}\}$$

```
In[892]:=  Names ["Experimental`*"] // Short
Out[892]//Short=
```

$$\{\text{Experimental`AngleRange}, \ll 47\gg, \text{Experimental`Wait}\}$$

Discussion

Strictly speaking, the Developer` context is not entirely undocumented, but rather consists of low-level access to underlying algorithms that are typically used in the implementation of higher-level, built-in functions. Here is an example of such a function and its documentation. However, you can see that the documentation is much more sparse than that of a function available in standard System` context.

```
In[550]:=  ?? Developer`PartitionMap
```

PartitionMap[f, *list*, n] applies f to *list* after
    partitioning into non-overlapping sublists of length n.
PartitionMap[f, *list*, n, d] applies f to sublists
    obtained by partitioning with offset d.
PartitionMap[f, *list*, $\{n_1, n_2, ...\}$] applies f after partitioning
    a nested list into blocks of size $n_1 \times n_2 \times ...$.
PartitionMap[f, *list*, $\{n_1, n_2, ...\}$, $\{d_1, d_2, ...\}$] applies f
    after partitioning using offset d_i at level i.
PartitionMap[f, *list*, n, d, $\{k_L, k_R\}$] specifies where
    sublists should begin and end.
PartitionMap[f, *list*, n, d, $\{k_L, k_R\}$, *padding*] specifies
    what padding should be used. .≫

```
Attributes[Developer`PartitionMap] = {Protected}
```

In contrast, expect to find little information about functions in the Experimental` context.

```
In[558]:=  ?? Experimental`ShortestSupersequence
```

Experimental`ShortestSupersequence

```
Attributes[Experimental`ShortestSupersequence] = {Protected}

Options[Experimental`ShortestSupersequence] = {IgnoreCase → False}
```

Even if you manage to figure out how these functions work, there is no guarantee the functions won't change or be removed in a future version, so use them with caution. Sometimes an experimental function will tell you it has been deprecated and direct you to an alternative.

```
In[559]:= Experimental`FileBrowse[]
```

```
Experimental`FileBrowse::obs :
 Experimental`FileBrowse has been superseded by
     SystemDialogInput, and is now obsolete. It
     will not be included in Mathematica version 8.
```

See Also

PartitionMap was used in Recipe 2.6.

18.4 Packaging Your Mathematica Solutions into Libraries for Others to Use

Problem

You have a nice collection of functions that are of general use within your organization or perhaps as a library that you want to distribute to others.

Solution

Mathematica provides a facility for defining custom packages that place functions in a unique namespace and also allow you to selectively expose some functions while leaving other low-level details hidden.

```
BeginPackage["CoolStuff`"]

Unique`::usage = "Unique[list] removes duplicates from a list (similar to
Union) but does not reorder elements of the list."

Begin["`Private`"]

Unique[list_List] := Module[{once},
    once[x_] := once[x] = Sequence[];x
    once /@ list]

End[]

EndPackage[]
```

Discussion

The solution follows a standard convention where actual definitions are placed in a Private context (Begin["`Private`"] ... End[]) while the function is exposed by defining its usage string (Unique`::usage) in the public part of the package. Having the definition of Unique inside Private does not mean you can't access it. What it does mean is that any symbols introduced inside the definition of Unique will not be exported when the package is read in. The context Private` does not have any special semantics, but it is a convention used by most Mathematica package authors, and it would be wise to follow suit.

If a package depends on other packages, you can list the dependents as a second argument to BeginPackage. Here, CoolStuff` needs SuperCool` and Essential`.

```
BeginPackage["CoolStuff`", {"SuperCool`", "Essential`"}]
```

You can defer loading other packages until you know they are needed by using DeclarePackage. The syntax is DeclarePackage["context`", {"name1", "name2", ...}]. Here you are telling Mathematica to execute Needs["context`"] contingent on the use of one of the symbols name1, name2, and so on (typically functions or constants).

```
BeginPackage["CoolStuff`"]

Cool`::usage = "Cool[list] does something cool."
Cooler`::usage = "Cooler[list] does something even cooler."
ReallyRadCool`::usage = "ReallyRadCool[list]does something too cool for words."

(*If functions Cooler or ReallyRadCool are used, then execute
Needs["SuperCool`"].*)

DeclarePackage["SuperCool`", {"Cooler", "ReallyRadCool"}]

Begin["`Private`"]

Cool[list_List] := Module[{},
    (*...*)
    ]

Cooler[list_List] := Module[{x,y},
    (*... uses something in SuperCool` context.*)
    ]

ReallyRadCool[list_List] := Module[{elvis, jamesdean},
    (*... uses something in SuperCool` context ...
      If I show you, I'd have to kill you.*)
    ]

End[]

EndPackage[]
```

See Also

See the tutorial for setting up Mathematica packages: *http://bit.ly/8Q9WIq*.

Some good advice regarding the creation of packages can be found here in the Wolfram Research MathGroup Archive: *http://bit.ly/7rZ60P*.

It is also worth reading Michael A. Morrison's "Mathematica Tips, Tricks, and Techniques" (*http://bit.ly/5Z5dI9*), although this is less about creating packages and more about using them.

18.5 Compiling Functions to Improve Performance

Problem

You have a function that is called frequently and you want to optimize its performance.

Solution

In many cases, you can remove a significant amount of overhead from your functions by compiling them. You can compile functions that take Integer, Real, Complex, Boolean arguments (True | False), or uniform vectors and tensors of these types.

```
magnitude1[vector : {__Real}] := Sqrt[Plus @@ vector];
magnitude2 = Compile[{{vector, _Real, 1}}, Sqrt[Plus @@ vector]];

vec = RandomReal[{0, 10}, 1000000];
Timing[magnitude1[vec]]
{0.485, 2236.01}

Timing[magnitude2[vec]]
{0.187, 2236.01}
```

Discussion

The syntax of Compile can be a bit confusing at first because it does not follow the traditional pattern-based syntax of an uncompiled function. This is partly due to the fact that Compile is far less flexible, and each argument must be entirely unambiguous in regard to its type. First note that Compile takes a list of argument specifications and that each argument specification is itself a list. The argument specifications must at minimum specify the argument name, but can also specify the type and the rank—if the argument is a vector (rank = 1), matrix (rank = 2), or tensor (rank > 2).

Table 18-1. Example argument specifications for compile

Argument specification	Description
{x}	x is some numeric type
{x, _Integer}	x is an Integer
{x, _Real}	x is a Real
{x, _Integer, 1}	x is a vector of Integers
{x, _Complex, 2}	x is a matrix of Complex
{x, _Real, 5}	x is a rank 5 tensor of Reals
{x, True	False, 1}	x is a vector of logical values

Note that functions that take strings or general symbolic arguments cannot be compiled. Also, if you specify a rank of two or higher, you must pass uniform arrays of the appropriate rank rather than jagged arrays (like {{1,2},{3}}), and you can't mix types in vectors or higher-ranked tensors. If you violate these constraints, the function may still work, but Mathematica will use an uncompiled form, which defeats the advantage of compilation.

18.6 Automating and Standardizing the Appearance of Notebooks Using Stylesheets

Problem

You find yourself frequently needing to tweak formatting in your notebook or you find formatting tedious. You may be frustrated that your notebooks do not have the professional appearance of your peers' or of notebooks you see at conferences or download from the Web.

Solution

Creating a basic stylesheet or modifying an existing stylesheet is easier than you might think, although there are some aspects that are tricky (or nearly impossible to figure out without help). The easiest way to proceed is to start with a built-in style. Starting with a new notebook, select Format, Stylesheet and select a style from one of the submenus. Figure 18-1 shows a notebook configured with the NaturalColor stylesheet, which is under the Creative submenu in Stylesheets.

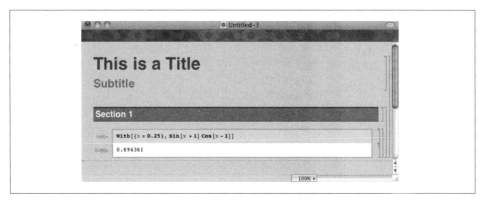

Figure 18-1. A notebook using the built-in Mathematica 7 stylesheet

Once you have a stylesheet selected that is close to how you want your notebook to look, you can customize it by selecting the Format, Edit Stylesheet menu. This will launch a special stylesheet notebook, shown in Figure 18-2. To modify an existing style, use the "Choose a style" drop-down menu. This will add a cell to the notebook that is styled in the selected style. By altering the style elements of this cell (using the Format menu), you update the stylesheet so this style now is associated with the style of the cell. Think of this as styling by example, which is a bit different than how stylesheets work in most word processors and certainly different than Cascading Style Sheets (*CSS*) used in web pages, but simple enough. You can also add a new style. In Figure 18-2, I add a style called Warning and give it a red font with gray background. New styles are added by typing their names in the "Enter a style" edit box and hitting Enter.

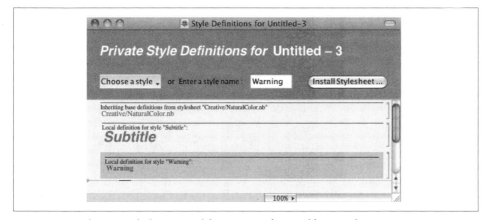

Figure 18-2. Editing a stylesheet to modify existing styles or add new styles

Discussion

Often when creating a new style you want to base it on an existing style. This inheritance of style attributes is a powerful capability because it reduces the effort for specifying a style and allows changes to the base style to automatically propagate to the derived. Creating derived styles involves getting your hands a bit dirty since you need to drill down into the underlying syntax of the stylesheet cells. As an example, imagine you want to create a base style called Note and a derived style called Warning. The intent is to use Note to provide some extra parenthetical information. Warning should derive from Note, but have a red font to emphasize that the extra information is cautionary.

When you select a cell (or cells) in a stylesheet and use Ctrl-Shift-E (or Command-Shift-E on Mac) you convert the cell to expression form, as shown in Figure 18-3. Here I show two cells that have been changed to expression form. The first cell defines the general properties I want to have for a note, including a special margin, bold font, and gray background. I'll discuss MenuPosition later.

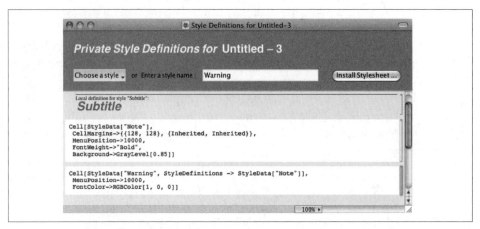

Figure 18-3. Editing style option in expression form

For now, consider the second style cell. Note in particular the expression for Style-Data. Here, in addition to the style's name, there is a rule StyleDefinitions, which indicates the base style is "Note". This is what you must type by hand to link a new style to its base since there is presently no other way to establish this relationship. Once the relationship is established, the Warning style will inherit all the attributes of Note but will be able to override or augment them. Here you can see that I augment Warning to use a red font. Once the inheritance is defined, you can revert the style cells back to their normal form (Ctrl-Shift-E again) since most other changes can be affected using the Format.

When you create new styles, they are integrated into the frontend menus (Format, Style) as well as the window's toolbar (assuming you show the toolbar; see Window, Show Toolbar). The position of the style within the choices is governed by the Menu-Position option in the stylesheet cell (Figure 18-3). You can set this value to whatever number you want, but a sensible scheme is to use either 1 or 10000 (the default). If you choose 1, the style will sort alphabetically within all styles that have the value 1. If you choose 10000, the style will appear after all styles with position 1, but again, sorted alphabetically. This sets up two groups, one for native styles (MenuPosition→1) and the other for custom styles (MenuPosition→10000). If you would like multiple groupings, use an intermediate value (like 5000), but don't attempt to assign a unique value to every style because this is not the intention of the option and will create maintenance headaches for your stylesheet.

There are a few style settings that are tricky to set up. One in particular is a numbered style for a heading. Here you typically desire a series of headings and subheadings with a hierarchical numbering system. The NaturalColor stylesheet has styles called ItemNumbered and SubitemNumbered, so let's look at these styles in expression form (Figure 18-4).

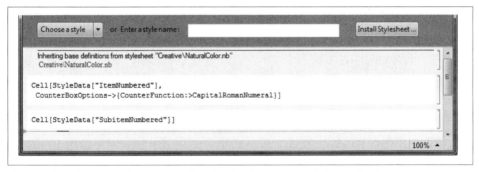

Figure 18-4. Expression form for numbered styles does not reveal the numbering options

Do you see anything that would indicate that these styles have some auto-numbering capability? No? Me either. These settings are magical. You need to select the cell and invoke the options inspector. Let's revert to normal cell form (important!) and use Ctrl-Shift-O to inspect options for ItemNumbered. Figure 18-5 shows how the item counters are maintained and Figure 18-6 shows how the displayed output is generated. These options are not visible in the stylesheet because they are inherited from the Default stylesheet. You can learn a great deal about Mathematica's stylesheet capabilities by studying the Default stylesheet, which is located in $InstallationDirectory <> "/SystemFiles/FrontEnd/StyleSheets/Default.nb". Default itself inherits from Core, so you should inspect that as well. You should avoid changing either Core or Default; rather, customize your own stylesheet based on these, as explained in the "Solution" section on page 728.

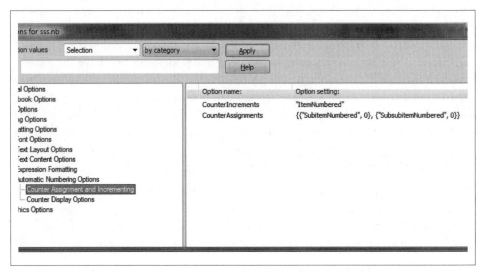

Figure 18-5. Options inspector for ItemNumbered *reveals numbering settings*

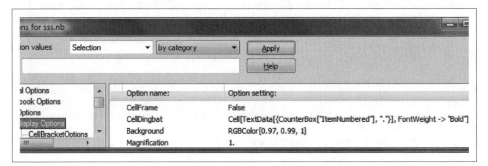

Figure 18-6. The CellDingbat option controls how the number is generated into the output

Armed with this information, you can create your own numbered styles.

1- This is h1 style.

1-1. This is h2 style.

1-1-1 This is h3 style.

18.7 Transforming Notebooks into Other Forms

Problem

You want to extract content from notebooks to create other kinds of documents that Mathematica does not support as a straight export. You may also want to extract information from notebooks for other purposes.

Solution

Like everything in Mathematica, notebooks are expressions and can be manipulated using the powerful expression manipulation facilities of Mathematica. Here is an example that takes a chapter of *Mathematica Cookbook* and creates a recipe cross-reference to native Mathematica symbols (those in the System` package).

```
In[518]:= crossRef[{_, code__}, {recipe_}] :=
            {StringJoin[ToString /@ {chapter, ".", recipe - 1}],
             Intersection[native, Cases[{code}, _String, Infinity]]}


          crossRefCookbookChapter[ch_Integer, path_String] :=
          Module[{nb},
            nb = NotebookOpen[path, Visible → False];
            crossRefCookbookChapter[ch, NotebookGet[nb]]]


          crossRefCookbookChapter[ch_Integer, nb_Notebook] :=
          Block[{native, chapter, cells, recipes, recipe = 0},
            chapter = ch;
            native = ToString /@ Names["System`*"];
            cells = Cases[nb, Cell[_, "Heading1" | "Input", __], Infinity];
            recipes = GatherBy[cells, Function[cell,
                If[MatchQ[cell, Cell[_, "Heading1", __]], ++recipe, recipe]]];
            MapIndexed[crossRef, recipes]
          ]
```

Here I run the transformation against Chapter 5's notebook.

```
In[521]:= crossRefCookbookChapter[5, NotebookDirectory[] <> "Strings.nb"]
```

```
Out[521]= {{5.0, {CharacterEncoding, FromCharacterCode,
         IgnoreCase, Input, NumberString, Partition, StringMatchQ,
         TableForm, ToCharacterCode, ToString, True, $CharacterEncoding,
         $CharacterEncodings, $SystemCharacterEncoding}}, {5.1,
         {Greater, GreaterEqual, Input, Less, LessEqual, Order, Protect, Unprotect}},
      {5.2, {Block, DateList, DatePattern, DatePlus, DateString,
         Except, FileNameJoin, IgnoreCase, Import, Input, InputForm, N,
         NotebookDirectory, NumberString, RegularExpression, Riffle, Shortest,
         ShortestMatch, StringCases, StringDrop, StringJoin, StringReplace,
         StringReplacePart, ToExpression, ToString, True, Whitespace}},
      {5.3, {All, Except, False, IgnoreCase, Input, Overlaps,
         RegularExpression, Repeated, Return, Shortest, StringCases,
         StringJoin, StringTake, TableForm, True, WordBoundary}},
      {5.4, {Array, Ceiling, Clear, Input, InputForm, Log, Mean,
         Nest, StringJoin, StringTake, Table, Timing}},
      {5.5, {DatePattern, False, FileNameJoin, FromDigits, Import,
         Input, Length, NotebookDirectory, NumberString, OddQ,
         Overlaps, Pick, Range, RegularExpression, SpellingCorrection,
         StringDrop, StringFreeQ, StringMatchQ, StringPosition,
         StringTake, TableForm, Transpose, True, With}},
      {5.6, {Blue, Bold, Brown, Except, FileNameJoin, FontColor,
         FontSlant, FontWeight, Import, Input, Italic, NotebookDirectory,
         Red, Row, StringSplit, Style, WhitespaceCharacter}},
      {5.7, {And, Block, Characters, Complement, DictionaryLookup,
         DistanceFunction, EditDistance, False, If, IgnoreCase, Input,
         Intersection, MapThread, MemberQ, Module, Nearest, SameTest, StringCount,
         StringReplace, StringReverse, Tally, Timing, True, WordData}},
      {5.8, {Apply, Cases, FileNameJoin, Head, ImageSize, Import,
         Infinity, Input, InputForm, List, NotebookDirectory,
         Symbol, TableForm, TreeForm, XMLElement, XMLObject}},
      {5.9, {Apply, Cases, ExportString, FileNameJoin, If, Import, Infinity,
         Input, Join, List, MatrixForm, NotebookDirectory, NumberString,
         Rule, StringMatchQ, StringReplace, ToExpression, XMLElement}},
      {5.10, {ClearAll, ExportString, FileNameJoin, Import, Input, List,
         Module, NotebookDirectory, Order, Rule, Sort, Split, StringJoin,
         StringReplace, ToExpression, ToString, XMLElement, XMLObject}},
      {5.11, {Append, Apply, Ceiling, Drop, First, Flatten, FoldList, Format,
         Hold, HoldAll, If, ImageSize, Infinity, Input, InputForm, Last, Length,
         List, Map, MemberQ, Module, N, Plus, RandomInteger, RandomReal, Rest,
         SeedRandom, SetAttributes, StringJoin, StringReplacePart, StringTake,
         Table, TableForm, Top, ToString, ToUpperCase, TreeForm, Union, While}}}
```

Discussion

The easiest way to get a notebook into another form is to leverage the conversions built into Save As. As of Mathematica 7, you can save a notebook as PDF, XHTML + MathML, plain text, Rich Text Format (RTF), and PostScript. However, if these formats are not what you're after, you should not be afraid to take matters into your own hands as I did in the solution.

The command NotebookOpen is used to load the notebook from disk and produce a NotebookObject. You use the option Visible → False to prevent the notebook from being opened in a new window. NotebookGet is applied to the NotebookObject to return the raw symbolic form of the notebook for manipulation. Here the bulk of the work is done by the second version of crossRefCookbookChapter. Cases is used to parse out Cell expressions with the style Heading1 or Input. The Heading1 cells represent the recipe titles, and the Input cells are the ones you want to cross reference. GatherBy groups input cells with their associated recipes, and then MapIndexed processes each recipe using the index and the chapter number to generate the recipe number. The mapped function, crossRef, extracts strings and uses Intersection to locate just those strings that are in the set of native System` symbols.

One of the handiest uses of notebook manipulation is to create small bulk conversion utilities. For example, imagine you had a large number of notebooks and you needed to change one style into another. This would be tedious to do by hand, but is a breeze with Mathematica. The converter would look something like this.

```
In[541]:= Clear[convertStyle];
          convertStyle[path_String, saveAs_String, fromStyle_String,
            toStyle_String] := Module[{}, NotebookSave[convertStyle[
              NotebookOpen[path, Visible → False], fromStyle, toStyle], saveAs]]

          convertStyle[nb_NotebookObject,
            fromStyle_String, toStyle_String] := Module[{},
          NotebookPut[NotebookGet[nb] /.
              Cell[c_, fromStyle, o___] :> Cell[c, toStyle, o], nb]]
```

Here I introduce NotebookPut and NotebookSave, which are used to modify the original notebook object and save it back to disk, respectively. Here is an example of usage:

```
In[543]:= convertStyle[NotebookDirectory[] <> "TestStyleConvert.nb",
          NotebookDirectory[] <> "TestStyleConvertOut.nb", "Section", "Subsection"]
```

See Also

Advanced notebook manipulations often require that you convert between strings, boxes, and expressions. See the *tutorial/ConvertingBetweenStringsBoxesAndExpressions* in the Mathematica documentation for details.

18.8 Calling into the Mathematica Frontend

Problem

You want to programmatically invoke functionality that is provided by the frontend rather than the kernel.

Solution

There are certain operations that are executed by the Mathematica frontend rather than the kernel. If you are running a program from the frontend, you generally don't need to worry about the distinction, because Mathematica is designed to make the distinction appear seamless. However, you can bypass the kernel when using the frontend with FrontEndExecute.

```
In[2]:= FrontEndExecute[
            FrontEnd`CellPrint[Cell["No Help From Kernel", "Emphasis"]]]
```

No Help From Kernel

You can also invoke actions typically performed via interaction with the frontend's menu. For example, the following will open the Font dialog.

```
In[5]:= FrontEndExecute[FrontEndToken["FontPanel"]]
```

Whereas FrontEndExecute is intended to be used in the frontend, UsingFrontEnd is intended to be executed from a kernel session to allow the kernel to invoke an operation in the frontend. The output here was created by executing the kernel directly on the command line.

```
In[1]:= nb = UsingFrontEnd[NotebookCreate[]]

Out[1]= -NotebookObject-
```

Note that a frontend must be installed on the system for this to work.

Discussion

You can see all the commands that can be executed directly in the frontend by executing

```
Names["FrontEnd`*"]
```

Sometimes you want to invoke features in the frontend that are not available via functions. For example, while doing some notebook manipulations a la Recipe 18.7, you wish to get the functionality available by selecting a cell and using CopyAs, Plain Text. You can do this like so:

```
In[885]:=  someCell = Cell[
              BoxData[RowBox[{"N", "[", FractionBox["1", "9999"], "]"}]], "Input"];
           First[MathLink`CallFrontEnd[
             FrontEnd`ExportPacket[someCell, "PlainText"]]]
Out[886]=  N[1/9999]
```

See Also

See the tutorial *ExecutingNotebookCommandsDirectlyInTheFrontEnd* for more details on frontend execution.

See *guide/FrontEndTokens* for tokens that can be used with `FrontEndToken` or `FrontEndTokenExecute`.

Also consult *tutorial/ManipulatingTheFrontEndFromTheKernel* for further commands useful for controlling the frontend from the kernel.

18.9 Initializing and Cleaning Up Automatically

Problem

You want to automatically execute code whenever the kernel or frontend starts. You may also want to execute code when the kernel is terminated.

Solution

There are several *init.m* files in which you can place function definitions or code you want executed automatically.

To execute code on kernel start for every user, modify the file given by

```
In[865]:=  ToFileName[{$BaseDirectory, "Kernel"}, "init.m"]
Out[865]=  /Library/Mathematica/Kernel/init.m
```

To execute code on kernel start for the currently logged-in user, modify the file given by

```
In[866]:= ToFileName[{$UserBaseDirectory, "Kernel"}, "init.m"]
Out[866]= /Users/smangano/Library/Mathematica/Kernel/init.m
```

To execute code on frontend start for every user, modify the file given by

```
In[867]:= ToFileName[{$BaseDirectory, "FrontEnd"}, "init.m"]
Out[867]= /Library/Mathematica/FrontEnd/init.m
```

To execute code on frontend start for the currently logged-in user, modify the file given by

```
In[868]:= ToFileName[{$UserBaseDirectory, "FrontEnd"}, "init.m"]
Out[868]= /Users/smangano/Library/Mathematica/FrontEnd/init.m
```

Clearly the results will vary depending on your particular OS.

Within these files, you can also modify the variable $Epilog to define code that executes right before the kernel exits.

Discussion

If you make frequent use of some utility functions or constants, you can make sure they are always available in every session. For example, if you always use a package called Essential`, you can add Needs["Essential`"] to the user-level version of *init.m* for the kernel.

Note that user-level initializations come after system-wide ones, so if you want to override some system-level definition, you can do so.

See Also

Recipe 18.10 shows a use case for *init.m* and $Epilog.

See *ref/file/init.m* in the Mathematica documentation for more information.

18.10 Customizing Frontend User Interaction

Problem

You want to hook into the processing performed by the frontend as you type and evaluate expressions.

Solution

You can intercept Mathematica's message loop at various stages by defining functions for $PreRead, $Pre, $Post, $PrePrint, and $SyntaxHandler. For example, as an educator, you might want to study students' experiences with learning Mathematica and log their interactions to a file. Here you can define $PreRead, which intercepts input before being fed to Mathematica; $SyntaxHandler, which is applied to lines with syntax errors; and $PrePrint, which gets the results before printing.

```
In[830]:= InitializeStudentMonitoring[] :=
            Module[{logFile, stream},
              logFile = $UserName <> DateString[{"Year", "", "Month", "", "Day",
                  "-", "Hour24", "", "Minute", "", "SecondExact"}] <> ".log";
              stream = OpenWrite[logFile] ;
              $PreRead = (Write[stream, "Input> ", #]; #) &;
              $PrePrint = (Write[stream, "Output> ", #]; #) &;
              $SyntaxHandler = (Write[stream, "Syntax:", #2, "> ", #1]; $Failed) &;
              stream
            ]

In[845]:= StopStudentMonitoring[stream_] := Module[{},
              $PreRead =.;
              $PrePrint =.;
              $SyntaxHandler =.;
              Close[stream]]
```

You can then place a call to InitializeStudentMonitoring[] in the *init.m* file and set delayed $Epilog to StopStudentMonitoring[Evaluate[stream]].

```
In[850]:= stream = InitializeStudentMonitoring[];
          $Epilog := StopStudentMonitoring[Evaluate[stream]]
```

Discussion

The solution shows a use case for capturing but not altering session input and output. However, you can also imagine advanced use cases where you want to use these hooks to do preprocessing or postprocessing. Here I use $PrePrint to force any string output into InputForm so I can see the quotes.

```
In[859]:=  $PrePrint = If[StringQ[#], InputForm[#], #] &;
```

```
In[860]:=  "SomeString"
Out[860]=  "SomeString"
```

Now revert to default behavior.

```
In[863]:=  $PrePrint =.
```

```
In[864]:=  "SomeString"
Out[864]=  SomeString
```

See Also

See the tutorial *tutorial/TheMainLoop* for more information.

CHAPTER 19

Debugging and Testing

Trying hard to speak and
Fighting with my weak hand
Driven to distraction
So part of the plan
When something is broken
And you try to fix it
Trying to repair it
Any way you can
I'm diving off the deep end
You become my best friend
I wanna love you
But I don't know if I can
I know something is broken
And I'm trying to fix it
Trying to repair it
Any way I can

Coldplay, "X&Y"

19.0 Introduction

Debugging and testing are not as romantic as solving a difficult partial differential equation, creating a breathtaking plot, or achieving a compelling interactive demonstration of a complicated mathematical concept. But, to loosely paraphrase Edison, Mathematica creation is often 10% coding and 90% debugging and testing. Mathematica's interactive development paradigm encourages incremental development, so often you proceed to solve a complex problem by writing little pieces, trying them, tweaking them, and repeating. In time, you will find yourself with quite a bit of code. Then, quite satisfied with yourself, you begin to feed your code real-world data and—bam!—something goes awry. Now what? Recipes 19.1 through 19.6 demonstrate various debugging techniques that you can use from within the traditional Mathematica frontend. Recipe 19.7 shows you how to use the powerful symbolic debugger provide by Wolfram Workbench.

Debugging skills are essential, but here frustration can begin to creep in. Mathematica code can often be difficult to debug, and if you've written a lot of it in a haphazard fashion, you might have your work cut out for you. There are two complementary techniques for maintaining your sanity when working with Mathematica on large projects. The first is knowing how to isolate the problem through debugging techniques, and the second is not getting into the problem in the first place. Clearly, the second is preferable, but how is it achieved? As convenient as interactive development inside a notebook can be, it is often a trap. How thoroughly can you test a complex function by feeding it a few values? Not very thoroughly. The solution is to write repeatable unit tests. Why is that better? First, test-drive development (part of what software developers call an agile development methodology) encourages breaking problems into small, easily testable pieces. In its purest form, developers are encouraged to actually write the test before the code! Having a test suite acts as documentation for the use cases of your function and is a godsend if you decide to enhance your implementation, because you can quickly see if you have broken existing functionality. Recipes 19.8 through 19.10 show how to develop unit tests within Wolfram Workbench. Recipe 19.11 shows how to adapt the underlying MUnit framework that is integrated with Wolfram Workbench for use in the frontend.

This chapter's workhorse function for illustrating debugging techniques is the Ackermann function. This infamous function has a simple recursive definition, but its pathological behavior makes it convenient for illustrating various real-world debugging problems (like stack overflows).

```
A[0,n_] := n+1
A[m_,0] := A[m - 1, 1]
A[m_, n_] := A[m - 1, A[m, n - 1]]
```

Figure 19-1. Ackermann function

 The Mathematica frontend has a debugger built into the Evaluation menu. I do not discuss this debugger in this chapter. I left it out for several reasons. The main reason is that I never use it, and when I have attempted to use it, I have found the experience quite unsatisfying. My impression is that, at best, the frontend integrated debugger is a work in progress. See *ref/menuitem/DebuggerControls* for description of the debugger.

19.1 Printing as the First Recourse to Debugging

Problem

You can't understand why you are getting a particular result but suspect it is due to a false assumption or bug in an intermediate calculation whose value is not visible.

Solution

Injecting a strategically placed `Print` statement can often be the quickest path to debugging a small piece of code. Suppose you forgot or did not know Mathematica's convention for choosing branches in the `Power[x,y]` function (it prefers the principal value of $e^{y \log(x)}$).

```
In[1]:= x = -1;
        y = Power[x, 1/3];
        If[ y == -1, "expected", "not expected"]
Out[3]= not expected
```

Here is the same code with a `Print` inserted so the value of y can be inspected. You will often want to force numerical conversion using `N[]` when inserting `Print`; otherwise you would get the symbolic value (in this case -1^(1/3)), which is quite unhelpful.

```
In[4]:= x = -1;
        y = Power[x, 1/3]; Print[N[y]];
        If[ y == -1, "expected", "not expected"]
```

```
0.5 + 0.866025 i
```

```
Out[6]= not expected
```

Discussion

Anyone who has spent even a day programming has come across this obvious debugging technique, so it may seem hardly worth a whole recipe, but please read on. Sometimes, injecting `Print` into code is very inconvenient, especially if you code in tight function style with few intermediate values appearing in variables. The problem is that you can't inject `Print` into functional code because `Print` does not return a value. Consider if the code for the value y did not exist because it was in-lined.

```
In[7]:= x = -1;
        If[ Power[x, 1/3] == -1, "expected", "not expected"]
Out[8]= not expected
```

You can't wrap the call to Power in a Print because it would change the behavior of the expression, which is not what you want to do when you are already contending with bugs. For these situations, it is handy to whip up a functional version of Print, which I call fPrint. This saves you the trouble of introducing temporary variables for purposes of debugging, thus leaving less mess to clean up after you have diagnosed the problem.

```
In[9]:= fPrint[x__] := (Print[x]; x)
        x = -1;
        If[ fPrint[N[Power[x, 1 / 3]]] == -1, "expected", "not expected"]
```

```
0.5 + 0.866025 i
```

```
Out[11]= not expected
```

A possible problem that can lead to lost or gray hairs when debugging with Print is when it seems to print nothing. This can take you down the road to hell by misleading you into thinking your code must be taking a different branch. For example, it is easy to miss the empty print cell created by executing this code.

```
In[12]:= x = Sequence[];
        Print[x]
```

This is not as contrived as it may seem: there are bugs that arise from failure to consider the fact that a sequence might be null, for example, when you use Apply (@@) on an empty list.

```
In[14]:= myFunctionThatIsBrokenForEmptySeq[x___] := Total[x]
        If[myFunctionThatIsBrokenForEmptySeq @@ {} == 0,
         "zero", "not zero", "something completely different"]
```

```
Total::argt :
  Total called with 0 arguments; 1 or 2 arguments are expected.
  >>
```

```
Out[15]= "something completely different"
```

Here an error was generated, and the output was "something completely different" because the expression in the If was neither True nor False. Pretend it was not immediately obvious to you what was going on (after all, you clearly see that you called Total with one argument x). You decide to use Print to get to the bottom of it. Notice that introducing Print into this code requires the whole thing to be wrapped in parentheses (another common debugging pitfall).

```
In[16]:= myFunctionThatIsBrokenForEmptySeq[x___] := (Print[x]; Total[x])
         If[myFunctionThatIsBrokenForEmptySeq @@ {} == 0,
           "zero", "not zero", "something completely different"]
```

```
Total::argt :
 Total called with 0 arguments; 1 or 2 arguments are expected.
  >>
```

```
Out[17]= "something completely different"
```

If you were confused before, you are now totally befuddled! Here is where your own little functional fPrint can help, but you need to tweak it slightly to expose two common ghosts you might encounter in the wild.

```
In[18]:= Clear[fPrint];
         fPrint[] := (Print["NullSequence!!"]; Unevaluated[Sequence[]])
         fPrint[""] := (Print["NullString!!"]; "")
         fPrint[x_] := (Print[x]; x)
```

Now the problem is revealed, and you also side-stepped the parenthesis mistake.

```
In[22]:= myFunctionThatIsBrokenForEmptySeq[x___] := Total[fPrint[x]]
         If[myFunctionThatIsBrokenForEmptySeq @@ {} == 0,
           "zero", "not zero", "something completely different"]
```

```
NullSequence!!
```

```
Total::argt :
 Total called with 0 arguments; 1 or 2 arguments are expected.
  >>
```

```
Out[23]= "something completely different"
```

See Also

There are other output functions (PrintTemporary, CellPrint, and MessageDialog) that may be useful in certain debugging situations. See the documentation for these functions. I use PrintTemporary as part of the solution in Recipe 19.5.

19.2 Debugging Functions Called Many Times

Problem

You have a function that is invoked thousands of times, but only a few of the calls produce an unexpected result, and it is difficult to determine which invocations are causing the problem. Print is a poor choice because of the unreasonable amount of data that may get printed before you identify the issue.

Solution

Use the Reap-Sow combination discussed in Recipe 2.10 to capture the data so you can analyze it using pattern matching or plotting. For example, imagine you have a function called func that is returning unexpected negative values and you are trying to understand the arguments that lead up to negative results. Here I use a contrived function for sake of the example. You can write a little wrapper around the function like so.

```
In[24]:= func[a_, b_, c_, d_] := If[a + 16 < b + c , 1 - d, b + c]
         funcWrapper[args__] :=
         Module[{r}, r = func[args] ; If[r < 0, Sow[{args}]]; r]
         {result, {problem}} =
           Reap[Table[funcWrapper[a, b, c, d], {a, 10}, {b, 10}, {c, 10}, {d, 10}]];
```

You can now see that there are 90 sets of arguments that caused the negative condition. Furthermore, you have the exact problematic values captured in a variable and can use the values to debug the function using techniques presented in other recipes in this chapter.

```
In[27]:= Length[problem]
Out[27]= 90
```

Invoking the function on these problematic arguments is a cinch using @@@.

```
In[28]:= func @@@ problem
Out[28]= {-1, -2, -3, -4, -5, -6, -7, -8, -9, -1, -2, -3, -4, -5, -6, -7, -8, -9,
          -1, -2, -3, -4, -5, -6, -7, -8, -9, -1, -2, -3, -4, -5, -6, -7, -8, -9,
          -1, -2, -3, -4, -5, -6, -7, -8, -9, -1, -2, -3, -4, -5, -6, -7, -8, -9,
          -1, -2, -3, -4, -5, -6, -7, -8, -9, -1, -2, -3, -4, -5, -6, -7, -8, -9,
          -1, -2, -3, -4, -5, -6, -7, -8, -9, -1, -2, -3, -4, -5, -6, -7, -8, -9}
```

Discussion

Reap-Sow are a powerful debugging tool because they can direct debug data into an arbitrary number of channels. By *channel*, I refer to the capability of Sow to specify a tag as a second argument such that all instances of Sow with that tag collect data into a distinct list. For example, imagine you want to detect when func returns zero but want to segregate those arguments from the arguments that cause negative results.

```
In[29]:= funcWrapper[args__] := Module[{r}, r = func[args] ;
            Which[r < 0, Sow[{args}, negative], r == 0, Sow[{args}, zero], True, 0]; r]

In[30]:= {result, {{n}, {z}}} = Reap[Table[funcWrapper[a, b, c, d],
            {a, 10}, {b, 10}, {c, 10}, {d, 10}], {negative, zero}];
```

Now you can use these values as separate test sets to understand these distinct behaviors.

```
In[31]:= func @@@ n
Out[31]= {-1, -2, -3, -4, -5, -6, -7, -8, -9, -1, -2, -3, -4, -5, -6, -7, -8, -9,
          -1, -2, -3, -4, -5, -6, -7, -8, -9, -1, -2, -3, -4, -5, -6, -7, -8, -9,
          -1, -2, -3, -4, -5, -6, -7, -8, -9, -1, -2, -3, -4, -5, -6, -7, -8, -9,
          -1, -2, -3, -4, -5, -6, -7, -8, -9, -1, -2, -3, -4, -5, -6, -7, -8, -9,
          -1, -2, -3, -4, -5, -6, -7, -8, -9, -1, -2, -3, -4, -5, -6, -7, -8, -9}

In[32]:= func @@@ z
Out[32]= {0, 0, 0, 0, 0, 0, 0, 0, 0, 0, 0}
```

See Also

Recipe 19.6 shows another common application of Reap-Sow in the debugging of built-in numerical algorithms or plotting functions.

Recipe 19.3 shows how to use Reap-Sow to take Stack snapshots.

19.3 Stack Tracing to Debug Recursive Functions

Problem

You have a recursive function that is unexpectedly violating $RecursionLimit and generating an error. Alternatively, you have a complex function with many function calls and you want to understand the sequence of calls that leads up to an error condition or erroneous value.

Solution

Use Stack[] to output a stack trace. Here I use Ackermann's function to illustrate the use of Stack because it will easily violate any sane recursion limit. Further, I create a function that will detect stack overflow before it happens and Throw the stack to caller. Specifically, I throw those expressions on the stack that match the function of interest by using Stack[A].

```
In[33]:= debugStack[] :=
            If[Length[Stack[]] + 1 ≥ $RecursionLimit, Throw[Stack[A]]];
          A[0, n_] := n + 1
          A[m_, 0] := (debugStack[]; A[m - 1, 1])
          A[m_, n_] := (debugStack[]; A[m - 1, A[m, n - 1]])
In[37]:= Catch[Block[{$RecursionLimit = 30}, A[4, 1]]]
Out[37]= {A[4 - 1, A[4, 1 - 1]], A[2 - 1, A[2, 5 - 1]],
           A[2 - 1, A[2, 4 - 1]], A[1 - 1, A[1, 7 - 1]],
           A[1 - 1, A[1, 6 - 1]], A[1 - 1, A[1, 5 - 1]], A[1 - 1, A[1, 4 - 1]],
           A[1 - 1, A[1, 3 - 1]], A[1 - 1, A[1, 2 - 1]], A[1 - 1, A[1, 1 - 1]]}
```

Discussion

If you want to take multiple snapshots of the stack during the progression of the function, regardless whether it overflows or not, you can use Reap-Sow.

```
In[38]:= Clear[f]

In[39]:= f[0] := Module[{}, Sow[Stack[Times]]; 1]
          f[x_] := Module[{}, Sow[Stack[Times]]; x * f[x - 1]]

In[41]:= Reap[f[3]]
Out[41]= {6, {{{}, {3 f[3 - 1]},
               {3 f[3 - 1], 2 f[2 - 1]}, {3 f[3 - 1], 2 f[2 - 1], 1 f[1 - 1]}}}}

Out[44]= {6, {{{}, {3 f[3 - 1]},
               {3 f[3 - 1], 2 f[2 - 1]}, {3 f[3 - 1], 2 f[2 - 1], 1 f[1 - 1]}}}}

Out[189]= {6, {{{}, {3 f[3 - 1]},
               {3 f[3 - 1], 2 f[2 - 1]}, {3 f[3 - 1], 2 f[2 - 1], 1 f[1 - 1]}}}}
           {6, {{{}, {3 f[3 - 1]},
               {3 f[3 - 1], 2 f[2 - 1]}, {3 f[3 - 1], 2 f[2 - 1], 1 f[1 - 1]}}}}
```

See Also

`StackInhibit` can be used to keep certain expressions from showing up in the evaluation stack. It can be helpful to insert this function into your code to control the amount of information in the stack. I use this function as part of Recipe 19.5.

19.4 Taming Trace to Extract Useful Debugging Information

Problem

`Trace` provides an extremely detailed account of the evaluation of an expression; however, for all but the most trivial expressions, this voluminous detail can be difficult to wade through.

Solution

Again, I use the Ackermann function to illustrate the issue, although this problem is not particular to recursive functions. Ackermann is convenient because it creates a large number of nested function calls and intermediate expressions. In addition, I purposefully throw a monkey wrench into this function to simulate a bug: "bug". Real-world bugs don't come so nicely labeled (if only!) but the point here is that in a real-world debugging situation you are looking for a particular subexpression that looks fishy based on your knowledge of the intended computation.

```
In[42]:= A[0, n_]  := n + 1
         A[m_, 0]  := A[m - 1, 1]
         A[m_, 2]  := ( "bug"; A[m - 1, A[m, 1]] )
         A[m_, n_] := A[m - 1, A[m, n - 1]]
```

If you attempt to trace this buggy Ackermann on even relatively tame inputs, you will quickly generate a lot of output that anyone but the most seasoned Mathematica developer would have trouble deciphering. In essence, what you are seeing is an expansion of the call tree, and thus, the problem is not only the amount of output but the deeply nested structure of the output. You could easily miss the "bug" in this data, and even if you spot it, you might still have trouble understanding what led up to its occurrence.

```
In[46]:= trace = Trace[A[2, 3]]
Out[46]= {A[2, 3], A[2 - 1, A[2, 3 - 1]], {2 - 1, 1},
          {{3 - 1, 2}, A[2, 2], bug; A[2 - 1, A[2, 1]],
           {{2 - 1, 1}, {A[2, 1], A[2 - 1, A[2, 1 - 1]], {2 - 1, 1}, {{1 - 1, 0}, A[2, 0],
             A[2 - 1, 1], {2 - 1, 1}, A[1, 1], A[1 - 1, A[1, 1 - 1]], {1 - 1, 0},
             {{1 - 1, 0}, A[1, 0], A[1 - 1, 1], {1 - 1, 0}, A[0, 1], 1 + 1, 2},
             A[0, 2], 2 + 1, 3}, A[1, 3], A[1 - 1, A[1, 3 - 1]],
            {1 - 1, 0}, {{3 - 1, 2}, A[1, 2], bug; A[1 - 1, A[1, 1]],
             {{1 - 1, 0}, {A[1, 1], A[1 - 1, A[1, 1 - 1]], {1 - 1, 0},
               {{1 - 1, 0}, A[1, 0], A[1 - 1, 1], {1 - 1, 0}, A[0, 1], 1 + 1, 2},
               A[0, 2], 2 + 1, 3}, A[0, 3], 3 + 1, 4}, 4}, A[0, 4], 4 + 1, 5}, A[1, 5],
           A[1 - 1, A[1, 5 - 1]], {1 - 1, 0}, {{5 - 1, 4}, A[1, 4], A[1 - 1, A[1, 4 - 1]],
            {1 - 1, 0}, {{4 - 1, 3}, A[1, 3], A[1 - 1, A[1, 3 - 1]],
             {1 - 1, 0}, {{3 - 1, 2}, A[1, 2], bug; A[1 - 1, A[1, 1]],
              {{1 - 1, 0}, {A[1, 1], A[1 - 1, A[1, 1 - 1]], {1 - 1, 0},
                {{1 - 1, 0}, A[1, 0], A[1 - 1, 1], {1 - 1, 0}, A[0, 1], 1 + 1, 2},
                A[0, 2], 2 + 1, 3}, A[0, 3], 3 + 1, 4}, 4}, A[0, 4], 4 + 1, 5},
            A[0, 5], 5 + 1, 6}, A[0, 6], 6 + 1, 7}, 7}, A[1, 7],
          A[1 - 1, A[1, 7 - 1]], {1 - 1, 0}, {{7 - 1, 6},
          A[1, 6],
          A[1 - 1, A[1, 6 - 1]],
          {1 - 1, 0},
          {{6 - 1, 5}, A[1, 5], A[1 - 1, A[1, 5 - 1]], {1 - 1, 0},
           {{5 - 1, 4}, A[1, 4], A[1 - 1, A[1, 4 - 1]], {1 - 1, 0},
            {{4 - 1, 3}, A[1, 3], A[1 - 1, A[1, 3 - 1]], {1 - 1, 0},
             {{3 - 1, 2}, A[1, 2], bug; A[1 - 1, A[1, 1]], {{1 - 1, 0},
               {A[1, 1], A[1 - 1, A[1, 1 - 1]], {1 - 1, 0}, {{1 - 1, 0}, A[1, 0],
                 A[1 - 1, 1], {1 - 1, 0}, A[0, 1], 1 + 1, 2}, A[0, 2], 2 + 1, 3},
               A[0, 3], 3 + 1, 4}, 4}, A[0, 4], 4 + 1, 5}, A[0, 5], 5 + 1, 6},
           A[0, 6], 6 + 1, 7}, A[0, 7], 7 + 1, 8}, A[0, 8], 8 + 1, 9}
```

Using Depth, you can see that there are 13 levels in the expression output by Trace (although this is inflated by the existence of HoldForm, as I explain later). In a real-world use of Trace, you could easily encounter output with depth an order of magnitude larger and an overall output several orders of magnitude larger still.

```
In[47]:= Depth[trace]
Out[47]= 13
```

To understand this solution, be aware that all the intermediate expressions output by Trace are wrapped in HoldForm to prevent their evaluation (which would of course defeat the purpose of Trace). You can see this by using InputForm. I use Short to suppress repeating the mess of output from above.

```
In[48]:=  trace // InputForm // Short
Out[48]//Short=
         {HoldForm[A[2, 3]], HoldForm[A[2
            - 1, A[2, <<1>>]]], <<8>>, HoldForm[9]}
```

One way to get a handle on the output of Trace is to linearize it so you get a flat structure that presents the sequence of operations as they occur in time. This can be done by using what amounts to a preorder tree traversal.

```
In[49]:=  Clear[traverseTrace, traverseTrace1];
         traverseTrace[x_]  := Flatten[Reap[traverseTrace1[x]]]
         traverseTrace1[{}]  := Sequence[]
         traverseTrace1[x_List]  :=
           (traverseTrace1[First[x]]; traverseTrace1[Rest[x]])
         traverseTrace1[HoldForm[x_]]  := Sow[HoldForm[x]]
```

This still produces as much raw data, but its linear nature makes it easier to visualize and manipulate.

```
In[54]:=  timeSequence = traverseTrace[trace]
Out[54]=  {A[2, 3], A[2 - 1, A[2, 3 - 1]], 2 - 1, 1, 3 - 1, 2, A[2, 2], bug;
          A[2 - 1, A[2, 1]], 2 - 1, 1, A[2, 1], A[2 - 1, A[2, 1 - 1]], 2 - 1, 1, 1 - 1,
          0, A[2, 0], A[2 - 1, 1], 2 - 1, 1, A[1, 1], A[1 - 1, A[1, 1 - 1]], 1 - 1,
          0, 1 - 1, 0, A[1, 0], A[1 - 1, 1], 1 - 1, 0, A[0, 1], 1 + 1, 2, A[0, 2],
          2 + 1, 3, A[1, 3], A[1 - 1, A[1, 3 - 1]], 1 - 1, 0, 3 - 1, 2, A[1, 2], bug;
          A[1 - 1, A[1, 1]], 1 - 1, 0, A[1, 1], A[1 - 1, A[1, 1 - 1]], 1 - 1, 0,
          1 - 1, 0, A[1, 0], A[1 - 1, 1], 1 - 1, 0, A[0, 1], 1 + 1, 2, A[0, 2], 2 + 1,
          3, A[0, 3], 3 + 1, 4, 4, A[0, 4], 4 + 1, 5, A[1, 5], A[1 - 1, A[1, 5 - 1]],
          1 - 1, 0, 5 - 1, 4, A[1, 4], A[1 - 1, A[1, 4 - 1]], 1 - 1, 0, 4 - 1, 3, A[1, 3],
          A[1 - 1, A[1, 3 - 1]], 1 - 1, 0, 3 - 1, 2, A[1, 2], bug; A[1 - 1, A[1, 1]],
          1 - 1, 0, A[1, 1], A[1 - 1, A[1, 1 - 1]], 1 - 1, 0, 1 - 1, 0, A[1, 0],
          A[1 - 1, 1], 1 - 1, 0, A[0, 1], 1 + 1, 2, A[0, 2], 2 + 1, 3, A[0, 3], 3 + 1,
          4, 4, A[0, 4], 4 + 1, 5, A[0, 5], 5 + 1, 6, A[0, 6], 6 + 1, 7, 7, A[1, 7],
          A[1 - 1, A[1, 7 - 1]], 1 - 1, 0, 7 - 1, 6, A[1, 6], A[1 - 1, A[1, 6 - 1]],
          1 - 1, 0, 6 - 1, 5, A[1, 5], A[1 - 1, A[1, 5 - 1]], 1 - 1, 0, 5 - 1, 4, A[1, 4],
          A[1 - 1, A[1, 4 - 1]], 1 - 1, 0, 4 - 1, 3, A[1, 3], A[1 - 1, A[1, 3 - 1]],
          1 - 1, 0, 3 - 1, 2, A[1, 2], bug; A[1 - 1, A[1, 1]], 1 - 1, 0, A[1, 1],
          A[1 - 1, A[1, 1 - 1]], 1 - 1, 0, 1 - 1, 0, A[1, 0], A[1 - 1, 1], 1 - 1, 0,
          A[0, 1], 1 + 1, 2, A[0, 2], 2 + 1, 3, A[0, 3], 3 + 1, 4, 4, A[0, 4], 4 + 1, 5,
          A[0, 5], 5 + 1, 6, A[0, 6], 6 + 1, 7, A[0, 7], 7 + 1, 8, A[0, 8], 8 + 1, 9}
```

Discussion

Once you have linearized the output of Trace, you can easily extract segments of the execution history or use patterns to extract specific segments of interest.

```
In[55]:=  timeSequence[[5 ;; 18]] // InputForm
Out[55]//InputForm=
          {HoldForm[3 - 1], HoldForm[2], HoldForm[A[2, 2]],
          HoldForm[bug; A[2 - 1, A[2, 1]]], HoldForm[2 - 1], HoldForm[1],
          HoldForm[A[2, 1]], HoldForm[A[2 - 1, A[2, 1 - 1]]], HoldForm[2 - 1],
          HoldForm[1], HoldForm[1 - 1], HoldForm[0], HoldForm[A[2, 0]],
          HoldForm[A[2 - 1, 1]]}
```

Here I use ReplaceList to find every occurrence of a call to A where the first argument was 0, and then output the expression computed immediately before and immediately after.

```
In[56]:=  ReplaceList[timeSequence ,
            {___, a_, HoldForm[A[0, z_]], b_, ___} :> {a, HoldForm[A[0, z]], b}]
Out[56]=  {{0, A[0, 1], 1 + 1}, {2, A[0, 2], 2 + 1},
           {0, A[0, 1], 1 + 1}, {2, A[0, 2], 2 + 1}, {3, A[0, 3], 3 + 1},
           {4, A[0, 4], 4 + 1}, {0, A[0, 1], 1 + 1}, {2, A[0, 2], 2 + 1},
           {3, A[0, 3], 3 + 1}, {4, A[0, 4], 4 + 1}, {5, A[0, 5], 5 + 1},
           {6, A[0, 6], 6 + 1}, {0, A[0, 1], 1 + 1}, {2, A[0, 2], 2 + 1},
           {3, A[0, 3], 3 + 1}, {4, A[0, 4], 4 + 1}, {5, A[0, 5], 5 + 1},
           {6, A[0, 6], 6 + 1}, {7, A[0, 7], 7 + 1}, {8, A[0, 8], 8 + 1}}
```

More to the point, here I do the same with the pattern that is the proxy for the buggy behavior. This shows the expressions that preceded and followed the bug.

```
In[57]:=  ReplaceList[timeSequence ,
            {___, a_, HoldForm["bug"; z_], b_, ___} :> {a, HoldForm["bug"; z], b}]
Out[57]=  {{A[2, 2], bug; A[2 - 1, A[2, 1]], 2 - 1},
           {A[1, 2], bug; A[1 - 1, A[1, 1]], 1 - 1},
           {A[1, 2], bug; A[1 - 1, A[1, 1]], 1 - 1},
           {A[1, 2], bug; A[1 - 1, A[1, 1]], 1 - 1}}
```

Clearly, linearizing loses some information that was in the original output of Trace. What you lose is the information that says a certain bunch of subexpressions were triggered by some parent expression. But, the act of debugging (or indeed understanding any complex data set) is the act of suppressing extraneous information until you can identify the area where there was a problem. Then some strategically placed debug code or Print functions can often get you the rest of the way to the fix.

A very similar result to this solution can be obtained using a variation of Trace called TraceScan along with Reap-Sow. The difference is that this expression will include a bit more extraneous detail because it shows the evaluation of every symbol and constant. Here is an excerpt using Short.

```
In[58]:= Reap[TraceScan[Sow, A[2, 3]]][[2, 1]] // Short
Out[58]//Short=
        {A[2, 3], A, 2, 3, A[2 - 1, A[2, 3 - 1]], A, 2 - 1,
         Plus, 2, <<450>>, 7, 1, 8, A[0, 8], 8 + 1, Plus, 8, 1, 9}
```

See Also

Trace has advanced features I did not cover here. Refer to *tutorial/TracingEvaluation* in the Mathematica documentation for details as well as a description of the related functions TraceDialog and TracePrint.

19.5 Creating a Poor Man's Mathematica Debugger

Problem

You tried debugging using Print, but your program creates too much output too quickly and it is difficult to identify the issue. You want to have more control of the debugging process.

Solution

Mathematica has an alternative print command called PrintTemporary that inspired me to create a sort of interactive debugger. PrintTemporary works just like Print except after the evaluation is complete the output is automatically removed. Further, PrintTemporary returns a value that can be passed to the function NotebookDelete to delete the output at any time. You can get an idea of what PrintTemporary does by evaluating the following line:

```
In[59]:= PrintTemporary["test"]; Pause[2]
```

If you could inject debug code into your ill-behaved programs that used PrintTemporary and then paused until you took some action (like pressing a button), you could effectively step though the code with the embedded prints acting like breakpoints in a real debugger. This can be done using a relatively small amount of code.

```
In[60]:= pmDebuggerInit[] :=
           Module[{}, $pmStep = False; $pmStop = False; CellPrint[Dynamic[Row[
               {Button["Step", $pmStep = True], Button["Stop", $pmStop = True]}]]]]
           pmWait[x___, t_] := (While[$pmStep == False && $pmStop == False,
               Pause[$TimeUnit]]; If[$pmStop, Abort[]]; NotebookDelete[t]; x)
           pmPrint[] := Module[{t}, $pmStep = False;
             t = PrintTemporary["NullSequence!!"];
             pmWait[Unevaluated[Sequence[]], t]]
           pmPrint[""] := Module[{t}, $pmStep = False;
             t = PrintTemporary["NullString!!"]; pmWait["", t]]
           pmPrint[x__] := Module[{t}, $pmStep = False;
             t = PrintTemporary[x]; pmWait[x, t]]
```

I explain this code further in the following "Discussion" section. For now, let's just try it out. Here I use an instrumented version of the Ackermann function as a test example.

```
In[65]:=
           A[0, n_] := pmPrint[n + 1];
           A[m_, 0] := A[m - 1, 1];
           A[m_, n_] := A[m - 1, A[m, n - 1]];
           test[] := Module[{}, pmDebuggerInit[]; A[4, 1]]
```

Executing test[] creates the debugging controls.

```
In[85]:= test[]
```

Step | Stop

3

Discussion

The code in the solution contains two user functions, pmPrint and pmDebuggerInit. Function pmPrint has the same features as fPrint from Recipe 19.1, but it uses Print-Temporary rather than Print. Further, it calls a function pmWait, which loops and pauses until a Boolean variable becomes true. These variables are initialized in pmDebuggerInit and associated with buttons that are used to control progress of the debugging session.

Often when creating little utilities like this, it's fun to see how far you can extend them without going too far over the top. There are a few deficiencies in the solution's debugging techniques. First, if you insert multiple print statements, there is no way to know which one created output. Second, it would be nice if you did not always have to step one print at a time. Third, it might be nice if you can also dump the stack while the program is paused. It turns out that using a bit of cleverness can get you all this new functionality using roughly the same amount of code.

```mathematica
In[69]:= Clear[pmDebuggerInit, pmWait, pmPrint];
        pmDebuggerInit[] :=
         Module[{}, $pmStep = 1; $pmStop = Function[False]; $pmPrintCells = {};
          CellPrint[Dynamic[
            Row[{Button["Step", (NotebookDelete /@ $pmPrintCells; $pmStep = 1)],
              Button["Step 10", (NotebookDelete /@ $pmPrintCells; $pmStep = 10)],
              Button["Stack", $pmStop = Function[
                StackInhibit[PrependTo[$pmPrintCells, PrintTemporary[Stack[]]];
                 $pmStop = Function[False]; False]]],
              Button["Stack Detail", $pmStop = Function[StackInhibit[
                PrependTo[$pmPrintCells, PrintTemporary[Most[Stack[_]]]];
                 $pmStop = Function[False]; False]]]
              Button["Stop", $pmStop = Function[Abort[]]]}]]]]
        pmWait[x___] :=
         (While[$pmStep == 0 && $pmStop[] == False, Pause[$TimeUnit]]; x)
        pmPrint[x__, tag_: ""] :=
         Module[{}, StackInhibit[$pmStep--; PrependTo[$pmPrintCells,
           PrintTemporary[Row[{tag, x}, " "]]]; pmWait[x]]]
        pmPrint[tag_: ""] := Module[{}, $pmStep--; PrependTo[$pmPrintCells,
           PrintTemporary[Row[{tag, "NullSequence!!"}, " "]]]; pmWait[""]]

In[74]:= A[0, n_] := pmPrint[n + 1, "n+1="];
        A[m_, 0] := A[pmPrint[m - 1, "m-1="], 1];
        A[m_, n_] := A[m - 1, A[m, n - 1]];
        test[] := Module[{}, pmDebuggerInit[]; A[4, 1]]

In[95]:= test[]
```

Step	Step 10	Stack	Stack Detail	Stop

```
n+1= 2
```

The trick here is to convert $pmStep to a counter instead of a Boolean and $pmStop to a function that can be changed by the buttons to either Abort or Print the Stack. I also introduce a new variable to collect multiple temporary print cells and move their cleanup to the button press for Step or Step 10. Finally, the pmPrint is refactored to take an optional tag to display so you can distinguish one debug output from another.

See Also

Recipes 19.1, 19.3, and 19.4 cover some of the functions used in this recipe in more detail.

19.6 Debugging Built-In Functions with Evaluation and Step Monitors

Problem

You are using various black-box numerical algorithms like FindRoot, NDSolve, NIntegrate, and the like, and you are getting puzzling results. You would like to get under the covers to gain insight into what is going on.

Solution

A classic problem with FindRoot (which uses Newton's method by default) is the possibility of getting into a cycle. If you did not know about this possibility, you might be confused by the error message generated. Here I suppress the message using Quiet because I have purposefully cherry-picked a misbehaved function. FindRoot has an option EvaluationMonitor that lets you hook every call to the supplied function. Here you use Reap-Sow to capture these values for analysis. Note that you must use RuleDelayed (:>) rather than Rule (->) with EvaluationMonitor.

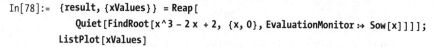

```
In[78]:=  {result, {xValues}} = Reap[
              Quiet[FindRoot[x^3 - 2 x + 2, {x, 0}, EvaluationMonitor :> Sow[x]]]];
          ListPlot[xValues]
```

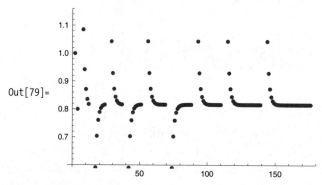

Out[79]=

Discussion

Sometimes a StepMonitor can also be useful for debugging. Whereas EvaluationMonitor shows each time a function is called, a StepMonitor is called only when the algorithm takes a successful step toward the solution. Stephen Wolfram explains the difference best:

> To take a successful step towards an answer, iterative numerical algorithms sometimes have to do several evaluations of the functions they have been given. Sometimes this is because each step requires, say, estimating a derivative from differences between function values, and sometimes it is because several attempts are needed to achieve a successful step.

In the solution example, StepMonitor is less informative than EvaluationMonitor.

```
In[80]:= {result, {xValues}} =
            Reap[Quiet[FindRoot[x^3 - 2 x + 2, {x, 0}, StepMonitor :> Sow[x]]]];
          xValues // InputForm
Out[81]//InputForm=
            {1., 0.8, 0.8178125000000002, 0.816037292480469, 0.8169240294396879,
            0.816480444471563, 0.8165081617635014, 0.8164943029060661,
            0.8164960352500287, 0.8164960352543595}
```

One reason you might use StepMonitor during debugging is to get a sense of how much computational effort an algorithm is expending to find a solution. One measure of effort would be the average number of function calls per step. Here you can see that the effort can vary widely for different algorithms and expressions.

```
In[82]:= Clear[x, y];
          Block[{stepCount = 0, callCount = 0},
            NDSolve[{y'[x] == y[x] Cos[x + y[x]], y[0] == 1},
            y, {x, 0, 30}, StepMonitor :> stepCount ++,
            EvaluationMonitor :> callCount ++]; N[callCount / stepCount]]
Out[83]= 2.14243

In[84]:= Clear[x, y];
          Block[{stepCount = 0, callCount = 0},
            NDSolve[{y'[x] == y[x] Cos[x + y[x]], y[0] == 1}, y, {x, 0, 30},
            Method -> "ExplicitRungeKutta", StepMonitor :> stepCount ++,
            EvaluationMonitor :> callCount ++]; N[callCount / stepCount]]
Out[85]= 16.039
```

```
In[86]:=  Clear[x, y];
          Block[{stepCount = 0, callCount = 0},
            NDSolve[{y'[x] == y[x] Cos[x + y[x]], y[0] == 1}, y,
              {x, 0, 30}, Method -> "Extrapolation", StepMonitor :> stepCount ++,
              EvaluationMonitor :> callCount ++]; N[callCount / stepCount]]
Out[87]=  49.25
```

See Also

Evaluation and StepMonitor are also useful outside a debugging context. For example, they can be used to visualize the behavior of an algorithm for educational purposes. See the Wolfram documentation for examples.

19.7 Visual Debugging with Wolfram Workbench

Problem

You are a Mathematica user longing for the kinds of visual debugging environments common in mainstream programming environments like Eclipse, Visual Studio, InteliJ, DDD, and others.

Solution

Use Wolfram Workbench, a Mathematica-specific extension to the Eclipse platform. When you launch Wolfram Workbench, you must first create a project. Use menu File, New, New Project. Give the project a name. I used the name Debugging for this example. Workbench automatically creates two files named after your project. In this example, I got a *Debugging.m* and a *Debugging.nb*. The *.m* file is where you would enter code that you want to debug. The *Debugging.nb* is a normal frontend notebook file. Here you would typically set up your test calls.

```
A[0,n_] := n+1
A[m_,0] := A[m - 1, 1]
A[m_, n_] := A[m - 1, A[m, n - 1]]
```

Figure 19-2. Debugging.m—functions being debugged

```
A[3,2]
```

Figure 19-3. Debugging.nb—place to exercise the functions to be debugged

Once you have these files set up, you can place a breakpoint by double-clicking on the left margin of the line of code you want the debugger to stop. In Figure 19-4 you see a dot appear in the margin to indicate the successful placement of the breakpoint. You can place as many breakpoints as necessary.

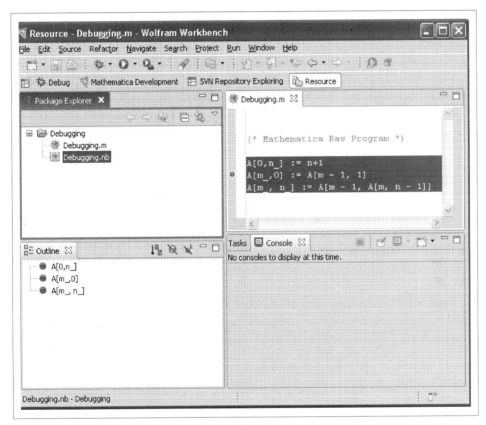

Figure 19-4. Wolfram Workbench showing breakpoints on `A[m_,0]`

Now right-click on the *Debugging.nb* file in the Package Explorer and select Debug As... Mathematica. You will be prompted to switch to the Debug perspective, which is recommended. Figure 19-5 shows what this perspective looks like. It will also launch the frontend with *Debugging.nb* active. Here you can use normal Shift-Enter evaluation to execute an expression. When a breakpoint is hit, you can switch back to the Workbench to continue debugging. Here you can inspect the call stack, see the value of variables, and set further breakpoints. You can step over or into further functions using F5 (set), F6 (step over) and F7 (step return). In short, you can perform all the operations you'd expect from a modern symbolic debugger.

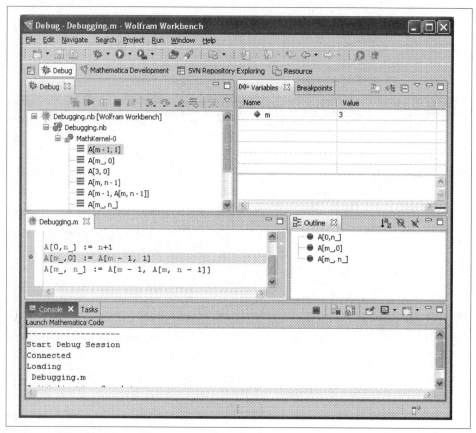

Figure 19-5. Wolfram Workbench in Debug perspective

Discussion

Many old-time Mathematica users feel that it is sacrilegious (or perhaps just frustrating) to leave the comfortable Mathematica frontend just to debug. If you don't have such a prejudice, your willingness will be rewarded. There is nothing like debugging within a real debugging environment! If you are a Java or C programmer who is used to such luxuries, the Eclipse-based Workbench environment is a must-have. Eclipse is an open source framework for building integrated software development environments (IDEs) that first gained popularity with Java developers. Wolfram used Eclipse to build an alternative development environment for Mathematica as an alternative to the traditional frontend. However, you don't need to abandon the traditional Mathematica interface to use Workbench to debug. In this section, I refer to Eclipse when speaking about generic features that are true about all Eclipse IDEs and Workbench when speaking about features of Workbench in particular.

If you have never used more traditional languages, such as Java, C, C++ and C#, then you are likely to find working in Workbench somewhat foreign. To avoid being frustrated, you should keep a few ideas in mind. First, because Workbench is built on top of Eclipse and Eclipse was built outside of Wolfram, you should not expect Workbench to have the same look and feel as the traditional frontend. You should approach it as you would approach any new piece of software—with an open mind and no preconceptions. For example, you should not expect to debug code that is written using all the fancy mathematical typesetting features available in a notebook. If you developed code solely using the *.nb* format, you should save your code as a *.m*, which is a pure text format. This is not to say you can't launch notebooks from Eclipse (the solution shows this is possible) but rather you should make all code that you wish to debug available in text format.

Another important concept of Eclipse is that it wants to manage all the source code under a project. Projects in Eclipse typically correspond to directories under a specific root directory you choose when Eclipse is installed. It is possible to specify other directories outside this hierarchy, but you will not automatically pick up files that happen to be in an existing location. You can use File, Import for that purpose.

In addition to source code-level breakpoints, Workbench supports message breakpoints that break when a function emits any error message and symbol breakpoints that provide a convenient way to place a breakpoint on an overloaded function name. For example, a symbol breakpoint can be used to put a break on all three variants of the Ackermann function A. The three types of breakpoints are accessible from the Breakpoints tab shown in Figure 19-6. The message break is set using , and is used for symbol breakpoints. There are also buttons for clearing selected breakpoints, , or all breakpoints, , and you can uncheck a breakpoint in the list to temporarily disable it.

Figure 19-6. Breakpoints tab has toolbar buttons for setting various types of breakpoints

See Also

If you are new to Eclipse, you should definitely check out the series of screencasts on Wolfram Workbench at *http://bit.ly/2srUoj*.

19.8 Writing Unit Tests to Help Ensure Correctness of Your Code

Problem

You want to write unit tests to help uncover bugs in a library of functions. Perhaps you are familiar with the unit-testing frameworks that exist in other languages, and you would like the equivalent for Mathematica.

Solution

Wolfram Workbench is nicely integrated with MUnit, a unit-testing framework for Mathematica. You create a unit test in a special file with extension *.mt*. The easiest way to create such a file is to right-click on your project and select New, Mathematica Test File (you should make sure you are in Mathematica Development Perspective, or you will have to navigate into the Other submenu to get to this feature).

The most convenient way to create your first test case is to type Test and then hit Ctrl-Space to trigger code assist, which automatically creates the test boilerplate.

```
(*Mathematica test file for Ackermann*)
Test[
    A[0,0]
    ,
    1
    ,
    TestID->"Test2-20090508-01L1K5"
]

Test[
    A[1,0]
    ,
    2
    ,
    TestID->"Test2-20090508-N4W7U7"
]

Test[
    A[0,1]
    ,
    2
    ,
    TestID->"Test2-20090508-F5F9A7"
]

(*This test will fail!*)
Test[
    A[1,2]
    ,
    3
    ,
    TestID->"Test2-20090508-L7N0S2"
]
```

Discussion

You can execute your unit tests at any time by saving the test file, right-clicking on it in the package explorer, and selecting Run As, Mathematica Test. This will generate a Test Report, as shown in Figure 19-7. The report shows which tests passed and which failed. Unique TestIDs are essential to this function, and Workbench has a feature that will help fix and duplicate IDs. Simply right-click on the file, select the Source menu, and then select Fix Test IDs.

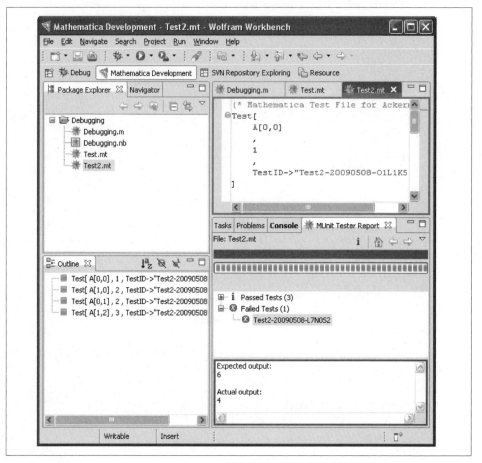

Figure 19-7. Test report generated after running the tests defined in the solution

Functions like Ackermann that return scalar values are easy to inspect in the failed tests section to investigate the difference between the expected and actual output. In Figure 19-7, you can see that the expected output is 6, but the actual output is 4. In this case, it is the test function that is wrong, because the correct output is 4. The more typical circumstance is that the function is wrong, but in either case you can quickly see that something is awry. With more complex outputs, it can be difficult to find the difference. A useful feature of Workbench is Failure Compare. Simply right-click on the failure test ID and select Failure Compare. This will open a dialog with a side-by-side tree view of the expected and actual expression (see Figure 19-8). You can expand the tree to inspect the branches that indicate differences (the X).

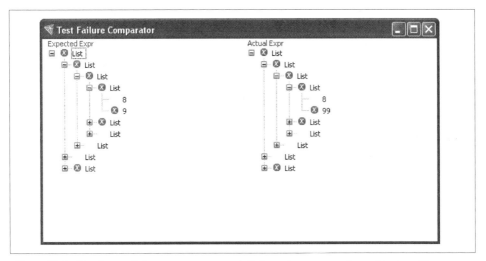

Figure 19-8. Use the test failure comparator to drill down into test results to detect problems

See Also

See the Wolfram Workbench unit-testing screencast at *http://bit.ly/dOJBL* for a step-by-step overview of unit testing.

19.9 Creating MUnit Tests Where Success Is Not Based on Equality Testing

Problem

Although the MUnit Test function is easy to use, it is not the most appropriate function for certain types of testing. For example, you may want to define your test in terms of pattern matching.

Solution

MUnit provides other test functions, including TestMatch, TestFree, TestStringMatch, and TestStringFree. TestMatch uses MatchQ to compare actual and expected results, and TestFree uses FreeQ. Likewise, TestStringMatch uses StringMatchQ, and Test-StringFree uses StringFreeQ.

```
TestMatch[
    {1,2,3,4,5}
    ,
    {__Integer}
    ,
    TestID->"TestOther-20090509-L8U9H1"
]

TestFree[
    {10,12,1/2,2/3,3/4,4/5,5/6}
    ,
    {__Complex}
    ,
    TestID->"TestOther-20090509-L8U9H2"
]

TestStringMatch[
    "Hello"
    ,
    "H" ~~ __ ~~ "o"
    ,
    TestID->"TestOther-20090509-L8U9H3"
]

TestStringFree[
    "Hello"
    ,
    "x"
    ,
    TestID->"TestOther-20090509-L8U9H4"
]
```

Discussion

You can create even more flexible tests by using the EquivalenceFunction option of Test to specify an alternative definition of success. The following test succeeds if the actual value is greater than 0.

```
Test[Cos[1]^2 + Sin[1]^2 - Sqrt[1 - Exp[-10]],
    0,
    EquivalenceFunction -> Greater,
    TestID -> "ID17"]
```

This option comes in handy when you are creating tests where exact equality is not useful. For example, you might want to use Round or Chop before comparing.

```
Test[
InverseFourier[Fourier[{2, 1, 1, 0, 0, 0}]],
  {2, 1, 1, 0, 0, 0},
  EquivalenceFunction -> (Chop[#1] == Chop[#2] &),
  TestID -> "ID42"
  ]
```

Of course, you can just as readily write the test with Chop applied to the actual computation, but I feel that EquivalenceFunction better documents the test designer's intention. Another example is when you are only worried about equality up to a specified tolerance.

```
Test[
(12/7) (2 Sqrt[2] - 1),
  Pi,
  EquivalenceFunction -> Abs[#1-#2] < 0.01,
  TestID -> "ID66"
```

19.10 Organizing and Controlling MUnit Tests and Test Suites

Problem

You have a complex test suite with many tests. The tests may naturally group into sections. Further, you want the ability to turn on and off test sections as well as state dependencies between sections, possibly to account for side effects. For example, you want to say, "only continue with this section if tests succeed, because further tests rely on results computed by earlier tests."

Solution

There are a few advanced MUnit features that are useful for organizing tests and managing test dependencies. You can organize tests into sections using BeginTest-Section[name,switch] and EndTestSection[].

```
(*Switches to activate and deactivate sections*)
Sect1Active = True;
Sect2Active = True;

(*Section 1*)
BeginTestSection["sect1", Sect1Active]

(*All tests in this section depend on first test success.*)
TestFree[str=OpenRead["SomeTestFile.txt"], $Failed,
EquivalenceFunction ->UnsameQ,
TestID-> "TestAdvanced-20090509-060603", TestFailureAction -> "SkipSection"]

Test[Read[str, Number], 5, TestID -> "IDS1_1"]

Test[Read[str, Word], "cars", TestID -> "IDS1_2"]

EndTestSection[]

(*Section 2*)
BeginTestSection["sect2", Sect2Active]
Test[2 + 2, 4, TestID -> "IDS2_1"]
EndTestSection[]
```

Discussion

If it does not make sense to continue tests after a failure, you can also specify Test-FailureAction → "Abort". This feature is available even if you do not use sections.

If you have a complex Mathematica library, you will want to organize it into separate test files. However, running each test separately would be tedious, so MUnit provides a TestSuite construct. First, you should place all your test files (.mt files) into a folder under the main project folder. Then create a test file that ties all the tests together into a suite, as shown in Figure 19-9.

```
        (*Mathematica TestSuite*)


        TestSuite[
            {
                "Test.mt",
                "Test2.mt",
                "TestAdvanced.mt",
                "TestOther.mt"
            }
        ]
```

Figure 19-9. `TestSuite` *is a test file that allows you to run other test files all at once*

19.11 Integrating Wolfram Workbench's MUnit Package into the Frontend

Problem

You would like to create unit tests but you prefer to work in the traditional frontend rather than Workbench.

Solution

You need a test driver to run the tests. This mimics the basic functionality of Workbench.

```
In[88]:= Needs["MUnit`"];
        TestDriver[tests__] :=
        Module[{testList = {tests}, numTests, failedTests},
          numTests = Length[testList];
          failedTests = Select[{tests}, ( FailureMode[#] =!= "Success") &];
          Print["Passed Tests: ", numTests - Length[failedTests]];
          Print["Failed Tests: ", Length[failedTests]];
          Print["Failed Test Id: ", TestID[#], "\nExpected: ",
            ExpectedOutput[#], " Actual: ", ActualOutput[#]] & /@ failedTests;
        ]
```

The MUnit package is not part of Mathematica 7, but you can still use it if you have installed Wolfram Workbench 1.1 or higher. You need to tell the kernel where to find the package. This will vary from system to system, but generally it will be under the Wolfram Research directory where Mathematica is installed. You want to find a directory called MUnit and add the path to that directory to $Path. On my Windows XP installation, I added the location to $Path by executing:

```
In[90]:= AppendTo[$Path, FileNameJoin[{"C:", "Program Files",
            "Wolfram Research", "WolframWorkbench", "1.1", "plug-ins",
            "com.wolfram.eclipse.testing_1.1.0", "MathematicaSource"}]]
```

```
Out[90]= {C:\Program Files\Wolfram
            Research\Mathematica\7.0\SystemFiles\Links,
          C:\Users\Sal Mangano\AppData\Roaming\Mathematica\Kernel,
          C:\Users\Sal Mangano\AppData\Roaming\Mathematica\Autoload,
          C:\Users\Sal Mangano\AppData\Roaming\Mathematica\Applications,
          C:\ProgramData\Mathematica\Kernel,
          C:\ProgramData\Mathematica\Autoload,
          C:\ProgramData\Mathematica\Applications, .,
          C:\Users\Sal Mangano, C:\Program Files\Wolfram
            Research\Mathematica\7.0\AddOns\Packages,
          C:\Program Files\Wolfram
            Research\Mathematica\7.0\AddOns\LegacyPackages,
          C:\Program Files\Wolfram
            Research\Mathematica\7.0\SystemFiles\Autoload, C:\Program
            Files\Wolfram Research\Mathematica\7.0\AddOns\Autoload,
          C:\Program Files\Wolfram
            Research\Mathematica\7.0\AddOns\Applications, C:\Program
            Files\Wolfram Research\Mathematica\7.0\AddOns\ExtraPackages,
          C:\Program Files\Wolfram
            Research\Mathematica\7.0\SystemFiles\Kernel\Packages,
          C:\Program Files\Wolfram
            Research\Mathematica\7.0\Documentation\English\System,
          C:\Program Files\Wolfram
            Research\WolframWorkbench\1.1\plug-ins\com.wolfram.eclipse.
            testing_1.1.0\MathematicaSource}
```

You can add this to *init.m* if you intend to use MUnit frequently. Alternatively, you can also copy the MUnit package into one of the locations in $Path.

Here is a simple example of using the driver. I purposefully made tests with ID2 and ID4 fail.

```
In[91]:= TestDriver[
         Test[1 + 1, 2, TestID → "ID1"],
         Test[1 + 1, 3, TestID → "ID2"],
         Test[2 + 2, 4, TestID → "ID3"],
         Test[2 + 2, 3, TestID → "ID4"]]
```

```
Passed Tests: 2
```

```
Failed Tests: 2
```

```
Failed Test Id: ID2
Expected: 3 Actual: 2
```

```
Failed Test Id: ID4
Expected: 3 Actual: 4
```

Discussion

The test driver used in the preceding "Solution" section is very basic and does not support all the features available when you build unit tests in Workbench. If you are ambitious, you can build a more sophisticated driver—even one that has more features than Workbench. It really depends on your needs. The main requirement is to become familiar with the MUnit API. Although documentation on MUnit is sparse at the time I am writing this, well-written Mathematica packages are self-describing. For example, you can find all the public functions in the package by using ?"MUnit`*". For the sake of space, I'll only list the functions that begin with the letter *T*. By clicking on the output, you can see what the function or option does. The most important functions are selectors, like TestID, because these allow you to extract information from a TestResultObject, which is the output produced by functions like Test, TestMatch, and so on.

```
In[92]:=  ? "MUnit`T*"
```

▼ **MUnit`**

Test	TestIndex	TestRunResultObject
TestCaveat	TestInput	TestRunTitle
TestCellEvaluationFunction	TestLog	TestStringFree
TestExecute	TestMatch	TestStringMatch
TestFailureAction	TestMemoryUsed	TestTags
TestFailureMessage	TestRequirement	TestTerminate
TestFree	TestResultObject	TestTimeUsed
TestID	TestResultQ	
TestIgnore	TestRun	

By inspecting MUnit's functions, I was inspired to create a test driver that supports the idea of test sections (see Recipe 19.10). However, instead of a BeginTestSection-EndTestSection pair, I use a single TestSection function. The TestDriver will work with multiple TestSections or multiple Tests but not mixtures of both. For this driver to handle skipping and aborting, it must be careful to evaluate a test lazily, hence, it uses Hold and the HoldAll attribute judiciously. It also uses Catch and Throw combinations. This is a feature of Mathematica I have largely avoided in the book, but it sometimes comes in handy as a way to terminate an iteration without cumbersome conditional logic. In this case, the function RunTest causes a test to evaluate and tests for failure. If the test does not succeed, it defers further decisions to OnFailedTest based on the test's FailureMode. OnFailedTest will either Throw or return, depending on the mode. Further, it uses the mode as a tag in the Throw, so the appropriate Catch handler can intercept the failure.

```
In[93]:= ClearAll[TestDriver, TestSection, RunTest, OnFailedTest];
        SetAttributes[{TestDriver, TestDriver2, TestSection, RunTest}, HoldAll];

        (*OnFailedTest simply returns the test if mode is Continue,
        otherwise it throws using mode as a tag.*)
        OnFailedTest[test_, "Continue"] := test
        OnFailedTest[test_, mode_] := Throw[test, mode]

        (*RunTest tests the failure mode and updates
          counters. It defers failure action to OnFailedTest.*)
        RunTest[test_TestResultObject] :=
          If[FailureMode[test] =!= "Success", failedTests++;
            OnFailedTest[test, TestFailureAction[test]], passedTests++; test]

        (*A TestSection has one or more tests, a name,
        and Boolean for enabling or disabling the section.*)
        TestSection[tests__, section_String, False] := {}
        TestSection[tests__, section_String, _ : True] :=
          Module[{},
            Catch[ReleaseHold[RunTest[#] & /@ Hold[tests]], "SkipSection"]]

        (*TestDriver2 valuates the results of tests.*)
        TestDriver2[tests__] := Module[{testList = {tests}, numTests, failed},
            failed = Select[{tests}, ( FailureMode[#] =!= "Success") &];
            Print["Passed Tests: ", passedTests];
            Print["Failed Tests: ", failedTests];
            Print["Failed Test Id: ", TestID[#], "\nExpected: ",
                ExpectedOutput[#], " Actual: ", ActualOutput[#]] & /@ failed;
          ]

        (*This instance of TestDriver executes sections.*)
        TestDriver[secs__TestSection] :=
          Block[{passedTests = 0, failedTests = 0},
            TestDriver2 @@ Flatten[ {Catch[ {secs}, "Abort"]}]]

        (*This instance of TestDriver executes tests.*)
        TestDriver[tests__] := Block[{passedTests = 0, failedTests = 0},
            TestDriver2 @@ Flatten[ {Catch[RunTest /@ {tests}, "Abort"]}]]
```

Here I put the driver through its paces demonstrating different failure scenarios.

In this scenario, the second test in sect1 fails with an Abort; hence, tests with test IDs "Sect1ID3" and "Sect2ID1" are not run.

```
In[103]:= TestDriver[
            TestSection[
              Test[1 + 1, 3, TestID → "Sect1ID1"],
              Test[1 + 1, 3, TestID → "Sect1ID2", TestFailureAction → "Abort"],
              Test[1 + 3, 4, TestID → "Sect1ID3"], "sect1"],
            TestSection[
              Test[1 + 1, 2, TestID → "Sect2ID1"], "sect2"]
            ]
```

```
Passed Tests: 0
```

```
Failed Tests: 2
```

```
Failed Test Id: Sect1ID2
Expected: 3 Actual: 2
```

In this scenario, the second test in sect1 fails with a "SkipSection"; hence, the test with test ID "Sect1ID3" is skipped, but a "Sect2ID1" runs.

```
In[104]:= TestDriver[
            TestSection[
              Test[1 + 1, 3, TestID → "Sect1ID1"],
              Test[1 + 1, 3, TestID → "Sect1ID2", TestFailureAction → "SkipSection"],
              Test[1 + 3, 4, TestID → "Sect1ID3"], "sect1"],
            TestSection[
              Test[1 + 1, 2, TestID → "Sect2ID1"], "sect2"]
            ]
```

```
Passed Tests: 1
```

```
Failed Tests: 2
```

```
Failed Test Id: Sect1ID2
Expected: 3 Actual: 2
```

Here sections are not used, but a `TestFailureAction` of `"Abort"` is still handled appropriately.

```
In[105]:= TestDriver[Test[1 + 3, 2, TestID → "Sect1ID1", TestFailureAction → "Abort"],
          Test[1 + 1, 2, TestID → "Sect1ID1"]]
```

```
Passed Tests: 0
```

```
Failed Tests: 1
```

```
Failed Test Id: Sect1ID1
Expected: 2 Actual: 4
```

See Also

The concept of test sections is native to MUnit when used with Workbench, but has a different syntax. This is covered in Recipe 19.10.

Index

Symbols

` (backtick), 7
! (escape character), 690–691
@ (prefix notation), 6, 49–50, 65
=== (SameQ), 91
(slot sequence), 34
(slots), 11, 35
| (vertical bar), 147–148
// (postfix notation), 6, 20–21, 49
/@ operator, 27
@@ operator, 27
@@@ operator, 27, 34
$CharacterEncoding, 182
$CharacterEncodings, 182
$MachinePrecision, 7
$MaxPrecision, 8–9
$MinPrecision, 8–9
$SystemCharacterEncoding, 182

A

AbsoluteThickness, 268
AccountingForm, 20–21
Accuracy, 8
accuracy of numeric results, 4–9, 10
Ackermann function
    as debugging illustration, 742
    debugging recursive functions, 748
    extracting debugging information, 749–753
    and recursion limits, 723
adaptive grid method, 575–577
Advanced Engineering Mathematics (Kreyszig), 439–440, 536

algebra problems, 413–414
    decomposing polynomials, 420–422
    dividing polynomials by other polynomials, 422–424
    finding polynomials from given roots, 415–416
    generating polynomials, 419–420
    solving equations, 414–415
    transforming expressions, 414, 416–419
algorithms (see also tree algorithms)
    rule-driven, 161–165
    running in parallel, 661–662
All, 481
alpha, 485–486
alternate tunings, 397–402
Alternatives, 147–148
American option pricing, 583–585
americanPutCompiled, 583–584
amplitude modulation, 392
anagram demonstration, 204–206
analysis of variance (ANOVA), 479–483
Animate
    creating self-running demonstrations, 627–629
    as key function for interactivity, 594
    relationship with Manipulate, 629
AnimationRate, 628
AnimationRepetitions, 628
AnimationRunning, 628
animations, 627–630
Animator, 629
annotation
    of 2D graphics, 269–270
    of 3D plots with 2D contours, 295–296

We'd like to hear your suggestions for improving our indexes. Send email to *index@oreilly.com*.

arrows, 270–273
  graph labels, 241–242
  interactive, 630–631
  legends, 260–263
annuity, 560
anonymous functions, 32
ANOVA (analysis of variance), 479–483
ANOVA` package, 479–480
Antidiagonal, 103
Apart, 417
Append, 87
AppendTo, 111–112
Apply
  level specifications, 117
  mapping multi-argument functions, 33–35
  operator notation, 26–27
  XML data, 212
apply (term usage), 26
approximate numeric results, 2–3, 5–7
approximate numeric values
  converting to exact, 19
  with mixed numerical types, 9–10
arguments, holding, 36
Array
  constructing lists, 86–87
  generating kernels, 48
ArrayPlot, 411–412
arrays
  packed and unpacked, 95–97
  sparse, 112–114
Arrow, 263–266
Arrowheads, 270–272
arrows
  in 2D graphics, 263–266
  customizing, 270–273
ASCII codes, use of, 181–182
AspectRatio
  overriding, 255
  with Plot, 244–245
  with PolarPlot, 249
associative functions, 30
associative lookup
  built-in, 130–134
  red-black tree implementation, 125–129
attributes, 29–30
Attributes, 29
audio and music processing, 373
  alternate tunings, 397–402
  applying an envelope to a signal, 394–397

chord notation, 380
chords and progressions, 378, 379, 383–384
exporting MIDI files, 389–390
Fourier analysis, 405–412
importing digital sound files, 403–412
musical notes, 374–375
percussion, 384–389
playing functions as sound, 390–391
rhythm, 376–377, 382
scales and melodies, 375–376
tremolo, 392, 394
vibrato, 393–394
volume, 377–378, 382
Axes
  overriding, 255–256
  suppressing plot axes, 240
AxesEdge, 278–279
AxesLabel, 240
axialForce, 545–547
axialStrain, 545–547
axialStress, 545–547

B

backtracking parsers, 235
Backus-Naur Form (BNF), 227, 232
balance, 128
Band
  synthesizing sparse functions, 113–114
  synthesizing tridiagonal matrices, 104,
    531–532
BarChar, 460
BaseForm, 12–13
bases other than 10, 12–13
BeginTestSection, 767–768
binary trees
  converting lists to, 89
  modeling, 121–123
  selective flattening, 90
BinarySearch, 100
BinCounts
  distributions of pseudorandom
    numbers, 460
  grayscale histograms, 341
bit vectors, 119–121
Black-Scholes formula
  finite difference method for, 578–582
  pricing European puts and calls, 565–572
  speeding up NDSolve, 574–578

Blank pattern constructs, 146–147, 148
Block, 66, 69–70
BNF (Backus-Naur Form), 227, 232
bonds, 551, 561–562
bookmarks, 618–619
Boslaugh, Sarah (see *Statistics in a Nutshell*)
BoundaryStyle, 280
box plots, 493–494
Boxed, 280–281
BoxQuantile, 493–494
BoxRatios, 280–281
BoxStyle, 280–281
BoxWhiskersPlot, 492–493
breakpoints, 761
buttons, 596

C

C and C++ functions, calling, 694–699
CAD, importing from, 326
calculus problems
    difference equations, 450–452, 519–521
    differential equations, 438–441, 537
    differentiating functions, 431–435
    generating functions for sequence
        recognition, 452–454
    integration, 435–438
    limits, 426–427
    minima and maxima problems, 441–443
    piecewise functions, 427–429
    power series representations, 429–431
    sum and product problems, 447–450
    vector calculus problems, 443–447
call options, 551, 566–567
Carlson, Chris, 306
Cartesian coordinates
    2D plots in, 239–247
    3D plots in, 276–282
Cases
    compared to DeleteCases, 153–154
    with Count, 156
    in coupled mass problems, 532
    extracting lines from 3D objects, 308
    extracting XML elements, 211
    filtering out MissingData entries, 512
    generating polynomials, 450
    level specifications, 117
    pattern matching, 151–152, 211
    querying databases, 172–173

taking lists apart, 88–89
    transforming notebooks, 735
    transforming XML, 213–214
cash flow value, 559–561
Catch, 772–773
categorical data, 483–486
CDF (cumulative density function), 461–464
Ceiling, 18–19
CellMeans, 483
center of mass, computing, 522–524
centerMass, 522–523
central limit theorem (CLT), 464–466
CentralMoment, 471
Cervantes-Pimentel, Ulises, 306
character encodings, 181–183
character manipulation, 188–192, 192–196
CharacteristicFunction, 464
ChemicalData source, 510–512
chi-square tests, 483–486
ChiSquarePValue, 485
choose, 227–228
Chop, 525
chords
    controlling voicings, 383–384
    creating, 378
    notation, 380
    playing progressions, 379
Circle, 263–266
cleaning up
    automatically, 737–738
    during incremental development, 720–721
Clear, 720–721
ClearAttributes, 29
Clip, 428
clone method, 68
closures
    in functional languages, 32
    implementing, 66–73
    transitive, 162–163
CLT (central limit theorem), 464–466
clustering solutions, third-party, 642
clusters
    grouping data into, 486–492
    and random number generation, 496–499
CMYK color space, 338
"CoarsestGrained", 659–660
Coefficient, 421
CoefficientList, 421
Collect, 418

colon syntax, 151
color directives, 266–267
color models, 335–340
ColorFunction
    highlighting distribution plots, 464
    imported image format, 330, 339
Column, 633–635
Combinatorica` package
    constructing graphs to use with, 134–140
    extracting information from graphs,
        140–143
    sorting lists, 98–100
command history, clearing, 721
command line programs, external, 690–691
comments, stripping, 190
CommonCompoundNames, 508
Commonest, 459
commutative functions, 29
Compile
    improving function performance, 727–728
    pricing American securities options, 583
compiling (computational finance), 550
Complement, 91, 278
complex numbers
    converting to other bases, 12–13
    as expression heads, 1–2
Composition, 63–66
computational finance, overview of, 549–551
Condition, 178
conditions, pattern, 149
ConsonantDistance, 208
ConstantArray, 86–87
constants, modifying, 721–723
continuations, 32
"Continued Fraction" (Weisstein), 63
continuously compounding interest, 560
ContourPlot3D, 292–294
contrast, image, 341–346
Control, 633–635
ControlActive, 602–603
controls
    creating custom, 625–627
    and dynamic updates, 605
    and graphics manipulation speed, 602–603
    intercepting output of, 607–609
    managing large numbers of, 633–639
    Manipulate's choice of, 595–596
    multiple, for single variables, 597
    types of, 595–596

convergence
    graphing iterations, 257
    of sums or products, 448
Core stylesheet, 731–732
Correlation, 467–468
correlation, computing, 466–468
CosineDistance, 488
Count, 155–156
coupled mass problems, 530–532
Covariance, 467–468
covariance, computing, 466
critical sections, 664, 665, 682
critical values, 485–486
CriticalSection
    diagnosing parallel processing
        performance, 685–686
    sharing resources in parallel evaluation,
        664–665
Cross, 443
CrossProduct
    solving vector calculus problems, 445–446
    and VectorAnalysis` package, 92
crossRef, 735
crossword puzzles, cheating on, 204
cumulative density function (CDF), 461–464
curl, of vector fields, 92, 446
Curry, 74–77
currying, 32, 73–77
cylindrical coordinates, 285–289

D

D, 432, 433
DAGs (directed acyclic graphs), 142–143
DamerauLevenshteinDistance, 488, 491
Dandelin demonstration, 304–305
data
    adjusting for outliers, 471–472
    categorical, 483–486
    generating multiple data sets in
        parallel, 658
    grouping into clusters, 486–492
    linear models, 472–474
    measuring shape of, 468–471
    nonlinear models, 475–477
    partitioning into parallel data sets,
        656–658
    plotting in 2D, 252–254
    plotting in 3D, 298–300
    sharing between parallel kernels, 662–663

data sources, curated
   ChemicalData, 510–512
   dictionaries, 202
   ElementData, 507–510
   FinancialData, 550, 552–557
   GenomeData, 516, 518–519
   ParticleData, 513–516
   PolyhedronData, 320–326
   ProteinData, 516–518
   value of, 506
Data specification, 403
databases (see also data sources, curated)
   querying with patterns, 171–177, 555
   storing results in, 714
   third-party, 690, 711–713, 715–717
"Data" element, extracting, 334–335
DataRange, 243
DataSourceNames, 715
Date, C.J., 171–172
debugger, built-in, 742
debuggers, creating interactive, 753–756
debugging, 741–742
   extracting useful information, 749–753
   function libraries, 762–765
   functions invoked many times, 746–747
   incremental development problems,
      720–721
   infinite loops, 165–167
   with Print, 743–745
   recursive functions, 747–749
   visual, 758–762
   XML transformations, 219
DecayModes, 516
DeclarePackage, 726
Default, 77–79
Default stylesheet, 731–732
default values
   compared to options, 81
   creating functions with, 77–79
definitions, custom, 28–29, 79–83
Delete
   level specifications, 117–118
   pattern matching, 154–155
DeleteCases
   excluding matching elements, 153–155
   extracting digits of a number, 15
   level specifications, 117
delimiters, changing, 190–191
delta (computational finance)

computing, 567, 569
   defined, 551, 567
   plotting, 569–570
Depth, 750
Derivative, 433
derivatives, computing, 431–435
derivatives, notation for, 431–432, 433
Developer` context, 723–724
Developer` package, 48, 96–97
Diagonal, 102–103
DiagonalMatrix
   compared to Table, 86
   constructing shift matrices, 106–107
   specifying matrix structure, 104
   synthesizing sparse equivalent of, 113–114
diagram, 543, 545
dictClear, 132
dictHasKeyQ, 132
dictionaries
   associative lookup, 131–133
   key-value, 130–134
   natural language, 202–209
Dictionary, 131, 133
dictKeys, 132
dictKeyValuePairs, 132–133
dictLookup, 132
dictRemove, 132
dictReplace, 132
dictStore, 131–132
difference equations
   modeling predator-prey dynamics, 519–521
   solving, 450–452
differential equations
   modeling electrical circuits, 537
   solving, 438–441
Digital Image Processing (Gonzalez and
     Woods), 331, 351, 359
DigitBlock, 21
digits, extracting, 13–16
directed acyclic graphs (DAGs), 142–143
directives (see graphics directives)
discount factors, 559–556
Disk, 263–266
Dispatch, 170–171
displacements, 542–543
Display, 680
display forms
   bit vectors, 119–121
   numerical expressions, 4, 20–22

DisplayAllSteps, 628
distance functions, 488, 490–492
DistributeDefinitions
    with map-reduce, 673
    with Parallelize, 651
distribution of processing (see parallel
        processing)
distributions, statistical
    central limit theorem, 464–466
    cumulative and probability density
        functions, 461–464
    measuring shape of data, 468–471
    nonuniform, 459–461
divergence (vector calculus), 446
Do
    non-functionality of, 31
    with ParallelEvaluate, 650
Dot
    compared to DotProduct, 445–446
    generating polynomials, 420
    with graphics matrices, 109
    solving vector calculus problems, 443, 444
    vector multiplication, 94–95
DotProduct, 445–446
downvalues
    inspecting with DownValues, 27–28
    synchronizing, 662
DownValues
    associative lookup, 132
    inspecting downvalues with, 27–28
Drakos, Nikos, 347, 351
Drop
    for composed invertible functions, 65
    taking lists apart, 88
drop-down lists, 596
DSolve
    compared to RSolve, 452
    limitations, 534
    modeling vibrating strings, 533, 534
    solving differential equations, 439–441
    with triangular waves, 538
duration of bonds, 561–562
Dynamic
    behavior of, 605–606
    creating closures, 70–71
    in dynamic updates, 604–606
    effect of Refresh on, 610
    intercepting control output, 607–609
    refresh rate, 610

segregating fast and slow operations, 620
speeding up interactive plots, 603–604
dynamic interactivity, overview of, 593–594
dynamic module variables, 624–625
dynamic updates
    with changing cell values, 604–606
    intercepting control values, 607–609
dynamic values, 609–610
DynamicModule
    balancing speed and space, 613–615
    creating wormholes, 624–625
    with Manipulate, 617, 622
    notebook representation of, 612
    scope of variables, 624
    as a scoping construct, 611–612
DynamicWrapper
    balancing speed and space, 613–615
    segregating fast and slow operations,
        620–621

E

Eclipse, 760–761
edgeDetectLOG, 362–364
edgeDetectSobel, 362–363
edges, detecting, 361–364
EditDistance
    creating spell-checkers, 207–208
    grouping data into clusters, 491
Eigenfaces for Recognition (Turk and
        Pentland), 367, 371
eigenImageElements, 368
eigenImageRecognition, 370
eigenImages, 368
eigenvectors (eigenimages), 365–371
electrical circuits, modeling, 537–539
ElementData, 507–510
engineering applications, overview of,
        505–506
EngineeringForm, 22
envelopes, applying to signals, 394–397
EquivalenceFunction, 766–767
errors, estimating, 16–18
EuclidianDistance, 488, 491
EulerianQ, 141–142
European option pricing, 551, 565–576,
        578–582
Evaluate, 62
evaluation after transformation, 168–169

evaluation monitors, debugging with, 756–758
EvaluationMonitor, 757–758
event propagation, controlling, 631–632
EventHandler, 630, 631–632
exact numeric values
    in expressions with mixed numerical types, 9–10, 11
    results as, 2–3, 5–7
ExampleData, 306
Except
    finding nonmatching values, 149, 151
    limitations of, 154
executable programs, calling, 690–691
Expand
    generating polynomials, 450
    transforming polynomials, 417–418
ExpandAll, 417–418
Experimental` context, 723–725
explicit methods, stability problems in, 585
expression evaluation, replacement and, 192
Extract
    level specifications, 117–118
    pattern matching, 152–153

F

FaceGrids, 281–282
FaceGridsStyle, 281–282
Factor, 417
FactorTerms, 417, 418–419
FDM (finite difference method), 578–582
FEM (finite element method), 539–547
fileDisposition, 677–678
Filling
    with ColorFunction, 464
    with Plot, 245–247
    with PolarPlot, 249
FillingStyle, 246–247
FilterOptions, 82
FilterRules, 81–82
financial data, importing from websites, 557–559
financial derivatives, 573
financial engineering, overview of, 549–551
FinancialData source, 550, 552–557
FindClusters, 486–492
FindFit, 475
FindGeneratingFunction, 453

FindMaximum, 442–443
FindRoot
    computing critical values, 485
    computing securities option volatility, 573
    debugging built-in functions, 756
    evaluation monitoring, 57–58
    solving algebraic equations, 415
FindSequenceFunction, 453
"FinestGrained", 659–660
finite difference method (FDM), 578–582
finite element method (FEM), 539–547
First, 88
first-class entities, 24
Fit, 473
fitness functions, in Java libraries, 703–706
FixedPointList, 164–165
Flat, 30, 152
Flatten
    collapsing unneeded nesting, 43
    restructuring lists, 89–90
    with SoundNote, 388–389
FlipView, 635
Floor, 18–19
flux, 444
Fold, 26
    as code generator, 63
    as recursion alternative, 53–56
foldl (Haskell), 54–55
FoldList, 26, 56
foldr (Haskell), 54–55
ForAll, 441
Format, 542
forms, for numerical expressions, 4, 20–22
Fourier analysis, on sound files, 405–412
Fourier series
    modeling electrical circuits, 538
    modeling vibrating strings, 534
Fourier transforms, in image processing, 356–361
fourierFilter, 357
fourierImage, 360–361
fractals, generating, 59–60
Frame, 242
FrameLabel, 242
FrameStyle, 242
FRatio, 480
frequency modulation (vibrato), 393–394
FromCharacterCode, 183
FromDigits, 15

frontend
    calling into, 736–737
    connecting to remote kernel, 692–694
    customizing user interaction, 739–740
    integrating MUnit` into, 769–775
    startup operations, 737–738
FrontEndExecute, 736
FullDecayModes, 516
FullForm
    debugging infinite loops, 167
    pattern matching, 152, 169–170
FullGraphics, 238
FullSimplify
    measuring securities option sensitivity, 571–572
    solving differential equations, 439
    transforming symbolic expressions, 417
function attributes, 29–30
functional notation
    for derivatives, 431–432, 433
    for numerical expressions, 6
functional programming languages, 31–32
functional programming style, 24–25
    compared to pattern-based programming, 145
    debugging with Print, 743–744
    and parallel evaluations, 654–655
functions (see also graphics primitives; primitive functions)
    associative, 30
    commutative, 29
    compiling, 727–728
    custom definitions, 28–29, 79–83
    debugging, 746–749, 756–758
    differentiating, 431–435
    distance, 488, 490–492
    finding series expansions, 429–431
    for image processing, 331
    indexed, 51–52
    for interactivity, 593–594
    interpolation, 477–478
    localizing within a Manipulate, 622–624
    locating undocumented, 723–725
    modifying built-in, 721–723
    packaging into libraries, 725–727
    piecewise, 427–429, 431–435
    playing as sound, 390–391
    recursive, 218–227, 747–749
    redefining with upvalues, 28–29
    region, 297–298
    repeated application of, 59–62
    for sequence recognition, 452–454
    vector, 91–92
functions, building
    accepting options, 79–83
    default values, 77–79
    downvalues and upvalues, 27–29
    for explicit currying, 73–77
    holding arguments, 36
    invertible, 63–66
    sequence recognition, 452–454
    through iteration, 62–63
functions, mapping over lists
    automatically, 37
    moving sublists, 43–48
    multiple arguments, 32–35
    multiple functions, 38–41
    tracking item indexes, 41–43
functions, plotting
    in Cartesian coordinates, 239–247, 276–282
    in polar coordinates, 247–249
    in spherical coordinates, 283–285

G

gamma (computational finance), 551, 567–568
GAs (genetic algorithms), 701, 706
Gather, 492
GatherBy
    with map-reduce technique, 676–677
    transforming notebooks, 735
GCD (greatest common divisor), 424
GenerateConditions, 437
GeneratingFunction, 453–454
generic programming, 99–100
genetic algorithms (GAs), 701, 706
GenomeData source, 516–519
geometric shapes, displaying, 263–268, 302–306
Global` context, 721
global matrices, 541
global variables, changing temporarily, 723
Glow, 313–314, 316
Gonzalez, Rafael, 331, 351, 359
gradient (vector calculus), 446
grammars, creating, 227–235

graph algorithms, 140–143
GraphData
    constructing graphs, 138–139
    querying databases, 175–177
GraphDifference, 136–137
Graphics, 330–331
graphics directives, 237
    color, 266–267
    combining with graphics primitives, 266
    lighting, 315–316
"Graphics" element, extracting, 333–334
graphics primitives
    combining with graphics directives, 266
    imported image representation, 330, 339
    three-dimensional, 237, 303–305, 408–409
    two-dimensional, 237, 263
    visualizing tree-based pricing
        approaches, 588
graphics, symbolic nature of, 276
graphics, three-dimensional (see also plots,
        three-dimensional)
    compared to 2D graphics, 275
    formats supported, 326
    geometric shapes, 302–306
    importing, 326–327
    lighting properties, 313–316
    polyhedra, 320–326
    surface properties, 313–316
    transforming, 317–320
    viewing perspective, 309–312
    wireframe models, 306–309
graphics, two-dimensional (see also plots,
        two-dimensional)
    annotating, 241–242, 269–270
    arrows, 270–273
    combining multiple graphics, 256–257
    format of imported images, 330–331
    geometric shapes, 263–268
    tree-based pricing approaches, 587–591
Graphics3D, 408–409
GraphicsArray, 258–259
GraphicsColumn, 238, 259–260
GraphicsGrid
    displaying related graphs, 258–259
    formatting 2D graphics outputs, 238
GraphicsRow, 238, 259–260
GraphIntersection, 136–137
GraphJoin, 136
GraphPlot, 161

GraphProduct, 136–138
graphs
    constructing for Combinatorica`
        algorithms, 134–140
    extracting information, 140–143
    interactive, 600–604
    transitive closure of, 162–163
GraphUnion, 136
GraphUtilities` package, 140, 161
Gray, Theodore, 610, 614, 615
"GrayLevels" element, 333–334
greatest common divisor (GCD), 424
greedy matching, 159–161
Greeks, 551, 567–572
grep demonstration, 199–200
Grid, 633–635
grid lines, on graphs, 241–245
Grid Mathematica, 641
grpath, 588

H

Halton sequence, 498
HamiltonianQ, 141–142
HammingDistance, 491–492
Haskell
    currying functions, 76, 77
    folding implementations, 54–55
    as functional language, 31–32
hasPath, 162–165
Head, 1–2
heads
    graphics, 275
    indexed, 51
    numerals, 1–2
    red-black trees, 125–126
    XML, 210, 212–213
HeapSort, 99–100
histogram equalization, 341–346
histogram specification, 347–351
histogramSpecification, 348–350, 352–354
history, clearing, 721
Hold, 30
    completing replacement before
        evaluation, 168–169
    currying, 75
    holding unique argument combinations, 36
    nonstrictness of, 32
    pattern matching, 152

HoldAll, 30
  creating grammars, 227–228
  implementing closures, 66, 70
  nonstrictness of, 32
HoldFirst, 30
  destructive changes to symbol values, 111–112
  effect on Dynamic, 605–606
  nonstrictness of, 32
HoldForm
  displaying polynomials in specific order, 420, 422
  with Trace, 750–751
HoldPattern
  associative lookup, 132
  completing replacement before evaluation, 168–169
HoldRest, 30, 32
HSV color model, 335–340
hue, 335–337
Hull-White method, 587–590
hyperspheres, volume of, 437–438
hypothesis testing, 483–486

I

identity matrices, 104
IdentityMatrix
  constructing lists, 86–87
  specifying matrix structure, 104
  synthesizing sparse equivalent of, 113–114
IgnoreCase, 200
IKernelLink, 709–711
Image, 330–331
image processing
  challenges of, 329
  converting RGB to HSV, 335–340
  correcting images, 347–351
  detecting edges, 361–364
  enhancing images, 341–346
  extracting elements, 332–335
  functions, 331
  image recognition, 365–371
  sharpening images, 351–361
  smoothing images, 356–361
image representation, 330–331, 336
ImageConvolve, 364
ImageHistogram, 346
images, imported, 330–331
imageVector, 368

ImplementJavaInterface, 704
Import
  extracting image information, 332–335
  image processing format, 330–331
  importing digital sound files, 403
  importing financial data, 557–558
  importing XML, 209–210
incUntilButton, 625
indexed functions, 51–52
infinite loops, debugging, 165–167
infix notation, 6
Initialization, 617–618, 622–623
initializing automatically, 737–738
Inner, 94–95, 420
InputForm, 237
Insert, 87
Inset, 272–273
Install (MathLink), 697
InstallJava, 700–701
InstallNET, 707
IntegerDigits, 13–15
integers, as expression heads, 1–2
IntegerString, 16
Integrate, 435–437
integration, 435–438
interactivePlot, 630–631
interactivity, 593–594
  animating expressions, 627–630
  balancing speed and space, 613–615
  controlling dynamic value updates, 609–610
  creating custom controls, 625–627
  creating custom interfaces, 630–633
  dynamic updates, 604–606
  improving Manipulate performance, 619–622
  intercepting control values, 607–609
  localizing functions in Manipulate, 622–624
  making a self-contained Manipulate, 615–618
  manipulating plots, 600–604
  manipulating symbolic expressions, 598–600
  remembering found values, 618
  scoping constructs in notebooks, 611–612
  sharing dynamic module variables, 624–625
  variable manipulation, 594–597

interest, continuously compounding, 560
interest rate sensitivity
    of bonds, 561–562
    of options, 567–572
    visualizing tree-based approaches, 587–591
interfaces, custom
    creating, 630–633
    managing large number of controls in, 633–639
interfacing with third-party tools, 689–694
internal rate of return, 560
Interpolation
    computing finite differences, 579–580
    creating interpolation functions from data, 477–478
InterpolationOrder
    in 2D plots, 253–254
    in 3D plots, 298–299
Intersection
    eliminating duplicate list elements, 91
    querying databases, 177
IntervalIntersection, 18
IntervalMemberQ, 18
intervals, estimating errors with, 16–18
IntervalUnion, 18
inverseEqualizationMap, 350
InverseFunction, 63–66
InverseSeries, 430–431
Item, 633–635
ItemNumbered, 731–732
iteration
    building functions through, 62–63
    computing with Nest functions, 59–62
    graphing convergence, 257

J

Java, 700–706
JavaBlock, 701
JavaScript closure solutions, 69–70
JLink` package, 700–701
Join
    composing new lists, 87–88
    transforming XML, 216

K

kernels
    as argument of ListConvolve, 45
    bypassing, 736
    clearing old definitions from, 720–721
    Laplacian, 352
    local, 643–646
    master, 642, 660, 665, 667, 668
    master-slave overhead, 660
    and .NET applications, 709–711
    in parallel computing, 642–650, 659–663, 686–688
    remote, 646–648, 692–694
    shared resource issues, 663–665
    sharing data across, 662–663
    slave, 642–646, 660, 665, 667, 668
    startup and termination operations, 737–738
    variable storage in, 612
Kernels, 649–650
keyToFilenamePrefix, 674–675
kinematics problems, 524–529
knapsack, 701–706
Koch snowflake demonstration, 59–60
Kreyszig, Erwin, 439–440, 536
Kurtosis, 469–470, 471

L

labels
    arrows, 272–273
    on graphs, 241–242
LabelStyle, 240
lambda functions, 32
language generators, creating, 232
Laplacian, 446
Laplacian of the Gaussian (LoG) algorithm, 361–362
Laplacian transforms, 351–356
Last, 88
LaunchKernels, 648
Lauschke, Andreas, 574, 578, 583
lazy evaluation, 32
LCM (least common multiple), 424
LeafCount, 156
least common multiple (LCM), 424
Legend, 263
LegendPosition, 261
legends, creating, 260–263
LegendSpacing, 261–263
LegendTextSpace, 261–263
Less
    creating functions that accept options, 80
    ordered associative lookup, 125–126

Level, 116–117
level specifications (levelspecs), 114
   counting matching elements, 155
   manipulating nested lists, 114–118
   in mapping multi-argument functions,
      34–35
   with ParallelMap, 655
   pattern matching, 152, 154
libraries
   creating, 725–727
   debugging, 762–769
Lichtblau, Daniel, 227, 232
Lighting
   controlling lighting of 3D graphics,
      313–316
   visualizing translucent surface
      coverings, 309
lighting properties, 313–316
Lightweight Grid Service, 642, 646–648
limits, computing, 426–427
Line, 263–266
line integrals, computing, 443
linear regressions, 472–474
linearElement, 539–540
linearElementMatrix, 540
LinearModelFit, 473–474
linguistic processing, 202–209
LinkObject, 689, 697
links, defined, 689
Lissajous curves, plotting, 249–250
List
   constructing lists, 85
   extracting matrix diagonals, 102
list functions, overview of, 85–90
Listable, 30
   mapping over lists automatically, 37
   vector math operations, 91–92
ListAnimate, 630
ListContourPlot, 410
ListConvolve
   computing finite differences, 579–580, 582
   image convolution, 352
   performing computations on sublists,
      44–48
ListCorrelate, 44–48
ListLinePlot
   in Fourier analysis, 409
   visualizing random walks, 500
ListPlot, 252–254

ListPlot3D, 298–300
lists
   building incrementally, 57–59
   converting to and from trees, 89, 127–128
   determining order without sorting,
      100–102
   eliminating duplicate elements, 91
   generating, 85–88
   manipulating nested, 114–118
   modeling tree data structures, 121–125
   numerical representation, 95–97
   processing functions, 85–90
   rearranging, 89–90
   restructuring, 89–90
   sorting, 97–100
   taking apart, 88–89
LoadNETType, 707–708
local kernels, 643–646
localMatrices, 541
locationVectors, 541
lock variables, 664–665
LoG (Laplacian of the Gaussian) algorithm,
      361–362
Longest, 159–161
"Lookup", 556–557
LowerTriangularize, 105

M

machine precision, 2–3, 7
MachinePrecision, 7
Macintosh computers, and remote kernels,
      693–694
makeAdaptiveGrid, 575–577
MakeGraph, 135
ManhattanDistance, 488, 491
Manipulate, 593–594
   controlling variable values interactively,
      594–597
   creating custom controls, 625–627
   creating custom interfaces, 633–635
   creating interactive graphs, 600–604
   creating tabbed and menu interfaces,
      637–639
   encapsulating startup definitions,
      615–618
   and graphics manipulation speed, 602
   improving performance of, 619–622
   localizing functions in, 622–624

measuring securities option sensitivity,
571–572
relationship with `Animate`, 629
remembering found values, 618–619
scope of control variables, 624
simulating kinematics problems, 526–529
varying symbolic expression structures,
598–600
with yield curves, 564–565
`Manual`, 698–699
`Map`
compared to `ParallelMap`, 654–656
creating scales and melodies, 376
effect of, 27
level specifications, 117–118
mapping multi-argument functions, 33–35
mapping multiple functions in a single
pass, 38–41
notations for, 26
playing chord progressions, 279
`mapAndStore`, 674
`MapIndexed`
level specifications, 117
parallel processing with, 652–653, 667
tracking item indexes, 41–43
transforming notebooks, 735
`mapper`, 676
mapping (see functions, mapping over lists;
`Map`)
`mapReduce`, 669–678
market cap, defined, 556
mass, computing, 522–524
master kernels
overhead, 660
in parallel computing, 642
in pipeline approach, 665, 667–668
matching (see pattern matching)
Mathematica in Action (Wagon)
3D graphics primitives demonstration,
304–305
iterative functions systems study, 52
`MathKernel`
connecting frontend to remote kernel,
693–694
creating a custom frontend, 711
`MathLink`, 689
installing programs, 697
types returned, 699
matrices, 93

diagonal, 104
global, 541
identity, 104
permutation, 105–106
shift, 106–107
sparse arrays, 112–114
tridiagonal, 104–105, 530
matrices, building, 103–109
matrices, manipulating
extracting diagonals, 102–103
modifying rows and columns, 110–112
non-numeric permutations, 109
permuting rows and columns, 105–107
transforming, 105, 319
with vector functions, 91–92
matrix computations
covariance and correlation, 466–468
normal modes, 530, 531–532
matrix functions, overview of, 93–95
maxima problems, solving, 441–443
`Maximize`, 441–443
`MaxIterations`, 165–166
`MaxRecursion`, 301–302
`Median`, 457
melody, 375–377
`MemberQ`
eliminating duplicate list elements, 91
emulating SQL subqueries, 174
level specifications, 117
testing repeated transformations, 163–164
"Members", 556
memory, freeing, 91, 112–114, 721
memory, shared, 682
`MenuPosition`, 731
`MenuView`, 635–637
`merge`, 676–677
`mergeAll`, 676–677
`Mesh`
constructing wireframe models, 306–307
highlighting plot points, 242–243
`MeshFunctions`, 300
`Method`, 659–661
`MethodOfLines`, 578
Microsoft .NET, 707–711
MIDI files, exporting, 389–390
minima problems, solving, 441–443
`MinimalPolynomial`, 415–416
`Minimize`, 441–443
`Mod`, 383–384

mode, computing, 459

Module
    compared to DynamicModule, 611–612
    implementing closures, 70

moment of inertia, computing, 522–524

MonomialList, 421–422

Monte Carlo method, 585–587

Monty Hall problem, 502–503

Moore, Ross, 347, 351

Most
    associative lookup, 132
    taking lists apart, 88

MousePosition, 630

MovingAverage, 44

MovingMean, 44

mprep preprocessor, 694–695, 699

MUnit` framework
    creating unit tests, 762–765, 765–767
    directing kernel to, 770
    functions, 772
    integrating with frontend, 769–775
    organizing and controlling tests, 767–769

music (see audio and music processing)

musical notes, creating, 374–375

N

N, 4–7

natural language dictionaries, 202–209

NDSolve
    evaluation monitoring, 57–58
    limitations, 534
    modeling vibrating strings, 533–534
    speeding up, 574–578

Nearest, 206–207

Nelson-Siegel function, 563–565

Nest, 26
    building functions through iteration, 62–63
    iterative computations, 59–60
    as recursion alternative, 56
    restructuring lists, 89

nested applications
    flattening, 30
    readability of, 48–51

nested lists, manipulating, 114–118

NestList, 26
    convergence through iteration, 257
    debugging infinite loops, 166
    generating lists of grid points, 579

iterative computations, 60

modeling population dynamics, 520

as recursion alternative, 56

NestWhile
    iterative computations, 60–62
    as recursion alternative, 56

NestWhileList
    iterative computations, 60
    as recursion alternative, 56

.NET, 707–711

NetImage, 325

NETLink` package, 707

NETNew, 707–708

networks
    configuring remote services kernels,
        646–648
    map-reduce technique for, 673
    parallel computing on, 642

nextUniqueFile, 674–675

ngon, 263–266

NIntegrate
    computing critical values, 485
    evaluation monitoring, 57–58

NMinimize, 57–58

nongreedy matching, 160–161

nonlinear models, 475–477

NonLinearModelFit, 475–477

nonparametric methods, 565

nonsinusoidal waves, 538–539

nonstrict languages, 32

nonticklish functions, 610

Normal
    converting sparse matrix to list form,
        104, 138–139
    forcing low-level primitive
        representation, 308
    generating series expansions of
        functions, 429

normal modes, computing, 530–532

notation, 3–4 (see also postfix notation;
        prefix notation)
    for bases other than 10, 12–13
    for derivatives, 431–432, 433
    functional, 6, 431–432, 433
    in GraphUtilities` package, 161
    for language grammars, 227
    musical, 380–384
    for numerical expressions, 3–4, 6
    for XMLObject, 210–211

Notation, 68
NotebookGet, 735
NotebookOpen, 735
NotebookPut, 735
notebooks
    extracting information from, 733–737
    formatting, 728–732
    SaveAs formats, 735
    saving and reopening, 615–616
    saving space in, 613–615
    transforming into other forms, 733–736
notebooks, interactive, 611–612
NotebookSave, 735
NSolve, 532
NSum, 57–58
Null, 174
NumberForm, 21
NumberFormat, 22
NumberPadding, 21
numbers, representation of (see also types,
        numerical)
    display forms, 20–22
    in lists, 95–97
    using other bases, 12–13
numeric results, precision of, 2–3, 4–9
numerical expressions, notation for, 3–6
numerical types (see types, numerical)

O

object-based programming, 541–542
octave divisions, 397–401
Ohm's law demonstration, 608–609
Opacity, 285, 295–296
OpenerView, 633–635
Options, 79–83
options, accepting, 79–83
options on securities, 551
    American pricing, 583–585
    computing implied volatility, 573
    European pricing, 551, 565–576, 578–582
    measuring sensitivity, 567–572
OptionValue, 79–80
Order, 187
ordered associative lookup, 125–129,
        133–134
Ordering, 101–102
Orderless, 29–30, 152
oscillations in tree methods, 585

Outer
    extracting financial properties, 555–556
    querying databases, 173
outliers, adjusting for, 471–472
overhead
    master-slave, 660
    of parallelization, 686–688
    tradeoffs, 652
Overlaps
    with StringCases, 195–196
    with StringPosition, 198, 200

P

packages, defining custom, 725–727
packed arrays, 95–97
PaddedForm, 21–22
PairwiseScatterPlot, 494–496
palindrome demonstration, 206
PaneSelector, 633–635
Parade magazine, 502
Parallel Computing Toolkit, 642
parallel primitives, 659
parallel processing, 641–643
    combining results of parallel data
            segments, 653–654
    debugging code for, 642
    distribution methods, 659–661
    mapping functions across lists, 654–656
    organizing operations, 665–668
    overhead of, 652, 686–688
    partitioning large data sets, 656–658
    performance problems, 678–686
    processing massive numbers of files,
            669–678
    race conditions, 663–665
    running commands on multiple kernels,
            648–650
    running different algorithms in parallel,
            661–662
    scope of, 641–642
    of serial expressions, 651–653
    sharing data between kernels, 662–663
ParallelCombine, 653–654, 659
ParallelDo, 659
ParallelEvaluate
    checking state of remote kernels, 650
    measuring overhead of parallelization,
            686–687

running commands on multiple kernels, 648–650
Parallelize, 651–653, 659
ParallelMap
  as alternative to CriticalSection, 665
  distributing computation across kernels, 659
  implementing data-parallel algorithms, 654–656
ParallelSubmit, 665–668
ParallelSum, 659
ParallelTable, 659
  as alternative to CriticalSection, 665
  partitioning large data sets, 656–658
ParallelTry, 661–662
parametric methods, 565
parametric plots, 249–251
ParametricPlot, 250–251
ParametricPlot3D, 290–292
  compared to RevolutionPlot3D, 288
  compared to SphericalPlot3D, 292
  constraining 3D plots to specified regions, 296–297
ParetoPlot, 494–495
parsers, 227–235, 670
Part
  accessing XML structure, 210–211
  compared to ReplacePart, 157–159
  taking lists apart, 88
partial derivatives, computing, 431–435
partial differential equations (PDEs), 534, 574–578
particleData function, 513
ParticleData source, 513–516
particleTable, 513–514
Partition
  converting linear list into 2D form, 258–259
  converting RGB images to HSV, 336–337
  relationship to ListConvolve, 47–48
  restructuring lists, 89–90
PassEventsDown, 631–632
PassEventsUp, 631
pattern-based programming, 145–146
pattern constructs, 146–150
pattern matching, 198–200
  counting matching elements, 155–156
  emulating unification-based matching, 178–180

excluding matching elements, 153–155
extracting substrings, 193
extracting XML elements, 211–212
finding longest or shortest matches, 159–161
finding matching values, 151–153
with genetic and protein data, 516–519
greedy and nongreedy, 159–161
manipulating 3D graphics, 326–327
manipulating patterns with, 169–170
order of processing, 28
primitives, 145–149
querying databases, 171–177
removing and replacing string characters, 188
replacing parts of an expression, 157–159
in strings and text, 183–186, 198–200
transforming matching values, 151–153
transforming XML, 213–214
using semantic relationships, 177–178
pattern tests, 149
patterns, defined, 146
PatternSequence, 148
PCA (principal component analysis), 365–367
PDEs (partial differential equations), 534, 574–578
PDF (probability density function), 461–464
Pentland, Alex, 367, 371
percussion grooves, 384–389
performance, improving
  compiling functions, 727–728
  dynamic modules, 613–615
  freeing memory, 91, 112–114, 721
  interactive graphics manipulation, 602–604
  interactivity, 613–615, 619–622
  parallel processing, 665, 678–688
  partial differential equations, 574–578
periodic table of elements, 508–510
permutation matrices
  constructing, 105–109
  sparse versions of, 114
perpetuity, 559–560
perspective, 309–312
perturbation, random, 498–499
Piecewise
  composing complex functions, 427–428
  creating envelopes, 394–397

piecewise functions
    composing, 427–429
    as result of Integrate, 437
PiecewiseExpand, 429
pipeline approach, 665–668
Play, 391
Plot, 239
    compared to ListPlot, 253
    compared to Plot3D, 278
    compared to PolarPlot, 248–249
Plot3D
    combining 2D contours with 3D plots,
        295–296
    compared to ParametricPlot3D, 291
    compared to Plot, 278
    constraining plots to specified regions,
        296–297
    plotting functions in Cartesian
        coordinates, 276–282
PlotLabel, 241
PlotLegends` package, 260–261
PlotPoints
    plotting 3D regions with satisfied
        predicates, 301–302
    speeding up interactive graphics
        manipulation, 602–603
PlotRange
    in interactive plots, 600–601
    overriding, 255
    specifying coordinates, 243–244
    viewing 2D contours with 3D plots,
        295–296
plots, general (see also graphs)
    combining slow and fast, 620–622
    interactive annotation, 630–631
    resolution and speed of interactivity, 602
plots, three-dimensional (see also graphics,
        three-dimensional; graphs)
    3D contour plots, 292–294
    building structural models from, 306–309
    in Cartesian coordinates, 276–282
    combining 2D contours with 3D plots,
        295–296
    constraining to specified regions, 296–298
    in cylindrical coordinates, 285–289
    interactivity, 600–604
    parametric, 290–292
    plotting data, 298–300
    regions with satisfied predicates, 301–302

in spherical coordinates, 283–285
plots, two-dimensional, 237–238 (see also
        graphics, two-dimensional; graphs)
    in Cartesian coordinates, 239–247
    central limit theorem, 464–466
    combining 2D contours with 3D plots,
        295–296
    combining multiple plots, 255–258
    combining slow and fast plots, 620–622
    of data, 252–254
    displaying related plots, 258–260
    distribution shapes, 468–471, 469–470
    formatting, 239–247, 259–260
    function gradients, 446–447
    interactivity, 600–604
    legends, 260–263
    limiting values, 426–427
    linear regressions, 472–474
    nonlinear models, 475–477
    parametric plots, 249–251
    in polar coordinates, 247–249
    probability distributions, 464
    pseudorandom number distributions, 460
    series approximations, 430
    statistical, 492–496
    stylizing, 269–270
    yield curves, 563–565
PlotStyle, 285
Plus, 34
polar coordinates, plotting in, 247–249
PolarPlot, 247–249
polyhedra characteristics, 320–326
PolyhedronData source, 175–177, 320–325
PolynomialMod, 423–424
PolynomialQuotient, 422
PolynomialQuotientRemainder, 422
PolynomialRemainder, 423–424
polynomials
    decomposing, 420–422
    dividing by other polynomials, 422–424
    extreme values, 441–442
    finding from given roots, 415–416
    generating, 419–420
    indefinite sums and products, 449
    transforming, 417–419
population dynamics, modeling, 519–521
Position
    with Count, 156
    level specifications, 117

manipulating nested lists, 114–116
pattern matching, 152–153, 154–155, 156
positions
    extracting substrings, 193–194
    removing and replacing string characters,
        189–190
Postfix, 51
postfix notation, 6
    with AccountingForm, 20–21
    and code readability, 48–51
    specifying precision, 7
power series representations, 429–431
Precision, 8
precision of numeric results, 6
    controlling, 2–3, 4–9
    with mixed numerical types, 11
    with mixed-precision values, 10
predator-prey dynamics, modeling, 519–521
Prefix, 51
prefix notation, 6
    and code readability, 48–51
    in rigid bodies problems, 522–523
Prepend, 87
prime notation, 432, 433
primes demonstration, 38–40
primitive functions, 25–27 (see also graphics
        primitives)
    color primitives, 335–336
    for decomposing polynomials, 421
    parallel primitives, 659
    pattern primitives, 145–149
principal component analysis (PCA), 365–367
Print
    compared to PrintTemporary, 753
    debugging with, 743–745
    with TraceHandler, 680
printing, as debugging technique, 743–745
PrintTemporary, 753–754
Private` context, 726
probability density function (PDF), 461–464
probability distributions, 461–464
procedural programming style, 24–25
products (discrete calculus), 447–450
ProteinData source, 516–519
prototype patterns, defined, 68
pseudorandom numbers, generating, 459–461
pure functional languages, 31–32
pure functions, 24, 32
put-call parity, 566

put options, 551, 566–567
PValue
    in ANOVA results, 480
    in chi-square tests, 484

Q

quadSwap, 359
Quantile, 457
QuantilePlot, 494–495
quantiles, 457
QuartileSkewness, 469
quasirandom generators, 496–499
querying databases
    for available entities, 715–717
    with patterns, 171–177, 555
    with SQLSelect, 711–713
Quiet, 756

R

race conditions
    in parallel evaluation, 643
    preventing, 663–665
Ramanujan, Srinivasa, 448
random numbers, 459–461, 496–504
random perturbation, 498–499
random walks, 500–502
RandomChoice
    adding rhythm to melody, 377
    defining indexed functions, 52
RandomInteger, 459
RandomReal
    generating random numbers, 459
    as nonticklish function, 610
Range
    composing lists, 86–87
    in grep implementation, 199
Raster, 330, 336–339
rational numbers
    converting to integers, 18–19
    as expression heads, 1–2
Rationalize
    converting approximate values to exact, 19
    finding polynomials from given roots, 416
readability, 48–51
ReadList, 690–691
real numbers
    converting to other bases, 12–13
    as expression heads, 1–2

RealDigits, 13–14
Reap
    building image transformations
        incrementally, 347–348
    building lists incrementally, 57–59
    debugging with, 746–749, 752, 756
Rectangle, 263–266
RecurrenceTable, 520–521
recursive descent parsers, 227–228, 235
recursive functions
    debugging, 747–749
    nonrecursive alternatives, 53–56
    transforming XML with, 218–227
red-black tree algorithms
    compared to built-in associative lookup,
        133–134
    ordered associative lookup, 125–129
Reduce, 415
reduce, 669–678
Refresh, 609–610
RegionFunction, 298
RegionPlot, 301–302
regions
    constraining plots to, 296–298
    plotting, 301–302
regular expressions
    common, 185–186
    extracting words from strings, 193
    standardization of, 183
    stripping comments from, 190
RegularExpression, 183
ReinstallJava, 700–701
ReleaseHold, 168–169
remote kernels
    benefits of, 693
    configuring, 646–648
    connecting frontend to, 692–694
Remove, 131
Repeated, 148
RepeatedNull, 148
Replace, 117–118
ReplaceAll
    changing heads of XML data, 212–213
    computing variance, 458
    creating functions that accept options, 80
    debugging infinite loops, 166–167
    eliminating complex numbers, 156
    evaluating difference equation solutions,
        452

querying databases, 174
transforming XML, 213, 223
ReplaceAllRepeated, 75
ReplaceList, 752
ReplacePart, 157–159
ReplaceRepeated
    querying databases, 173–174
    testing, 165–167
Resolve, 441
Rest, 88
Reverse, 89
RevolutionAxis, 289
RevolutionPlot3D
    constraining 3D plots to specified
        regions, 296–297
    plotting surfaces in cylindrical
        coordinates, 286–288
RGB color model, 335–340
rho (computational finance)
    computing, 568
    defined, 551, 568
    plotting, 571
rhythm, 376–377, 382
Riffle, 87–88
rigid bodies problems, 522–524
roman numerals, converting, 15
Root objects, 441–442
Rotate
    labeling arrows, 272–273
    rotating 3D graphics, 318–319
RotateLeft, 65, 89
RotateRight, 65, 89
Round, 18–19
rounding rational numbers, 18–20
Row, 633–635
RSolve, 451–452
rules, 146, 150
    completing replacement before
        evaluating, 168–169
    implementing algorithms, 161–165
    optimizing, 170–171
    transforming matched values, 151
    transforming XML, 213–218
    using patterns as a query language, 171–177
Run, 690–691

S

SameQ, 91, 156
SameTest

finding duplicate list elements, 91
querying databases, 177
saturation, 336
Save, 680
SaveAs, 735
SaveDefinitions, 617, 622–624
saveDirectory, 674–675
saver, 674–675
scalar operations, 17
scalars, defined, 93
Scale, 317
scales, musical, 375–376
Scan, 117–118
scientific applications, overview of, 505–506
ScientificForm, 22
scoping constructs, 611–612
scratch variables, 613–615
SeedRandom, 500
Select
    extracting matching strings, 196
    filtering points in kinematics problems, 525
    taking lists apart, 88
SelectionSort, 98–99
semantic pattern matching, 177–178
sequence, 227–228
sequence recognition, 452–454
serial expressions, parallelizing, 651–653
Series, 429
SeriesObject, 429
Set
    creating downvalues, 28
    differentiating functions, 432
    finding series expansions, 429
set functions, overview of, 91
SetAttributes, 29
SetDelayed
    creating downvalues, 28
    differentiating functions, 432
    finding series expansions, 429
SetEdgeWeights, 139–140
SetPrecision, 7
sets, defined, 91
SetSharedFunction, 662
SetSharedVariable, 662–663
shape, 523–524
shared memory performance, 682
SharedMemory tracer, 682
Sharpen, 356
ShearingTransform, 320

shift matrices, constructing, 105–109
Short, 15
Shortest, 160–161
Show
    combining 2D contours with 3D plots, 295
    combining plots in a single graph,
        255–258
ShowLegend, 263
Sign, 428
Simplify
    deriving cash flow arrangements, 559–560
    solving differential equations, 439
    transforming symbolic expressions, 417
simulations
    kinematics problems, 526–529
    power of, 502
    stochastic, 499–504
Sin functions, 426–427
single-assignment, 31
SkeletonGraph, 175
Skewness, 468–469, 471
slave kernels
    checking status of, 645
    configuring, 643, 644–646
    overhead, 660
    in parallel computing, 642
    in pipeline approach, 667, 668
sliders, 595–596, 625–627
SlideView, 635–636
Sobel edge-detection method, 361–364
Solve
    compared to NSolve, 532
    computing normal modes, 530–531
    differentiating functions, 432
    solving algebraic equations, 414–415
Sort
    animated demonstration of, 628
    compared to Ordering, 101
    compared to SelectionSort, 98
    identifying outliers, 471
    with ParallelCombine, 653–654
    restructuring lists, 89
    sorting lists, 97–100
    in structure-adding transformations,
        224–226
SortBy, 97
sorting (see also Sort; SortBy)
    customizing quick sorts, 79–80
    lists, 97–100

Sound
  creating scales and melodies, 375–376
  playing digital sound files, 403–404
sound files, digital, 403–412
SoundNote
  creating chords, 378
  creating musical notes, 374–375
  playing chord progressions, 379
  specifying percussion instruments,
      385–388
  syntax, 388–389
sounds (see audio and music processing)
Sow
  building image transformations
      incrementally, 347–348
  building lists incrementally, 57–59
  debugging with, 746–749, 752, 756
sparse arrays, 112–114
SparseArray
  conserving space, 91, 113–114
  in statistical analysis, 457
  synthesizing tridiagonal matrices, 104,
      531–532
specificationMap, 347–348, 350–351
spectrograph demonstration, 411–412
Specularity
  controlling lighting of 3D graphics,
      313, 316
  visualizing translucent surface
      coverings, 309
spell-check demonstration, 206–209
spherical coordinates, 3D plots in, 283–285
SphericalPlot3D
  compared to ParametricPlot3D, 292
  constraining 3D plots to specified
      regions, 296–297
  plotting surfaces in spherical coordinates,
      283–284
Split, 224
SQL
  database connectivity, 713–717
  query equivalents, 171–177
Stack, 748
stack tracing, 747–749
StackInhibit, 749
Start (Windows), 691–692
stateless approach, 667
statistical analysis, 455–456
  central limit theorem, 464–466

common functions, 456–459
common plots, 492–496
covariance and correlation, 466–468
grouping data into clusters, 486–492
hypothesis testing, 483–486
interpolation functions, 477–478
linear models, 472–474
measuring data shapes, 468
nonlinear models, 475–477
outliers, 471–472
probability distributions, 461–464
pseudorandom number generation,
    459–461
quasirandom number generation,
    496–499
statistical significance, 479–483
stochastic simulations, 499–504
Statistics in a Nutshell (Boslaugh and
    Watters), 455
  central limit theorem, 465
  chi-square demonstration, 484
  testing for statistical significance, 479–480
StemLeafPlot, 494
step monitors, debugging with, 756–758
StepMonitor, 757–758
stochastic rounding, 19–20
stochastic simulations, 499–504
strict languages, 32
String, 380–381
string expressions, 183–185, 193
string patterns, classes of, 183–186
StringCases, 193, 195–196
StringDrop
  compared to StringTake, 194
  matching and searching text, 200
  removing and replacing characters, 189
StringExpression, 183–184
StringFreeQ, 198, 199–200
StringJoin
  duplicating strings, 196–197
  extracting characters, 194
StringMatchQ
  extracting matching strings, 196
  matching patterns, 198, 199–200
StringPosition, 198, 200
StringReplace, 188–192
StringReplacePart, 189–190
strings, 181–186
  comparing, 187

converting, 15–16
duplicating, 196–198
extracting substrings from, 192–196
removing and replacing characters, 188–192
stripping comments from, 190
StringSplit
  listing polyhedron attributes, 321–322
  tokenizing text, 201–202
StringTake, 193–194, 200
Style, 269
StyleData, 730
StyleDefinitions, 730
stylesheets, 728–732
SubitemNumbered, 731
Subscript, 420
subscripts, 51
Subsets, 91
substrings, extracting, 192–196
Sum
  generating polynomials, 420
  solving discrete calculus problems, 448–450
SumConvergence, 448
sums (discrete calculus), 447–450
surface integrals, 444–445
surface properties, 313–316
surfaces, plotting, 285–292
Svensson model, 565
symbolic expressions, manipulating, 598–600
symbols
  assigning attributes to, 29
  in expressions with mixed numerical types, 9–10
  modifying meaning of, 723
symbols, undefined, 27
syntax, 6
  colon use, 151
  Dictionary, 133

T

Table
  creating a moving window for mapping, 44
  generating lists, 86–87
  mapping multiple functions in a single pass, 39–40
  with ParallelEvaluate, 650
  representing numerical lists, 95–96
TableType, 716

TabView, 635, 637–638
TagSet, 29
TagSetDelayed, 29
Take
  mapping a function over a moving sublist, 44
  running commands on multiple kernels, 648–649
  taking lists apart, 88
Tally
  adjusting for outliers, 472
  counting matching elements, 156
  in linguistic processing, 205–206
  in statistical analysis, 459
tempered tuning, 397, 400, 401–402
tensor functions, 93–95
tensors, defined, 93
Test, 766–767
TestFree, 765–766
TestID, 763, 771
testing, 742
  creating tests with alternate criteria, 765–767
  creating unit tests, 762–765
  organizing and controlling MUnit tests, 767–769
TestMatch, 765–766
TestSections, 772–775
TestStringFree, 765–766
TestStringMatch, 765–766
TestSuite construct, 768–769
Text
  annotating 2D graphics, 263, 269–270
  labeling arrows, 272–273
text annotations (see annotation)
text strings, 181–186
  changing delimiters in, 190–191
  matching patterns in, 198–200
  tokenizing, 201–202
theta (computational finance)
  computing, 568
  defined, 551, 568
  plotting, 570
Thickness, 268
three-dimensional graphics (see graphics, three-dimensional; graphs; plots, three-dimensional)
Through, 457
Throw, 772–773
ToCharacterCode, 182

ToExpression
    expression evaluation, 192
    transforming XML, 213–214
tokenizing text, 201–202
ToolTip, 512
ToString, 182
Towers of Hanoi puzzle, 451–452
Tr, 102–103
Trace, 749–753
TraceHandler, 679–680
TraceList, 680–686
Tracers, 679–680
TraceScan, 752–753
transform, 225–226
transformation functions, symbolic, 319–320
transformation matrices, 319–320
transformations
    after evaluation, 168–169
    images, 347–348
    polynomials, 417–419
    structure-adding, 224–226
    trigonometric, 419
transitive closure, computing, 162–163
transitiveClosure, 162–163
Translate, 318
Transpose
    formatting property lists, 517–518
    in Fourier analysis, 411–412
    in grep implementation, 199
    interlacing percussion elements, 387–388
    restructuring lists, 89
traversal algorithms, 121–125
tree algorithms
    interest-rate sensitivity, 587–591
    option pricing, 585, 587–590
    red-black, 125–129, 133–134
    traversals, 121–125
tree data structures
    converting to and from lists, 89, 127–128
    modeling with lists, 121–125
    selective flattening, 90
tremolo, 392, 394
TriangleWave, 538
tridiagonal matrices, 104–105, 530
TrigExpand, 419
TrigFactor, 419
trigonometric transformations, 419
TrigReduce, 419
trimmed mean, computing, 471

trinomial scheme, 583–585
truss structures, modeling, 539–547
trussGraphicNodes, 544–545
TrussModel, 541–547
tunings, alternate, 397–402
Tuples, 14–15
Turk, Matthew, 367, 371
two-dimensional graphics (see graphics,
        two-dimensional; graphs; plots,
        two-dimensional)
types, numerical
    compiling functions, 727, 728
    converting between, 18–20
    identifying database support for, 716
    indicated by Head, 1–2
    mixing, 9–11
    with .NET applications, 707–708, 710
    returned by MathLink, 699

U

unbiased rounding rule, 19–20
uncertainty, 16–18
undo operation, 65
Unicode, 181
unification-based matching, 178–180
uniform distributions, 465–466
unify, 179–180
Union
    eliminating duplicate list elements, 91
    ordering extracted nodes, 541
Unique
    associative lookup, 131
    with Private, 726
uniqueFileName, 674–665
unit tests
    in frontend, 769–775
    organizing and controlling, 767–769
    writing, 762–767
UnitStep, 428
unpacked arrays, 95–97
unprotecting operations, 722–723
UnsavedVariables, 613
UpperTriangularize, 105
UpSet, 28–29
UpSetDelayed, 28–29
upvalues, 28–29, 65
UpValues
    displaying bit vectors efficiently, 119
    redefining functions, 28–29

user-customized functions, 28–29, 79–83
UsingFrontEnd, 736

V

value (brightness), 336–337
Value-at-Risk (VaR), modeling, 585–587
van der Corput sequence, 497, 498
variables
    controlling values interactively, 594–597
    dynamic module, 624–625
    global, 723
    labeling, 597
    scoped, 611–612
    scratch, 613–615
    storage of, 612
Variables, 421
variance, computing, 458
vector calculus problems, solving, 443–447
vector functions, overview of, 91–92
VectorAnalysis` package, 92, 445
VectorPlot, 446–447
vectors, 93
    bit, 119–121
    Boolean, 488–491
    computing covariance and correlation, 466–468
    eigenvectors, 365–371
vega (computational finance)
    computing, 568–569
    defined, 551, 568
    plotting, 571
Verbatim, 169–170
vibrating strings, modeling, 533–536
vibrato, 393–394
ViewAngle, 312
ViewCenter, 311–312
ViewPoint, 310, 312
ViewVector, 312
ViewVertical
    controlling viewing perspective, 312
    plotting surfaces in cylindrical coordinates, 289
volatility, implied, 573
volume, 377–378, 382

W

Wagon, Stan, 52, 304–305
Wang, Ruye, 351

Watters, Paul (see *Statistics in a Nutshell*)
Webber, Thomas, 578, 582
Weisstein, Eric, 63
wget (GNU), 690–691
Windows programs, launching, 691–692
WinMain, 695–697
wireframe models, 306–309
With
    binding locally defined variables, 648–650
    measuring securities option sensitivity, 571–572
    with ParallelSubmit, 668
    varying electrical circuit input values, 537
Wolfram Workbench
    integrating into frontend, 769–775
    visual debugging, 758–762
    writing test units, 762, 764–765
Woods, Richard, 331, 351, 359
WordData, 208
wormholes, 624

X

XML
    heads, 210, 212–213
    importing, 209–213
    removing markup, 191–192
    stylizing, 201–202
    transforming with patterns and rules, 213–218
    transforming with recursive functions, 218–227
XMLElement, 210, 212–214
XMLObject, 209–210, 212–213
XSLT
    compared to Mathematica, 218, 226–227
    grouping constructs, 224
    transformation rules, 221

Y

Yahoo! URL structure, 557–559
Yale Face Database, 367–371
yield curves, 563–565
yield to maturity, 561

Z

Z-transforms, 449

About the Author

Sal Mangano has been developing software for over 12 years and has worked on many mission-critical applications, especially in the area of financial-trading applications. Unlike many XML/XSLT developers, he did not approach the technology from the standpoint of the Internet and Web development but rather from the broader need for a general-purpose, data-transformation framework. This experience has given him a unique perspective that has influenced many of the recipes in his book, the XSLT Cookbook. Sal has a Master's degree in Computer Science from Polytechnic University.

Colophon

The animal on the cover of *Mathematica Cookbook* is a solarium (genus *Solarium*) known more commonly today as a sundial or perspective shell. It serves as protection for marine snails of the genus *Architectonica* (a Latin name which modern scientists also use to refer to the shells). While usually found in the tropical Indo-Pacific region, the solariums also live in warmer waters near North and South America. As the snails prefer shallow habitat, their shells often wash ashore and are an easy find for beachgoers.

There are approximately 40 species, and while texture, coloration, and markings vary accordingly, all solariums have a spiral pattern. On their flattened circular shells, this radiating effect is evocative of the sun, and likely how the animal got its name. Most solarium decorations are vivid, including such motifs as bold lines, grooves, alternating colors, or blotches. Viewed from below, the shell's deep interior is lined with corrugations that resemble a winding staircase.

The direction in which a snail's shell coils, interestingly, is comparable to left- or right-handedness in a human. In their larval stage, *Architectonica* snails begin to develop soft left-coiling shells. However, when the snail enters its adult stage, the solarium reverses direction and spirals to the right as it grows. The majority of gastropods have dextral (right-facing) shells.

The cover image is from Dover Pictorial Archive. The cover font is Adobe ITC Garamond. The text font is Linotype Birka; the heading font is Adobe Myriad Condensed; and the code font is LucasFont's TheSansMonoCondensed.

Get even more for your money.

Join the O'Reilly Community, and register the O'Reilly books you own.It's free, and you'll get:

- 40% upgrade offer on O'Reilly books
- Membership discounts on books and events
- Free lifetime updates to electronic formats of books
- Multiple ebook formats, DRM FREE
- Participation in the O'Reilly community
- Newsletters
- Account management
- 100% Satisfaction Guarantee

Signing up is easy:

1. **Go to: oreilly.com/go/register**
2. **Create an O'Reilly login.**
3. **Provide your address.**
4. **Register your books.**

Note: English-language books only

To order books online:

oreilly.com/order_new

For questions about products or an order:

orders@oreilly.com

To sign up to get topic-specific email announcements and/or news about upcoming books, conferences, special offers, and new technologies:

elists@oreilly.com

For technical questions about book content:

booktech@oreilly.com

To submit new book proposals to our editors:

proposals@oreilly.com

Many O'Reilly books are available in PDF and several ebook formats. For more information:

oreilly.com/ebooks

O'REILLY®

Spreading the knowledge of innovators   www.oreilly.com